ANOTHER PLACE, ANOTHER TIME:

A U-BOAT OFFICER'S WARTIME ALBUM

U-74 manoeuvring in the harbour at La Spezia, Italy. (WH col.)

ANOTHER PLACE, ANOTHER TIME

A U-BOAT OFFICER'S WARTIME ALBUM

Werner Hirschmann

with Donald E. Graves

Foreword by Timothy P. Mulligan

Maps by Christopher Johnson

ROBIN BRASS STUDIO   CHATHAM PUBLISHING
Toronto   London

Published in Canada 2004 by Robin Brass Studio Inc.
www.rbstudiobooks.com

Published in the UK 2004 by Chatham Publishing
Park House, 1 Russell Gardens, London NW11 9NN
Chatham Publishing is an imprint of Lionel Leventhal Ltd
www.chathampublishing.com

ISBN 1-896941-38-9

Printed and bound in Canada by Friesens, Altona, Manitoba

National Library of Canada Cataloguing in Publication

Hirschmann, Werner

Another place, another time : a U-Boat officer's wartime album / Werner Hirschmann with Donald E. Graves ; foreword by Timothy P. Mulligan ; maps and diagrams by Christopher Johnson.

Includes index.
ISBN 1-896941-38-9

1. Hirschmann, Werner. 2. World War, 1939-1945 – Naval operations – Submarine. 3. World War, 1939-1945 – Naval operations, German. 4. World War, 1939-1945 – Prisoners and prisons, Canadian. 5. World War, 1939-1945 – Personal narratives, German. 6. Immigrants – Canada – Biography. 7. German Canadians – Biography. I. Graves, Donald E. (Donald Edward). II. Title.

D811.H567 2004   940.54'51'092   C2004-900118-3

CONTENTS

LIST OF MAPS

FOREWORD

by Timothy P. Mulligan

I met Werner Hirschmann while researching a book on the men who served in the German U-boat arm during the Second World War. Over the course of extended interviews during several visits to Toronto, Werner patiently and graciously answered my questions and shared his experiences and insights as a former U-boat engineering officer. In addition to his incredible memory for events and attitudes of the period, he offered a unique perspective in several ways. First was his Canadian identity, reflecting a remarkable adaptability that bridged wars, continents and cultures. The skills he brought with him helped modernize Toronto's traffic control system and other public utilities in the 1960s and 1970s, and he became a welcome participant in meetings with Royal Canadian Navy veterans.

Second, Werner belonged to a select group within one of the Second World War's combat elites. During that conflict Grand Admiral Karl Dönitz's U-boat crews lost well over half their men killed in action, a casualty rate unmatched by any service branch of the major powers; thus simple physical survival represented a badge of distinction as well as good fortune. In a reality where the most common experience of a German submariner

was to die on his first patrol, Werner Hirschmann served three years aboard U-boats in the Mediterranean, the Baltic and the Atlantic. He merits special consideration, however, as the engineering officer aboard a snorkel submarine for the war's final three months, a taxing responsibility that demanded constant vigilance, anticipation and ingenuity, all in addition to the standard duties associated with the submarine's propulsion and technical systems. No more than a handful of U-boat chief engineers successfully mastered these tasks and possessed both the skill and luck to evade destruction.

That Werner Hirschmann himself dismisses such assessments testifies to his distinctive personal qualities. An interviewer quickly becomes aware of his candour, sense of humour, modesty and, above all, clarity. Through all the filters of selective human memory, the propaganda images of the U-boat service, and contemporary attitudes, he retains a remarkably vivid picture of his life and times as a German submariner, buttressed by his wartime diary. Werner evades no questions, has little concern for interpretative orthodoxy, and presumes to speak for no one but himself, yet conveys throughout an understanding of human conduct and frailty too often overlooked by professional historians.

Finally, his story is enhanced by an extensive collection of personal photographs from the period. Published here for the first time, they not only supplement his narrative, but provide a new source for the study of the U-boat service. Each photograph constitutes a historical document itself, recording the everyday life of what Winston Churchill later acknowledged as the "only thing that ever really frightened me during the war."

We are all indebted to Canadian historian Donald E. Graves on two counts, both for convincing Werner Hirschmann to publish his story and for assisting in editing his wartime diary. Mr. Graves, who has already written extensively on the War of 1812, now follows his recent account of the Royal Canadian Navy's role in the Battle of the Atlantic with a German perspective of that conflict. Moreover he has added an authoritative profile of a Type IXC U-boat's interior.

The result of their efforts lies before you, a unique look inside the German U-boat service and the record of one man's passage through the world's greatest conflict. Grateful for Werner's assistance to my study, I am honoured to contribute this brief foreword to that account.

TIMOTHY P. MULLIGAN
Washington, March 2004

INTRODUCTION

More than a half century has passed since the events described in this book took place. In those intervening years, most of which I have spent in a new country and a new society, my youth as a German naval officer receded into the dim past and it was only with some reluctance that I undertook the task of revisiting these early chapters of my life. Once I had started this task, however, I was gratified to see that the passage of time had given me a certain detachment from my youthful life and I was able to be more dispassionate and reasoned about my experiences during the Second World War than I would have been if this book had been written earlier.

Before I discuss what this book is about, I want to be clear about what it is not about. It is not a history of anti-submarine warfare in the Second World War, nor is it a study of the German *U-Boot-Waffe* and its weapon systems. These subjects are well covered in a considerable and ever-growing literature that provides the details of losses and successes, technological developments and the role of the outstanding personalities on either side. Although I have included some historical background to

place my own story in proper context, the reader looking for a new aspect of the struggle in the sea lanes waged by the Allied navies and the *Kriegsmarine* between 1939 and 1945 will be disappointed, as the pages that follow contain only the story of one rather insignificant participant in that great conflict.

That story is very much the same as the stories of many of my comrades who served in the U-boat service during the war – including the nearly 30,000 German sailors who were killed in action. Most books about the men of the *U-boot-waffe* (with a few notable exceptions) concentrate on the senior commanders and leading aces; they ignore the humbler members such as myself who, too often in the postwar literature, are reduced to faceless ciphers whose sole purpose was to assist those commanders and aces increase their scores in the tonnage war.

Although it seems only natural to assume that a war of the magnitude of that waged between 1939 and 1945 must have governed every hour of every day of all those who lived through it, I would like to emphasize that, after the initial shock, one had no other choice but to accept war as simply a new set of conditions under which

ANOTHER PLACE, ANOTHER TIME

one still had a daily life with the same desires and problems one had in peacetime. We needed sleep, we were hungry and thirsty, we wanted to laugh and we fell in love – in short, we tried to satisfy the most basic and normal human instincts. There is a certain analogy with the weather, as one is affected by it, whether one curses or enjoys it, but life goes on since there is nothing one can do about it. Even in action at sea, my job was not to win the war but to fulfill my duties as a chief engineer to the best of my abilities, namely, to keep the engines running, to dive and surface the boat as required and to keep it in good repair – just as would have been required of me if there had been no war.

The reader will probably note variations in the amount of detail present below in the different periods of the war. I kept a number of diaries during those years but not one of them deals with actual U-boat missions. They covered only those events that were out of the ordinary for a sailor, including the courting of my future wife, as to me these were the things important enough to be recorded in writing. The U-boat patrols were full of long periods of boredom, occasionally interrupted by some action, and it was often very mundane and not worth recording for posterity.

Although this book is a personal story and not a political analysis, I should explain how we young Germans regarded the nation for which we fought. For those of us who grew up in the difficult years after the First World War, Nazism meant a re-awakening of pride in our country and the promise of a better future. Hitler enjoyed incredible popularity, and in that sense I can probably say that in those days we were all Nazis. To us before the war Nazism did *not* mean concentration camps, war, master race, and it certainly did not mean world domination. During the war civilization became a victim everywhere. We were disappointed to be at war with England since we always had considered that country to be our natural ally in the affairs of the world. We practically remained Anglophiles through the war and looked at our combat at sea more as a competition than as a clash of ideologies.

We had a saying in the German navy that this or that well-known hero was just "too dumb to feel fear," and there weren't many of those around. I believe that the vast majority of us had to fight the fear that threatened to overcome us. Worse and more immediate was the fear of being considered a coward by our comrades and therefore there was always an internal imperative to do what was necessary or desirable, if not always rational. You simply acted, almost automatically, in ways which, when you thought about it later, seemed utterly impossible. In that way, quite unintentionally, you might or might not become a hero. I have been told that to be a hero is to make a choice, but I believe that in many combat situations there is no opportunity to think about choice – you just act. I also do not believe in the commonly accepted definition of a hero, as it is voiced time and time again – namely the man who goes to war to make supreme sacrifices and to give his life for his country. Such a man does not lose his life because he offered it – he loses it because he cannot prevent it being taken from him. He does not sacrifice – he is sacrificed.

We submariners were human beings who experienced the full spectrum of joys and tragedies, of triumphs and disasters, both personal and professional. We were also very young, and what follows is really the story of a young man who wanted to be a naval officer but who, because of the time and place, became caught up in one of the longest and most desperate conflicts in naval history and was fortunate to survive it.

This book would not have been written without the invaluable help of both my editor, Donald E. Graves, and publisher, Robin Brass. Both took great efforts to shape my ramblings into a form that might appeal to the reader. Furthermore, I must thank Dr. Timothy P. Mul-ligan of the National Archives in Washington and Mr. Michael Whitby, Senior Naval Historian, Department of National Defence, Ottawa, for going through these chapters and offering valuable criticisms.

I am grateful to three former members of the crew of my last submarine, *U-190:* Werner Müller, Rudi Rauch and Rudi Bartsch, who have helped to refresh my memory on certain questions. Ultimately, however, these are my memories and I am responsible for their content, including occasional lapses.

WERNER HIRSCHMANN
Toronto, March 2004

EDITOR'S NOTE

I knew of Werner Hirschmann more than two decades before I met him as we had a mutual friend who had informed me of the existence of a former U-boat officer in Toronto. While researching my book *In Peril on the Sea: The Royal Canadian Navy and the Battle of the Atlantic* (Robin Brass Studio, Toronto, 2003), I contacted Werner and he provided me with excerpts from an unpublished memoir of his wartime service. When he later showed me his photograph albums and wartime diaries, I was able to convince him, after much discussion, that he should consider making this trove of historical material available to a wider audience. The result is *Another Place, Another Time: A U-Boat Officer's Wartime Album.*

The first part of this book, Werner Hirschmann's personal story, is based on his memoir but it was fleshed out by other sources. Between June 1944 and May 1945 he kept a diary and this was the paramount source for the chapters that cover that time, but this diary was highly personal in subject matter and did not include his experiences at sea. For his training and for three of his four wartime patrols, we were able to make use of some of his course material which he had preserved and the *Kriegstagebücher* or logs of *U-190* and *U-375*, on which he served. The *Kriegstagebüch* of the last patrol of *U-190* was destroyed before that boat surrendered in May 1945 but use was made of Canadian naval documents, including the interrogation reports of the boat's officers and material found on board when it was taken over by the Royal Canadian Navy. All this material, together with other wartime primary sources, and interviews with three of Werner Hirschmann's former shipmates, was used to verify and expand Werner's memories. A complete list of all the sources on which this book is based is contained in the bibliography.

When it came to visual sources we were blessed not only with the author's large personal collection but also many fine views of *U-190* and *U-889* taken in 1945 which are now in the National Library and Archives of Canada. This turned out to be such a rich vein that it led to the decision to include a photographic tour of the Type IXC 40 U-boat in this book.

All of these sources have been utilized for *Another Place, Another Time,* but, as Werner emphasizes, this is not a history of submarine warfare in the Second World War, nor is it a history of the German *U-Boot-Waffe.* It is

12

the story of a young man who cherished a lifelong ambition to be an officer in his country's navy and attained that ambition – that his country was Germany and that he served in U-boats between 1942 and 1945 is of historical interest but it really is incidental because Werner would have become a naval officer, in peace or in war.

In closing I would like to acknowledge the spendid assistance given to me by Dr. Timothy P. Mulligan of the National Archives in Washington and Mr. Michael Whitby, Senior Naval Historian of the Department of National Defence in Ottawa. Their expert research help and critical comments on early drafts of the text considerably eased my burdens.

DONALD E. GRAVES
Ottawa, April 2004

In the summer of 1940 we did our best to prepare for service in the navy. Fortunately, we did not have to row into battle. (WH col.)

I was born in Düsseldorf, Germany, on 2 March 1923. At the time of my birth, life in my country was still very much affected by the consequences of Germany having lost the First World War. Parts of the country were occupied by foreign powers, the economy was reeling under the burden of wartime reparations that had to be paid to other European nations, and inflation was rampant. In fact, it was so uncontrollable – and such was the rate of devaluation of the currency – that workers were taking their wages home in wheelbarrows, or spending it before going home, as within a matter of hours banknotes might lose half their purchasing power. I myself was, of course, not aware of these conditions in my early years but I mention them to emphasize a factor that contributed heavily to later political developments in Germany – the consequences of which led to this book being written.

My father came from a very strict Bavarian family in Nürnberg. His mother ruled with such an iron fist that, before the outbreak of the First World War, his two older brothers ran away from home, joined the merchant marine and roamed the oceans. When war came in 1914, they were both drafted into the Imperial German Navy and my father, hearing his brothers recount their adventures, joined the same service. He served as a sailor on board a battleship of the High Seas Fleet and, while on shore leave in Kiel, Germany's largest naval base, he met a charming secretary who became his wife a few years later, and my mother a few years after that. This gave me grandparents in Kiel as well as Nürnberg.

After the war ended in 1918, my father became a manager in a professional association that had branches across Germany. Although he was employed throughout the bitter economic times that his country experienced in the postwar years, it meant that when I was growing up in the 1920s and 1930s we moved constantly as my father was transferred to the various offices of his employers. By the end of my school years I had lived in Essen, Münich, Leipzig, Stuttgart and Berlin. In Germany at that time, there were a great number of regional dialects and, although benefiting from my exposure to different cities, I was keenly aware of the disadvantages of this nomadic life because when I arrived in a new place and a new school speaking the dialect of my previous residence, I promptly became a laughing stock to my classmates. As quickly as I could, I learned to speak the

Still carefree at age five in 1928, here I am enjoying the beach at the River Isar in Munich with my parents, Willy and Erna Hirschmann. (WH col.)

new local dialect, only to repeat the process a few years later. In the end I claimed Berlin as my home town since that is where I became aware of the important difference between boys and girls, and from where I ventured into the wider world.

There is one incident in my childhood that I do remember quite vividly and which I should record as the result may be noticeable in the photographs of me in this book – the origins of the circular scar on my forehead. When questioned about that scar I would love to be able to say, "Ah well, there was this affair that led to a duel" or something romantic like that. Unfortunately, I have to confess that, at the age of six, while riding my bicycle I went full speed ahead into a parked truck and received

the entire impact of the collision on my forehead. I was taken to the hospital for repairs while a friend took the remains of my bike to my mother and reported that her darling son had been transformed into a bloody mess. I spent a week in hospital, where I was neatly stitched up, before being released, and when I came home, I found, standing in front of our house, a brand new bicycle waiting for me, bought by my parents. I learned a valuable lesson – do not dwell on the past because the future starts today.

Other than that incident, my memories of my early years are rather hazy and only gain some focus after Adolf Hitler and the National Socialist Party came to power in 1933. I must admit, however, that this important event in the history of my country hardly registered on my mind when it happened but when I look back now, most of my early memories stem from the period after 1933. The change in government was noticeable since, shortly after it occurred, there were fewer unemployed men in the streets as the economy seemed to undergo a quick revival – yet I showed about as much interest in politics as any kid of my age in any country, because my mind was consumed with an unwavering ambition to become a sailor.

I can trace the origin of this ambition to my father. He was proud of his service in the Imperial German Navy during the First World War and the fact that he had fought in the famous 1916 battle of Jutland. He occasionally talked about his experiences in public – however, as is usually the case with veterans, he spoke more of the good than the bad. I became fascinated with Jutland, the largest naval engagement in modern history, and read every book I could find on the subject. In fact, I became such an expert on this famous action that I was soon able to correct my father when his memory committed the odd error. Through my father's influence, I became interested in all matters maritime and as I grew older I expanded my reading to include numerous books on naval history. My childhood heroes were not knights, kings, great generals, cowboys or Indians but naval commanders such as Hawke, Nelson and De Ruyter. My childish imagination was enthralled by images of large battleships with at least four funnels belching smoke and I very much wanted to be part of it all. I never dreamed of a career as a fireman or a pilot – I wanted to be a sailor!

I nurtured these ambitions by spending many happy hours building scale models of battleships, sailing ships, submarines and armed merchant cruisers. After they were finished I would then, much to my mother's distress, devise ways of turning my creations into battle casualties by setting them on fire. My mother tolerated my obsession with naval warfare but she was really more concerned about the progress of her only child's manda-

Above are some of the ship models I built in the late thirties: On the right the battleship *Derfflinger* and at the left the armoured merchant cruiser *Wolf*, both of First World War fame. Below is a model of a pre-war type IA U-boat. (WH col.)

1938: Our folk dancing group in the *Hitlerjugend* together with our partners, the girls of the BdM *(Bund deutscher Mädchen)*. (WH col.)

Like almost every boy in Germany I played football. Here, second from the left, I appear in the uniform of the Berlin club "Victoria 89" in 1938. (WH col.)

ously about a career: I wished to spare my parents the expense of a university education; I hoped to play soccer against British sailors in such far-off and exotic ports as Shanghai and Hong Kong; and I suffered terribly from hay fever! Being rather a romantic young man, I also had this far-fetched theory that a sailor's marriage would never suffer from that deadly enemy of romance called boredom and, after long absences, there would be a wonderful renewal, a starting all over again. Unfortunately, having had my navy career terminated rather prematurely before I married, I was never able to test this theory and perhaps that is just as well.

When I began seriously to think about a naval career, I decided to choose the engineering branch. I did so because I was technically inclined and because I also wanted to get professional training that would be useful

tory violin lessons. (After having developed enough maturity to make my own decisions, I abandoned the violin and switched to the accordion.) In between violin lessons, I studied naval tactics by carrying out fierce battles in the bathtub using fleets of half walnut shells filled with wax, sticks and paper sails. An opportunity to go sailing with friends of my parents was my introduction to wind, waves and water, and I was fascinated.

It would seem from my earliest recollections that I was destined to become a sailor. There were also more practical considerations that came into play when I approached the end of my high school education and had to think seri-

Having finally managed to escape the mandatory violin lessons, I taught myself to play the accordion. (WH col.)

Even though I was crowned "King of the May" for 1939 in my home town, it did not relieve me from having to scrub my royal carriage to make it suitable for the ceremonies. (WH col.)

Flanked by our retinue of maidens of honour, my May Queen and I arrive in our carriage at the May Pole. (WH col.)

in peacetime maritime commerce, other than navigation. For this reason, guns and torpedoes were of no interest to me. Of course, when I entered the navy I did not know there were disadvantages to being an engineer officer which I discovered later during my service in the *U-Boot-Waffe*.* Rather facetiously it was claimed that when a U-boat was successful, its commanding officer got all the medals, whereas lack of success was the chief engineer's fault.

Since a great deal of my activities as a teenager were connected with the *Hitlerjugend*, or Hitler Youth, I should talk about my experience in that organization. It seems that, according to modern popular opinion based on films and television, the boys who belonged to it were a bunch of robot-like, unthinking and unfeeling fanatical followers of the *Führer*, engaged in preliminary training to become the future soldiers of Germany's planned attempt at world conquest. Period films and photographs show German boys of my age at that time wearing brown uniforms, carrying flags or torches in military formation and shouting their support of the Nazi party at massive public events and staged political rallies. Pictures do not lie and these things did, of course, take place, but it should be realized that the participants in these demonstrations represented only a very small part of the Hitler Youth. The vast majority of its members were never involved in such spectacles.

What I remember about the *Hitlerjugend* is that we

---

* The *U-Boot-Waffe* was the submarine service of the German navy during the Second World War.

had a marvellous time in what was, until the war years, really another name for an organization not unlike the Boy Scouts. Apart from such scouting activities as hiking, camping and swimming, we also had a choir, a folk-dancing group in conjunction with the *BdM** and a popular string quartet, in which I played second violin. We went on week-long bicycle trips during which we camped, did some target shooting (but it was not in any sense of the word military training) and played a lot of sports. We also did social volunteer work, including assisting the local farmers with their harvest (an activity I hated because of my hay fever), raising funds for the needy, and acting as helpers in any kind of emergency. We were part of every community event and we learned about self-discipline, dedication, loyalty, honesty, sacrifice and clean living.

My memories contrast with the established modern view of the *Hitlerjugend* and I do not recall that we had any discussions on National Socialist philosophy or any other such indoctrination. We did discuss history and the latest technical developments such as the fastest aircraft, racing cars or speedboats. We also spent some time talking about culture but rarely did any of our discussions have any political content. Our organization was a movement without drugs, sex, nicotine or alcohol and the Nazi leaders played the same role in our lives as the principal of our school – in other words we did very nicely without their involvement and did our best to avoid them.

Frankly, I liked being in the *Hitlerjugend* as it was fun, and by the time I was 16 I had become a senior leader in Blankenfelde, our 10,000-strong dormitory town outside Berlin. My most memorable experience was being selected to play the "May King" who, with the "May Queen," led the traditional festivities around the May Pole in our small community. This involved dancing a solo waltz in the three restaurants in Blankenfelde, which was one of the more trying "firsts" in my life. My part in this celebration, however, taught me that rank hath its responsibilities as well its privileges as I personally had to clean out the farm wagon which, suitably decorated, served as the royal couple's chariot.

In September 1939 the series of political and international crises, of which my friends and I had only dimly been aware, boiled over when Germany invaded Poland. This caused Britain and France to declare war against Germany and brought about the second great conflict of the 20th century and the loss of millions of lives. This, of course, did come to our attention as it caused immediate changes in our lives, but I should emphasize that there were no great outpourings of patriotic fervour in Germany in September 1939 – the country had suffered too much in the previous conflict. Instead I would characterize the German attitude to the outbreak of war as being almost fatalistic. When the Polish campaign was brought to a quick and victorious conclusion by the German army, there was great hope that peace negotiations would ensue and that the war would end. When this did not happen, Germans resigned themselves to a long struggle.

---

* *Bund deutscher Mädchen*, the female equivalent of the *Hitlerjugend*.

My family became caught up in this conflict when my father, at that time 44, was called up by the *Kriegsmarine*, or German navy. He was posted to the coast artillery, which under the German system was a naval organization. At almost the same time, I transferred to the *Marine-Hitlerjugend*, the naval branch of the Hitler Youth, which is perhaps best described as being the equivalent to the modern Canadian Sea Scouts. I now learned sailing, rowing, flag signalling, maritime history and spent much of the winter of 1939-1940 ice-boating on one of the larger lakes near my home. My new white and blue naval-type uniform was a welcome change from the previous rather drab brown uniform of the Hitler Youth, and learning to look after it properly prepared me for things to come.

After having switched to the *Marine-Hitlerjugend* in the autumn of 1939 I enjoyed wearing the new uniform which gave me a foretaste of my future profession. (WH col.)

I now looked like a sailor (on certain days) but to accomplish my long-cherished ambition of becoming one, which had by now become refined into wanting to be an officer in the *Kriegsmarine*, I had to undergo a rigorous selection process. I had decided on a naval career before the Second World War began and the fact that my country was at war when I entered the *Kriegsmarine* did not in any way change my career plans. It was really as simple as this – when you are a young man and your country is at war, you go to war because you cannot just sit at home and let others fight or, worse, come home in fancy uniforms and impress all the girls. Above all, there was the challenge of adventure, which for a young man is an irresistible attraction. Finally, in those far-off days, there was nothing dirty about nationalism or patriotism and as a European I knew that wars had been common events throughout history. War or no war, I was going into the navy.

For me, the process of becoming a naval officer started in late 1939 with the submission of my written application, complete with supporting documentation. I had to endure months of waiting before this application was even acknowledged and, even then, it was not until the summer of 1940 that I was directed, with the other applicants of my age group, to report to the naval base in Kiel to undergo a series of tests to assess my suitability as an officer candidate.

On the appointed day, we all arrived in Kiel and the examinations began. I had weak sight in my left eye and I was very worried that this might jeopardize my chances but nothing was said about this defect during a very thorough medical examination.

A *Mutprobe*, or test of elementary courage, followed the medical examination. We were taken to a gym where each candidate, in succession, was ordered to assume a

We had our own, rather primitive iceboat (above) on a lake near Berlin that was one of two centres of European ice-boating. I am leaning against the mast. The iceboat at the left is an open 15 m² racing yacht built for international competition, the letter *G* on its sail indicating its German nationality. (WH col.)

position on a high bar about 10 feet off the ground, balancing on his arms. We were then ordered to pull our legs and feet up over the bar and jump feet-first to a thin, padded mat situated on the floor on the opposite side of the high bar. I had never done such a gymnastic act before, had no idea how to do it and was not very enthusiastic about the process. But since this was not so much a matter of skill but of courage, and knowing my life's ambition hung in the balance, I pulled my feet up and over the bar and made the jump. Unfortunately, my feet

caught the bar and, instead of coming down feet first, I fell head first toward the mat at great velocity. Fortunately for my naval aspirations (and my physical well being), I was caught in the strong arms of two waiting sailors posted there for just such an eventuality. Nothing was said about my clumsiness and I began to hope that the instructors had mistaken it for simple blind courage.

This was only the beginning. The next day we were required, without warning or preparation, to stand in front of the assembled herd of applicants and present a five-minute speech on any topic of our choice. Here my studies of the Battle of Jutland came in handy and after about three minutes of rapid-fire dissertation about the origins and course of the battle, I was just warming to my subject when I was rudely interrupted by the officer in charge with a shout of "Okay, that's enough. You obviously know your stuff." For the remainder of the day,

I had to listen to speeches of varying or, in some cases, little quality.

That night I was told, without any further comment or elaboration, that I could return home on the following day. This news came as an enormous shock as I was prepared to travel with the rest of the group to Hamburg for a series of psychological tests. Completely deflated and worried sick, I sat abjectly in the train taking me back to Blankenfelde, convinced that I had failed to gain entrance to the *Kriegsmarine* and that my naval ambitions had come to an inglorious end. I spent the next four weeks in a state of despair which was only relieved by the arrival of an official letter informing me that I had been accepted as an *Offiziersanwärter*, an officer-candidate, and was to report in late September 1940 to Stralsund for basic training.

To this day, I have no idea why I was singled out for a premature departure from Kiel and why I was allowed to avoid the psychiatric testing – perhaps it would be just as well to not inquire too deeply. Reflecting on it now, I think that either the testing officers were enormously impressed by my talents and dedication, or they were scraping the bottom of the barrel and concluded that a blindly brave fool with a good knowledge of naval history might, after considerable ef-

In my *Marine-Hitlerjugend* (M.H.J.) uniform with the word *Teltow* indicating the *Kreis* or county in which Blankenfelde was located. (WH col.)

fort, make a useful officer. In my own defence, I can say that, of about 3,000 applicants in my group, only about 1,000 were selected for further training, so possibly I can discard the second hypothesis.

As might be expected, I was elated and looked forward to the formal beginning of my naval career. My *Abitur*, or final high school examination, necessary to gain admission to a university, was not due until the spring of 1941 but a new regulation allowed the school system to confer this diploma without examinations to students who went into military service, as long as their academic standing at the time of leaving school was up to the requirements for the *Abitur*. This unexpected bonus naturally put a big smile on the faces of those of my schoolfriends who had decided on military careers when talking to those unfortunates who had not yet joined one of the armed services. My mother, who, with some sadness, had seen my father drafted into the *Kriegsmarine*, was happy that my dreams had become reality, although it no doubt added to her worries. Nevertheless, she put on a good face about events over which she had no control.

My enthusiasm was, of course, tempered by the knowledge that my country was at war. The successes in the west in the spring of

1940 had created renewed optimism in Germany that there would be a negotiated end to the conflict but these hopes were doomed.

Almost all of us wartime German naval officers, for whatever reasons, simply loved naval life, although whether these reasons made sense must remain questionable. It must also be said that, although the armed forces in Germany had always been proud of being completely apolitical, we who served did not think that we were fighting for an unjust cause. As an aside, I would like to note that most of us seemed to be from inland areas, many from Austria, and there were relatively few from coastal areas, perhaps because maritime people were much more aware of the realities of life at sea than inlanders, whose knowledge of naval service was gained mainly from books.

At the age of 17, however, having been accepted in the *Kriegsmarine* as an officer-aspirant, and with the certainty of a glorious career ahead of me, all such matters were secondary.

Cutter rowing was one of the skills taught in the *Marine-Hitlerjugend.* Some of the crew were new members and had not yet acquired their uniforms. (WH col.)

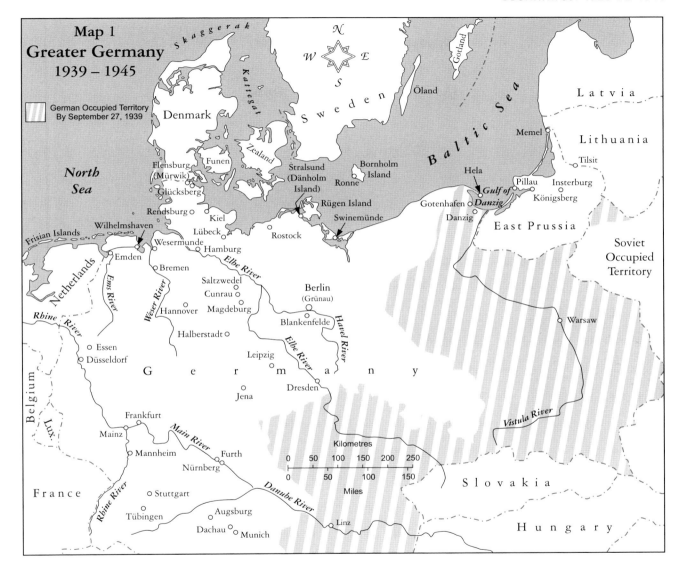

Map 1
Greater Germany
1939 – 1945

German Occupied Territory
By September 27, 1939

After a lot of work, we finally learned to stand at attention in a straight line at the Dänholm. I am the sixth recruit from the left. (WH col.)

FROM BLANKENFELDE TO THE BISMARCK: OCTOBER 1940 TO MAY 1941

On 26 September 1940 I walked with my mother from our house in Blankenfelde to the train station at nearby Dahlewitz to catch a commuter train into Berlin. There, at the Anhalter *Bahnhof* I boarded a train for Stralsund on the Baltic to report for basic training.

This was to be the first of many wartime train journeys and I found that train travel in Germany changed according to the fortunes of war. Inter-city railway carriages had a corridor along one side, feeding into individual compartments for up to six or eight people – sometimes one could stretch out in a compartment, and sometimes there was standing room only in the corridor. The compartment benches in Third Class were wooden but in Second Class they were upholstered. There was no First Class. I don't recall there being a dining car on these trains and we usually took snacks with us. Not yet an officer, only a humble *Offiziersanwärter*, I travelled to Stralsund on a Third Class ticket, sitting on a wooden bench and wearing civilian clothes.

September 1940 was supposedly a good time in the war for Germany. The campaigns in Poland, Norway,

France and the Low Countries had been brought to a successful conclusion, although not without losses, and the only enemy remaining was Britain. There was, however, no euphoria over the recent victories as they did not appear to have led to a satisfactory conclusion – if Germany had won, why was there no peace agreement with Britain? This was typical of the German attitude to the war, as I recall it – there was no great excitement over the "good" times, just as there was no great anxiety when things started to go downhill and disaster loomed. Individuals reacted, on the other hand, according to their personal experiences and/or tragedies. At this point in my life I was excited at finally beginning my long-cherished ambition of a naval career, although my feelings were tempered with a certain apprehension about what was awaiting me in challenges and hardships.

In the *Kriegsmarine* all officer cadets joining at the same time formed what was called, using the English word, a "crew," or class, and each crew was identified by the year and, sometimes, the month of joining – not by the year of graduation as is the case with the United States Navy. I was about to became a member of Crew 40 but ahead of me stretched months and years of training and many hurdles to overcome before I became a commissioned officer. The first obstacle was to get through the *Schiffsstammabteilung*, or boot camp.

If there is one thing that unites western nations, it is the military boot camp, which, contrary to popular belief, is not an exercise in furthering human dignity or the building of self-esteem. The process of basic training is the same in most armed forces – the recruit is isolated from civilian society, subjected to rigid and often not very logical discipline, and taught the basics of service life: how to wear and care for a uniform, how to salute and whom to salute, how to drill and march in formation, how to fire weapons and how to suffer through much strenuous physical exercise. For reasons that I (and probably anyone else who has had the misfortune to undergo this process) have never been able to understand, much of it is accomplished "at the double," accompanied by frequent loud, shouted orders. The essential purpose of this process is to make the recruit realize he is no longer a sloppy, happy-go-lucky civilian but a disciplined and self-sufficient cog in a greater machine, to teach him that he is now part of a community, and that he must learn to live with others in barracks.

I and my fellow officer-aspirants of Crew 40 underwent this process at the 7. *Schiffsstammabteilung*, the naval basic training camp on Dänholm Island near Stralsund.* The camp was a mixture of modern buildings and structures dating back to the First World War, when it had been used for a similar purpose. My training unit was housed in one of the older buildings, which needed more effort to keep clean as we soon discovered, and for which we were pitied by those of our comrades who were fortunate enough to be accommodated in the more modern barracks built around a large drill square. We were housed six to a room, slept in standard military bunks and performed our ablutions in the one large communal washroom in each building. When the time came to clean the barracks, however, I was excused from this fatigue as I provided entertainment for my perspiring comrades by playing current hit songs on my accordion. Meals were taken in a very large mess hall with everyone picking up their food from a line of kitchen staff. There was little enthusiasm for the rather bland food, which we were convinced was spiked with liberal doses of potassium nitrite (or saltpetre) to keep our libidos under control.

Although we were destined to become naval officers, our time at the Dänholm was largely concerned with learning how to be infantrymen. We received field-grey army uniforms which were differentiated only by our naval brass buttons from those worn by the *Heer*, or German army (which had aluminum buttons), and we also received military *Arbeitspäckchen* or fatigue dress. We were, however, supplied with a blue sailor's uniform for formal parades and occasional – but rare – leave in nearby Stralsund. During my time at the Dänholm there

---

* For reasons that are obvious, this basic training organization was never called the *Schiffsstammabteilung* but simply "the Dänholm." As most officers and the sailors in the *Kriegsmarine* passed through it at one time or another, a simple reference to "the Dänholm" was all that was necessary in conversation about this place.

was a shortage of naval instructors and as a result army NCOs served in this capacity, and one of these was in charge of my training unit. Surprisingly – and thankfully – he was rather gentle and rarely lost his composure or temper, in distinct contrast to most of the other instructors.

Behind the city of Stralsund can be seen Dänholm, the island on which was the camp where I received basic training from October to December 1940 at the 7. *Schiffsstammabteilung*, the *Kriegsmarine* training centre. (WH col.)

The standard of 7. *Schiffsstammabteilung.* (WH col.)

Fahne der 7. Schiffsstammabteilung

I am now a sailor in the *Kriegsmarine* although some people, seeing this picture, might suspect I had joined the Vienna Choir Boys. (WH col.)

(Below) I believe I never again looked as warlike as in this picture, which shows me on guard duty. (WH col.)

Playing the accordion gave me the advantage of entertaining my comrades while they cleaned the barracks before inspection – better to play than work. (WH col.)

Our Guard of Honour marches past Admiral Marschall, the Inspector of the *Bildungswesen* (the *Kriegsmarine* training organization) shortly after our oath-taking ceremony on 27 October 1940. We did not find the *Parademarsch* or "goose-step" all that useful at sea. (WH col.)

Enlisted personnel, as well as officer cadets, also underwent basic training at the Dänholm, but during the time I spent there in October and November 1940, we were all officer-aspirants because the two groups never trained at the same time. Our days certainly did not end at 5 P.M. and when they did end, we were much too tired to do anything, particularly to get into trouble. I cannot remember much about what we did in our limited spare time but we probably talked, read, played cards and so on.

Near the end of October we experienced the most important day of our short time in service when we underwent the solemn swearing-in ceremony. This day began with a moving service at the magnificent Nikolai Church in Stralsund, where the navy chaplain delivered a sermon that left a deep impression on me. It contin-

ued with the administration of the oath under the eyes of *Admiral* Wilhelm Marschall in the big drill square.[*] After swearing our loyalty to our country, we finally felt we had become real soldiers.[**]

From this day on, we were entitled to "shore leave" and we received our first pass to get out of camp for a few hours, which we did in our blue dress sailors' uniforms. We went no farther than Stralsund and did little more than go to a restaurant and have a good meal,

---

[*] *Admiral* Wilhelm Marschall (1886-1976) joined the Imperial German Navy as a cadet in 1906 and won the *Pour Le Mérite*, the highest German decoration during the First World War, as a U-boat commander. He rose steadily in rank and by 1941 was inspector of training in the *Kriegsmarine*. He held a series of important operational commands from 1941 to 1944 and survived the war.

[**] The German custom is to use the word *Soldaten* to include not only members of the army but also the navy.

because at this point we were very aware of the importance of proper behaviour while ashore and, therefore, the consumption of alcohol and the pursuit of females were considered rather dangerous and (reluctantly) avoided.

On 4 December 1940, my training unit had its final inspection by the commandant of the Dänholm, and after a satisfactory performance, we handed in our infantry uniforms and equipment and packed our bags. A large and very happy farewell party marked the end of this, the first chapter of our service careers, and then those of us in the engineering branch boarded a special train to Flensburg to begin our First Workshop Course.

It took us 28 hours to travel the 210 miles to Flensburg-Mürwik, where we were to receive our initial technical training. We were met by a *Leutnant* and some sailors and ordered to load ourselves and our luggage onto trucks for the trip to the nearby *Marineschule*, the German naval academy and the equivalent of the United States Naval Academy at Annapolis. Our Workshop Course was not actually part of the *Marineschule* curriculum; we just used its facilities. Our quarters were on board the passenger liner *Caribia* moored in Flensburg harbour, and this was typical of the wartime *Kriegsmarine*, as most of Germany's passenger vessels were tied up in various ports to serve as accommodation ships for the personnel of a rapidly expanding service. For us, however, living on a passenger liner was a welcome change from the drafty huts at the Dänholm and I had a cabin (not very large) all to myself!

The *Caribia* in better times as a passenger liner of the Hapag Line. (WH col.)

The first days of our Workshop Course were occupied in getting familiar with our new environment. If we thought life was going to get any easier, we quickly learned that our time at the Dänholm had actually been rather carefree and it had now come to an end. The Workshop Course was intended to put both our intellect and technical dexterity to the test. The daily routine consisted of lectures in the morning and workshop practice in the afternoon, interrupted periodically by sports, rowing, infantry drills, watchkeeping (or guard duty) and other activities regarded as necessary for the proper education of a young officer. The morning lessons began with rather basic lectures in physics that most of us knew already from high school, but soon progressed to more advanced topics such as marine engines, boilers, turbines, pumps, generators and the characteristics of electricity. In addition, we were taught how to behave on board a warship, received lectures on German naval history, and were also compelled to attend certain social events at which our behaviour was closely observed.

There was much practical work on the curriculum. Our first experience at the metalworking shop involved being issued a set of files and being told to produce a perfect cube out of a ball of steel, which was quite a shock for those of us who had more theoretical than practical backgrounds. The eight weeks of the Workshop Course were evenly divided into training in the metalworking shop, welding shop, blacksmith's shop and finally a shop where we learned to operate a lathe. All the pieces we produced had to be designed, documented with

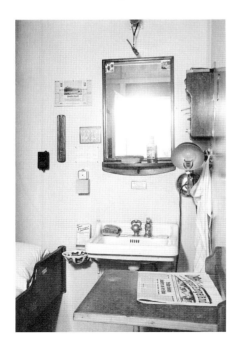

After three months in the navy, I finally had my own cabin aboard the *Caribia* in Flensburg, where we started our first workshop training in December 1940. Spartan, but mine! (WH col.)

For the first time I am posing in naval dress, although still an ordinary sailor. (WH col.)

Classroom lectures during our assignment to the first workshop training from 14 December 1940 to 16 February 1941 by the officer in charge of our group, *Leutnant (Ing)* Löblich. (WH col.)

drawings and certified by the group officer. All of it, of course, was interesting and satisfying work although it required much labour.

If we thought that long hours spent doing military drill were behind us, we were rudely reminded on the first day at the *Marineschule* that we were in the navy. While we were in the workshop, our group officer inspected our cabins on the *Caribia* and was not happy about what he found, as we had not been living up to the standard expected of would-be officers – to put it plainly, our cabins were a mess. The result was that we now became acquainted with the hoary old German naval tradition known as the *Maskenball* (masquerade ball) or "Signal Flag Lucie."

This involved having to report to the group officer on the deck of the *Caribia* with all our bed linen neatly folded for inspection, then being given five minutes to return to our cabins, remake our bunks, and be back on deck in work clothing. We then got another five minutes to report back in pyjamas, followed by another five minutes to be back in blue uniform, and finally five minutes to report in gym clothes. Slightly out of breath, we realized that, if we wished to become officers in the *Kriegsmarine*, discipline and neatness were important matters. "Flag Lucie" was an off-duty entertainment we were subjected to quite frequently, often for small digressions committed by various individuals, as the ruling principle was "one for all and all for one."

It did not help that on 20 December 1940 we received a week of home leave. This was, of course, the highlight of our naval careers so far, but on our return to Flensburg we apparently had, as it was pointedly made clear to us, reverted to our sloppy civilian ways again and the appropriate remedies were immediately applied.

During the winter of 1940-1941 the weather was not always very pleasant and sometimes the ice in Flensburg harbor was so thick that the boat service from the *Caribia* to the shore had to be suspended. One of our watchkeeping duties consisted of spreading salt over the ice-covered expanse of the landing quay at the *Marineschule*, a job we could have done without.

Halfway through the Workshop Course we held our *Bergfest*, a ceremony to celebrate having reached the peak of the mountain, and the fact that we could now look forward to an easier descent. On this occasion *Admiral* Marschall again visited us and delivered a speech about the required traits of a naval officer. To be a leader, he told us, we had to acquire three things: experience, judgement and instinct. The first could only be gained in the practical environment provided by service on a warship – and this would therefore be the next part of our training – while the other two would develop after many years in various commands. The admiral also emphasized the importance of a sound relationship between an officer and his subordinates. It was necessary that *both* sides display absolute respect for the other and *both* sides had to accept the fact that no human being is perfect.

After this professional and spiritual enlightenment, however, the powers-that-be decided that we still need-

At New Year's Eve our officers displayed some surprising human attributes for such ogres. (WH col.)

ed some physical strengthening and we immediately received more infantry training. The infantry drills of the Workshop Course, for which we were issued rifles, made us long for the rather harmless exercises we had carried out on the Dänholm, and after some exposure to them and various rugged sports, we were usually ready to collapse. Dance parties, visits to the theatre and informal conversations with our officers, though, did help to make us feel human again.

In the middle of February 1941 our First Workshop Course came to an end when, after a final and satisfactory inspection, we were promoted to *Kadett* (naval cadet). We now turned in our well-thumbed textbooks and had a grand farewell party because the next chapter of our training was sea duty.

In peacetime, the tradition had been that, following their initial studies, cadets served for several months on board one of the full-sail training barks, *Gorch Fock*, *Horst Wessel* or *Leo Albert Schlageter*, which sometimes made long cruises to foreign ports. For Crew 40, unfortunately, the war meant that our seagoing time would be shorter and spent on operational warships. Of course, no one asked for our preferences about our choice of vessel and it was therefore with great delight that I learned on 16 February 1940 that I was to report on board the destroyer *Hans Lody* (*Z.10*)* at Wesermünde near Bremen. I was elated about being assigned to a destroyer since we

---

* The destroyer *Hans Lody* was named after an intelligence officer of the Imperial German Navy who had been executed by the British as a spy in the First World War. This vessel survived the Second World War and was turned over to the Royal Navy in 1945.

My first seagoing assignment, on 16 February 1941, was to the destroyer *Hans Lody*. (WH col.)

Kadetten always preferred smaller warships because of the closer and less formal relationship of the crew than on a *Dickschiff*.*

Late in the evening of a very wintry day I reported to the *Hans Lody* at Wesermünde with a comrade from the Workshop Course. I well remember being somewhat awestruck when I first saw her tied up at the dock – finally, my childhood dreams had come true and I was about to go to sea. I was fascinated by the activities on the ship, its noise, the steam escaping from somewhere and also the unique smell of a warship. This initial impression was so strong that it has remained with me

for the rest of my life. Decades later when I drove each morning to work along Lakeshore Boulevard in Toronto and passed the Second World War Canadian destroyer HMCS *Haida** at her dock at Ontario Place, I would get a strange but strong urge to turn off and show up for duty.

Stepping on board the *Hans Lody* and reporting to the officer of the watch was a rather informal affair but we were immediately made aware of the insignificance of our status when we were turned over to a petty officer, who showed us to the *Kadett* quarters and then left. Rather tired, I stumbled over some sleeping bodies, and

---

* Literally "thick ship" or big ship, meaning a battleship, battlecruiser or cruiser.

* HMCS *Haida*, the last Tribal Class destroyer in the world, was a museum ship on display at a berth in Toronto for many years. She has since been moved to Hamilton, Ontario.

Wesermünde was a major naval base although this picture shows another aspect, its beach. (WH col.)

and later that evening we cadets celebrated our recent promotion on the after deck and invited some of the ship's officers as well. Even the commanding officer, *Korvettenkapitän* Werner Pfeiffer, joined us and at midnight used the opportunity to start celebrating his birthday. It was 2 A.M. before we fell asleep but the next morning our cadet officer, *Oberleutnant z.S.* Carlheinz Vorsteher, who was also the ship's gunnery officer, thought it prudent to get us back to life with a two-hour session of strenuous sport.*

If we thought that being on an operational warship was going to be easier than the Dänholm or the Workshop Course, we were soon disabused of that notion. We *Kadetten* quickly learned that service on a warship was absolutely no excuse for neglecting to keep ourselves and our surroundings neat and tidy. When I had first looked at the size of my locker, I wondered how I could get all my stuff into it, but in the end I squeezed it all in – but not according to naval standards. *Oberleutnant*

with effort located a hammock and a place to string it up. I just wanted to sleep.

We *Kadetten* were accommodated in the large aft sailors' messdeck and, like many German sailors, we slept in hammocks. Around the periphery of the messdeck were nooks with tables accommodating six to eight men and one was assigned to our group of six *Kadetten*, two aspiring engineer officers and four aspiring *Seeoffiziere* or executive branch cadets, the latter having arrived straight from the Dänholm.

The next morning we were kept busy running from one officer to another to inform each of our existence. We were then sent ashore to the station to pick up our *Seesäcke* or duffel bags, which had been left there the night before. Back on board we were assigned our duties

---

* In the *Kriegsmarine*, the junior ranks of the *Seeoffiziere*, or executive branch officers, added the qualifier "*zur See*" after their rank. In this book, the abbreviation "*z.S.*" will be used for this qualifier. Engineer officers were denominated by the abbreviation "(*Ing*)" for "*Ingenieur*" after their rank.

z.S. Vorsteher inspected our lockers and was not happy about what he discovered. My comrades being found similarly negligent, we spent an hour being chased around the *Lody* until we were totally out of breath – all in the name of officer education.

Untidy lockers were not our only transgression. There was a standing order on the destroyer for the crew not to leave any personal items in their jackets when they hung them up but we only found out about this regulation when *Oberleutnant z.S.* Vorsteher searched our jackets and removed their contents. We got them back, one by one, by a process similar to "Signal Flag Lucie," receiving one item at a time from Vorsteher after having reported to him in a different uniform. At the Dänholm or the Workshop Course, we had become inured to such rituals but we could not understand why we had to undergo them on board a fighting warship.

Not that the *Hans Lody* made a very great contribution to the German naval war effort. After my arrival, it took many weeks before this ship even moved for the first time as there were seemingly endless problems with the destroyer's machinery, which was repaired, only to be followed by tests and further problems. The *Hans Lody* was a Type 34A destroyer, the first class of destroyers constructed by the *Kriegsmarine* after the lifting of the tonnage restrictions imposed by the 1919 Treaty of Versailles. The Type 34 vessels were 374 feet in length, 37 feet in beam, displaced 3,190 tons and had a crew of 283 officer and sailors. They were armed with five 12.7 cm (5-inch) guns in single turrets, four 3.7 cm and six 2 cm anti-aircraft guns, and eight 53.3 cm (21-inch)

torpedoes. Since I was an engineer *Kadett*, however, I was more concerned with the propulsion machinery and this consisted of six Benson steam boilers and two Wagner geared turbines which nominally gave the *Lody* a top speed of 36 knots.

The high-pressure Benson boilers represented experimental propulsion plants and were notorious for their temperamental operation and poor service record. A few years ago I acquired a copy of a 1941 technical assessment, done by the *Kriegsmarine* itself, of the quality of German surface warship design, and it was disastrous. Our destroyers were, on average, unserviceable about 42% of the time they were in commission and of the twelve Type 34 ships in our navy, only four were ready for sea at any given time. We engineering *Kadetten* on the *Lody* were uncomfortably aware of the problems posed by the Benson boiler and of the rather unpleasant consequences of any leaks or damage to our steam pipes – a pin-size hole in a pipe would produce a jet of high-powered steam that would go right through a human body in its way. We were therefore very alert when on duty, as were all the engine room personnel.

Our daily routine was a constant succession of watches in the engine rooms, cleaning and maintenance of the propulsion plant, lectures, tests and exams, sleeping, eating, interrupted sometimes by sports or infantry drills and the occasional recuperation provided by rare visits ashore. On a warship there are no weekends, holidays or nine-to-five days, and our shipboard life was dominated by the requirement to learn, and learn. At one time the navy had obviously discovered that keeping clean the

Map 2
Western Europe,
The Mediterranean
And Norway

NOTE: Map Depicts Modern National Borders

floor plates in the engine rooms of a warship was not a very pleasant job and we believed that this was about the same time they invented the *Kadett*, because cleaning floor plates occupied an inordinate amount of our time. Guess who received this dirty job and who was required to climb into a boiler and clean the insides? I remember that, while cleaning the boilers, I had to emerge every ten minutes to let the soles of my shoes cool down before returning to work, so hot was the interior. By trading some watches with a stoker I was, however, able to have two half days free so that I could go ashore to celebrate my 18th birthday with my mother, who travelled from Blankenfelde to Wesermünde for the occasion.

On board the *Lody* we were also taught that part of our officer education was to learn how to drink properly. We did not acquire this knowledge, as we would have liked, on shore in civilian establishments, nor did we learn it in the wardroom, the officer's mess of the destroyer. Being humble *Kadetten*, the lowest form of life on board (so we were often told), we were not permitted the privileges of that establishment. Our training in this respect was not neglected, however, because one evening *Oberleutnant z.S.* Vorsteher appeared in our mess, accompanied by sailors carrying cases of beer, and invited us to drink with him. There was no way of avoiding this activity as it was a direct order from a superior and therefore bottle after bottle was consumed until Vorsteher was the only one still functioning, and not a few of us *Kadetten* were resting comfortably under the table. But *Oberleutnant z.S.* Vorsteher was an officer without mercy and early next morning he scrutinized each of us

carefully, and if there were any signs of dysfunction, we were addressed in very unpleasant terms. These sessions, which occurred more than once, fell under the heading of "necessary officer training" and valuable training it was, because we in the *Kriegsmarine* were proud of the fact that we were about the only large navy in the world of which there was rarely a complaint concerning the behaviour of its officers and men ashore in foreign ports.

In the middle of March 1941 the *Lody* finally got up steam and left Wesermünde for Kiel. I found this journey interesting as we went through the very scenic Kiel

A training session to teach us how to drink into the wee hours and still be functional at 0530 the next morning. At the back on the right is our cadet officer, *Oberleutnant* z.S. Vorsteher. (WH col.)

Canal to get from the North Sea into the Baltic. Unfortunately I also found out that, while sailors on deck could admire whatever sights came before their eyes, as a stoker I was confined most of the time to the engine rooms which did not have scuttles, or portholes. For engineering personnel at sea it was six hours on watch and six off, but the latter hours were spent taking care of the rest of our needs which – if we wanted to eat – included peeling many potatoes.

On German warships there was a system of individual small units (the equivalent to a British or Canadian navy "mess") usually consisting of the men at each table in the living quarters. Each mess peeled their own potatoes which then were transferred to the *Kombüse* or galley in a net container clearly labelled with the mess's identity. After cooking, this net with the potatoes was brought back by a mess member together with the remainder of the meal – meat, soup, fish, sausages or whatever. The amount of food we consumed was therefore to some extent determined by the industry we devoted to peeling potatoes.

At Kiel our ship was subjected to a seemingly endless series of technical inspections and tests in dock, in a shipyard or at sea. In between I had a few days shore leave during which I visited my grandparents on my mother's side, and also spent some time with my parents, who made a visit. I remember that, during this leave, an evening at the opera was a welcome diversion. However, all was not so pleasant as in Kiel we *Kadetten* were subjected to an exhausting two-hour infantry exercise complete with full battle dress and rifles as the very

reasonable compensation for one *Kadett* having misbehaved while ashore.

Having at long last got her machinery in working order, the *Hans Lody* now started to carry out exercises in the Baltic with two other destroyers, *Karl Galster* and *Hermann Schoemann*. While undergoing this training, we wore leather gear, gas masks and life preservers and it involved simulated torpedo attacks, target shooting with our main guns, ASW (Anti-Submarine Warfare) attacks with depth charges and formation exercises. After dropping depth charges we usually came to a stop, lowered all boats and provided personnel on deck with potato nets and waste paper baskets – all in the quest for a delicious meal provided by hundreds of fish, floating on the surface either killed or stunned by the blast. Hits by the "enemy" were simulated on our ship and I found myself carrying "terribly mutilated bodies" on stretchers to the ship's sick bay. I was amazed how much the massive machinery in the engine rooms shook when the ship fired a full salvo from its 12.7 cm main guns. I also had to struggle with my first attacks of seasickness, but they never prevented me from carrying out my duties – I just delivered up my offering to Neptune and became hungry again. These exercises were interrupted by a brief visit to Danzig, where I took the opportunity to see some relatives.

Just before Easter in April 1941, we returned to Wesermünde, and as the *Lody* entered the harbour, we passed the sad sight of the large and once proud ocean liner *Bremen* which had been reduced to a burned-out hulk after a crew member had set it on fire. We now

The destroyer *Karl Galster* practising manoeuvres with *Hans Lody* in the Baltic in the spring of 1941. (WH col.)

commenced another period of repairs, as defective machinery was removed and replaced with new equipment. The Easter holidays were recognized with a general easing of duties and additional goodies for our meals, but holidays they were not, and I remember having to stand watch outside the ship's arrest cell! During the evening of Easter Monday, however, I was finally allowed ashore and saw a performance of *Die Fledermaus* at the opera.

We *Kadetten* now commenced writing a series of examinations leading towards our eventual promotion to *Fähnrich* (midshipman). While writing these tests, we were required to wear dress uniform, which puzzled us,

but by now, having been six months in service, we knew better than to complain.

Towards the end of April 1941, *Hans Lody* returned to Kiel, to the crew's deep disappointment, as we had all hoped that we would go into action in the North Sea. In Kiel I was sad to see the widespread destruction British bombers had recently inflicted on the city and I wondered what the cities in England looked like. Again we engaged in various tests and exercises and practised more battle evolutions, mostly in very heavy seas that made it impossible to get from the engine rooms to the aft messdecks without getting drenched. Visits to places like Rønne on

Hans Lody exercising in the Baltic, being followed by the destroyers *Karl Galster* and *Hermann Schoemann* in the spring of 1941. (WH col.)

A rough sea with winds of force 8 in the Baltic in the spring of 1941. No wonder I had my first bouts of seasickness! (WH col.)

Our ship's mascot, "Norge," who was spoiled by the entire crew of the *Hans Lody*. (WH col.)

the delightful Danish Island of Bornholm and the harbours in Swinemünde and the Island of Rügen were a pleasant change from both training and rough seas.

The war, meanwhile, had heated up again in the spring of 1941 when German forces were deployed in southern Europe and North Africa to assist our Italian allies. Although we could follow the progress of the campaigns in the Mediterranean theatre, it all seemed rather remote to us and we wondered when we would get a chance to go into action. Our opportunity finally came on 19 May 1941 when the *Lody* was ordered to raise steam and proceed to sea.

Just before we left Kiel I had the good luck to see my father, who was now serving as an *Unteroffizier* in a naval anti-aircraft battery in Denmark. He had some leave and came on board and met both my captain and my group training officer. I suppose he was just checking up on me!

On 19 May, we slipped from our anchorage after night had fallen and at 11 P.M. rendezvoused with the battleship *Bismarck*, the heavy cruiser *Prinz Eugen* and the destroyers *Z 23* and *Friedrich Eckoldt*, and then set a course due north. In the darkness the shadowy silhouettes of the big ships made them look like threatening ghosts. In the open sea we assumed cruising formation with *Hans Lody* leading, *Z 23* on starboard and *Friedrich Eckoldt* on port with the big ships side by side in the middle, the whole force steaming at 27 knots. I have learned from postwar reading that our force was sighted by a Swedish cruiser on 20 May but I have no recollection of this being reported in the ship at the time, and, of course, I would have had no realization of the significance of this event.

Late next morning (20 May 1941) we approached Bergen in Norway and for the first time I saw the majestic mountains and fjords I had read so much about. But of course, as usual, most of the time I was cooped up in the engine room. The destroyers moved deep into the scenic harbour at Bergen to take on fuel and water. Again, from postwar reading I have learned that our ships were photographed by a British reconnaissance aircraft on this day but we were not aware of it at the time. At 1900 hours we moved back to the area where the big ships had anchored and continued our journey. By now, the weather had turned misty and windy.

Next morning at 0500 hours the *Bismarck* released her escort destroyers and we altered course for Trondheim in Norway, where we arrived about five hours later. Once again we took on fuel and water to be ready for

In May 1941 when my destroyer accompanied the battleship *Bismarck* on her first (and last) operation, she was one of the most powerful warships in existence. The top picture is an official photo of the ship. Before her first mission her hull was camouflaged, as is evident on the pictures I took of her in the Baltic. The view of her bow gives a good idea of the enormous size of this ship. (WH col.)

(Above) Distant views of the *Bismarck* taken after the *Lody* and two other destroyers joined her and the *Prinz Eugen* to escort the two ships out into the Atlantic. (WH col.)

The picture above is an official photo of the heavy cruiser *Prinz Eugen* taken after she was commissioned. At left she can be seen accompanying the *Bismarck* on her last mission, and has also acquired new camouflage. It has often been claimed that these warships were difficult to distinguish at a distance, something neither I nor my comrades found hard to do, but then maybe our eyes were trained. (WH col.)

further orders. In the meantime we were given leave to explore the city and we were also given some Norwegian money. Except for some coffee and cake, however, there was nothing to buy. But a warm sun was shining and the population did not display any animosity towards us, so it was a very pleasant experience. We were looking forward to another day of leisure when on 24 May our hopes were rudely dashed with the shout, "Be ready to depart at 0100 hours!" In the afternoon we learned that the *Bismarck* had sunk the British battlecruiser HMS *Hood* but had herself been slightly damaged. We were now prepared, if required, to sortie from Trondheim and bring the *Bismarck* back to Norway, but when I came back on watch next morning, I checked the compass and it showed a course of 190 degrees or nearly due south, which meant we were on our way home.

The sea became so rough that day that movement across the deck was dangerous. In the afternoon of 24 May we returned to Bergen and as we approached the city we were overwhelmed by the beauty and peace of the sight in front of us. Someone mumbled, "To live here…," which expressed everyone's feelings. After a short while, however, our tender returned from the city and almost immediately our propellers started to turn again.

We now travelled through the inner passage between the Norwegian coast and the islands, and it was almost like a river journey. Sometimes we seemed to be surrounded by mountains, but the Norwegian pilots we brought on board knew their business and always found the correct route. They left us near Stavanger and, on the afternoon of the next day (25 May 1941), while passing through the Skagerrak, the other two destroyers headed for Kiel while we continued on to our home port of Wesermünde. On our way we learned that the beautiful and mighty *Bismarck* had been sunk by superior British naval forces and we felt terribly guilty for not having been there to defend her. In this connection it is worth mentioning a story widely known in German naval circles during the war. It concerns an officer who also wanted to protect the *Bismarck* but failed, through no fault of his own, to do so.

Kapitänleutnant Herbert Wohlfarth was a well known officer in our submarine service whose nickname was "*Parzival*" after the heroic medieval knight.* In the spring of 1941, Wohlfarth (whose name literally translates into "welfare") took over a new U-boat, *U-556*, and was at Gotenhafen working up at the same time as the *Bismarck*. The story goes that one day when both vessels were exercising in the Baltic, Wohlfarth signalled the captain of the battleship: "CO to CO. You have a mighty fine ship." He then dived the *U-556*, came up on the other side of the *Bismarck*, and signalled a second time: "CO to CO. Question: Can you do that too?" He received a serious dressing down for his impertinence from *Kapitän z.S.* Ernst Lindemann, the captain of the *Bismarck*, but the two later became friends after Lindemann sent his

---

* Herbert Wohlfarth (1915-1982), a member of Crew 33, was a very successful U-boat commander in the early years of the war. On 31 June 1941, however, his command, *U-556*, was sunk by the Royal Navy although Wohlfarth survived to spend the remainder of the war in a Canadian prison camp.

During our escort operation, the three destroyers needed to refuel and we therefore put into Bergen in Norway on 20 May 1941 for that purpose. *Friedrich Eckoldt* and *Z 23* are following *Hans Lody*. *Bismarck* can be seen in the distance. (WH col.)

ship's band to play at a ceremony involving *U-556*. In return, Wohlfarth prepared a medieval-looking document which stated that his boat would always guard the battleship from all enemies, complete with a drawing of "*Parzival*" deflecting torpedoes from the *Bismarck* with his sword. Lindemann liked this document so much that he had it framed and hung it in the battleship's wardroom.

In one of those ironic incidents that happen in war, Wohlfarth was returning from his first patrol in *U-556* when, during the evening of 25 May 1941, his bridge lookouts sighted two large warships immediately ahead. Wohlfarth crash dived to periscope depth and when he looked through his periscope, found himself staring at the British aircraft carrier HMS *Ark Royal* and the battlecruiser HMS *Renown* steaming directly at him. Unfortunately, Wohlfarth had expended all his torpedoes and could do nothing but watch helplessly as the two enemy warships passed by him just a few hundred yards away. That evening the *Ark Royal* launched an air strike on the *Bismarck* which crippled the German ship's steering gear and ultimately doomed her to destruction. Wohlfarth followed the two British ships on the surface to become a distant spectator of this action and could actually see the *Bismarck's* gun flashes before he was forced to turn away for France as he was short of fuel. Such are the fortunes that fate sometimes has in store.

To return to the *Hans Lody*, after our arrival in Wesermünde, we *Kadetten* were warned of another inspection on the following day which required an immediate trip to the barber. This inspection – really a test – involved

us reciting what we had learned and we passed with flying colours. This marked the end of our assignment to the *Hans Lody* and we packed our things and said farewell to the many friends we had made, seamen as well as officers. We were all somewhat sad to leave a ship that had been our home for the last three months and envied those that could look forward to seeing more action in her. After leaving the *Lody* I sent my bag straight to Flensburg-Mürwik, where I had to report to the *Marineschule* – but only after five glorious days of leave at home in Blankenfelde!

After having been released by the *Bismarck*, the three destroyers returned to Norway and on 24 May tied up in Trondheim to wait for further developments. Here we enjoy some sunshine and rest. (WH col.)

On 27 September 1941, we graduated from the *Marineschule*. The picture shows one of the four companies forming Crew 40, my class. I am the *Fähnrich* at the far left of the seated front row. (WH col.)

THE ROTE SCHLOSS AND THE U-BOOT-WAFFE: JUNE 1941 TO MARCH 1942

3

On 3 June 1941, full of my mother's good home cooking, I arrived at the *Marineschule* at Flensburg-Mürwik, my country's naval academy, where every German naval officer since 1910 had received his academic training.* The *Marineschule* was a ten-minute drive from Flensburg, and although my fellow engineer officer cadets of Crew 40 had used its facilities for our First Workshop Course the previous winter, we were now formally enrolled as students at this august institution.

When I first entered the main building, an imposing brick structure often referred to as the *Rote Schloss* or red castle, I was overwhelmed by the sense of tradition emanating from the many pictures and plaques along the halls honouring the memory of former students. The *Rote Schloss* was located close to the Baltic and at the opposite end of the parade ground very wide stairs

led down to a 200-yard waterfront with its boating and swimming facilities. Once I saw this, I decided that no matter what lay ahead I was going to enjoy my time at the academy.

Very quickly, however, our enthusiasm was dampened when we learned that, due to the war, there was a vastly increased demand for naval officers and the old cadet quarters were too small to accommodate the greatly-expanded student population. Adjacent to the main grounds of the school, a new compound of simple one-storey barracks had recently been constructed and that was where I was assigned my living quarters, a room that I was to share with three fellow cadets. But this new accommodation block was clean and modern and our disappointment at not being able to live at the *Schloss* quickly faded.

Crew 40, my class, was subdivided into groups of approximately 40 students, all from the same branch, whether *Seeoffiziere*, engineers, weapons officers, etc. Each group was under the control of a group leader, an officer who was either an *Oberleutnant* or a senior *Leutnant* and who seemed to have been selected, not so much because of his outstanding service record, but

---

* Completed in 1910 to train officers for the Imperial German Navy, the *Marineschule* at Mürwik, just outside Flensburg, is the German Annapolis. In May 1945 it briefly became the seat of the German government, which was transferred there from Berlin. Its spacious grounds and lovely buildings were not destroyed or damaged during the war and today all officer cadets for the *Bundesmarine*, the modern German navy, receive their training at the *Marineschule*.

Two views of *Marine-schule* Flensburg-Mürwik, Germany's "Annapolis," where I commenced my academic training on 3 June 1941. (WH col.)

because he possessed the kind of personality that made him a suitable mentor of the young. Long before we arrived at the school, common wisdom among engineering cadets held that, if one wanted to enjoy life at the *Schloss*, one should avoid ending up in a group led by *Oberleutnant (Ing)* Heinz-Günther Stockfleht, who had a reputation for being able to make a cadet's time at the academy a living hell.

Well, I ended up with tall, lanky *Oberleutnant* Stockfleht as my group officer, and although he would make us undergo "Flag Lucie" at the slightest violation of the rules, Stockfleht proved to be an excellent teacher. He was a strict disciplinarian but an even-tempered man

and, in contrast to the well-known service practice of establishing authority by screaming, he never raised his voice, but had perfected an icy stare that often had a far more devastating effect on a miscreant *Kadett*. Such was *Oberleutnant* Stockfleht's quality that by the end of our time at the *Schloss* every cadet in our group would have gone through fire for him and he was one of the most respected officers I ever served with during my time in the *Kriegsmarine*.

Our days at the *Schloss* were occupied by lectures, all given by experts in their field. The curriculum was geared to the different branches of the service – which meant that we engineers did not learn anything about

The wartime officer cadet crews had grown so large that the prewar buildings of *Marineschule* could no longer accommodate all the students and a group of modern barracks were built, called the *Memellager*. This is where I was quartered during my time there. (WH col.)

Drafting lessons were a minor part of our education. (WH col.)

weapons and navigation while future *Seeoffiziere* were kept ignorant of the intricacies of marine machinery. Most of the classrooms were in the main building, and the technical classrooms in which engineering subjects were taught, such as mechanical theory, drafting, electrical installation, chemistry, physics, mathematics, ship design and so on, were well appointed. Non-engineering classes in naval and military history, leadership, social behaviour and sports were conducted by our group officers. We were kept very busy but one bright feature was that we no longer had to do military drills.

The cadet day began with a roll call on the parade square between the barracks, followed by a good breakfast. Then came the morning classes, each lasting about 45 minutes with 15-minute breaks between. During the lunch break, which lasted an hour, I was usually able to squeeze in a much-needed and useful 15-minute cat-nap on my bunk. Afternoons were a mixture of classes and sporting activities like sailing and rowing, where

my experience in the *Marine-Hitlerjugend* proved useful and afforded me a certain authority, and swimming, diving or team games in the water. Instruction in firing handguns and handling the officer's ceremonial sword provided a welcome break in the round of lectures. In peacetime, cadets had also received instruction in driving a car (in those days driving was not as common a skill in Germany as it was in North America) and horse-back riding, but these interesting occupations were now considered unnecessary frills. Our classroom instruction was also varied with group trips to shipyards and to factories manufacturing naval weapons and equipment.

Evenings were mainly taken up with study and preparing for the following day's lectures but we did have a modest private life as well as the occasional evening leave in nearby Flensburg. This activity, however, was limited by our meagre cadet's pay. There were a number of nice dining establishments in Flensburg where one could meet young ladies for drinks and conversation, and naval cadets were regarded as acceptable because Flensburg's social life was heavily influenced by the presence of a large naval community. Some of my classmates annoyed me with their boastful and exaggerated tales of easy conquests among the local young women, which they recounted in colourful detail and which were most likely complete fabrications.

In August 1941, most of us *Kadetten* having passed a series of exams, we were promoted to the rank of *Fähnrich* or midshipman. This meant exchanging our sailor's uniform for a made-to-measure officer's dark blue uniform complete with white shirt, tie and a peaked cap. We were now entitled to wear an impressive accessory, the ceremonial naval dirk, with our uniforms. For summertime we received a white uniform but, regardless of the weather, when ashore we always had to wear grey gloves. As yet, we had no officer's stripes on our sleeves; silver epaulettes on our shoulders were our badge of rank. This was a momentous and important event for every member of Crew 40 for it meant that we had moved an important step closer to commissioned rank and – at a considerable distance on a foggy evening – might even be mistaken for officers by those unfamiliar with naval uniform and rank insignia.

There were actually two ranks of midshipman, and once we got accustomed to our new and exalted status, we began to look forward to the next step, becoming an *Oberfähnrich*, or senior midshipman. The *Fähnrich* wore his dirk without a *Portepee,* an embroidered knot on the hilt, whereas the *Oberfähnrich* was entitled to this mark of status (chief petty officers also wore the *Portepee* on their dirks). Apparently, the tradition was, and I believe it, that the word of honour of a man who wore the *Portepee* was accepted at face value but, of course, he was also obligated to keep it when given. Midshipmen, when serving on a warship, carried out the duties of an *Unteroffizier* or petty officer, whereas senior midshipmen occasionally acted as junior commissioned officers. I was now a *Fähnrich (Ing)* and proudly presented myself in my new uniform to my parents when they showed up in Flensburg to check on the progress of their only child. A number of our classmates who failed their exams found to their dismay that they had to con-

tinue wearing the sailor's uniform but most had a second chance to redeem themselves by writing the exams again and so remain members of Crew 40.

Our promotion resulted in some rather undisciplined merriment on the part of Crew 40 because it was a tradition at the *Schloss* that each crew marked this event by playing some ingenious prank. The day after we became midshipman, the faculty officers on their way to breakfast found that the mess furniture had been neatly placed on top of their mess building with an effigy in an old sailor's uniform hanging from a nearby yardarm. This wasn't our only prank. One of our faculty officers, known to be a heavy drinker, awoke one morning after a long night in the officers' mess, in his room but sleeping in a dinghy instead of his missing bed. On another occasion the big bronze statue of the famous *Admiral* Bromme, which stood at the foot of the steps from the

Our promotion meant we exchanged our enlisted sailor's uniform for one more closely approximating that of an officer, complete with jacket, tie and peaked cap. Our old uniform was ceremoniously "hung" on the roof of the *Memellager*. (WH col.)

On 1 August 1941, my crew was promoted from *Kadett* to *Fähnrich*. In our exuberance mischief was in order and the next morning the officers of the *Memellager* found their wardroom furniture had been moved to the roof of their building. (WH col.)

shore to the main building, disappeared to be replaced by a sign explaining that the admiral had "gone ashore."*

Actually our pranks were rather harmless compared to those played by other crews. A story went round that a prewar crew, on the occasion of its graduation, found the moving vans of the commandant of the school, who was being replaced, standing at the top of the above-mentioned steps leading down to the water, and pushed them slightly, so that they rolled down into Flensburg Bay. It was said in my time at the academy in 1941 that this crew was still paying for their fun. On another occasion, the senior officers and guests at a festive dinner in

the first floor dining room were bombarded through the open windows by projectiles of meat salad fired from the ancient naval guns which decorated the grounds of the *Schloss*. These more elaborate pranks, however, took place in peacetime – Crew 40 was a wartime crew and we behaved with more decorum.

As newly-minted midshipmen we were all on top of the world and had to prove it. I particularly remember a group trip to Hamburg to visit a factory, a trip made memorable for me not so much for its educational experience as its social value. Having arrived in the city in the morning, we were scheduled to return to Flensburg in the evening and we spent much time discussing the opportunities available in the free hours between the end of our official duties and our departure. In a rather dubious fit of self-confidence I assured my comrades that I would appear that evening at the train station in the company of an attractive woman.

My attempts to live up to this boast proved unavailing. Late in the afternoon while sitting alone in a famous cafe on the shore of the Alster, a scenic body of water in the centre of Hamburg, I contemplated my foolish words and wondered how to get out of this situation without looking a complete fool. As I pondered my dilemma, I noticed a somewhat older but very pretty woman sitting reading alone at a nearby table. I gathered all my courage, walked over and asked if I could sit down for a moment. The lady didn't seem to mind so I sat down and explained my problem to her. She listened attentively, and with obvious amusement, so I asked whether she would have the time and the goodwill to

* *Admiral* Karl Rudolf Bromme (1804-1860) commanded the first German naval fleet which was created by the states of the North German Federation to fight against superior Danish naval forces during the conflict waged in 1848-1849 over possession of the Duchy of Schleswig-Holstein. He may rightly be called the "father of the German navy."

help me out by accompanying me to the station. She took pity on a troubled young naval *Fähnrich* wearing her country's uniform and, to my utter amazement, agreed with a smile to accompany me. When we arrived at the station, I basked in the envious looks of my friends at this clear sign of triumph

Here I am with the lady who saved me from my embarrassing boast. (WH col.)

on the part of an almost-officer. Unfortunately, after this nicely staged encounter, I never saw the lady again.

At the *Rote Schloss*, we were required to attend a number of arranged social events where our behaviour was carefully observed and evaluated. Good manners were regarded as a hallmark of the naval officer and it was simply astounding just how much time was spent on teaching us proper etiquette. As a result, we soon became real snobs. We learned all about the proper conduct of a visit to the home of a senior officer and the all-important deployment of calling cards: for example, one was definitely not to shove the card under the door after leaving; it had to be presented in person. We were told that, if we went bowling, we might as well do it in shirtsleeves as it was a less-than-acceptable leisure activity for an officer and gentleman. We learned that flowers were never to be presented to ladies still wrapped in their paper – the wrapping had to be removed and the

blossoms presented stems down (which, of course, left us with the problem of how to dispose of the paper). Finally, we were cautioned most strongly about our choice of female partners for important social occasions and were told in no uncertain terms that we were not to bring a young person to a dance attended by officers and their ladies if there was a chance that this same young person might be dressing the hair of our captain's wife the next day. Although it was less important to us at this time in our lives, we also learned that a naval officer's choice of a wife and his engagement were carefully scrutinized by his superiors before they granted him permission to marry.

I must say, however, that a certain attractive chivalry was present in all this rigorous social training. To illustrate the *Kriegsmarine*'s attitude towards women, let me remark that a German naval officer was never introduced to a lady by his rank, only his name – it was always "Meet *Herr* Johann Schmitt," never "*Leutnant* Johann Schmitt." This was because a woman was not supposed to be involved in service matters and she therefore had to judge a man by his personality and manners (and perhaps his looks) but never by his rank or achievements. It is a curious thing but today all these important social strictures are more engrained in my memory than the rest of what I learned at the *Rote Schloss*. However, I hasten to add

(Left) The beer keg was a vital piece of life-saving equipment. (Right) One of the sailboats available for excursions was the *Planet* shown here. (WH col.)

that we regularly but secretly violated almost of all of these sacred taboos so that we could have a little fun. The fact that in those days I dated the gorgeous daughter of one of the more prominent members of Flensburg society and the owner of a fabulous restaurant, kept me in good graces with the naval establishment and myself in enduring bliss.

After official lectures and activities ended, we were permitted to use the many different types of sailboats moored at the school docks. We spent entire weekends, with or without supervision, but always with a barrel of beer, exploring the nooks and crannies of Flensburg Bay complete with attempts to supplement our food with eggs obtained from local farmers. On such occasions, my accordion supplied some of the entertainment. Whether it was the influence of beer or the vagaries of nature I am not sure, but on one voyage we went thoroughly aground and had to spend a night on board before be-

Here I am in an evening regatta at the helm of a 35m² National Cruiser with a reefed mainsail. My sailing experience from my time in the *Marine-Hitlerjugend* provided me with a certain authority in these events. (WH col.)

ing towed off the next day by a naval tug. Fortunately, this was one of the excursions supervised by our beloved *Oberleutnant* Stockfleht. Regatta sailing became one of our favourite pastimes and this passion has remained with me, for I still regularly sail my 26-foot sloop on Lake Ontario.

I wish to make it clear that our newly acquired snobbishness in social matters did not extend to our later relationship with our sailors. It was pounded into us at the *Schloss* that an officer's paramount concern was the welfare of his men. German naval officers ate the same food as their men, polished their own shoes and ironed their own uniforms. The idea of an officer having an enlisted man as a valet, common in other navies, was abhorrent to us. Another difference between the *Kriegsmarine* and the Royal Navy was that all German naval officers, regular or reserve, wore the same uniform and rank insignia. We did, however, maintain some distance

The fate of Germany is in good hands…

(Below) Minutes later we ran aground but no pictures were taken of this event. This time I am at the helm of our largest boat, the *Paul Beneke*, on an overnight cruise, under the guidance of my group officer, *Oberleutnant (Ing)* Stockfleht. (Both, WH col.)

between the various branches of the service and there was always slight tension between the *Seeoffiziere*, or executive branch, midshipmen and those destined for the engineering branch. The future *Seeoffiziere* regarded themselves – with totally unwarranted arrogance – as being slightly higher in the pecking order than those who were concerned with oily machinery. This tension, however, was often expressed in a humorous way and we engineers, of course, would always tell the aspiring *Seeoffiziere* that without us they would be unable to go very far.

After a rousing farewell party, the *Fähnrichslehrgang*,° my midshipman course ended on 26 September 1941. During the formal dinner in the great dining hall of the school we were presented with the ultimate test of our ability to function in polite society. This test involved the dessert, which was a bowl of so-called *Seekadettenprüfungsbirnen* ("Cadets' Testing Pears"), pears too large to be gulped in one piece and too hard to be divided into smaller pieces with a desert spoon. Rejecting the dessert was severely frowned upon and so it happened occasionally that one of the pears was accidentally launched into the lap of the commandant or another officer. Having solved this problem without mishap was an indication that we were finally fit to graduate from the *Schloss* and mingle, without their embarrassment, in the company of our superiors.

We engineer cadets were now subdivided into smaller classes of about 20 students and moved to our former quarters on the liner *Caribia* in preparation for our Second Workshop Course, which would take place using

Our teachers display a sense of humour during our graduation dinner at the end of September 1941. (WH col.)

the facilities of the *Marineschule*. I was very happy to retain *Oberleutnant (Ing)* Stockfleht as my group officer during this course. For the next two months we returned to the workshops and produced practice pieces of a more sophisticated nature than in our first practical course. Our knowledge of electrical welding, working on a metal lathe, and electrical wiring were subjected to severe and exacting tests.

We continued our social life by holding our own events. We organized a fancy ball aboard the *Caribia* and spent days producing nearly a thousand paper cherry blossoms that transformed the liner's ballroom into a Japanese tea garden. We invited an appropriate number of young ladies from Flensburg society, who had to be ferried by boats to and from the *Caribia* because it had broken from its moorings a few days earlier and was now anchored out in the bay. The ladies were duly im-

I moved back to the *Caribia* for my second workshop training from 1 October to 17 December 1941. Here my comrades and I are decorating the ballroom for a social event with a thousand paper cherry blossoms, which took many hours of labour to produce. The clean-up the next day was made worse by our hangovers. (WH col.)

pressed by our attempts to create an exotic environment and this social event of the year proceeded to everyone's satisfaction. Our hangovers, however, did not make the clean-up job any easier the following morning.

On another weekend we had a lovely nine-mile walk to Glücksburg, where we met *Oberleutnant* Stockfleht's wife and little daughter and found, much to our surprise, that our feared "Ogre" was completely dominated by his two ladies. Coffee and cake in a beautiful white castle, situated nearby and surrounded by water, completed the afternoon. Fortunately for the blisters we had acquired during our lengthy morning walk, a merciful fate intervened and provided a number of boats to take us back to the *Caribia* by sea. Lest the reader get the impression that life in the *Kriegsmarine* was nothing but

fun, it should be remembered that one usually recalls the days when the sun shone and never when they poured with rain – one recalls mostly the good things rather than the bad. These memoirs are certainly affected by this human trait.

Toward the end of our Second Workshop Course came the moment we had been waiting for – when we learned to which branch of the *Kriegsmarine* we would be assigned. Being a lover of broad horizons and far distant seas, I had been hoping for an assignment to a destroyer or *Schnellboot* (motor torpedo boat) or better still, to one of our armed merchant cruisers which roamed the globe. I was therefore rather disappointed to learn that I was going into the *U-Boot-Waffe*, the German submarine service. Having read the memoirs of such famous U-boat officers from the First World War as de la Perrière, von Forstner and Valentiner, I had no wish to serve in what was basically a large steel tube that sailed (if that is the word) under the surface.* In the navy, however, orders are orders and in the first week of 1942 I travelled to the small Baltic port of Pillau in East Prussia (now Baltiysk, Kaliningrad Oblast, a part of Russia) to begin my submarine training.

My assignment to the *U-Boot-Waffe* was not a haphazard one, as this branch of the German navy was be-

---

* *Kapitänleutnants* Lothar von Arnauld de la Perrière, Max Valentiner and Georg-Günther Freiherr von Forstner were three highly successful U-boat commanders from the First World War who published memoirs of their service in that conflict. De la Perrière, a member of Crew 4 in 1906, became the most successful U-boat commander in history, sinking 194 ships totalling more than 450,000 tons and winning the *Pour Le Mérite*. He rejoined the *Kriegsmarine* in the 1930s.

Our second workshop class with me seated on the left side of our group officer, *Oberleutnant (Ing)* Stockfleht, who is seated in the centre of the second row. Note that Stockfleht, as an officer, does not wear his rank insignia on his shoulders as do we midshipmen. (WH col.)

ing greatly expanded and there was a need for personnel. As the rest of my wartime service was spent in submarines, I think it would be useful at this point to discuss the history of that branch of the *Kriegsmarine* and the course of its wartime operations up to the point when I joined.

During the First World War Germany had been a leader in the use of submarines as commerce raiders and had nearly brought Britain, a maritime power, to its knees before technical developments and the hasty introduction of the convoy system saved that nation. Under the terms of the Treaty of Versailles which ended the war, Germany had to scrap its submarine fleet and was forbidden to possess this weapon. During the 1920s and 1930s, the *Reichsmarine* (the official title of our navy until 1935 when it was changed to the *Kriegsmarine*) continued submarine development clandestinely using foreign shipyards in anticipation of the fact that Germany would sometime in the future again be allowed to commission such vessels.

After Hitler came to power and the German armed forces began a program of re-armament, *Kommodore* Karl Dönitz was placed in charge of the newly created *U-Boot-Waffe* in 1935. That same year Germany commissioned her first postwar submarine, the *U-1*, and by the outbreak of war in 1939 Dönitz commanded a force of 47 operational U-boats as *Befehlshaber der U-Boote* or *BdU* pronounced "Bay-Day-Ooh"). He would continue in this position to the end of the war, even after he was promoted to commander-in-chief of the German navy in 1943. In the late 1930s, Dönitz developed a new system of U-boat tactics, based on group attacks by submarines acting in concert against single convoys. By these means, he hoped to be able to bring Britain to its knees in a future conflict, but when war broke out in 1939, he did not have enough operational submarines to carry out these tactics successfully. It was not until the late summer of 1940, after the *Kriegsmarine* took over French bases on the Atlantic coast, that German U-boats were able seriously to threaten Britain's seaborne lifeline.

Thus began a critical phase in what would later be called the Battle of the Atlantic, the attempt by Germany to use her submarine force to sever Britain's maritime communications. Operating from French bases in late 1940 and early 1941, the *U-Boot-Waffe* began to sink increasing numbers of merchant ships in the waters around the British Isles. Ace commanders such as Otto Kretschmer, Günther Prien, Joachim Schepke, Erich Topp and others began to accumulate high scores in a

tonnage war to sink merchant vessels faster than they could be replaced – Kretschmer alone sank 42 ships totalling 238,327 tons in 1940-1941 – and were rewarded with Germany's highest decorations and lionized by the press. This period in the greatest and most cruel maritime campaign in history was later referred to by the men of the *U-Boot-Waffe* as the *"Glückliche Zeit"* or "Happy Time," and it came to an end in the late spring of 1941 when increasing numbers of British and Canadian warships and aircraft offset U-boat successes and many aces, including Kretschmer, Prien and Schepke, were either killed or captured.

Threatened with disaster and struggling alone except for her empire, Britain fought back hard and the advent of increasing numbers of aircraft flying from the British Isles forced the U-boats to move continually west into the middle reaches of the North Atlantic beyond the range of aircraft. In late June 1941, a few weeks after I entered the *Marineschule*, Germany invaded the Soviet Union and Britain no longer stood alone. I remember thinking at the time that "we have now lost the war" as my country was committed to fighting on two fronts, thus repeating a mistake that had been made in the First World War. In the latter half of 1941, while I had been completing my term at the *Marineschule* and attending my Second Workshop Course, the Battle of the Atlantic had hung in the balance as both sides committed increasing numbers of ships and submarines to the contest. German U-boats steadily moved farther and farther to the west.

Ultimately, this brought the United States into the

During our stay on the *Caribia*, I took this photograph of the light cruiser *Nürnberg* moving into the harbour. (WH col.)

struggle because, although America was officially neutral, President Franklin D. Roosevelt committed the United States Navy to the protection of convoys in the western Atlantic. Ironically, although very few Americans knew it at the time, the United States was at war with Germany many months before the official declaration of hostilities. Despite strict orders from *BdU* to all U-boat commanders to avoid attacking American warships, given the circumstances it was inevitable that German U-boats and American warships would come into contact. On 31 October 1941, *Kapitänleutnant* Erich Topp in *U-552* fired at what he believed was a British or Canadian destroyer escorting a convoy southeast of Greenland and sank the USS *Reuben James*, with the loss of 115 of her crew – America's first fatal casualties in the Second World War.

On 7 December 1941, the Japanese attack on Pearl Harbor and the subsequent German declaration of war against the United States brought that powerful nation into the conflict as a major partner in the Allied coalition. But the United States was not prepared for war in late 1941 and early 1942 – particularly against the U-boats, which were unleashed against American coastal shipping. The result was a second "Happy Time" for the *U-Boot-Waffe* as German submarine commanders ranged the length of the American Atlantic coast and found easy pickings; some targets were sunk within a mile of brightly-lit coastal ports which had no blackout.

Thus, when I arrived at the 1 *U.L.D.* (*U-Boot Lehr Division* or Submarine Training School) at Pillau in the middle of one of the coldest winters in recent European history, the Battle of the Atlantic appeared to be going well for Germany. Attached to the *U.L.D.* was the 21. *U-bootsflottille* under the command of *Korvettenkapitän* Otto Schuhart, which was a training flotilla of old and very small Type II U-boats that we called "*Einbaum*" or "canoes," and a few Type IV craft. We *Fähnriche* came under Schuhart's command. The weather during that winter of 1941-1942 – the same winter that German troops were fighting in the outskirts of Moscow – was so bitterly cold that every morning we faced the difficult task of extricating our boats from the icy grip of the frozen harbour. The one bright point was that we were accommodated in the elegant East-Asia liner *Pretoria* and enjoyed its luxurious environment after returning from the day-long trips on the "canoes," which rolled so mercilessly on the surface that even the most experienced and salty veterans suffered from seasickness.

We were again subdivided into small groups and my own was under command of *Oberleutnant (Ing)* Heinz von Haefen, who turned out to be a very approachable and understanding superior. Every morning we engineer midshipmen were assigned to one of the Type II boats and spent the day learning about the functions of diesel motors, electric engines, valves, pipes and the operation of the diving and surfacing mechanism. To my surprise, my very first dive in a submarine had already taken place long before I, stationed in the diesel room, became aware of it. At the time, it didn't seem to be a very difficult task to dive a submarine from the surface to a depth of a hundred feet but later experience showed this assumption to be a bit premature. Many weeks went by before we achieved a certain degree of confidence in operating a submarine and began to regard being under water as just as normal as being on the surface. We also gradually became acclimatized to the unique environment of a submarine – the smells, wetness and the closeness of all personnel aboard – and such was the cold that

From 5 January to 29 March 1942, while attending the U-Boat school in Pillau in East Prussia, we lived on board the *Pretoria*, one of many German liners used as accommodation ships during the war. (WH col.)

we learned to appreciate the grey leather submariner's working uniform that was issued to us.

Our group officer, *Oberleutnant* von Haefen, made sure that there were diversions from the daily routine by organizing handgun practice and marches through the wintry landscape, which sometimes developed into spirited snowball fights with our group officer right in the middle of it.

Korvettenkapitän Otto Schuhart, the commander of the 21. *Flottille*, was a strict disciplinarian, and if I had any doubt about it, I soon learned the hard way. I had an uncle who owned a well known restaurant in Insterburg, a city about 80 miles east of Pillau. Since he also had two delightful teenage daughters, I gave in to the temptation of a great meal and the company of my relatives, and took the train to spend a weekend's leave in Insterburg. My female cousins were most impressed with the sudden appearance of a dashing *Fähnrich* from the *Kriegsmarine* in their midst, and felt duty bound to present this warrior to all their girlfriends, whom they invited to a dance party in one of the private rooms at my uncle's restaurant. Being the centre of all this female attention was a very welcome boost for my ego, and although we all knew that public dancing had been prohibited in Germany for the duration of the war, we felt this was a private affair that lay outside the rules. I therefore succumbed to the young ladies' blandishments and danced with as many as I could. Unfortunately our party was not regarded as a private affair by the municipal police, who suddenly burst into the room, took the names of everybody and left after delivering a stern warning

that we had broken the law and would be hearing more about the matter. The mood of the evening was thoroughly spoiled and slowly everyone went home.

This disaster, however, was somewhat lessened when the elder of my cousins thought she might benefit from my presence and worldly experience and promptly asked me to teach her how to kiss properly. As a result the visit was not a total loss.*

Afraid that the Insterburg police would inform the *U.L.D.* of the incident, immediately after my return I reported to *Korvettenkapitän* Schuhart to confess my sins. The result was a lengthy and blistering tirade in which I was told in no uncertain terms that not only had my improper act put the entire national war effort in peril but that I had thoroughly disgraced the uniform and reputation of the *Kriegsmarine* and the *U-Boot-Waffe*. By the time I received permission to leave Schuhart's office, I felt very small – about three feet high – and just managed to slink out of the door. I was fortunate, however, that no other punishment was meted out and my service record remained unblemished.

At the end of March 1942 our course at 1. *U.L.D.* ended and my group received their seagoing assignments for the next phase of our training. I was ordered to report to the 29. *U-bootsflottille* at La Spezia in Italy, an order that I was only too pleased to obey as, having just experienced one of the most wretched winters on record, I was delighted to be on my way to sunny climes.

---

* When I next met my cousin again, it was 1964 and my first words to her were "You still haven't learned it!"

(Above) A hand-driven scheduled ferry service across a small river in Pillau. In the background can be seen the camouflaged *Pretoria*. (WH col.)

(Left) The winter of 1941-42 was bitterly cold with temperatures dropping as low as -37°C (-35°F). This picture shows a group of six small Type II training boats tied up to a supply and support ship. We often had to fight our way through thick ice to get out to sea and it was not easy. (WH col.)

A typical scene at our base in La Spezia shows one Type VIIC boat, *U-97* under command of *Kapitänleutnant* Friedrich Bürgel, tied up after just having arrived, while, in the background, *U-372* under command of *Kapitänleutnant* Heinz-Joachim Neumann departs. (WH col.)

SUNSHINE, CHIANTI AND ICE CREAM: ITALY, APRIL TO JULY 1942

What an exciting prospect lay ahead – an escape from icy East Prussia to warm and sunny Italy! An additional bonus was that my best friend, *Fähnrich (Ing)* Otto Luft, who had been with me since the *Marineschule* at Flensburg, was also posted to the 29. *U-bootsflottille*. The two of us boarded a train at Pillau bound for the south, crossed the Alps and, after a stopover in Bologna, arrived at La Spezia on the Gulf of Genoa, one of Italy's largest naval bases, on 1 April 1942.

At La Spezia, we found that a long pier on one side of the harbour, with two adjacent buildings, had been assigned to the 29. *Flottille*, which had been operating in the Mediterranean since the previous September. The larger building provided living quarters for the crews and the smaller one housed the flotilla administration and officers' mess. There were always two or more U-boats tied up at the pier, vessels that either had just returned from patrol or were preparing for one. Otto and I were somewhat surprised to find eight *Fähnriche z.S.* from our own Crew 40 already at La Spezia, some of whom we knew, and they gave us a hearty welcome. The flotilla command, however, did not consider our arrival such a momentous event,

and although we were allowed to eat in the officers' mess, it was made very clear that we *Fähnriche* were still very insignificant members of the *U-Boot-Waffe* and had a long way to go before we achieved a status worth noting. After a few days, Otto and I received our assignments to *Frontboote* – Otto to *U-74* and me to *U-375*, both Type VIIC craft as were all the U-boats in the Mediterranean. We were happy to become members of a crew.

We now became very busy familiarizing ourselves with the intricacies of the machinery of Type VIIC U-boats, as this vessel was new to us, most of our training having been on the little Type II boats. Part of our instruction took place at the shipyard of the *Regia Marina*, or Italian navy, across the harbour from the *Flottille* base where our U-boats were repaired. We observed the work being done on several boats but our attempts to communicate with the yard workers were frustrated by our lack of Italian, although we were surprised to discover to what extent some of the German U-boat personnel had become proficient in that language. We learned some words very quickly – particularly *"domani"* or "tomorrow," which seemed to be the routine response to any question about when a job would be finished. We came

This view of the naval base at La Spezia shows a number of Italian auxiliary naval vessels. (WH col.)

to know that this word actually meant *"dopodomani,"* – "in a few days" or "the day after tomorrow" – and that it could also be translated as "probably never."

In our free time we explored La Spezia and some of the surrounding mountains, although I do not recall anything memorable about the nightlife in this port. To emphasize the friendly relationship that was supposed to exist between Germany and Italy, we were not permitted to wear our ceremonial dirks off the base when in dress uniform. On the base, meals in the officers' mess were usually very formal affairs, served by Italian waiters wearing white gloves (with their thumbs often showing

traces of the soup of the day). One local custom that did take some getting used to was the serving of red wine throughout the day – much as water would be in North America.

The Mediterranean was not a good place for U-boats. Beginning in September 1941, our submarines had been sent into that theatre at the express order of Hitler to assist our forces fighting in North Africa – much against Dönitz's wishes as he wished to concentrate on the North Atlantic. Altogether 64 U-boats operated in the Mediterranean during the war and all became casualties. For the *U-Boot-Waffe,* the Mediterranean quickly developed a reputation as an extremely dangerous body of water. It had the disadvantage of being small in area compared to the Atlantic – there was little room to plan attacks and little time to carry them out. Land-based Allied aircraft could cover almost the entire area of that sea and this, only too often, had unpleasant consequences for our boats.

Some felt that the danger in the Mediterranean was partly due to the water, which was much clearer than in the Atlantic. But we also thought another explanation might be the fact that, from our impression, half of the bombs dropped on us came from German aircraft. There was absolutely no cooperation of any kind between the *Kriegsmarine* and the *Luftwaffe* in the Mediterranean and our aircraft were never informed about the locations of the U-boats. I do not claim that any U-boat submarine was actually sunk by German aircraft, but I am trying to convey our sceptical and sarcastic attitude towards the other German fighting services – and I can honestly say that in the *U-Boot-Waffe*, we always felt a much closer affinity to the Allied navies than we did to our own *Luftwaffe* or *Heer* (army). Our three serv-

Having both been assigned to the 29. *U-bootsflottille* in Italy in April 1942, *Fähnrich* Otto Luft and I are shown here exploring the city of La Spezia, one of the largest Italian naval bases and the home of our flotilla. (WH col.)

An artist's rendition of the commanding officer of the 29. *Flottille, Kapitänleutnant* Fritz Frauenheim. (WH col.)

ices differed so much in their attitudes that they were often referred to as the "Republican" army, the "Nazi" air force, and the "Imperial" navy (and we sailors did not at all mind being called "Imperial"). Cooperation with the *Regia Marina*, the Italian navy, was not much better – one of our U-boats was rammed and sunk by an Italian destroyer at the entrance to Salamis harbour in Greece, our other submarine base in the Mediterranean.[*]

In the last week of April 1942, the crew of Otto's boat, *U-74*, commanded by *Oberleutnant z.S.* Karl Friedrich, began loading torpedoes and provisions in preparation for its next mission. After being fully armed and stored, *U-74* went out for a lengthy stationary test dive inside the harbour – which Otto Luft was ordered by his CO to photograph, and which I include in this book – and then Otto bid me goodbye and I wished him a safe return. *U-74* departed from La Spezia at the end of April and a few days later my boat, *U-375*, began its own patrol.

---

[*] This is a reference to the sinking of *U-557*, rammed and sunk by the Italian torpedo boat *Orione* on 16 December 1941.

The Type VIIC boat *U-74* undergoing a routine diving test before embarking on a mission. Otto Luft, my friend and a member of the crew, was ordered to take the two sequences of pictures on this and the facing page from a dinghy. (WH col.)

My commanding officer on *U-375* was *Kapitän-leutnant* Jürgen Könenkamp, a tall, lanky and somewhat aloof individual. My position on board was supernumerary, at the level of a leading seaman, and I reported to the *Leitender Ingenieur*, or *LI*,[*] not to the *Wachoffiziere*, or watch officers who were responsible for all the non-

mechanical functions of the boat.[*] I was on *U-375* to master all the technical details of the propulsion and other mechanical systems of the Type VII, and also to gain experience in maintenance, diving, damage control

---

[*] The *Leitender Ingenieur,* commonly abbreviated as *LI* (pronounced "Ell-ee"), was the engineer officer on a U-boat.

[*] There were normally two *Wachoffiziere* on a U-boat. The *Erster Wach-offizier*, commonly abbreviated as I.WO, was usually an *Oberleutnant z.S.* and functioned as the executive officer of the boat, although in the on-board hierarchy the *Leitender Ingenieur* ranked somewhat higher and the *Zweiter Wachoffizier* (II.WO), usually a *Leutnant z.S.*

1

2

3

4

5

and surfacing, without actually having to assume any responsibility for these functions. My accommodation was not in the wardroom, or officers' quarters, but in the *Unteroffiziereraum*, or petty officers' quarters. Basically, my job was to learn as much as I could while keeping out of everyone's way.

My first war patrol, so the *KTB* (*Kriegestagebuch* or war diary) of *U-375* reminds me, began late in the afternoon of 28 April 1942 when we left La Spezia bound for the western Mediterranean. As soon as we had emerged

(Above) *Oberleutnant z.S.* Fritz Guggenberger, commanding officer of *U-81*, departing on another mission, after having sunk the British aircraft carrier HMS *Ark Royal* on 13 November 1941. Guggenberger was later transferred to Dönitz's staff and then given command of the Type IXC boat *U-513*. It was sunk on 13 July 1943 but Guggenberger was rescued and survived the war. (WH col.)

Oberleutnant z.S. Guggenberger and his crew enjoying some farewell wine from a set of pewter goblets given to his boat as a present from the flotilla. (WH col.)

U-81 departing La Spezia on Easter Sunday 1942. The goblets can be seen in their case by the conning tower. (WH col.)

At the upper left, *U-375* approaches the pier, prepared to take on torpedoes, as can be seen by the open torpedo hatches halfway along her aft deck and in front of the gun. At the upper right, a floating crane lowers a torpedo down to the deck. The lower pictures demonstrate the activity of placing the torpedo on a slide to move it below deck. The gear at the right controls the speed of the movement. (WH col.)

The *Techniker*, or technical, division of *U-375* assembled on 27 April 1942, the day of our departure on patrol from La Spezia. I am on the far left of the rear rank. (WH col.)

The CO of *U-375, Kapitänleutnant* Jürgen Könenkamp, receiving a toy duck as a mascot. He was lost with his entire crew when this boat was sunk on 30 July 1943. (WH col.)

from the harbour, *Kapitänleutnant* Könenkamp carried out drills intended to test the crew's reaction to an *Alarmtauchen* or crash dive. Almost immediately, we began to have trouble with the starboard diesel, which took us four hours to fix, but after that problem was solved, we continued on the surface west across the Gulf of Genoa. On 29 April, the CO held another alarm drill and late in the evening of that day he received a radio message from *FdU Italien** ordering *U-375* to patrol the south half of grid square 75, which was about midway between Spain and North Africa, 60-70 miles south of the Spanish city of Almeria.** When this message reached us, we were already west of the island of Sardinia as we had made good time running on the surface.

Our luck, however, did not hold. On the morning of the following day, 30 April 1942, enemy aircraft forced *U-375* to crash dive twice. A few minutes later the starboard diesel failed again. At almost the same time we received a message from *FdU Italien* that our agents had reported that a British aircraft carrier, cruiser and five destroyers had left Gibraltar at 6 A.M. that morning and *Kapitänleutnant* Könenkamp therefore altered course, hoping to be able intercept

---

* *Führer der Uboote Italien*, the commander of German submarine forces in the Mediterranean, who was at this time *Fregattenkapitän* Viktor Oehrn.

** During the Second World War, the *Kriegsmarine* planned and carried out operations by means of a global grid chart in which the entire water surface of the world was divided into square sections or "*Quadrats*," which were in turn subdivided into smaller square sections. By making use of this system, fairly accurate deployment and operational orders could be issued to German warships.

U-375 alongside at La Spezia in Italy loading provisions for the patrol which was to be my first submarine operation. (WH col.)

U-573, which had been caught by British aircraft on the surface just off the Spanish coast and had been so badly damaged that it could not submerge. Our CO estimated that, given the reported position of *U-573* and our current surface speed, which had been reduced to about 12 knots rather than the normal 17 by the malfunctioning starboard diesel, it would take us nearly five hours before we could reach the beleaguered *U-573*.

We proceeded at our best speed but at about 8 P.M. in the evening of 1 May we were forced to crash dive twice by a Sunderland flying boat, which in the event did not attack. Shortly before midnight we reached the reported position of *U-573* but there was nothing to see and by radio our CO requested clarification of the damaged boat's position from *FdU*. We then altered course for the Spanish coast near Alicante and while on passage, received a warning from *FdU* that we could expect to encounter numerous British aircraft in the coming daylight hours. Shortly before dawn, we received a second message calling off our rescue mission as German and Italian aircraft and Spanish warships were expected to reach and assist *U-573* that day.*

this enemy force early the next day. During the evening and night of 30 April we passed south of Majorca, but our troublesome starboard diesel reduced our surface speed, and in the late afternoon of 1 May it failed completely. Within a half an hour, we altered course a second time after receiving an order from *FdU* to go to the assistance of

---

* The captain of *U-573* was able to bring his badly damaged boat into the Spanish naval base at Cartagena, where it was transferred to the Spanish navy, and the crew was permitted to return to Germany. Spain was only nominally neutral during this period of the war.

The warning about enemy air activity turned out to be entirely accurate. In the late morning of 2 May, British aircraft forced us to crash dive twice and this day turned out to be a very difficult one for *U-375*. We were now under orders to patrol in the north half of Grid Square CH 81, or the Spanish coast off Cartagena, which was fortunate for us as we happened to be near that area. At almost the same time, the clutch between the port diesel and port electric motor began to malfunction, making it very difficult for us to recharge our batteries. As if this were not bad enough, just after 2 P.M. we were spotted by a British flying boat but managed to dive before it dropped two bombs, which missed us by a considerable distance. The CO observed the movements of this aircraft, a Catalina, through the periscope and although it flew away, it was shortly replaced by two more aircraft of the same type which carried out an attack that resulted in between 10 and 20 bombs being dropped (it was hard to make an exact count) in our vicinity.

Kapitänleutnant Könenkamp now began a submerged run to the south to seek deeper water. As our starboard diesel had failed completely by now, Könenkamp wisely decided that his best course of action was to abort the patrol and return to La Spezia because *U-375* was clearly in no condition to continue. We therefore altered course to the east and as soon as darkness had fallen, surfaced. At 10.20 P.M., however, an enemy destroyer appeared directly ahead, and although Könenkamp tried to outmanoeuvre him on the surface, the enemy spotted our wake and altered course towards us. We crash dived and went down to a depth of 60 metres (180 feet) but the

Oberleutnant Friedrich and two of his officers racing toy cars in the flotilla officers' mess at La Spezia. (WH col.)

depth charges soon began to fall, and although none came closer than 150 yards, the enemy kept up the attack for nearly two hours. Könenkamp recorded in the *KTB* that, in all, 13 depth charges came our way but we suffered only minor damage.

The enemy destroyer abandoned the hunt about midnight, and when the CO was sure he had gone, we surfaced. It was now 3 May and as we had received permission from *FdU Italien* to return to base, we made course for La Spezia, running on the surface as much as possible. It still took us three days to get home but finally, at 8 A.M. on 6 May 1942, we made fast at a berth in the U-boat base. My first war patrol, which had lasted only eight days, was now over.

As soon as I returned, I learned some bad news: my friend Otto Luft's boat, *U-74*, was overdue from its scheduled return. Later we heard that it had been sunk and that there were no survivors.* I was devastated by

Oberleutnant z.S. Karl Friedrich, who had just taken command of *U-74* in April 1942. (WH col.)

Otto Luft (in the centre) and crew members of *U-74* on the day of departure on a patrol that ended on 2 May 1942 when his boat was sunk with all hands. (WH col.)

this news as this was the first time during the war that I lost a close friend. Sometime later I received a large parcel from his father, who operated a photo laboratory; the package contained good prints of the pictures that Otto had taken that recorded our time at the *Marineschule* and in Italy up to the day he departed on his ill-fated patrol. His father, knowing I was Otto's friend, thought I might like to have these prints as a keepsake, and thanks to this generosity I am today able to illustrate my naval career from Flensburg to La Spezia.

It was clear to everyone that *U-375* needed major repairs to its diesel and electric motors but we shortly discovered that the boat had even worse problems. When we attempted to draw the torpedoes from the forward tubes, we found that the tubes had become so warped that the pistons which pushed the torpedoes out of them could no longer move. A defect of this nature could not be fixed, all four tubes would have to be replaced and the boat would therefore be out of action for months.* As was customary, while this work was in progress, the crew was sent to a hotel maintained by the *Kriegsmarine* in Viareggio, one of the most popular resorts on the Gulf of Genoa.

For two weeks we lay on the beach, drank ourselves through numerous bars, went sightseeing to places like Florence and Pisa and attended a performance at the opera house in Lucca, with our officers being officially honoured by seats in the royal box. I also enjoyed the

---

* On 2 May 1942, *U-74* was spotted running on the surface by a British Sunderland flying boat which summoned two British destroyers, HM Ships *Wishart* and *Wrestler*, which sank *U-74* with the loss of all on board. *U-74* had been the former command of U-boat ace *Kapitänleutnant* Eitel-Friedrich Kentrat.

* *U-375* had been badly depth-charged and heavily damaged when it had attempted to pass through the Straits of Gibraltar into the Mediterranean the previous autumn and this may have contributed to the boat's mechanical problems.

On patrol – a view from the *Wintergarten* of the bridge of *U-375* while surfaced in the Mediterranean. (WH col.)

After we returned to La Spezia from our patrol, the most important task was catching up on our mail, read here by the I.WO and an NCO. (WH col.)

The I.WO (first watch officer) of *U-375*, Oberleutnant z.S. Heintze, in a picture taken from atop the periscope housing. (WH col.)

hospitality of an Italian business tycoon who invited me to spend a weekend with him and his family at his estate on beautiful Lake Como near Milan. During my time in Italy, it was noticeable to me and my comrades that there were almost no indications that this nation was at war. In the three months I was posted to La Spezia, I never saw an Italian warship enter or leave the base, while at

the ritual evening promenade in Viareggio young men of military age strolled up and down, a dozen abreast and arm in arm, seemingly without a care in the world.

After a few weeks at Viareggio, I returned to La Spezia, and the remainder of my time in Italy was spent in trying to assist in the repairs on *U-375*. A better knowledge of Italian would have been helpful but, by now, I had become only too familiar with *"domani"* and *"dopodomani"* which, in most cases, were the stock replies to almost every question asked about progress.

I was not there when the boat was finally ready because, after a few more glorious weeks of sunshine, Chianti and ice cream on the shores of the Mediterranean, it was time to return to the *Marineschule* at Kiel for more specialized technical classes. The train trip north, which I made with a *Fähnrich z.S.*, was interrupted by a sightseeing visit to Parma. After we had recrossed the Alps, the soft pastel colours of the landscape and the overcast weather were almost a welcome relief from the eternally blue sky, the aquamarine Mediterranean and the strong reds and greens that dominate the scenery of Italy.

U-375 continued to serve in the Mediterranean until 30 July 1943 when, still under Könenkamp's command, it was sunk with all hands near Pantellaria.*

In 1942, most Type VII U-boats still carried an 88 mm gun on the foredeck. These guns were later removed because constantly increasing Allied airpower forced German submarines to travel less and attack less on the surface and because, since diving time was crucial during an air attack, the boats could no longer afford to have crew on deck before an alarm dive. (WH col.)

---

* *U-375* was sunk by the American patrol craft *PC-624* on 30 July 1943, after it tried to attack Allied shipping supporting the invasion of Sicily.

The shipyard of La Spezia where *U-375* spent many weeks having the damage repaired that was suffered during the last mission from 27 April to May 6. Apart from *U-375* there are two other Type VII boats in the shipyard. (WH col.)

The *Fähnrich (Ing)* of *U-375* in May 1942 – that is to say, me. (WH col.)

With another *Fähnrich* from Crew 40 I am returning from the shipyard to our quarters using a novel form of transportation. (WH col.)

On the beach of Viareggio, a famous Italian resort city, where U-boat crews were sent for recuperation. It was not hard to take. (WH col.)

Some of the attractions available at Viareggio. This is a commercial postcard but we lived in hope. (WH col.)

On a guided excursion from Viareggio to the small town of Lucca we were entertained and fed by a group of our Italian military hosts. (WH col.)

The Type VIIC *U-331*, under *Kapitänleutnant Freiherr* von Tiesenhausen, at La Spezia after returning from a mission. Note the sea serpent insignia which was this boat's emblem. (WH col.)

As the *Kriegsmarine* battle ensign is hoisted on 31 May 1943, indicating that *U-612* is in commission, the crew comes to attention and salutes. Evergreen garlands around the conning tower create a decorative and festive atmosphere. (WH col.)

On my return from Italy in late June 1942, I rejoined my comrades of the engineering group of Crew 40 at the *Marineschule* at Kiel. We commenced a whirlwind of courses lasting six months which taught us the finer points of diesel engines, electric motors and generators in Kiel, and the technicalities of U-boat manoeuvre in Königsberg, East Prussia, with some additional training on how to operate and repair gyro compasses.

We also took a course – and it was one we enjoyed very much – in the diving tank in Gotenhafen to become familiar with the Dräger *Tauchretter*, a submarine escape device. The *Tauchretter* consisted of an airbag worn on the chest with a mouthpiece through which one breathed in and out, while a clip closed off the nose. The exhaled air went into the airbag through a chemical scrubber (potash) to clean it of carbon dioxide. The cleaned air could then be breathed in again, supplemented if necessary with a dose of oxygen from a steel bottle in the bottom of the airbag. The *Tauchretter* was like using scuba diving gear but without the bubbles, and its purpose was to enable submariners trapped in their sunken boat to reach the surface safely.

The escape procedure in a sunken submarine was to open the bottom valves to allow water to enter the boat until the pressure inside the boat equalled the pressure of the surrounding water. The crew would breathe the air trapped inside the boat in air pockets close to the ceiling. The main hatch could then be opened and every survivor put on his Dräger lung, dived underneath the open hatch and ascended to the surface. There was, however, a problem. If the user surfaced too quickly, he could suffer from the "bends" and might not survive. We were advised to surface very slowly, with the help of a line attached to a float sent to the surface first, which had a series of equally-spaced knots at which the escaping submariner was supposed to make stops to allow his body to adjust to the diminishing water pressure. Frankly, we wondered if anyone, under the stress of escaping death, would have enough presence of mind and rational thought to stop his ascent for several minutes at each knot instead of shooting straight to the welcoming light of the surface.

Survival also depended on the physical constitution of the individual. There is one known case where a submariner shot to the surface without a *Tauchretter* from

From 6 July to 24 September 1942 my group was sent on a course in submarine machinery at the Naval School in Kiel, where we were accommodated aboard the Hapag liner *New York*. (Many ships of the German Hapag line had names relating to American or British geography). Here I am with a fellow student in my stateroom. (WH col.)

a depth of more than 200 feet without damage to his health, but this must be considered an exception. When one ascends to the surface without stops, a *Tauchretter* might not be needed at all.

To us, however, this was schoolroom theory because we were quite sure that we would never need the *Tauchretter* since our boat would, of course, never become a casualty of war. But to roam around weightless in the diving tank at Gotenhafen while practising all kinds of contortions was great fun and the shouted order to "come out" was always obeyed with reluctance.

At the end of December 1942 we entered our final period of training with an organisation called *Agru-Front*, standing for *Ausbildungsgruppe Front*. This took place at Hela in East Prussia and was the most feared of all training courses for future submariners and *Frontboote*. As

From 26 September to 22 November 1942, my group was sent to Königsberg, the capital of East Prussia, for further practical training on submarines. Part of this course involved learning how to use the *Tauchretter* device (above) to escape from a sunken submarine that was not too deep. There

was no accurate figure for the depth limit at which this device could be used successfully but escapes were made from depths as deep as 70 metres (230 feet). (WH col.)

Our practical training took place on the small Type II craft such as *U-3* shown here. Like all the other boats of that type, it had become obsolescent and had been withdrawn from combat and was used only for training purposes. (WH col.)

individual engineering students we were subjected to a very intense and often humiliating three-month course in simulated operational conditions to prepare us for the most demanding duty of the *Leitender Ingenieur* on a U-boat, namely that of diving officer. In the *Kriegsmarine*, unlike other major navies, the engineer officer of a submarine was responsible for diving, surfacing and underwater manoeuvre. Since the *Agru-Front* organization was under intense pressure to produce capable and effective engineering officers in the shortest possible time, this meant that we attended diving exercises on

board boats at sea during the day and took classes during the evening, often resulting in assignments that had to be completed during the night. For us, there were no weekends or holidays. Each day a group of four of five of us students was assigned to a training U-boat, where, in turn, we practised diving manoeuvres under the stern eye of *Agru-Front* instructors. Our mistakes and weaknesses were ruthlessly exposed and criticized in public and not in very gentle terms. Our egos, which had received a tremendous boost on 1 January 1943 when we had all been commissioned as *Leutnants (Ing)*, finally achieving the goal we had been working towards for more than two years, were shredded without mercy.

At the beginning we learned to carry out a dive, to rectify imbalances in trim and ballast, and to take the boat to periscope depth. The difficult task was to keep it steady at this depth without letting either the bow or stern stick out of the water. We also learned how to keep the periscope head just above the surface to allow the commanding officer to have a clear view of the horizon, but not higher than necessary so as to prevent detection by the enemy. This was as much an instinctive job as a scientific one and success really depended on acquiring the ability to anticipate the movements the boat might make, so that countermeasures could be taken in time. I believe some of us became quite good at this, whereas others never perfected the necessary skills.

Being full of mischief, we once carried out an experiment. One of us consumed such an intake of alcohol that he had difficulty standing straight without holding on to the periscope guide wires. After observing his performance, we came to the conclusion that his ability to maintain the boat at periscope depth exceeded everything we had ever been able to muster. Unfortunately the results of our scientific research were never properly acknowledged by the naval authorities.

A few weeks into our course we encountered what we called the "*Fünfte Kolonne*."* This was a group of very experienced U-boat officers who provided advanced training by creating real war conditions on board by simulating depth charge effects and damage at the most undesirable moments. When, for example, one of us had just executed an *Alarmtauchen*, or crash dive, and found himself diving at the correct angle, all hell would suddenly break loose – noisy detonations occurred, followed by valves being opened which permitted seawater to pour into the boat, while fuses were removed so that only dim emergency lighting remained, and tanks and bilges mysteriously filled with water, completely destroying the balance of the boat, and, finally, compartments became filled with smoke – all this while going down at full speed! More than once, a boat buried its bow in to the bottom of the Baltic, which was thankfully soft in the training area, and this would result in some acid commentary from the "*Fünfte Kolonne*."

At times we novices were so discouraged that we became convinced that we would never learn the intricacies of handling a U-boat under water. By the end of the course, however, we attained our goal and so thorough was our training that we became convinced that as long as the pressure hull remained intact, there was nothing the enemy could do that we could not handle. We were very proud when we finally held our certificates as diving officers in our hands – and the picture on the certificate is an apt indication of just what we endured to receive it. It was now mid-March 1943 and we newly-minted engineer officers were ready to make our contribution to the war at sea.

Although we did not know much about it at the time,

* "Fifth column," meaning agents or saboteurs working for the enemy. This term, which was used by both sides during the Second World War, originated during the Spanish Civil War when Fascist forces announced that they were besieging Madrid using four columns attacking from outside the city while a "fifth column" attacked from within.

that war was not going well for the *U-Boot-Waffe*. While I had been serving on *U-375* and attending the *Marine-schule* at Mürwik in the latter half of 1942, the Battle of the Atlantic had entered a critical stage. In the autumn of 1942, Dönitz had concentrated his submarine forces in that ocean in the "air gap" between Ireland and New-foundland which could not be patrolled by aircraft op-erating from land bases. This deployment brought good results, and by the end of 1942 Allied shipping losses had reached alarming levels. The result, however, was a mas-sive redeployment of enemy naval forces as both Britain and the United States realized that the sea lanes to Brit-ain had to be secured before any other major operation could take place against Germany, on land or sea.

Over the winter of 1942-1943, the battle seesawed back and forth as both sides gathered their strength. By March 1943, the scales of victory appeared to be tipping in favour of the U-boats when they sank 108 vessels, although German losses were also very high. In the fol-lowing month, however, the tide began to turn when the Allies closed the air gap with long-range aircraft and, more importantly, completely cracked the German naval code which they called "Enigma," giving them the price-less advantage of being able to locate our U-boats at sea and either steer convoys around them or destroy them using the newly-formed British "support" or American "hunter-killer" groups. These were often built around escort carriers and were not assigned to a particular con-voy but would reinforce the escorts of any threatened convoy. These measures brought victory to the enemy when the climax of the battle was reached in May 1943

Like all officers destined to become a *Leitender Ingenieur* on a U-boat, I received an advanced and concentrated course at the *Agru Front* from 15 December 1942 to 11 March 1943, to enable me to handle a submerged boat under the most difficult conditions and with every imaginable simulated damage. I received this diploma upon graduation. It contains not a single swastika – but the treat-ment of the student illustrated in the diploma was not far removed from reality. The document reads: "Master Diving Diploma – We Masters of the Guild of Trim Tamers and Chief Engineer Tortur-ers herewith make known that the most worshipful *Leutnant (Ing)* Hirschmann today before the undersigned took a submarine of medium size undamaged below the surface without danger to the galley and the training officer's nap and moved same in moderate oscillations up and down so that now he has been found worthy and is admitted into the brotherhood of the glorious diving boat people." (WH col.)

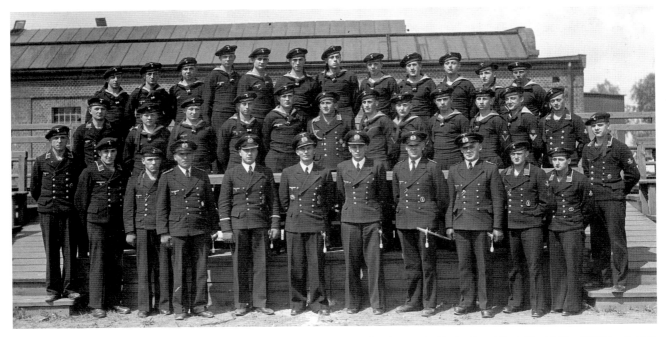

On 1 January 1943, after more than two years of training, I was commissioned and promoted to *Leutnant (Ing)*. On 15 May 1943 I was sent to the Schichau shipyard in Danzig to take up an appointment as *Leitender Ingenieur* on the Type VIIC submarine *U-612*. This boat had been sunk in a collision the previous year but had been raised and repaired. This picture shows the crew of *U-612* on the occasion of the boat's commissioning, which took place on 31 May 1943. I am in the front rank, fifth from the right, and on my right is the commanding officer, *Oberleutnant z.S.* Theo Petersen, who is wearing the German Cross in Gold on the right side of his jacket. (WH col.)

– during that month 33 U-boats were lost, nearly a third of our operational strength in the Atlantic, in return for very few merchantmen sunk. Dönitz could not continue to take such losses and ordered our U-boats out of the North Atlantic. Although they returned briefly in the autumn of 1943, our submarines were never again to pose a serious threat to the lifeline of Britain.

As for me, I was just happy to receive orders in mid-March 1943 to report to the Schichau shipyard in Danzig to take up an appointment as *Leitender Ingenieur*

on *U-612*. This was a Type VIIC boat that had a rather checkered past. While still in acceptance trials in August 1942, it was rammed by another U-boat and sunk in about 120 feet of water with, fortunately, the loss of only one crew member. It was subsequently raised and towed to the Schichau yard in Danzig, where it was repaired, a process that had almost been completed when I arrived.

When a U-boat was in the final stages of its construction, its crew was assigned to the boat to familiarize themselves with the vessel before it was commissioned. This process was termed *Baubelehrung* (literally "construction training"), where the crew learned all there was to know about their boat while it was still in the shipyard. When I came on the scene, somewhat late, at Danzig, most of the crew, including the commanding officer, *Oberleutnant z.S.* Theo Petersen, were already there, but the watch officers were still on the way. *Oberleutnant* Petersen was a veteran who had risen from *Obersteuermann*, or navigator, to I.WO on three boats commanded by our second most successful wartime U-boat commander, *Korvettenkapitän* Wolfgang Lüth,* and had been awarded the *Deutsche Kreuz in Gold* for his achievements.** Despite his reputation, I found him to be one of the most pleasant superiors I encountered during my naval career and, together with the I.WO, *Leutnant z.S.* Pieper, who arrived after me, we three formed a most relaxed but efficient trio on *U-612*. Unfortunately, when the II.WO arrived a few weeks later, he did not fit very well into this happy wardroom.

---

* Born in 1913 and a member of Crew 33, Wolfgang Lüth was one of the most successful U-boat commanders of the Second World War, sinking 47 ships totalling 225,756 tons, for which he was awarded Germany's highest decorations. Lüth survived years of operations as a submarine commander, including one long patrol lasting 205 days. In September 1944 he was promoted *Fregattenkapitän* and appointed to the faculty of the *Marineschule* at Flensburg. He survived the war only to be tragically shot in an accident five days after it ended.

** The *Deutsche Kreuz in Gold,* or German Cross in Gold, ranked between the Iron Cross, 1st Class, and the Knight's Cross. It was instituted to reward those who did not qualify for the Knight's Cross. Many U-boat engineer officers, petty officers and ratings received this medal rather than the *Ritterkreuz,* which was largely awarded to *Seeoffiziere.*

Together with my two technical *Oberfeldwebel*, or engineer chief petty officers, I roamed *U-612* from stem to stern, becoming familiar with every pipe, hose, instrument, coupling, valve, tank, pump and anything else that needed to be checked to ensure that it was in working order and our boat could fulfil its intended function. In our quarters, which were in some very spartan barracks in Danzig, we pored over drawings, plans, handbooks and other technical literature. At the same time we trained our enlisted engine room personnel because our success and even survival depended as much on their abilities as our own. Most had never been on a submarine and only a few wore medals earned in front-line action, but all were eager to learn and, with one or two exceptions, showed such promise that we were able form an effective technical division on *U-612*. All of us in this division put much effort into ensuring that the damage suffered during the boat's previous sinking had been properly repaired and all signs of that earlier catastrophe removed.

On 31 May 1943, we commissioned *U-612* for the second time. As usual, this event was a mixture of military formalities and enthusiastic celebration. Everyone in the crew did his best to turn out in spotless uniform and we officers wore our white, formal dress belts – for me the first and last time I did so in my naval career. When the crew was formed on the afterdeck, *Oberleutnant z.S.* Petersen, standing on the *Wintergarten*, gave the order to hoist our ensign and his CO's pennant. He then stepped ashore and reported to the commanding officer of the base that *U-612* was ready for service. With

The crew of *U-612* is formed up on the deck during the commissioning ceremony at Danzig, 31 May 1943. I am the officer at the left and this was the first and only time I got to wear my ceremonial officer's white dress belt. (WH col.)

The officers of *U-612* host officials of the Danzig naval base at a champagne breakfast held in the bow torpedo room of the boat with myself seated at the right hand corner. This was the only time during my service in U-boats that the bow compartment looked as civilized as this! (WH col.)

the official part of the ceremony now ended, the invited guests came on board and assembled in the forward torpedo room, where chairs and tables, covered with proper white cloths, had been set out, with a battle ensign decorating the hatches of the four forward torpedo tubes. Our sailors served snacks and champagne and it was a happy occasion, although all of us knew that this compartment would never again look so festive. Speeches were made expressing the hope that *U-612* would enjoy a successful career, and in the afternoon a second reception followed on board the liner that served as the accommodation ship for the Danzig naval base. The next day submarine life started in earnest for the crew of *U-612*.

A newly-commissioned U-boat had to undergo a series of acceptance trials and tests which usually showed up any flaws, sometimes very serious, that had to be repaired. We therefore returned to the shipyard for a few days. Demagnetization was an important process to protect us from magnetic mines. When the boat appeared to be in the best condition possible, we spent several weeks practising dives, firing torpedoes and shooting our anti-aircraft guns.

Before being assigned to the *Frontflottille*, however, we still had to pass the final hurdle – the dreaded *Agru-Front*. This time the boat and crew, as a unit, were subjected to the well-known exercises I had gone through as an individual just a few months earlier. Forewarned

A view from the bridge of *U-612* through the deck hatch down into the conning tower. Beneath the crew member can be seen the ladder down into the *Zentrale* or control room of the boat. If an alarm occurred, the entire bridge watch, except the watchkeeping officer, grabbed the rails of the ladders and, without touching any rungs, let themselves fall all the way into the *Zentrale*, and then quickly moved aside so as not to be trampled by the next man coming down. The watchkeeping officer then went into the conning tower far enough so that he could close the hatch and declare the boat ready to dive. After many weeks of drill, we could disappear from the surface in just 25-30 seconds. (WH col.)

is forearmed and I knew what to expect. We passed with flying colours, and as a sign of our final certification a small decal was fixed to the side of the conning tower as a declaration that *U-612* was *Frontreif* – ready for operational deployment.

Our enthusiasm over this triumph did not last long. To our deep disappointment *U-612* was assigned to the 24. *Ubootflottille* in Memel, the most easterly port in Germany, to serve as a training boat. The 24. *Flottille* was what we called a *"Schiessflottille"* ("shooting flotilla"), a training unit that instructed future commanding officers in how to carry out torpedo attacks by day or night while facing any kind of opposition. Apart from about 15 Type VII boats, the flotilla also had several target ships and numerous escort, torpedo recovery and service vessels. The escorts, mostly older but fast torpedo boats* acted as protectors of the target ships, simulating actual war conditions. At Memel, we were accommodated in a simple one-storey barrack while the flotilla command staff was housed in greater luxury on board the *Daressalam*, an older Africa Line passenger liner tied up in the harbour.

At any one time there were about 25 students attending a course, which lasted four weeks and permitted each student to fire between 35 and 50 torpedo shots. At the beginning, most of our students had been *Wachoffiziere* on *Frontboote* and therefore came to us with considerable experience. This changed, however, in the latter part of 1943 when heavy losses and the resulting need for new commanding officers meant that the students were often officers transferred from the surface fleet who had no submarine experience whatsoever. Meanwhile, the

---

* The torpedo boat was a type of surface warship common in the *Kriegsmarine* and other European navies which was encountered only rarely in the British or American navies. Torpedo boats were small, fast, surface vessels about the size of a British frigate or an American destroyer escort, with a smaller gun armament than a destroyer, but with the full torpedo armament of that class of warship.

The gun crew drilling with the single 20 mm anti-aircraft gun on *U-612*. In combat the anti-aircraft defences had little success after a few initial surprises and the best chance for survival lay in a constant air watch and readiness to crash dive. (WH col.)

"target" ships, all civilian merchantmen, were under the command of their normal peacetime masters, whose enthusiasm for naval service was not at all high.

Every morning the training boats, with one or two students on board, left Memel at about 7 A.M. for the practice area, together with the target and torpedo recovery ships, as well as the escorts. When the students had completed their torpedo firing it was usually about 3 P.M. and the U-boats returned to the base, while the recovery ships picked up the air-driven torpedoes, whose location was indicated by the bubbles in their wake. After the U-boats arrived at the base, they rafted up alongside a torpedo supply ship to prepare for the night shooting exercise, while, on the other side of that same ship, the recovery ships returned the torpedoes they had picked up. At dusk the entire squadron of surface vessels and submarines went out again for the night exercise, returning about 1 A.M. to reload torpedoes for the next day's exercise. For us on the training boats, three or four hours of sleep became the norm, six days a week. We got no holidays but we did get Sunday off, although it was usually occupied completing all the necessary maintenance we never had time to do during the week. Rarely have I ever been, before or since, so intensely involved with any professional activities as at that time.

When returning from the training area to reload torpedoes, all the U-boats went as fast as possible so as to get closer alongside the torpedo supply ship and thus cut down the waiting time until it was their turn to reload. The last and outside boat had to wait, of course, the longest, and yet, when *U-612* arrived, we always found a place had been left for us to sneak in, somewhere in the middle of the waiting boats, with as many ahead as behind us. The reason was that, through some connections, I had been able, against all odds in war-torn Germany, to accumulate a most impressive and very rare record collection of the most popular songs. Among them was the favourite of the *Kriegsmarine,* which was *"Sing, Nachtigall, Sing,"* by the popular Evelyn Künnecke, which was a catchy, haunting tune that told the story of a young girl waiting for her boyfriend to return.* As soon as *U-612* tied up, we fixed the bridge speaker and tried to meet the requests that came from the boats on both sides of us, so that their crews had music while reloading torpedoes. The most popular song was always *"Sing, Nachtigall, Sing."*

Sing, Nachtigall, sing
Ein Leid aus alten Zeiten
Sing, Nachtigall, sing
Rühr mein müdes Herz

Ach, sing, Nachtigall, sing
Ein Lied aus alten Zeiten,
Bring, Nachtigall, bring
Mir mein Glück zurück.

[Sing, nightingale, sing
A song from the old days
Sing, nightingale, sing
Sooth my troubled heart.

Oh, sing, nightingale, sing
A song from the old days
Bring, nightingale, bring
My love back home to me.]

For this, if no other reason, *U-612* was the most popular boat in the 24. *Flottille.**

With the change of students every few weeks as their courses ended, I had the privilege of becoming acquainted with many of the U-boat commanders of the late war period, and all too often over the next two years, when I heard about a U-boat having been lost, I could remember the CO from his time with our flotilla.

Service in the 24. *Flottille* proved to be a hardworking and interesting period and it was not without its dangers. While a student was at the periscope during a submerged daytime attack, our CO, *Oberleutnant z.S.* Petersen, knew very little of what was going on at the surface. This could be rather dangerous since occasionally, when the escorts located a periscope, they immediately left their target ship and steamed toward us for a ramming attack, this being what the student had to expect in actual war conditions. If he did not dive fast enough, there often came a noisy crash and one knew that one had either lost another periscope or the bridge superstructure had suffered a crumpled railing. This did not happen to *U-612* but did happen to other boats in the flotilla, and collisions between boats or between

---

* *"Sing, Nachtigall, Sing,"* or "Sing, Nightingale, Sing," by Evelyn Künnecke, was the signature song of the 1941 German film *Auf Wiedersehen, Franziska.*

* So popular was *"Sing, Nachtigall, Sing"* that when my copy of the record broke when I was serving on *U-190,* my engine-room staff lovingly glued it back together and we kept listening to it, albeit with new and unintended percussion passages provided by the cracks in the record.

boats and surface vessels were not uncommon. At least one boat of our flotilla was lost at the cost of some members of the crew.*

We did get every fourth weekend off and we took full advantage of it to make up for an otherwise deprived social life. In my case one of these weekends was spent taking a 15-hour train trip to Berlin to attend a party for four hours, followed by a 15-hour return trip to Memel. My main attraction in Berlin was Dolores, who was nine years my senior and taught me a few things that had not been on the curriculum of the naval academy.

Dolores, who was nine years my senior, taught me things that were not on the curriculum of the naval academy. (WH col.)

On the return journey I had a strange experience that would probably only occur in wartime. The train was so packed that I had to stand in the corridor of the carriage. At some point, a lady boarded the train and ended up beside me. A very pleasant conversation ensued and a few hours later, when she got off at her home town of Tilsit, I knew her name and her address. I had, however, only a vague idea what she looked like because our meeting had taken place in complete darkness as we were travelling through a totally blacked-out country with no light penetrating the railway carriage. We stayed in contact by letter until, on one of my next returns from

Berlin, I interrupted my trip in Tilsit to finally meet her. We spent a very pleasant two hours before I had to continue my journey. I was not disappointed when I finally saw her and we stayed in touch for another year or so before the relationship fell victim to the circumstances of time and distance.

If we officers did not leave the base at Memel on our free weekends, we often joined the flotilla chaplain at the bar of the *Daressalam* for what we referred to as the Sunday morning "Church Cocktail." This is a concept I carried over into my postwar civilian life with enjoyable results for all my invited guests.

The crew of *U-612* were a lively and intelligent group of men. Sometime after our commissioning ceremony, they produced a mimeographed memorial album entitled *"Bierzeitung 612"* ("612 Beer News"), which was largely composed of doggerel poems about our boat and those on board. I have kept my copy ever since and, glancing through it, I still chuckle over what the crew said in verse about the leading personalities on the boat. Almost every important crew member was described in somewhat comical, if flattering terms – but always with an emphasis on the motto of the *U-Boot-Waffe*: *"Einer für alle – alle für einen."*

As satisfying as the results of our activities were in

---

* This is no idle statement – during 1943 and early 1944, at least 7 U-boats were lost in training accidents in the Baltic.

the 24. *Flottille*, a certain monotony began to creep into our lives as we on *U-612* wanted to make our contributions to the war in a more substantial way. After all, the lengthy practice of diving and manoeuvring a submarine under water, which had earlier seemed to present such insurmountable difficulties, had now made that skill second nature to me. I believed I was ready to serve on a *Frontboot* and waited anxiously for the call.

It came on 12 January 1944. That day I was relieved of my duties on *U-612* and ordered to report to the *Deutsche Werft* shipyard in Hamburg to join the *Baubelehrung* of a new boat. I was elated at this news because it meant that after nearly seven months in a training flotilla in the Baltic, I would shortly be joining the war.

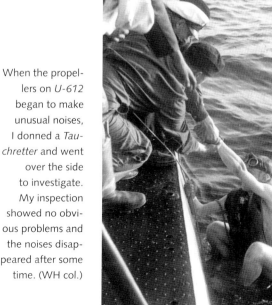

When the propellers on *U-612* began to make unusual noises, I donned a *Tauchretter* and went over the side to investigate. My inspection showed no obvious problems and the noises disappeared after some time. (WH col.)

During the summer of 1943 *U-612* was assigned as a training boat to the 24. *Flottille* in Memel, which trained future commanding officers in torpedo shooting. The practice target convoys were accompanied by fast *Geleitboote* which, when sighting the periscope of an attacking submarine, did their best to ram it. These pictures show the consequences of not avoiding contact – the crumpled bridge and a broken periscope on another U-boat in the flotilla which bear witness to such altercations. *U-612* was lucky enough to avoid encounters such as these. (WH col.)

I am on the right on the *Wintergarten* of *U-612* with the I.WO, *Leutnant z.S.* Pieper, enjoying a cigarette break from our relentless training schedule. Smoking was not permitted inside a U-boat due to the potential hazard of igniting battery gases and causing an explosion. (WH col.)

This periscope became another victim of an over-eager escort when a pupil could not get away fast enough. (WH col.)

Wearing a white summer jacket, I am being admired by my mother during a visit on leave to our home in Blankenfelde. (WH col.)

In quieter moments and in sunshine I was able to entertain myself and others by playing the boat's accordion on the bridge of *U-612*. (WH col.)

The old battleship *Schlesien* of pre-First World War vintage. It was already obsolete by the time of the Battle of Jutland of 1916 but was one of the few battleships allowed to Germany in the terms of the 1919 Treaty of Versailles. My father served on this vessel's sister ship *Schleswig-Holstein* in the Battle of Jutland. (WH col.)

A Type 39 torpedo boat at high speed in the Baltic in 1943. Although called a torpedo boat, this type of warship was actually a small destroyer with the same torpedo armament as a destroyer but lighter gun armament. (WH col.)

An unidentified Type IX boat returns to Lorient from patrol to be greeted by the usual large crowd composed of U-boat crews, flotilla staff and other military and naval organisations stationed there. Why there are no members of the *Blitzmädchen* (civilian female communications employees, who got their name from the lightning insignia on their sleeves) visible in this photo is a mystery as they were usually the first-line greeters with flowers and kisses for the returning commanding officer. In the background can be seen the First World War cruiser *Strassburg*, which was turned over to France as part of Germany's reparations. (WH col.)

FRONTBOOT U-190: JANUARY TO JUNE 1944

On 13 January 1944, I boarded the train at Memel for Hamburg. When I arrived at the latter place, I was distressed to see the destruction caused by the heavy RAF bombing of the previous July which had killed more than 40,000 civilians and rendered half the population of the city homeless. Hamburg was not the only German city that had suffered such devastation and the German people had slowly become so conditioned to accepting these terrible sights that we actually became somewhat numb. The mood in devastated Hamburg was grim but the bombing had not seriously affected the shipyards and at the *Deutsche Werft* I found several Type IXC/40 boats in the final stages of construction. It was not, however, a very happy time and I still remember making the daily ferry trip from the east side of the Elbe River to the opposite bank, where the yard was located, with the cold and the fog penetrating my clothing, my breath visible and destruction apparent wherever one looked.

My assignment at the *Deutsche Werft* was as a temporary relief for another engineer officer, but after only a few weeks I received fresh orders to join the 3. *Ubootsflottille* in La Rochelle, France. I was happy about this posting as it now appeared that I would finally join a *Frontboot*. On my way to take up my new assignment, I had an opportunity to spend a few days in Paris, a time I enjoyed to the fullest, including, of course, an evening at the famous Folies Bergères. Going shopping and visiting such landmarks as the Arc de Triomphe, the Champs Elysées and the Louvre were among the more memorable experiences of my wartime service. When I arrived at La Rochelle I discovered that, for reasons never explained, there was no position for me in the 3. *Flottille* and I was ordered to report to the 2. *Flottille* at Lorient to take up an assignment as *LI* on the Type IX boat *U-190*.

I arrived in Lorient on 9 February 1944. This port, situated on the southern coast of the Brittany peninsula, was one of the five U-boat bases in western France, the others being Bordeaux, Brest, La Rochelle and St. Nazaire – from which *BdU* had been conducting the Battle of the Atlantic for nearly four years. In the summer of 1940, when the first U-boat began to operate from Lorient, it was a large fishing port and a secondary French naval station. By the time I arrived in February 1944, it had been transformed by massive construction projects into the largest German submarine base in the west, manned

Massive U-boat pen under construction at Lorient. The Royal Air Force kindly refrained from bombing these buildings until their roofs were finished, at which point they were bombproof. (Editor's collection)

by a navy, army and air force population of more than 10,000 men and women.

Lorient lies on the Atlantic at the junction of the Skorff and Blavet Rivers, several miles from the mouth of the Blavet. Beginning in 1941, the *Kriegsmarine* began to build a series of large bunkers, some wet (in that U-boats could float in them) and some dry (in that the boats had to be transported into them). There were six such submarine bunkers in Lorient. At the junction of the Skorff and the Blavet was the Skorff-Bunker, a wet bunker, and about a mile and a half to the west, around Point Keroman, were the two cathedral-like *Dom* Bunkers and three huge structures known as the Keroman I, II and III bunkers. Keroman I was a dry bunker with one wet slip for hauling submarines out of the water,

Keroman II was dry, and Keroman III was wet. Boats were moved into Keroman II by means of a unique transportation system. To get to this bunker, a U-boat first entered the wet pen in Keroman I, where it was positioned on a cradle that was then hauled by a small railway engine along a system of tracks to Keroman II, which lay inland. This entire process, by which a U-boat weighing more than 1,000 tons could be transported onto dry land, took only 90 minutes and was a much faster method of carrying out repairs on the hull than using a conventional drydock.

The construction of these six bunkers, which could shelter more than 30 U-boats, took nearly three years and they were massive structures. The concrete roof of the Keroman III Bunker, for example, was between 15

(Above) At Lorient the crews and administrative staff of the 2. *U-Bootsflottille* were housed in these barracks, called *Lager* Lemp, located some 16 miles north of the city. Here they were relatively safe from the incessant air attacks on Lorient. (WH col.)

(Left) Some of the camouflage protecting *Lager* Lemp. (WH col.)

and 20 feet thick and the other bunkers were nearly as well protected. When the war ended, the French government realized it would be too expensive and time-consuming to demolish these memorials to the Battle of the Atlantic and they can be seen today in Lorient and the other former U-boat bases in France. But the boat bunkers were not the only results of the *Kriegsmarine*'s efforts: scattered around the naval base between the larger buildings were dozens of smaller but just as strongly-built structures, including torpedo, personnel, machinery and administrative bunkers. Curiously enough, the Royal Air Force did very little to interfere with this building project, which rivalled those of the pharaohs of ancient Egypt in magnitude, and it was only after most of the main bunkers had been completely roofed that the British began to bomb them. Repeated bombing attacks in 1943 and 1944 had not damaged the bunkers – at worst, the concrete of the roofs was cratered – but they had caused the near-total destruction of the surrounding civilian town.

Fortunately for the U-boat crews, we were not required to live in the naval base. The quarters of the 2. *Flottille* lay 16 miles north of Lorient at *Lager* Lemp, named after the commanding officer of the first submarine to operate from the port.* *Lager* Lemp consisted of a number of plain one-storey wooden buildings that served as quarters for the officers and sailors of the 2. *Flottille*, plus administration buildings, sports fields and dining facilities, all situated in lush and picturesque countryside. There was a large pond inside the camp that was covered with a large camouflage net to disguise it, since it was a highly visible aiming point for uninvited and unwanted British aerial visitors.

One of the nicest features of Camp Lemp was the *Alte Mühle,* an old mill that had been taken over as the officers' mess. Completely refurbished, it contained lounges and that necessary adjunct to naval morale – a well-stocked and comfortable bar. Many of the commanding officers of the flotilla had carved their names in the aged wooden beams that supported the roof, and the bar served as a memorial to those that had not returned.

Lorient was the home base of the 2. *Ubootsflottille,* to which *U-190* belonged, and the 10. *Ubootsflottille*, both of which operated Type IX U-boats. *U-190*, my new boat, was a Type IXC/40 submarine, which was larger than Type VII craft such as *U-375* and *U-612* on which I had previously served, displacing some 1,144 tons on the surface to the Type VII's 770 tons. In some of the postwar literature on German submarines, I have read many negative comments about the Type IX boat, which has been criticized for being too large, too unwieldy, too complicated and fragile, and for having a slower diving time than the Type VII, which supposedly made it more vulnerable to air attack.

In my experience, and I served as an *LI* on both the main types of U-boats, I found few differences between the two worth mentioning, and in terms of handling both types behaved very much the same. While it was true that the Type IX took longer to submerge, this was of less importance than it had been during the high point of the Battle of the Atlantic, as by early 1944 German U-boats were spending less and less time on the surface. In terms of machinery, there was nothing more complicated on a Type IX than on a Type VII. The Type IX also possessed some assets – being larger it was marginally more comfortable for the crew and it had more torpedo tubes, a larger fuel capacity (and thus longer range), more diving tanks (making it less vulnerable to damage) and more powerful engines which gave it a superior surface speed. Since I made three war patrols on a Type IX/C40, I may be prejudiced in favour of this craft but it should be noted that 14 of the 20 top-scoring

---

* *Kapitänleutnant* Fritz-Julius Lemp. Although he is notorious in the English-speaking world for sinking the liner *Athenia* on 3 September 1939, Lemp was actually a very audacious U-boat commander who torpedoed the British battleship *Barham* in December 1939 and sank 19 merchant ships on four war patrols before being killed in action in May 1941.

The bar in the flotilla wardroom at *Lager* Lemp was located in an ancient building, the Old Mill. The custom was for the COs of the boat in the flotilla to carve their names into the wooden ceiling beams and in this picture one can recognise the signatures König, Winter, Gelhaus, Heyse, Mohr, Witt, Kuhnke, Stockhausen, Abel, Markworth. Carving one's name into the beams seemed to have the effect of protecting the writers against evil: Most of these officers survived the war. (WH col.)

U-boats of the Second World War were Type IX boats.*

U-190 was a veteran boat commanded by a veteran officer, *Käpitanleutnant* Max Wintermeyer, a tall and somewhat aloof man. Wintermeyer, a 30-year-old member of Crew 34 at the *Marineschule*, had commanded *U-62* before commissioning *U-190* in September 1942 and had commanded it during three previous patrols, but had not enjoyed much success. Like their CO, most of the crew had been with the boat for a long time and it was obvious to me that, as a newcomer without much *Frontboot* experience, I would have to work hard to establish myself and earn the confidence of the crew,

---

* The top scoring Type VII boats were *U-46*, *U-47*, *U-48*, *U-96*, *U-99* and *U-552*. The top Type IX boats were *U-38*, *U-66*, *U-68*, *U-103*, *U-107*, *U-123*, *U-124*, *U-129*, *U-130*, *U-155*, *U-160*, *U-172*, *U-181* and *U-515*. However, it must be said that most Type IX craft operated in distant theatres where merchant shipping was not as strongly protected as in the Mediterranean and North Atlantic. The Type VII boats bore the brunt of the battle in those important theatres and suffered the bulk of the losses.

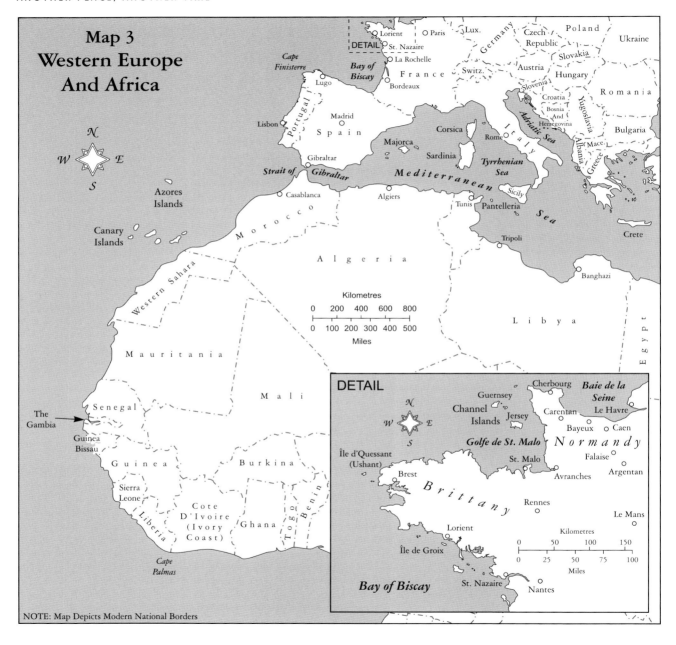

Map 3
Western Europe
And Africa

N
W · E
S

Cape Finisterre
Lugo
Lisbon
Portugal
Madrid
Spain
Gibraltar
Strait of Gibraltar

Azores Islands
Canary Islands

Casablanca
Morocco

Western Sahara

Mauritania

Mali

The Gambia
Senegal

Guinea Bissau
Guinea
Sierra Leone
Liberia
Cote D'Ivoire (Ivory Coast)
Burkina
Ghana
Togo
Benin

Cape Palmas

Lorient
Paris
Lux.
Germany
Czech Republic
Poland
Ukraine
St. Nazaire
DETAIL
Slovakia
Austria
Hungary
Slovenia
Bay of Biscay
Switz.
Croatia
Bosnia And Herzegovina
Yugoslavia
Romania
La Rochelle
France
Bordeaux
Italy
Adriatic Sea
Albania
Mace.
Bulgaria
Greece
Corsica
Rome
Majorca
Sardinia
Tyrrhenian Sea
Mediterranean
Sicily
Sea
Crete
Algiers
Tunis
Pantelleria
Tripoli

Algeria

Banghazi

Kilometres
0   200   400   600   800
0 100 200 300 400 500
Miles

L i b y a

E g y p t

DETAIL

N
W · E
S

Cherbourg
Baie de la Seine
Guernsey
Channel Islands
Jersey
Carentan
Le Havre
Bayeux
Caen
Golfe de St. Malo
Normandy
Île d'Quessant (Ushant)
St. Malo
Falaise
Argentan
Brest
Avranches
Brittany
Rennes
Le Mans
Lorient
Kilometres
0   50   100   150
Île de Groix
0 25 50 75 100
Miles
Bay of Biscay
St. Nazaire
Nantes

NOTE: Map Depicts Modern National Borders

especially that of my two *Obermaschinisten*, or chief engineer petty officers, Holtmann and Krüger, who were not only older than I, being 27 and 29 respectively, but had been on *U-190* since its commissioning. As both men were excellent at their duties, I left them alone and did not interfere with their responsibilities.

Although at this point in my service in the *U-Boot-Waffe* I had not experienced much action, I would like to make a few general comments about our morale in the last years of the war. When I joined *U-190* in February 1944, the so-called *"Glückliche Zeit"* or "Happy Times" were long past and we were experiencing what we U-boat personnel called the *"Saure Gurkenzeit"* or "Sour Pickle Times," which were entirely different. During the early years of the war, U-boats had spent much of their time on the surface – the type of action for which our submarines were actually designed – and usually dived only to escape pursuit or make a daytime torpedo attack. By 1944, such were the numbers of Allied warships and aircraft deployed against us that we had very much become the hunted, rather than the hunters. The odds against our survival were getting steadily worse and we all knew it, yet it rarely became a subject of discussion among us – in our minds, it would always be the other boat that wouldn't make it, not our boat. The flotilla administration, however, looked at the matter in a somewhat different way; to lighten their burden when a U-boat was lost, before departing on a patrol we were required to pack our personal belongings in a wooden box and address it to our next of kin. If we did not return, the flotilla simply sent the box to the addressee. End of story.

In the last week of February 1944, we began to prepare *U-190* for one of the long patrols typical of Type IX boats. The loading of provisions, torpedoes and ammunition were the responsibility of the two watch officers, whereas I was concerned with filling the fuel and fresh water tanks and ensuring that all machinery on board was operating at peak efficiency. I also satisfied myself, after the boat had been fully loaded and I had calculated the changes in weight throughout the vessel, that it was properly balanced and ballasted. Once this was confirmed by a test dive, I could then report the *Techniker*, or engine division, of *U-190*, ready for patrol.

After *U-190* was fully armed and loaded, it was moved to the Skorff-Bunker, northeast of the Keroman complex. Because of its small size (only two wet bays), the Skorff-Bunker was normally used as the departure bunker for boats going on patrol, leaving the larger Keroman bunkers to berth returning boats and for work on those under repair and maintenance.

The night before our departure there was the usual farewell gathering at the *Alte Mühle* for the officers of *U-190* and another boat, which shortly would also be leaving on patrol. I include some photographs of this small party, and in my experience such affairs – in contrast to what is often portrayed in postwar films and novels – were rather subdued occasions, not without humour but affected by thoughts of whether those present would ever see each other again. That particular evening, which I remember well, our quiet but competent French mess waitress, Simone, added an even more dignified tone to what was really a very civilized occasion.

On 9 March 1944 the 2. *Flottille* gave a farewell party for the officers of *U-190* and another boat that were about to depart on patrol. The dress code for an event like this was dress blue uniforms, except for members of the two departing crews, who had already packed their uniforms away and can be identified in this photo by their grey service dress. I am sitting in the middle in the upper photo. On the beam above our heads in the lower picture can be seen the carved signatures of comrades. These pictures, which depict a very civilized atmosphere, provide a realistic contrast to the drunken orgies so popular in films about the wartime U-boat service. (WH col.)

In the early evening of 7 March 1944, *U-190* left the Skorff-Bunker and, with the crew lining the deck and the officers on the bridge, acknowledged the waves of those who had gathered to wish us well and moved slowly down the Blavet River. The passage down the Blavet to its mouth at the Atlantic was a somewhat treacherous stretch to navigate due to its shallow depth, shoals and tricky combination of current and tide, which required constant vigilance on the part of the helmsman. We arrived at its mouth without incident, however, and picked up our escort of small surface vessels from the *Vorposten Flottille** that would take us out into the open sea of the Bay of Biscay.

By early the next morning, we were in deep water and *Kapitänleutnant* Wintermeyer ordered a test dive. It quickly became apparent that we had a serious problem – the hatch in the aft torpedo compartment leaked – and there was nothing for it but to return to Lorient. We made fast again in the Skorff-Bunker at 8 P.M. that evening. The dockyard staff worked on the hatch for two days and then, on 11 March, we again left Lorient in the early evening, picked up an escort and headed for the Atlantic. Another test dive gave conclusive proof that the hatch leak had not been fixed and was, if anything, worse. Back we went to the Skorff-Bunker – this time the repairs took four days and it was not until 16 March that we set out for the third time. Thankfully, the twice-repaired hatch proved sound and we dropped our escort

at 7 A.M. on 17 March 1944 and proceeded into the Bay of Biscay.

For U-boats operating from the bases in France, traversing the Bay of Biscay was always a very dangerous proposition as it was constantly patrolled by radar-equipped Allied aircraft. Since its last patrol, however, *U-190* had been equipped with a radar detector that gave us warning of enemy aircraft and we got many such contacts during our "*Biskayamarsch*" – the eleven days it took us to get across the Bay and out into the open Atlantic – and we were neither sighted nor attacked.* Progress was slow because we only surfaced briefly during the hours of darkness "*zum Laden und Lüften*," to recharge our batteries and change the air in the boat, and we did not tarry long above water as it was extremely dangerous. Thus, we crept slowly along the coast of France and then the northern coast of Spain, occasionally obtaining faint hydrophone and visual contacts, until by 28 March we had reached *Quadrat* CF 35, 100 miles west of Cape Blanco. We were now in the open Atlantic.

On 29 March, we received a signal from *BdU* ordering us to patrol *Quadrat* EU, the area immediately west of Cap Palmas off the Liberian coast of Africa. Accordingly, we continued to make our way south for nearly four weeks, passing west of the Azores and Canary Islands. The farther we got from Europe, the more time we ran on the surface using our diesels, usually spending

* *Vorposten Flottille* were composed of small escort vessels, usually converted trawlers, that escorted U-boats and convoys in coastal areas.

* The *KTB* for this patrol provides information that indicates that this device was most probably the Telefunken *FuMB 7 Naxos* detector, coupled with the dipole aerial codenamed "*Fliege*," which could provide warning of radar-equipped aircraft within a three-mile range.

the darkness hours above water and the daylight hours below, but it was not until 23 April, just over five weeks after leaving Lorient, that we reached our assigned patrol area.

In all, we spent nearly a month in the waters off Liberia, Sierre Leone and the Ivory Coast and it was not at all a profitable time. Glancing at a copy of the *KTB* or log for this patrol today, I see that the entries are minimal – a typical day, 8 May 1944, informs me of the location of our boat and provides the following information:

0634 *Getaucht* [submerged]
2020 *Aufgetaucht* [surfaced]

Etmal [summary of distance traveled]
Über Wasser [surfaced]   74 sm. [nautical miles]
Unter Wasser [submerged] 14 sm.
                            88 sm. [total]

Day after day, the same brief entries appear because nothing much happened. While this is not exactly the stuff of dramatic sea fiction, it must always be remembered that wars are rarely as dramatic as novelists portray them – basically they consist of long periods of fatigue and boredom punctuated by brief moments of sheer terror.

During the time we spent off Africa, the heat on board was brutal, rarely below 40° Celsius (104° Fahrenheit) with extremely high humidity. Most days, we were bathing in our own sweat and yet it was a serious disciplinary offence to expose one's body to the airflow of one of the many fans on board without protection of one's kidneys. I am not sure why this was so – the *Kriegsmarine* medical staff who issued this decree never bothered to explain their reasoning – but in practical terms it meant we had to wear special woollen waist bands all the time. When we surfaced at night, the CO permitted the crew to come up in shifts to the *Wintergarten*, the platform at the rear of the conning tower where our anti-aicraft guns were mounted, to cool off – that is to say, enjoy temperatures of only 95° Fahrenheit or so. While doing so, we could smell the continent of Africa which, although it was out of sight, wafted to us on the breeze.

I was relaxing on the *Wintergarten* one dark night when a curious incident occurred that still comes readily to mind after all the intervening years. Our bridge lookouts spotted a neutral passenger ship steaming on an opposite course – which was not hard to do as the vessel was fully lit. It passed close by us, completely unaware of the dark marauder, moving a few thousand yards away on the surface. Through our binoculars we could actually see a party in progress with elegantly-dressed couples talking, drinking and dancing on the afterdeck, all the while being serenaded by the ship's orchestra. The contrast between this happy peacetime social scene and our own situation on a tiny steel platform and facing an unknown fate, was nearly overwhelming.

And so we passed long days patrolling off West Africa. Occasionally, the bridge watch reported lights or smoke but always too far off to investigate. In the late evening of 12 May 1944, however, our lookouts spotted a small freighter of about 5500 BRT* about 2.5 miles off our starboard bow and moving fast. We immediately went to action stations and steered towards it at high speed on the surface. When we were within range, *Kapitänleutnant* Wintermeyer fired a single T5 *Zaunkönig* acoustic torpedo** and then ordered an *Alarmtauchen*. A few minutes later, our sound man heard a large explosion and then, as the *KTB* records, came *"Sinkgeräuschen (Rauschen und Knacken)"* or the sounds made by the collapsing bulkheads of a doomed ship as it slid beneath the waves. Shortly after this, all contact was lost with the target and when we surfaced 15 minutes later, there was nothing to be seen except a smoke pall hanging over the water where we assumed our target had gone down.***

An *Alarmtauchen*, or crash dive, might originate from the sighting of an aircraft (and in the Atlantic, this was almost always an enemy aircraft), the radar detector providing a warning that the boat was being probed by radar pulses, the bridge watch sighting an enemy vessel – or it might simply be ordered by the CO. Regard-

less of its cause, an *Alarmtauchen* was usually initiated by the shouted order "Alarm!" from the bridge into the conning tower below and the ringing of a loud electric warning bell. Normally there were four men on the bridge: the *Wachoffizier* or watch officer; an *Unteroffizier* and two seamen – all four covering a quarter of the horizon – and the CO might be there as well. Once the *Alarmtauchen* commenced, all occupants of the bridge, except the senior officer, dropped quickly through the conning tower hatch into the conning tower and then through the *Zentrale* hatch into the *Zentrale*, or control room, itself. They moved quickly, as if they did not, the next man coming down would trample them. Once in the *Zentrale*, the *Unteroffizier* and one of the two sailors immediately occupied the two hydroplane positions and the *LI*, if he was not already in the *Zentrale*, moved there and took up a position behind them. The diesel engines were now stopped, the clutches to the electric motors opened allowing those engines to go at full speed, and the various air intake valves were closed. Other assigned crew members readied themselves to open and close vent and air valves on command.

As the last man off the bridge entered the conning tower, he secured the hatch, shouting *"Turmluk is zu!"* (Tower hatch closed!) before he had actually finished locking it. It was only after hearing this shout, which he had been waiting for, that the *LI* would order *"Fluten!"* (Flood!) and the diving process would commence.

The above procedure was really the "normal" procedure for any type of dive but rarely was an *Alarmtauchen* normal because whatever could go wrong often did go

---

* Brutto Registered Tons, a measuring system for the cargo-carrying capacity of merchant ships, from which insurance, port and harbour fees were calculated. One BRT was taken to equal 100 cubic feet or 2.83 cubic metres of cargo-carrying capacity.

** The German T-5 *Zaunkönig* ("Wren") acoustic torpedo, which homed in on the noise created by the propellers of target ships, was introduced in the latter half of 1943. It was effective but was soon countered by noise-maker decoys towed by warships.

*** Allied records do not confirm the sinking of a vessel of this size in this location on 12 May 1944. The fact that the records did not confirm a sinking reported by a U-boat CO was very common as it was extremely hard, in many cases, for the boat commander to positively establish his success.

wrong. For example, the boat might be reluctant to leave the surface because of the influence of rough seas. Or it might be under air attack. Or it might be reluctant to level out from its dive, a problem caused either by the salinity and temperature of the water or an over eager *LI*. The possible variations of result in an *Alarmtauchen* were almost endless.

To return to *U-190* off Africa, the inconclusive action of 12 May was the only truly notable event during a long, fatiguing and really rather boring patrol. Two days later, after spending just over three weeks in his operational area, *Kapitänleutnant* Wintermeyer decided to return to base, a decision impelled by the fact that, due to the delay caused by the repairs to the aft hatch, we had exhausted nine days of our food supply before we had even set out, and we had not had an opportunity to re-provision. We altered course to the north and *U-190* began the long and slow return journey to Lorient – two weeks later, we were still southwest of the Canary Islands, but as we neared the Bay of Biscay we began to spend less and less time on the surface as our radar detector came alive to warn us of enemy aircraft.

It was standard procedure while on patrol for our radioman to record all the messages he picked up, whether intended for our boat or not. On numerous occasions during this long African patrol, we heard messages from other U-boats informing *BdU* that they were being attacked by enemy warships or aircraft and, too often, these messages were the last anybody ever heard from the boats involved. During our return voyage we picked up a message from *U-505* of our own 2. *Flottille* that

it was under attack and then nothing more so we presumed this boat was lost. We did not know it at the time, of course, but in fact *U-505*, which had been crippled by air attack, was captured intact on 4 June 1944 by a daring American boarding party from a task force centred on the escort carrier USS *Guadalcanal*. It can be seen today on display in the city of Chicago in the United States.*

On 6 June 1944, the *KTB* informs me that we formally commenced the *Biskayamarsch*. That, of course, was a famous day in history and, at 5.43 A.M., we received a short radio message from *BdU* stating that the Allies had landed in Normandy. A longer message came in at 7.05 A.M. addressed to *"alle Kommandanten in See"* from *Grossadmiral* Dönitz that stressed the seriousness of the situation and urged the sailors of the *U-Boot-Waffe* to take "the most extreme measures," and

to abandon the normal precautionary measures. Each enemy vessel useful for landing is to be subjected to all out attack, even when there is danger of losing your own U-boat. Every enemy soldier and enemy weapon destroyed before landing diminishes the enemy's prospect of success. In this crisis I know that I can rely on my trusted men of the *U-Boot-Waffe* – who have been tried in the toughest battles.

---

* The Type IXC boat, *U-505,* which was captured by the American navy in 1944, is currently on display at the Chicago Museum of Science and Industry.

Since at that time none of us were fully aware of the historical significance of this event, we looked at it as just another phase of the war and optimistically talked about the failed landing that had taken place at Dieppe in 1942. We had quite enough to do to survive the homeward voyage and we concentrated on our own problems.

Progress across the Bay of Biscay was slow because of the ever-present threat of aircraft and we spent most of our time running submerged. A week after the Normandy landing, we were still west of Cape Finisterre in Spain when we received a message informing us that we were one of four boats inbound for Lorient and that among the others was *U-505* (which was actually now in the hands of the United States Navy). We crept along the northern coast of Spain and then north until finally, at dawn on 20 June, we picked up our *Vorposten* escort and proceeded into Lorient. With the entire crew lining the deck as we approached the Skorff-Bunker, we could see the usual welcoming committee of senior naval officers, various personnel of the *Kriegsmarine* and *Heer* from the garrison and, of course, a female contingent from the *Blitzmädchen* or "Lightning Girls."*

After we tied up and the gangway was placed, *Kapitänleutnant* Wintermeyer formally saluted the senior officer in the welcoming delegation, reported *U-190* back from its mission, and received the traditional gift of a bouquet of flowers from one of the *Blitzmädchen*. In a rare show of emotion I noticed the eyes of our

Kapitänleutnant Max Wintermeyer, the CO of *U-190*, is shown here on his bridge on 20 June 1944, the day the boat returned to Lorient from a patrol to African waters. Note the salt corrosion covering the metal surfaces of the boat; in some places one could poke one's finger right through the metal. The white pennant indicates the sinking of a freighter of 5,500 tons on patrol but this assumed success was never confirmed. U-boat commanders always had problems confirming their sinkings and often, mostly unintentionally, exaggerated these numbers. (WH col.)

flotilla chief, *Fregattenkapitän* Kals, fill with tears when he came on board. During the 96 days we had been away, very few of the other boats from 2. *Ubootsflottille*, which had been out on patrol at the same time, had returned.*

---

* Members of the *Kriegsmarine* women's communication service, somewhat equivalent to the British Wrens but civilian, not service personnel. Their nickname came from the lightning flash insignia on their uniforms.

* During the period March to June 1944 the 2. *Flottille* lost 7 boats (*U-66*, *U-68*, *U-125*, *U-505*, *U-801*, *U-856*, and *U-1224*). Another boat, *U-545*, which had departed on patrol before *U-190*, was lost shortly before Wintermeyer set out while *U-154*, which departed after *U-190*, was lost within a week of Wintermeyer's return. The strength of a *Flottille* was not fixed but the loss of these nine craft would have been well over half of Kals's operational strength.

U-190 returning to Lorient from its fourth patrol on 20 June 1944. The water deflector on the bridge superstructure shows damage from heavy wave action. Note the khaki tropical uniforms worn by the crew – they were needed in African waters. (WH col.)

Some photos from my album…

(Top) The battle cruiser *Gneisenau*, of 31,600 tons displacement with a main armament of nine 11-inch guns, was commissioned in 1938. During the war she sank a number of British ships, including the auxiliary cruiser *Rawalpindi* and the aircraft carrier *Glorious*. In February 1942 she participated, with her sister ship *Scharnhorst*, in the "Channel dash" and arrived in Kiel where she was heavily damaged by bombing that put an end to her active career.

(Centre) The light cruiser *Nürnberg,* of 9,040 tons displacement and 6-inch main armament, was commissioned in 1934 and survived the war only to be taken over by the Soviet Navy in 1945. She was scrapped in 1961.

(Bottom) On the left is the fleet tender *Grille* with a displacement of 3,430 tons. Built in 1935, she served during the prewar years as the host ship for Hitler's naval visits and during the war as a minelayer and headquarters for the U-boat command in Norway. In the postwar period she briefly became a cruise ship in the Mediterranean before being scrapped in 1951. On the right is the pocket battleship *Admiral Scheer,* a diesel-powered warship armed with six 11-inch guns built under the restrictions of the Treaty of Versailles to be faster than stronger opponents and stronger than faster opponents. *Scheer* served throughout the war but was sunk by bombing in Kiel in April 1945.

Submariners at their best! Practising emergency power drill at
Lorient in the summer of 1944. (WH col.)

The welcoming ceremonies behind us, the elation of having returned from a long patrol against all odds began slowly to ebb away. I felt as if I could spend hours lying on my stomach on the grass, revelling over the sight and smell of those green blades that were part of another world while we were at sea. Coming home, however, had some disadvantages. We reacted to the first cigarette in more than three months like teenagers who had never smoked before and felt slightly ill, but of course that did not last long and we were soon ready to indulge again in all the minor vices civilisation had to offer.

The fighting in Normandy, which had been going on for nearly a month when we returned, was too far away to affect us in Lorient and slowly we became reaccustomed to the daily routine of a naval base. In my case it began with making an inventory of repairs required for *U-190* and then conferring with the dockyard technical staff about scheduling this work. Since we had not had any encounters with the enemy during the last patrol and had suffered no damage, the nature of this work was largely routine maintenance, such as the cleaning, testing and replacement of aging equipment, and painting.

We were informed, however, that *U-190* would be fitted with a *Schnorchel*, a breathing device that would permit us to run our diesels at periscope depth and both recharge our batteries and renew the air in the boat, while still remaining submerged. We were intrigued by this innovation as we would be able to avoid surfacing and, given growing numbers of Allied warships and aircraft, this would considerably improve our chances for survival. As the *Leitender Ingenieur* on *U-190* I would be responsible for the operation and maintenance of this device and I would therefore have to learn how to use it. After some inquiries I found out that I was to attend a three-day *Schnorchel* course in Danzig to be held in the first week of July.

Our commanding officer, *Kapitänleutnant* Max Wintermeyer, who had commissioned *U-190* in 1942, was scheduled to be replaced by his former I.WO, *Oberleutnant z.S.* Hans-Edwin Reith, expected to arrive shortly from the *Kommandantenschule* (commanders' school) to take over the boat. As my business with the dockyard staff was settled, I did not wait for Reith's arrival but said goodbye to Wintermeyer and proceeded on leave to Berlin.

After a four-day journey through France, I reached home in Blankenfelde on 30 June 1944. The sun was smiling in the sky, the morning promised a wonderful summer day and, better still, I had three weeks of leave ahead of me! I felt I deserved them after my time in African waters suffering from the heat, without seeing daylight. Our faces were yellow and green when we returned to Lorient and, even now, ten days later, my white face contrasted oddly with the colour of my khaki tropical uniform, newly decorated with the *U-bootsabzeichen* or submariner's combat badge which I was now entitled to wear as I had spent more than 45 days on combat patrol. Before I left Lorient, I availed myself of the opportunity to stock up with bottles of cognac and liqueurs, perfume, silk stockings and other luxuries not readily available in Germany but which might be bought by U-boat crews and which felt heavy in my suitcase. Once at home, I enjoyed a great breakfast cooked by my mother and was eager to get going. In the evening I visited my friend Hannes, an engineer who did not serve in the military because he was employed on essential war work. Hannes was the only one of my friends still around; the others were in the armed forces on one front or another – or they were dead or seriously wounded. When he asked me about my plans for the weekend and heard that I had none, Hannes suggested I join him and his girlfriend the next day, and assured me that he would provide a date for me as well.

On the following day, a Saturday, when the two of us stepped out of the station at Grünau, a part of Berlin famous for its lakes and woods, I met Reni, a very vivacious young lady who was Hannes's girlfriend, and the three of us waited for the remaining member of the party. I was told that lack of punctuality was one of the outstanding characteristics of this person but that it could be partially explained by her obligations at work because she was employed in an important government office. We only waited a quarter of an hour, however, before the lady in question, an attractive, blue-eyed, blonde girl, arrived and was introduced to me as Ruth.

After coffee and cake first and dinner later, Hannes and I walked with the ladies along the shore of the lake in the dusk of the evening. I asked my companion about her work (how imaginative!) and she told me she was a secretary to a high official in the Reich Chancellery. I was impressed since she seemed to be rather young for such a position. Before she and I said goodbye we agreed to get together again in a few days and I had to admit to myself that I was very attracted to this intelligent and pretty young lady.

I managed to get another date with Ruth before I had to leave for Danzig to attend my *Schnorchel* course. I must confess that, while on this three-day course, my mind was more occupied with Ruth than my duties. Arriving back in Blankenfelde after the course had ended, I immediately called her and we had dinner together. A few days later, Hannes arranged a little party at Reni's home in Eichwalde, to which I invited Ruth. I arrived, loaded with bottles and full of expectations, and Reni's mother, a lively but elderly lady, joined us and mixed in well with the youthful company. She asked me quite a few questions about my activities and as I elaborated

During a leave to Germany after my return from the African patrol on *U-190*, I was introduced to Ruth Ehlers, who was destined to become my wife. (WH col.)

a little about my existence as a submariner, my pride in being a *Leitender Ingenieur*, and the peculiarities of submarine warfare, I was happy to see Ruth was an attentive listener.

Late in the afternoon Ruth and I found ourselves alone on the terrace. It was a beautiful summer day and the fragrance of the garden flowers and the music from the radio – and just being by ourselves – made this a special moment. Sitting beside Ruth on a garden bench I told her of my days and months at sea, I described intoxicating tropical nights under the incredible clear sky of the southern ocean, but also how, even on a crowded U-boat, one can feel very lonely.

Unfortunately, a few hours later, our lovely dinner party was rudely interrupted by the Royal Air Force when the air raid sirens began to howl. The revellers did not feel like going into the basement on such a beautiful summer evening and so we went out into the garden and watched as searchlights probed upward and anti-aircraft shells burst

in the night sky. Finally, the raid ended and we all danced and talked and laughed until the approach of dawn.

A few days later I met Ruth's parents and the two of us enjoyed each other's company for the remainder of my leave, but the shadow cast by its approaching end began to intrude into our happiness. I tried to console Ruth with the promise that I would be back in three to four months, although it occurred to me that such a promise was really rather reckless as I was not going out on a vacation cruise when I returned to my boat – at least not in the summer of 1944 when, on average, for every three U-boats that departed, only one returned. On the other hand, I had never had any doubts about coming back myself and it was no different now – of course I would make it back to Ruth!

On Wednesday, 19 July 1944, I was on the platform of the station early to make sure I got a decent seat on the train for Paris. After I had stowed my suitcase I went back to the gate to meet Ruth, who had promised to see me off. She arrived and we walked up and down the platform arm in arm while she courageously tried to hide her sadness. One had so much to say and yet, at a moment like this, suitable words were hard to find and all too soon we were interrupted by the shout, "Board the train! Close the doors!" There was time for one last kiss and then the train started moving. Looking back out of my compartment window, I watched Ruth wave from the end of the platform for a long time.

It was at this time that I began to keep a diary, fragments of which survive, and I can now refer to it for an account of my return trip to Lorient.

20 July 1944

The trip from Berlin to Paris takes much longer than scheduled. After many delays the train rolls into the Gare du Nord twelve hours late. It's evening now and I check into a hotel near the Madeleine.* where I have stayed before. It has the advantage of not being too far from the Quai d'Orsay where I want to visit a young lady who works there for the German Embassy.

Since the landing in Normandy there is a curfew for German soldiers at 10 o'clock at night. As it is already after nine I will have to hurry. The way leads past the Place de la Concorde along the Seine to the gigantic building, where to my dismay I learn that the lady left several weeks ago to return to Germany. Disappointed, I walk back to my hotel.

21 July 1944

I do some shopping and make inquiries about how to continue my trip from here. I am lucky – in the afternoon two buses will leave for Lorient. Then I have lunch in the very elegant *Offiziersheim* [Officers' club], write a letter to Ruth, and saunter over to the headquarters of *Marine Gruppenkommando West* where the buses are waiting. There I run into a comrade of mine, a watch officer of one of the boats in my flotilla and I am glad not to be completely alone on the trip.

Right on time at five in the afternoon we depart from Paris. The way leads us past completely destroyed Orléans towards Angers. Outside Tours – it is now two in the morning [of 22 July 1944] – we have a break to give the drivers some rest. I can't sleep in the uncomfortable seat and have a stroll through the warm summer night. I settle down under one of the bridges across the Loire and dream ……

A thought hits me, when I see one of the bridge sentries approach. I stop him and give him a hastily scribbled note with my regards for a nurse who works at the railway station and whom I met on my way to Germany. Well – one's duties never end! (Of course I'm fully aware of the fact that I will probably never see the nurse again in my life.)

In Angers we spend the night in the lovely little castle, occupied by the *FdU West** – known for assembling the most beautiful female staff in the whole of France. I enjoy a few glasses of champagne and write some words to Ruth.

The journey continues [on 23 July 1944] via St. Nazaire and after a few interruptions caused by air attacks, our buses finally reach Lorient. Since it is Sunday I can't report back to my flotilla until tomorrow and I therefore drive straight to *Lager* Lemp where we live, far away from the naval base. The welcome from my comrades lasts until late into the night.

I recall that the main topic of conversation on the night of my return was the recent assassination attempt on Hitler. This had occurred on 20 July, just as I was passing through Paris, and I had heard rumours about the event.

---

* The area in Paris around the Madeleine Church square, a few minutes walk from the Champs Elysées.

* *Führer der U-boote West* or Commander of Submarines, West, the officer in command of administrative and disciplinary matters relating to the U-boat flotillas based in France although operational command was always retained by *BdU*. In the summer of 1944, the *FdU West* was *Kapitän z.S.* Rudolf Rösing, who had his headquarters at the Château de Pignerolles in the suburbs of Angers.

We naval officers were in agreement that the army officers involved in this attempt on our leader's life may have had honourable motives but had carried them out by very dishonourable methods. We could not understand how these officers could break their oath of loyalty and become traitors to their country and we could not condone their actions. Although the years that have gone by since have opened my eyes to better understanding the motivation of the conspirators, I must still condemn their actions, particularly the manner in which they were carried out.

At the base, however, life went on as before and I found the work on *U-190* was in progress as expected. I now met my new commanding officer, *Oberleutnant z.S.* Reith, who was 24 years of age and a member of Crew X/39. At our first meeting, I was not particularly impressed with him but I deferred my final judgement to a later date.

About a week after my return to Lorient, life at the base began to change following the American breakthrough on the Normandy front. By the last days of July, American armoured columns were pushing into Brittany and it looked very much as though Lorient would shortly be on the front line. By the first days of August 1944, life in Lorient suddenly became rather exciting as is described in the diary I kept during that summer long ago:

While waiting for a Japanese submarine to arrive in Lorient, on 1 August 1944 the 2. *Flottille* at Lorient entertained a Japanese officer who had been sent from Berlin. On the right is the chief of staff of the flotilla, *Korvettenkapitän* Friedrichs. (WH col.)

The commanding officer of the 2. *U-Bootsflotille*, *Fregattenkapitän* Ernst Kals at the same reception, which preceded his 38th birthday celebrations on the following day. (WH col.)

Tuesday, 1 August 1944

4.30 A.M.: What a lovely time to begin a new day! In the middle of the night one is chased out of bed. A Japanese submarine* is expected to arrive. There isn't even time for breakfast and we are on our way to the harbour.

In the bunker, in which the Japanese submarine is to tie up, preparations have been made in the form of waiting dignitaries, flowers, band, girls, etc. And we wait ......

6.15 A.M.: The Adjutant brings the news, that our escort vessels have come back without the Japanese. Well – we'll try again tomorrow – getting up at four thirty, etc.

6.30 A.M.: On our return to Camp Lemp we meet the Japanese delegation sent from Berlin. They come with us and in the camp, in honour of our guests, a hearty breakfast is served to us half-starved ordinary sailors.

11.30 A.M.: My CO, *Oberleutnant z. S.* Reith, and I have to return to the harbour again – our boat is scheduled to come out of the dry dock very shortly. The weather is marvellous. The sun is so warm that I'm determined to go swimming tomorrow with our crew.

3 P.M.: Coming back to camp from the dockyard we enjoy the delicious lunch that was kept warm for us.

7 P.M.: The afternoon nap did some good. A bit short, though, since as Duty Officer I am expected to look after the affairs of the camp. After a good dinner we sit contentedly on the terrace and are looking forward to the nightly festivities in the Old Mill.

Shortly after nine, the Chief of our 2. *Flottille*, *Fregatten-kapitän* Kals, suddenly returns from Lorient and, with a serious face, approaches the Japanese delegation sitting at a slight distance from the rest of us. Politely they rise immediately. "Bad news, Gentlemen. You have to pack at once and be ready to leave in half an hour at the latest." The gentlemen from the Far East accept the news calmly and their permanent, inscrutable smile does not fade for one second. I'm flabbergasted!

I grab the Adjutant and ask him, "Hey, what on earth is the matter?" "The Americans are at Rennes," is the reply. For the moment that doesn't mean very much to me. He offers, "Come, I'll show you on the map." Then I too realize the seriousness of the situation.* The Chief-of-Staff comes running: "All boats report at once the strength of their complements!"

9.30 P.M.: We are all ordered to pack immediately, abandon the camp and move into a personnel bunker at Lorient. The bus for our crew will leave in one hour. I go to my room and pack what I unpacked only a few days ago on my return from my three weeks of leave in Berlin.

10.50 P.M.: The bus is loaded and then we realize that half the luggage is still outside. I guess we'll have to go twice. I remain behind with ten men to deliver the remain-

---

* This is a reference to the Japanese submarine, *I-52*, commanded by Commander Uno Kameo, which departed Japan in March 1944 bound for France with a cargo of 2.2 tons of gold. On 24 June 1944 *I-52* was sunk by American naval aircraft near the Cape Verde Islands with the loss of all on board. On 30 July, however, a coded signal was received by the *Kriegsmarine* in France that the vessel was inbound for Lorient, hence the preparations to meet her. This signal was later determined to be false and on 30 August 1944 the *Kriegsmarine* officially declared the vessel as presumed sunk. *I-52* was the last Japanese submarine to attempt to reach Europe.

* The general military situation in early August 1944 resulted from Operation COBRA, a massive attack made by the 1st US Army on the western end of the German lines in Normandy. This attack resulted in a breakthrough and the 3rd US Army, under Lieutenant General George S. Patton, was then tasked with exploiting it. On 1 August, the spearhead American formation, the 4th Armoured Division, drove south and reached Rennes, well behind the German front lines, creating a serious situation for the German forces in Brittany as their communications were nearly severed.

der in another hour. After the bus has left, I'm overwhelmed with questions from the men. I know very little and try to calm their excitement. I ask two men to play cards with me. I have lots of luck – but only with cards.

11.30 P.M.: The electric power has failed and so has my card game. I go for a walk. Everywhere there is plenty of activity. With a lot of yelling, bags, suitcases and crates are loaded, and one bus after the other leaves the camp. I approach the Chief-of-Staff, *Korvettenkäpitan* Friedrichs, and request to be relieved as Duty Officer of Camp Lemp. Granted.

Shortly before midnight our bus returns. Fifteen minutes later our stuff is loaded and we depart – two men on the fenders, two more on the roof as lookout for aircraft and the remainder in the bus, ready to evacuate at a moment's notice. In this fashion we race through the moonlit night.

Wednesday, 2 August 1944

12.30 A.M.: The crew is occupied making the residence bunker their home. After I have stowed my things in my cubbyhole I go to *Haus Schneider*,* where the Chief [*Fregattenkapitän* Kals] has just begun to celebrate his birthday. There is a small group of about ten officers, and the mood is rather subdued in keeping with the circumstances. I congratulate the Chief and am invited to enjoy a glass of champagne. At 1.30 in the morning: the Chief calls it a day.

At 4.30 A.M. we have to get up for the reception of the Japanese submarine – again. Once more we wait in vain. The whole effort is wasted – the Japanese didn't come. Af-

ter breakfast I have the pleasant task of accompanying the *O.T. (Organisation Todt)** girls to their quarters.

9 A.M.: Great excitement in the dockyard! The dockyard workers are all transformed into soldiers and will now abandon their work places. Our boat will not be finished. Only a few others are being prepared for a quick departure. Our crew is made available to fill the gaps in other crews due to crew members not having returned from leave. We have no new information about the military situation but everything has calmed down a bit and the tension has also diminished.

5 P.M.: The birthday of the Chief is now officially being celebrated over coffee and cake. Afterwards he receives his presents, some of them absolutely beautiful. He is quite moved and drinks toasts to continuing successful team work. (Who knows for how long?) After the birthday dinner the drinks are getting more alcoholic. We younger officers have formed our own group and entertain ourselves with old sailors' songs and we are in a very pleasant mood. At the next table the Chief sits with the other senior people and enjoys himself. At midnight he takes his leave since tomorrow – oh no! – we have to report for the reception of the Japanese submarine. I too withdraw from the festivities – the ever present alcohol is going to ruin me!

---

* The naval officers club in the Lorient base.

* The *Organisation Todt* was created under Dr. Fritz Todt in 1938 to complete the construction of fortified line known in Germany as the *Westwall* and to the Allies as the Siegfried Line. During the war, its work groups were employed on the construction of the U-boat pens at the French bases and also on the construction of the defensive fortifications on the Channel coast. As Lorient was one of the largest U-boat bases, with continual construction in progress, the *Organisation Todt* maintained a large labour force at the port.

Thursday, 3 August 1944

8 A.M.: Only now do I wake up and I hear that the Japanese boat again didn't arrive. The Japanese delegation, by the way, left yesterday in a great hurry. After all – it is getting a bit uncomfortable here. The soldiers of the base have now occupied the outlying posts, as the infantry in charge of these posts is marching against the enemy.

10.30 A.M.: Good news – our boat is now expected to be finished after all. During the afternoon, I wonder where the incredible number of infantrymen came from who are suddenly populating the city.*

6.30 P.M.: I'm sitting with two friends at *Haus Schneider* when the Chief enters and says "Bad news." We fall silent. We find out that the army's high command had to abandon its headquarters when American motorized troops approached. And that's just 50 km [30 miles] from here!**

Slowly the situation is becoming serious. The Chief-of-Staff is on the telephone continuously. All our camps around the city are to be abandoned. The perimeter of Lorient is being fortified. Nobody is permitted to leave the city. In between we suddenly hear loud detonations: our airfield, built during the last three years, is being blown up with all its installations.

---

* The garrison of what was termed *Festung* Lorient was created around the staff of the XXV. *Armeekorps*, commanded by *General* Wilhelm Fahrmbacher. The major component was formed by units from the 265. *Infanteriedivision* but there were also miscellaneous *Kriegsmarine*, *Luftwaffe* and *Heer* (army) personnel. Fahrmbacher's total strength was about 26,000 all ranks armed with 197 artillery pieces.

** By 3 August 1944, the lead elements of the 4th US Armoured Division had swept around Rennes and were heading west into Brittany although the divisional commander was more interested in driving east into the German rear areas than west to secure the Brittany ports as was his mission.

10 P.M.: Small groups of officers sit quietly at *Haus Schneider*, quiet and occupied with their own thoughts. The Chief paces restlessly back and forth, waiting for further news. Time passes and nothing happens apart from the sound of explosions from the airfield which cause the windows to clatter in their frames. I can't stand the tension any longer and go to bed.

Friday, 4 August 1944

8 A.M.: The night passed without interruption. I learn at the dockyard that work on our boat has stopped again. Three boats will be made ready, then the workers will reach for their rifles.

9 A.M.: We are told that the enemy has occupied Nantes.* That means that we are now cut off at the land side. A little joke in the midst of it all: The *FdU West* calls from Angers to find out whether we can tell him something about the general situation! (Do they know anything?)

10 A.M.: Another call – our beautiful rest home in Pont Callek has been attacked by the guerillas.** The administrator wants instructions. He is told to withdraw immediately to Lorient.

The infantrymen are taking up more and more room and sit in the dockyard bunkers without doing anything. They answer our sarcastic comments with: "Well – we haven't got a single armour-piercing weapon!" What a lovely war!

7.30 P.M.: The administrator of our other home in Vannes

---

* This was not accurate information as the 4th Armoured Division did not reach Nantes until 12 August. On 4 August 1944 its spearheads were southeast of Rennes and probing in the direction of St. Nazaire and Lorient.

** The Free French Forces of the Interior, popularly known as the "Resistance."

arrives and reports having abandoned it. That beautiful interior! (And all the beautiful bottles!) Everything is falling into the hands of the guerillas – that's what they are until now. But they are actually capable of negotiating the surrender of our regular troops and enforcing the conditions of that surrender.

During the evening I'm informed that work on our boat has been resumed again. But will we be ready in time? The mood improves in leaps and bounds. We begin to fill the gaps in our crew from the personnel reserve.

8.30 P.M.: At the dockyard I listen to the complaints of the dockyard staff about the behaviour of the members of the A.O.K. (Army High Command).* They behave as if they have no other reason for existence than to enjoy life as much as possible in the yard bunkers. Instead of weapons of any kind they brought complete home furnishings for their personal comfort!

Saturday, 5 August 1944

8 A.M.: There has been no change in the situation. One has become used to it already – that never takes very long – and the mood isn't nearly as depressed any more. Life has become routine again: work throughout the day, *Haus Schneider* in the evening. There life has picked up. In the current atmosphere of a going-out-of-business sale everything is being given away for free! Since we probably won't have very much use for our French francs anyway this doesn't really make all that much difference to us. One guy pays, the other doesn't.

2.30 P.M.: Though it's rather early, I am sitting at *Haus Schneider*, enjoying some wine and entertaining myself with my own "*Wunschkonzert*"* of records on the gramophone. As I'm all by myself, I can play my favourite excerpts from "Tosca" over and over again without getting on anybody's nerves. Then I write home. That isn't easy – what can one write? At the moment everything is still quite all right. With our beautiful weather – the sun is shining brightly – and peace and quiet all over the area one has to force oneself to realize that war is suddenly very close – a condition we as submariners ashore have never experienced before.

In the afternoon four sailors are decorated with the *Deutsche Kreuz in Gold* (one of them has had more than 700 days at sea!). The ceremony is simple but very nice. At the same time we have a farewell party for our flotilla dentist as she will go by boat to a more southerly, as yet not threatened, base. I take the opportunity to give her my letter for delivery.

The Chief has visited the A.O.K. and expressed the indignation of the Navy about the fact that the entire area just outside Lorient was turned over to a ridiculously small number of guerrillas without any fight. Nothing could have inflicted more severe damage to our reputation – not too great to begin with! He offered to prove with his sailors that there are still German soldiers in existence. The A.O.K. in the person of a Chief-of-Staff reacted in a quite embarrassed fashion and hesitantly granted permission for an assault on the guerrillas by the Navy base support company. Homeric laughter in the submariners' messes!

---

* *Armeeoberkommando*, in this case probably the staff of the German coastal defence command responsible for this area of the Atlantic wall.

* A reference to the "*Wunschkonzert für die Wehrmacht*," a popular German wartime radio programme which played requests from listeners.

7 P.M.: We observe two army battalions leave the fortress to harass the guerrillas. We are heavily involved in our own preparations for our martial adventure. Unfortunately the crews from the U-boats are not permitted to participate. Pity!

Our men leave around nine o'clock in the evening. Three trucks, one car with our Chief-of-Staff, who is in command, two 2 cm guns, several machine guns, hand grenades and bottles filled with kerosene to smoke the guerrillas out of their nests – a really impressive show of fighting power!

Sunday, 6 August 1944

In the morning we find out about the night's excursion. Our guns did a very effective job in clearing out some of the resistance positions, but at the cost of several wounded, among them the explosives expert who dies the same day.

At the yard I once again have to listen to the bitter complaints about the behaviour of the *A.O.K.* On a bright sunny day two scantily-dressed French girls are promenading up and down among the workers of the yard, as if this were the most natural event one could expect. Everybody stops and stares at the somewhat unusual sight. Satisfying our curiosity we discover that the soldiers have brought a whole cavalcade of these camp followers – considered a necessity for the well-being of the soldiers – into the protection of the bunkers. Note: With approval of the commanding general! Just like the Middle Ages! But, of course, our armies haven't been doing anything else here in France but playing house for three solid years! What a sad picture our famous army presents!*

And then the climax: An army officer asks the *Kriegs-marine* to replace the wounded, sick and the nurses, scheduled to leave the fortress on the next departing U-boat, with forty of these French girls so as to not expose the poor things to the cruelties of the expected battle! A rather peculiar attitude displayed by the gentlemen of the *Heer!* By the way – throughout this time I haven't seen more than ten soldiers with any kind of war medal, apart from countless *K.V.K.s.* (a medal for services outside the war zones).**

11.30 A.M.: I have to eat early as I want to participate in the test of some equipment on a U-boat that is going to undergo a diving test in Keroman III, a wet bunker. A driver takes me to the officer's mess and there I find out that the whole building has been abandoned and the mess has been transferred to the yard bunker. I'm puzzled – just minutes ago the Chief made his car available to me to get here! Had he known about this he certainly would have told me! Now I'm standing here and the car is gone. Rather miffed I make my way to the yard. Twenty minutes it takes me to get there, only to be told that the whole kitchen facility was actually here for a little while but has now been returned again to the officer's mess building. My collar is getting tight

---

* In fact these rather unkind words are probably a fairly accurate assessment of the 265. *Infanteriedivision*, which was raised in 1943 for occupation duties in France and formed parts of the garrison of both Lorient and St. Nazaire in 1944. The formation consisted of older men and its senior staff were taken from another low-quality occupation division. The division sent its two best battalions to the Eastern Front in the autumn of 1943 and they were replaced with two battalions of former prisoners from the Soviet Red Army who had volunteered for German service.

** The *Kriegsverdienstkreuz* or War Service Cross was awarded to noncombatants for achievements in their respective services. The fact that army officers who composed the garrison of Lorient did not seem to possess any gallantry medals is an indication of the fact that many of them had served only in the occupation forces.

around my neck! I'm just on the verge of exploding when the Flotilla Engineer comes by in his car and cheerfully offers me a lift to the officer's mess, so that I can eat. (I'm starting to wonder about the state of our navy.)

3.30 P.M.: The tests on the U-boat start two hours late. About two hours have gone by while being submerged inside the bunker when all of a sudden several heavy explosions rock the boat. Almost like depth charges. The tanks are blown immediately and raise the boat to the surface. On the bridge we can hardly see a thing because of dust and smoke. Somebody yells "Air attack!" *

At the boat entrance of the bunker the sky can be seen as a faint rectangle. As soon as a gangway has been pushed onto the deck I jump ashore and illuminate my way with a flashlight through the crowds of people on the narrow pathways of the bunker. The beam of my light hardly reaches the ground in front of me. Slowly I work myself through to the entrance where the air is getting much better.

The street outside is covered with mud, rocks and other debris and is hardly distinguishable from the surroundings. The entrance of the bunker on the opposite side is collapsed and nearby is a giant crater in the ground.

The bomb attack has ceased and our anti-aircraft guns have stopped firing. My first thought is: "My boat and the launching ramp!" I run across the square, when the guns open fire again and I hastily take shelter in a nearby bunker. But there is no further attack and I continue my run to

bunker Keroman II (an enormous garage-like building, away from the water, with space for six U-boats) where my boat sits high and dry in its cradle. This bunker and the next, Keroman I, as well as the tracks in front of them, don't seem to have suffered any damage. When I climb up to the deck of *U-190* the sentry receives me with "No special events to report." He heard the noise but nothing happened here.

I breathe easier. There seem to be no obstacles to the launch of our boat, planned for tomorrow.

Returning to Keroman III, I learn that the diesel motors creating the electricity for the cradle and track system will have to be switched off as the cooling water supply has been damaged. This puts our launch in question again. The outcome will not be known until late into the night.

There is nothing I can do now and I walk home. The car of the Flotilla Engineer that stood outside the bunker has simply been blown away. Not a trace is left of it.

At Keroman I, the beautiful *Heer* vehicles are neatly squeezed flat against the wall. The collapsed entrance covers some more. Apparently there have been no casualties here, but at the entrance to the dockyard a small anti-tank bunker with about twenty soldiers has been completely torn apart. Only a heap of rocks and iron rods remains. It is a grim sight and I turn away in horror.

Outside the dockyard there are a few fires. I'm warned of bomb duds but I'm far too tired to make cautious detours. Together with the Torpedo Officer of the Flotilla, who spent the entire attack lying outside on the ground and is covered with mud, I go to *Haus Schneider* to recuperate with a cognac.

Our fear that because of the late hour – it is now eleven at night – there might not be anybody there is quite un-

* On 6 August 1944, 12 Lancaster and 3 Mosquito bombers of No. 617 Squadron RAF bombed Lorient. This squadron (the famous "Dambusters") was British Bomber Command's special operations unit. No aircraft were lost and two direct hits were reported.

founded. We don't even have to enter since the whole happy gang sits in front of the door on the street and drinks – beer! BEER, a pleasure unknown to us for weeks! But, of course, we come just in time to see the contents of the last bottle disappear and have to settle for champagne to rinse down the dust and dryness of our throats.

I can't get into the proper mood to participate any longer and go to sleep.

Monday, 7 August 1944

8.30 A.M.: We are told that the tracks have been damaged after all, and spend the morning waiting for the repair. In between the guns start shooting again and everybody takes shelter in the bunker. Then we find out that the guns are firing against approaching American tanks. At this time I have the opportunity to see the Commanding General in person – and I'm no longer surprised about anything!* Around noon: The big guns on the Île de Groix** open fire. I'm crossing the waters of the harbour in a small launch and can observe the flashes of the guns all the way around. Thick dark clouds of smoke rise into the sky. The thunder of the guns continues without pause.

1 P.M.: At lunch the Chief tells us that work on the U-boats has been stopped once again but that he has pointed out to the dockyard *Admiral* that, according to a *BdU* order, Lorient is to be considered a U-boat base first and that all

boats are to be made ready as soon as possible. The admiral agreed to consider it.

3 P.M.: When I arrive at our boat I notice that in fact all workers have been withdrawn and have been moved into our trenches as soldiers. I approach the Engineer in charge and recount the conversation between our Chief and the admiral. He just shrugs and knows only that no further work will be done on our boat.

Slowly I'm being gripped by despair. Together with the CO, I try to talk the responsible authorities into at least agreeing to launch our boat, since, after all, we are able to float and one more bomb into the tracks means our boat will never get into the water again.

4.30 P.M.: We spend the afternoon sitting in the sun outside the bunker together with the officers of three other boats that will depart tonight. We envy them.

We talk about the air attack. According to British reports we were the first targets for their so-called earthquake bombs, especially designed for our bunkers.* One of the bombs produced a crater three metres [10 feet] deep on top of the bunker I was in but with the existing thickness of seven metres [23 feet], that didn't mean much.

The sun is beautiful, the sky is blue, the men are swimming. The shooting has stopped. A picture of peace. And it may take only seconds to transform this serenity into hell.

* Possibly this was *General der Artillerie* Wilhelm Fahrmbacher, commanding the XXV. *Infanteriekorps,* which held Brittany, and had his headquarters at Lorient at this time. Fahrmbacher was 57 years old in 1944.

** There was a *Kriegsmarine* coast artillery battery on this island a few miles from Lorient. It was firing at the lead elements of the 4th Armoured Division, which were beginning to probe the outer defences of Lorient.

* In fact, 617 Squadron were using the newly-developed 12,000 lb. "Tallboy" bomb designed by Barnes Wallis, the man who designed the bombs that this squadron used to attack the Mohne and Eder dams. This was not the first use of the "Tallboy" on U-boat pens, the previous day 617 Squadron had attacked the *Kriegsmarine* facilities at Brest and reported six direct hits. However, none of the U-boat pens or bunkers in France, that possessed a completed protective roof system, were ever penetrated by any bomb in the Allied inventory.

10 P.M.: The Chief has finally established, after long battles, that *U-190* will be launched. At eleven we are aboard and the boat actually starts to roll. We are half way out and the sirens announce an air attack. We are pushed back into the bunker and wait. We are ready to climb the wall!

Half an hour later the alarm is over, but the electricity is gone. We wait …… Finally the boat starts moving again and rolls out into the open air of the night.

Tuesday, 8 August 1944

About 1.30 A.M.: The boat has arrived at the ramp in Keroman I. I feel a lot better. The most dangerous part of the operation is behind us. A few more hours and we will be afloat.

A yard director arrives and announces that an order has been received to resume work on the boats in full force. At noon the workers will be aboard again. I feel like a child at Christmas and go to sleep more contentedly than I have for some time.

9 A.M.: The boat is afloat and we move to a wet bunker. I hardly leave the boat any more and I am busy urging on the workers.

2 P.M.: We take on fuel. We don't get very much as there isn't much left in the fortress. After a few minor problems the task is completed.

During these activities we hear new explosions that cause everything to grind to a halt. They are hits of enemy artillery shells. Soon it's over and we proceed.

Wednesday, 9 August 1944

9 A.M.: We take on torpedoes. The guns have resumed their fire and in the north we see thick clouds of smoke: It seems our Camp Lemp goes up in flames. In front of the residence bunker we note a martial sight: An armoured vehicle is moving back and forth. It is, though, the only vehicle of this kind that is available in the whole fortress. It's a French machine, the turret of which has been removed and all it's good for is towing away disabled cars.

A bit later: Surprise, surprise! There is actually a 3.7 cm gun passing by. Is it really possible? Our chances are rising rapidly!

10 P.M.: The administrator of our Camp Lemp arrives with his men, exhausted but elated, and describes his withdrawal from the approaching Americans. They were dangerously close, when they left the camp, which was already falling under the fire of our own guns. (We don't, after all, approve of the use of our Old Mill for the recreation of American officers!)

Our men had to avoid the villages on the way, as on the steeples of some of them they could already see the French tricolour and the Stars and Stripes. But they made it. Great guys!

Thursday, 10 August 1944

There is another sale on. I get all my goods for our canteen for nothing. Everybody can take whatever they want out of the clothing inventory, without paying a *Pfennig*. Everywhere our men are admiring themselves in their brand new outfits. Why should all that fall into the hands of the Americans? We are busy stowing our supplies. Normal provisions for sixteen weeks, but no fresh food.

The day goes by quietly – disturbingly quiet. After an exploration it is reported that the entire area surrounding

Lorient has been deserted by the enemy! It's hard to believe. What does it mean?

In the evening our diesels make their first hesitant turns and then assume their old steady rumble. What a lovely sound! It's like music in my ears.

10 P.M.: *U-270* departs under the command of *Oberleutnant z.S.* Schreiber. It's an old, already decommissioned boat, made barely seaworthy. The small crew has been assembled from the remainders of other boats. It has thirty passengers – and no *Schnorchel*. The CO has never commanded a U-boat. He looks unsure of himself. And although he is only to take the boat south to Bordeaux, everybody knows he faces a difficult task, perhaps too difficult. Only the Chief Engineer is, at least outwardly, cheerful and optimistic. Let's hope they'll make it!*

Friday, 11 August 1944

9 A.M.: We complete an engine test run and are very satisfied with the results. All that's left now is to finish loading the boat and we are ready.

2 P.M.: After several busy days, I can afford to take a few hours off and I sit in the officers' mess of the other U-boat flotilla, the 10th. Why not at *Haus Schneider*? Is it because of the lovely quiet here or because of Janine, the dark-haired ballet dancer serving the drinks?

The Chief of the 10th Flotilla is also here and plays the

---

* *U-270* left Lorient under the command of *Oberleutnant z.S.* Heinrich Schreiber. While running on the surface, possibly because it could not submerge, it was attacked and sunk early in the morning of 12 August 1944 by an aircraft of the Royal Australian Air Force. Of the 81 persons on board, 71, including Schreiber, were rescued that same day by HMC Ships *Ottawa II* and *St. Laurent*.

piano. The only interruption in our peaceful existence is the occasional scream of enemy bombers that, ignoring the anti-aircraft fire, carry out their dives, unload their bombs and disappear again. At first one still ducks under something, but then one gets used to it and watches the spectacle from the window. One has to admire the courage of the flyers.

Saturday, 12 August 1944

10 A.M.: We cast off for the trial run. Great to once again have a floating platform underneath! Everything works out fine, even the first trial dive.

In the afternoon we finish loading, then there is a rest for the crew. I spend more time than permissible, without creating suspicion, in the officers' mess of the 10th.

Sunday, 13 August 1944

Morning: As we are also expected to transfer to Bordeaux first, we receive a complete *Schnorchel* system as cargo. Our deck, so nicely cleaned up, is a mess again.

Noon: We have invited the upper ranks of flotilla and dockyard to a small farewell lunch. The menu consists of soup, ham, fried eggs, white asparagus and potatoes. Wine and then champagne and coffee complete the meal. The atmosphere is very pleasant and our guests are appreciative.

Early afternoon: We practice our *Schnorchel* drill and then take it easy.

9 P.M.: Five of us sit in the mess of the 10th together with Janine and have some lively conversations. The talk drifts to war and politics and we have an opportunity to experience first hand the effects of British propaganda on the French population. We admire Janine's passionate defence of her

Most of the French girls serving in our officers' wardrooms and messes at Lorient were highly-educated artists and performers. I became friends with the ballet dancer Janine, but our relationship ended with her farewell words written on the back of this picture: "ne m'oublie pas. Ta petite Janine. Le 14 août 44" ("Don't forget me, your little Janine."). (WH col.)

points of view – in her own mind the only valid ones. We try hard to hold our own but I don't think we are succeeding. The pause after Janine's last words "only my France" is being filled by soothing sounds from a guitar. In the darkness of the room our combative mood changes back to the peace and quiet we had before. Janine also displays a more conciliatory spirit and we get along fine again. We are happy about it and the evening gets longer and longer until …

Monday, 14 August 1944

… until suddenly a man appears with a flashlight, directs the beam at our faces and says in a sharp tone not to be misunderstood "Gentlemen, closing time is at 2300 hours. Please!" The man wears the *Ritterkreuz** around his neck. Silently we file out of the room, somewhat bitter about that sad end to a lovely evening, our last evening. Tonight we depart.

The morning passes with a lot of confusion. We are supposed to take 25 passengers to Bordeaux. I feel some weakness in my stomach. So many people in that confined space and so little fresh air!

Noon: Finally everything is ready.

2 P.M.: We are just embarking on a final trim test dive of the boat when we get orders to unload our *Schnorchel* cargo and our passengers. Although I once again curse the organization, or the lack of it, I am of course quite happy to be rid of the additional weight.

It is rather laughable. As U-boat officers we can't show

---

* The *Ritterkreuz* or Knight's Cross of the Iron Cross was the premier gallantry medal in wartime Germany. To receive it, a serviceman had to already possess the Iron Cross, 1st Class. There were several grades of the Knight's Cross.

our faces anywhere without being approached by all kinds of people, young and old, army, naval dockyard personnel, uniformed and civilian, with the request to take them with us. But of course, that's not the Navy way of recruiting its personnel. We refer everybody to the flotilla though we are quite sure of the futility of such attempts. It's amazing how popular all of a sudden a submarine trip seems to be without anybody, of course, having any idea of the real meaning of it.

4.15 P.M.: All that can go wrong does go wrong on our final trim test dive. Slowly I start to despair. The Flotilla Engineer does everything to drive me crazy. When finally we report the malfunctioning of a torpedo tube flap, he orders the postponement of the trial.

While returning to the bunker I'm crawling through the bow compartment to help isolate the cause of the trouble, when the boat seems to bang into something and I almost lose my balance. I race up to the bridge, just in time to see the boat get clear of the bunker gate.

Trying to test the forward diving plane we discover that it can't be moved any longer. We are forced to return to the dock for repairs. With this new problem our departure is now definitely postponed!

I'm fed up with it all and leave the boat as soon as we are tied up.

9 P.M.: I sit again in the officers' mess, and after it closes at ten, I go for a long walk with Janine. It is once again a lovely warm summer night …

11 P.M.: Renewed artillery fire interrupts the peace and shortly after we see our fortifications light up bright red with thick smoke rising into the dark sky. Janine and I try to ignore it.

Tuesday, 15 August 1944

In the dry dock we discover considerable damage to our diving plane. The CO himself is eagerly supervising the repairs, so that I feel slightly superfluous and, after an hour of instruction for my men, the II.WO and I go swimming. The cool water feels great, but less great is the bomb dud that suddenly decides to explode and shower us with its fragments.

The evening we spend at *Haus Schneider*. A strange mood pervades the room. The people of the flotilla who have to stay here know that sooner or later, they will have to defend this place to the last man. I must admit that I can't see any other possibility either and that I'm glad not to be part of them, and will be leaving in a few days like a rat leaving the sinking ship. I try to put myself into the place of those that face the bitter end here but it's difficult.

The thought that my chances at sea may not be any better doesn't bother me. On the one hand the people staying here give us their last letters to their loved ones, but on the other hand we may only get the second or third copy of such letters whereas the originals may be entrusted to others whose chances of reaching their destination may be as good or as bad as ours. But what good are these contemplations! Let's have another drink, resort to nostalgia and ignore the future!

Wednesday, 16 August 1944

I don't have very much to do as the CO looks after everything himself.

11 P.M.: We leave *Haus Schneider* to board our boat. We are scheduled to leave the dock at three in the morning.

Aboard we celebrate the birthday of one of our men and get little sleep.

Thursday, 17 August 1944

4 A.M.: Somebody wakes me up and I have a rather sizeable hangover. The manoeuvre proceeds without problems and so does the final trim trial. We are ready. Departure is scheduled for tonight from the Skorff Bunker.

2 P.M.: I'm told to unload one third of my fuel supply. It will be needed for two other boats that arrived this morning delivering armour-piercing weapons for the soldiers.

I'm getting used to sorrow. Let's get rid of the fuel again! I'm afraid I'm not very cooperative as I have no interest at all in losing my precious fuel. I'm not quite sure how far the remainder will take us. Our destination is now Norway!

Afternoon: We visit the doctors of the flotilla who have transferred their operating rooms into the residence bunker and who are now quite busy. Every day new wounded are brought in and the hospital is already overcrowded. But the doctors still have time for a farewell coffee hour.

Evening: The officers of our boat split up to pursue their respective interests: The CO again with the doctors, the II.WO at *Haus Schneider*, together with the I.WO, and I – at the officers' mess of the 10th Flotilla, where Janine presents me with a picture of herself with some warm words written on the back, closing with "ne m'oublie pas."

10 P.M.: When I get aboard an hour before departure time, not even half of the fuel destined for the other boats has been unloaded. We line up anyway and our Chief makes a short farewell speech. Then: "Dismissed to manoeuvre and aircraft alarm stations!"

The hoses are removed and we say goodbye to our friends with whom we have spent many a happy hour here in Lorient. They give us their greetings for the homeland and I ask one of them to pass on my own good wishes …

The removal of the oil barge causes a slight delay, the Chief yells at the Flotilla Engineer, the Flotilla Engineer yells at me and I'm glad when the lines have been hauled in and the tug tows us out.

11.15 P.M.: The motors start and after a last cheer for the flotilla we wave once more to our comrades until we disappear in the darkness.

Whether we will see each other again remains to be seen?*

---

* In fact, *Festung Lorient*, which was never seriously attacked by Allied land forces, held out until 10 May 1945 when Fahrmbacher surrendered the fortress to American forces. After the losses suffered in attacking the German bases at Brest and Cherbourg in 1944, Eisenhower wisely decided to let the other Atlantic bases "wither on the vine."

Oberleutnant z.S. Reith, the CO of *U-190*, listens on a long lead to the GHG passive sonar listening device while the operator, *Funkobergefreiter* Kurt Petereit, searches for more contacts using the handwheel which traversed the device. This picture was taken while we were under attack by Allied surface vessels. (WH col.)

HEIM INS REICH – ESCAPE FROM LORIENT: AUGUST TO OCTOBER 1944

We were happy to be out of Lorient bound for Norway and eventually "*Heim ins Reich*" (back home to Germany) but less than two hours from the base it became apparent that *U-190* had serious mechanical problems. One of the diesels, which had been overhauled while I was on leave, began to smoke badly as the packing around one bearing had been incorrectly installed. While my engineering staff worked on this problem, we submerged and tried out our newly installed *Schnorchel*. The operation of this device, which permitted our U-boats to survive during the last 18 months of the war, fell within my area of responsibility and therefore merits a detailed description

The *Schnorchel* consisted of a 28-foot mast, reaching as high as the extended periscope. Inside it were two tubes, one to permit fresh air to enter the boat and another to vent diesel exhaust gases at about two feet below the surface. The device was hinged at the bottom and in its resting position was carried in a bay in the deck of the boat. When the *Schnorchel* was raised, a large opening about seven feet above deck level connected with a similar large opening in an air intake tube that had been attached to the outside of the conning tower and led into the diesel room. The intake tube had a float valve at the top, which closed when it became submerged. This meant that the incoming air was cut off but the engines continued to operate, creating a not very pleasant but temporary partial vacuum in the boat. The worst effect this vacuum ever had on our crew happened when the cork was sucked out of a large glass container with acetic acid and splashed some of its content over the floor. Anybody near the splash started crying due to the biting effect of the acid. One disadvantage of the *Schnorchel* was that it restricted a U-boat's speed to about 5-6 knots due to vibrations in the periscope at higher speed, and it also created a blind spot behind the periscope. The operation of the *Schnorchel* left us to some extent vulnerable but we still felt much safer than we would have if we had had to surface to charge the batteries and renew our air, making discovery almost a certainty.

The *Schnorchel* also left a small but visible wake on the surface and its head could be picked up by some of the Allied naval radars. We quickly became aware of this problem as we had deployed the device for less than 30 minutes when an enemy aircraft, equipped with a Leigh

On 17 August 1944 *U-190* left Lorient bound for Germany. This grainy picture taken in the boat's wardroom shows, from the left, myself (with my face half cut of), our cook, the CO, *Oberleutnant z.S.* Hans-Edwin Reith, and the I.WO, *Oberleutnant z.S.* Friedrich Schmidt. (WH col.)

Light, a powerful searchlight, located our *Schnorchel* head and homed in on the boat causing *U-190* to go to alarm stations and me to retract the device. About an hour later, our sound operator picked up, using the GHG,* the propeller noises of three enemy destroyers and several smaller craft searching for us. Fortunately, they hunted in vain and gradually drew away.

We continued on our way submerged and, convinced that the enemy were now out of contact, deployed the *Schnorchel* for 30 minutes shortly after dawn, after which I went off watch. About six hours later I got out of my bunk and immediately noticed that nearly the entire crew was unconscious. I quickly realized that we must have an excessive amount of carbon monoxide in

the submarine and remembered that, while using the *Schnorchel* earlier, I had found it difficult to maintain the correct depth and keep the *Schnorchel* head just above the surface. The head had been submerged a few times for limited periods and the exhaust gases from the diesels could no longer overcome the increased water pressure and thus emptied through the safety valves, located at the engines, into the boat. We did have a kit aboard that indicated the level of carbon monoxide in the boat by the change of colour of a chemical in a vial but unfortunately the explanation of the meaning of the colour changes had been left behind in Lorient! Just in time, we surfaced in broad daylight to ventilate the interior. This was a particularly nerve-wracking experience as we were only too aware that Allied aircraft and warships had been deployed to block the escape of U-boats leaving the French bases.

To even the odds, we deployed a new piece of equipment – an *Aphrodite* radar decoy. This was a hydrogen-filled balloon, to which were attached aluminum foil strips, suspended by a wire from a small floating buoy. The buoy was thrown overboard and the balloon was suspended a few yards above the surface – the aluminum strips returned a strong radar echo, very similar to that of a surfaced U-boat. Once the device was deployed, we moved away from it at high speed on the surface while we ventilated the interior of the boat. Fortunately, there was no enemy contact.

I soon encountered worse problems with the *Schnorchel*. It had become clear that, probably due to the poor workmanship of the French maintenance staff at

---

* *Gruppen-Horch-Gerät*, the highly accurate sound location equipment on U-boats.

Lorient, the device had not been properly installed and it began to leak badly at its junction point on the conning tower. This, combined with the diesel problem, forced me on 19 August to recommend to my CO, *Oberleutnant z.S.* Reith, that we put back to Lorient for repairs. He concurred and we immediately reversed course, trying to run at high speed on the surface as much as possible but we were soon forced under by numerous sound and radar detector contacts with enemy aircraft and vessels. We managed to get off a *Kurzsignal** and an escort was waiting for us at the arranged rendezvous point. At 8.30 A.M. on 21 August, we made fast in the Skorff-Bunker in Lorient.

A hectic 36-hour period followed while emergency repairs were made to the *Schnorchel* and the malfunctioning diesel and then, at 8.45 P.M. on 22 August, we set out again. Within ten minutes of dropping our surface escort, we got multiple radar contacts with enemy forces and dived. Two hours later our sound man picked up propeller noises from five destroyers which began to search for us with Asdic from positions all around the boat. Inside the boat the metallic pinging on the hull made by the Asdic pulses was a very disconcerting sound since it was almost always an announcement of depth charges to follow. Our CO went to the bottom which was very shallow at this point, about 225 feet, and there we remained for 12 hours until there were no more sound contacts.

We then went on our way, mostly travelling submerged, occasionally surfacing, *"zum Laden and Lüften,"* but mainly depending on the *Schnorchel*. We usually deployed it twice a day, according to conditions – that is, the absence or presence of sound contacts – for anywhere between 30 minutes to an hour. Our course lay due west from Lorient along the northern coast of the Bay of Biscay and then out into the Atlantic.

We were very aware that Allied naval task forces were not only blockading our bases on the Bay of Biscay but actively searching for *U-190* and the other boats attempting to leave them. There were constant sound contacts with enemy ships and aircraft and we could often hear the detonations of *Flibos** and *Wabos.*** In the early morning of 25 August, three days after we left Lorient for the second time, we had reached a point southwest of Ushant and here we were hunted for a couple of hours by four enemy destroyers but managed to elude them. Our *KTB* or log indicates that 25 August 1944 was a busy day for the Allied navies and air forces, as our sound man recorded the detonation of no less than 50 *Flibos* – thankfully all at a distance.

On 27 August, we were hunted by an enemy surface force of four destroyers and pinned down for more than three hours while they tried to establish our exact location by Asdic. This time they came closer and launched four depth charges.

At this point, I would like to make a comment about

---

* A *Kurzsignal* was a coded radio message sent in a short burst, rarely more than a few seconds. Allied radio detection equipment could pick up longer radio messages and possibly triangulate and locate the position of a U-boat.

* *Fliegerbomben* or aircraft bombs.

** *Wasserbomben* or depth charges.

The CO of *U-190, Oberleutnant z.S.* Hans-Edwin Reith, in his so-called cabin, which consisted of a bunk, some cupboards and a desk with a washbasin underneath, separated from the rest of the boat by a curtain which was never closed. (WH col.)

the films that portray life on submarines during the Second World War, including the famous German epic "*Das Boot.*" Motion pictures have to be entertaining and dramatic – otherwise nobody would pay to watch them – while actual life on a submarine is usually as visually interesting as watching paint dry. You can't sell tickets to a film that shows life on a sub as it actually was, or is. When depth charges explode, people inside the boat must be falling all over each other, if not desperately hanging onto something to keep themselves upright, while the boat rolls through 30-degree arcs.

In reality that submarine isn't moving a fraction of an inch as it is a mass of a thousand tons, surrounded by an almost solid mass of water. In my experience, an exploding depth charge felt like a blow with a giant hammer on an immovable object – valve shafts break, fuses blow, light fixtures shatter, but the boat doesn't move. One may have the understandable inclination to duck, but one has to wonder why. The chaos, the panic, the screaming portrayed by the crew in "*Das Boot*" was entertaining and interesting to watch but had no connection with reality. In addition, none of us engineering officers in real life would have had the talent and the abilities of the chief engineer in that film – truly a superman of our profession – otherwise we would have lost very few boats during the war, and I, for one, am still puzzled as to how he got that damaged boat back to the surface. While the film was true to life in many of its aspects, especially the depiction of everyday life on a U-boat and also with respect to the characters portrayed, most of the battle scenes were overdramatized and defy any logic.

However, let us return to reality. The moments between the sound man's report of a depth charge splash in the water and the explosion were truly terrifying. Cold sweat breaks out and, personally, I always had a terrible urge to have a bowel movement, but of course I couldn't as, with your subordinates watching you, an officer must stay cool and put up a brave face, even make a joke. Then the charge exploded, and before you realized you were still alive the next charge was on its way. During this time the utmost silence had to be maintained throughout the boat – all conversation was reduced to a minimum and then only in the form of whispering, while shoes were replaced with specially made socks to avoid any noise when moving through the boat. Coughing or sneezing was considered more criminal than high treason and had to be avoided at all costs.

Between depth charges the operator of the *GHG* or hydrophone listening device attempted to analyze the movements of the ship above while the pinging pulses of the Asdic indicated that the enemy was still in contact. But when another explosion reverberated through the boat and something broke, there was no time for fear as one was too busy taking care of the damage to worry. This pounding could go on for ten hours or more before you were finally able to slink away and hope they had lost you. Then you were full of bravado and felt assured once again that, at a depth of 600 feet, nothing could touch you. At this depth the boat had lost about a ton of its volume due to external pressure. Steel can take this compression comfortably, but the wooden interior made awful creaking noises due to this deformation. In other words, even without enemy action, being down there was not a comfortable feeling, especially since our boats were officially certified only to a depth of about 300 feet.

As for our knowledge that the enemy was deliberately hunting us, I must return briefly to Lorient to relate why we were so certain of this fact. The Nazi party regarded American jazz as degenerate and forbade it from being played, or broadcast on German radio. Despite this official proscription, we often switched our radios over to the prohibited British stations, particularly the popular propaganda station *Soldatensender Calais*,* which al-

The *Zentrale,* or control room, of *U-190* provides the venue for a chess game during some quiet times during our journey from Lorient to Germany in the late summer of 1944. (WH col.)

ways had good jazz and pop music. However, before we had first set out from Lorient, our pleasure in listening to such fine musicians as Glen Miller and Benny Goodman was rudely interrupted by somewhat disconcerting announcements along the lines of: "To the men of U-190. We hope you are enjoying your last day ashore and wish you a happy departure. We will be waiting for you and will meet at …" followed by a certain latitude and longitude. When we returned briefly to Lorient, there came another ominous announcement, again interrupting the music: "Too bad, U-190, that you had to go back for now, but don't worry, when you leave again, we will be ready to welcome you."

We were well aware of the probable source of this kind of information – the young women who served as hostesses and waitresses in our bars and dining rooms. They were usually highly educated and intelligent pro-

---

* *Soldatensender Calais* was a British radio station which broadcast good modern music and propaganda to German service personnel in occupied Europe. Its programming resembled that of conventional German military radio stations.

A breakdown of important equipment in the electric motor room required many hours of work to fix that could only be carried out during those periods when we were sure that there were no Allied warships nearby as the repairs were very noisy. (WH col.)

Having arrived at Faresund in Norway on 1 October 1944, the I.WO, *Oberleutnant* Schmidt, and I can finally relax. Behind us can be seen another Type IXC boat which had just returned from patrol. (WH col.)

fessionals, mostly in the arts, whose careers had become derailed by the war and who made a living by taking the jobs offered by the *Kriegsmarine*. We had many intriguing conversations with them as they all had a very good command of the German language. They always had a smile for us, and some developed quite genuinely warm relationships with some of our officers, although most of these encounters were of necessity short, and ended abruptly when the officer failed to return from a patrol. At the same time these very patriotic girls did a terrific job for the Allied cause by passing on important intelligence and, for our part, we found it difficult to refuse their proffered warmth.

The enemy, however, was only one of our problems. By the first days of September, we were about 500 miles due west of Brest and far out in the Atlantic. It was clear that we had broken through the blocking forces looking for us as sound and radar detector contacts began to decline. On 4 September, however, matters got worse when one of our compressors – necessary to fill the high pressure air bottles used to blow out the diving tanks – failed. A cylinder push rod in the compressor had broken and in doing so had lifted the crankshaft out of its bearings, bending it to an angle of a few degrees and shattering one of the bearings. Repairing a major fault like this normally required the machinery and staff of a naval base and was therefore a serious matter because, without a functioning compressor, our survival was very much in question.

At least this was the opinion of my two chief petty officers, *Obermaschinisten* Holtmann and Krüger. Both of these veterans declared the compressor situation to be

Enjoying the first sunshine after living many weeks under water are my two technical chief petty officers, *Obermaschinist* Werner Holtman from the *E-raum* on the left and *Obermaschinist* Willi Krüger, responsible for the diesels. They had served on *U-190* from the time of its commissioning in 1942, and being in their late 20s, were the oldest men on board. Men of this experience and ability were indispensable for the survival of a U-boat. (WH col.)

The II.WO of our boat, *Leutnant z.S.* Herbert Rogge, who became I.WO on our next mission after *Oberleutnant* Schmidt was given another assignment. Schmidt had been sent on board our boat at Lorient with other personnel from the flotilla reserve as half our crew were on leave in Germany and had been cut off from returning by advancing Allied forces. (WH col.)

(Below) Engine room personnel of *U-190* enjoying the sun after our arrival in Norway. The large tube at the left is the container for spare barrels for our anti-aircraft guns. (WH col.)

Approaching the Norwegian coast in late September 1944, this picture shows the I.WO of *U-190*, *Oberleutnant* Schmidt, and one of the lookouts, as seen from the front of the bridge. The specially formulated sunglasses worn by the lookout were valued by their owners and became precious souvenirs after the war. I kept and used my pair until the 1970s when they finally broke. (WH col.)

To everyone's amazement, the compressor worked long enough to replenish our high-pressure air sufficiently to get us to Norway, although it failed and was repaired twice more during the journey. The dockyard technical staff who later examined this jury-rig were amazed that the thing had held together at all. As from the beginning my two *Obermaschinisten* had given me the feeling that the single gold ring on my sleeve did not justify my authority over these old veterans, this incident earned their respect. It took a certain tension out of our relationship, but of course they didn't realize how lucky I had been.

By the time the compressor was repaired, we had altered course and started to run north, out in the Atlantic and west of Ireland, to circumvent the British Isles. By 16 September we were between Iceland and the Orkney

hopeless. If I had had their experience I would probably have agreed with them – but I was too young to know what I didn't know, so I therefore exerted my authority and insisted that we try to repair it. I ordered the shaft to be removed, heated, and hammered back into a reasonably straight line. This was a painstaking and laborious process – and it was also a lengthy one as we had to cease work whenever our sound man picked up a contact and sometimes it was hours before we could resume banging on the shaft. In the end it took 12 days of agonizing work to complete this task. When we were satisfied that the shaft was reasonably straight, the broken bearing pieces were put round it and wired together.

More crew members enjoying sun and fresh air in the *Wintergarten* after many weeks of deprivation during our journey from Lorient. The man at the right shows his loyalty to the boat by displaying a miniature of *a* compass rose at his cap. The compass rose was the insignia of *U-190* and was painted on the boat's conning tower. (WH col.)

Islands but enemy contacts increased as we turned east toward our eventual goal, a friendly base in Norway. The following day, we received a warning in the form of a radio message that there were strong enemy naval forces in the area through which we were sailing, and more and more we resorted to the *Schnorchel*. On 20 September our sound man got a strong contact with an enemy destroyer proceeding on a course that would bring him right across our bows. The Allied ship was clearly not searching for us as he was moving at very high speed and our CO, observing him through the periscope, contemplated firing a conventional torpedo. In the event, however, the destroyer was too fast and Reith chose not to shoot.

While on the surface during the approach to Norway, all crew members on the bridge or on deck were ordered to wear their life vests in expectations of sudden air attacks or the chance of hitting a mine. The binoculars seem to be somewhat out of place on a *Leitender Ingenieur* such as myself. (WH col.)

(Below) As *U-190* approaches the entry to the harbour of Kristiansand in Norway on 1 October 1944, we follow another boat. The white cap at the left indicates that the wearer was the captain of the vessel, in this case *Oberleutnant* Reith. The wearing of white caps by German naval commanding officers became a habit during the war although it was not specifed by regulations. (WH col.)

By the last week of September we were approaching the Norwegian coast south of Trondheim. On 24 September, we received a radio message ordering us to make for Kristiansand and four days later we rendezvoused with German patrol boats, who brought us into Faresund, ending an extremely hazardous 38-day journey of 2,438 sea miles (2,807 land miles). At this point I will continue the story by inserting an excerpt from the diary that I resumed shortly after our return. It begins at Faresund on 30 September 1944:

This picture of the wardroom of *U-190*, taken during the 1944 voyage to Germany, shows, from the left, myself, *Oberleutnant* Reith, the CO, and the I.WO, *Oberleutnant* Schmidt. The little doll hanging from the lamp was thoroughly drenched with Chanel 5 before coming aboard to serve as a reminder of more pleasant times in the past and, hopefully, in the future. (WH col.)

Aboard we have a boisterous party and then, for the first time in weeks I can sink into my bunk to enjoy a deep, undisturbed sleep. But I think I must have shown a happy smile on my face. I'll see my girl again – after all!

Next morning, in a few hours of easy travel, we transfer to Kristiansand. We take on fuel – we arrived in Norway with a thimble of fuel left – fresh food and water and then leave for Germany.

I have had a marvellous day in Kristiansand. First the lovely warm late summer day enticed me on a long walk into the surroundings of the harbour. For hours I could soak in the fabulous sights of the fjord below me, the shimmering water and the steep mountains. Then I had a long soothing bath ashore and enjoyed a quiet afternoon in the abode of a comrade, with gentle music and the newest papers. A big cigar and a cup of coffee completed the paradise.

The following night five U-boats (four others have joined us in Kristiansand) meet – in the bright moonshine – a ghostly-looking squadron of German warships. It's the cruiser *Emden* and several destroyers which pass at high speed

pretty close to us. Unnoticed we continue on our way.

On 4 October we arrive in Flensburg. We are the first *Frontboote* to come to this port and we are accordingly celebrated. *Korvettenkapitän* Schewe, chief of the 33. *Flotilla*, receives us with a speech of welcome.

We now begin ten days of uninhibited enjoyment. One party follows another and our behaviour is not always exemplary but we generously manage to overlook that fact.

Quite a few important tasks have to be taken care of. After a ceremony on the occasion of my promotion to *Oberleutnant (Ing)* and investiture with the *Eiserne Kreuz* II [Iron Cross, Second Class], I feel a need to visit all my old teachers at the *Marineschule* who made such an effort to make my life as midshipman as miserable as possible. It's now quite a satisfying experience to be able to give them a friendly slap on the shoulder without fear of incurring the wrath of undermined authority!

Then we visit all the old hunting grounds in the city where the randy pupils of the *Marineschule* robbed – and probably still do – the peace of mind of mothers with nubile daughters. The girls serving in these places are still the same. Among the *M.W.P.s*,* though, the new blood has become noticeable.

On 13 October the fun comes to an end and, together with another boat, we leave Flensburg to go to Bremen. While travelling

After having secured at Flensburg on 4 October 1944, we were assigned to the 33. *U-Bootsflottille* stationed there and were welcomed by its chief, *Korvettenkapitän* Georg Schewe. (WH col.)

through the Kiel Canal there is a stopover in Rendsburg and seven young U-boat officers, bearded and impudent, try to pump some life into the sleepy little town. First assignment is a visit to the famous *Kolonialschule*** for girls. The director of the school shows little enthusiasm for our plans and so we depart under mumbled curses aimed at these "behind-the-front bureaucrats" and "war prolongers."

We then invade the most elegant cafe in town where by midnight we have solicited the appropriate number of female partners to create a lovely dance party in a quickly

requisitioned separate room, lasting into the morning hours. It is a minor miracle that at the time of casting off the lines of our boats, all of us are actually back aboard.

We don't worry much about the consequences we leave behind. Girls just aren't looked after as well any more as they used to be. How does the saying go? "Everything is getting worse in this war, only one thing is getting better and that is that morals are getting worse."

Unfortunately, all this fun – well deserved in our opinion – came to an end when we departed from Rendsburg to go to Bremen. A day later we tied up in Bremen at the shipyard of Deschimag A.G. where our boat had been built more than two years before. The fifth operational mission of *U-190* had now ended.

---

* *Marinewanderpreise* or navy challenge trophies, the prizes for service competitions, here being applied to easily available girls.

** A preparatory school founded in 1926 to prepare young women to become the wives of German missionaries and farmers in the former German colonies in Africa.

After *U-190* returned to its home shipyard, Deschimag in Bremen, for extensive modifications, we had time on our hands. I was invited to attend the commissioning of *U-3021*, one of the new so-called *"Elektro"* Type XXI boats that possessed a vastly-increased battery capacity and had a higher speed underwater than on the surface. Any hopes for winning the submarine war hinged on the quick replacement of our obsolete Type VII and IX boats with these new craft – but the end of the war came before that could happen. The I.WO on this boat was my old comrade Pieper from *U-612,* who can be seen on the right of the first rank on the boat, while I am observing behind the other officers at the bottom of the picture. (WH col.)

LOVE IN THE RUINS OF THE REICH: OCTOBER 1944 TO FEBRUARY 1945

Our arrival at Bremen was part of a general reorganization of the *U-Boot-Waffe* caused by the loss of the French bases during the previous summer. Until a new generation of advanced "elektro-boats" entered service, Dönitz planned to continue operations using *Schnorchel*-equipped Type VII and Type IX craft operating from Norway. The 2. *U-bootsflottille*, which had been our unit in Lorient, was now disbanded and *U-190* was transferred to the newly-created 33. *U-bootsflottille* with headquarters at Flensburg. In the future we could expect to sail from Germany to Norway to mount our patrols, but before we left on our next mission, *U-190* was to undergo a major modification. For this reason we had returned the boat to the Deschimag shipyard.

This modification involved cutting away much of the forward deck where there was an external compartment to store four torpedoes. This large flat area created undesirable adhesion to the surface of the water when trying to break through during the diving process. Under normal conditions, it took a Type IX boat up to 45 seconds to completely submerge, and it was expected that reducing the amount of deck to be submerged would result in a reduction in the time required, an important advantage as by this period in the war we faced overwhelming numbers of Allied aircraft and warships. As opportunity presented itself, many Type IX boats had been thus modified and it was now the turn of *U-190*. This was a major job that was expected to take between six weeks and two months to complete.

I was busy immediately after our arrival getting the boat ready to be turned over to the shipyard. After a few days, preparations for this work had progressed to the extent that I could go on leave and after a call to my mother I was on a train to Berlin. I was hoping that Ruth would be at the station to meet me but I was disappointed. We got together, however, a few days later and she was duly impressed with the shiny new star on my epaulettes marking my recent promotion to *Oberleutnant*. For the remainder of my leave we spent nearly every evening together – I would pick her up at her office at the Reich Chancellery, buy her dinner at the Riviera Restaurant in Grünau where we first met, and afterwards take her home. At this time I introduced Ruth to my mother, who liked her very much.

Although we were as happy as circumstances permitted, I caught Ruth one evening with tears in her eyes. When I asked what the matter was she began to tell me hesitantly that she had been thinking about the time when I would soon be gone again and that she knew, given the way the war was going, which was not good at all, that the Russians must one day get to Berlin. I assured her that even though I would have to leave again, everything would be the same on my return. I am not so sure she was convinced.

Such, however, is the resiliency of youth that at this time I visited the *Oberkommando der Marine*, the Naval High Command in Berlin, and applied for a transfer to the *Kleinkampfverbände*, the special attack units of miniature submarines and manned torpedoes which had been formed under the command of *Vizeadmiral* Helmuth Heye. The *Kleinkampfverbände* was an elite force but, as is so often the case with such forces, often suffered high losses. Despite my own worries, I think I was searching for some excitement. Certainly Ruth became very angry when she learned of what I had done as, with good reason, she considered my current duties to be dangerous enough.

During my last week in Berlin I was glad that my father came home on leave for a few days. He too met and liked Ruth, but all too soon it was time to return to Bremen and yet another goodbye scene ensued at the train station. My parting gift to Ruth was a copy of my diary of the siege of Lorient and the miniature *U-bootsabzeichen* that I usually wore on my civilian clothes on leave – it was intended as a good luck charm for her while I was absent. Then the train started rolling and

there was just time for a last kiss.

In Bremen I found that the completion of the modifications to *U-190* had been delayed and it was now expected that the boat would not be ready for service until the middle of December. I therefore found myself with little to do. I spent a couple of days convincing my superiors that my presence in Bremen was superfluous and fortunately I soon held a 10-day leave pass in my hands. This time Ruth met me at the station and we were happy to see each other. However, I was not feeling all that well and my mother insisted on calling our doctor, who diagnosed influenza and prescribed a week in bed, which was a disastrous turn of events. The only consolation was that Ruth came daily to visit. Inevitably, the time came to return to Bremen and we parted once more at the station after I promised her that I would try and return for her birthday on 14 December.

Back in Bremen, I discovered that Deschimag had put back the modifications yet again and the boat would not now be ready until January 1945. Since the shipyard was handling this job, there really was not much for the crew to do and we led rather a carefree life. I spent many a happy hour drinking with Herbert Rogge, who shared my rooming house. He had been our II.WO on the previous mission but had now become the I.WO. I am sure that sometimes innocent bystanders were worried about our ability to find our way home but one of us was always able to function well enough to navigate a return to base. On one occasion, Herbert had to make a dedicated effort to keep me inside a moving street car when I was trying to abandon ship, while on another occasion it was

I who had to sort out whose legs belonged to whom, and that in the middle of the Bremen *Marktplatz!* The consequences were usually king-size hangovers the next morning – which we attempted to cure, not always very successfully, with more alcohol.

Between these misadventures I wrote long letters to Ruth. While the fairer sex played an important role in Herbert's plans and activities, I had, to my own surprise, renounced other women altogether as I did not want Ruth to have any reason for complaint. Apart from my rather harmless flirtation with Janine in Lorient, I had actually been leading an admirably unblemished life in that respect.

On 12 December I got a lucky opportunity to travel to Berlin on navy business. When I arrived, Ruth immediately dragged me to a photographer's studio to get some formal portraits done. The following morning my CO, *Oberleutnant z.S.* Reith, arrived in Berlin and I accompanied him to the UFA, Germany's largest film production company, where, through Ruth's connections, they agreed to produce a great number of prints of photographs taken on our last patrol. At Ruth's invitation, we had lunch with her in the cafeteria of the Reich Chancellery, where the sight of two uniformed naval officers must have been rare, as we attracted many interested glances.

The next day, which was Ruth's birthday, I visited her office to present my presents – some silk stockings, a decorative pot containing a cyclamen, a bottle of fine liqueur and a box of chocolates. Any plans on my part to deliver the fine speech I had prepared for the occasion were interrupted, however, by numerous telephone calls and the arrival of a *Luftwaffe* major who wanted to wish Ruth a happy birthday and was only got rid of with great difficulty.

To my annoyance, I found that Ruth had many admirers. A few days later, my plans to take her to dinner were frustrated by her wish to invite an old flame to join us, a former *Leutnant* in the *Heer* who was badly wounded on the Eastern Front. At her office a few days later, while I was in the middle of trying to convince her to spend the Christmas holiday with me in Bremen, our conversation was interrupted by yet another admirer – this time a *Luftwaffe* officer who was passing through Berlin and took the opportunity "to just pop in and say hello." This was about the last thing I needed as I myself was leaving in a few hours, but Ruth did accompany me to the station, where we said good-bye for the fourth time – but with the hope on my part that we would be together for Christmas.

In Bremen I got caught up in all kinds of festivities, including the commissioning of new boats and celebrating comrades' birthdays. We were frequently disturbed by enemy aircraft but they mostly just flew over on their way to Berlin, which was being heavily bombed at this time, a fact that caused me much concern for my family. I was always glad when, via a telephone conversation arranged by Ruth, who, unlike most Germans, had access to the government phone system, I could calm my worries about my family suffering in the incessant bombing raids.

Christmas was now approaching and the officers of *U-190* began to make preparations for the holiday. We reserved a hall in the *U-bootheim** for a crew party to which the ladies of the crew were invited. Among them was Ruth, for whom I managed to get a military permit to use the railway system. On 23 December the sister and fiancée of our CO, *Oberleutnant* Reith, arrived for the festivities and that evening Reith, Herbert and I sat with the ladies waiting for a courier who was expected to deliver the prints from UFA. With painstaking efforts, Reith had fabricated a small photo album for each of the nearly 60 men in his crew into which we would paste 50 photos taken during our last patrol. When the courier finally arrived, we began this laborious task which was only completed by noon on Christmas Eve. We were dead tired but there was no opportunity for sleep as Herbert and Reith had to finalize the preparations at the *U-bootheim* while I had to meet Ruth at the station.

Her train was late but finally it arrived. I had arranged for her to stay in the house of a relative of the Reith family, and after she had changed at that place I accompanied her and Reith's sister and fiancée to the *U-bootheim* for the party. Since there were no streetcars running we had to walk all the way and it took almost an hour.

When we arrived, everyone was assembled and waiting. The candles on the Christmas tree were lit and a festive mood filled the hall. Reith made a short speech and then we enjoyed an opulent meal, followed by cake and punch. The crew, dressed in meticulously clean dress uniforms and wearing their decorations, looked terrific and were on their best behaviour although the younger

sailors were a bit shy in the presence of the ladies. The high point of the evening, of course, was the appearance of Sankt Niklaus, who, with a long white beard, a heavy sack on his back and a switch in his hand (intended for use on the officers), looked absolutely genuine. When he made his entry speech, only the crew recognized the voice of our *Nummer Eins,** *Bootsmaat* Alois Feldbauer, who had a gift for everyone, which he presented along with suitable personal remarks. At about 8 P.M., the official part of the festivities ended and the II.WO, *Leutnant z.S.* Werner Müller, who had recently been assigned to *U-190*, assumed the role of master of ceremonies. Reith, Herbert, our ladies and I now left to have our own party and also to give the sailors a chance to let their hair down. As our navigator, *Obersteuermann* Dombrowski, was alone at Christmas, we invited him to join us at the house where Ruth was staying and where we had another exchange of gifts. Ruth presented me with a beautiful framed picture of herself which I really appreciated, while the navigator received a lovely little doll for his daughter that she had brought from Berlin. We sat around the tree in the light of the flickering candles until late into the night, and so passed Christmas Eve 1944 for the crew of *U-190*.

On the following morning Reith, Herbert and the ladies left for Hamburg, from which place Herbert would continue on to Berlin. I had a pass for Berlin but the next train that Ruth and I could catch did not leave until the

---

* A club and billeting establishment for U-boat personnel on leave.

* The *"Nummer Eins"* or "Number One" was the nickname of the coxswain of a U-boat, in charge of the seamen, as opposed to the engine-room and technical personnel.

following day, so we remained alone in the house. Ruth felt uncomfortable about this because she feared that people "might talk," but I, of course, was delighted.

Next morning early, we went to the station. We got two good seats side by side and by mid-afternoon we were in Berlin, where I took Ruth directly to her parents, who were glad to get their daughter back safe and sound. The evening before my return to Bremen I spent at Ruth's home. She was planning to celebrate New Year's Eve with her brother in Cunrau in the Altmark and I suggested she accompany me in my train as far as Salzwedel, halfway to Bremen, and then change for Cunrau. Just before Rogge and I returned to Bremen, she showed up with a travel bag and squeezed herself between us and we had a fun-filled trip as Herbert regaled us with many amusing stories. We soon reached Ruth's destination and once more we had to say good-bye.

Back in Bremen Herbert and I went in desperate search of a suitable New Years's Eve party to crash. On the morning of 31 December 1944, however, I had a brilliant idea. I suggested that I sign two passes for Herbert and me, and we could then take off for Berlin and be back before anyone noticed our absence. He agreed with this stroke of administrative genius and I immediately called Ruth and arranged to meet her in Salzwedel. At the train station, I was worried that the ever-watchful *Kettenhunde** would carefully inspect our passes and discover that the bearer of my pass was also

the same officer who had signed it. Fortunately, there were no problems.

Ruth was waiting in Salzwedel and the three of us continued on to Berlin. I managed to convince Ruth that her going home first would be an awful waste of time, and after some hesitation, she agreed. Herbert was dropped at the Friedrichstrasse Station and we then continued on to Blankenfelde.

Ruth and I celebrated New Year's Eve with my mother and her lady friend from next door. At midnight we toasted the new year, 1945, and wondered what it had in store for us. Certainly, the future did not look good for Germany. In the west, the Allies had pushed our forces out of France and most of the Low Countries and were poised on the Rhine, ready to invade our territory. A few weeks before, our army had mounted a counter-offensive in the Ardennes but its progress, at first promising, now appeared to have bogged down. Matters were even more serious in the east – the Soviets, who had launched great offensives during the previous six months, were on the borders of Germany, and although the Eastern front was currently static, everyone knew that this was just the lull before the storm.

We pushed all this out of our minds and tried to be as happy as we could, as we knew not what the future would bring. In honour of the moment I decided to go outside and fire a few rounds from my service pistol, a Mauser 7.65 mm automatic, into the winter sky. After the first shot I handed the weapon to Ruth but when she tried, it jammed. Disappointed, we returned to the house just as the telephone rang – it was Herbert wish-

* Literally "chained dogs" – the military police. This nickname was occasioned by their insignia, which was a metal shield worn on the chest and suspended from a chain around the neck.

ing us a happy New Year and it was clear that he was not suffering any great pain either.

Ruth and I took a short walk through the winter landscape. We stomped through the deep snow and dropped in at the home of the parents of Ulrich, my best friend from my school days, who had failed to return from a reconnaissance flight in the Arctic, to present his mother with our best wishes. However, when Ruth and I, the picture of carefree happiness, stood before this sorely afflicted woman, the tears welled in her eyes as she would never again she see her son and would never have a daughter-in-law. In vain I tried to cheer her up but eventually we walked back home, somewhat depressed.

Ruth and I at a party in Berlin. Atop the two rings indicating my rank of *Oberleutnant* can be seen my submariner's badge. (WH col.)

When Herbert and I returned to Bremen, we found our absence had not been noticed. The following week, the shipyard's work on *U-190* was approaching completion and it was clear that we would soon be returning to sea. One evening Herbert and I got into a discussion about our chances of surviving the next patrol and we both were surprised to learn that the other had the same sentiment – namely that we might not return. This mutual fear was somewhat strange as, since the introduction of the *Schnorchel*, U-boat losses had appeared to lessen. We both thought that the reason for our disquiet was our concern about our CO, Reith, in whom we had very little confidence. But, on the other hand, we also realized that, as the senior officers on the boat, we had considerable influence on the course of events.

At this time I was disappointed to learn that my application for a transfer to the *Kleinkampfverbände* had been refused. I thought bitterly that at least Ruth would be happy.

Our first trial run with the boat took place in the middle of January and passed without problems. Our day of departure from Bremen was now fixed for 24 January and I wanted desperately to get back to Berlin just one more time. After some negotiations with Reith, both Herbert and I received leave for the weekend of 19 January. We got to Berlin without any trouble and on the Saturday night I had a farewell party at home in Blankenfelde with my mother, one of her friends and, of course, Ruth. Ruth and I suffered a bit under the torture of not being alone. However, I was pleased just to be with her and when I opened the window and the cold winter air hit my face, I inhaled deeply and thought the world a beautiful place.

On the Sunday afternoon, Ruth and I travelled into Berlin, where we met Herbert and his girlfriend on the platform of the Lehrter Station. We learned that our train had been cancelled as the situation in the east was extremely desperate because, just a few days before, the Soviets had unleashed a great offensive. They had penetrated East Prussia and overloaded refugee trains were arriving continuously from that area. In Germany in January 1945, trains rarely operated according to schedule and Herbert and I therefore abandoned the idea of returning to Bremen that day and went our separate ways with our ladies. Ruth took me to the Reich Chancellery, where we spent the night drinking champagne and dancing.

When we returned to the station next morning, Herbert and I were forced to wait for any train that might even take us in the general direction of Bremen. As this looked like it might take hours, we invaded a train signal shack where, after a generous distribution of our cigarette ration, we got permission to warm ourselves near the red-hot coal stove. Despite the general chaos in the rail system, the Berlin railwaymen had not lost their traditional caustic sense of humour and we had a lot of fun. Finally, in the afternoon, we were able to board a refugee train bound for Bremen, where we arrived several hours later, to be strongly reproached by Reith for overstaying our leave.

We now became very busy as we prepared the boat for its next patrol. We took on provisions while the workers of the Deschimag yard were still putting the finishing touches to the bow modification.

Shortly after 2 P.M. on 24 January 1945, we cast off and passed through the Kiel Canal to Kiel to load fuel, ammunition and torpedoes. Kiel was crowded with refugees who were constantly arriving by ship and train. The situation in both the city and naval base was very disorganized and the harbour was filled with warships waiting for orders, and almost every day brought air-raid warnings. Under these circumstances we were informed that it would be at least a week before we could load torpedoes.

While we waited, I ran into an acquaintance, another *LI*, who told me that he now had a second engineer on board for training purposes so that he could be relieved after his next patrol to take over one of the new Type XXI U-boats coming out of the shipyards. This struck me as an eminently good idea and I immediately visited the personnel office of the naval base. There, after an interview with a *Kapitänleutnant* who did not know me, conducted with some slight exaggeration on my part, I received permission to select an officer to assist me as *Wachingenieur* with the understanding that, after our next patrol, I would leave *U-190* and transfer to one of the new Type XXI craft. A few days later, *Leutnant (Ing)* Ernst Glenk joined our wardroom.

Having learned from Ruth that she might possibly be able to manage one last trip to Kiel, I spent considerable time in the telephone booth of the liner *Milwaukee*, the headquarters of the 5. *U-bootsflottille*, to which *U-190* was attached for administrative purposes, discussing arrangements. Finally we agreed that Ruth would come to Kiel on Saturday, 3 February 1945. On the day before her arrival, however, an order was issued that, owing to the refugee chaos in the city, all naval shore leave was cancelled, married men excepted. I spent some time pleading my case with the adjutant of the 5. *Flottille* but got nowhere and was on the point of going ashore without a pass when, in the evening, *U-190* was moved across the harbour to a civilian shipyard, far from the naval base and the prying eyes of the calcified bureaucrats on the flotilla staff.

My next problem was to find a place for Ruth to stay, in a chaotic and overcrowded city. It cost me a bottle of rum from my liquor ration to convince the desk clerk of the *Bahnhofhotel* that he did indeed have a room available. Ruth's train arrived at 2 A.M. and, after the usual loving greetings, she informed me that she was lucky to be on it as there had been a very bad air raid that day in Berlin and she was forced to spend hours in the basement shelter of the Chancellery and only managed to make it to the station through streets blocked with debris by hitching a ride on a fire engine.

The next morning we managed to get a good breakfast but the area around the train station was crowded with masses of refugees looking for ways to continue their journey. I was deeply shocked by their indescribable misery and to get away from such sights I took Ruth down to the port and showed her the inner harbour, which was not at all inviting as fog had descended and everything was clad in the same monotonous grey. The noise of the hammers from the shipyards on the opposite shore filled the air while the many welding torches dimly illuminated that side of the harbour with a pale, flickering light.

It began to snow, and Ruth replaced her hat with a kerchief as I pointed out the four mighty Hamburg-Amerika liners, *Deutschland*, *Hamburg*, *Hansa* and *New York*, moored in the outer harbour. As we walked through the gate into the naval base I told her that my next patrol would be my last on *U-190* and that, after I returned, I would spend at least six months ashore before my new

Type XXI boat would be ready for operations. Naturally, this news made Ruth extremely happy.

As we strolled along the piers of the naval base, where many U-boats were secured, I was constantly greeted by officers that I knew, one of whom informed me that my friend Pieper from *U-612* was the I.WO of a boat moored nearby. We walked over and I asked the watch on deck to call the I.WO, who promptly appeared and greeted me effusively. I asked Pieper to help me locate *U-190,* which had, in my absence, been moved from the shipyard back to the base, and he ordered the bridge watch to locate a Type IX boat with a "blue star" (the blue compass rose which was the boat emblem of *U-190*) on the conning tower. The watch scanned the harbour for a few minutes and then reported my boat's location, which was not far away. We bade goodbye to my friend and continued on to *U-190,* which appeared totally deserted.

The bridge watch informed me that the crew had gone to the *Milwaukee* to hear an announcement. I contemplated taking Ruth down to the wardroom to get away from the rather unpleasant weather but since the traditional superstition among U-boat crews was that, if a woman comes on board, it brings bad luck, I did not do so. I was relieved from my dilemma at that moment because our crew returned from the *Milwaukee.* Inviting Ruth on board, however, was declared unacceptable by an unanimous vote of my comrades despite the fact that wet snow was falling heavily. I accepted their arguments and had a bottle of cognac delivered to the dockside where, at the end of the pier, there was a bit of a roof. Under its cover, Herbert Rogge, the II.WO, Werner

Müller, my *Wachingenieur*, Ernst Glenk, and we two consumed one cognac after the other while, in between, the occasional chocolate was shoved into Ruth's mouth. The alcohol warmed her up and she became quite lively despite her pitiful resemblance to a drenched cat.

An idea occurred to me and I took our *Nummer Eins*, the inimitable *Bootsmaat* Feldbauer, aside. A few days before, he had told me that he knew of a room available not far from the base and I asked him if it was still available. He replied that he could find out but he had pressing duties to perform, so I asked Herbert if he could spare Feldbauer for a few minutes and the I.WO, who was more interested in entertaining Ruth than his job, immediately granted permission. Feldbauer returned in less than 30 minutes to inform me that the room was available and that the landlady was expecting us, and coffee was on the stove, awaiting our arrival.

Ruth and I therefore said good-bye to the officers and together with Feldbauer, we went to the room, which was in a house on nearby Knorrstrasse. En route, Ruth was not pleased to learn from Feldbauer that the only way he was able to procure the room was by telling the landlady that it was needed, not for a single woman, but for a married naval officer and his wife, although I assured her that in this regard I was totally innocent. The landlady, a pleasant woman, was not suspicious, however, and proved very solicitous about the poor, bedraggled, young naval wife and served us coffee. Feldbauer, glad of the break, stayed on to help us drink the coffee and it was arranged that we would return to the hotel that night and move into our new accommodation in the

morning. After an hour of not unpleasant walking – as neither one of us were feeling any discomfort – through the wet, foggy evening we reached the Bahnhofhotel. I had thoughtfully picked up some food from the boat so we were able to have supper in our room.

Next morning early, I took a street car back to the base, leaving Ruth to move to Knorrstrasse later. Meanwhile I began the job of getting the boat ready for its next mission. At the end of the day, however, I took one of my chief petty officers aside and borrowed his wedding ring so that when I returned to Knorrstrasse, I was in proper marital uniform. When I did return "home," I was pleased to find that my "wife" had prepared my evening meal.

For Ruth and me, our last days together passed amid a whirlwind of work on the boat as we struggled to take on torpedoes, ammunition and provisions. I was glad to have the assistance of a *Wachingenieur,* but even so it was usually 6 or 7 P.M. each evening before I appeared at Knorrstrasse. In the evenings we talked to the landlady, who was glad to receive some of my liquor ration, and on one occasion we held a little dance party, to which the I.WO came, although it was interrupted by an air raid. It was now accepted that Ruth and I were formally engaged and I wrote my mother to tell her so.

The time approached when the crew of *U-190* had to return to the war after our pleasant four months' break. Our original departure was scheduled for Friday, 9 February 1945, but after loud protests from the crew – since German sailors consider it unlucky to sail on a Friday – it was postponed to the following day. All of us officers, not knowing what the immediate future held, decided to take our dress uniforms and personal kit on this patrol as we feared they might be lost in the increasingly chaotic conditions in Germany.

I spent my last evening at Knorrstrasse, drinking and dancing with Ruth, and at 10 A.M. on Saturday she accompanied me to the naval base as I didn't know whether I would be able to return again. We said good-bye at the gate although the presence of the nearby sentry kept our farewell embraces somewhat stiff – but what could we say to each other at this moment anyway? Words would be small things relative to the pain of having to part.

When I arrived at *U-190*, preparations for departure were almost complete and by noon I found myself with little to do so I decided to go back and see Ruth just one last time. When I returned to the base I took her with me all the way to the boat. However, from far down the pier I could hear the CO screaming, "*LI*, where the hell are you? We have to leave immediately for a test dive. Hurry up!" I was therefore forced to abandon her again. The test dive was completed very quickly – I just dropped the boat to the bottom of the harbour and then immediately surfaced. The hatch was hardly open when I was on deck and hailing a safety launch which came alongside in an impressive manoeuvre. Telling the bridge watch I was leaving the boat for a short period I hopped a ride on the launch over to the Scharnhorst Pier, hoping to catch Ruth, but she was already out of sight.

I returned again to *U-190* only to learn that the departure of our boat and the two others going out with us had been delayed for two hours. On a whim I asked Reith if I could take the I.WO and II.WO back to Knorrstrasse and say goodbye to my fiancée. He agreed somewhat reluctantly but insisted we be back by 3.30 P.M. Ruth, of course, was pleased to see us and quickly made coffee, which we consumed with some liqueur, but all too soon it was time again to go. Again, I took Ruth back to the boat so that she could witness our departure and the four of us returned to *U-190*. At the boat I had to leave Ruth on her own for a few minutes when the crews of the three departing submarines were brought together to hear the final remarks of the flotilla chief, but I was soon back with her. In the meantime, the mother and wife of the CO, who had married a few days before (although he did not invite his officers to the ceremony), arrived and I introduced Ruth to the CO's mother. As the two other boats began hauling in their lines, in readiness to depart, we stood together on the pier beside *U-190*.

Then it was our turn. I reported the boat ready to the flotilla engineer before becoming the last crew member to go on board. The gangway was removed and, accompanied by a stirring military march played through our bridge loudspeaker, we cast off. The diesels sprang to life, spitting and rumbling, and we eased out into Kiel harbour and headed for the open sea. Glancing back from the bridge, I watched the pier getting smaller, but for some time I could see Ruth waving until only her white handkerchief was visible and finally even that disappeared from view.

More pictures from my album…

The sail training ship *Horst Wessel* tied up to the Blücherbrücke in Kiel. Built in 1936 with a displacement of approximately 1,750 tons, *Horst Wessel* served during the war as an accommodation vessel. Turned over to the United States, she became the Coast Guard training vessel *Eagle*.

This picture of the cruise ship *Wilhelm Gustloff,* of 25,484 tons, was taken during a trip to East Prussia in 1939. Constructed for the "Strength through Joy" organization in 1937, she took thousands of passengers on peacetime cruises, but during the war served as a transport, a hospital ship and an accommodation ship. On 30 January 1945, while carrying more than 10,000 people, mostly refugees from East Prussia, the *Wilhelm Gustloff* was torpedoed by a Soviet submarine in the Baltic and sank with the loss of 9,343 souls, the worst maritime disaster in history.

HMCS *Esquimalt*, the Bangor-class minesweeper that was the last Royal Canadian Navy ship sunk in the Second World War. The RCN used this class and the Algerine class minesweepers as inshore ASW escorts. *Esquimalt* had a crew of 6 officers and 77 ratings, displaced 592 tons and was armed with one 12-pdr gun and two 20 mm AA guns. She was commissioned in October 1942. (RCN photo/NAC/ PA-116954)

It took nearly a week for *U-190* and the two boats that travelled with us to move cautiously through the Kattegat and Skagerrak to reach our bases in southern Norway. The Allied navies, which possessed the matchless advantage of being able to intercept and read the coded radio communications between *BdU* and U-boats at sea, were fully aware of the movements of most German submarines at this time but, owing to the presence of German land-based aircraft, the enemy could not risk surface warships in these shallow waters. The nearer we came to Norway the more active enemy air patrols become and not only did aircraft, equipped with highly accurate radars, search for U-boats at sea; they also mined the approaches to our bases.

We became aware of this threat on 17 February 1945 when our three boats entered the Oslofjord near Horten. *U-1273*, a new Type VIIC boat on its first patrol, was travelling behind *U-190* when it hit a mine and sank immediately, taking 43 of its 51-man crew with it, including the boat's CO, *Kaptänleutnant* Helmut Knollmann. The sight of this disaster, which was witnessed by our bridge watch, deeply affected us, particularly since we had squeezed ourselves between *U-1273* and the pre-

ceding boat instead of following *U-1273* as we had done before. We were convinced that the mine could have been the "counting" type, a mine that lets a number of targets go by before exploding at a set number, meaning that *U-1273* had been destroyed by a mine meant for *U-190*. This tragedy, however, did not affect our activities as, after a brief stop at Horten, we continued on to Kristiansand South, from where we would depart on patrol.

By this late period in the war, the *U-Boot-Waffe* had nearly been swept from the North Atlantic. The attempts of our commander, Dönitz, over the previous nine months to hamper the Allied invasion of Europe and the resulting build-up of enemy troops and supplies on the mainland had been frustrated by overwhelming air and sea forces and we had suffered heavy losses in boats and crews. But *BdU* did not give up the struggle as it was Dönitz's intention to continue fighting with our obsolescent Type VII and Type IX boats until the new "elektro boats" entered service, hopefully in the spring of 1945. We were told that the purpose of our missions was to tie up Allied forces by forcing them to disperse and fight us wherever we showed up. It was reckoned that any ship or aircraft occupied in chasing us was one less warship or aircraft that could be used to directly attack Germany. By continuing our operations, we also forced the Allied navies to maintain the very uneconomical (in terms of the warships and personnel it required) convoy system and this, in itself, was considered worthy of our best efforts. This attitude was reflected in the words of a flotilla chief who, bidding goodbye to a submarine, was heard to say, "Never mind sinking ships, please just come back."

Thus, the *U-Boot-Waffe* went on waging what had by now become a very unequal struggle. *Schnorchel*-equipped Type VII boats were sent to the waters around the British Isles but the larger Type IX boats, such as *U-190*, with their greater range, were as usual ordered on long-range missions to distant areas, particularly North America. Between February and April 1945, 19 U-boats, all Type IX craft, were sent west across the Atlantic – and 10 were destroyed. Our boat's objective, as we learned when we docked at Kristiansand Sud on 18 February 1945, was to head for the western Atlantic. We took the opportunity to top up our fuel tanks and then, at 6 P.M. on 21 February 1945, *U-190* departed from Kristiansand for what would be its sixth patrol.

Our course lay across the North Sea, then north of the Faeroes, through the Faeroes-Iceland Gap and finally southwest into the Atlantic until we reached the area on the German naval grid denominated as CB (Caesar-Bruno) 20, which lay about 150 miles southeast of Halifax on the great circle route. In all it took us more than six weeks to reach this point because we

spent most of our time travelling submerged, using *U-190's* electric motors, which would only provide an economical speed of 1.5 knots – or, in plain words, a crawl. In the first two weeks of the patrol, during the time we were in the North Sea and traversing the Faeroes-Iceland Gap, we surfaced rarely. After we were well out into the Atlantic, we ran on the surface for longer periods at night, sometimes for as much as ten hours but our progress was still not swift as we kept our speed down to conserve fuel.

In the middle Atlantic, *Obersteuerman* Dombrowski, our navigator, piloted by using radio beams provided by the *Kriegsmarine Elektra-Sonne* navigational system, which was very similar to the Allied Loran system. Various land stations in Norway, in our bases in France that were still holding out, and even in Lugo in Spain, transmitted radio beams on fixed bearings but different frequencies that created a lattice pattern across the Atlantic. We had a small dipole antenna attached to our *Schnorchel* and, after receiving these beams and identifying them, we could triangulate them to arrive at a rough estimate of our position. When we ran on the surface for longer periods, it gave Dombrowski a chance to shoot the stars.

At set times during the day, usually in the evening hours, our radio man listened for messages broadcast from the *BdU* transmitter at Magdeburg codenamed "Goliath," which we could sometimes pick up while running just under the surface. We usually timed our use of the *Schnorchel* to coincide with the scheduled time for us to receive radio messages.

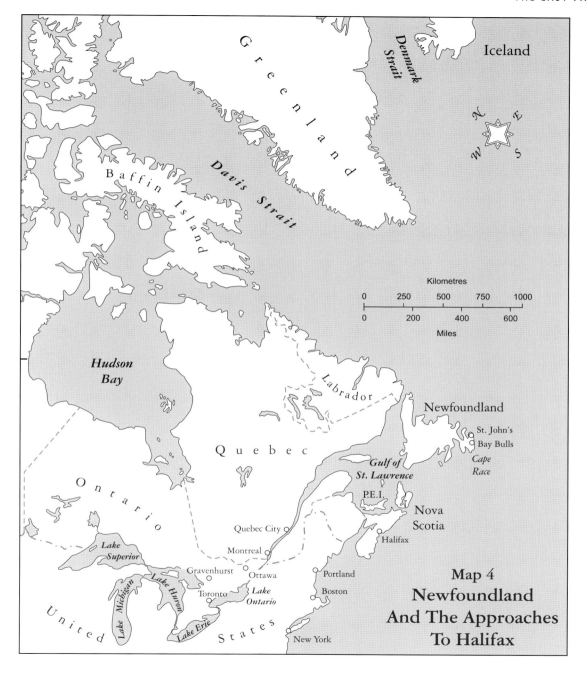

Kilometres

| 0 | 250 | 500 | 750 | 1000 |

| 0 | 200 | 400 | 600 |

Miles

Greenland

Denmark Strait

Iceland

Baffin Island

Davis Strait

Hudson Bay

Labrador

Newfoundland

St. John's
Bay Bulls
Cape Race

Quebec

Gulf of St. Lawrence

P.E.I.

Nova Scotia

Halifax

Ontario

Lake Superior

Quebec City

Montreal

Gravenhurst

Ottawa

Toronto

Lake Ontario

Lake Michigan

Lake Huron

Lake Erie

United

States

Portland

Boston

New York

Map 4
Newfoundland
And The Approaches
To Halifax

From *BdU*, we learned, after leaving Norway, that our operational area was to be off Halifax harbour in Canada. This came as no surprise, as late in 1944 two boats, *U-806* and *U-1232*, had carried out very successful patrols in this area, sinking a number of vessels, including a Canadian warship.* The result was that Dönitz, feeling the enemy defences around Halifax were not quite as vigilant as at other areas of the North American coast, had dispatched a number of boats, including *U-190*, to hunt in the entrance to a port that was one of the major mustering points for the North Atlantic convoys.

During our crossing of the Atlantic we had a few encounters with enemy (probably American) surface vessels which pursued us for hours with a tenacity that evoked our admiration, as the rough seas would have sent German destroyers home very quickly. We were fortunate that their depth charges only rattled our nerves and never came close enough to cause any damage.

Possibly our worst enemy during this slow and lengthy voyage was boredom. Much has been made of the horrifying conditions U-boat crews had to endure during the war and certainly it was no picnic, but the reality was not nearly as bad as has been made out because, except for the occasional bursts of action, our life on long patrols such as this was rather tedious. During this seemingly endless voyage I remember spending countless hours reading books and playing in chess tournaments. We seized on anything that might provide amusement – we held competitions for inventing the most stupid joke and we developed an interesting social intercourse with a solitary fly that appeared in mid-ocean and which, after fierce debate, was christened "Emma." We later speculated about the subsequent miraculous appearance of Emma's daughter. We also engaged in an intense analysis of, and debate about, the growth of the only other living matter aboard *U-190* – mildew. Philosophical discussions about anything and everything were geared to compensate for the somewhat stupefying effects of long periods of inactivity in a closed environment 200 feet below the surface, as we were well aware that atrophy of the brain was one of our biggest problems. There were, however, some subjects we never talked about – politics, war aims or the reason for being out there in the first place.

Cooped up in close confinement for such a long period meant that personal habits, which might under normal conditions have been only a minor annoyance or even the subject of a joke, became unbearably irritating. I remember that one of the strains of my daily life was watching my friend, Herbert Rogge, the I.WO, undertake his very peculiar method of brushing his teeth. After watching this for the hundredth time I developed an unreasonable but ardent desire to murder him, since there was absolutely no practical way to escape this ritual which became a daily torture to me.

If you lie down, you use less oxygen than when you stand up or move, and if you sleep, you use less oxygen

---

* In December 1944, *U-806*, under *Kapitän z.S.* Klaus Hornbostel, sank the freighter *Samtucky* and the minesweeper HMCS *Clayoquot* in the approaches to Halifax. A few weeks later in January 1945, *U-1232*, under *Kapitän z.S.* Kurt Dobratz, sank five freighters in the same area, winning Dobratz the *Ritterkreuz*. Both officers reported to *BdU* that the naval forces defending this area appeared to be weak and uncoordinated.

than when you are awake. On this long patrol we tried to sleep as much as 20 hours a day to save oxygen and electricity. We had a few bottles of oxygen on board but never used them within a 24-hour period so as to save them for real emergencies, and the same was true of our potash containers, which filtered out carbon dioxide. Although we were not supposed to have a level of carbon dioxide higher than 2.5 percent, we lived regularly with double that amount and none of us seemed to suffer any permanent damage as a result. After 24 hours, however, lack of fresh air made itself noticeable with heavier breathing and more sluggish activities. For this reason, the use of the *Schnorchel* was welcomed on board and when we employed it, we arranged our ventilation system so that incoming fresh air was channelled first to the bow compartment from where the diesels sucked it, without any use of pipes back through all the forward compartments and then into the engine room in the aft part of the boat. By this method, all the crew, except those aft of the engine room, got an immediate whiff of what was to us, the most sweet-smelling air.

On the last day of March 1945, we began to operate completely underwater and the surviving records of the patrol show that we only surfaced three times in the next 40 days. Finally, early in April we entered our operational area off Halifax. I clearly remember that the temperatures near the coast were much colder – in *U-190*, the temperature outside the engine room rarely crept above 40° and often sank to only 34° Fahrenheit. But we regarded this as only a minor inconvenience, because we knew it was worse on the surface.

Close in-shore, we navigated by using our *Echolot* depth finder or by taking advantage of the convenient navigation points provided by the Sambro Light Ship and the lights of Halifax. That city had no blackout, and although we could not see its lights from the open sea we knew exactly where it was because their glow was clearly visible on the western horizon. We did not sight any convoys, only single merchant vessels, and these were usually small coastal vessels not worth wasting one of our 14 torpedoes on. As the *LI*, I wasn't too involved in tactical matters, but it appeared that all commercial traffic in the area had come to a halt. On the other hand the Royal Canadian Navy must have suspected that we were in the area, because they seemed to carry out constant Asdic searches for us.* Occasionally, depth charges were dropped on our supposed location, which was fortunately far away from our true location. Few came close enough to cause more than minimal damage and even fewer presented any real danger.

A more disconcerting effect on our nerves was created by the noise of the CAT** gear streamed or towed by surface warships for protection against our acoustic torpedoes. It consisted of two iron bars that, when dragged through the water behind a warship, produced

---

* This suspicion on the part of the crew of *U-190* was accurate as the RN Operational Intelligence Centre report for 19 to 28 March 1945 states that three U-boats were known to be operating off Nova Scotia with another two east of Newfoundland but on passage to that area.

** CAT, or Canadian Anti-acoustic Torpedo gear, was a noisemaker towed behind warships to act as a decoy for the German T5 acoustic torpedo. It was so loud under the water that many U-boat crew were convinced that its purpose was to make life miserable for them.

a rattle far louder than the vessel's propellers and therefore served as an effective decoy to divert our T5 acoustic torpedoes from their intended target. Long before an enemy warship could be seen or heard by our listening gear, the noise of CAT gear alerted us to the presence of the enemy because it sounded in our submerged boat like a *Kreissäge*, or an ear-piercing circular saw, and that was the name we gave the contraption. For years after the war was over, a noise as innocent as the humming of a bee would instantly bring back unwelcome memories of that devilish device.

Any time the situation became too uncomfortable we crept close in-shore and spent some time on the bottom. Here we felt relatively safe because the very poor Asdic conditions in this area and the many wrecks made it difficult for the enemy to find us. We also knew that prevailing wisdom in the Allied navies held that a U-boat would seek deep water for safety and they therefore looked for us farther out to sea and, by hiding in the shallows, we were able to thwart them. We, of course, did not know it at this time but the depredations on Allied shipping made the previous December and January by *U-806* and *U-1232* had resulted in the major eastbound convoy assembly points being switched from Halifax to Portland, Maine, and Boston, Massachusetts, and this was the reason for the scarcity of targets in our patrol area.

On 12 April 1945, we received our last distinct message from *BdU* in Germany. After that we heard nothing more from "Goliath" (which had been overrun by Allied troops) and from here on we were on our own. That same day (or the next, as the *KTB* for this patrol did

not survive the war and one day submerged off Halifax was much like another) *Oberleutnant* Reith fired a total of four torpedoes at a freighter and a steamer which he claimed to have spotted by periscope. He did not witness the destruction of these vessels but later stated that he had heard the torpedoes exploding and was certain he had hit both.* We did not wait around, however, to find out whether we were successful but immediately went to the bottom, which was quite shallow in this area, to hide from the inevitable antisubmarine sweep, which we were sure would follow.

Nothing happened, however, and we continued our patrol. On 16 April, we had just finished our midday meal (early morning local time) in the wardroom when we heard the pinging of Asdic against our hull. Reith went to periscope depth and, raising that device, spotted a small warship rapidly approaching from astern. Convinced we had been discovered, he decided to defend the boat by firing a T5 acoustic torpedo from a stern tube. A short period later, we heard an explosion, followed by "*Sinkgeräuschen*," the noises made by a sinking ship as its bulkheads collapsed. We had not been able to identify our target nor did we loiter around to investigate what was clearly a victory for *U-190*, but moved away and hid on the bottom. Strangely enough, there was no immediate reaction on the part of the enemy to this attack, although it was clear that we had sunk an Allied warship.

Much later I learned that our victim was HMCS

---

* Canadian records reveal no attacks on merchant shipping in the area on either 12 or 13 April 1945.

Esquimalt, a Bangor-class minesweeper carrying out an antisubmarine patrol in the approaches to Halifax harbour. Postwar research indicates that, despite standing orders, *Esquimalt*'s captain was neither zig-zagging nor towing the CAT gear with which his ship was equipped. He had also switched his radar off, and although his Asdic operators were searching for possible contacts, it is not clear whether they had actually detected *U-190* before Reith fired. Our torpedo hit *Esquimalt*'s starboard side and she sank in less than four minutes, giving her radio operator no opportunity to send a distress call to alert other ships that she was sinking and that there was a U-boat in the area.

Esquimalt went down so fast that her crew had no time to launch her whaler and managed to get only four of the vessel's six Carley floats into the water. Most of them, however, were able to leave the doomed vessel and swim to the floats but their ordeal was by no means over. No other Canadian warships or shore establishments knew that *Esquimalt* had been sunk and the survivors, not warmly dressed, were forced to spend six hours on the North Atlantic while aircraft flew overhead and ships steamed by at a distance, ignoring their desperate attempts to summon help. By the time they were rescued, many had tragically succumbed to hypothermia and exhaustion and, in the end, of the 70 officers and sailors in the minesweeper's crew, 44 lost their lives. HMCS *Esquimalt* was the last Canadian warship to be sunk during the Second World War.

At the time, of course, we knew nothing of the consequences of our actions. This was typical of the submariner's war as rarely did we become aware of the human suffering we caused – during the entire war I did not see a single dead person, nor any blood. In the end, we believed, we would either come home happy and healthy or we would not come back – there was nothing in between. Within the next ten hours, however, we became fully aware that the enemy, now alerted to our presence, was hunting for us. American and Canadian warships began a sweep around the approaches to Halifax and continued this activity for several days. Over the next week they were reinforced by more vessels, but the enemy, convinced that we would seek deep water, hunted farther out to sea while during most of this time we were close in-shore and on the bottom.

We thus escaped retribution from the enemy, but three days after the sinking of *Esquimalt* we nearly sank ourselves. On 19 April, just after having terminated our nightly use of the *Schnorchel*, I had gone into the wardroom to eat, leaving the completion of the operation to my *Wachingenieur*, Ernst Glenk. I suddenly felt the boat going down rapidly by the stern and my plate slid off the table. I raced to the *Zentrale* and found to my horror that the *Schnorchel* had been lowered into its horizontal storage position without the huge valve in the connecting pipe outside the conning tower first being closed. As a result, tons of water had flooded the engine room and short-circuited our main switchboards, producing flames and smoke. There was absolutely no alternative but to blow the tanks and surface.

So there we were, sitting ducks on a brightly moonlit night in sight of the Sambro Light Ship at the mouth of

Halifax harbour and quite unable to move. We immediately set about the task of pumping out the water and getting our electrical system back into shape, a process that required nearly two hours work. The crew's nerves were very much on edge and *Oberleutnant* Reith on the bridge naturally became impatient, several times urging me to hurry up with the repairs. I refused, however, to be hurried because I wanted to be absolutely sure that the boat was safe before taking it down again. Finally I decided it was safe enough to dive and we submerged only to face more hours of work cleaning up the mess in the engine rooms. Today, I find it hard to believe that we could spend that much time on the surface near one of the busiest ports in the world and not be discovered.*

By the last days of April 1945, having prowled off Halifax harbour for a period of nearly three weeks, our fuel and food began to run low and Reith contemplated a return to Norway. On 29 April we therefore turned east and commenced the long journey home but on the following day Reith claimed to have spotted a frigate or destroyer and fired three torpedoes at this vessel, all of which apparently missed.** At this time, I should mention that, although we were not receiving radio transmissions from *BdU*, we did occasionally get scraps of information from North American radio broadcasts and the news was not good. The Russians were fighting

in the streets of Berlin and close to my parents' home in Blankenfelde, while the American, British and Canadian armies had penetrated deep inside western Germany.

To lift our sagging spirits, we decided to stage a rather unmilitary interlude. The 1st of May was Germany's National Holiday, our equivalent to the American Fourth of July or the Canadian Dominion Day. We knew that, no matter what the future held in store for us, 1 May 1945 might be the last opportunity we would have for some time to celebrate the occasion in style and we decided to do so.

In normal times, U-boat crew members received a generous monthly ration of alcohol in the form of several bottles of liquor. These bottles were usually left at the base to be taken to our homes after we returned from a patrol, but when we left Kiel in February 1945, we were not altogether certain that we would be coming back to that particular port, and to prevent these desirable items from falling into the wrong hands, we had taken them along on our patrol, just as we had our dress uniforms. As the outlook for future parties to enjoy this liquid cargo appeared rather poor, we decided to live up to our responsibilities and have a rousing National Holiday party right then and there, at a depth of 200 feet somewhere between Halifax and southern Newfoundland. Despite the fact that the war was still being fought, we paid little attention to other happenings in the world and even hoped that Allied seamen were also having a holiday.

In *U-190*, from stem to stern the party got noisier and noisier and ever more boisterous. I had delegated responsibility for keeping proper depth to the forward

* While discussing this incident a few years ago with the former Senior Officer of the RCN Escort Group 27 charged with finding and destroying *U-190*, he explained jokingly that: "I believe on that day, my entire group was in dry dock!"

** Canadian naval records bear no mention of this incident.

planesman, who at that time happened to be our *"Nummer Eins," Bootsmaat* Alois Feldbauer. As the party progressed, I went to check on him and asked him how it was going. He replied with great satisfaction, "Boat holds steady, *Herr Oberleutnant,*" tapping the depth gauge which was, indeed, not moving at all. Unfortunately it was not the depth gauge but the clock.

One of our youngest sailors who had not had enough training in the naval art of holding one's liquor without becoming sick, became very sick indeed. He climbed into the conning tower above the *Zentrale* and made quite a mess. When he had recovered somewhat, he was ordered to take a pail of seawater into the tower and clean up, an order he did not seem to find unreasonable. Staggering up the ladder with his pail he had almost reached the conning tower when he lost his grip on the pail and it came crashing down – unfortunately at exactly the same moment as the CO was passing underneath. Reith, thoroughly drenched, was not at all amused. Our CO was rather a pompous man and not well liked by his officers (who were almost inclined to award the hapless sailor a medal) or by the ordinary crew members who

detested his habit of twisting their ears or pulling their hair to enforce his authority. On his orders, a pro-forma court-martial was immediately convened, which was hampered by the fact that no sober participant could be found. The culprit, having a very bad conscience, was eager to do penance and stammered to the CO, *"Herr Oberleutnant,* I deserve punishment and I think that you should shoot me with a torpedo! There are enough left over." This response drew suppressed laughter from the court, but by the time we found a solution to the problem, we had all sobered up again, and the incident was mercifully forgotten. The chuckles, however, went round the boat for days afterwards.

When we had recovered, we continued on our way home. We were still fighting the war because we did not know it had ended on 2 May when the German armed forces surrendered to the Allies. Indeed, Hitler had committed suicide in his bunker beneath the Reich Chancellery the day before our party under the sea. On 8 May 1945, while we headed northeast towards Norway, Germany formally signed the surrender documents and the Second World War came to an official end.

Shot from one of the RCN Motor Launches (patrol craft) which met us, this photograph shows *U-190*, escorted by the frigate HMCS *Victoriaville*, entering Bay Bulls on 14 May 1945. (NAC/PA-145581)

FLYING THE BLACK FLAG: SURRENDER, MAY 1945

T he war was over but *U-190* was still at sea although my days as an active *Kriegsmarine* officer were shortly to draw to a close. The best description of these days is contained in my wartime diary, which I began to keep again as soon as I learned the war in Europe had ended.

11 May 1945

After eleven weeks at sea we are on our way back to our homeland. For weeks we have lost radio contact with our country. Only American stations can be heard and they leave no doubt about the hopelessness of our situation.

An uncontrollable urge drives us home. The uncertainty is unnerving. We have now been submerged for nearly 50 days and we try again and again to take the boat as close as possible to the surface to perhaps receive some instructions.

Finally, finally we pick up a somewhat garbled message from *BdU*. It orders us to surface, to set a black flag, to throw overboard all our ammunition and to wait for further orders. So – that's the bitter end!

Shortly after midnight – we are again at a depth of 60 metres [190 feet] – the officers meet to discuss the situation.

It is not easy to follow these last orders and to deliver our battle-proven boat to the Allies. We ponder all kinds of options: scuttling the boat, Spain, South America, Germany – nothing is a viable solution. We will, after all, obey, as always!

The CO calls the crew together into the *Zentrale* and makes a short speech explaining the situation. Then, "At 0900, at dawn, we will surface. Everybody will have packed his basic necessities and be ready to abandon ship. Any questions?" Silence. "Dismissed!"

Again we sit in the wardroom and talk about non-important matters. The mood is tense. Artificial gallows humour helps to overcome the bitterness of the situation.

Then it's time for our preparations. The II.WO, *Leutnant* Müller, stows all secret books, papers and matters in bags and weighs them down with heavy objects. They are destined to go overboard. The torpedo artificer prepares his eels* for firing. Ammunition is being lugged to the *Zentrale*. And the men are busy collecting their belongings.

I find myself standing around, somewhat helplessly, as I don't quite know what to do with myself. Joining the others in packing my things? Abandoning what has been my world

---

* German naval slang for torpedoes.

for more than a year? The full meaning of the events has not sunk in yet.

At 0855 the order "Diving stations!" Slowly I raise the boat to periscope depth. The CO takes a look around, then "Ready to surface!" The order is passed on throughout the boat. While I am contemplating that this will be my last surfacing manoeuvre ever and therefore the end of my career as a U-boat engineer officer, responses are coming in from both ends: "Ready to surface." I report to Reith: "Lower deck ready to surface! – Starboard diesel." "Surface!"

With maximum revolutions the propellers start to churn and the boat shoots upwards. I order "Blow" and report "12 metres, boat rises, 10 metres, 8 metres, 6 metres – bridge is clear! Blow out with diesel!"

Slowly the engines turn over and then fire up and I leave the rest to my *Wachingenieur*. I climb the ladder up to the bridge. Bright sunshine and a leaden sea. For the first time in 83 days we see daylight but the light is far too intense and hurts our eyes. The first bags with secret material arrive on the bridge. One bursts while hitting the water and, shining brightly, the red confidential books float on the surface. The CO curses.

The torpedoes are reported ready. They are expected to go down immediately after launching. The I.WO fires one after the other. Shortly thereafter heavy detonations rock the boat. Once, twice, three, four – five!

I shout down the conning tower "Check all valves and bilges!"

After a short pause there is the report "All valves tight and bilges dry." Well – we just missed sinking ourselves!

The torpedo artificer is called to the bridge. Reith barks:

"How was that possible?" After some discussion we come to the conclusion that the pressure of very deep water must have blown up the batteries and then, in turn, the warheads.

Two sailors inflate our rubber boats. One never knows whether some Allied aircraft might try and collect some last laurels. In the meantime our radio operators are trying to establish contact with the homeland. Again and again they call – but no success. Nobody seems to hear us. We are now southeast of Newfoundland and will continue on our course to Norway – as long as they'll let us!

The off-duty crew slowly assembles on the bridge and soaks up the beautiful sunshine. What a sight they are! Their faces seem to be green and yellow. The long lack of fresh air does leave its traces. The lovely weather, however, helps to raise our spirits a little. One sailor plays the accordion. All those familiar German songs we won't hear for some time to come. Our flag is still flying proudly from its staff at the aft end of the bridge. With a bit of imagination we could be on a training cruise in the Baltic.

In the afternoon the last crates with ammunition go overboard. And still nothing to see or to hear!

At 5.30 P.M. Rogge and I are having dinner – with a few cognacs to aid the digestion – when our radio operator establishes contact with the outside world. Unfortunately it is not the homeland that answers but Cape Race in Newfoundland.

In English language we are given new coordinates to steer to. We jump to the chart: It is Newfoundland.* We are not enthusiastic! We have had quite enough cold during the last

---

* At this time, Newfoundland was an independent colony and not part of Canada.

months. Well – let's enjoy the sunshine while it lasts, since in two days we will be once again within the ice limits.

On the bridge again I notice that the sun has moved from starboard to port. We are on our new course: destination Newfoundland. It will take us about three or four days.

The news we receive from American radio stations affects us deeply! We learn that Germany is to be divided into parts, each to be occupied by one of the Allied powers.

We could not know it at the time but on 11 May, after receipt of our radio message giving the position and course of *U-190*, the Canadian corvette HMCS *Thorlock* and the frigate HMCS *Victoriaville* were ordered to leave the convoy they were escorting just off the coast of Newfoundland and to proceed to our reported position. According to Canadian naval records, these two ships spotted our navigation light at 11.05 P.M. on 12 May 1945 and their arrival quickly became known on board our boat as I describe below.

[12 May 1945]

Midnight – I had just lain down on my bunk – when I wake up to a slight touch on my shoulder. *"Herr Oberleutnant, lights ahead."* Out of the bunk, into my boots and up to the bridge – it's all one move.

It is pitch black. I ask Rogge: "Herbert, what's up?" He points ahead. "There! The shadow. He signalled. Seems to be a destroyer." Slowly my eyes adjust to the dark. Through the binoculars I see the faint outlines of a vessel. "One funnel" I hear the I.WO say. Reith appears on the bridge, ready to receive, white cap on his head.*

Our engines have stopped. The ship is now quite close.

Suddenly a searchlight brightens the night, crawls along the water surface, catches us in its beam and is switched off. Blinded we stare into the darkness which has returned.

Again the searchlight comes on, but illuminates its own bow. Now we see a cutter emerge from the other side of the ship, manned by about fifteen sailors. We observe them row the boat over to us. All are wearing steel helmets.

Slowly the cutter approaches. Now we recognize the gold rings of an officer. Reith orders some sailors down to the deck to assist the boat as it awkwardly comes alongside. Our men help the visitors onto our deck. Our bridge is immediately occupied by heavily armed men and some climb down the conning tower into the boat. An enemy naval officer appears on the bridge. He asks "Where is the commanding officer?"

Our CO identifies himself and the officer – also with the rank of lieutenant** – requests Reith to accompany him down into the boat. The CO in turn asks me to come with him.

"I.WO, you stay here!" he tells Rogge.

Down below the foreign sailors have spread out over the boat. A big chain hangs down from the bridge into the *Zentrale*.*** It seems they don't trust our peaceful intentions

---

* It was the custom in the *U-Boot Waffe* for the commanding officer of a boat to wear a white cap to distinguish him from all other personnel on board.

** Canadian naval records identify this officer as Lieutenant R.O Blackford, RCNVR, from HMCS *Thorlock*.

*** The chain was a security measure to prevent *U-190* from being submerged as the open hatch could not now be closed.

After our surrender on 12 May 1945 the Canadian warships HMCS *Thorlock* and HMCS *Victoriaville* sent a boarding party onto *U-190* and most of our crew was taken aboard the two Canadian ships except for myself, my two technical chief petty officers and nine ratings who were kept aboard to help the Canadians to run the boat. On our arrival in Bay Bulls, Newfoundland, on 14 May I can be seen at the front of the bridge with Canadian sailors in the *Wintergarten* behind me and a few of my leather-coated men. The boat is now flying the White Ensign of the Royal Navy and Royal Canadian Navy. (WH col.)

and suspect we may dive away with them. They are Canadians and apparently don't feel all that comfortable in their new environment.

Reith shows the Canadian officer to his quarters. I just stand by and happen to see the II.WO and *Wachingenieur* crawl out of their bunks, still half asleep and with surprise on their faces.

With the help of an English-German questionnaire, the Canadian officer poses a few questions and gives a few instructions. He inquires about our weapons and ammunition, but he answers right away himself "Thrown overboard, I'm sure." We confirm. Our handguns are still in our possession and he collects them immediately. (I'm angry with myself, that I didn't throw mine overboard as well.)

We are told that an armed guard will remain aboard and that we are not to use our radio transmitter. (We didn't have any doubt about that!) The CO in the meantime has offered his guest a cognac and so we drink to our mutual health. The Canadian then wants to light a cigarette but that we cannot permit down here. Apparently there are some doubts about what to do with us, since nothing is happening. All of us go back to the bridge and smoke our cigarettes in silence.

Suddenly the II.WO reports a second vessel abeam on port, and soon another cutter comes alongside. Several officers climb aboard, among them a very energetic red-haired lieutenant, who confers with his ship by way of a portable radio* and who, after much pandemonium, finally creates order.

He asks me how many men I'll need to operate the boat.

I don't quite understand and reply, "All, of course." He explains that he is only talking about the three days we will need to take the boat to Newfoundland and also informs me that the Canadians will provide navigation and deckhands.

After some consultation with one of my chief petty officers officers we arrive at six technicians for the engine room, three sailors for the engine telegraph and rudder and also my two chief petty officers. We are told that all other men and all officers are to leave our boat and transfer to the Canadian ships. Upon my question, "For how long?" the answer is: "Take necessary items for three days."

I go down below to pack. Next door, in the CO's quarters there is quite a commotion – even with help from a sailor Reith has difficulties first deciding what to take and then to find ways to carry it all.

While I'm waiting for him, a few Canadian officers have joined me, among others a rather hefty engineering lieutenant* with glasses who seems to be cordiality in person. He is perspiring just from watching our CO, but then it is really hot down here inside the boat. The Canadian smiles and makes a pitying gesture in the direction of Reith. I can only shrug.

In the meantime our energetic officer-in-charge has become rather impatient and he leaves no doubt about his feelings in his request to the CO to hurry up. But Reith doesn't even notice since he is far too busy trying to convince a Canadian sailor that all these things are his private property, although the Canadian is not interested nor does he understand.

---

* Canadian records identify this officer as Lieutenant F.S. Burbidge, RCNVR, of HMCS *Victoriaville*, which arrived after *Thorlock*.

* Chief Engine Room Artificer Stanley Dean, RCNVR, from HMCS *Thorlock*.

Finally we make it up to the bridge. All our officers are already sitting in one of the cutters – the CO and I board the other one. Hardly have I sat down, when the Canadians order me back aboard. They have decided to keep me on the boat and I'm happy about that change.

Well – here I am, with 11 German sailors, 5 Canadian officers and about 25 Canadian sailors aboard our U-boat – and all waiting for things to happen. The two cutters with our crew have disappeared into the darkness.

All of a sudden I find it difficult to suppress a chuckle. I poke one of my chief petty officers and point to our flagstaff. There flies, of course, the White Ensign, the flag of the Royal Navy and Royal Canadian Navy, but on top of the staff sits still our brass eagle clasping the swastika – a most peculiar combination!

Smoking again one of the cigarettes offered by the Canadians – they taste great – I talk to our guests about terminology for boat speed and manoeuvring. As none of the Canadians understands a single word of German and as I have forgotten most of my school English, it isn't simple! Thanks to the existence of a nautical dictionary we manage somehow to communicate. Having clarified the issues I request our diesels and soon, after a three-hour interruption, they again roar to life.

I'm still standing on the bridge and contemplate with sadness the changed circumstances of my life. My comrades are somewhere aboard Canadian warships and I am on our boat with a Canadian crew, and feel rather lost. The Canadians are quiet too and may have similar thoughts. If we had met only 24 hours ago, it would have meant, it's either you or us! Each side would have done the utmost to destroy the other. And now we sit together peacefully on our bridge, smoking cigarettes, listening to music from our record player, and thinking: "The war is over."

I go down below and have somebody make coffee. On a walk through the boat I look at my men. Thank goodness I can't see a sign of depression. All are standing straight at their engines, full of self-confidence, with an expression on their faces telling the rather helpless-looking Canadians "What do you know about running a U-boat! Without us you wouldn't get very far, despite your big peashooters." Some efforts at humour on my part result in a grin on their faces, making the Canadians even more unsure of themselves in their strange surroundings.

The boat is one big mess! The hasty departure has left its traces. In the officer's quarters I make an effort to clean up a bit and put cups and saucers and cookies on the table. Back on the bridge I invite the officers down to a steaming cup of real coffee. The engineering lieutenant and two of the other officers follow me happily down the conning tower.

The smell of the coffee creates a peaceful mood. The hot liquid warms us up. We get to know each other a bit and I find my former enemies are rather nice guys. Very politely they inquire where they may sit down, and express their thanks for anything I have to offer. They pay me compliments for my fragmented English and make every effort to speak slowly so that I can follow.

Main topic is, of course, the war at sea. They are amazed that we have been at sea for more than eighty days and that we have spent almost the last fifty submerged without any interruption. They admire the boat and its equipment. Engineering officer Dean is particularly full of praise.

The conversation drifts to personal matters. Their first question is whether I'm married. I answer "No" and add that I just turned 22 two months ago. I show them some photographs and Lieutenant Webb* asks me for a small passport picture of myself.

I learn that they are all reserve officers, as are most officers of the Canadian escort ships. Most of them are former university students.

Two of the officers take their leave and relieve the watch on the bridge. Now Lieutenants Burbidge and Stirling** enjoy the coffee. The cognac they all refuse. I put on a record of "*Die Fledermaus*" and, of course, they know it too and request all the other Strauss records as well.

Gradually we get tired. Some of the officers lie down for a sleep and I play a game of chess with Webb. I win easily and tell him that it's probably a bit late for this game. My watch still shows German time*** and I reset it to Newfoundland time. It's now four o'clock in the morning.

After a short sleep I wake up again and climb up to the bridge. The sea has become rough. It is bright daylight with clear visibility. To port is the frigate *Victoriaville* and to starboard the corvette *Thorlock*, some distance away. We are abeam of each other and cruise at 11 knots.

I talk with the Canadian officers about anything and everything and am amazed how well we can communicate. *Obermaschinist* Krüger also tries to utilize his knowledge of English, acquired on many long trips. He is, though, rather busy flipping the pages of his dictionary and less so in actual talking. I learn that Lieutenant Blackford, who was the first officer to come aboard, is from the *Thorlock*, whereas all the others are from the *Victoriaville*.

The hours of the morning pass quickly with much laughter about various misunderstandings. The flagstaff has now been changed. After lunch the sea gets pretty rough and the first breakers come through the open hatch. I equip the Canadians with wet weather gear, while I myself withdraw into the comfort of the boat. Webb loses the return chess match too.

One of my mates reports that one of the Canadians didn't close the appropriate valves in our head so that our aft compartments slowly but surely started to fill with seawater. Now my men are busy pumping the water out of the boat again. It's rather ironic. When, a short time before, I blew out our diving tanks – a periodic routine – I suddenly felt the muzzle of a rifle in my ribs. One of the Canadian sailors obviously didn't trust me and didn't want to see me scuttle the boat.

We lose a cylinder on our port diesel. I tell my men to ignore it as we'll get to Newfoundland on 8 cylinders just as well. Our low-pressure air system is also out of service and will remain so.

On my inspection of the boat I notice the growing understanding between the Canadians and our men. With the help of gestures and sign language they carry out a lively conversation. In the *Zentrale* the officers admire our Zeiss binoculars and admit that their own don't compare. One of the officers is full of praise for his Kine-Exacta camera, and

---

* Sublieutenant Arnold Webb, RCNVR, from HMCS *Victoriaville*.

** Lieutenant A. Stirling, RCNVR, from HMCS *Victoriaville*.

*** German warships always kept German time and did not alter their timekeeping to local time.

overall, they all are quite willing to acknowledge positive German achievements.

During a conversation between the German and Canadian sailors, in which I function as well as I can as interpreter, a Canadian petty officer replies to my question as to the general opinion in Canada about Germany with: "Oh – the German people are very clever, but the Nazis …" and illustrates his meaning with a throat-cutting gesture. I tell him that we are all Nazis, since National Socialism did a lot of good for our country in the years before the war. He doesn't believe me and insists that all Nazis are criminals whereas we here are really easy to get along with. And with respect to the anti-German hatemongering in the press – well, that's the way newspapers make a living and few reasonable Canadians are taken in by it.

When the conversation gets to discussions of the present situation in Germany, the same petty officer suggests to Krüger that he should remain in Canada – it would be quite easy for him to get a job in his factory. "And my family?" asks Krüger. "They'll follow, of course."

The next morning [13 May 1945] I notice that my medals and ribbons have disappeared from my uniform jacket which was hanging in the radio room. Shortly thereafter my two chief petty officers report the same. Their shoulder straps have also been cut off their jackets. I immediately complain to Lieutenant Stirling, a very nice young man, who is sitting at the table in the officer's wardroom area. He is visibly disturbed by this discovery and promises to stop this quest for souvenirs by his men at once and assures me that everything taken will be returned. Very soon I see several of the officers questioning and searching their men. It's quite

a commotion, but by the next day all the missing items are neatly lying on the table in the wardroom. Lieutenant Stirling expresses his regrets and continues to apologize for the behaviour of his men. He complains about having to go to sea with sometimes less than virtuous men, but during wartime one can't be too choosy. He still looks very unhappy after he notices my apparent lack of understanding. But deep down I'm actually rather amused and smiling about his eagerness.

Another incident occurred that caused the Canadian officers much anguish. After our party beneath the sea, our sailors had apparently poured the remainder of their alcohol supplies into their canteens. The canteens had stayed behind after their owners' hasty departure, and I was not aware of their contents. At one time I noticed that most Canadian sailors had a German canteen hanging from their belts and didn't think very much about it until I heard a Canadian petty officer suddenly yell at the top of his voice at some of his men who he had found lying in the bow torpedo compartment – in a state of happy contentment and not quite sober. The interest of the Canadian sailors in requisitioning our canteens became quite understandable to me. The temptation had been irresistible.

The Canadian officers now become very strict with their men and voluntarily promise me that each and every one of their sailors will be subject to a body search upon leaving our boat.

With the increasingly heavy weather it has become very, very cold. We have passed the ice limits and the effects are felt by all. It is close to freezing point and everybody digs up some woollies from somewhere. The Canadian supervision has become rather slack and automatic rifles and bayonets are hanging everywhere around the boat. We are hardly watched at all any more.

The difference in appearance between our own and the Canadian sailors is very notable. The Canadians look a bit dishevelled – shirts hanging out front or back, left foot a slipper, right foot a shoe, tears in their not very clean clothing.* Our men, on the other hand, make a tremendous effort to look neat and clean – but only since the time our "guests" arrived aboard!

In the afternoon we reduce speed so as to arrive at our destination just at day break. Later we even stop for a while. We are close to land now and, when darkness falls, there are some lights visible ashore. Once again Webb, Stirling, Dean and I are on the bridge in a somewhat romantic mood in the moonlight, stars in the clear sky and listening to recorded music recalling homeland, family and shore leave. It is nice and reflective, but terribly cold. The hours pass by and only shortly before dawn [on 14 May 1945] do I lie down for some sleep.

Soon after I am being awakened again by one of our sailors. "*Herr Oberleutnant*, how about it?" He is holding a whole plate full of gorgeous smelling Bratwurst under my nose. I'm enthusiastic. There is peak activity in our galley as all our men are being generously supplied out of our leftover stores. I don't take the time to find fork and knife but, with a sausage in one hand and a piece of bread in the other, I gorge myself in the galley with an amazing appetite. I finally decline an offer of a fourth serving – I'm full!

Lieutenant Burbidge comes down from the bridge and looks longingly at our meals and of course he is invited to participate. He and his fellow officers are surprised how well we still live on our boat – much better than they expected. A can of delicious peaches concludes our feast.

Some time later, climbing up to the bridge, I note that we are entering a large bay surrounded by mountains. In the distance, for the first time, I see some huge icebergs. The two escorts are circling around us. Ahead there are some patrol boats, like our *R-boote*.* We have arrived in Bay Bulls, Newfoundland.

Dean and I have some discussions concerning the upcoming manoeuvres. The Canadians are not familiar with our engine telegraphs and procedures. Answering a question I point out the rather difficult manoeuvring characteristics of a submarine. Close to the entrance of the harbour we stop the diesels. One of the couplings has almost seized up and, lacking our low-pressure air system, it takes quite some time until the electric motors start humming.

More and more small craft are circling our sub. A motorboat with a group of photographers aboard comes quite close. There is a girl on board and I must have stared a bit too intensely as Burbidge feels inclined to smile and drop a teasing remark. I explain: "The first girl in three months." He nods understandingly.

A boat comes alongside and a group of officers and sail-

* In fairness to the Royal Canadian Navy, the custom on Canadian escort vessels was to permit the sailors to wear whatever they wanted while at sea and items such as hockey sweaters were much in vogue. On land, it was another matter entirely.

* In fact, these were Canadian Fairmile B Motor Launches, fast patrol craft.

This picture, taken at Bay Bulls, shows Fairmile B Type Motor Launch Q-95 guiding U-190 to its mooring buoy while a small boat tied alongside our vessel has transferred additional Canadian sailors. (WH col.)

ors, dressed in immaculate blue uniforms, come aboard. One of the officers speaks some German and has spent some time in Germany. He also is a submariner and takes over the command from Lieutenant Burbidge. He shows me a chart and points to the buoy where the boat is to be moored. I suggested carrying out the manoeuvre myself and he agrees.

With *Bootsmaat* Wehle at the helm I now execute my first and my last mooring manoeuvre with *U-190*. We still have to pass a net barrier, then we are in the inner harbour. The surroundings leave a god-forsaken impression. A few wooden shack-like houses are perched on the rocks and the harbour area looks just as primitive. Our two escorts have already tied up at a wooden pier.

We are now close to our mooring buoy. Canadian sailors are on deck to handle the lines. Both engines have stopped and we glide slowly towards the buoy. "Both engines half astern!" Once again the waters are churning around our stern, then: "Both engines stop! Final stop! Boat is tied up! Dismissed from stations!" No more "Ready for action" – ever. "Assemble on deck." The last war patrol of *U-190* has finished – and it was quite different from our expectations 85 days ago on our departure from Germany.

The war was over and I was fortunate to survive it, particularly after I learned the fatality statistics for the *U-Boot-Waffe*. They were chilling – of the more than 40,000 men who served in that branch of our navy between 1939 and 1945, 28,000 were killed. I had done my best to serve my country in time of war but, looking back more than half a century later, I think that perhaps my proudest achievement was to help ensure that the 57 officers and sailors on *U-190* survived that awful conflict.

After *U-190* had secured to the buoy, the I.WO, *Oberleutnant z.S.* Herbert Rogge, came back on board to supervise the unloading of the crew's personal belongings. Here he can be seen standing between my two technical chief petty officers – on the left, *Obermaschinist* Krüger, and on the right, *Obermaschinist* Holtmann. (WH col.)

U-190 at the mooring buoys in Bay Bulls, Newfoundland. This was our first close look at North America and we were surprised by the barrenness of the landscape. (RCN photo)

My last duties on board *U-190* ended on 14 May 1945 and I was officially no longer an active officer in the *Kriegsmarine* but a prisoner of war of the Royal Canadian Navy. I was to remain a prisoner for nearly 26 months, a period of my life that was both interesting and frustrating. I shall commence the story of this part of my life by returning to my personal account.

14 May 1945

Our men now come up through the hatch and look around at their new environment. They are obviously glad, that this kind of operation is over – they had very little sleep during recent days as the lack of a full crew made itself felt.

One of the last officers to come aboard, a lieutenant in the special service, speaks German fluently, without any accent. Only rarely does he search for the right German word. When I ask him about this he tells me that he studied at the University of Hamburg until 1938 and that he is now acting as an interpreter. I'm told to stay aboard, together with my two chief petty officers, whereas the remainder of my crew are to join their comrades aboard the escort vessels.

In the meantime more Canadian navy personnel have come aboard. They are trained in submarine operations and, in contrast to their friends from the escort vessels, are very impressive. I am interrogated with respect to our boat. They ask only general questions and then want me to demonstrate our diesels. I decline with the explanation that it is a job for more people than just me, and in addition, they wouldn't be able to remember the procedures anyway. After all, a German crew goes through a training period of six months and more. So the questions come to a quick end.

The officers who boarded us at sea now return to their respective vessels and, one by one, approach me to say goodbye. Everyone offers a firm handshake with best wishes and assurance that I will probably be home in six months at the latest. They try to console me about becoming a prisoner-of-war and express confidence that we will be treated very well in the camps. (I'm not so sure about all this!) Dean regrets that he can't offer me his bathtub as promised, as I won't be coming to his ship. He assures me that none of our personal belongings have been taken by his men since they were all searched.

Coming up to the bridge of *U-190* again I find myself face to face with Herbert Rogge, the I.WO. After a lively exchange of greetings and backslapping he informs me that he has come aboard with a small detail to collect the belongings of the entire crew. The other crew members will not be allowed back on our boat.

While we are packing the personal effects of our officers, he tells me a bit about the happenings of the last days. They didn't suffer any more than I did – but received very decent treatment, comfortable quarters and good food. To my question "What's going to happen to us now?" he tells me that our crew has been transferred to another frigate, the *Prestonian*, and that we will be taken to Halifax, whereas our boat will remain here. We spend a long time talking while trying to consume as much of the remaining canned fruit as possible. And a few Canadians participate.

All our luggage is now loaded on a boat that has come alongside. We are standing on our aft deck and take a last look at our *U-190*. Then we step into the small boat and are taken to the frigate, HMCS *Prestonian*.

The weather has turned beautiful again. It's warm, it smells like spring, the sun is shining and against the blue sky we see an airplane. Strange to be able to listen to the noise of a plane without getting a somewhat uncomfortable feeling – something we had become very used to in Germany. A Catalina circles overhead, quite harmlessly.

After we come alongside the *Prestonian*, Rogge and his people go aboard immediately, while I and my two chief petty officers still have to wait. All around us are people who stare at us as if we were one of the wonders of the

The warship at the left is HMCS *Thorlock*, escorting *U-190* into Bay Bulls, Newfoundland. In the background can be seen a Fairmile B Type Motor Launch. (NAC/PA-145580)

world, and take a lot of pictures. (I am amazed, how many people inhabit this little village.) But we do look a bit wild – the chief petty officers in their grey leather jackets and I, though in my blue coat, with red kerchief and a 12-week old beard.

Then we follow a few sailors on board the frigate. On our way below decks we pass through two rows of heavily armed soldiers and I can't help smiling – I don't think we are nearly as dangerous as they seem to think we are. Then we have to empty our pockets, but I am allowed to keep everything, even my pocket knife.

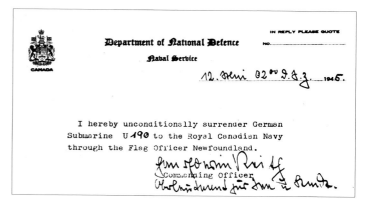

Our commanding officer, *Oberleutnant z.S.* Reith, signed this prepared document of surrender when requested to do so by the Canadian officer who took charge of *U-190*. (WH col.)

I want to digress briefly to comment on a legend that has arisen from the circumstances of the surrender of *U-190*. This event attracted considerable attention, as the numerous photographs taken at the time (many of which are included here) attest. For years after the war ended, eyewitnesses who were supposedly present when our crew was searched claimed that streetcar and cinema tickets from Halifax were found in their pockets – proof that we had secretly gone ashore in Canada during our last patrol. As late as 1989, a reputable Canadian magazine printed a letter from a veteran of the RCN who insisted that when he searched us he found not only the proverbial streetcar tickets but also Canadian cigarettes, Canadian-made rubber boots, maps of Canadian cities and even pictures of Canadian girls that crew members had dated in Halifax. As if this was not ludicrous enough, this same correspondent claimed that some of the sailors from *U-190* had grown up in Canada and spoke fluent English. Such statements are pure in-

vention, the product of an overactive imagination, and, worse still, this myth has been compounded and exaggerated over the years and the story has grown in the telling. Yet, this legend of the "German U-boat sailors who went ashore in Halifax" simply refuses to die and can still be encountered.

Let me resume my narrative:

Our next destination is *Prestonian's* sick bay, where a medical officer asks me about any illnesses and, after my negative reply, I am reunited with the officers of our boat in a small officer's cabin. They are in a great mood and the loud bidding of their card game shows that they feel quite at home. My two chiefs have been put together with the rest of the crew.

We move over to the officers' wardroom, after it has been cleaned up. It's quite comfortable, but very wartime spartan. The first thing that hits our eyes is an enormous portrait of our special friend, Mr. Churchill. Quickly an animated conversation develops between the ship's officers and us and we get along just fine. They are all university students and somewhat older than us. We are offered Coca-Cola and cigarettes. We notice the ports being closed and soon we hear the hum of the engines and feel the motion of the sea – we are under way.

For lunch we join the captain* of the frigate, and his officers take a later sitting. We are amazed about the rich variety of food. In the afternoon we are taken back on deck to pick up our bags from the big heap belonging to our crew. We are asked to open the bags and after a rather superficial inspection everything is taken down into a room near the officer's wardroom.

Then the aforementioned interpreter, who is accompanying us, once again goes over our belongings. Several written notes are taken from us, as is my radio and a photo of a Japanese submarine in my album. "We may have some use for this," says the interpreter. Everything else, letters, pictures etc. we can keep, including our ceremonial uniform dirks.

Right afterwards we are offered the use of a bath and the services of the ship's barber. How absolutely lovely, to be clean again after twelve weeks, and to have a clean-shaven face! We feel like the newly born and admire ourselves in a full-size mirror – now wearing our dress uniform. The Canadians can't believe their eyes when they see us so transformed. They claim to hardly recognize us.

In the wardroom there are illustrated magazines containing many pictures of pretty girls and much anti-German invective. In our conversations with the Canadians we talk about war and origins of war. They accuse us, i.e. our government, of having broken its word after the Munich agreement, when we attacked Poland. When we talk about cause and effect, the Canadians change the subject. They do everything to avoid confrontation with us, and continue to assure us that we are all very reasonable people, as is probably the whole population of Germany. But the evil Nazis brought disaster to the world and after their elimination, there would be no reason at all not to get along well with Germany.

Then we talk about warfare at sea. They explain the methods used by their ace submarine chaser Captain Walker,* and how he achieved his successes. We in turn tell them our ways to elude the anti-submarine forces. It is an interesting dialogue between opponents who respect each other, after the battle is over.

The captain of the frigate, a St. Lawrence river pilot – a magnificent, bearded figure – plays a game of cards with one of his officers. We watch with interest and soon understand the game of cribbage. I ask Lieutenant Fox for a game, which he promptly loses. I have incredible luck with the cards. After the fourth loss Fox has had enough and I can't get him to play another game for the rest of the trip.

For the night the ship's sick bay has been made available to us. Only our CO sleeps somewhere else. A steward supplies us with mattresses and blankets. He is a young guy

---

* Lieutenant-Commander G.N. Downey, RCNR.

* Captain Frederick Walker, RN, was the most successful anti-submarine officer in the Allied navies and is credited with sinking more U-boats than any other naval officer in the Second World War.

While my two chief petty officers, Holtmann and Krüger, have their backs to the camera I am standing in front of the conning tower smoking a cigarette that was very welcome at the time. Above me is the outboard air intake tube of the *Schnorchel* with its inlet at the right which connected to the upper mast. Note the effects of salt corrosion on the superstructure. (WH col.)

(Below) The nine crew members who helped bring *U-190* into Newfoundland are seen here about to be transferred to the Canadian frigate, HMCS *Prestonian*, which took our entire crew to Halifax. (WH col.)

who has seen a lot of the world. He sits with us until almost midnight and recites wondrous adventures from his life. Finally he leaves and we get some sleep. Outside there is a sentry but he lets us walk in and out as we please.

The following day is very quiet. We play cards or chess and read newspapers. In between we have an opportunity to go up on deck for fresh air, where we meet the men of our crew. They are no worse off than we are, and are in good spirits. One of them shows us a photo of himself arm in arm with a Canadian sailor. We are amazed about how fast the two groups make friends!

We watch a strange-looking piece of equipment being lowered over the stern. We assume it is the infamous *Kreissäge or* "circular power saw" which made life hell for us for so many weeks.

The weather is lovely and we feel almost like being on a holiday cruise. Only the zigzag course of the frigate indicates the uncertainty of the situation as there may still be a German U-boat lurking below the surface, having had no contact with *BdU* and carrying on the war on its own!

Next morning we notice that we are very close to shore. The frigate is expected to tie up at Halifax at 8 A.M. This is the same harbour we have looked at for five weeks through our periscope and where we have sunk our victims.* We learn that we will not tie up at a shore pier but will make fast at a mooring buoy for the purpose of avoiding the attention of the population of Halifax which has been informed about our arrival through the press. We are not to disembark until later in the evening.

Shortly after the mooring manoeuvre, several high-ranking Canadian naval officers come aboard for, as we soon find out, the task of interrogating us. One after the other we are taken to a cabin where several of the interrogators have assembled. When I enter the room, the first thing I see lying on the table is the manual containing our top secret standing war orders issued by *BdU* – are they ever well informed! They are not interested at all in military matters but ask only questions of a political nature. I convey my ideas honestly to them whereupon they, in lengthy elaboration, explain to me that it is now up to me to decide on which side I want to be in the coming conflict between Communism and Democracy. And with that I am dismissed. The other officers have a more difficult time, especially the CO (at least according to his stories when he comes out). He must have been squeezed terribly!*

In the afternoon the II.WO, Werner Müller, and my *Wachingenieur*, Ernst Glenk, are taken up on deck for a presentation to the press. They have interesting and amusing details to tell about the theatrical performance on deck.**

At 5 P.M. a small boat takes us ashore. The officers of the *Prestonian* bid us goodbye and the captain assures us that all our conversations will not leave the confidentiality of the

---

* In retrospect, there was only one victim: HMCS *Esquimalt*.

* The Canadian naval intelligence officers who interrogated the CO of *U-190* came to the conclusion that Reith, who claimed to have fired at several merchant ships and perhaps to have hit one, had simply expended his torpedoes so that he could end his patrol and return to Germany sooner.

** Glenk and Müller were featured in an article published in the *Halifax Chronicle Herald* titled "Spent Last 50 Days Down Scared to Death of Radar." The article makes much of the two officers' support for Hitler and the Nazi party and includes a comment from the Canadian interpreter that my two comrades "say that National Socialism is so right that whatever was done was the right thing."

The I.WO, *Oberleutnant s.Z.* Herbert Rogge, and the II.WO, *Leutnant s.Z.* Werner Müller, are seen here following a Canadian officer on to HMCS *Prestonian*. (RCN photo)

Eight members of the German crew that brought *U-190* into Newfoundland, having collected their belongings, are ready to go aboard HMCS *Prestonian*. (RCN photo)

officers' wardroom. He also expresses his deep regret that the unpleasantness of a political interrogation had to take place on his ship. We have now become charges of the Canadian Veterans Guard and our treatment by this home-based organisation is much stricter than that afforded to us by our real adversaries in the war at sea. We have to laugh when we step ashore at a pier in Halifax. Several hundred heavily armed soldiers with their hands on their weapons stand in grim anticipation of – what, we are not quite sure. An army of criminals? Behind the shelter of the guards is the population of Halifax, jostling for a good spot to see the Germans. We are required to open our bags and are bodily searched for concealed weapons. During this operation my little pocket knife disappears into the big pockets of a grim-looking sergeant. (I hope he's going to cut his thumb with it!)

The luggage is loaded on a truck. We, the officers, climb aboard one bus and our crew boards two others. In a long convoy we are driven through Halifax. Our driver, who is new in the city, loses his way and some time goes

The CO of *U-190*, *Oberleutnant z.S.* Reith is seen here boarding HMCS *Prestonian* with his hand raised to the *Deutsche Gruß* (or "Hitler salute") that replaced the traditional military salute after the assassination attempt on Hitler's life in July 1944. In the photo to the right he is seen landing in Halifax from a tender.(RCN photos)

The officers of *U-190*, having disembarked in Halifax from HMCS *Prestonian* in Halifax have set foot on Canadian soil and are waiting to be moved to a prisoner-of-war camp. From left the CO, *Oberleutnant s.Z.* Reith, me, the II.WO, *Leutnant s.Z.* Werner Müller, *Oberfähnrich* Martin Oldenstädt and, crouching, the I.WO, *Oberleutnant s.Z.* Herbert Rogge. The suitcase in front of me followed me throughout my life and is still in my possession today. (RCN photo)

by before a very angry officer on a motorcycle catches up with us and leads us back to the path of the righteous.

We are not impressed with the sights of the city considering its importance for Canada. We drive directly to the main station. With us is a soldier who speaks some German and eagerly tries to utilize his knowledge. At the station we board a waiting train, bound for Montreal. We officers have an entire Pullman car to ourselves, whereas our crew occupies the carriages that follow. An officer approaches us and offers us less strict treatment if we give our word of honour not to escape. We give our word of honour. After that only one or two soldiers sit with us in a far corner of the carriage and completely ignore us. Later we again see our well known interrogators, who will accompany us to Montreal. They occupy a little compartment of their own. About seven o'clock the train starts moving and rolls out of Halifax.

Later during the evening an officer asks us to follow him to dinner. We walk through several cars and end up in the dining car of the train, where we sit down at two tables among the Canadian civilian passengers. At first we seem to be unrecognized as Germans, and the conductor persistently demands to see our tickets, until the situation is explained to him and he leaves us in peace. Now we become subject to curious glances from the other tables, but our appetite is not adversely affected. Once again we feel like we are on a holiday excursion. And I don't think we look all that repulsive in our dress uniforms.

After dinner we return to our car and talk until late into the night, before the black Pullman porter finally makes up our beds. They are marvellously comfortable. We sleep deeply as we haven't done in months in our narrow, hard U-boat bunks.

Next morning – it is hard to believe – we stay in bed as long as we want, but then breakfast calls, served by our porter. And we really enjoy the sights of the passing countryside. Endless woods alternate with vast steppes, rarely do we see a human settlement. The train doesn't stop often. Very few people leave or board. Soon we reach the St.Lawrence river. Ponderously the waters roll along the wide river bed and we think about the fact that some of our U-boats were able to penetrate right up to here.

In the afternoon we reach Quebec City. On the opposite river bank we notice a magnificent building.* We learn that Roosevelt and Churchill had an important meeting there, affecting the outcome of the war. The French character of the city is noticeable with its inscriptions, advertisements and signs written in the French language. A few weeks ago on our patrol we read a book dealing with the battles between the British and the French in this area. We didn't expect to see the battlefields so soon in person.

About nine o'clock we approach Montreal, the only city with more than a million inhabitants in Canada. Long before our arrival we notice the glow of its lights in the sky. The city presents an impressive sight with its brightly illuminated bridges crossing the river and the brilliance of colourful advertisements of a size and quantity we hardly knew in peace time. We haven't seen anything like that for nearly six years.

---

* The Château Frontenac hotel, the site of the Quebec Conferences of 1943 and 1944 at which Allied leaders met to discuss wartime strategy.

We change trains in Montreal. We are now separated from our crew and only the CO receives permission to say goodbye to our men. The interrogators also leave us here and we are turned over to the Military Police. A major with several soldiers takes over and leads us to a train on an adjacent track.

Here, to our astonishment, we meet three German U-boat officers. Following our custom of saluting them arouses the ire of the major, who declares such a salute as prohibited and warns us of dire consequences, should we violate his rules.* When our CO addresses him, quite innocently, as "Captain," his self control takes a leave of absence. He almost bursts with indignation, explains that he is a major, that we are to take our hands out of our pockets, when we talk to him and if we expect to be treated correctly we have to behave correctly.**

The three officers are from *U-889*.*** They surrendered their boat just before us. They are the LI, the II.WO and a *Kapitänleutnant* who was aboard as a commanding officer trainee.**** This boat was still on its way to the operations area and had not seen any action. These officers had much worse experiences in comparison to us. Every piece of personal property was confiscated and they were not treated nearly as well as we were.

As we have noticed already – here blows a different wind. We are only allowed to sit on two specific benches and when we have to follow a human urge, a guard comes with us and keeps an eye on us. Any conversation containing politics is strictly prohibited. While we lament this unpleasant change for the worse, our friends from *U-889* claim they have never had it so good since their surrender, as now here on their journey from Shelburne to Montreal.

Shortly thereafter the train starts moving and we leave Montreal. The curtains are drawn and we are not allowed to look out of the windows. At nine o'clock we are ordered into our bunks. Everyone of us is in an upper berth with a Canadian in the lower. The curtains must stay open and the lights are left on all night.

Early in the morning we have to get out of bed and receive breakfast in our seats – but no knives! On the title page of a newspaper somebody is carrying through the compartment we see a picture of our two "interviewees," *Leutnants* Glenk and Müller. Our request to get a copy of the paper is passed on to the major. We finally receive the picture, cut out from the paper, without any text. Maybe even the major himself isn't too convinced of the reliability of newspaper reports. After a while, however, he joins us in our compartment and all of a sudden he is quite human. Very soon we carry on a lively conversation.

In the early afternoon we reach our goal – Gravenhurst in the province of Ontario. It's a small but well known tourist town. On a hand cart we transport our substantial luggage through the station to a truck which takes us to Camp 20,

---

* Obviously, the officers used the *Hitlergruss* or raised arm salute.

** In point of fact, Reith was being generous as his intention was probably to call the Canadian officer a naval captain, equivalent to an army colonel.

*** *U-889*, which had been sent to North American waters a few weeks after *U-190*, surrendered to Canadian warships near Shelburne, Nova Scotia, a few days after that boat.

**** The three officers from *U-889* were *Kapitänleutnant* Arthur Muersinsky, the trainee CO, *Oberleutnant (Ing)* Wilhelm Eve, the *LI*, and *Leutnant z.S.* Edmund Jaeger, the II.WO.

a few miles outside the town. After a quarter of an hour we arrive at a barracks where we are subjected to another inspection of our luggage and a search of ourselves. This time we lose our naval dirks.

We approach a high fence and the barbed wire fence closes behind us – we wonder for how long?

We need not have worried because Camp 20 turned out to be a very pleasant place. Built around a former tuberculosis sanatorium near the shore of a lovely lake, it had all the comforts of life (with the exception of female company) and we prisoners were treated like guests of the country. We had our own dance band, playing mainly big band "swing" music, our own symphony orchestra, our own internal university and six first-run American films every week, which in summer were shown under the trees. There was a library with about 3,000 books of all categories in many languages, with bookbinding equipment to repair damaged volumes. We had a tennis court inside the barbed wire, while outside there were two hockey rinks and our own fenced-off swimming area in nearby Lake Muskoka with diving tower and water-polo basin. Farther away we had a farm with chickens, pigs, horses, potato fields and maple trees. Eaton's catalogue challenged us to splurge our financial allowance, which was $20 a month. A beer ration was provided officially by the Canadian authorities but spirits were produced illegally and our still was protected by an elaborate alarm system.

I can't imagine any tourist resort being busier than Camp 20. The typical response of any prisoner you wanted to talk to was "Sorry – I'm busy – see me tomorrow some time," and then he hurried off to his next activity. Despite our worries about conditions in Germany, the general mood in the camp was similar to that at a modern resort. Conversations between Monday and Thursday dealt almost completely with the bridge tournament that had taken place the previous Sunday. On virtually any Friday evening, after allocation and the trading back and forth of our beer ration, you could find a rousing party that went on into the morning, when the hangovers were cured with some more beer. Rogge, Müller and I from *U-190* spent weeks converting our room into an authentic dimly-lit North European harbour tavern, with fishing nets covering the ceiling, fishing implements on the walls, nautical lanterns swinging from above (I have no idea where we got all that stuff from) and then invited our friends (our CO, *Oberleutnant* Reith, was not among them), all of whom had saved at least four weekly rations of beer, amounting to about a gallon each. How many uninvited guests came – and they filled the room to overflowing – is not known. The reverberations lasted for months and everybody talked about "the *U-190* party of the year."

For the activities outside the barbed wire, like hockey, swimming or visiting the farm, we had to leave the camp perimeter and therefore had to give our parole not to escape. We did this by presenting a wooden tag, with our name and signature on it, at the main guardhouse. Our outside behaviour was, of course, governed by certain regulations. Our signature was given back to us when we returned and it was commonly accepted wisdom that

(Above) Our prisoner-of-war camp in Gravenhurst in Ontario was situated in the beautiful resort region of the Muskokas, providing us with access to the beach on Lake Muskoka for recreational swimming. (Courtesy, Gravenhurst Archives)

(Left) On a farm in Gravenhurst allocated to the prisoners we maintained two horses, a hundred chickens and built a cottage for storage, meals and shelter. (WH col.)

as long as our signature, or our word of honour, was with the guards, we were as safe to our captors as any mechanical means could make us. As soon as we got our signatures back, all bets with respect to escape were off.

Every morning our "farmers" assembled outside the gate and were accompanied by a few guards on the half-hour march to the farm. There the prisoners had built a log farm house for protection from inclement weather. At lunch time the guards delivered the camp's meal by jeep. Many tasks had to be looked after, including feeding and caring for the three horses and the one hundred chickens, planting and harvesting vegetables and potatoes. But one could also get involved in a game of soccer or get away from it all by having a leisurely hour-long walk around the farm. Another activity was collecting maple sap in a nearby sugar bush. For a few weeks we tended to the containers at the trees, shipped them to the camp with the guards' jeep and spent many hours, day and night, stirring the sap in enormous kettles over the fires in the kitchen, until it had evaporated enough to become syrup and was a welcome addition to our breakfast. The day at the farm ended in the evening when, after roll call, the guards led us back to the camp.

One event occurred at Gravenhurst that was perhaps not so pleasant but, in retrospect, was necessary. During the last two patrols of *U-190*, the relationship between the boat's CO, *Oberleutnant z.S.* Hans-Edwin Reith, and his officers had seriously deteriorated due to Reith's indecisiveness and his inability to control difficult situations, combined with an ever-increasing pomposity. After our arrival in Camp 20, the officers of *U-190*,

that is, the I.WO, *Oberleutnant z.S.* Herbert Rogge, the II.WO, *Leutnant z.S.* Werner Müller, the *Wachingenieur*, *Leutnant (Ing)* Ernst Glenk and myself, petitioned the *Lagerführer*, the German senior officer at Gravenhurst, *Oberst* Meythaler, to formally dissolve the command relationship between Reith and the officers of *U-190* because we had lost all respect for the man and found it distasteful in the extreme to have to salute him. A subsequent board of inquiry held at Gravenhurst resulted in the granting of our request with an option to re-open the matter of Reith's behaviour, if there should ever be an opportunity within a new German navy. There was no more social intercourse between Reith and us and I never exchanged any communication with the man after that time.

Although Germany had surrendered and the war was over, life in Gravenhurst continued much as it had before May 1945. We did have a few characters (like a certain *Hauptmann* Hamacher) in the camp who, immediately after hostilities ended, took off their uniforms and asked the more junior officers not to salute them and to address them with the familiar "Du," etc. The vast majority of us had nothing but contempt for such behaviour. Unfortunately for the would-be "civilians," their initiatives were squashed when the Canadian commandant addressed us and made it quite clear that, as long as we were at Camp 20, we were German officers and he expected us to behave as such, including wearing uniforms and medals! Since the war, some commentators have exaggerated these small and quite unimportant acts of personal behaviour into a general description of imagined conflicts in the camp, but such a por-trayal is not accurate. There were some strange people in the camp as there are in any collection of human beings anywhere, and one just had to get used to them. As far as most of us were concerned, our war would be over when we finally went home, and until then we continued to behave as officers.

We were all shocked after we were exposed to evi-dence of the concentration camp horrors and the Holo-caust. For many weeks we denied that these things could have taken place under German authority and some of us ascribed this information to well-honed Allied prop-aganda. Knowing how in Germany we had been subject-ed to very effective and skilful wartime propaganda, we felt that here in Canada we were being exposed to more of the same and that the horrors we were now being told about had no greater credibility. We discussed the mat-ter among ourselves and decided that the truth seemed to lie on a path straight through the middle of the con-trasting claims. Finally, most of us came to accept this shameful chapter in the history of Germany and thus had to learn how to carry a burden that would remain with us for the rest of our lives. Not having known of these atrocities during the war did, however, allow us to live with our own personal consciences in respect to having fought for Germany, not for the regime that car-ried out these unspeakable horrors.

Because of the immediate postwar conditions in our war-ravaged homeland, mail from Germany ceased dur-ing the first few months after our arrival at Gravenhurst. When it resumed, I received one of the first letters and

The main building of Camp 20 at Gravenhurst where about 300 officers of all branches of the German armed forces lived. (NAC/PA-181222)

it was from Ruth – an event that was one of the big sur-prises of my life! I had no idea how she found out that I was still alive and a prisoner in Canada. We began to correspond regularly and this exchange nourished our hope for a happy reunion in Germany – whenever.

Our relations with our Canadian captors were al-ways very good. As an example, I should mention our camp interpreter, Captain Michael Chramtchenko, and his contribution to amity between former enemies. When we finally began to receive parcels from home, they were examined by the camp staff, who were some-what puzzled by the fact that so many prisoners were receiving bottles labelled "hair tonic" which, of course, entered without problems and provided the recipients with a nice dose of Schnapps. It did not take long for the staff to figure out what was going on and such contain-ers began to be tested. On one occasion, when Captain

SKIZZEN VOM LAGER 20
UND MÖSERICH

A budding artist, a member of my Crew 40, rendered this depiction of the building in which we lived. At the bottom is our swimming area, with "Möserich," a dog who belonged to one of the senior German officers in the camp. (WH col.)

Chramtchenko was the tester, he opened a number of suspect bottles, sniffed the contents and pronounced clearly, "This is hair tonic!" and the Schnapps continued on to the grateful recipients. Chramtchenko was an engaging man whose sense of humour reverberated throughout the camp.

During the time I spent at Gravenhurst, all of us in the camp were anxious for our repatriation to Germany. In the meantime, we kept busy. Since many of the prisoners were reserve (or wartime only) officers and had civilian professions, a very effective university had been created in the camp and there were very few disciplines that did not have courses given by experts in their fields – the products of our forestry classes were visible outside the former camp for many years afterwards. A number of these POW courses were granted a credit at some German universities. I took lessons in mathematics and physics to prepare for my own professional development after my return home. In June 1946, however, our idyllic existence came to an end when we learned that we were to be transferred to a camp in Britain. Our response to a survey made a few months before, in which the majority of all prisoners voiced their desire to remain in Canada instead of returning to Germany, had been ignored.

Our beloved boat, the *U-190*, did remain behind and, as we learned much later, had an interesting postwar career. It was commissioned into the Royal Canadian Navy as His Majesty's Canadian Submarine *U-190* and used for evaluation and trials. Its first voyage under the White Ensign was a publicity tour of the ports along the St. Law-

(Above) A display about *U-190* at the Canadian War Museum, Ottawa. (WH col.)

In July 1945, *U-190* was sent on a tour of Canadian ports along the St. Lawrence in an effort to raise funds in support of the Royal Canadian Sea Cadets. Note that the boat has been repainted in a lighter shade of grey. (RCN photo)

(Left) This picture of *U-190* was taken by a Canadian aircraft while the boat was on its way to Newfoundland. Note the low buoyancy of a submarine, with its entire body becoming invisible in a heavy sea. (NAC/PA-154011)

(Below) *U-190* enters the harbour of St. John's, Newfoundland. (NAC/PA-145576)

I have become a number in the Canadian prisoner-of-war system. This document followed me through my entire time in captivity with all transfers being entered on the other side. (WH col.)

rence River in August 1945, and thousands of fascinated Canadians waited in line for hours to get an opportunity to visit a German U-boat, an authentic "gray wolf of the sea," about which they had heard so much during the war. HMCS *U-190* continued in Canadian service until July 1947 when it was declared surplus and paid off.* Rather

than ending its life in a scrapyard, our boat came to a more spectacular end.

On Trafalgar Day (21 October) 1947, *U-190* was towed to approximately the same position where HMCS *Esquimalt* had been sunk in April 1945, to become the target in Exercise "Scuppered." The plan for this event called for Canadian naval aircraft – Fireflies armed with rockets and Seafires armed with bombs – to attack *U-190*, which would be followed by gunfire from two Tribal-class destroyers, HMC Ships *Haida* and *Nootka*, which would actually sink our old boat. As it was going down, an escort vessel would then administer the *coup de grace* by firing Hedgehog depth charges. As it happened, matters got somewhat confused – the destroyers opened fire first and straddled the boat and then the Fireflies attacked with rockets, after which *U-190* sank rapidly, stern first. It now lies on the ocean floor, not far from its former opponent, HMCS *Esquimalt.**

To return to Camp 20, in the evening of 10 June 1946 we were marched to the railway station in Gravenhurst to board a train. We travelled via North Bay and Montreal to Halifax, where we arrived two days later and there boarded the liner *Aquitania* for the voyage across the Atlantic. This ship had served as a troop transport during the war and we lived in stacked bunks in the holds but were allowed on deck a few times each day. On this voyage I met one of our most famous U-boat aces, *Fregattenkapitän* Otto Kretschmer, who was taken

---

* *U-889*, which also surrendered to the RCN in May 1945, was turned over to the USN in January 1946 and, a year later, expended as a target vessel.

* Before *U-190* was sunk, its periscope was removed and fixed in the Crowsnest Club in St. John's, Newfoundland, where it can be seen today.

prisoner after his boat, *U-99*, had been sunk in early 1941.*

When we stepped ashore in Southampton, in England, we quickly learned that the British had a different attitude than the Canadians toward German prisoners. I was not wearing my decorations but those who did had them rudely ripped off their uniforms by a grim-looking sergeant when they came down the gangway. England, of course, had suffered much more than North America during the war and this attitude was perhaps understandable. We were loaded into a train that took us to a camp near Sheffield, where we spent several months in drafty Nissen huts, mostly in pouring rain, before being shifted to other camps and finally, in February 1947, we were settled at Llanmartin, near Newport in Wales.

There we were allowed to leave the camp for walks but were told not to fraternize with British civilians. About this time, the effects of wartime suffering in England seemed to abate and our treatment by the authorities became much more relaxed, although our food remained rather plain and just sufficient to prevent starvation. We often thought wistfully of Camp 20 at Gravenhurst.

The order not to fraternize was disobeyed by both British and Germans. One day my former *Wachingenieur*, Ernst Glenk, and I met an English-

---

* Kretschmer is credited with having sunk more tonnage than any other German U-boat commander during the war – 42 ships totalling 238,327 tons.

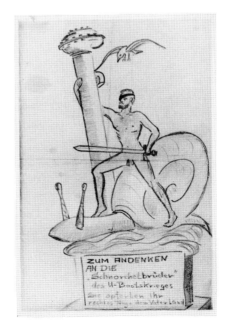

Our I.WO, *Oberleutnant z.S.* Herbert Rogge, was a talented cartoonist with a developed sense of humour and tried to capture the submariner's spirit in his work. At the left, the caption translates: "*Now* I can see something!" indicating the difficulties we had seeing around the *Schnorchel* head and its wake when it was in use. The other caption reads: "In memory of the snorkel brethren of the submarine war – they gave their right eye for the fatherland." The latter sketch combines the *Schnorchel*, our snail-like speed while it was in use, injured right eyes that had been glued to a periscope and, finally, our fighting spirit. (WH col.)

man who told us that he owned a Jaguar car but that he could not drive it as its motor was disassembled and he did not know how to get it running. Since he could not find anyone to do the necessary work, he offered the job to two former U-boat engineer officers and for two weeks Glenk and I walked every morning to the residence of our new employer and exchanged our uniforms for overalls he provided (because he did not want to be caught having German prisoners working for him as this was illegal). We took the engine of the vehicle apart, cleaned it, re-assembled it, installed it in the Jaguar, adjusted the ignition and turned the key. It ran most smoothly and we informed our employer that our task was finished – but I do not think he completely trusted us as he asked us to take the car for a test drive. The result was that two German officers enjoyed a fine drive through the beautiful Welsh countryside in a Jaguar and were able to report that the car ran beautifully.

My British employer was highly pleased and we became frequent guests at his house for afternoon tea. It was about this time that Howard Hughes's notorious film "The Outlaw" was released. It had been banned in the United States because it displayed Jane Russell's generous and lovely shape in rather scanty clothing, and also depicted her behaving in an amoral fashion. It was, however, shown in British cinemas, including the local theatre in Newport. For obvious reasons, it was of great interest to all the prisoners, starved of female company, and one day my host loaned me a suit belonging to his son, gave me the price of admission and sent me off to Newport to satisfy my curiosity. I spent a very pleasant few hours admiring Miss Russell's physique.

I was already quite familiar with the town of Newport since a few days earlier another naval officer and I, in full *Kriegsmarine* uniform and in defiance of rules and regulations which forbade us entering it, had paid the place a visit. When we arrived in the downtown area, we had asked a policeman for directions to the harbour and he showed us the way. When we arrived at the very wide entrance to the port area, we found one guard house on the left side and another on the right. We simply walked straight through the middle and nobody challenged us. Newport was so full of seamen of all nationalities that our German uniforms did not attract any attention. After an hour of exploring quays and ships, we turned to go home again and at that very moment a harbour police jeep came to a screeching halt beside us. Our concern was not justified – the policemen simply offered us a lift back to the city and we graciously accepted.

By the summer of 1947, after nearly a year in Britain, we still had no indication of when we would be permitted to return home and I started to get very restless. All this time Ruth and I had been corresponding and making plans for the future. She had moved to Tübingen, a university town south of Stuttgart, where she had found a job and where I hoped to study at the university. I was anxious to get back to her and my parents so, in the late summer, I decided to do something about it.

Throughout my childhood and youth, I had suffered from asthma when exposed to certain substances such as dust or straw. The heating in our barracks was by coal-fired ovens, and by manipulating the exhaust gases and breathing them, I was able to manufacture a very genuine asthma attack. After I had demonstrated my clearly fading state of health to the military doctor, he became concerned and sent me for an examination to a hospital in Chepstow. By the time I arrived there, I no longer had any symptoms, but on the other hand my claim to be very sick couldn't be totally disproved. I was therefore extremely happy to be told in September 1947 that I was being repatriated to Germany – considerably ahead of any of my comrades from *U-190*.

I was transferred to Hull, where I boarded a ship transporting POWs across the North Sea to Cuxhaven. Since I was the only prisoner wearing a navy uniform instead of the normal drab prisoner garb which had a bright red fabric disk sewn onto the back of the jacket, I was mistaken for a member of the ship's crew, which I found quite amusing. In Germany I was forced to spend another two weeks in a transition camp in Munsterlager before finally being released in Dachau, the location of the infamous concentration camp.

On 20 August 1947, after more than two and a half years of separation, Ruth was waiting at Tübingen *Bahnhof* when my train arrived. Our joyful reunion was complete on 18 October when we were married in a small village church high in the mountains of the Schwarzwald, where her parents had found a place of refuge from the turmoil of postwar Germany.

At long last, after seven years as a naval cadet, U-boat officer and prisoner, the war had ended for me and a brighter future beckoned.

On 16 April 1995, at the 50th anniversary of the sinking of the minesweeper HMCS *Esquimalt*, I was welcomed by the survivors of that ship and made an Honorary Life Member of their Esquimalt Memorial Association. The president of the association, Frank Smith, is shaking my hand in front of the cairn erected in honour of the *Esquimalt*. Former enemies had become friends. (WH col.)

ANOTHER PLACE,
ANOTHER TIME

After a few years in the turmoil of postwar Germany, I developed a longing for the open spaces of Canada and the fairness and tolerance Canadians had shown to me during my time in that country as a prisoner of war. I therefore resolved to emigrate to Canada. I did not expect a return to my resort hotel existence in Gravenhurst but I thought I had learned enough about Canada that after overcoming initial difficulties as an immigrant I could make a better future in a new country. North America beckoned and I was surprised how easily Ruth agreed to this major change in our lives, and I therefore applied for an immigration visa. It took some time to be approved, but in 1952 I was able to board a ship bound for Quebec City to begin a new life, and Ruth followed me with our infant son in 1953. With the initial assistance of a member of my Crew 40 and another U-boat veteran, Eberhard von Ketelhodt, who had arrived six months earlier, I settled in Toronto. In the beginning, life was certainly not easy but over the years I managed to build a rewarding career in the field of computer systems design.

One of the first adventures Ruth and I embarked on after our arrival in Canada was to visit my old POW camp at Gravenhurst. During the trip by car from Toronto, which lasted two hours, we were impressed with the rustic beauty of the countryside and I had no difficulty locating the camp, which was now the Gateway Hotel, a popular summer resort. With some apprehension I introduced myself to the management and was gratified by the warm reception we received. They showed us the rooms I had shared with my comrades in 1945-1946 and were full of curiosity about the events of the past. Ruth and I were given free rein to explore the property. We visited the prisoners' beach and swimming area and I was pleased that the trees planted by our forestry classes had grown into fine mature specimens. With some amusement, however, I pointed out to Ruth that many of the cement foundations of the posts for the barbed wire that had kept us inside were still in existence.

Despite all our initial hopes, the problems of beginning a new life in a new country put such strains on our marriage that Ruth and I went our separate ways in 1958. We remain friends, however, a relationship unaffected by my second marriage.

As the years and then the decades passed, I gradually

In 1953 I returned to Gravenhurst for a visit with my wife Ruth and our small son. The former camp had by now become one of the most popular summer resorts in the Muskoka region. (WH col.)

naval officer whose mother lived in East Germany. With thanks for my interest, therefore, the navy sent me its sincere regrets.

Six years later, in 1960, I talked to the German naval attaché in Ottawa, who was then actively trying to recruit former *Kriegsmarine* officers living in Canada to join the newly-established *Bundesmarine*, the Federal German navy. By this time, however, I had become far too used to the relaxed ways of North American life and had grown comfortable talking with my hands in my pockets or walking around with my jacket unbuttoned, to again subject myself to the old Prussian codes of behaviour. I now realized that I had become too much of a Canadian square peg to ever fit back into the German round hole and I declined the offer with thanks.

In the following year, my friend Eberhard von Ketelhodt and I visited Chicago and took the opportunity of calling on the staff of the Museum of Science and Industry in the hope of getting a tour of *U-505*, the Type IX boat from my old *2. U-bootsflottille*, which had been captured by the USN in 1944 and was now on display outside that institution. The staff arranged for us to meet two officers from the USS *Silversides*, a submarine stationed in Chicago, and the four of us had lively conversations on board both *U-505* and *Silversides*. Eberhard and I, comparing the two boats, found the living quar-

became more Canadian than German, although occasionally my past life as a *Kriegsmarine* officer intruded into my new life. In 1954 I learned that the Royal Canadian Navy was in need of personnel for their submarine force. Believing the RCN could not find a recruit better suited for that service than myself, I approached the naval establishment in Toronto to plead my case. To my utter astonishment, I was received with interest and after having been subjected to a series of medical examinations and an "Officer's Selection Board," was found suitable for acceptance into the RCN for a position equivalent to my old rank. Unfortunately both for myself and the RCN, the Royal Canadian Mounted Police, at that time responsible for security matters in Canada, objected to the commissioning of a former German

ters of the American vessel much more impressive and wondered whether American naval architects actually intended to facilitate the occasional dance party on board!

In 1993 my earlier life as a U-boat officer suddenly and markedly came to the fore. In that year, which was the 50th Anniversary of the high point of the Battle of the Atlantic, I was invited to speak about my wartime experiences to a large reunion of naval veterans in Halifax. During the course of that event, I was asked if I would like to meet one of the 26 survivors from HMCS *Esquimalt*, the Canadian ship that my boat had sunk in April 1945. I replied that I would consider it an honour and, following a somewhat hesitant handshake, which was transformed into an embrace, I met Joe Wilson, who was *Esquimalt*'s Asdic operator on that fateful day, 16 April 1945. It was an emotional and moving encounter for both of us and the media, always on the look-out for stories, pounced on the event. A well known Canadian radio personality who interviewed us was incredulous when he saw how well we got along with each other, but Joe Wilson explained why this was so: "We just did our duty, Werner was lucky, I was not."

A year later another *Esquimalt* survivor, Stoker Jack Ware, a lumberjack by profession, invited me to visit him in Comox, on Vancouver Island on the Pacific coast, and I spent a delightful weekend with him at his small cottage high on Mount Washington. Some time later I received a beautiful clock, fashioned out of a slice of wood from a tree, with a dedication and Jack Ware's

In August 1960 a business trip took me to Chicago, where, on a visit to the Museum of Science and Industry, I had an opportunity to tour *U-505*, captured in the Atlantic by a USN task force on 4 June 1944 not far from where *U-190* was operating at the time. My friend Eberhard von Ketelhodt, ex-commanding officer of *U-712*, is second from the left, and the two USN Lieutenants Brown and Willis, both submariners, have joined me on deck. The person on the right is a museum employee. (WH col.)

naval identification document glued to the back. When he learned that I was in contact with my old II.WO, Werner Müller, in Germany, Jack asked for his address and made a similar clock for him.

In 1995, on the 50th anniversary of the loss of *Esquimalt*, I travelled to the town of the same name in British Columbia and met more members of the Memorial Association. I laid a wreath in the name of the crew of *U-190* at the cairn dedicated to the warship and was simply overwhelmed when the Association made me an honorary life member. People, whose entire knowledge of the history of the Second World War stems from read-

On 16 April 1995 I laid a wreath at the war memorial in the town of Esquimalt, BC, accompanied by *Esquimalt* survivor Jack Ware. (WH col.)

After the official ceremonies in the town of Esquimalt on 16 April 1945 some of the surviving participants of that encounter in April 1945 got together to share our experiences. I am sitting at the head of the table on the left. (WH col.)

ing and watching films and documentaries, find such a development rather strange but sailors do not, and that is because a sailor's first enemy is the cruel sea itself. Those who have faced this enemy are automatically members of a global fraternity, regardless of nationality. Thus, the *Esquimalt* survivors and I have become good friends.

Shortly after this trip, I received a very disturbing letter from a young lady whose uncle had died on the *Esquimalt*. She had learned of my existence, and after many months of hesitation, finally decided to contact me because she was curious to find out what kind of man would have killed her beloved relative. This lady mentioned that for many years anything German had been absolute anathema to her and she felt she needed some help in finding peace of mind. I responded with a long letter of my own, expressing my hope that she would meet me and we did so. This meeting evolved into a close friendship. I introduced her to the *Esquimalt* survivors, who talked to her about her uncle, and I travelled with her to reunions and took her and her small son sailing on Lake Ontario. Standing by her side at one of the reunions, a reporter from the *Hamilton Spectator* became aware of our relationship and the next day, 20 May 1997, that paper published an article with the headline, "Slain sailor's niece stands with the man who helped to sink her uncle's ship."

I made my last visit to a U-boat in 1997 when the American PBS network funded a documentary about the discovery of the wreck of *U-869* off the coast of New Jersey. I was invited to come to Chicago to give a stem to stern tour of *U-505* to the producers, and I thus renewed my acquaintance with the only surviving Type IX U-boat that is close to its wartime condition. I found this visit very interesting but not a little embarrassing as, in the intervening years, I had forgotten many technical details such as which valve was which, and which electrical or air line led where – things that were once as familiar to me as my own face.

All these activities have led to my becoming involved in a number of marine organizations. I became a member of the Naval Officers Association of Canada, a member of the officers' mess of the Canadian Forces College in Toronto, and other similar groups. I have been a guest speaker at naval mess dinners and, even more pleasing to me, have made dives on submarines of the modern Canadian navy (now known as Maritime Command) and have been accorded the status of "Honorary Canadian Submariner." Sharing the occasional drink with serving naval officers gives me a comforting feeling of having returned to my beginnings – of going back to the navy.

Through all the years since the war, however, I have never lost my love of boats, wind and water and that love is now expressed by sailing my 26-foot sloop on Lake Ontario, with or without crew. For me, sailing is the best way to get away from it all, to think about the past and to recall the events that are worth recalling – and perhaps some that are not. When I am out on the water, with the waves slapping against the hull and the wind singing through the sails, my youth as a U-boat officer seems very distant and, in truth, it is – for it was very much another place and another time.

In May 1993 I first met a survivor from HMCS *Esquimalt*, the vessel's Asdic operator, Joe Wilson, in Halifax during a convention of Canadian naval veterans. Our meeting became a major media event with coverage by Canadian television, newspapers and resulted in a radio interview broadcast nationwide. (WH col.)

In September 1997, I enjoyed looking through the periscope of HMC Submarine *Okanagan* after a dive in Lake Ontario. (WH col.)

***U-190* and *U-889*, the "Canadian" U-boats, Halifax, June 1945**
View of the after decks of *U-889* (left) and *U-190* (right). Canadian
crews have moved on board both boats, as shown by the washing
hung up to dry and the fact that three sailors appear to be alongside
U-190 in one of the boat's inflatable rubber emergency rafts. This
photograph shows minor differences between the two craft – *U-190*

does not have a grating hatch over the aft torpedo loading hatch nor
the containers for the emergency life rafts which are found at the
rear of the superstructure of *U-889*. There is also a slight difference
between the two boats in the shape of the *Schutzbügel* or guard
rail for the *FlaK M42U* 3.7 cm gun which is noticeable in this photo.
(WH col.)

THE TYPE IXC/40 U-BOATS *U-190* and *U-889:*
A PICTORIAL TOUR

I n May 1945 the two Type IXC/40 German submarines, *U-190* under the command of *Oberleutnant z.S.* Hans-Edwin Reith, and *U-889* under the command of *Kapitänleutnant* Friedrich Braeucker, surrendered to the Royal Canadian Navy in the northwest Atlantic. The pictorial tour of these boats which follows is largely based on the many high-quality photographs taken of them (most of which have never been published) immediately after their surrender. The two boats had different fates. *U-889* was turned over to the USN in late 1945 and was scuttled the following year. *U-190*, as described in Werner Hirschmann's memoir above, served in the RCN as a trials boat until October 1947 when it was destroyed in a very dramatic fashion not far from the resting place of HMCS *Esquimalt*, the Canadian minesweeper it sank in April 1945.

Development and operational history of the Type IX U-boat

The origins of the Type IX U-boat are found in a specification issued by the German Naval High Command in 1935 which called for the construction of a submarine type larger than the medium Type VII, with in-

creased range, speed and torpedo armament, that could either be used as a long-range fleet boat or minelayer. This proposal was not popular with *Kommodore* Karl Dönitz, commanding the U-boat service, because he favoured the Type VII, which he regarded as more useful in the North Atlantic. The design of the Type IX, as the new submarine was designated, was based on an experimental vessel, the Type IA, which speeded up development time, and late in 1935 contracts were let for the construction of 13 Type IX craft. Only eight were actually completed when an improved model, the Type IXB, somewhat larger and with increased range, was introduced in 1937. Fourteen Type IXB boats were laid down before the war and the last was commissioned in 1940 just as a new model, the Type IXC, a further development with additional fuel capacity and even longer range, was introduced. Fifty-four Type IXC boats were constructed, the last being commissioned in 1942. The Type IXC/40, which began to come into service in that year, continued the development of the class and had increased range and surface speed over its predecessors. A total of 87 Type IXC/40 boats were constructed and commissioned between 1940 and 1944: *U-190* was one of the first to enter service in 1942 while *U-889* was one of the last in late 1944.

After 1942, most of the Type IX U-boats were deployed with either the 2. or 10. *U-bootsflotille* in Lorient. It became clear, because of their heavy losses, that these boats were at a disadvantage in the North Atlantic, where their slower diving time made them vulnerable to air attack. They were usually employed on long-range patrols to North America, the Caribbean, the southern Atlantic, the Indian Ocean and the Orient. Under the right captain, in waters where their size was not a disadvantage, the Type IX was very successful and of the top scoring 20 U-boats of the war, no fewer than 14 were Type IX craft of different variants. *U-123*, a Type IXB, was the highest-scoring boat of the class, sinking $41\frac{1}{2}$ ships, totalling 209,817 tons in 1941-1942. In 1945, with war almost at an end, Dönitz launched a miniature offensive in North American waters using 19 Type IXC and IC/40 boats; of these, 10 were sunk and 9 surrendered – 2 to the Royal Navy, 5 to the United States Navy and 2 (*U-190* and *U-889*) to the Royal Canadian Navy. It is the latter two boats that are described in the pictorial essay that follows.

Technical data for Type IX/C40 U-Boats *U-190* and *U-889*

N.B.: Note that the boats varied slightly.

Dimensions

Length overall	249.5 feet
Length at the waterline	245.5 feet
Maximum beam	21.9 feet
Maximum height (keel to bridge)	31.2 feet

Diving depth

Constructor's depth	325 feet
Proof depth	536 feet
Est. maximum depth (crush depth):	812.5 feet

Fuel oil carried

For a long patrol, about 245 metric tons (319,725 lb)

Batteries

Two 62-cell batteries weighing 74.9 tons (165,154 lb)

Diesel engines

Two M.A.N. 9-cylinder, 4 cycle, M9V 40/46 engines with Büchi superchargers generating 2200 hp and capable of a maximum output of 2500 hp for short periods

Electric motors

Two Siemens Type 2GU 345/34 motor/generators capable of up to 500 hp for short periods

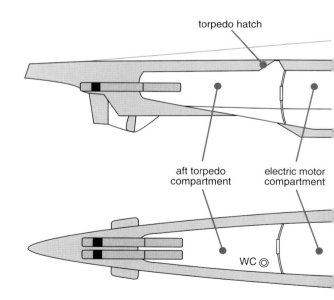

torpedo hatch

aft torpedo compartment

electric motor compartment

WC

NOT TO SCALE

Torpedoes

The number and types of torpedoes carried on a patrol varied. On their last mission, *U-190* carried 14 x 53.3 cm (21-inch) torpedoes comprising:

    8 x TVb *Zaunkönig II* acoustical homing torpedoes
    6 x TIIIa *Lut II* (*Lagen unabhängiger Torpedo*) independent running torpedoes

The *U-889* carried six TIIIa *Lut II* and six TVb *Zaunkönig II* torpedoes.

The TVb weapon had a speed of 21.5 knots and a range of 44 miles. Its warhead contained 602 lbs of explosive and and could be fitted with the Pi-2, Pi-3 or Pi-4c magnetic proximity pistols.

The TIIIa *Lut II* weapon had a speed of 30 knots and a range of 41.6 miles. Its warhead contained 616 lbs of explosive and could be fitted with the Pi-2 magnetic proximity pistol.

Guns

2 x *FlaK M42U* 3.7 guns on the *LM42U* twin mount with 2000 rounds of ammunition situated on the after platform of the *Wintergarten.*

4 x *FlaK 38* 2 cm guns on two *LM43U Flak-Zwilling* twin mounts with 8000 rounds of ammunition situated on the forward (upper) platform of *Wintergarten.*

Schnorchel

Type 1 *Schnorchel* with head coated in *"Alberich"* rubber compound and mounting an *FuMB 3 Bali I* rundipole antenna. Extendable 28-foot mast mounted in bay on starboard side of deck forward of bridge.

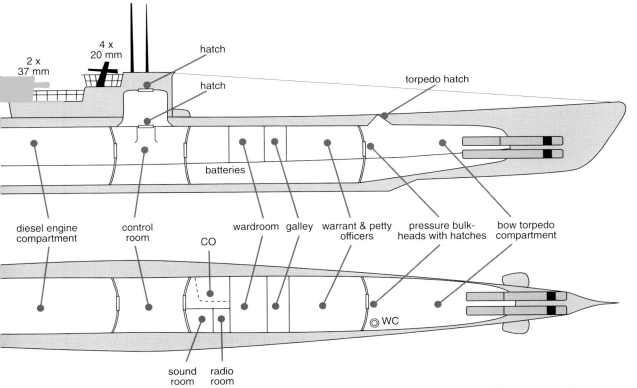

Type IX U-boat – simplified cross-section

Radios

1 x Telefunken S406S 200-watt short-wave transmitter
1 x Telefunken Spez. 2113IS 150-watt long-wave transmitter
1 x Lorenz Lo 40K 39C short-wave transmitter
1 x Telefunken E 437S marine receiver
1 x Telefunken emergency receiver

Radar and radar detectors

1 x *FuMO 61U Hohentwiel* radar with mattress antenna
1 x *FuMB 28 Naxos-ZM*4 radar detector with 2 x *FuMB 3 Bali I
    Rundipol* antennae, one on *Schnorchel* and one on bridge
1 x *FuMB 26 Tunis* radar detector with antenna array

Sound, sonar, direction and depth-finding equipment

1 x Atlas ANG 301 *Gruppen-Horch-Gerät* device in a *"Balkon"*
    mount
1 x *S-Gerät* passive sonar
1 x Lorenz or Telefunken Direction Finder
1 x Atlas *Echolot* depthfinder
1 x Atlas *Elektrolot* depth estimator with 100 charges
1 x U/T (*Unterwasser Telephonie*) device

Maximum range

13,450 sea miles (15,487.5 miles) at 10 knots using diesels
128 sea miles (147.3 miles) at 2 knots using electric motors

Fresh water storage capacity

4.16 cubic metres

Displacement (fully loaded)

1096.74 metric tons (241,831.7 lbs)

Crew

Varying number, but usually between 55 and 60 officers and sailors.

Rumpf (hull)

Unlike the Type VII, the "saddle" fuel tanks outside the Type IX's pressure hull were encased by the outer skin of the hull, giving it a more streamlined and pleasing appearance than its smaller cousin.

In the lower bow area were mounted the *Gruppen-Horch-Gerät* or sound location receivers, the U/T underwater telephone equipment and the *Echolot* depthfinder equipment. Both *U-190* and *U-889* had their *GHG* receivers arranged in a *"Balkon"* (literally a balcony), a small gondola attached to the forward part of the hull ahead of the keel, a late-war modification that resulted in improved sound reception. *U-889* also had a *Zwiebel* or "Onion" dome mounting 15 sound receivers on the upper deck at the point of the bow.

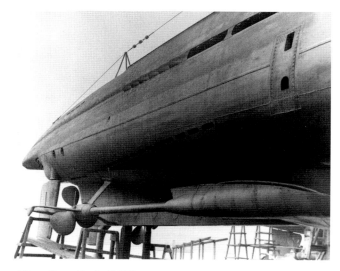

Aft portion of hull, *U-889*.
Quarter view looking aft of the stern section of *U-889*, showing propellor farings and the starboard rudder. (RCN photo/R. Bucharest/Halifax/26 June 1945/NAC/PA-179181)

Bow, *U-889*, showing *"Zwiebel"* structure.

U-889 was the only Type IX U-boat to have the *"Zwiebel"* or "on-ion" dome at the point of its bow. Inside the dome was an additional sound listening device with 15 crystal receivers used to listen on a 60 degree arc on the bow when the boat was using its *Schnorchel* as the latter device interfered with normal use of the *GHG* equipment. (RCN photo/R. Bucharest/Halifax/26 June 1945/NAC/PA-179187)

After part of hull, *U-889*.

View of the stern of *U-889*. Note the the half opened hatches for the stern 53.3 cm (21-inch) torpedo tubes, the double rudders and the two 3-bladed propellors behind the stern hydroplanes. Each of the massive propellors weighed 1356 lb. and the aft torpedo tubes were positioned so as not to be affected by interference from the propellors and rudders. The more powerful diesel engines of the Type IX U-boats gave them a higher surface speed than their smaller consort, the Type VII, despite their having a greater displacement. (RCN photo/ R. Bucharest/Halifax/25 June 1945/NAC/PA-179184)

(Right) *"Balkon"* installation, *U-889*.

The *"Balkon"* or "balcony" installation on *U-889* for the *GHG* sound locating equipment. Beginning in late 1943, the 48 sound receivers of this device were collected into a gondola mounted on the lower bow, at the front of the keel. Both *U-190* and *U-889* were fitted with this installation, which permitted sound bearings to be obtained from almost all directions, except for a sector to the stern. (RCN photo/R. Bucharest/Halifax/25 June 1945/NAC/PA-178980)

Bow and forward torpedo tube hatches, *U-889*.
View of lower bow of *U-889* showing the four forward torpedo tubes and the *"Zwiebel"* dome on the point of the bow. The streamlined appearance of the outer hull of the Type IX, which, in contrast to the Type VII, enclosed its fuel tanks, is apparent. (RCN photo/R. Bucharest/Halifax/26 June 1945/NAC/PA-179183)

Aussenschiff (deck)

The size of the Type IXC/40 U-boat meant that it was a larger and more comfortable craft than its smaller consort, the Type VII. It paid a price, however, in having a slower diving time – about 40-45 seconds to completely submerge – which left it at risk when operating within range of enemy aircraft. To increase survivability, many Type IX boats (including *U-190* but not *U-889*) were modified by cutting away the forward portion of their upper deck (where an outside torpedo storage compartment had been located in the original design) in an attempt to reduce the diving time of the boat. Evidence is contrary as to whether this modification had any practical effect.

From the upper deck, which was constructed of East Prussian Scotch Pine planks, each about 20 inches wide and 1.5 inches thick, five pressure hatches led to the interior of the boat (the forward torpedo loading hatch, the galley hatch, the bridge hatch, the diesel room hatch and the aft torpedo loading hatch). Above the pressure hatches were grating hatches on the wooden upper deck (*U-190* was missing some of these outer hatches but *U-889* had them all) which also could be opened to permit access and egress.

(Right) **Stern, *U-889*, looking aft.**
View of *U-889* looking aft from the lower *Wintergarten* platform. Note that the aft torpedo loading hatch is open. (RCN photo/G. Gadde/25 May 1945/ NAC/PA-178880)

(Left) **Forward deck, *U-190*, looking aft.**
The deck of *U-190* looking aft from the bow at Bay Bulls, Newfoundland, on 14 May 1945 after the crew of the boat had been transferred to HMCS *Prestonian*. Their belongings can be seen piled on the deck while nearby an RCN rating mounts guard with what appears to be a Lanchester 9 mm submachine gun. In the foreground, on the starboard side, the closed galley hatch is visible. This photo shows clearly the modification of cutting away the upper deck to reduce diving time. (RCN photo, author's collection)

(Above) **Stern, *U-190*.**
This view shows clearly the two AA platforms of the *Wintergarten*. Note that the twin *Flak M42U* 3.7 cm and twin *FlaK 38* 2 cm guns have been raised to maximum elevation – an indication of the usefulness of this type of weapon for defence against aircraft, if German U-boats had not been simply overwhelmed by Allied airpower. (RCN photo, author's collection)

***U-190* alongside a Canadian frigate, 1945.**
This photograph shows the modification carried out by Deschimag at Bremen between October 1944 and January 1945, during which this boat's upper deck was cut away in an attempt to reduce the diving time of the boat. Note that the boat has been repainted in a lighter shade of grey by the RCN. (RCN photo/A. F. Tigerstedt/15 May 1945/NAC/PA-133131)

Schnorchel (snorkel)

Both *U-190* and *U-889* were equipped with a Type 1 *Schnorchel*, an extendable air mast, by which a boat could run on its diesel engines and recharge the batteries for its electric motors while submerged. The *Schnorchel* was invented by a Dutch naval officer and examples were captured by the *Kriegsmarine* when Germany occupied the Netherlands in 1940, but it was not until 1943, when increasing numbers of radar-equipped Allied aircraft were inflicting heavy losses, that its use was seriously considered. Beginning in the winter of 1943/1944, an attempt was made to equip all operational U-boats with *Schnorchel* equipment, and although there were some reluctance at first to use the device, it eventually became popular as it increased survivability.

There were problems with the *Schnorchel*. It could only be deployed at speeds of less than 5-6 knots which meant that U-boats had to spend longer getting to and from their operational areas and thus had less time on patrol. The *Schnorchel* also obscured vision from the periscope and it was detectable at close ranges by the centimetric radar which Allied navies began to introduce in 1943-1944. In addition, great care had to be taken with the *Schnorchel*, as if the head dipped deeply below the surface for a period, it might lead to the poisoning of the crew by diesel exhaust as indeed did happen on *U-190* in August 1944.

Schnorchel stowage bay, *U-889*, looking forward.
View of *U-889* looking forward, showing the stowage bay on the starboard side of the forward deck for the 28-foot-long *Schnorchel* mast. This mast, with its streamlined cross-section, was raised hydraulically from within the *Zentrale* and connected by means of a water-tight coupling to an air intake tube fixed to the starboard side of the conning tower. Farther forward on the deck can be seen the open hatches of the bow torpedo compartment and the galley. Note the raised deck grate over the galley hatch. (RCN photo/G. Gadde/Halifax/25 May 1945/NAC/PA-134168)

Schnorchel head, U-889.
View of the *Schnorchel* 1 head as fitted on *U-889* coated with "*Alberich*" rubberized material to reduce radar echo. This picture shows the *FuMB Ant. 3 BALI* I Rundipol antenna mounted on the head for use with the *FuMB 28 Naxos ZM 4* radar detector. A second antenna of this type was on the periscope housing on the bridge. (RCN photo/G. Gadde/Halifax/25 May 1945/NAC/PA-178856.

Schnorchel intake, U-889, quarter view, looking forward.
View of the starboard bridge superstructure of *U-889* showing the lower air intake mast piping from the junction point with the upper mast aft to where it is fed into the diesel vents below the forward *Wintergarten* platform. (RCN photo/G. Gadde/Halifax/25 May 1945/NAC/PA-178879)

Mittelschiff und Turm (midships and bridge superstructure)

Often called, rather inaccurately, the conning tower, the bridge superstructure of *U-190* and *U-889* had been enlarged to mount the increased anti-aircraft armament carried in the late war period. Both boats were armed with four 20 mm guns and two 37 mm guns, all in twin mounts.

When the boat was running on the surface, it was controlled from the open bridge but, in 1944-1945, U-boats were spending very little time on the surface because of Allied airpower.

Bridge superstructure, U-190, looking aft from bow.
Note the deflectors on the front of the bridge – the lower is for water and the upper for wind – and the damage from salt spray. The protruding housing at the base of the superstructure contains the magnetic compass. Visible on the starboard side is the lower, or air intake, section of the *Schnorchel* with the watertight coupling for the upper mast, which can be seen lying in its bay on the deck. (RCN photo/A.F. Tigerstedt/St. John's/17 May 1945/NAC/PA-134169)

(Above) *Wintergarten, U-190,* **looking aft.**
View of *U-190* looking aft from the upper platform of the *Wintergarten*, showing the lower platform and the breech of the *FlaK M42U* twin 3.7 cm gun on its *LM42U* mounting. This accurate and highly effective weapon, which could fire 180 rounds per minute, was introduced in a single version early in 1944. A twin version began to be installed on Type IX craft in the autumn of that year but, by this time, it was somewhat redundant as very few U-boats were engaging in surface duels with Allied aircraft. There were also problems with this weapon as it was delicate and required regular maintenance that had to be done on the surface. (RCN photo/A. F. Tigerstedt/St. John's/late May or early June 1945/NAC/PA-178938)

(Above) *Wintergarten, U-190,* **looking forward.**
View of *U-190* from the stern looking forward and showing the lower or aft *Wintergarten* platform and the twin 3.7 cm *FlaK M42U* gun on the *LM42U* mounting and, on the upper platform, the four *FlaK 38* 2 cm guns on their *LM43U (Flak-Zwilling)* mountings. The 2 cm weapons have been removed from their mounts. At the foot of the ladder from the upper to the lower *Wintergarten* platform can be seen one of the five waterproof and pressure-resistant ammunition containers; this one is for 2 cm rounds. The *Schnorchel* mast has been raised and locked into place and also visible are the loop aerial for the direction finder and the two periscopes: the navigation periscope or *Luftzielsehrohr* (forward) and the attack periscope (aft). (RCN photo/D.J. Thorndick/Sydney/5 September 1945/NAC/PA-134173)

Bridge superstructure, *U-190,* **from port bow quarter.**
This view shows the *Schnorchel* mast raised and locked into place. It appears that the four *FlaK 38* 2 cm guns, removed by the German crew before the boat surrendered, have been remounted by the RCN. Note the open grating leading to the galley hatch immediately forward of the Canadian sailor. This photo provides good detail of the modified bow portion of *U-190*. (Editor's collection)

***Wintergarten, U-889*, looking forward.**
This view shows one of the two storage containers for the inflatable 5-man rubber emergency rafts opened and its contents displayed. In the foreground can be seen the grating hatch, underneath which lies the pressure hatch to the aft torpedo compartment. (RCN photo, author's collection)

***Wintergarten, U-889*, looking forward.**
The forward or upper *Wintergarten* platform and the four *FlaK 38* 2 cm guns on their *LM43U (Flak-Zwilling)* mounts. Note the water-resistant ammunition containers at the rear of the platform and in the foreground. (RCN photo/G. Gadde/Halifax/25 May 1944/NAC/PA-134165)

Bridge superstructure, *U-190*, starboard side.
The *Schnorchel* mast is raised and locked in place. Note that the air intake tube is continued around the starboard side to the diesel intake at the rear of the bridge. The fact that sunlight appears under the hull immediately forward of the bridge gives the impression that the lower half of the hull is missing but this light is actually coming through the *Schnorchel* bay, which had no bottom, and shining through the hull drainage slots. (RCN photo, author's collection)

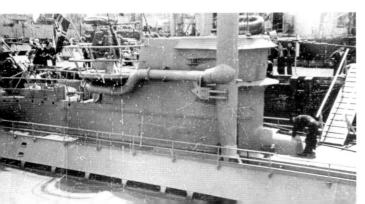

***Wintergarten, U-889*, looking forward.**
View of the aft *Wintergarten* platform of *U-889* showing the twin 3.7 cm *FlaK M42U* gun on the *LM42U* mounting. The containers under the platform contain rubber emergency rafts. Note the *Schutzbügel* or guard rail which prevented

the gun from being depressed too low. (RCN photo/G. Gadde/Halifax/25 May 1945/NAC/PA-178872)

(Above) Radar detector antenna head, *U-889*.
Antenna head for the *FuMB* 26 *Tunis* radar detector on *U-889*. This equipment was not waterproof and had to be mounted when the boat surfaced and removed before it submerged. (RCN photo/G. Gadde/Halifax/25 May 1945/NAC/PA-178914)

Bridge, *U-889*, looking aft.
This photo shows, on the port side, the watertight casing for the mattress aerial of the *FuMO* 61 *Hohentwiel U* radar and, on the starboard side, the mounting for the *UZO* (*Unterseeboots Ziel Ortungsgerät*), the sighting apparatus for torpedo firing. On the front of the periscope housing is the holder for the antenna head of the *FuMB* 26 *Tunis* radar detector and direction finder. Between the two periscopes is the *FuMB Ant.* 3 *BALI* I dipole antenna for the *FuMB* 28 *Naxos ZM*4 radar detector. A second antenna of this type was mounted on the *Schnorchel* head. (RCN photo/G. Gadde/Halifax/25 May 1944/NAC/PA-134166)

Radar antenna, *U-889*.
Radar antenna head for the *FuMB* 26 *Tunis* radar detector erected on the bridge of *U-889*. Behind the operator is the radio direction finder loop. To the left can be seen the *FuMB Ant.* 3 *BALI* I *Rundipol* antenna mounted on the periscope housing. This was hooked up to the *FuMB* 28 *Naxos ZM* 4 radar detector. (RCN photo/G. Gadde/Halifax/25 May 1945/NAC/PA-137697)

(Left) Bridge superstructure, *U-190*, port side.
Interesting view of the port side of the superstructure of *U-190* showing clearly the boat's emblem – a blue compass rose edged in white. The number below, which appears on no other photos of *U-190*, is a Canadian addition made after the craft surrendered. This photograph shows *U-190* during the period it was commissioned in the RCN as HMCS *U-190* as the boat has been repainted a lighter shade of grey and only one 2 cm gun is mounted in each of the twin mounts. (RCN photo, author's collection)

Bugraum (bow torpedo compartment)

This 75-square-foot area was the largest compartment on the Type IX U-boat and at the beginning of a patrol was normally cluttered with crew bunks and torpedoes stored on the deck plates. The bow torpedo compartment was the major fighting component of a U-boat and during an attack was an extremely busy place. Up to 25 enlisted sailors worked, ate and slept in this compartment, with two or even three men sharing a bunk. Collectively, they were known by the English term as "Lords" but they certainly did not live like their namesakes. In the aft part of this compartment, immediately forward of the pressure bulkhead, was located the forward torpedo loading hatch, which opened onto the deck.

Bow torpedo compartment, *U-190*, looking forward.
Normally this area was cluttered with bunks and torpedoes but they were gone when this photo was taken. Note the folding leaf tables and benches for dining that were stowed when not in use. Also note the wooden lockers on either side of the compartment where the men stored kit and foodstuffs at the beginning of a patrol. (RCN photo/A.F. Tigerstedt/St. John's/late May or early June 1945/NAC/PA-178941)

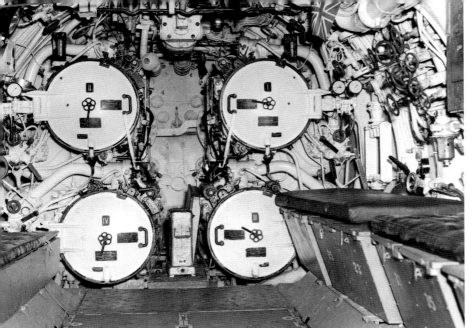

Bow torpedo compartment, *U-190*, looking forward.

The hatches of the four bow tubes are clearly visible. The metal surfaces of the living quarters throughout the boat were painted flat white or flat ivory. There is what appears to be an electric heater between the lower Tubes III and IV, but this may have been brought on board after the boat had surrendered, as was certainly the small Union Jack lodged in the pipe near Tube IV. This shot, taken after all torpedoes had been fired and crew possessions and bunks removed, shows this compartment at its most spacious and provides good detail of the equipment lockers which formed platforms for the bunks on which crew members slept. (RCN photo/G. Gadde/Halifax/25 May 1945/NAC/PA-178849)

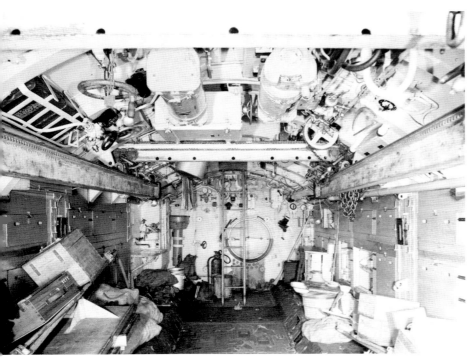

Bow torpedo compartment, *U-889*, looking aft.

This view shows the pressure hatch leading to the *Unteroffizieresraum*, or warrant and petty officers' quarters. On the deckhead can be seen the mobile I-beams set up to facilitate torpedo handling. The position of the torpedo loading hatch is marked by the moveable aluminum ladder fixed below it. This picture was taken just after *U-889* had surrendered and her crew had been removed. Boxes containing equipment, personal possessions, and mattresses and duffel bags are scattered about the deck. Note the difference in construction of the wooden lockers from those on *U-190* – all U-boats differed slightly in their fittings. The use of wood on German submarines was notable – it was lighter and more attractive than metal but absorbed light and its use surprised Allied inspectors of captured boats. (RCN photo/G. Gadde/Halifax/25 May 1945/NAC/PA-178861)

Bow torpedo compartment, *U-190*, looking aft from mid-compartment.

A closer view of the pressure hatch leading to the *Unteroffizieres-raum*. There were four of these hatches, of 23.6 inch maximum diameter, in the Type IXC, and all were provided with grab handles to facilitate swinging through them. Note that the torpedo loading hatch on the deckhead is open and daylight can be seen streaming through it. In the aft starboard corner is the door to the forward WC 2 toilet. The electric heaters may belong to the RCN, not the *Kriegsmarine*. (RCN photo/A.F. Tigerstedt/probably St. Johns/early June 1945/NAC/PA-179006)

Bow torpedo compartment, *U-190*, view of aft bulkhead.

This view, taken shortly after *U-190* was constructed in 1942, provides good detail of the pressure hatch leading into the *Unteroffizieresraum*. This bulkhead was the first of four watertight bulkheads that divided the interior of the Type IXC/40 into five separate areas: the bow torpedo compartment; the petty officer and officers' quarters; the *Zentrale*; the diesel and *E-maschine* compartments; and the aft torpedo compartment. On the starboard side, just in front of the door to the WC 2 toilet, are hatches for two folding washbasins built into the bulkhead for the men who lived in this compartment. (Editor's collection)

(Left) Bow torpedo compartment, *U-190*, looking forward.

Two RCN officers pose beside *U-190*'s four forward 53.3 cm (21-inch) torpedo tubes, numbered I-IV clockwise from the upper port (or left) tube. This photo gives a good idea of the size of this compartment, the most forward in the Type IX boat. (RCN photo, author's collection)

Wasserklosett (head)

There were two toilets (often called "*Rohr* 7" or "Tube 7" by the crew) on the Type IX boat: *Wasserklosett* 2 was at the starboard aft corner of the bow torpedo compartment while *WC* 1 was in the starboard forward corner of the aft torpedo compartment. *WC* 1 was usually used as a storage area during the first weeks of a patrol, so for much of the time a boat was at sea, *WC* 2 was the only plumbing available for the 55-60 crew members. Accessing the toilet could be a problem, particularly for crewmen in the aft compartments, so most U-boats had a system of announcing when the facility was clear. This toilet, which was operable only to a depth of 100 metres (300 feet), functioned by means of a complicated pressure system that necessitated the user opening and closing a number of levers. Accidents were not infrequent.

Unteroffizierswohnraum (warrant and petty officers' quarters)

A pressure bulkhead separated the bow torpedo compartment from the after part of the boat, and stepping through the watertight hatch in this bulkhead, one entered the warrant and petty officer's quarters. Between 14 and 16 men ate and slept in this compartment, which was considerably more comfortable than the sailors' crew spaces in the forward and aft torpedo rooms; rank does have its privileges. This compartment was usually ruled by the four men who, after the officers, were the most important crew members: the *Obersteuermann*, or navigator; the two *Obermaschinists* responsible for the diesel engines and electric motors; and the "*Nummer Eins*" or chief petty officer responsible for the dress, discipline and conduct of the enlisted personnel.

Toilet, *U-190*.
WC 2, the forward toilet of *U-190*, photographed just after the boat's construction in 1942. Located on the starboard side just off the aft bulkhead of the bow torpedo compartment, this device was the only plumbing available for 50-60 crew members at the beginning of a patrol as the aft WC 1 toilet was usually used for food storage. (Editor's collection)

Unteroffizierswohnraum, U-889, looking aft.
Through the open door can be seen the edge of the electric range in the galley. Note the wooden table with a folding top. The upper bunks above the table were hinged and could be swung back and locked flat against the bulkhead to convert the lower bunks into benches during meal times. (RCN photo/G. Gadde/Halifax/25 May 1945/NAC/PA-178863)

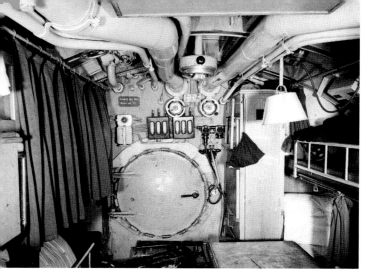

Unteroffizierswohnraum, *U-889*, looking foward.
This view shows the pressure hatch on the bulkhead that separated this room from the bow torpedo compartment. The curtains, which could be drawn across the bunks, provided a bare minimum of privacy – although privacy was not an important consideration on a U-boat. (RCN photo/G. Gadde/Halifax/25 May 1945/NAC/PA-178862)

Galley, *U-190*, forward part.
The forward portion of the galley taken shortly before the boat commissioned in 1942, showing the lever for the fresh water hand pump and various taps and faucets for fresh and salt water, and waste

water. Fresh water was crucially important on board a U-boat and the Type IXC/40 was fitted with an evaporator in the *E-Raum* which could distil 8 litres (1.76 gallons) of fresh water per hour. This was stored in four tanks and piped throughout the boat as required. (Editor's collection)

Küche (galley)

One of the smallest compartments on a Type IXC U-boat, but one of the most important, was the galley. In this tiny area, with a floor space measuring only 59 by 27 inches, the boat's *Smutje* or cook, assisted by assigned crew members, prepared meals for the 55-60 members of the crew. Meals were planned in consultation with the *Obersteuermann* and U-boat crews took the business of eating very seriously. For long patrols, between 14 and 15 tons of food were stored throughout the Type IX craft in just about everywhere it could be placed – including the aft toilet. In the deckhead above the passageway that divided the cooking appliance in the galley from the main provision storage area was a pressure hatch that opened onto the deck for convenience when loading foodstuffs.

Galley, *U-190*, after part.
The aft part of the galley as it appeared just before commissioning in 1942, showing the electric range with its three hot plates and, below, the two baking ovens. The ring fitting to the right of the range held the separately-heated

40-litre (10.6 gallon) cooking pot, a necessary appliance as the diet was heavy on potatoes. Note the moveable aluminum ladder leading to the galley hatch above and the doorway aft to the wardroom. The galley's central position was useful for distributing food to the living quarters fore and aft. (Editor's collection)

(Left) **Wardroom, *U-190*, looking aft.**
This photo shows the pressure hatch leading into the *Zentrale*. The lighting fixture was not a standard fitting, but a gift from the father of the *Leitender Ingenieur* of *U-190*, *Oberleutnant (Ing)* Werner Hirschmann, which he wired into the boat's electrical system. Note the folding stools stacked on the port side of this compartment – junior officers sat on these when eating as they often had to move out of the way when crew members came through. Senior officers sat on the more comfortable bunks on the starboard bulkhead which served as benches because rank has its privileges. The jacket at right belongs to an officer of the RCNVR. Through the passageway can be seen the sliding doors to the sound and radio cabins which were aft. (RCN photo/A.F. Tigerstedt/St. John's/June 1945/NAC/PA-137698)

Wardroom, *U-889*, looking forward.
Note the bunks on the right and the curtain across the passageway to the next compartment aft – the CO's quarters. Also note the many hooks on the lockers and bulkheads, used to hang clothing, which cut down even more on the available space. The personal lockers were also used to store food during the early weeks of a patrol. On the deck of the next compartment can be seen the hatch to one of the two battery storage compartments, each of which held 62 batteries. In the background is the pressure hatch leading into the *Zentrale*. (RCN photo/G. Gadde/Halifax/25 May 1945/NAC/PA-178864)

Offizierswohnraum (wardroom)

The wardroom was possibly the most cheerful area in a U-boat, if that word is appropriate when referring to a submarine. Normally, it was the quarters for the I.WO, the II.WO and the *Leitender Ingenieur*, but if a boat was carrying midshipmen or supernumaries such as trainee commanders, journalists or technical officers, as many as six or seven men might eat and sleep in this area. On *U-190*'s last patrol from February to May 1945, there were four officers in the boat's wardroom.

The commanding officer took his meals in the wardroom but a wise CO made a point of getting out of earshot of his officers from time to time so that they could gripe about him without being overheard.

Kommandantenraum (commanding officer's quarters)

The most spacious and comfortable individual crew space on board the Type IX/C40 was the Commanding Officer's quarters, located on the port side, immediately forward of the *Zentrale* or control room. Space and comfort are relative terms when talking about a U-boat – for example, the captain's bunk, an artificial leather mattress, which he had the privilege of not having to share with anyone else, was only 52 inches long.

Across the passageway from the captain's quarters were the sound (forward) and radio (aft) cabins. Their close proximity was important as it was crucial that the CO have quick and easy access to the crucial functions carried out in these cabins.

Commanding officers's quarters, *U-889*, looking aft.
Although he had the most personal space, the captain was still fairly cramped as his quarters consisted of only a small area on the port side, as seen here on *U-889*, that could be curtained off for privacy. Into this was fitted a bunk, lockers and a small desk. Above the desk is a locked cupboard where drugs, navigation instruments and books were stowed, while below the desk surface is a built-in wash basin and two more cupboards. The middle locker of the three seen on the bulkhead above the bunk held a small metal safe in which confidential material was secured. Across the passageway can be seen the sliding doors to the sound and radio cabins and, looking forward through the open doorway to the wardroom, the edge of the officers' folding table is visible. (RCN photo/G. Gadde/Halifax/25 May 1945/NAC/PA-178865)

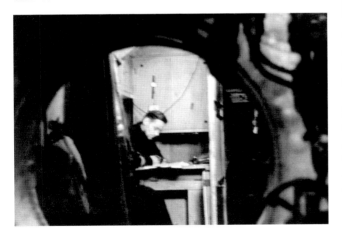

Kommandant of *U-190* at his desk, 1944.
Oberleutnant z.S. Hans-Edwin Reith, the CO of *U-190*, at his desk in his quarters on the port side of the boat. This picture, taken through the pressure hatch from the *Zentrale*, gives a good idea of the crowded conditions on a Type IX U-boat. (Hirschmann collection)

Horchraum (sound cabin) and *Funkraum* (radio cabin)

Manned 24 hours a day, these two small cabins contained the GHG sound listening device, the S-Gerät active sonar, radios, radio detection and ranging equipment, radar, and radar detector equipment. The Schlüssel M coding and decoding device, more commonly known as the Enigma machine, was kept in a locked cabinet in the radio cabin.

(Above) **Radio cabin, *U-889*, forward part.** This view shows: (a) the *200 W-Kurzwellensender*; (b) the tuner for the *Kurzwellensender*; (c) the 150 *W-Langwellensender*; and (d) the *Kurzwellen* receiver. Below the latter is the wooden cupboard for the *Schlüssel M* (Enigma) coding device. Above the fuse box on the bulkhead is a shelf for holding coding books and manuals. (RCN photo/G. Gadde/Halifax/25 May 1945/NAC/PA-178905)

(Below) **Radio cabin, *U-889*, aft part.** This view shows: (a) the Telefunken direction finder receiver; (b) the boat's secondary gyro compass; (c) the oscilloscope or sighting device for the *FuMO 61 Hohentwiel-U* radar; and (d) the handwheel for turning the *Hohentwiel* mattress antenna mounted on the port side of the bridge. The *FuMO 61* radar, which was standard equipment on U-boats in the last year of the war, could detect aircraft at 12 miles range and ships at 6 miles. (RCN photo/G. Gadde/NAC/PA-178910)

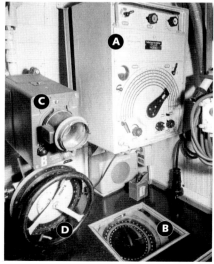

(Above) **Radio cabin, *U-889*, aft part.** This photo shows: (a) the transmitter of the *FuMO 61 Hohentwiel-U* radar; (b) the *Hohentwiel* receiver; and (c) a volt meter. Beneath the table near the bulkhead can be seen two antennae heads for the *FuMB 26 Tunis* radar detector, which were erected on the bridge when required. Note the coding and instructional books and papers stored in the shelf built into the deckhead. What looks like a fuse box fixed to the starboard bulkhead is a fuse box. (RCN photo/G. Gadde/Halifax/25 May 1945/NAC/PA-178909)

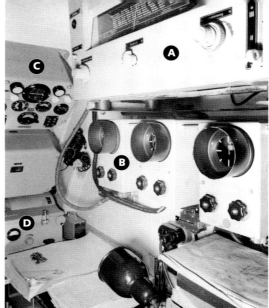

Sound cabin, *U-889*, aft part.
This view shows: (a) the Telefunken marine radio receiver above; and (b) the three circular screens for the *FuMB* 28 *Naxos-ZM4* radar detector for picking up enemy radar signals on the 9 cm wave band. On the bulkhead behind is (c) the tuner for the Telefunken all-frequency/marine radio (underneath), while below (d) is the shortwave receiver. (RCN photo/G. Gadde/Halifax/25 May 1945/NAC/PA-178904)

(Above) **Sound cabin, *U-889*, forward part.**
This photo shows the compensator and amplifier of the Atlas *AN 301 Gruppen-Horch-Gerät* sound device. Note the headset and the additional lead plugged into this equipment. The *GHG*, which consisted of 48 sound receivers mounted in a *"Balkon"* or "balcony" or gondola beneath the boat's keel, was automatically switched from receiver to receiver as the handwheel was turned, providing critical bearings from almost all directions, except a narrow sector astern. Depending on conditions, the *GHG* could detect the underwater noises of a single ship at 12 miles and a convoy at between 50 and 60 miles but its performance was adversely affected by the acoustic conductability of the water and it was also vulnerable to depth charges and could not be used while snorkelling. The *GHG* was a passive sonar device but the Type IX boat was also fitted with an active sonar, the *S-Gerät*, which had a maxium range of 6 miles. In the corner is a locked wooden cabinet for the storage of confidential material. (RCN photo/G. Gadde/Halifax/25 May 1945/NAC/PA-178907)

***Kriegsmarine Schlüssel* M.**
This coding machine, known to the Allies as the "Enigma" machine, is a late war version with the fourth rotor. When not in use, it was kept in a locked cupboard. The Allies' achievement in breaking the codes generated by this device was a major factor in their eventual success in the Atlantic as it allowed top-secret German radio traffic to be read almost simultaneously after transmission. (Courtesy, Steve Fahie)

Zentrale (control room) and *Turm* (conning tower)

Stepping through the hatch, about 26 inches in diameter, on the pressure bulkhead that separated it from the officers' quarters, one entered the *Zentrale*, or control room. The *Zentrale* was the nerve centre of a U-boat and from this compartment the submarine was commanded, manoeuvred, navigated and fought. A fairly spacious compartment, measuring about 17 by 13.5 feet at its outside extremities, the *Zentrale* was crammed with a confusing array of handwheels, gauges, instruments, equipment and controls, many of which were colour-coded as to function. Its cramped interior was made smaller by the well of the attack periscope and the ladder to the hatch that led to the *Turm* or control tower above. If the boat was submerged, the *Zentrale* was the normal action station of the boat's CO, *Leitender Ingenieur* and *Obersteuermann*, who could communicate with any compartment by voice tubes and telephones.

The conning tower, basically a separate pressure compartment located above the *Zentrale* and accessed by a ladder from it, was the compartment from which underwater attacks were made. The captain manned the attack periscope and gave his instructions and target data to an officer who fed them into the torpedo attack calculator. The CO was often assisted in the *Turm* by crewmen who manned various controls or communicated messages. In the deckhead above was the main pressure hatch that led to the open bridge.

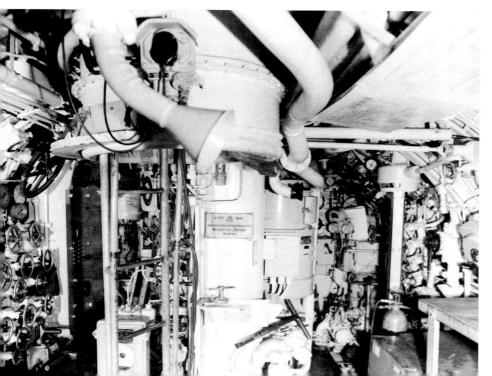

***Zentrale*, *U-889*, looking aft from centre of compartment.**
This interesting photo, taken from just inside the hatch leading to the next compartment forward, shows the middle section of the *Zentrale*. On the starboard bulkhead are the various valves for controlling compressed air for the diving tank and the auxiliary switchboard. In the centre is the ladder leading to the hatch to the *Turm*, and thus to the bridge – note the skirting around the hatch, which was a safety measure, and the housing for the main periscope. The voice tubes can be seen above. On the port side is the navigator's chart table and, aft of it, the main oil pump. (RCN photo/G. Gadde/Halifax/25 May 1945/NAC/PA-178867)

Zentrale, U-889, looking forward.
This view from the port side of the compartment shows the forward pressure bulkhead and forward starboard corner of the _Zentrale_. Note the repeater compass immediately to the right of the hatch, housing for the gyrocompass below and the engine RPM indicator gauge. To the left can be seen the navigator's chart table and, in the foreground, the bicycle seat often used by the _LI_ to rest his weary legs after standing for hours behind the planesmen. This photo gives a good idea of the crowded nature of the _Zentrale_, in which 8-10 men were on duty when the boat was at action stations. (RCN photo/ G. Gadde/Halifax/25 May 1945/NAC/PA-178866)

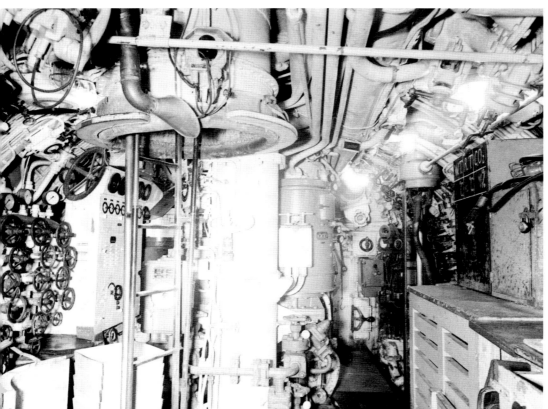

Zentrale, U-190, general view looking aft.
Taken from some distance inside the compartment, this photo provides a good view of the port bulkhead of the _Zentrale_, including the navigator's chart table and chart lockers, the oil pump, the ladder and hatch to the _Turm_ and the housings for the two periscopes. An idea of the narrow size of the _Zentrale_ can be gained from this view. (RCN photo/A.F. Tigerstedt/Halifax/May or June 1945/NAC/ PA-179011)

(Left) **Starboard side of *Zentrale*, *U-190*, looking aft.**
In the deckhead can be seen the skirting of the hatch to the *Turm* above, although the ladder is not fixed. On the housing of the periscope, below the large name plate, is the knot indicator. From left to right, can be seen the aft hydroplane control and, above it and to the left, are the panels which indicated the status (open or closed) of all outboard openings, vent valves and internal compartments. To the right of the hydroplane wheel are the valves for blowing out the various tanks – the main valve for blowing the diving tanks is the large handwheel above the bank of valves. Beside it is the auxiliary switchboard. (Editor's collection)

(Above) **Hydroplane control station, *U-190***
This view, taken before the boat was commissioned, shows the hydroplane control station on the starboard side of the *Zentrale*. This was the action station of the *Leitender Ingenieur*, who stood behind the two hydroplane operators to control the depth of the boat. The planes were operated electrically with two small pushbuttons in front of the planesmen. The wheels were only used in an emergency after the electricity failed. On either side of the depth indicator between the two wheels are the position indicators for the hydroplanes. Above the left indicator are the two engine RPM gauges and above the right are two depth indicators. (Editor's collection)

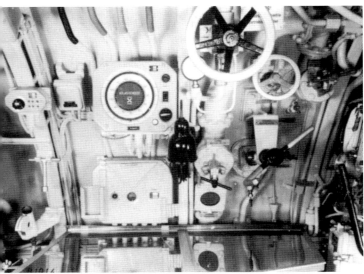

Echolot* installation, *U-190
The Atlas *Echolot* depth sounding and finding installation was mounted over the navigator's chart table on the port side of the *Zentrale*, immediately aft of the pressure bulkhead. This equipment measured the response to sound pulses sent out by transmitters which were then picked up by receivers, both senders and receivers being mounted in the lower hull. This depthfinding equipment was important for U-boats operating, as *U-190* did, in shallow waters. The photo is from 1942. (Editor's collection)

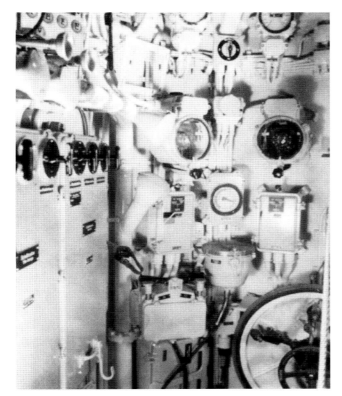

Interior of *Turm*, *U-190*, looking forward

This photo, taken in 1942, shows some of the equipment mounted in this small and crowded space, including the removable auxiliary rudder stand on the deck to the left of the open hatch to the *Zentrale*, the repeater compass above the hatch, a switchboard, an engine RPM gauge and, above that, indicator lights for the six torpedo tubes. (Editor's collection)

Dieselmotorenraum (diesel engine compartment)

Stepping through the hatch on the pressure bulkhead that separated it from the *Zentrale*, one entered the diesel engine compartment. This long compartment, just over 33 feet in length, was the kingdom of the *Diesel Obermaschinist*, a chief petty officer who reported directly to the *LI* for its operation. In the forward port section of this compartment was a lathe and work bench at which minor repairs might be carried out on board.

This compartment was entirely dominated by the two M.A.N. M9V 40/46 9-cylinder diesel engines which, with Büchi superchargers, were each capable of producing 2200 HP for long periods and 2500 HP for very short periods – under optimum conditions, they could propel a Type IX boat at 18-19 knots on the surface. The diesels were fuelled by the 250 or so metric tons of oil carried in the boat's oil tanks.

Communication between the *Zentrale* and the diesel mechanics at the throttle position for each engine was by means of the engine telegraph which was graduated in various speeds. The forward speed commands were:

KF (*Kleine Fahrt*), "Dead Slow:" about 170 rpm

LF (*Langsame Fahrt*), "Slow:" about 240 rpm

HF (*Halbe Fahrt*), "Half Speed:" about 300 rpm

HHF (*Zweimal Halbe Fahrt*), both engines half speed: about 390 rpm

GF (*Grosse Fahrt*), three-quarter speed: about 414 rpm

GGF (*Zweimal Grosse Fahrt*), both engines three quarter speed: about 455 rpm

(Left) **Diesel room, *U-889*, looking forward.**
This good shot of the diesel room of *U-889* gives some idea of the length of this large compartment and the size of the diesel engines. (RCN photo/G. Gadde/Halifax,/25 May 1945/NAC/PA-178913)

(Above) **Diesel room, *U-190*, forward section.**
View of the pressure hatch leading to the *Zentrale* taken in 1942. From left to right can be seen storage lockers for engine parts and tools, the work bench, various engine, oil and cooling pumps. Note the step in front of the hatch. (Editor's collection)

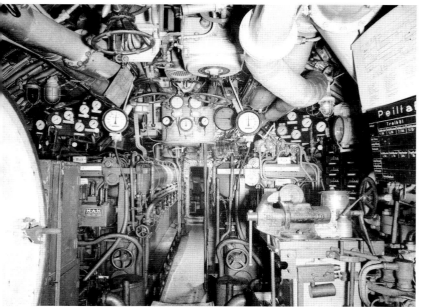

(Left) **Diesel room, *U-190*, looking aft.**
One of the larger compartments on the Type IX U-boat was the *Dieselmotorenraum*, or *D-Raum*. This view, taken from just inside the *Zentrale* (note the open hatch on the left side of the photo), shows the starboard and port MAN 9-cylinder engines that could provide a maximum surface speed of 18 knots. Note the workbench in the right foreground, the skirting for the diesel room hatch on the deckhead and, immediately in front, the two hand wheels for closing the lower diesel air valves. (RCN photo/A.F. Tigerstedt/Halifax/June 1945/NAC/PA-179010)

Port diesel, *U-190*, looking aft.
Chief Engine Room Artificer G.R. Benham, RCN, poses proudly at the throttle position of "Puck," the port M.A.N. 9-cylinder diesel engine. Directly above his left hand is the revolution indicator of the port engine and, immediately to the right of that device, can be seen the oil and air pressure gauges. The engine room telegraph is immediately behind his head, while mounted on the deckhead in the upper left of the photograph is a depth gauge. Note the work bench immediately behind Benham, with a vise mounted on it. (RCN photo, editor's collection)

E-Maschinenraum (electric motor compartment)

The diesel engine compartment was separated from the electric motor compartment, which lay aft, by a watertight door. The *E-raum* contained the two 500 hp Siemens Type 2GU 345 electric motor/generators, powered by two 62-cell batteries located under the floorplates of the second watertight section (the officers and petty officers' quarters, galley and sound and radio cabins), which propelled the Type IXC/40 boat while submerged. At emergency speed, these motors could produce up to 7 knots but only for very short periods; to conserve batteries, slower speeds were more normal. This compartment was the province of the *Elektro Obermaschinist*, or chief petty officer in charge of the electric motors. As in the diesel compartment, commands were communicated by means of a telegraph and the common speeds were:

> KF (*Kleine Fahrt*), "Dead Slow:" about 90 rpm
>
> LF (*Langsame Fahrt*), "Slow:" about 120 rpm
>
> HF (*Halbe Fahrt*), "Half Speed:" about 180 rpm
>
> GF (*Grosse Fahrt*), three-quarter speed: about 220 rpm
>
> AK (*Aüsserste Kraft*), "Full Ahead:" about 250 rpm

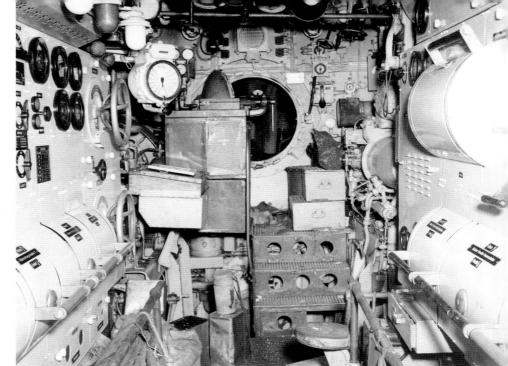

E-Raum, U-190, looking aft.
The aft pressure bulkhead on *U-190* with the steps leading up to the hatch into the aft torpedo compartment. Note the depth gauge in the upper left deckhead. This photograph, taken after the German crew had left *U-190* in May 1945 and before a Canadian crew took over, shows miscellaneous boxes and containers piled around the steps. (RCN photo/A.F. Tigerstedt/ St. John's/May or June 1945/ NAC/PA-179008)

E-Raum, U-190, looking forward.
The *E-Raum* or electric engine room on *U-190* showing the two Siemens electric motors on both sides and, behind them near the open door to the diesel room, the main switchboards. These switchboards and another in the *Zentrale* fed all electical systems on board that were not connected directly to the motors, including systems for cooking, heating, lighting, communication and the gyro compass. (RCN photo/A.F. Tigerstedt/ May or June 1945/NAC/PA-179009)

Hecktorpedoraum (aft torpedo compartment)

Stepping through the hatch on the pressure bulkhead located aft of the *E-Raum*, the visitor comes to the final space on the Type IX boat – the aft torpedo compartment. About 55 square feet in size, this compartment was the working, eating and sleeping space of between 10 and 12 men. Three torpedoes were usually stored on the floor plates until needed and the crew had to live around them (and on them) until they were loaded into the two aft tubes. One of the few advantages of the aft torpedo compartment was the close proximity of the WC 1 toilet, which was located in the starboard forward corner, but since this was usually used as a temporary storage area at the beginning of a patrol, it was only free after a few weeks into a patrol.

In the forward part of this compartment a pressure hatch, used for loading torpedoes, led to the deck above.

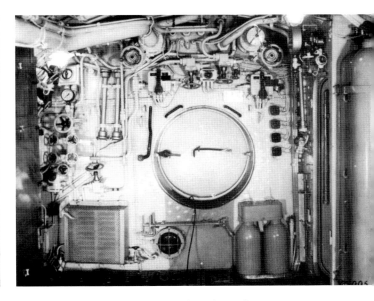

Aft torpedo compartment, *U-190*, looking aft.
This view, taken in late 1942, shows the aft 53.3 cm (21-inch) aft Tubes V and VI. Under Tube V is the well for the stern planes while over in the upper right foreground is the emergency rudder equipment. On the deckhead at upper left can be seen the chain tackle for handling the torpedoes in the compartment. (Editor's collection)

Aft torpedo compartment, *U-190*, looking forward.
This photo, taken shortly before *U-190* was commissioned in 1942, shows (immediately below and to the right of the watertight door to the *E-Raum*) two 50-litre oxygen bottles. Some 13 similar containers were situated in the forward and aft torpedo compartments which were used to refresh the air on board during extended submerged periods. To the right of these bottles is the door to the aft toilet on the starboard side of the compartment, known to the crew as "*Rohr* VII," or "Tube VII." (Editor's collection)

(Left) **Aft torpedo compartment, *U-889*, looking forward.** Note the bunks fixed above the three torpedoes stored on the deck. On the deckhead can be seen the I-beam rails by which torpedoes were moved in and out of the tubes and the ladder leading up to the aft torpedo loading hatch. On the bulkheads are the wooden lockers in which the men who worked, ate and slept in this compartment stored their kit and personal possessions. Torpedo compartments were always crowded and busy places and, as the torpedoes carried in the tubes had to be removed for inspection and maintenance periodically, they were worse at the beginning of a long patrol. At the end of such a patrol, with all torpedoes fired, the I-beam rails removed and stowed, and the aft toilet free for its intended purpose, this compartment was almost comfortable if comfort is a term that be used in connection with U-boats. (RCN photo/G. Gadde/Halifax/25 May 1945/NAC/PA-178912.

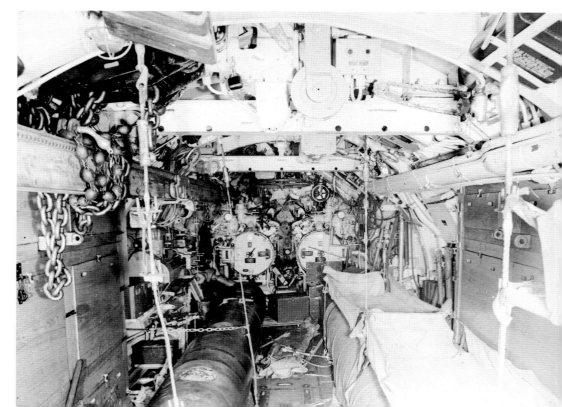

Aft torpedo compartment, *U-889*, looking aft. In addition to the two torpedoes carried in the tubes, three might be stored on the deck of this compartment and the "Lords" slept on them. Note the I-beams mounted on the deckhead and the heavy tackle used to shift torpedoes within the compartment. (RCN photo/ G. Gadde/Halifax/25 May 1945/NAC/PA-178906)

LIFE ON A U-BOAT

Werner Hirschmann

Though some of the topics I write about here may be touched on elsewhere in the book, this personal postscript brings together some of my recollections about our day-to-day lives in U-boats and our morale. W.H.

The crew

The crew of a submarine of the large, ocean-going Type IXC/40 of approximately 1,000 tons consisted of the *Kommandant* or Commanding Officer (CO), the *Leitender Ingenieur* or Chief Engineer (*LI*, pronounced "ellee"), *Erster Wachoffizier* or First Watch Officer (*Eins-WO* or *I.WO*), *Zweiter Wachoffizier* or Second Watch Officer (*Zwo-WO* or *II.WO*), three chief petty officers and about 50 petty officers, sailors and stokers. Occasionally, as on the final patrol of *U-190*, an officer-in-training or a midshipman complemented the wardroom. Patrols for this type of boat lasted anywhere from two to four months, the return to base being determined by the remaining fuel and/or food.

The seamen were on a "three-watch system." A bridge watch consisted of one of the watch officers, a petty officer and two seamen as lookouts. The third watch was run by the *Obersteuermann* or Chief Helmsman, usually the most senior non-commissioned officer of the crew. The *I.WO* was responsible for the weapons systems aboard whereas the *II.WO* looked after communication systems and provisioning.

In the *Kriegsmarine*, the *LI* was the diving officer on the submarine and was practically in charge of operations when submerged, following only general directions from the *Kommandant*. He was also responsible for the operation of all propulsion and diving machinery. The *LI* was the undisputed master of the control room and second in seniority to the CO.

Two of the chief petty officers, the *Obermaschinisten*, were in charge of the diesel and electric machinery respectively. The technical personnel were divided into two watches, with six hours on and six hours off during the night, followed by three four-hour watches during the day. German submarines stayed on German time and did not switch to local time.

Diving a submarine

As a submarine has relatively low buoyancy, it usually drives through the waves rather than floating on top of them. In heavy weather the bridge watches would frequently get drenched and the hatch leading into the boat was often thrown shut to prevent a heavy sea from flooding the conning tower and the control room beneath. Buoyancy is, of course, what keeps the boat on the surface and it has to be eliminated to enable the boat to dive. This is achieved by venting the diving tanks, allowing the air in them to be replaced by water entering the tanks through openings in the bottom.

While the boat is below the surface, its weight ideally should equal the weight of the water it displaces. Only then will the boat float at a certain depth without rising or sinking. Although the sub is equipped with regulation tanks and pumps necessary to achieve this state, it will always be ever so slightly lighter or heavier than desired. If the boat is too light by the smallest amount, it will rise, and this in turn will let the boat expand due to lower outside pressure and make it even lighter, causing it to rise with ever-increasing speed until it pops out of the water like a cork. If, on the other hand, it is slightly heavier, the reverse happens, the volume of the boat will shrink, and it will sink until its hull collapses under the pressure of the water. An exception to this may be offered by the boundary layer between water of different densities or temperatures, where the boat can float without moving. These layers are not often to be found when they are needed.

To maintain the known weight and balance of our boat, every change due to consumption of any matter had to be recorded, as well as the movement of items from one place in the boat to another. Every man moving from one end of the boat to the other had to announce his intended movement to the control room. The consumption of fuel oil had only a minor effect on the weight of the boat since it was replaced by sea water, and only the difference in specific weight between oil and water had to be compensated for.

The control of the depth of the sub was therefore maintained dynamically through propulsion. At high speed the submerged submarine was steered up and down with a set of planes at the stern not unlike the elevator of an airplane, and the sub moved in the direction its nose pointed. At low speed the boat used both front and stern planes to move both ends up and down, parallel to the surface. The movements of the planes were controlled by orders from the Chief Engineer standing behind the two planesmen.

The design depth of the submarines was 100 m but the boats routinely went down to 200 m, at which depth they felt relatively safe from depth charges, which were thought to be limited to higher depths.

To surface the boat, it was moved dynamically up to periscope depth, and after the CO had assured himself that it was safe to surface, a short burst of compressed air into the top of the diving tanks took the boat up high enough that the CO could open the hatch leading to the bridge. The remaining water in the diving tanks was then driven out by diesel exhaust gases directed into the tanks. The boat had returned to its full buoyancy again.

Vitally important equipment for the operation of the submarine were the two compressors used to fill the high-pressure air bottles to blow out the diving tanks.

One of these compressors was driven electrically and could be used while being submerged, although this was done only in case of emergencies. The other compressor was powered by diesel oil, injected into the gap between two horizontally opposed pistons. Unfortunately this type of compressor was unreliable and often kept the technical personnel occupied with repair work.

Food and drink

Provisioning a U-boat had its own particular problems because our submarines were not designed for storing food for 60 men for three to four months. At departure every nook and cranny was filled with cartons, cans, sacks and other containers, while dried salami sausages hung from the ceiling throughout the boat, looking like stalactites. The floors of the crew's living quarters in the bow and stern rooms were covered with food packages, which severely limited the head room for the crew until the food had been consumed.

The cook always had trouble finding what he was looking for. The various cans or packages were identified by numbers only, so that only the cook knew their contents. This decreased the temptation of the crew to help themselves to delicacies. Fresh food such as meat, eggs, vegetables and fruit usually lasted only two weeks and from then on most perishables, including bread, came out of cans. Fresh potatoes lasted about six weeks and then they too came from cans, as did hard sausages and hams. Lemons were freely available but vitamins were unknown to us; however I never heard of a case of malnutrition or scurvy and I can't even remember com-

plaints about the food, which might have been expected because of its monotony, although our wartime calorie consumption by far exceeded that of the ordinary German citizen.

The boat had one water evaporator to keep us provided with drinking and cooking water and to produce distilled water for the batteries. The breakdown of this piece of equipment was far more serious than most other damage. Drinking water, including an allocation for cleaning teeth, was strictly rationed and amounted to about two to three cups a day. Thirst was a problem, especially in tropical temperatures, and was eased with an additional supply of lemonade. For washing we used seawater and special seawater soap, but as we could not rinse off the sticky salt residue from the water, this procedure was not very satisfactory. Shaving and showering were postponed until we returned from a patrol. Quite honestly, I don't remember how we handled our laundry and I am not sure I want to remember.

General conditions

Temperatures aboard varied with the area of operations. Off the Gold Coast of West Africa in May 1944 the temperature rarely fell below 40° Celsius (104°F) with extremely high humidity. We were literally sleeping in our own sweat. On the other hand, off Halifax in March 1945, the temperature outside the engine room rarely crept above 10°C (50°F) and often sank to only 2°C (35°F) – but that was only a minor inconvenience.

Since open flames were strictly prohibited due to the probable presence of battery gases, there was never any smoking inside the boat. To allow only the few privileged – those assigned to bridge watches – to smoke would have been unfair and smoking was therefore banned altogether, and it was surprisingly easy to get used to it as nobody was smoking.

Daylight we saw when we departed, and the next time when we returned, except the officers who occasionally peered through the periscope. Even this we got used to without problems but upon our return even a cloudy day had the blinding effect of the sun.

On a U-boat we did have some problems with waste. There were two toilets but for half the trip only one was used since the other served as storage space for food. There was sometimes a line-up for the toilet and the inquiry *"Frage rot?"* ("Question red?") could often be heard throughout the boat. This referred to the red light at the door to the toilet indicating that it was occupied. Emptying the toilet bowl with varying outside water pressures required a well-rehearsed routine, which some seemed unable to master. Occasionally the contents of the bowl went forcefully the wrong way – a cause for much mirth among onlookers and fury on the part of the victim. Beyond a certain depth the toilet could not be used at all as the outside pressure became too great to be overcome by the pumps.

A crew of nearly 60 men could produce an awful amount of waste and it could only be accumulated inside for a short time before it became necessary to get rid of it. The only way to do this was to launch it through a torpedo tube, after the torpedo had been temporarily removed, the latter being a routine activity for the purpose of servicing the torpedoes. Of course, it was always an uncomfortable feeling to leave visible evidence of our presence floating around on the surface.

All U-boats had one or two crew members trained in first aid, but to become sick during a mission was not recommended. We found that a man who would have been declared unfit by a doctor ashore continued to function on board, simply because he had to. Our main remedies for various health complaint were aspirin and castor oil. There were a few supply submarines, called "milk cows," that had complete medical facilities with a doctor, but that, of course, was far from ideal. Our very large Type IXD2 submarines, operating in the Indian Ocean and beyond, had a doctor aboard and one of these boats stayed at sea for more than seven months.

At one time our high command ordered us to fight attacking aircraft with anti-aircraft guns instead of diving to escape, and the result was that many members of the gun crew were badly wounded. An attempt was made to assign a medical doctor to every U-boat operating in areas susceptible to air attack but the idea was abandoned quickly when so many doctors were lost on service.

I was told that the smell on the boat was unbearable but we all know that you get used to the worst smell in a few minutes. When the *schnorchel* head became submerged for a few seconds due to heavy seas or the inattention of the *LI*, the diesels sucked their air out of the boat and created a slight vacuum. I was told that we suffered terrible pains in our ears due to that condition, and yet I never became aware of it in myself or anybody else aboard

Stress and morale

After the war much fuss was made about this German officer who was the youngest captain of a submarine or that officer who was the youngest chief of a flotilla. Such more or less unsubstantiated claims have been used as an indication of exceptional talents or dedication. To me, however, this is only an indication of the pitiful state of the German submarine service – I became a Chief Engineer at the age of 20 because there were few experienced 30-year-old engineering officers left alive. During the war, kids were called upon to do a man's job and they weren't always successful at it.

With a single exception I have never heard of a mental breakdown on a sub in action. Recently I had an interesting discussion with a former squadron leader of RAF Bomber Command, whose speech about combat stress outlined the tremendous effects of battle fatigue, which often led to the total inability of men to continue the daily attacks on Germany with their extraordinary losses. Although our losses were greater than those of Bomber Command, battle fatigue was not known to us in the submarine service. The reason seems to be that, unlike Allied airmen, even during a mission we always had long periods to recover from the strains of action, and after the return to base we spent almost as much time on leave as we spent at sea. We called this rest the "refuelling" of the psyche.

Those of us who survived did so not least because we had an outstanding complement of chief petty officers. Despite constant admonitions from High Command to replenish the diminishing numbers of experienced sub-marine officers by sending capable chief petty officers to Officer's School, it rarely happened. No submarine commander in his right mind would dare lose the skill and experience of a long-serving chief petty officer if that commander wanted to survive the war. But there were a few duds among the chief petty officers and they were sometimes the ones who were sent off to Officer's School.

The spirit in the *U-Boot-Waffe* was buoyed by the knowledge that we belonged to an elite service which had its perquisites, and these we thoroughly enjoyed. During operational patrols we had three good meals a day and a warm bunk, kept so by the man who just had gone on watch. When we came back after a long patrol, the boat was usually in need of an extensive overhaul and so we got weeks of leave, far more than any other branch of the German armed forces. We were also better paid than the other branches and we received favoured treatment with respect to goods in short supply – alcohol, coffee, butter, silk stockings, etc. – to take home to our families, wives or girlfriends. We ate better than almost anyone in Germany and, finally, after nearly every patrol, there was usually a ceremony at which medals were distributed, swelling our already sizeable egos. All in all, despite the odds against us, I do not think any of us would have exchanged his existence with anyone else in the German armed forces, particularly not with an infantryman on the Eastern Front.

It was true that the chances of coming back from a patrol became slim late in the war, when many U-boats did not even survive their first mission. Time and again we had to accept that one of our close friends had gone, never to return. But the shock lasted briefly, then over another drink we switched the conversation to more mundane topics. It was quite astonishing how we began to lose all sensitivity to the occurrence of death and came to regard it as a natural consequence of our choice of work. Perhaps our attitude really had nothing to do with morale and (a sign of the times) was sheer fatalism. If we were fatalists, however, we did our best to enjoy today and let tomorrow take care of itself.

It has been said, quite truthfully, that our morale never faltered, and I don't think that anxiety or uneasiness dominated our lives. At no time did I consider the possible sacrifice of my life as a valuable contribution to the welfare of the human race, and under attack I never lost fear for my life. I learned, however, to put up a good front and I think we approached everything with the same nonchalance one has when one does one's job in peacetime, whatever it may be. We grumbled, we enjoyed ourselves, we complained, we laughed and found it sometimes difficult to take the whole Human Comedy too seriously. The fact that we could lose our lives was only a rather unfortunate and unavoidable side effect of our choice of profession. We kept on doing our job, and to us at sea the CO of the corvette chasing us was a colleague pursuing another aspect of the same trade as we did, and his performance was often subjected to a running critique from us.

Immediately after leaving port we looked forward, like all sailors, to returning to base, but today I find it almost beyond belief that after a few weeks at home with our families or in specially dedicated recreation centres, we became edgy, got ants in our pants and couldn't wait for the moment of departure for the next mission. Such is the foolishness of youth.

BIBLIOGRAPHY

Unpublished Sources

Directorate of History and Heritage, Department of National Defence, Ottawa.

DHH 79/446. *Kriegestagebuch, Befehlshaber der Unterseeboote,* 1942-1945.

German Navy Research Reports by D.E. Graves compiled for the official history of the Royal Canadian Navy in the Second World War .

G 2c: "Glossary of German Naval Terminology, Codenames and Abbreviations." November 1991.

G 3: "German Navy Radar, 1939-1945: Overview and Descriptive Catalogue." November, 1990.

G 4: "German Navy Radar Detectors, Radar Foxing and IFF Equipment, 1939-1945: An Overview and Descriptive Catalogue." November 1990.

G 5: "Descriptive Catalogue of German Navy Sonar and Sonar Foxers, 1939-1945." November, 1990.

G 6: "German Navy U-Boat Torpedoes, 1939-1945: Overview and Descriptive Catalogue." November 1990.

Naval Historical Section 1650 "Ship" Files.

NHS 1650 HMCS *Esquimalt.*

List of Casualties and Survivors in the loss of H.M.C.S. *Esquimalt.*

NHS 1650 HMCS *"U-190."*

Documents Relating to Surrender, May 1945

"A German Sub Surrenders" by Sgt. Frank Bode, YANK Field Correspondent, Newfoundland.

HMCS *Victoriaville,* Report of Proceedings on *U-190,* May 1945.

Nominal Roll of U-190 (surrendered off Newfoundland 12.5.45).

Report on an Interrogation of some members of the crew of U-190, which formally surrendered to H.M.C.S. "Thorlock" and "Victoriaville" on 12th May, 1945. N.I.D. 3 [22 May 1945].

Report on U-190, surrndered off Newfoundland on 12th May, 1945, being supplementary to the interrogation report issued on 22nd May, 1945.

U-190 Fuel Consumption Table – Sixth Patrol.

Documents Relating to Service of *U-190* in RCN and Exercise "Scuppered," October 1947.

List of Commanding Officers. HMC Submarines U-190 and U-889.

RCN Press Releases: 15 June 1947; 18 October 1947; 27 October 1947.

Memorandum on Sinking of Former German Submarine "U. 190."

Other Documents

Memorandum from Captain J.A. Heenan, RCNR (Retd.) to E.C. Russell, 27 June 1962, subject: "Interview with Ex-German Naval Officers who served in "U" Boats in Canadian waters, World War II.

Werner Hirschmann Papers, Toronto.

Diaries and Memoirs .

Diary, 30 June -17 August 1944; 20 October 1944-7 February* 1945; 11 May-20 May 1945.

Memoir, "Memories of a Submariner," Various drafts, 1993-2001. Final draft, October 2002.

Memoir of Surrender of *U-190*, May 1945, written c. June 1945.

Praktikant-Werkarbeiten Buch Nr. 1, 16 December 1940 to 25 November 1941.

Personal Papers.

"Bierzeitung! 612," mimeograph newsletter, c. May 1942

Copy of Surrender Document of U-190, dated 12 May 1945.

Photograph Albums.

Prewar, c. 1923-1940.

Wartime, 1940-1947.

Interviews and Correspondence.

Interviews and correspondence with D.E. Graves, 2002-2003.

Correspondence, 1991-2002 with historians Michael Hadley, Timothy P. Mulligan and Douglas Maclean.

Transcript of Interview with Documedia Group, 1997, for "Secrets of War."

Library of Congress, Manuscripts Division, Washington

"German Submarine Materials."

Box 5, Reel 81, U-505.

Bücherausgabe (Library catalogue of boat), March-May 1944.

Schallplattenverzeichnis (record catalogue), March-May 1944.

Box 12, Reel 82, U-858.

Schallplattenverzeichnis (record catalogue).

National Archives and Record Adminstration, Washington

MS B-490.

Oberstleutnant Fritz Ziegelmann, "III. Final Phase. An estimate of the situation with a concluding description about the fighting on the Invasion-Front up to the 31st July 1944."

MS B-619.

Generalmajor Julius Kuse, "Operations in Brittany near Lorient."

MS-B-731.

General der Artillerie Wilhelm Fahrmbacher, "Background and Development of the Atlantic Wall in the Brittany Area, Summer 1942 to 1 June 1944."

Record Group 38, Records of Office of Chief of Naval Operations.

Office of Naval Intelligence, Special Activities Branch (Op-16-Z).

"U-Boat Bases, 1942-1945."

"U-Boat Bases … for the Use of Interrogating Officers. Information as of 5 July 1943.

Interrogation Reports, (Op-16-Z).

Report on the Interrogation of Survivors from *U-515* sunk 9 April 1944 and U-68 sunk 10 April 1944.

Report on the Interrogation of Survivors from *U-128.* Sunk, on May 17, 1943.

Report on the Interrogation of Survivors from *U-172,* Sunk 13 December, 1943.

Report on the Interrogation of Survivors from *U-604* and *U-185* Sunk 11 August 1943.

Report of Interrogation of the Crew of *U-805* Which Surrendered to the USS *Varian* on 13 May 1945 off Cape Race.

Report on Interrogation of the Crew of *U-873* Which Surrendered to the USS *Vance* on 11 May 1945.

A Summary of Inspection and Interrogation Reports by Officers of the D.N.I, D.O.R., D.S.D., and D.W.T., who were present at the formal surrender of U-889 … at Shelburne, N.S. on 13th May 1945.

Report on Interrogation of the Crew of *U-1228* Which Surrendered to the USS *Neal A. Scott* on 11 May 1945.

Interrogation of Survivors from *U-1229.* Sunk 20 August 1944. September 1944.

Final Report on the Interrogation of Survivors from *U-1229.* Sunk on 20 August 1944.

Record Group 242, Seized Enemy Records, 1942-1945.

Kriegestagebuch, U-190, 14 January-20 June 1944; 20 June-4 October 1944.

Kriegestagebuch, U-375, 19 April - 7 May 1942.

Microfilm Publication T1022, reel 3987, PG 33966b.

Denkschrift der Seekriegsleitung über Forderungen für den künstigen Kriegsschiffbau auf Grund der Erfahrungen des 1.Kriegsjahres … 4 February 1941 .

Other Unpublished Sources.

    Interviews and questionnaires completed by Rudi Bartsch, Werner Müller, Germany, and Rudi Rauch, Canada, with Donald E. Graves, September-November 2003.

    Jobst Schaefer, "Die Ernährung des U.- Bootsfahrers in Kriege," unpublished Phd. dissertation, Christian-Albrechts University, Kiel, 1943.

    "Portsmouth Report": Technical Report on German Submarine Type IXC, held at the Museum of Science and Industry, Chicago.

Published Sources

Books

Admiralty, Historical Section. *The Defeat of the Enemy Attack on Shipping 1939-1945: A Study of Policy and Operations. Volumes IA and IB*. London: Admiralty, 1957.

Ballard, Robert D. *The Discovery of the Bismarck*. New York: Time-Warner, 1990.

Blair, Clay. *Hitler's U-Boat War. Volume I: The Hunters, 1939-1942. Volume II: The Hunted, 1942-1945*. New York: Random House, 1996 and 1998.

Blumenson, Martin. *Breakout and Pursuit. United States Army in World War II. The European Theatre of Operations*. Washington: Center of Military History, 1961 and 1989.

Burgess, John and Ken Macpherson. *The Ships of Canada's Naval Forces 1910-1985. A Complete Pictorial History of Canadian Warships*. Toronto: Collins, 1985.

Dönitz, Karl. *Ten Years and Twenty Days*. New York: Da Capo, 1997.

Douglas, Alec, Roger Sarty and Michael Whitby. *No Higher Purpose. The Official Operational History of the Royal Canadian Navy in the Second World War, 1939-1943. Volume II, Part I*. St. Catharines: Vanwell, 1993.

Fahrmbacher, Wilhelm, and Walter Matthiae. *Lorient: Enstehung and Verteidigung des Marine-Stützpunketes, 1940/1945*. Weissenburg: Prinz-Eugen Verlag, 1956.

Gannon, Michael. *Operation Drumbeat: The Dramtic True Story of Germany's First U-Boat Attacks Along the American Coast During World War II*. New York: HarperCollins, 1990.

———. *Black May: The Epic Story of the Allies' Defeat of the German U-Boats in May 1943*. New York: HarperCollins, 1989.

Graves, Donald E. *In Peril on the Sea: The Royal Canadian Navy and the Battle of the Atlantic*. Toronto: Robin Brass Studio, 2003.

Hadley, Michael. *U-boats against Canada: German Submarines in Canadian Waters*. Montreal: McGill-Queen's University Press, 1985.

———, *Count Not The Dead. The Popular Image of the German Submarine*. Montreal: McGill-Queen's University Press, 1995.

Hughes, Terry and John Costello. *The Battle of the Atlantic*. New York: Dial Press, 1971.

Kemp, Peter, ed. *The Oxford Companion to Ships and the Sea*. Oxford: Oxford Univerity Press, 1988.

Kennedy, Ludovic. *Pursuit. The Chase and Sinking of the Bismarck*. London: Collins, 1974.

Köhl, Fritz and Axel Niestlé. *Vom Original zum Modell: Uboottyp IXC*. Koblenz: Bernard & Graefe Verlag, 1990

Lynch, Thomas G., ed. *Fading Memories: Canadian Sailors and the Battle of the Atlantic*. Halifax: Atlantic Chiefs and Petty Officers Association, 1993.

Mulligan, Timothy P. *Lone Wolf: The Life and Death of U-Boat Ace Werner Henke*. Westport: Praeger, 1993.

———. *Neither Sharks nor Wolves. The Men of Nazi Germany's U-Boat Arm, 1939-1945*. Annapolis: Naval Instiute Press, 1994.

Neitzel, Sönke. *Die deutschen Ubootbunker und Bunkerwerften. Bau, Verwendung und Bedeutung verbunkerter Ubootstützzpunkte in beiden Weltkriegen*. Coblenz: Bernard & Graefe Verlag, 1991.

Rössler, Eberhard. *The U-Boat. The Evolution and Technical History of German Submarines*. Annapolis: Naval Institute Press, 1981.

Malmann Showell, Jak P. *Hitler's U-Boat Bases*. Annapolis: Naval Institute Press, 2002.

Schmeelke, Karl-Heinz & Michael. *German U-Boat Bunkers*. Atglen, PA: Schiffer Military/Aviation, 1999.

Syrett, David. *The Defeat of the German U-boats: The Battle of the Atlantic*. Columbia: University of South Carolina, 1994.

Terraine, John. *The U-Boat Wars, 1916-1945*. New York: Henry Holt & Co., 1989.

The U-boat Commander's Handbook ("U.Kdt.Hdb."). Gettysburg: Thomas Publication, 1989.

Westwood, David. *Type VII U-Boat*. Annapolis: Naval Institute Press, 1984.

Whitley, M.J. *Destroyer! German Destroyers in World War II*. London: Arms and Armour Press, 1983.

Newspaper and Magazine Articles

"Achtung! Meet the German Navy's youngest captain," *St. John's Evening Telegram*, 17 April 1982.

"City under observation by U-boat's periscope," *St. John's Evening Telegram*, n.d. (c. May 1963].

"Flying Sailors Sink German Sub," *Halifax Daily Star*, 23 October 1947.

"Its 'Up Periscope' at the Crow's Nest," *Crowsnest*, July 1963.

"Lest We Forget 'Esquimalt,'" *Victoria Daily Times*, 17 February 1965.

Marsh, Ron, "Eight Tubes of Death on U-190, She Sought Canadian Shipping," by Ron Marsh, Montreal *Gazette* [n.d., c. 28-29 July 1945].

Mulligan, Timothy P., "German U-boat Crews in World War II: Sociology of an Elite," *Journal of Military History* 56, no. 2 (April 1992): 261-281.

Paterson, T.W., "Death Struck the 'Sweeper," *The Islander*, 25 April 1965.

———, "We Captured the Sub That Sank Esquimalt," *The Daily Colonist*, 30 May 1965.

"Spent Last 50 Day Down Scared to Death of Radar," *Halifax Chronicle Herald.*, n.d. [c. 18 May 1945].

Young, Scott, "Newfie Has Real V-Day as German U-Boats Quit," *St. John's Evening Telegram*, n.d. [possibly 16 May 1945].

Websites

NB: *Internet websites often change their addresses. Those below were accurate at the time of publication of this book in May 2004.*

"HMCS Esquimalt" <http://members.rogers.com/manuel> A website, created by one of the survivors, dedicated to the memory of HMCS *Esquimalt*, sunk by U-190 on 16 April 1945.

"Feldgrau" <http://www.feldgrau.com> A website specializing in the history and organization of the German armed services during the Second World War. Contains much good information on the *Kriegsmarine.*

"Grey Wolf" <http://home.t-online.de/home/grey-wolf> A German language website which offers much useful information about U-boat technical matters, construction types, boat histories and life on board.

"Lexikon der Wehrmacht" <http://www.lexikon-der-wehrmacht. de> A German-language site which contains much useful information on the history, organization and personalities of the German armed services during the war, including the *Kriegsmarine.*

"U-505" <http://www.msichicago.org/exhibit/U505> An excellent visual tour of *U-505*, the Type IXC boat at the Museum of Science and Industry in Chicago, which is both informative, interesting and educational.

"U-Boat Archive" <http://www.uboatarchive.net> An excellent site offering copies of photographs and original documents relating to the destruction of U-boats by Amercan naval forces during the Second World War.

"U-Boat Net" <http://uboat.net> A comprehensive and very useful site offering information on all aspects of the *U-Boot-Waffe* in the Second World War and the German submarine service in the First World War, including biographies of commanders, boat and formation histories, articles on specialized subjects, and reviews of literature on anti-submarine warfare. This site is a first and important stop for the researcher.

INDEX

NASA
SKYLAB

1969 to 1979 (all modules)

Dedication

Dedicated to the late Raymond Loewy, with whom the author discussed Skylab interior layouts at the NASA Marshall Space Flight Center, Huntsville, Alabama. His work changed the way we all thought about interior design – of space stations!

First published in February 2018

A catalogue record for this book is available from the British Library.

ISBN 978 1 78521 065 5

Library of Congress control no. 2017948762

Published by Haynes Publishing,
Sparkford, Yeovil, Somerset BA22 7JJ, UK.
Tel: 01963 440635
Int. tel: +44 1963 440635
Website: www.haynes.com

Haynes North America Inc.,
859 Lawrence Drive, Newbury Park,
California 91320, USA.

Printed in Malaysia.

NASA
SKYLAB

1969 to 1979 (all modules)

Owners' Workshop Manual

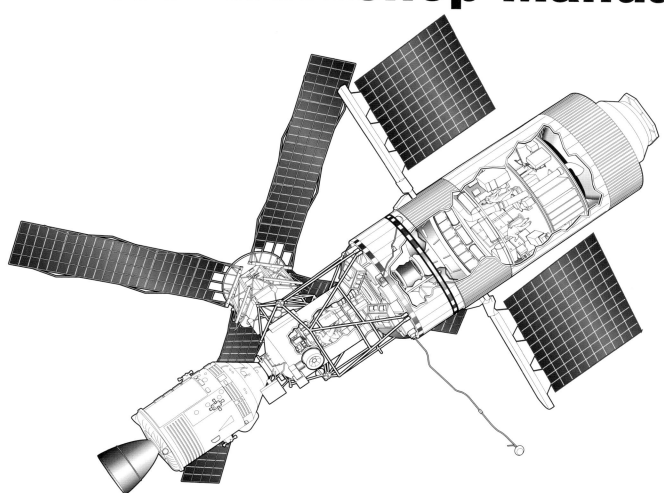

An insight into the history, design, development and operation
of the first US manned space station

David Baker

Contents

ABOVE From left, astronauts Parl Weitz, "Pete" Conrad and Joe Kerwin, the crew of the first manned visit to Skylab. Had it not been for their efforts at setting out a parasol shade for the exposed hull of the Orbital Workshop and freeing debris preventing the remaining Solar Array Wing from deploying, the station would have been a useless hulk. *(NASA)*

OPPOSITE Lift-off for the SL-4 mission on 16 November 1973, the last crewed visit to the Skylab space station. *(NASA)*

Introduction

In 1973 and 1974, NASA operated the world's first fully operational space station capable of hosting successive visits by separate crews of astronauts. Expanding the human presence in Earth orbit and pioneering the operation and management of an orbiting facility for experiments in science, technology and engineering, it was a unique example of optimum use of existing hardware. Using Apollo spacecraft and rockets developed to support Moon landings, Skylab became a one-of-a-kind research laboratory and gave NASA an early start in the management and operation of a manned space station in low Earth orbit.

Although Skylab was unique, and one of a kind, the fact that it did not mature into an evolved set of hardware fails to detract from its inherent usefulness, and in a legacy value built in to future research facilities for humans in space it was special. While the Russians began to develop long-duration flights themselves after Skylab was retired, NASA focused on a reusable transportation system, using Apollo-era ballistic capsules. This was capable of supporting research facilities in Spacelab modules from 1983, eventually playing the dominant role in building the International Space Station from 1998.

Many challenges faced by flight controllers and crew were unique to Skylab, however. Without the advantage of tracking and data relay satellites in geostationary orbits, the station was within range of any one of the 13 ground stations for only one-third of total flight time, with sustained periods of communications between only two and eleven minutes at most. This situation was exacerbated by the much higher orbital inclination for Skylab than for any of the previous Earth-orbiting missions for which the ground networks had been built. This took its toll on data harvesting and on systems monitoring.

Nevertheless, with a six-fold increase in NASA flight duration for a single crew, the Skylab contribution to understanding the physiological consequences of long-duration flight was significant. The ability of humans to operate effectively over long periods was also demonstrated, workloads increasing proportionate to the length of the mission. Moreover, without a human presence it would not have been possible to protect the hull of the Orbital Workshop from solar radiation after the meteoroid shield had been torn off shortly after launch; nor would it have been possible to remove debris from the sole remaining solar wing and achieve a 20% increase in man-hours spent aboard the orbiting complex over that planned pre-flight.

There are many ways of assessing the performance of any space programme and of measuring its value, but one way is to examine its legacy for future engineering, technology and scientific applications. On all those levels Skylab

OPPOSITE Clearly lacking a Solar Array System wing on the port side of the Skylab cluster, the Multiple Docking Adapter and Apollo Telescope Mount point toward the camera as the Apollo spacecraft conducts a fly-around inspection. *(NASA)*

BELOW Incorrectly labelled by NASA, the mission badges denoting Skylab I, II and III shown here referred to the manned launches. However, the official mission designations began with the unmanned launch of Skylab (SL-1) and progressed through successive manned flights (SL-2, SL-3 and SL-4. *(NASA)*

achieved a high performance and made a very important contribution to the development of computer and software programmes for the Shuttle era. Skylab began flying 17 months after the formal start of the Shuttle programme and provided a funded development platform for the computer systems that would be introduced on that vehicle.

Environmental data collection and Earth resource management became a hot topic in the United States during the 1970s. With the emergence of the world's first major commitment to reduce toxic pollutants and limit the indiscriminate use of natural systems on a global basis, resource inventories and land use management were greatly assisted by Skylab's Earth Resources Experiments Package (EREP) which partnered with the Landsat satellite series

began as the Earth Resources Technology Satellite (ERTS). Together, EREP and ERTS made a major contribution to awareness outside America that the planet's resources are finite and threatened by indiscriminate use.

Tentative experiments previously carried out aboard Apollo spacecraft led to interesting speculation on the ability to produce new materials and carry out research on the possibility of better and more targeted pharmaceutical products for combating major diseases. This work was conducted through a major series of experiments carried out for the first time aboard Skylab, with promising results. New mechanisms for using weightlessness as an asset were developed, pointing to the positive effects of zero-g rather than its negative effects, on human physiology for instance.

RIGHT The last Skylab crew look down upon the Orbital Workshop and the Apollo Telescope Mount, with the two protective solar shades installed by the first and second crews shielding the hull of the station from powerful solar arrays. *(NASA)*

The study of the physiological effects of weightlessness on the human body, establishment of a space-based environmental monitoring service and the possibilities opened up by microgravity research into materials processing were all tested and developed in the 12,351 man-days of space flight hosted by Skylab. All this work would feed directly into the Shuttle programme and to Spacelab, the joint endeavour between NASA and the European Space Agency, before application on the International Space Station.

Many books have been written about Skylab and there are copious accounts of the development and operating story of America's first space station – in fact, the *only* one built and operated solely by the United States. There are fewer books that explain in detail the engineering philosophy behind Skylab. This book provides what the author intends as the most detailed look yet at the design, layout and materials used in its fabrication and assembly, providing a detailed explanation of its constituent elements and the performance of the overall cluster.

There will probably never again be a single-launched space station, and Skylab was unique. Yet it was the first in several generations of habitat used by scientists, engineers and technicians, in space and on the ground, to better understand the space environment and to chart ways in which space flight could become routine, pointing the way forward to a permanently manned facility. Today, that facility is the International Space Station. And it all began with Skylab.

LEFT Alan Bean conducts an EVA, epitomising the breadth of scientific investigations at the Skylab space station, inside the separate modules and in the array of solar telescopes at the Apollo Telescope Mount *(NASA)*

Chapter One

Genesis

Humanity has sought to visit the planets and eventually travel to the stars from time immemorial. But the opportunity to live and work in space came only with the advent of the Space Age, when serious studies really began.

OPPOSITE Only through adaptation of the Saturn V developed for the Apollo missions to the Moon was the dream of building a station in space finally realised in the 1970s. *(NASA)*

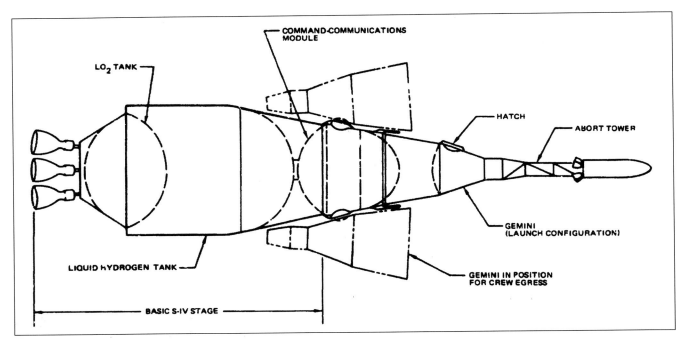

LO$_2$ TANK

COMMAND-COMMUNICATIONS MODULE

HATCH

ABORT TOWER

GEMINI
(LAUNCH CONFIGURATION)

LIQUID HYDROGEN TANK

GEMINI IN POSITION
FOR CREW EGRESS

BASIC S-IV STAGE

ABOVE Early proposals for the use of spent rocket stages for habitation after propellants had been vented and the tank pressurised began with the early large rockets, as depicted here by a proposal to use the spent cryogenic S-IV stage of a Saturn I rocket, with Gemini spacecraft employed to ferry crew and cargo between Earth and the makeshift space station. A Gemini spacecraft would be launched with the S-IV and a Command-Communications Module carried on top of the two-stage propellant tanks.
(Douglas Space Division)

Space stations have been implicitly linked to space travel from the earliest collective writings about reaching other worlds. Arguably the earliest published idea of a space station dates to the 16th century, when Romanian artillery officer Conrad Haas proposed a three-stage rocket capable of lifting a 'house' in which travellers could ride through space and observe the Earth – an extraordinary proposition for its day, illustrated and imagined in copious writings based on his knowledge of gunnery and Chinese rockets.

Ideas flourished and concepts far beyond any known technology of the day were developed. In 1897 the German Kurd Lasswitz spoke of a broad space programme in which humans would live in orbiting stations and in 1903 the Russian mathematics teacher Konstantin Tsiolkovsky developed the basic technical principles for rocket motors, multi-stage launch vehicles and orbiting space

stations. Taken further, in Germany in 1923 Hermann Oberth wrote down the first rudimentary theory for operating stations in space and by 1929 he had developed his station in great detail, adding construction methods and assembly techniques.

During the late 1920s and early 1930s space flight organisations were formed in the US, Russia, the UK and Germany, some carrying out practical tests in the development of rocketry, others carrying out theoretical studies and basic research while promoting the idea of space travel – astronautics. Immediately after the Second World War, one of the first exponents of space stations was the British Interplanetary Society (BIS), formed in 1933.

In 1945, BIS co-founder Arthur C. Clarke published in the magazine *Wireless World* his description of three manned orbiting platforms spaced at 120° intervals around the equator, relaying radio signals around the globe; later Clarke said these platforms could be unmanned and operated automatically. Three years later, in 1948, Harry E. Ross – another BIS Fellow – completed initial studies on a station concept based on a rotating, dish-shaped structure for the specific purpose of meteorology and astronomy. It was described in the January 1949 issue of the Society's journal.

By the dawn of the Space Age on 4 October 1957, when Russia launched Sputnik 1, scientists and engineers were already thinking about space stations. After the National Aeronautics & Space Administration (NASA) was established on 1 October 1958, and President Kennedy had committed America to sending men to the Moon in a speech to a joint session of Congress on 25 May 1961, serious planning for space stations got under way through what NASA called the Apollo Applications Program (AAP), in which a used rocket stage – the S-IVB, upper stage for the Saturn IB launch vehicle – could be fitted out in orbit and operated as a space station.

Known as a 'wet' workshop, because it would first propel itself into orbit before visiting crews would adapt it into an orbiting laboratory, it would be capable of supporting three crews and separate modules, some of which would support solar observations through an Apollo Telescope Mount (ATM). A special docking module would be attached to the top of the S-IVB stage through which astronauts could pass to access the spacious interior of the spent rocket stage.

By 1968 the AAP 'wet' workshop was seen as too limited for the objectives of what was emerging as a wide range of activities during and after the Moon missions, Apollo's primary purpose. The concept of a 'dry' workshop emerged in which the first two stages of a powerful Saturn V rocket would lift an S-IVB stage converted on the ground into a fully functional space station, the vastly greater lifting capability of the two-stage Saturn V allowing expansive growth in the size and weight of the modular attachments, especially the Apollo Telescope Mount.

Toward the end of the 1960s, with Kennedy's Moon goal clearly in sight, NASA looked more favourably at the 'dry' concept and the great advantages that would accrue from launching on a single rocket all the various elements of the AAP concept, versus the difficulties of converting a spent rocket stage in orbit. On 18 July 1969, two days after the launch of Apollo 11 – the first Moon landing mission – NASA Administrator Thomas O. Paine decided to make the shift to a 'dry' workshop, launched on a Saturn V, now redundant from the lunar landing initiative.

The plan now was to launch the workshop

cluster on the first two stages of AS-513, the 13th of 15 Saturn Vs built, and to send up three crews one at a time, the first visit lasting 28 days and the last two 56 days, with unmanned periods between visits. On 17 February 1970, with two Moon landing missions accomplished, NASA renamed the Apollo Applications Program as Skylab. Crews would visit the Skylab cluster in Block II Apollo Command and Service Module spacecraft launched by two-stage Saturn IB rockets, five of which had flown

BELOW During the evening of 19 August 1966, NASA manned space flight boss George Mueller penned this sketch of a converted S-IVB stage, a more power and re-engined successor to the S-IV. It depicts a converted Lunar Module used as an Apollo Telescope Mount (ATM) connected to the adapted stage by fluid and oxygen lines so that it could operate independently of the main station. *(NASA)*

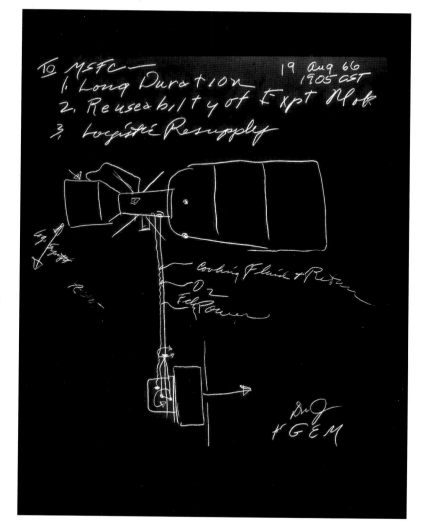

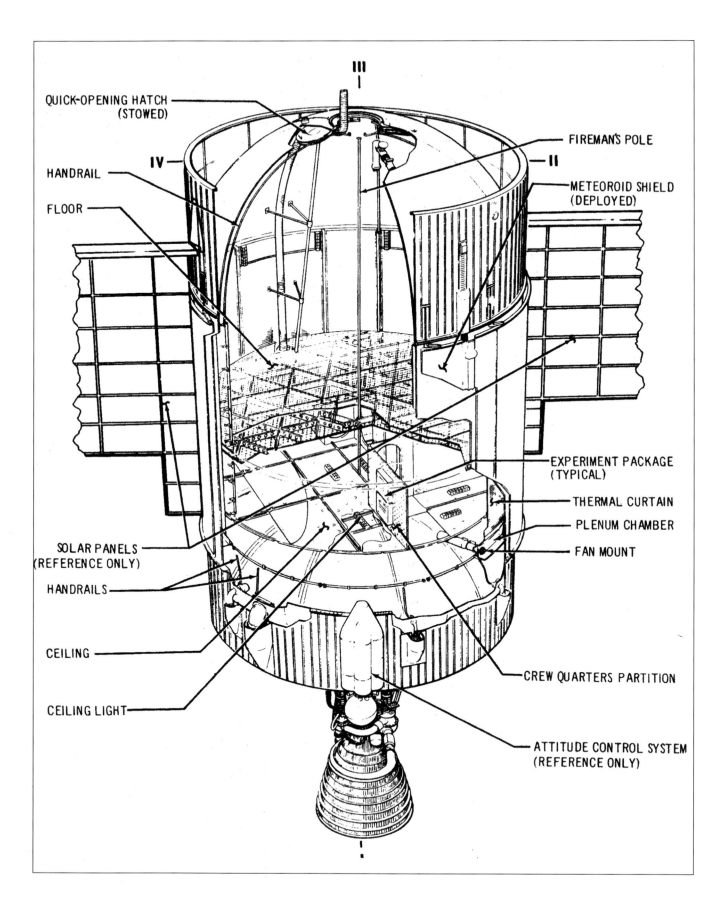

QUICK-OPENING HATCH
(STOWED)

HANDRAIL

FLOOR

III

IV

FIREMAN'S POLE

II

METEOROID SHIELD
(DEPLOYED)

EXPERIMENT PACKAGE
(TYPICAL)

THERMAL CURTAIN

PLENUM CHAMBER

FAN MOUNT

SOLAR PANELS
(REFERENCE ONLY)

HANDRAILS

CEILING

CEILING LIGHT

CREW QUARTERS PARTITION

ATTITUDE CONTROL SYSTEM
(REFERENCE ONLY)

before and most recently carried Apollo 7, the first manned spacecraft of this type, into orbit in October 1968.

The Block I version of Apollo had been used for unmanned tests and was to have carried the first Apollo crew into space, but they died in a tragic fire at Cape Canaveral on 27 January 1967. Modifications were made to improve quality control and safety and all subsequent Apollo spacecraft were of the Block II configuration. The outstanding weight-lifting capability of the Saturn V liberated engineers from the strictly limited capacity of the Saturn IB, relegating that smaller launch vehicle to lifting Apollo spacecraft and their three-man crews.

OPPOSITE The evolved concept envisaged a spent S-IVB stage, propelled into orbit off the spent first stage of a Saturn IB by a single J-2 engine, converted in space to a habitable workshop, pressurised with a breathable two-gas atmosphere, its liquid hydrogen tank divided into two sections for work (above) and for living (below). Note the configuration of the Solar Array System panels and the vertical interior poles thought necessary for controlling movement around the interior. *(Douglas Space Division)*

BELOW This 1966 artwork shows the configuration of the 'wet' workshop, so-called because it would have been launched with propellants to power the rocket motor that would propel it to orbit. Note the Apollo Telescope Mount with the square-shaped array of solar cells launched separately and docked to a radial port, opposite another module for long-duration Earth-pointing experiments and the Apollo spacecraft at the forward axial port. *(NASA)*

MS-G 93-4-66
15/AA 696

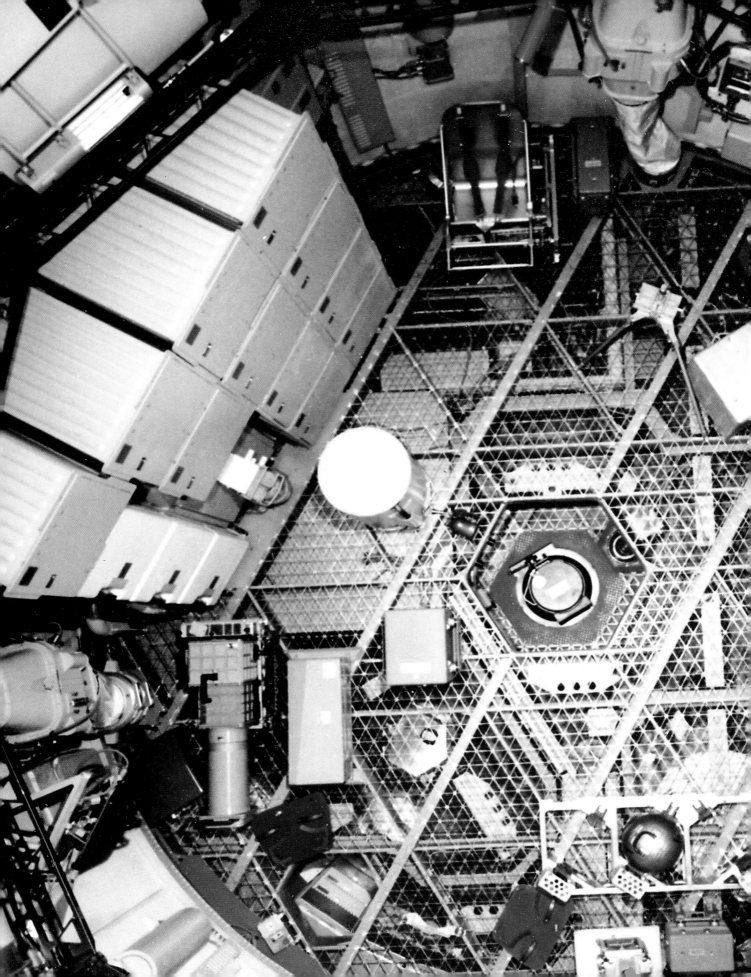

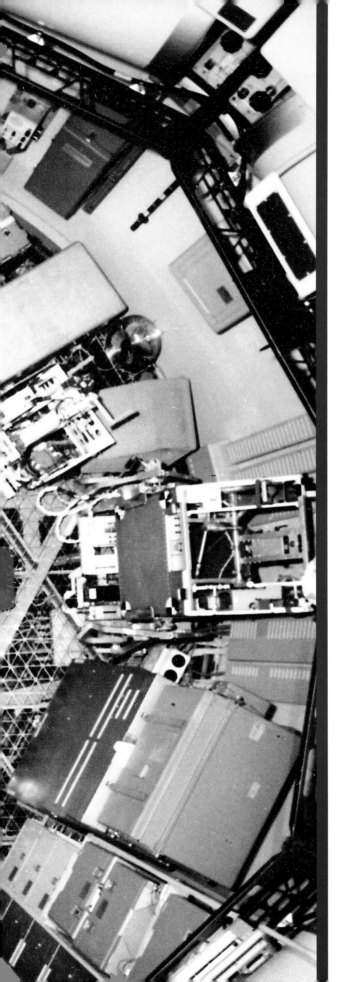

Chapter Two

Skylab
(1969–74)

— (●) —

America's first space station was a purpose-built facility, created out of the shell of a redundant rocket stage to which was added several unique modules and structures that would transform this use of Apollo hardware into a stunning success.

OPPOSITE A view looking down from the dome of the forward compartment, as might be seen when entering the OWS from the Airlock Module, with food lockers, storage bins and water tanks visible around the periphery. *(NASA)*

RIGHT The overall configuration of the 'dry' workshop with dimensional properties and primary elements carried into orbit by a two-stage Saturn V. Fully outfitted for immediate habitation and with provisions for 420 man-days of occupation, the definitive Skylab was a considerable advance in capability over the 'wet' workshop previously planned. *(NASA)*

RIGHT The overall configuration of the 'dry' workshop with dimensional properties and primary elements carried into orbit by a two-stage Saturn V. Fully outfitted for immediate habitation and with provisions for 420 man-days of occupation, the definitive Skylab was a considerable advance in capability over the 'wet' workshop previously planned. *(NASA)*

BELOW Manufacturer of the S-IV and S-IVB rocket stages, Douglas had considerable experience with studying the potential application of these stages as habitats for human occupation in space. This drawing was part of a 1960 configuration schematic with a lifting-body type ferry vehicle on the front. *(Douglas Space Division)*

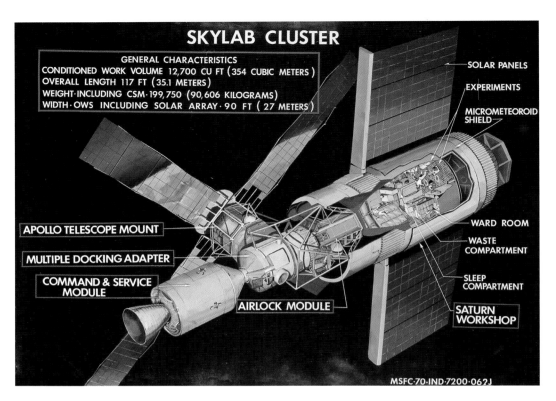

SKYLAB CLUSTER

GENERAL CHARACTERISTICS
CONDITIONED WORK VOLUME 12,700 CU FT (354 CUBIC METERS)
OVERALL LENGTH 117 FT (35.1 METERS)
WEIGHT·INCLUDING CSM·199,750 (90,606 KILOGRAMS)
WIDTH·OWS INCLUDING SOLAR ARRAY·90 FT (27 METERS)

SOLAR PANELS
EXPERIMENTS
MICROMETEOROID SHIELD
WARD ROOM
WASTE COMPARTMENT
SLEEP COMPARTMENT
SATURN WORKSHOP
AIRLOCK MODULE
COMMAND & SERVICE MODULE
MULTIPLE DOCKING ADAPTER
APOLLO TELESCOPE MOUNT

MSFC·70·IND·7200·062J

The Integrated Cluster

Skylab consisted of an Orbital Workshop (OWS), an Airlock Module (AM), a Multiple Docking Adapter (MDA) and an Apollo Telescope Mount (ATM), together with a truss assembly for securing the ATM to the cluster and a purpose-built Payload Shroud encapsulating the structures on top of the OWS. It would be launched on the first two stages of Saturn V AS-513 in an integrated configuration as Skylab-1 (SL-1), followed by three manned visits, SL-2, -3 and -4.

To appreciate the significance of opportunities afforded by shifting from the 'wet' OWS, launched by Saturn IB, to the 'dry' OWS on a two-stage Saturn V, in July 1969 the near-definitive AAP Saturn IB cluster provided a payload capability of 17,780kg (39,200lb) to an orbit of 407km (253 miles) at an inclination

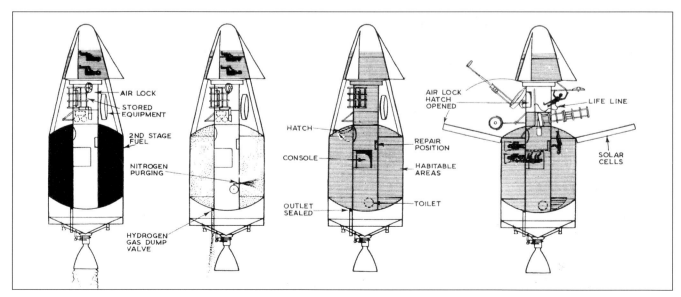

AIR LOCK
STORED EQUIPMENT
2ND STAGE FUEL
NITROGEN PURGING
HYDROGEN GAS DUMP VALVE

HATCH
CONSOLE
OUTLET SEALED

AIR LOCK HATCH OPENED
REPAIR POSITION
HABITABLE AREAS
TOILET

LIFE LINE
SOLAR CELLS

of 29°; in February 1972, the Saturn V provided a predicted payload capability of 96,492kg (212,725lb) to a 434km (270 miles) orbit at 50°.

Conversely, as expected, the Saturn IB lost some payload capability by going to the higher inclination orbit for crew delivery on SL-2, -3 and -4, presenting a limit of 16,880kg (37,200lb) to an initial orbit of 222 x 150km (138 x 93 miles). From there the Command and Service Module (CSM) would separate and begin rendezvous manoeuvres to arrive at the Skylab cluster. But this was more than sufficient for the CSM, which did not need to carry as much propellant as that required for a lunar mission, due to the much reduced demand placed on the Service Propulsion System.

Skylab was an integrated cluster of several separate elements and its support systems were dispersed across the four essential structures. Their detailed description can be found in the following relevant sections, but they were designed to operate as a single unit.

Electrical power for Skylab was provided by the Saturn V AS-513 Instrument Unit (IU), by the Apollo Command and Service Modules (CSM) and by the Skylab cluster itself. Power from the IU was provided for all activity from power-up on the ground to orbital insertion and separation from the launch vehicle, while the CSM provided electrical energy for each of the three manned visits from power-up on the ground until shut down to a quiescent state awaiting power-up for returning the crews to Earth. Power for Skylab throughout its mission came from the OWS-Solar Array System (OWS-SAS) attached to the Orbital Workshop and by the Apollo Telescope Mount Solar Array System (ATM-SAS), both of which would provide power generation.

Environmental control was likewise obtained by a set of systems and subsystems distributed between the Airlock Module and the OWS, an open-cycle system in which consumables were not reclaimed or reused. The habitable areas were pressurised to 34kN/m² (5lb/in²) by a mixture of 74% oxygen and 26% nitrogen. This mixture was based on the minimum pressurisation level for compatibility with the structural design of the cluster and the physiological requirement for a nitrogen admix so as to satisfy the requirements of the human body over periods of up to 56 days, envisaged

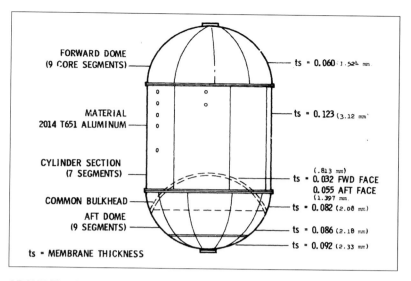

ABOVE The development of the S-IVB grew out of the S-IV, the world's first cryogenic rocket stage to be launched and operated in space, its essential elements being the liquid hydrogen and liquid oxygen tanks separated by a common bulkhead. *(Douglas Space Division)*

BELOW To the basic tank structure were added a forward skirt and an aft skirt carried on all S-IVB stages, but for Skylab the J-2 rocket motor would not be carried and dedicated elements such as the Solar Array System, the Thruster Attitude Control System and the space radiator were added. *(NASA)*

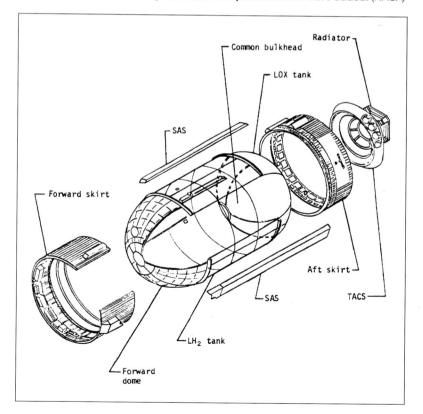

Sky lab

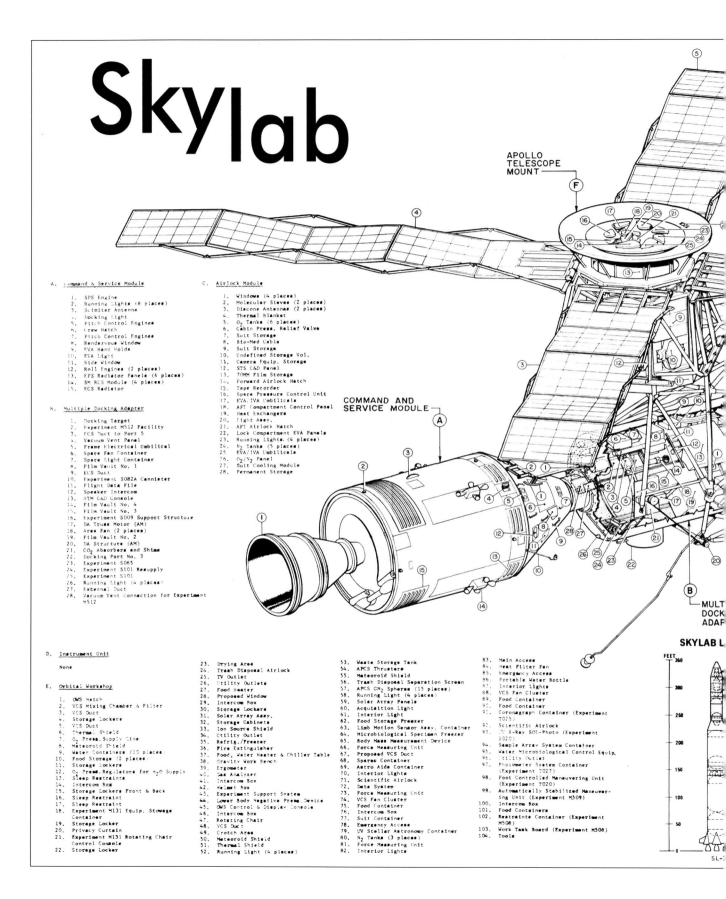

APOLLO
TELESCOPE
MOUNT — (F)

COMMAND AND
SERVICE MODULE — (A)

COMMAND AND
SERVICE MODULE

MULT
DOCK
ADAP — (B)

A. Command & Service Module

1. SPS Engine
2. Running Lights (8 places)
3. Scimitar Antenna
4. Docking Light
5. Pitch Control Engines
6. Crew Hatch
7. Pitch Control Engines
8. Rendezvous Window
9. EVA Hand Holds
10. EVA Light
11. Side Window
12. Roll Engines (2 places)
13. EPS Radiator Panels (6 places)
14. SM RCS Module (4 places)
15. ECS Radiator

B. Multiple Docking Adapter

1. Docking Target
2. Experiment M512 Facility
3. ECS Duct to Port 5
4. Vacuum Vent Panel
5. Frame Electrical Umbilical
6. Spare Fan Container
7. Spare Light Container
8. Film Vault No. 1
9. ECS Duct
10. Experiment S082A Cannister
11. Flight Data File
12. Speaker Intercom
13. ATM C&D Console
14. Film Vault No. 4
15. Film Vault No. 3
16. Experiment S009 Support Structure
17. DA Truss Motor (AM)
18. Area Fan (2 places)
19. Film Vault No. 2
20. DA Structure (AM)
21. CO₂ Absorbers and Shims
22. Docking Port No. 3
23. Experiment S065
24. Experiment S101 Resupply
25. Experiment S101
26. Running Light (4 places)
27. External Duct
28. Vacuum Vent Connection for Experiment M512

C. Airlock Module

1. Windows (4 places)
2. Molecular Sieves (2 places)
3. Discone Antennas (2 places)
4. Thermal Blanket
5. O₂ Tanks (6 places)
6. Cabin Press. Relief Valve
7. Suit Storage
8. Bio-Med Cable
9. Suit Storage
10. Undefined Storage Vol.
11. Camera Equip. Storage
12. STS C&D Panel
13. 70MM Film Storage
14. Forward Airlock Hatch
15. Tape Recorder
16. Spare Pressure Control Unit
17. EVA/IVA Umbilicals
18. AFT Compartment Control Panel
19. Heat Exchangers
20. Light Assy.
21. AFT Airlock Hatch
22. Lock Compartment EVA Panels
23. Running Lights (4 places)
24. N₂ Tanks (5 places)
25. EVA/IVA Umbilicals
26. O₂/N₂ Panel
27. Suit Cooling Module
28. Permanent Storage

D. Instrument Unit

None

E. Orbital Workshop

1. OWS Hatch
2. VCS Mixing Chamber & Filter
3. VCS Duct
4. Storage Lockers
5. VCS Duct
6. Thermal Shield
7. O₂ Press. Supply Line
8. Meteoroid Shield
9. Water Containers (10 places)
10. Food Storage (2 places)
11. Storage Lockers
12. O₂ Press. Regulators for H₂O Supply
13. Sleep Restraints
14. Intercom Box
15. Storage Lockers Front & Back
16. Sleep Restraint
17. Sleep Restraint
18. Experiment M131 Equip. Stowage Container
19. Storage Locker
20. Privacy Curtain
21. Experiment M131 Rotating Chair Control Console
22. Storage Locker
23. Drying Area
24. Trash Disposal Airlock
25. TV Outlet
26. Utility Outlets
27. Food Heater
28. Proposed Window
29. Intercom Box
30. Storage Lockers
31. Solar Array Assy.
32. Storage Cabinets
33. Ion Source Shield
34. Utility Outlet
35. Refrig./Freezer
36. Fire Extinguisher
37. Food, Water Heater & Chiller Table
38. Gravity Work Bench
39. Ergometer
40. Gas Analyzer
41. Helmet Box
42. Intercom Box
43. Experiment Support System
44. Lower Body Negative Press. Device
45. OWS Control & Display Console
46. Intercom Box
47. Rotating Chair
48. VCS Duct
49. Crotch Area
50. Meteoroid Shield
51. Thermal Shield
52. Running Light (4 places)
53. Waste Storage Tank
54. APCS Thrusters
55. Meteoroid Shield
56. Trash Disposal Separation Screen
57. APCS GN₂ Spheres (15 places)
58. Running Light (4 places)
59. Solar Array Panels
60. Acquisition Light
61. Interior Light
62. Food Storage Freezer
63. Limb Motion Sensor Assy. Container
64. Microbiological Specimen Freezer
65. Body Mass Measurement Device
66. Force Measuring Unit
67. Proposed VCS Duct
68. Spares Container
69. Astro Aids Container
70. Interior Lights
71. Scientific Airlock
72. Data System
73. Force Measuring Unit
74. VCS Fan Cluster
75. Food Container
76. Suit Container
77. Suit Container
78. Emergency Access
79. UV Stellar Astronomy Container
80. N₂ Tanks (3 places)
81. Force Measuring Unit
82. Interior Lights
83. Main Access
84. Heat Filter Fan
85. Emergency Access
86. Portable Water Bottle
87. Interior Lights
88. VCS Fan Cluster
89. Food Container
90. Food Container
91. Coronagraph Container (Experiment T025)
92. Scientific Airlock
93. UV X-Ray Sol-Photo (Experiment S020)
94. Sample Array System Container
95. Water Microbiological Control Equip.
96. Utility Outlet
97. Photometer System Container (Experiment T027)
98. Foot Controlled Maneuvering Unit (Experiment T020)
99. Automatically Stabilized Maneuvering Unit (Experiment M509)
100. Intercom Box
101. Food Containers
102. Restraints Container (Experiment M508)
103. Work Task Board (Experiment M508)
104. Tools

SKYLAB L

FEET
360
300
250
200
150
100
50
0

SL-

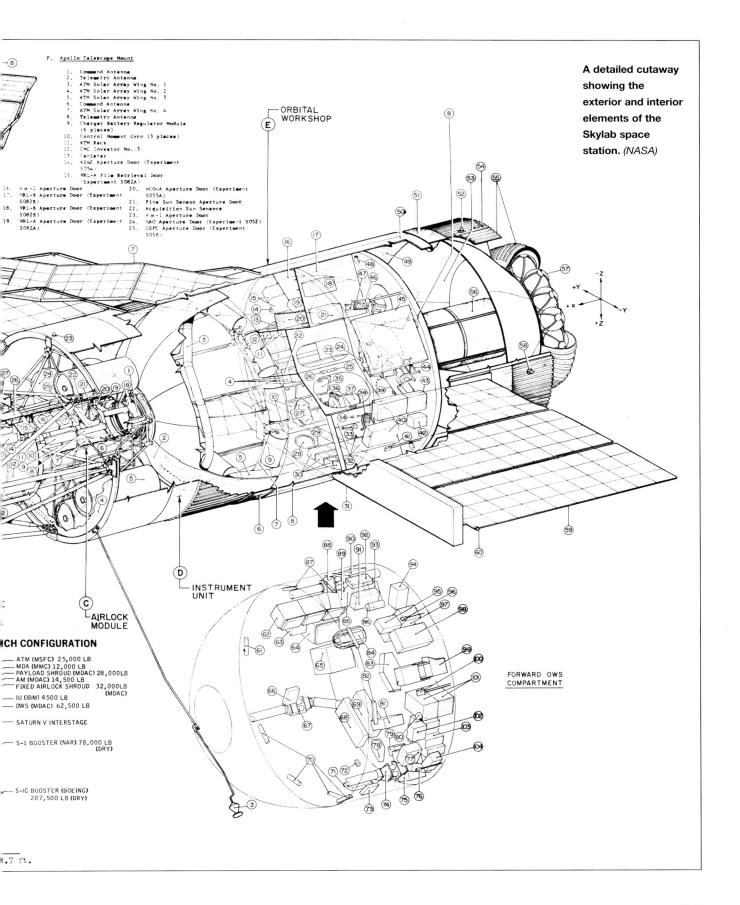

F. Apollo Telescope Mount

1. Command Antenna
2. Telemetry Antenna
3. ATM Solar Array Wing No. 1
4. ATM Solar Array Wing No. 2
5. ATM Solar Array Wing No. 3
6. Command Antenna
7. ATM Solar Array Wing No. 4
8. Telemetry Antenna
9. Charger Battery Regulator Module (6 places)
10. Control Moment Gyro (3 places)
11. ATM Rack
12. CMG Inventor No. 3
13. Canister
14. AS&E Aperture Door (Experiment S054)
15. NRL-A Film Retrieval Door (Experiment S082A)
16. Hα-2 Aperture Door
17. NRL-B Aperture Door (Experiment S082B)
18. NRL-B Aperture Door (Experiment S082B)
19. NRL-A Aperture Door (Experiment S082A)
20. HCO-A Aperture Door (Experiment S055A)
21. Fine Sun Sensor Aperture Door
22. Acquisition Sun Sensors
23. Hα-1 Aperture Door
24. HAO Aperture Door (Experiment S052)
25. GSFC Aperture Door (Experiment S056)

— ORBITAL
  WORKSHOP

E

A detailed cutaway showing the exterior and interior elements of the Skylab space station. *(NASA)*

D — INSTRUMENT
    UNIT

C
 — AIRLOCK
   MODULE

CH CONFIGURATION

— ATM (MSFC) 25,000 LB
— MDA (MMC) 12,000 LB
— PAYLOAD SHROUD (MDAC) 28,000LB
— AM (MDAC) 14,500 LB
— FIXED AIRLOCK SHROUD 32,000LB (MDAC)

— IU (IBM) 4500 LB
— OWS (MDAC) 62,500 LB

— SATURN V INTERSTAGE

— S-1 BOOSTER (NAR) 78,000 LB (DRY)

— S-IC BOOSTER (BOEING) 287,500 LB (DRY)

.7 ft.

FORWARD OWS
COMPARTMENT

RIGHT The scientific
purpose of Skylab was
to satisfy investigators
in solar astronomy,
Earth resources and
materials processing,
and in the effects of
long-duration flight
on the human body.
(NASA)

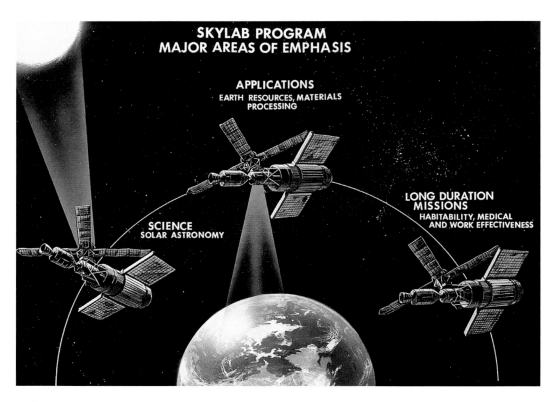

at the outset as the maximum duration. Relative humidity would be controlled to about 26% at 30°C (86°F), while the carbon dioxide level would be kept to a maximum pressure level of 0.70kN/m² (0.0115lb/in²), or 0.23%. Maximum sound levels in all areas would be limited to a summed total of 72dB, about the level of a busy office.

Because Skylab was a scientific laboratory designed to study the Sun, the Earth and celestial space, instruments for these experiments were located at places that could provide proper viewing directions with a minimum of manoeuvring. Active and continuous control of attitude was designed in from the outset, so that instruments pointed in the desired direction during operation, while allowing the energy-producing solar arrays to point so as to gain acceptable, if not maximum, solar energy for as long as possible.

The most demanding pointing requirements for the instruments in the Apollo Telescope Mount were obtained by gimbal mounting of the ATM canister within the ATM rack, with the attitude of Skylab controlled by the Attitude Control & Pointing System (ACPS). Its function included rotating the cluster to the desired orientation, holding that alignment for as long

as necessary, and providing high-precision pointing control for the ATM. To achieve this, the ACPS employed sensors to reach existing attitude with respect to reference directions and a mechanism to change the attitude in a controlled fashion.

To achieve this, Skylab carried rate gyroscopes measuring the rate of angular rotation of Skylab around each of the three principal axes, and by integrating these rates over a given time the angular changes could be obtained. Reference directions were provided by the Sun and star seekers, the former monitoring the solar reference direction aimed at the centre of the solar disc, the latter aiming at one of three stars, preferably Canopus in the southern constellation Argus.

Changes in cluster attitude could be made by either the Control Moment Gyroscope (CMG) system, or the nitrogen-fuelled Thruster Attitude Control System (TACS). Located in the Apollo Telescope Mount, the CMG system – consisting of three large gyroscopes mounted with mutually perpendicular axes – was the primary method of control. The TACS system controlled Skylab in the more conventional manner of using thrusters to change attitude, expelling gas and inducing a reaction according to the axis in the reciprocal direction to the line of thrust. The TACS system was mounted at the base of the Orbital Workshop.

The amount of data that was to be gathered by the instruments aboard Skylab, and which had to be returned to Earth, posed a complex problem divided into two challenges: the transfer of film, tapes, emulsion plates, surface samples, biomedical specimens, log books and notes to the ground; and the transmission of data such as audio crew communications, telemetry and video signals. Physical data could be brought back in the Apollo Command Module (CM), with electronic information sent through a system of transmitters and receivers on Skylab and in the Spacecraft Tracking and Data Network (STDN).

The STDN consisted of 13 tracking stations, 11 of them fixed, one shipborne and one airborne. Real-time telemetry would be available about 25% of the time, with an average contact duration of 6.5 minutes per station; delayed time data and voice would be recorded on board and transmitted over a ground station. The playback system had the ability to dump two hours of data in 5.45min. Periodic TV transmission for the five ATM cameras and for the portable TV cameras would be achieved through the frequency-modulated S-band link on the Apollo CSM. A video tape recorder was available in the Multiple Docking Adapter, and the portable colour cameras – either hand-held or bracket-mounted – had 525-scan lines at 30 frames per second, capable of operating over a wide range of light levels.

In every critical element of electrical power, habitability, attitude control and data gathering, Skylab posed unique challenges and introduced technology new to the science and engineering of manned space vehicles. The challenges posed by the need to provide sufficient food for the planned 420 man-days were unique and would never again be so difficult to overcome. Breaking away from the unsavoury combinations of visually unrecognisable food that passed the test for human consumption in Mercury, Gemini and Apollo, Skylab crew members would receive culinary delights that were unprecedented.

The pioneering departure from tube-squeezed food prevalent in Apollo came with

the flight of Borman, Lovell and Anders to lunar orbit at Christmas 1968. A surprise food package gave each Apollo 8 crew member a welcome festive meal of natural turkey, brown gravy, bright red cranberry apple sauce and a conventional spoon with which to eat it. That 'experiment' from the NASA food laboratories

BELOW Unlike previous manned space flight on Earth-orbit missions, Skylab would fly with a higher orbital inclination to cover larger areas of the inhabited planet for resource monitoring. This compromised the sustained communications when the station flew away from the network of ground stations previously set up for earlier missions in the Mercury and Gemini programmes. *(NASA)*

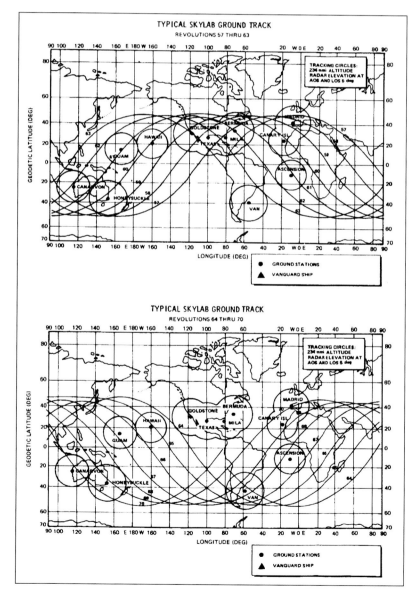

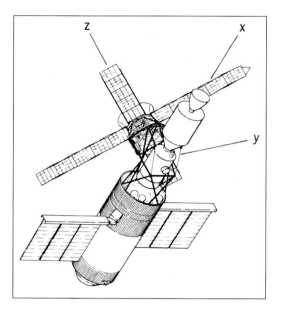

RIGHT The attitude reference for Skylab adopted the same conventions as those used for earlier space vehicles, with pitch, roll and yaw axes as displayed here. (NASA)

BELOW Saturn IB was the launch vehicle employed to deliver the three crew members on each of the three manned visits to Skylab. The launch vehicle was a developed version of the Saturn I and had flown five times previously, testing unmanned Apollo spacecraft, lifting the first unmanned Lunar Module and flying the first manned Apollo mission. (NASA)

broke new ground and proved that it was possible to serve tasty, familiar food and to eat it with conventional utensils in zero gravity. Following on the heels of that breakthrough in food technology, Skylab crew members would have a relatively attractive menu typically including cold cereals, potato salad, shrimp cocktail, filet mignon, mashed potatoes, pie and liquids such as coffee, tea, instant breakfast, grape and orange drink, cocoa and lemonade. The fluids were served up on squeezable containers and sipped through drinking tubes.

Areas of habitation would divide the cluster into a dedicated living space and a succession of connected workspaces forward, for dedicated activities and stations where crew members could carry out complex scientific and engineering activities impossible to conduct in any space vehicle launched to this date. Life would be as normal as it ever could be in a weightless environment, with a galley containing food compartments, refrigerators, freezers and food trays, a table where three crew members could meet and eat, and a toilet more conventional than anything flown before, offering a degree of normality to the essential functions of living and working in a confined space.

For habitability and the examination of physiological and psychological response to extended stays in orbit, Skylab was an experiment uniquely placed to afford large areas for functional and recreational activity similar to that envisaged for space stations that were planned to follow it into space. Much would be learned, about the ability of humans to spend long periods in orbit, about the design of future stations and the optimisation of work schedules, flight plans and the division of labour into 'housekeeping' functions, general maintenance and science activity. Only the very median level of concerted planning could be laid out before flight, because nobody knew how the mission would unfold across the three separate expeditions.

Considerable attention was given to the aesthetic appearance of the interior, consideration being given to the psychological welfare of the crew and to the need for a relaxed environment during off-duty hours. For that reason, a permanently located tape recorder was provided for monaural or stereophonic playback of pre-recorded tape cassettes through speakers or headsets. For individual use, headsets with headphones were provided with earpieces for connection to the tape player, a total of 48 cassettes of material selected by the crew being launched aboard Skylab.

For relaxation, four decks of playing cards were provided along with five card deck retainers to permit card playing in zero gravity. The retainer held the cards in place as a deck, or individually for player use, the cards being played normally at the food table with the tabletop in place. In addition, 36 paperback books selected by the crew made up the on-board library. For fun, 12 darts and a dartboard were stowed. The darts were standard darts with Velcro hooks substituting for the pointed shaft and the dart board was fitted with Velcro hooks for attachment at selected locations, the front face being a Velcro pile superimposed on a standard target face.

In addition to the bicycle ergometer for exercise (which see), each crew member was provided with an isometric exerciser for in-flight exercising. Six hand exercisers, shaped to fit the hand, were available for frequent use as a means of maintaining hand-grip strength in weightlessness. A pair of binoculars was available for casual viewing of the Earth below, and plastic-covered foam balls were available that would prove popular with some crews.

Its spacious volume dictated by the capacious liquid hydrogen tank of the S-IVB stage, adapted and supplemented by additional fixed structures to expand the habitable space available for work and rest, Skylab afforded a unique opportunity to carry out its primary function: unprecedented levels of scientific work and investigation. But it also placed demands on the ground support infrastructure, both through the planning phases for each expedition and on the day-to-day timeline worked out by Mission Control and prosecuted by each crew. It was to place unprecedented demands on Mission Control, if only due to the extended duration of each mission.

Whereas the timelines of previous Apollo lunar flights were dictated largely by the dynamics of the mission and the relative phasing of the Earth and the Moon, Skylab

crew members would operate on a rhythmical timeline keeping step with Houston local time on a 24-hour cycle. Each 'day' of 24 Earth hours would typically consist of eight hours for experiment and work, eight hours for eating, personal hygiene and general systems housekeeping duties, and eight hours for sleep and rest. Some shifting in these cycles would be required during periods when, for instance, a particular crew member was required to attend to a specific instrument.

The crew were also expected to conduct Extra-Vehicular Activity (EVA), to retrieve or replace cassettes of film and other instruments outside the pressurised volume, most notably on the Apollo Telescope Mount. Advance planning, conceptual at best due to the shifting requirements of long-duration activities, envisaged a single EVA on Day 26 of the first (28-day) visit to retrieve an experiment designed to study the effect of the vacuum of space on thermal coatings, as well as to change ATM film. Additional EVAs were anticipated for changing film, three on the second (56-day) expedition and two on the third (56-day) visit. Each spacewalk would involve two suited crew members, one to go outside and the other to stand by ready to assist.

Uniquely, Skylab had a backup plan in case the astronauts were in danger of being stranded if an Apollo spacecraft that had carried a crew to the cluster, and remained docked thereafter until called upon to return them to Earth, should

ABOVE In this dual exposure, the AS-513 Saturn V (left) was the only one to fly in a two-stage configuration and had conducted 12 launches prior to carrying Skylab into orbit, its last mission. For supporting the three crew-delivery flights, the second Saturn V launch pad was used to send the Saturn IB/Apollo into space, carried on a 'milk stool' to make the upper elements compatible with the upper swing arms of the launch tower. *(NASA)*

scenarios where a second Saturn V/Apollo assembly could have been launched to rescue a crew stranded in lunar orbit, for instance.

For cost and scheduling reasons, it had not been possible to provide a rescue system during the Moon landing programme and it had not been implemented; the multiplicity of ways a crew could become stranded would call for a specifically and uniquely configured launch vehicle and spacecraft and in the time available to activate such a rescue the consumables on the imperilled Apollo would have run out. The nearly disastrous mission of Apollo 13, however, reintroduced the possibility of mounting a rescue for the Earth-orbiting Skylab programme.

Skylab's ample supplies and long-duration life-support capability made it possible to use the cluster as a safe haven while a resident crew waited out the period of time necessary to effect a rescue. The only contingency which could be met, however, was that of a failed CSM docked to the cluster, either by it being unable to operate at all, or because it could not de-orbit and return the crew. In either instance, a rescue Apollo CSM modified to carry five crew members back from Skylab would be launched with a two-man crew. This would require removal of storage lockers and the installation of two additional crew couches beneath the three existing seats.

The amount of time required to mount a rescue would depend upon the time when

ABOVE Control functions for the launch vehicle were administered by the Instrument Unit, mounted on the top of the S-IVB forward skirt assembly and containing computers and electronic equipment for managing the sequence of events required to deliver the station to orbit. Each IU varied. This one was flown on the first Saturn V launched on 9 November 1967. *(NASA-KSC)*

prove inoperative when needed. There had been historical concerns about astronauts stranded in space, and the Apollo Moon programme had supported several mission

RIGHT Unsung heroes of almost every mission ever launched by NASA, the Goddard Space Flight Center is the home of the agency's space tracking and data network, without which the scientific value of Skylab would have been considerably reduced. Established in 1959, it is the core of NASA's space science and Earth observations programmes. *(NASA)*

the emergency developed, and if it happened on the first day of occupying Skylab it would take 48 days to launch a rescue, including 22 days required to refurbish the launch tower at LC-39B at the Kennedy Space Center. During this period the specially modified rescue kit would be installed in the CSM, a task that would take about eight hours. The amount of preparation time would reduce down to 28 days at the end of the first manned visit, or 10 days at the end of the third mission.

For the first two expeditions the next vehicle in flow would be rapidly prepared for a rescue, and for the third visit a backup Saturn IB/CSM would be on standby should it be required. Prior to arrival at the cluster, the Skylab crew would install a special spring-loaded device to separate the disabled CSM from the axial port of the MDA. But this was not essential because the rescue vehicle could dock at the radial port on the Multiple Docking Adapter (which see) and, if necessary, conduct a full rescue activity from there, despite it being a contingency location.

Orbital Workshop

The primary structure of the Skylab cluster was the Orbital Workshop (OWS), the converted Saturn S-IVB stage designed and manufactured by McDonnell Douglas Astronautics Company's Western Division for the Saturn IB AS-212 launch vehicle. A second S-IVB, produced for the Saturn V AS-515 vehicle, was outfitted as a backup, albeit with the original intention of flying it as Skylab B. In the event that a second Skylab was flown, it would have been launched on the first two stages of Saturn V AS-515.

The function of the OWS was to provide living and work accommodation for the crew,

experiment installation, stowage for supplies and to support approximately one half of Skylab's electrical power. It also supported the Thruster Attitude Control System (TACS) for primary attitude control through the Control Moment Gyroscopes (CMGs) installed on the Apollo Telescope Mount. Because it had to be adapted from a stage already manufactured, it had to receive various modifications to convert it to the special requirements of the Skylab programme, as noted overleaf.

LEFT The S-IVB selected for conversion to the Orbital Workshop was the stage assigned to AS-212. It can be seen here with the paint patterns together with an excellent view of the TACS spheres and the radiator. With assembly completed in 1967, by McDonnell Douglas at Huntington Beach, California, S-IVB-212 received the J-2 engine assigned to it (J-2103). However, it was never test fired in the stage, which remained in storage between 3 November 1967 and 26 March 1969, when the J-2 was removed and modifications began for its conversion to the OWS. *(NASA)*

RIGHT The size of the liquid hydrogen tank of the S-IVB is evident from this view showing technicians at work removing cryogenic insulation panelling. All equipment fitted to the interior of the tank would have to come through the 101.6cm (40in) circular opening that would allow crew access from the Airlock Module, most of it in sections to be assembled on the inside of the OWS. *(Douglas Space Division)*

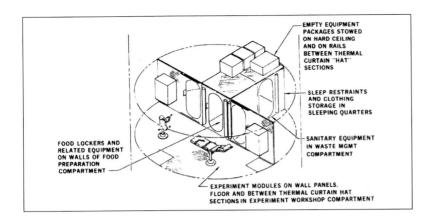

EMPTY EQUIPMENT
PACKAGES STOWED
ON HARD CEILING
AND ON RAILS
BETWEEN THERMAL
CURTAIN "HAT"
SECTIONS

SLEEP RESTRAINTS
AND CLOTHING
STORAGE IN
SLEEPING QUARTERS

SANITARY EQUIPMENT
IN WASTE MGMT
COMPARTMENT

FOOD LOCKERS AND
RELATED EQUIPMENT
ON WALLS OF FOOD
PREPARATION
COMPARTMENT

EXPERIMENT MODULES ON WALL PANELS,
FLOOR AND BETWEEN THERMAL CURTAIN HAT
SECTIONS IN EXPERIMENT WORKSHOP COMPARTMENT

As the second stage of the Saturn IB and the third stage of Saturn V, the basic S-IVB rocket stage had a length of 18m (59.1ft) and a diameter of 6.64m (21.67ft). It consisted of two separate propellant tanks, the larger of the two designed to contain liquid hydrogen fuel, which occupied the forward section, and the lower tank with liquid oxygen. The two were separated by a common semi-hemispherical bulkhead, with hemispherical domes occupying each end of the S-IVB. The stage was equipped with a single Rocketdyne J-2 engine with a

ABOVE For comparisons with the definitive interior, this layout was an early proposal before specialist interior design consultants were employed to suggest a better and more functional distribution of the four essential areas in the lower compartment: sleeping quarters, galley, waste management area and experiments section. *(NASA-MSFC)*

RIGHT This sectional cutaway of the Orbital Workshop shows the layout as fitted to Skylab, including the general arrangement of the converted hydrogen tank for habitation and the use of the oxygen tank as a waste compartment. *(NASA-MSFC)*

ENVIRONMENTAL
CONTROL SYSTEM

SKYLAB STUDENT
EXPERIMENT
ED-52 WEB FORMATION
OPERATIONAL MODE

FOOD FREEZER

FORWARD
COMPARTMENT

FRENCH
ULTRA-VIOLET
EXPERIMENT

EARTH OBSERVATION
WINDOW

WARD ROOM

SKYLAB STUDENT
EXPERIMENTS

FOOD TABLE

EXPERIMENT
COMPARTMENT

WASTE DISPOSAL

SHOWER

ENTRY HATCH &
AIRLOCK INTERFACE

LOCKER STOWAGE

WATER SUPPLY

WASTE MGT ODOR
FILTER

BODY WEIGHT DEVICE

WASTE
MANAGEMENT
COMP
FECAL-URINE
SAMPLING

SLEEP
COMPARTMENT

WASTE TANK

MICROMETEROID
SHIELD

RADIATOR

thrust of 1,000.8kN (225,000lb), to provide the terminal propulsion phase for achieving orbit. This engine was also used, in a cluster of five, for the second stage of the Saturn V and would be responsible for placing Skylab in orbit – the first D-II stage to do so.

As the OWS for Skylab, the essential structural configuration remained the same as that for a rocket stage but with different functions. The pressurised interior of the OWS was divided into a forward compartment and a crew compartment, separated by an aluminium open-grid floor/ceiling with a central cut-out for movement between the two. The total volume was 292m³ (10,426ft³). The forward and aft dome assemblies were 6.64m (21.67ft) in diameter and fabricated from 2014-T651 aluminium.

The cylinder of the main tank was of similar diameter and had a length of 8.82m (22.38ft), machined from 2014-T651 aluminium with integral machined ribs to form a 45° waffle pattern for stiffening. The common bulkhead between the two propellant tanks was 6.64m (21.67ft) in diameter as a partial hemisphere

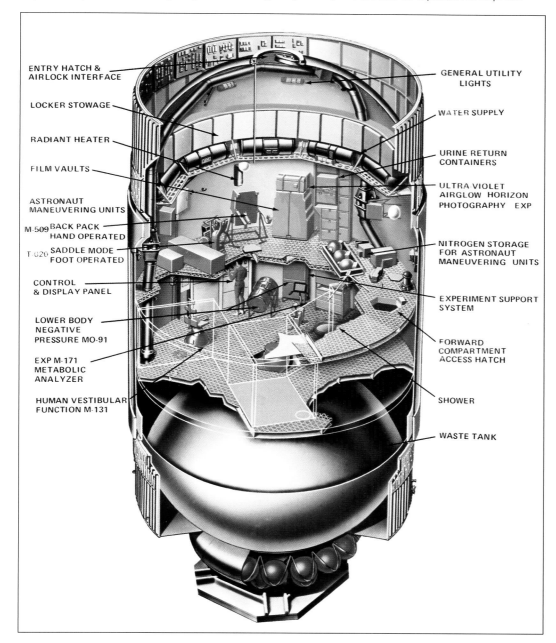

ENTRY HATCH & AIRLOCK INTERFACE

LOCKER STOWAGE

RADIANT HEATER

FILM VAULTS

ASTRONAUT MANEUVERING UNITS

M-509 BACK PACK HAND OPERATED

T-020 SADDLE MODE FOOT OPERATED

CONTROL & DISPLAY PANEL

LOWER BODY NEGATIVE PRESSURE MO-91

EXP M-171 METABOLIC ANALYZER

HUMAN VESTIBULAR FUNCTION M-131

GENERAL UTILITY LIGHTS

WATER SUPPLY

URINE RETURN CONTAINERS

ULTRA VIOLET AIRGLOW HORIZON PHOTOGRAPHY EXP

NITROGEN STORAGE FOR ASTRONAUT MANEUVERING UNITS

EXPERIMENT SUPPORT SYSTEM

FORWARD COMPARTMENT ACCESS HATCH

SHOWER

WASTE TANK

LEFT Viewed from the other side, this cutaway displays the experiments in the living area and those in the forward compartment together with associated systems and subsystems as described in the following chapters. *(NASA-MSFC)*

with a forward and aft face of 2014-T651 aluminium separated by 4.445cm (1.75in) thick layers of 0.445cm (0.18in) hexcell fibreglass honeycomb bonded to each face. This was attached to the aft dome and separated the habitable area from the lower (oxygen) tank that was adopted as a waste tank.

The main skin of the cylindrical tank section was 3.12mm (0.123in) thick and assembled from seven circular segments, but each of the hemispherical end domes was fabricated from nine segments (gores). The top dome had a thickness of 1.524mm (0.60in) while the lower dome at the base of the oxygen tank was divided into three separate circular sections. The topmost section, where it mated with the main cylindrical tank, had a thickness of 2.08mm (0.082in), the middle section was 2.18mm (0.086in) thick, while the lower domical section was 2.33mm (0.092in) thick.

The walls of the habitation area were insulated with 3D polyurethane foam tiles, while the forward face of the common bulkhead was covered in 1D foam and added, on top of the 3D foam, to the aft dome and the lower 50.8cm (20in) of the cylinder. Special flammability requirements, heightened as a result of the Apollo fire, imposed a fire-retardant coating of 0.076mm (0.003in) aluminium foil bonded over the insulation in the forward dome and the cylinder. The aft dome and the common bulkhead insulation were covered with 0.127mm (0.005in) foil, and the foil on the

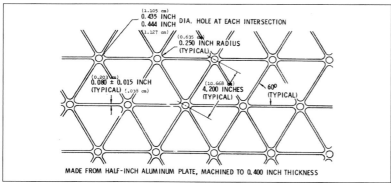

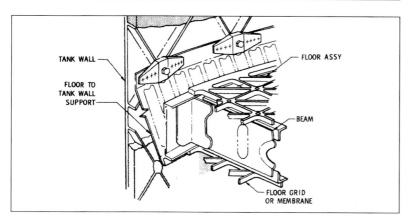

SATURN WORKSHOP 1-G TRAINER
CREW QUARTERS

WARDROOM/GALLEY

EXPERIMENTS OPERATION AREA

WASTE MANAGEMENT

SLEEP COMPARTMENT

LEFT This overhead view of the living compartment mock-up and facilities trainer shows the general distribution of the facilities and the arrangement of fixed experiment equipment. They were arranged in a logical sequence from sleep, to wash, to eat, to work. *(NASA-MSFC)*

forward dome and cylinder was coated with coloured Teflon for interior colour plans.

Attachment of floor supports, water bottles, Active Control System (ACS) fan supports, equipment supports and electrical bonding strap attachment holes were drilled in the waffle rib intersections to a maximum depth of 1.687cm (0.625in), these being tapped for threads for bolts or studs. Phenolic discs with a nutplate attachment were bonded to the insulation with

CENTRE Several features of the Skylab interior displayed lessons applied as a result of the Apollo fire, and flexible and rigid troughs were provided to maintain safety for electrical bundles and pipes and conduits. This view shows the configuration of a rigid trough connection. *(NASA-MSFC)*

RIGHT Here, both rigid and flexible trough paths are displayed with typical locations. Rigid troughs have fireproof metal covers, flexible troughs have bellows-like covers which are also fireproof. *(NASA-MSFC)*

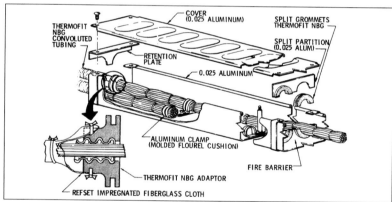

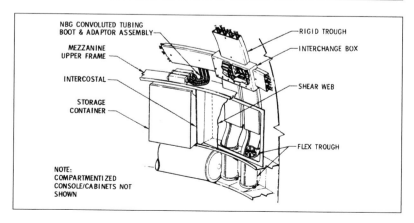

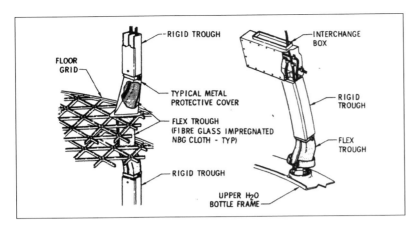

OWS, was 90.17cm (35.5in) by 132cm (52in), retained by 224 bolts.

Openings into the cylindrical and domical structure occasioned by its use as a rocket stage were sealed or had the capability of being re-sealed once opened. Two electrical feed openings were included in the forward dome. In addition, specific to Skylab, the OWS had unique openings for two scientific airlocks, a viewing window, an access panel, six helium ports and a refrigeration feed. The existing helium ports were closed off and sealed, four of which were covered with 2.54cm (1in) thick 3D foam insulation and then covered with a layer of fibreglass cloth, a layer of 0.127mm (0.005in) aluminium foil and a single layer of Teflon-coated foil. A single blind flange had a tube welded in to provide access to a water line.

One port provided for a TV coaxial cable installed in a hole in the blind flange, with insulation provided by a box assembly of 6061-T6 aluminium filled with a flexible polyurethane foam. The sixth helium port was closed by a refrigeration line attached by a Marman gasket and coupling. The existing ports had a local skin thickness of 0.541cm (0.213in), and a 16.179cm (6.37in) diameter circular hole was cut in the wall and had a special fitting installed using lock bolts and a silicone sealant.

Several penetrations in the aft dome were closed off. The lower (liquid oxygen) tank would be used as a waste container, taking trash from

ABOVE Trough routes through the floor grid (left) and at the upper section of the forward dome where the water containers were attached to a bottle frame penetrated for flexible trough routing. *(NASA-MSFC)*

adhesive to which other equipment, wiring, conduits and experiments could be supported. Two layers of fibreglass liner were bonded over the discs, approximately 1,450 being bonded to the habitation tank wall area.

The external surface area of the cylinder was covered with a gold-coated, pressure-sensitive Polyimide tape, except for the area underneath the main tunnel, the inner surface only of which was also covered with this tape. A side access panel was designed into the stage to allow personnel to enter the OWS during manufacture and pre-launch activity so as to install and assemble equipment, service the station and conduct checkout and provisioning activity. There was to be no entry when the vehicle was on the launch pad but the design allowed for contingency access. The panel itself, allowing access to the lower accommodation area in the

RIGHT Crew quarters with (left to right) the galley, waste management compartment and sleeping quarters. This diagram and others in this chapter are from photographic files documenting various levels of finish and relative location of equipment. *(NASA)*

SKYLAB WORKSHOP
CREW QUARTERS

crew activity through an airlock in the floor of the habitable section. It had a total volume of 62.5m³ (2,233ft³) and vent ports were installed 180° from each other, 131.445cm (51.75in) aft of the dome cylinder joint and 18° from position I towards position II and from position III towards IV (see diagram on page 34). These vent ports were fabricated from 6061-T651 aluminium, attached to the aft dome waste-tank wall with adhesives and lock bolts. These were sealed with a silicone sealant, and the vent system sealed with an O-ring. Attached by bolts, the vent system was supported by a port fitting extending through a hole in the aft skirt, with directional adjustment provided by two tapered rings.

A forward entry hatch to the OWS was located centrally in the forward dome, providing access to and from the Airlock Module and serving as a structural element, carrying pressure loads during the boost phase to orbit. It also acted as the aft airlock hatch during EVAs and had a diameter of 101.6cm (40in). Located in the centre of the hatch it was operated manually using one hand, requiring a load of 11.3kg (25lb), its two functions being pressure equalisation and the latching and unlatching action. Pressure equalisation was achieved through nine 0.06cm (0.025in) diameter holes. The release handle locked and unlocked the hatch handle to prevent inadvertent activation.

In normal operating mode, pressure equalisation both sides of the hatch was required prior to opening the hatch proper, which was designed to swing into the habitation area and lock into its stowed position on the forward dome wall. Because the habitation area was sensitive to pressure differentials, redundant check valves in the hatch itself would crack at a pressure differential of 1.378 x 105N/m² (0.2lb/in²) when the pressure in the AM was greater than that in the OWS.

The wardroom window was designed to provide protection from meteoroid impact, impact from internal equipment, and to protect from ultraviolet and infrared radiation, with a heating capability for de-fogging, a metal cover to resist boost pressures and a shade to prevent unwanted light intrusion on crew equipment or activity. It was installed from the inside and was flush with the exterior mould

line. Windowpanes carried a small differential pressure during the boost phase, the cavity between being vented by the crew during initial OWS activation. Loads from the cylindrical tank ran around the window reinforcing ring to which the assembly was attached, providing a 45.72cm (18in) clear-view opening.

One pane of the window carried an electro-conductive coating to inhibit fogging, designed to maintain the inner surface of the window within a range of 12.8°C (55°F) to 40.6°C (105°F). To prevent contamination and inhibit outgassing, all window silicone and Viton rubber seals, cushions and spacers were cured at high temperatures.

The two scientific airlock (SAL) assemblies accommodated a number of separate experiment packages which were required to have some part of them exposed to the space environment, one on the solar side and the other diametrically opposite on the exterior of the cylindrical hull. Each experiment was contained within a pressure cell with an external flange that mated with, and sealed against, the inboard side of the airlock. Each had a metal plate window and was sealed in a similar manner. The inboard face had an opening that could be sealed by an experiment or window, the outer door being closed whenever an experiment or window was installed or removed, so as to isolate the cabin from the exterior environment. After installation, the pressure vessel of the experiment became

BELOW The forward compartment provided storage for food, freezers, refrigeration systems and the waste management ventilation unit. The bottom of the forward dome provided a mounting position for the water tanks. *(NASA)*

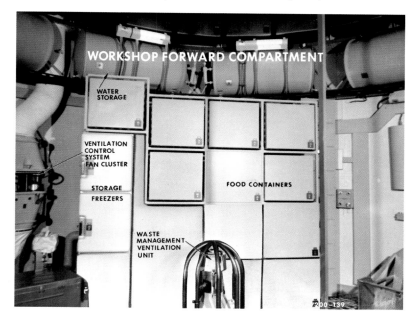

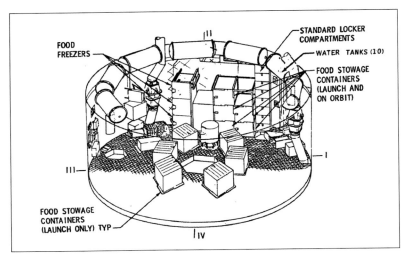

ABOVE The forward compartment provided storage for a wide range of essential items for the three periods of habitation. The weighty food containers were arranged in a torus around the central access hatch to the living/experiment area below and were relocated to their wall-mounted positions during the first visit. (NASA)

part of the airlock pressure vessel so that the outer door could be opened and the experiment deployed.

Apart from individual thermal coatings the two airlocks were identical, each being 21cm (8.25in) square and bolted direct to a flange on the wall of the OWS. Each had a vacuum-fitting at the top, a latching handle on the right-hand side, a pressure gauge at the centre and a crank at the lower left for opening the outer door. An indicator showed the operator the relative position of the door between fully open and fully closed, with a lock to prevent accidental rotation of the crank. A valve on the left-hand side of the airlock permitted venting

the airlock cavity either overboard or directly back into the OWS.

The experiment and window latching mechanism was enclosed in the square tubular structure with roller dogs emerging through openings which engaged the flange of the experiment window, pressing the rubber seals on the flange against the airlock sealing surface. The solar and anti-solar window positions for these airlocks were installed in containers for launch, removed during on-orbit activation after the release of restraint bolts and installed in the airlocks, where they remained, except when an experiment was installed in the SAL, at which time the airlock was returned to its pre-launch container until the experiment was removed.

The forward compartment of the OWS was divided into three main sections for identification of locations: the experiments area, the stowage area, and the dome. The experiment area was essentially the cylindrical section of constant diameter from the open-grid floor to the stowage area, where 10 water containers and 25 lockers were secured to a stowage ring. The main items in the dome section of the OWS included the entry hatch and the ventilation control system mixing-chamber and ducts. The stowage ring was the point where the cylindrical forward experiments area joined the dome.

As with all consumables on board Skylab, the water available for providing the requirements of three men for a planned 140 days of occupation had to be carried up in the initial cluster and stored on board for intermittent use over a period of almost one year. The water was required not only for consumption but also for reconstituting food, crew hygiene, urine separator flushing, thermal control and conditioning. Water was also necessary for the EVA suit loops, the ATM caution and warning panel and EREP cooling loop, the M512 materials processing facility and the crew shower.

The water was stored in ten stainless steel tanks each having a capacity between 289.57kg (638.4kg) and 300.28kg (662lb), depending on the specific tank. Quantities capable of being expelled, and therefore available for use, varied from 259.64kg (572.4lb) to 270.34kg (596lb) for a usable total of 2,683.36kg (5,915.7lb) out of a tanked load of 2,982.73kg (6,575.7lb).

BELOW The water tanks were arranged around the inner circumference of the forward cylindrical tank section and just below the dome, retained by an installation that also provided support for the 25 lockers by attachment to the stowage ring. (NASA)

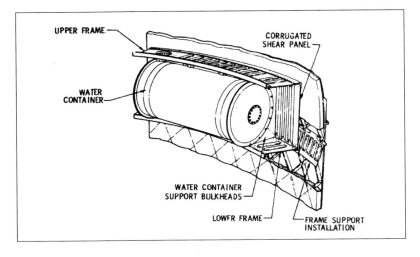

The expellable volume allowed for the loss of a complete tank without compromising the water budget and drawdown from the coolant system for unimpeded cluster operations.

The ten tanks were numbered sequentially around the circumference of the stowage ring and each had a dedicated allocation: tanks 1, 2, 3, 4, 5 and 10 were assigned to the wardroom; tanks 7 and 8 were connected to the waste management compartment (WMC); and tanks 6 and 9 were for contingency use and were capable of being directed to either application in the event of a malfunction in the dedicated supply to that compartment or excessive consumption to depletion.

Internally, each tank contained a sealed metal bellows which allowed nitrogen gas to pressurise and maintain water supply pressure for water expulsion, the bellows expanding as the volume of water was reduced. Each tank also had two electrical heater blankets wrapped around the circumference to protect against freezing. The blankets were controlled by an electronic module and a backup thermostat to ensure that water temperature remained at 13.3–15.6°C (56–60°F) during uninhabited periods, but in reality – due to the elevated temperatures during the first mission – they were not used.

Water purification was provided by equipment inside a metal container mounted on the forward compartment wall under tank 2 and consisted of two water samplers, two reagent containers, two iodine injectors and their containers, one colour comparator and one waste sample container. The duplicated items were divided into primary and secondary groups. Each of the ten tanks was initially charged with iodine until the concentration reached 12ppm.

Over time, with normal depletion of iodine, the concentration would fall to a maximum of 2ppm at the point of consumption. In this case, iodine reactions would form iodides while in contact with various metal surfaces, and also while passing through the cation (deionisation) cartridge. The crew would periodically sample the iodine levels and, if necessary, recharge the water tank with 30,000ppm iodine solution from the water purification equipment iodine container. The amount to be injected was determined by using a reference chart that

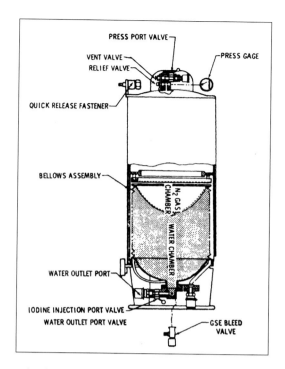

LEFT A typical water tank with iodine injector and cutaway section showing the nitrogen gas chamber for positive expulsion in the weightless environment. (NASA)

scheduled water-tank volume (in per cent) and iodine concentration. For safe drinking the concentration had to be 0.5ppm or greater.

The nitrogen distribution network in the Airlock Module provided a regulated gas supply to each of the water tanks, this gas being used to operate the storage tank bellows. The source of the nitrogen distribution was the tanks in the AM, pressurised to 27,580kPa (4,000lb/in²) but regulated to 1,034kPa (150lb/in²) in the AM and to 241.3kPa (35lb/in²) in the OWS. In addition, a portable water tank was provided for sterilisation of the water distribution system during the second and third crew visits. Mounted on a wall bracket below tanks 1 and 2, it also served as a

BELOW With safety features driving the design, the wardroom viewing window consisted of several coatings to protect eyes from ultraviolet light, and adjacent insulation. (NASA)

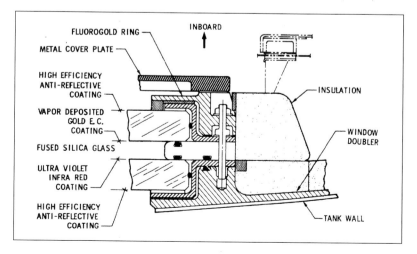

RIGHT The location of the viewing window and configuration of the metal cover, detached when occupied, and the impact shield installed during the first visit. *(NASA)*

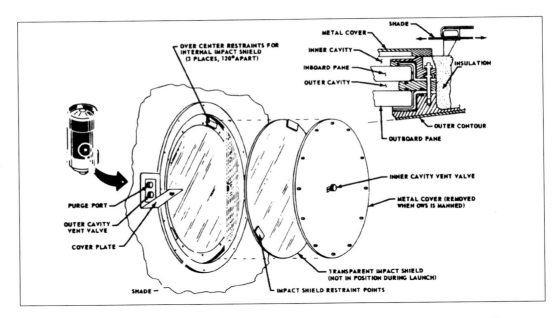

OVER CENTER RESTRAINTS FOR INTERNAL IMPACT SHIELD (3 PLACES, 120° APART)

SHADE

METAL COVER

INNER CAVITY

INBOARD PANE

OUTER CAVITY

INSULATION

OUTER CONTOUR

OUTBOARD PANE

INNER CAVITY VENT VALVE

METAL COVER (REMOVED WHEN OWS IS MANNED)

TRANSPARENT IMPACT SHIELD (NOT IN POSITION DURING LAUNCH)

IMPACT SHIELD RESTRAINT POINTS

PURGE PORT

OUTER CAVITY VENT VALVE

COVER PLATE

SHADE —

contingency water supply in the event of failure of the normal water distribution system and could be unclipped and taken to the area where it was required and secured to the grid surface by a quick-release fastener.

The portable tank was launched with the iodine solution containing 30,000ppm, and when filled with 11.79kg (26lb) of water

the concentration would be 100ppm. The solution was then injected into the water distribution system for a biocide soak. The cation deionisation cartridge consisted of a stainless steel container holding approximately 1,081.7cm³ (66in³) of ion exchange resin, the function of which was to remove metal ions from the water as it passed through the resin

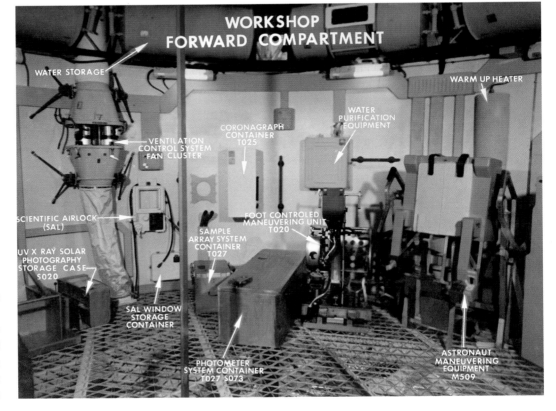

WORKSHOP FORWARD COMPARTMENT

WATER STORAGE

WARM UP HEATER

VENTILATION CONTROL SYSTEM FAN CLUSTER

CORONAGRAPH CONTAINER T025

WATER PURIFICATION EQUIPMENT

SCIENTIFIC AIRLOCK (SAL)

UV X RAY SOLAR PHOTOGRAPHY STORAGE CASE S020

SAMPLE ARRAY SYSTEM CONTAINER T027

FOOT CONTROLED MANEUVERING UNIT T020

SAL WINDOW STORAGE CONTAINER

PHOTOMETER SYSTEM CONTAINER T027 S073

ASTRONAUT MANEUVERING EQUIPMENT M509

RIGHT The general arrangement of equipment in the forward compartment above the living/experiment compartment, with a wide range of equipment and experiments including the M509 manoeuvring unit. *(NASA)*

bed. This bed was pre-treated prior to flight and at the end of each mission to compensate for the absorption of iodine, which would have adversely affected the water system.

The wardroom distribution system consisted of a flex line from the designated water storage tank to a hard line on the upper wall of the habitation area. The hard line extended down the wall to the crew quarters floor, underneath the floor to the wardroom table, where it branched to both the water heater and chiller. The heater was connected to a food and beverage reconstitution dispenser and three individual drinking guns.

The waste management system water distribution equipment supported crew requirements for personal hygiene and urine flushing, the former supplied by a flexible line from the appropriate tanks via a hard line network extending to the personal hygiene locker, where it was connected to a water heater. The urine flush system consisted of a supply network from water tank 6 to a dispenser in the waste management compartment that could meter 50-milligram increments of a water/iodine solution necessary to flush the urine separators each day.

The location of the water containers was important from a flight dynamics and control standpoint in that it was necessary to minimise the mass moment of inertia for the cluster to maintain the capabilities of the Control Moment Gyroscopes (CMGs). This made it preferable to locate the heavy water containers as close to the Skylab centre of gravity as possible, and since that was forward of the OWS this dictated an extreme forward location.

The water container support ring was designed to transfer all loads from the ten water storage containers and the 25 stowage containers to the habitation tank cylindrical shell. The structure consisted of two basic elements: the circular ring structure providing the actual support and the conical load distribution ring transferring loads from the ring to the OWS shell. The circular ring was designed to react to applied loads so that primarily shear loads were transmitted to the shell. Container loads in the vehicle thrust direction tended to cause the circular ring cross-section to roll. However, due to its high circumferential stiffness little rotation

occurred, and there was, therefore, negligible radial deflection of the joint between the circular and conical rings and the load transmitted to the shell was shear.

Container loads in the lateral, radial or tangential directions resulted in a sinusoidal shear distribution in the circumferential plane, with peak shears occurring 90° to the direction of the applied load. The conical ring was designed to transmit container loads to the shell while minimising radial restraint of shell growth due to internal pressurisation.

The circular ring structure was made of ten frame segments in two basic configurations. Four had a constant cross-section while the other six were modified at one end to provide an opening for a ventilation duct to pass through. The upper frame of each segment consisted of two extruded angle caps riveted to a beaded sheet-metal web. The lower frame was similar to the upper except that the outboard cap was a modified tee with one leg machined at a skewed angle for the interface with the conical ring. The conical ring itself was composed of thin aluminium sheet sections spliced together to form a continuous assembly, one edge attached to the habitation tank shell and the other to the smaller diameter circular ring.

Two intercostals for each container support bulkhead were installed to react to container axial loads and were aligned at 45° with respect to the water container centreline. They extended from the container support bulkhead to the

ABOVE Alan Bean occupies a little of his time on the second crew visit to demonstrate the voluminous space available for the most comprehensive display of weightless acrobatics possible in any space station ever assembled, including the International Space Station, which has a maximum diameter of 4.5m for all modules compared to 6.6m for Skylab. (NASA)

frame stabilisation bulkhead. The intercostals provided added stiffening to the support bulkheads and a more uniform load distribution on the water container support flange.

The upper and lower frames were joined on the outboard edge by a vertical corrugated sheet-metal web with Hi-lock fasteners, two machined bulkheads for each water container being installed parallel to each other. In addition to the container support bulkheads there were two intermediate machine bulkheads required per frame segment to maintain support structure cross-sectional stability.

The conical ring was composed of 21 beaded sheet sections spliced together to form a continuous ring assembly. The inboard flange of the ring was attached to the shell with bolts on approximately 34, 29cm (13.5in) centres. The spacing corresponded with the intersection of the waffle-pattern integral tank skin stiffeners. This intersection was selected to take advantage of the load distribution capabilities in that the conical ring tended to chord between attachments. As the chording occurred, hoop tension in the ring was reduced, effectively increasing the ring flexibility. Beading the sloped portion of the ring in the meridional direction offered little restraint to expansion, while maintaining the capability of taking compressive loads from vehicle dynamic transients. In order to prevent condensation on the tank wall and conical support ring on the cold side of the OWS, a series of heat-pipe thermal conductors

were attached by supports that used the same tank wall attachment as the conical ring.

The stowage-container support structure was a circular ring attached to the forward frame of the water-container support structure. It consisted of a cap and web horizontal frame, vertical and canted webs, and 26 vertical machined bulkheads spaced around the ring between the containers. Machined toe fittings were attached to each bulkhead to provide the interface with the water-container support structure, which was located in a horizontal circular plane in the forward experiment compartment adjacent to the forward dome.

Because the support structure was added to the forward dome at a late date in the programme, minimum impact on manufacturing and optimum load distribution was accomplished by attaching the stowage-container support structure to the water-container support structure upper frame outboard cap at 26 discrete points. These points corresponded to the bulkhead locations and picked up existing fasteners in the frame cap.

The stowage-container support structure was designed to transfer all loads from the 25 stowage containers to the water container support structure, which was composed of five elements, consisting of a horizontal circular cap and web frame vertical bulkheads, vertical webs, inclined webs and bulkhead end fittings. The circular frame was designed to react to radial load inputs from the containers and the bulkheads were designed to react to vehicle thrust direction loads and to shear out circular frame reactions. The vertical and inclined webs were designed to carry lateral loading through shear. All container loading was eventually dumped into the outboard cap of the upper frame of the water container support structure through the bulkheads and bulkhead end fittings, the transferred loads being shear and tension, or compression.

The structure of the crew quarters was to provide two floors, one above the other, to provide living quarters for the crew and a support area for equipment and experiments, most of the latter being mounted on the forward surface of the forward floor. The loads from all equipment installations were distributed floor to floor through the compartment walls, which

BELOW In the foreground the bicycle ergometer, and beyond it the lower body negative pressure device for determining the effects of weightlessness on the human body. *(NASA)*

acted as tension, compression and shear members between the two. These loads were then transferred to the cylindrical tank wall through the support cones at the periphery of each floor. The cones acted as tension members for aft loads, as compression members for forward loads and as shear members for radial loads. The cones were also designed to accommodate the growth of the habitation area tank cylinder due to internal pressurisation.

The compartment walls divided the crew quarters into four sections, identified as the wardroom, experiment, waste-management and sleep compartments. The crew quarters' internal walls consisted of four double-grid panel walls and four single-grid panel walls. The structure for the double-grid walls was built from 7.62mm (3in) wide formed and extruded aluminium channels, the horizontal channels at the top and bottom being bolted to the forward and aft floors to form an integral load-carrying structure. The intermediate, horizontal, vertical and diagonal channels divided the large grid panels into small segments, and to prevent buckling under shear loads the edges were attached to the end of the double-grid walls.

The walls had three door openings, that to the wardroom being covered by a soft, sliding curtain. This was a single accordion-pleated fabric panel held taut between floor and ceiling tracks. One vertical edge was permanently attached to the wardroom wall and the other was stiffened with a full-length aluminium tube that served as the handhold for operating the curtain. In its stowed or folded position it was retained by three loop straps, and a single strap on the tube was snapped to the wardroom wall to hold it in the fully deployed position. The curtain fabric was TFE (tetrafluoroethylene) coated beta glass with a sewn-on matrix of stainless steel yarn for grounding electrostatic charges. Glass-filled TFE ball-sliders were used in aluminium tracks to reduce friction and prevent binding. A breakaway feature was added by attaching the curtain to the sliders with snaps and to the vertical tube with Velcro.

The door to the waste management compartment was a two-piece folding type with an integral skin grid construction, folding in the centre with a full-length hinge and guided by struts running in tracks located at top and

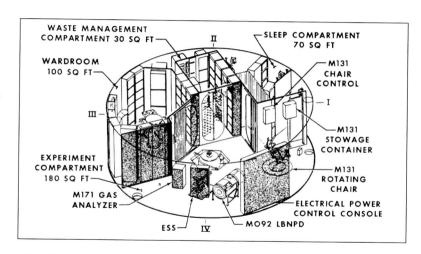

ABOVE This cutaway shows the orientation of the OWS axes by position references in Roman numerals at 90° intervals. The general configuration of the OWS and its equipment served as a template for the much larger space station planned by NASA. With a diameter of 10m and also launched on the first two stages of a Saturn V, the 12-man station envisaged as a successor to Skylab would have had an initial complement of 12 crew members. (NASA)

bottom. The strut track follower had a built-in emergency breakaway feature in the form of a ball and socket track follower held in place in the strut by a ball plunger detent. The resistance of the detent was set such that a load of 22.65–47.65kg (50–105lb) at the centre of the door would disengage the followers from the tracks and allow the door to open without folding.

The waste management system was designed to collect, sample, process and store all crew metabolic waste. Its main function

BELOW The overall and general arrangement of the waste management compartment configured for personal hygiene, toilet facilities and body washing. (NASA)

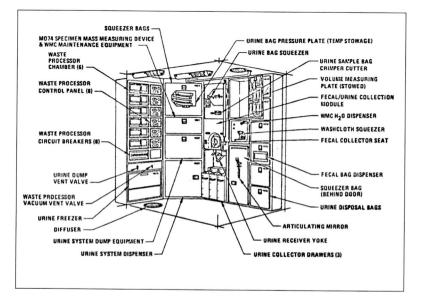

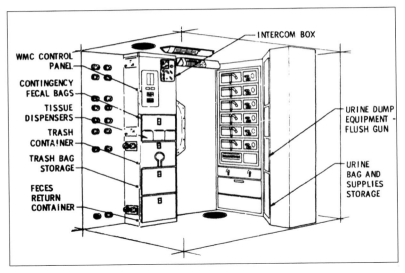

Labels on diagram:
- WMC CONTROL PANEL
- CONTINGENCY FECAL BAGS
- TISSUE DISPENSERS
- TRASH CONTAINER
- TRASH BAG STORAGE
- FECES RETURN CONTAINER
- INTERCOM BOX
- URINE DUMP EQUIPMENT - FLUSH GUN
- URINE BAG AND SUPPLIES STORAGE

ABOVE Supporting the several separate provisions in the waste management compartment, lockers, storage boxes, dump lines and towel supplies were integrated with efficient storage allocation that had become the normal way of designing the interior of much smaller spacecraft and paid dividends with Skylab. *(NASA)*

BELOW Urine cleaners, faecal dump bags and venting provisions shared space with controls and adapters for maintaining personal cleanliness and a tidy station. *(NASA)*

was to provide a comfortable means by which the crew could perform their daily faecal and urine discharges and to provide a means of preserving material for return to Earth in the Command Module for biocidal analysis. The system consisted of a faecal/urine collector, collection and sample bags, odour-control filters, blower, waste processor, urine freezer and associated equipment. The faecal/urine collector used airflow as a substitute for gravity

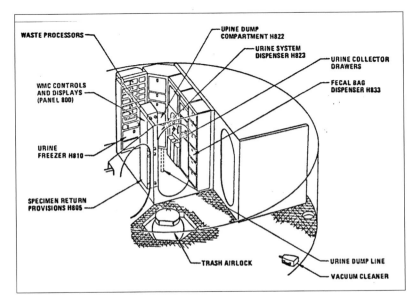

Labels on diagram:
- WASTE PROCESSORS
- UPINE DUMP COMPARTMENT H822
- URINE SYSTEM DISPENSER H823
- URINE COLLECTOR DRAWERS
- WMC CONTROLS AND DISPLAYS (PANEL 800)
- FECAL BAG DISPENSER H833
- URINE FREEZER H810
- SPECIMEN RETURN PROVISIONS H805
- TRASH AIRLOCK
- URINE DUMP LINE
- VACUUM CLEANER

to separate waste material from the body. Urination would be performed standing or sitting as preferred, with both urination and defecation being carried out simultaneously if required.

The faecal/urine collector was a wall-mounted unit incorporating a single faecal bag and three urine drawers, one for each crew member to be able to store the urine for 24 hours in a chiller. It incorporated a blower that provided suction to withdraw faecal material from the rectum, filtered it to remove odour and removed it to the collector for storage. The faecal bag was removed from the collector and replaced with a fresh bag before the used bag was weighed using a mass-measuring device before vacuum-drying in a waste processor for storage. The amount of drying time required was determined by the mass of the used bag and could be controlled by the user. The bags were then removed and placed in a storage area for return to Earth.

The collection of urine was accomplished by one of two methods: suction airflow through a receiver and hose to a centrifuge unit for air and urine separation and then to a collection bag; or by a 'roll-on' cuff much like the application of a condom to the penis but for urination directly into the collection bag without airflow suction. A sample was taken from the bag every 24 hours and then the collection bag was replaced, the sample being placed in the urine freezer and returned to Earth at the end of the mission. Each crewman had a separate urine collection system in one of three drawers.

A 120–130ml sample was drawn from each crew member's daily collection. For this the urine bag was attached to the front of the upper faecal/urine collector door and a sample bag connected to the urine bag with an interconnecting hose. The sample bag was then placed in a crimper/cutter mechanism and filled by applying pressure to the urine bag with squeezer handles. The interconnecting hose was then cut and crimped and the sample frozen in the urine freezer and maintained until return to Earth.

Located below the waste processors, the urine freezer contained 42 sample containers for two weeks' accumulation in separate compartments. Two urine trays, with an integral thermal capacitor of dodecane (heat sink) wax, were stacked in the freezer. The urine freezer stored both urine and blood samples and reduced the temperature of the sample to below -2.7°C (27°F) within three hours, to -17.7°C (0°F) within six hours and to below -19.2°C (-2.5°F) within eight hours. After thermal conditioning, the wax was kept at -10°C (14°F) during the return to Earth in a urine sample container.

Particulate matter, excess water and debris was removed by a portable vacuum cleaner, a self-contained unit powered from a convenient high-power accessory outlet, utilising a debris bag for disposal. The vacuum cleaner was kept in a stowage locker in the forward compartment together with attachment, hose and caddy. A beta fabric caddy enclosed the cleaner and provided stowage, restrained by a waist tether around the caddy. A short strap provided stowage of a 4.6m (15ft) accessory cable. Three attachments were provided, including a surface tool for screen cleaning and the collection of loose or floating debris, a crevice tool for cleaning confined areas, and a brush attachment for removing dirt and debris sticking to surfaces.

A 1.2m (4ft) flexible hose connected the vacuum cleaner inlet fitting and provided a tool/hose adapter with a locking feature for tools. The hose and vacuum cleaner combined provided a 6.1m (20ft) radius of operation from the power outlet. A vacuum bag access door was hinged to the blower unit through the use of one latch which was used to install and remove the debris bag when full, or at weekly intervals. Airflow retained the debris in the bag while the air exited through the vapour port. The power switch could be set to operate for short or extended periods. The inlet adapter of the vacuum cleaner was removable to allow the blower to be interchanged with other blower units.

Personal hygiene was given high priority, to ensure the health of the crew member, to prevent microbial or bacterial infections, to lower the probability of medication being necessary, and to sustain the operational value of the crew member for general housekeeping duties and scientific tasks. The extended duration of the Skylab visits required special attention to health and comfort and to the control of microorganisms that could threaten the mission.

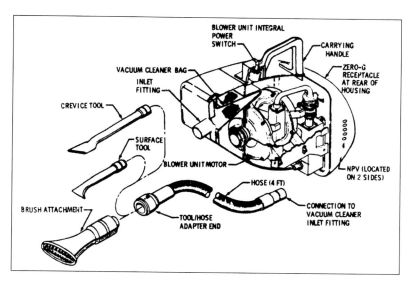

Unlike previous space flights, even a modest level of physical discomfort was unacceptable for long missions, and the requirement to make the life of the astronaut as comfortable as possible was judged an essential prerequisite for efficiency.

Partial body cleanliness was ensured by a water module locker in the waste management compartment, consisting of a hot water dispenser, valve and washcloth squeezer. A washcloth was placed in the squeezer and the handle pulled down to remove excess water from the cloth and into the bag. The collected water was drained through a filter into the waste tank by the normal vacuum-dump system. A total of 55 soap bars were provided, 11 for the first crew, but in fact one bar lasted for the entire duration of the first manned visit.

One of the unique devices for personal hygiene was the whole body shower (WBS), which required considerable engineering ingenuity due to its operation in weightlessness, necessitating the use of a positive airflow to move water over the crewman. For use, a 2.72kg (6lb) water bottle was filled from the waste management compartment water heater, pressurised with nitrogen gas that expelled water through a transfer hose to a crew-operated, hand-held spray nozzle. A dispenser containing 8ml of liquid soap was available for each shower, fastened to the ceiling with Velcro. A suction head removed water from the crewman and the interior of the shower. The suction head was connected by hoses to the centrifugal separator that deposited the water

ABOVE An innovation for spacemen but a necessity on a station where crew members would spend several weeks living and working, a vacuum cleaner with appropriate attachments proved a useful multipurpose device. *(NASA)*

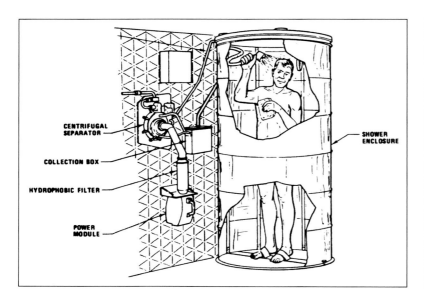

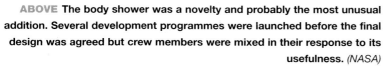

CENTRIFUGAL SEPARATOR

COLLECTION BOX

HYDROPHOBIC FILTER

POWER MODULE

SHOWER ENCLOSURE

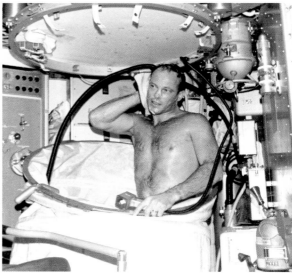

ABOVE The body shower was a novelty and probably the most unusual addition. Several development programmes were launched before the final design was agreed but crew members were mixed in their response to its usefulness. *(NASA)*

ABOVE RIGHT SL-3 crew member Jack Lousma demonstrates the use of the body shower during the second manned visit. A marvel of ingenious design, never again would a space station provide such pseudo-luxury! *(NASA)*

into the collection bag, from where the blower pulled the air from the separator through a hydrophobic filter that protected the blower.

The shower enclosure consisted of two end ring enclosures and a translucent Beta cloth skirt with stiffening rings. The floor closure ring was attached to the floor grid in the crew-quarters area. During stowage, the other ring – the ceiling enclosure – was attached coaxially to the floor closure with quick release fasteners, and in this condition the skirt was compressed between the two ends. For operation, the ceiling closure would be raised, extending the aft skirt, and attached to the ceiling with quick-release fasteners. The ceiling ring closure included the spray nozzle, the suction head and the associated flexible hose and quick disconnect couplings. The skirt had straps for handholds and restraints.

The separator was gear-driven by a brushless direct-current motor with a maximum of 1,100ml/min. The pressure drop across the separator was a maximum 10.16kg (4in) of water at a flow rate of 0.140m³/min (5.0ft³/min)

and an inlet temperature of 21.1°C (70°F). The collection box had an elastomeric bag replaced after each use of the shower, containing a maximum 3,000ml of water. The hydrophobic separator prevented any waste water from entering Skylab and had a minimum water retention capacity of 81.9cm³ (5in³).

The food management system (FMS) consisted of provisions for three crew members, with a 140-day supply of food and beverages, and assumed the use of the wardroom as a kitchen. Food was stored in boxes, galley trays, food freezers and chiller. A galley, components of the food table, food trays and utensils were provided for the preparation and consumption of meals.

Food was provided at ambient or frozen temperatures, the ambient food consisting of dehydrated products, thermos-stabilised (pre-prepared and moisturised), dry bites and puddings. The frozen food consisted of thermos-stabilised food, some of which had to be heated prior to consumption. Food for all three manned visits had to be carried up on SL-1, except for a supplementary stock carried up on SL-4 for the extended mission. Ambient temperature foods were vacuum-packed in single-meal portions in cans. Beverages were stored in the dehydrated state in packs that collapsed, accordion style, to facilitate storage and drinking. Each can and beverage pack was labelled with its contents and the quantity of water required for rehydration.

The refrigeration system was designed as

LEFT The diameter of the upper and lower shower cover discs was determined by the requirement to pass it through the forward hatch ring. Here technicians begin its assembly. *(NASA)*

a low-temperature thermal control system that used Coolanol-15 in a closed-loop circuit, dissipating heat through a ground heat exchanger during pre-launch operations and by the external radiator in orbit. It provided for freezing of food and urine and for chilling food, urine and potable water. Specifically, it controlled temperatures through a range of 5.5 to -28.9°C (42 to -20°F) by way of a dual coolant loop and redundant components, for reliability.

Each of the cooling circuits contained four pumps, with any one pump capable of applying normal flow. The circuits were basically identical and independent of each other, except for the common application of the radiator, ground cooling heat exchanger, thermal capacitor, freezers and chillers, although these components had separate coolant paths.

The single-phase Coolanol-15 was a mixed blend of 50% ethylene glycol antifreeze and 50% deionised water, to inhibit rust and provide corrosion protection. (It is used today for aluminium and magnesium motorcycle engines.) In Skylab's refrigeration service it circulated through the freezers and the chillers to absorb heat, which was rejected to either an external space radiator or a thermal capacitor. The capacitors consisted of three in-series, phase-changing wax compound heat sinks which absorbed thermal energy when the temperature of the radiator exceeded the system operating temperature and could no longer be used for rejecting heat.

If the radiator surface temperature reached -9.4°C (15°F), a control circuit driven by

LEFT A development model of the body shower curtain enclosure is tested in a laboratory at the Marshall Space Flight Center. *(NASA)*

BELOW This simple schematic displays the working elements of the full body shower, with water delivered through a shower head and sucked back from the enclosure through the suction head to the separator, where air and water go their separate ways. *(NASA)*

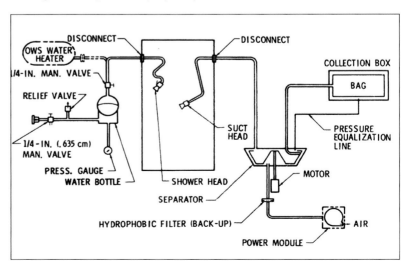

a temperature transducer on the radiator assembly switched the radiator bypass valve to the bypass position. This diverted coolant flow past the radiator and directly to the thermal capacitor units, where heat transfer from the coolant to the thermal capacitor occurred at essentially the constant temperature of -25°C (-14°F). When the radiator surface temperature dropped to -17.8°C (0°F), the radiator temperature transducer caused the radiator bypass valve to open to the radiator position, allowing full flow of coolant through the radiator.

The coolant from the radiator outlet passed through the thermal capacitor, which regenerated the phase-change in preparation for the next warm cycle. During this period a maximum temperature of -25°C (-14°F) was maintained at the thermal capacitor. As the radiator temperature decreased and the stored heat was absorbed from the capacitor, the temperature of the coolant between the first and second thermal units eventually reached -36.9°C (-34.5°F). At this temperature the radiator bypass valve was actuated to cause the coolant to flow directly to the thermal capacitor units and bypass the radiator. This mode of operation continued until the temperature of the coolant between the first and the second thermal capacitor units increased to -24.9°C (-14°F) and the radiator bypass valve was actuated to direct the coolant back through the radiator.

A 243kN/cm² (34lb/in²) relief valve was installed across the radiator to maintain a constant pressure differential at that value through the radiator in the event of a coolant blockage, which could occur when extremely low-temperature coolant was in the radiator. From the outlet to the last thermal capacitor unit, the coolant flowed in series through the urine freezer, the wardroom food freezers and the food storage freezers. The coolant was then controlled to 3.9°C (39°F) by means of the chiller thermal control valve, three regenerator heat exchangers and a 75W heater.

This fluid temperature control at the outlet of the chiller control valve was achieved by proportional flow mixing of the regenerator outlet and the freezer outlet. The flow through the three regenerator heat exchangers was warmed by a counter-flowing coolant path from the regenerator heater, the coolant being routed in parallel paths through the chilled food compartment and urine chiller. The paths united and a single path was routed to the pump assembly.

The pump assembly was essentially two twin-pump packages in parallel. The twin-pump unit consisted of two parallel pumps with discharge check valves and pump differential pressure transducers, a 0.868mm³ (53in³) accumulator and a 689.4kN/m² (100lb/in²) bypass relief valve. The pump assembly outlet was routed through a 15-micron filter through the inverter and heater control cold-plate and to the regenerator heater. This provided heat which allowed coolant temperature regeneration to reach 2.2°C (36°F) under the coldest design conditions. From the regenerator heater, the flow passed through the three heat exchangers and to either the radiator or thermal capacitor for rejection. A transducer located between the chiller thermal control valve inlet and the regenerator heat exchanger cold side outlet, caused the regenerator heater to energise and de-energise as the temperature reached 2.8°C (37°F).

This system as flown for the 'dry' workshop was greatly simplified compared to the original concept for the 'wet' OWS, which required four separate systems, but because not all were introduced at the same time unique systems were developed to integrate with preceding elements as they evolved. Moreover, all the equipment had to be portable and capable of being installed by hand after being passed through the 1.09m (43in) diameter liquid hydrogen

BELOW The greater volume for living activities and the additional weight allowed for personal requirements enabled engineers to permit a greater weight per astronaut of food items that were impossible to include on previous spacecraft. Trays with heated sections and specially prepared contents were integral to the galley allowing a semblance of social normality in coming together for meals. (NASA-JSC)

RIGHT Essential elements of the galley are shown in this diagram, with stowage lockers and freezers contained around the circular curvature of the wall. Note the observation window, an important viewing space epitomising the first attempt in any space vehicle to create an aesthetic connection with surroundings inside and outside the structure. This was particularly emphasised as a necessity by NASA manned flight boss George Mueller. *(NASA-MSFC)*

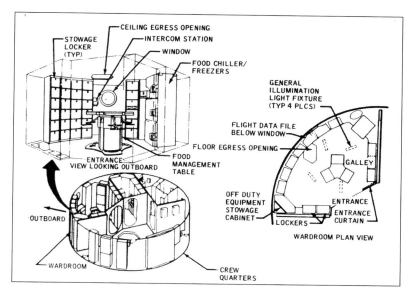

tank forward dome hatch. The techniques developed to achieve temperature control were liquid ammonia evaporation, sublimation and thermoelectric heat pumps. With the change to a 'dry' workshop the equipment no longer had to be portable and all systems could be, and were, permanently mounted to the OWS, creating a more technically refined and superior system with greatly enhanced reliability.

The selection of suitable menus for each crew member was made on the basis of age and body mass, but would ensure a daily intake of 750–850mg of calcium, 1,500–1,700mg of phosphorous, 3,000–6,000mg of sodium, 300–400mg of magnesium and 90–125g (3.17–4.4oz) of protein, to within 2% per person. Some 950kg (2,100lb) of food and accessories for all three manned visits was stowed on the OWS prior to launch.

The frozen food items were contained in the five food freezers with a total volume of 0.3m³ (10.6ft³). Each freezer was 33.1 x 42.1 x 43.3cm (13.03 x 16.56 x 17.07in) in size and supported a maximum food load of 45.4kg (100lb). The other food items were contained in lockers on the floor of the OWS for launch and relocated by the SL-2 crew after entering the cluster. The 11 food lockers had a combined volume of 2.5m³ (88.3ft³). The single refrigerator had a physical envelope of 33 x 42.2 x 43.2cm (13.00 x 16.60 x 17.00in).

Each crew member taste-tested the more than 70 food items carried and the emphasis was on preparing meals that would closely approximate food on Earth as far as possible, consideration being given to taste, aroma, shape, colour, texture and temperature. The dehydrated food had the moisture level at no greater than 3%, with intermediate pre-cooked

food possessing a moisture content of 10–20%. Thermostabilised food had the temperature reduced to -23°C (-10°F) before launch so as to slow the rate of spoilage, while pre-cooked frozen food was reduced to lower than -40°C (-40°F) for the same reason. Rehydratable drinks included black coffee, tea, cocoa, cocoa-flavoured instant-breakfast drink, grape drink, limeade, lemonade, orange drink, grapefruit drink, cherry drink and apple drinks.

BELOW The galley contained within the wardroom provided all the meals required by a total of nine crew members over a planned 140 days of occupation. Meals were colour-coded per crew member and situated within the pantry along with large and small food cans, beverage trays and storage spaces. *(NASA)*

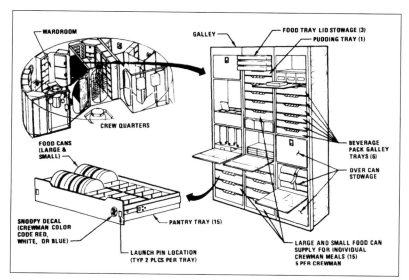

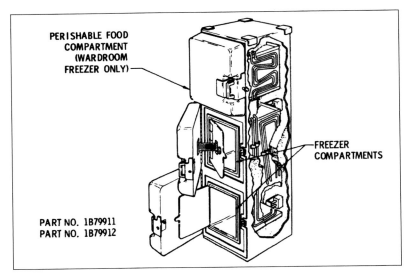

PERISHABLE FOOD COMPARTMENT (WARDROOM FREEZER ONLY)

FREEZER COMPARTMENTS

PART NO. 1B79911
PART NO. 1B79912

large and small food cans, pudding cans, or beverage packs in partitioned segments. Galley tray identification for each individual crew member was by a 'Snoopy' decal. In total, 18 trays stowed 360 large and small food cans.

The galley trays held food in overcans – sleeves that provided protection from its heated containers – and on removing the food cans and beverage packs from these the overcans were transferred to three of the stowage compartments within the galley allocated to storing empty cans. Six of these empty overcans were installed in the food can disposal wells in the galley, a facility which held six wells, three for large overcans and three for small overcans, which were accessed through separate spring-loaded hinged lids. Empty food cans and beverage packs were disposed of in their appropriate size overcans in the disposal well, and when full these were placed in a disposal bag and replaced by empty overcans. A utensil stowage compartment in the galley stowed the eating utensils for all crewmen and a supply of food supplements. Two tissue dispensers were also provided to support the cleaning of the various food implements and the galley equipment.

The daily cycle of life aboard Skylab required all three crew members on each visit to eat together at the same time, with the galley able to accommodate all three in a comfortable environment. One astronaut would be assigned 'chef' for the meal on a rotational basis, but the design of the system required no longer than five minutes for food preparation at each meal.

The food table pedestal provided three eating stations at 120° intervals and also housed the water chiller, with water dispensed via three personalised water guns, and the wardroom water heater. The wardroom water heater provided hot water via a dispenser and valve unit attached to the upper surface of the table and this was used for reconstitution of dehydrated food. Each eating station had a foot and thigh restraint for anchoring the body in weightlessness.

A food tray that heated a crewman's food

The food was carried in 22 galley trays with five trays per crew member for their individual meal choices, one tray per crew member for snacks (dry bites) and another tray for beverages. One galley tray was for the weekly pudding supply of 18 cans for all crew members. Each tray slid out on a track and could be completely removed from the galley. Each galley tray held 20 items including

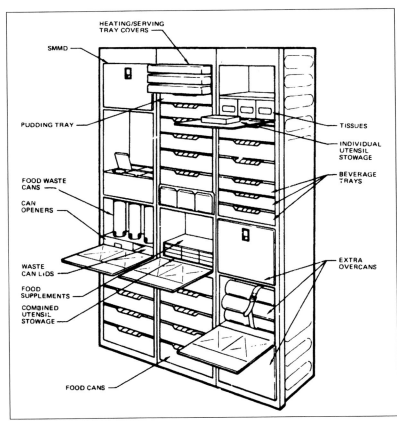

HEATING/SERVING TRAY COVERS

SMMD

PUDDING TRAY

FOOD WASTE CANS

CAN OPENERS

WASTE CAN LIDS

FOOD SUPPLEMENTS

COMBINED UTENSIL STOWAGE

FOOD CANS

TISSUES

INDIVIDUAL UTENSIL STOWAGE

BEVERAGE TRAYS

EXTRA OVERCANS

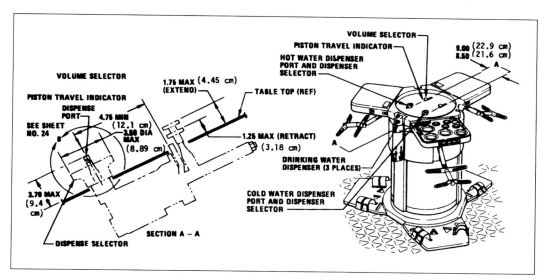

was provided with a mounting at each eating station with electrical power from OWS Bus 1 and Bus 2 for power selection at a particular eating tray. Each food tray contained eight cans, equally divided between large and small, with three of the can cavities heated with individual power switches and a timer controlling the heater. A removable food tray lid was used when the food was heating and this was stowed in the food tray lid stowage area in the galley when not in use. Each of the three food trays and their lids were colour-coded with 'Snoopy' decals. Two dial-type latches were located on the food tray to secure it to the food-table mounting.

A single set of utensils was allocated to each crew member, with three additional sets per crewman as spares, ie 12 in all. A utensil set consisted of a knife, spoon and fork, all three-quarter size, made from magnetic stainless steel so that they would remain in place against a metallic surface. The knife had a pointed tip to pierce and slice the flexible membranes in some food cans. All utensils were retained against the food trays with magnets, and in the utensil stowage container in the galley or the personal preference lockers with utensil restraints. Disinfectant-moistened pads, obtained from a galley tissue dispenser, were used to cleanse the utensils after each use.

Some special tools were required, specifically an overcan removal tools and a can crusher. Two sets of removal tool were supplied for opening the screw-type overcan lid in the event that they were too tightly screwed on, one

set for large overcans and one set for small overcans. These were stowed in the galley just below the waste cans. The can crusher was a contingency tool in the event that the trash airlock became disabled. With this tool it would have been necessary to dispose of opened food cans by storing them in empty stowage freezers. To ensure adequate volume, the food cans would have been smashed flat in the manually operated can crusher.

The OWS provided three individual sleep compartments each containing a sleep support system, including: 3 sleep restraint assemblies; 27 stowed comfort restraint/top blankets; 12 stowed bottom blankets; 27 stowed pillow covers; 12 stowed large body straps; 24 stowed small body straps; 3 privacy curtains; 3 light baffles; and 3 privacy partitions. The sleep restraint frames were installed in a vertical position and were mounted to the floor and ceiling with spring snaps and webbing assemblies, enabling them to be used and supported in a variety of locations, such as the forward compartment, the Multiple Docking Adapter and the experiment compartment. Each frame was approximately 91.5 x 183cm (36 x 72in) and was of welded tubular aluminium construction.

The thermal back assembly combined Teflon-coated glass fabric, durrette batting, PBI (polybenzimidazole, a fireproof material) fabric and fluorel-coated webbing, materials that provided crew thermal protection. This was attached to the sleep restraint frame by one of the two rows of snaps located around the

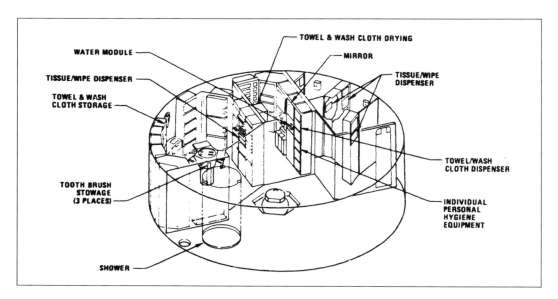

periphery, the second row providing options for adjustment. The comfort restraint was essentially a sleeping bag made from PBI loose-knit fabric, which provided limited ventilation to the crewman. A stretchable-knit fabric provided the upper, or top, blanket. The crewman's head was placed through the expandable opening that allowed the blanket to be spread over the shoulders and the chest area.

The restraint and top blanket were attached to the thermal back by two zippers, one around each side of the periphery. The 27 available for each crew member allowed for a change every 14 days for the sleep restraint. The bottom blanket was made from heavy PBI fabric that incorporated two 'vee' panels and was attached to the bottom of the thermal back by two zippers. The blanket was designed with a

zippered pouch, located near the bottom of the frame. The pouch restrained the blanket during launch and when not in use. The provision of 12 such blankets provided a change-out every 28 days for each sleep restraint. Pillow inserts consisted of a PBI-covered, heat-resistant foam panel with six installed inserts at launch. These were kept in place by an attached restraint cover and the crewman had the option of selecting the number of panels he preferred for personal comfort.

The pillow cover was made to stretch over the number of panels selected by an individual crew member. Made of PBI loose-knit fabric, it was attached by a zipper to the thermal back and also prevented the head from drifting during sleep. The restraint was placed over the forehead, or even the entire head if preferred, with one side

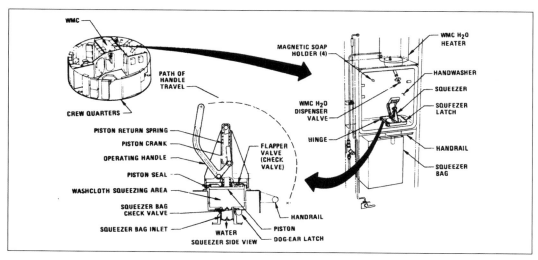

attached to the pillow cover and the other side by Velcro secured by the crewman.

Three body straps were provided for each sleep restraint and these were fabricated from stretch-knit PBI fabric, spandex, PBI webbing and fluorel-coated webbings. The design of these belts allowed them to stretch as the crewman changed sleep position, adjustment in length being possible by releasing buckles. The straps were used to restrain the crewman's body while inside or outside the comfort restraints. Soiled straps were periodically changed, removal being accomplished by releasing the buckles at one end and disengaging snaps at the other. The 12 large and 24 small body straps allowed a change every 28 days, one of each size being required for each sleep restraint.

Each crewman had a Teflon-coated glass fabric privacy curtain which, when not in use, was stowed against a locker wall that allowed the crewman in and out of the sleeping area. In the used position, the curtain separated each sleep compartment from the passageway and also served as a light barrier against lit areas elsewhere. Each curtain was held in the closed position with Velcro, which mated to Velcro on the lockers or walls. In addition, a fabric light baffle was provided for each sleep area, a device designed to be supported by snaps and Velcro that mated to snaps on the ceiling and Velcro on the walls and lockers. When installed, it provided a barrier against illumination from the forward compartment. The baffle in the centre sleep area had a section the size of the emergency escape exit, fastened with Velcro for a breakaway emergency exit.

The light baffles were fabricated from two layers of fabric, the inter-layer (the side facing the sleep compartment) being white Teflon-coated glass fabric and the layer facing the ceiling being black Teflon-coated glass fabric. The louvres contained four layers of these fabrics, which provided stiffness. Two privacy partitions were provided in the sleep area, the one between compartments one and two consisting of an aluminium corrugated panel and a standard stowage locker. The second partition was installed between compartments two and three and was made up with the installation of two standard stowage lockers adjacent to each other.

Several unbreakable mirrors were provided for the crew, a single 25.4 x 38.1cm (10 x 15in) mirror on the rear of the top locker door at each sleep station and a 30.0 x 40.0cm (12 x 16in) mirror on the waste management compartment wall above the indentation opposite the faecal/urine collector. There was an additional mirror covering the upper door of the waste management compartment (WMC) locker.

General-purpose tissues and utility wipes were contained in fireproof aluminium-foil lined pasteboard packages, containing 11 tissue packages each with 392 tissues, providing for a budget of 12 per man-day with a 10% contingency. Tissues were used for cleaning equipment, for personal use and for small cleaning jobs. Each tissue was fabricated from Kimberley Clark 'Kay Dry' material measuring 12.7 x 20.6cm (5 x 8.11in), the packages having tear-out panels front and rear. Utility wipes were in identical packages, each with 23 wipes providing a minimum 196 per package for a budget of ten per man-day with a small contingency. These were of the same material as the tissues, 12.7 x 41.8cm (5 x 16.45in) in size.

Five biocidal wipe packages, each with 70 wipes, were also supplied in aluminium-foil lined pasteboard containers providing a usage rate of two per man-day, each wipe being 16.5 x 19.0cm (6.5 x 7.5in) of Webril cotton containing 12ml of Betadine solution with 5,000ppm of iodine. Each wipe was wrapped in Conolon 6000 film before packaging.

A total of 840 washcloths were packaged in 30 sheet aluminium boxes, each 300mm²

BELOW Three washcloth modules provided towels and wipes on the wall dividing the waste management compartment from the sleep cubicles. (NASA)

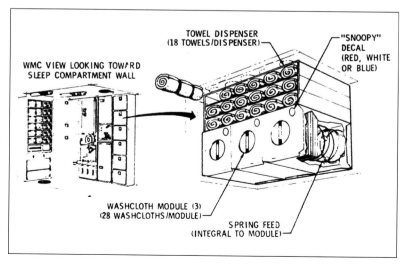

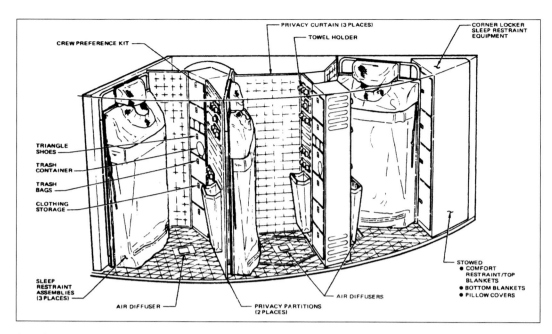

(12in²) in area, fabricated from rayon polysonic terrycloth. Each washcloth was edged with the crewman's colour code and had a 76mm (3in) diameter hole in the face that allowed retrieval. A special spring-feeding device in the back of the container advanced remaining washcloths to an accessible position at the front. Three removable boxes, each colour-coded per crewman, were located in the WMC in the stowage compartment adjacent to the hand-washer.

After washing, and disposal of the cloths, crew members had a total supply of 330 towels stowed in two lockers, with five three-tier aluminium dispensers each containing 18 stored towels each measuring 36 x 81cm (14 x 32in). This supply provided a usage rate of one per man-day, fabricated from rayon polysonic terrycloth and edged with the crew member's colour code. One dispenser was in the WMC, the others in the wardroom stowage compartments. After use the towels were transferred to the washcloth and towel drying area in preparation for another use, or dispensed with at the end of the day in a trash bag.

The forward compartment floor consisted of a 20.32 (8in) beam and intercostal structure sandwiched between an open triangular pattern with intermediate intercostals where required to concentrate loads from floor-mounted equipment such as film vault, food containers, experiments etc. Where peak loads were likely, bathtub fittings were added to beams

and intercostals to provide maximum load-carrying capability. The open pattern allowed the atmosphere to be circulated through the habitation area and to provide a mobility aid for crewmen and a mounting surface for various types of portable restraints and mobility aids.

The floor and ceiling grid was provided for the crew to use as both handholds and so that crew members could secure themselves at a fixed location by means of triangular locking devices on the soles of their shoes (see below). The grids were equilateral cut-outs machined from a 1.27cm (0.5in) thick aluminium plate to a thickness of 1cm (0.4in). Each grid intersection had a single hole 1cm (0.4in) in diameter, with each arm of the equilateral triangle having an included angle of 60° to its neighbour. It originated as a concept from the 'wet' workshop, when it would have been pre-installed for crew occupation after the liquid hydrogen had been used during the launch phase and the single J-2 engine had consumed the propellants.

The aft surface of the upper floor had a 0.635mm (0.025in) thick aluminium sheet attached to the grid in the area of the waste management compartment to seal it from particulate migration. One 106.68cm (42in) hexagonal opening in the centre of the floor provided ingress or egress from the crew quarters. Two smaller openings in the floor, above the sleep compartment and wardroom, provided emergency egress from the crew quarters.

The crew quarters floor was located 1.98m (6.5ft) aft of the bottom of the forward compartment floor and was similar but with a 1.016mm (0.040in) thick aluminium sheet on the aft surface in place of the grid panels. This formed a plenum for the air circulation system. The floor had three openings similar to the forward compartment, the 106.68cm (42in) hexagonal opening in the centre providing access to the trash airlock and the two smaller openings (opposite the emergency egress openings in the forward compartment floor) providing access to the aft compartment. These two openings were covered to maintain a closed plenum. The forward surface of the floor had a 0.635mm (0.025in) thick aluminium sheet attached to the grid in the area of the waste management compartment to seal it from particulate migration to match the similar sheet on the upper floor.

The portions of the OWS normally viewed by the crew were specially designed to enhance both crew comfort and interior illumination while meeting thermal, toxicity and durability requirements. Most materials were left in their natural finishes, such as stainless steel and fabrics, or integral colour finishes as in the case of aluminium anodise. Since the optical reflectance of these metallic finishes was relatively low, off-white paint was applied to stowage locker faces in the wardroom and forward dome areas to improve internal illumination and on the electrical

control panels to provide adequate legibility of control markings.

The overall finish of the interior was a compromise between these specified criteria and the aesthetic preference for a suitable colour balance to ensure a passive visual impact on the crew. Attention to the need to satisfy aesthetic sensibilities in ensuring the psychological wellbeing of long-duration crews was ensured by the early intervention of NASA's George Mueller, who was appalled at the lack of attention to this aspect of station life. Mueller introduced the noted design house of Loewy and Snaith Inc, responsible for designing Studebaker cars and the celebrated Coca-Cola bottle, to advise him on colours and general layout of the OWS so as to provide the maximum degree of visual comfort for the astronauts.

In March 1968, when the 'wet' workshop was the chosen concept, Loewy and Snaith recommended specific materials, colours and other devices to retain a sense of wellbeing amid the isolation that the crews would experience. In so doing, they brought examples of challenges to submarine crews, who benefitted from similar arrangements of colour and design features. At that meeting the company suggested a library of books to allow crew members to focus their attention on non-station-related subjects and to gain cerebral relaxation from cultural pursuits.

This effort extended to discussion with

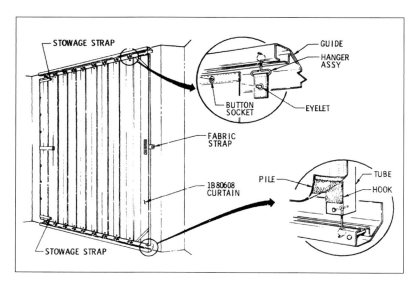

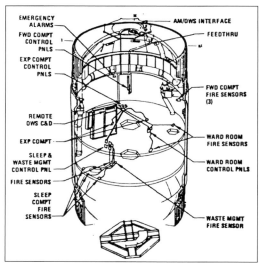

prospective crew members for their opinions. These were most difficult to incorporate within the analyses due to their training, which braced them to withstand stressful work experiences and long periods of isolation in good faith, mixed with a reluctance to suggest ameliorating additions, which some considered an unnecessary intrusion. Moreover, NASA had no experience in the psychological reaction crews would have to very long periods of such isolation, simply because there had been no flights longer than 14 days. It would take three Skylab missions to fully explore the consequences of those pressures, lessons that would be learned and applied to the next generation of astronauts aboard the International Space Station.

Some of the technical imperatives would intervene in disallowing the advice received from Loewy and Snaith. In April 1969, at a meeting held at the Manned Spacecraft Center, a special paint developed at the Marshall Space Flight Center (MSFC) was found to be flaking under exposure to cryogenic temperatures. Several presentations were made and a green alodine was finally selected for the fire retardant liner, and it was on this basis that Loewy and Snaith proceeded to work up some recommended schemes. Their drawings and suggestions were met with interest and some enthusiasm and would never have happened had it not been for the initial urging of George Mueller, who discussed with the author the essential nature of an aesthetically configured station using layouts still in the author's possession.

Engineering the interior of the OWS also had to be considerate of the requirements of the crew to move around and to access various locations, as well as to remain restrained from weightlessness when working at a specific location. They were required to conduct EVAs to retrieve film canisters from the Apollo Telescope Mount and to be prepared to go outside to carry out emergency repairs or to fix problems within their ability to correct. But these capabilities were not easily achieved because NASA had little experience with working outside. The experiences of spacewalking in the Gemini programme demonstrated the difficulty of remaining at a specific location without tethers, restraints, handholds and foot grips.

Five Gemini astronauts (White, Cernan, Collins, Gordon and Aldrin) had depressurised their two-man capsules and physically departed from the re-entry module on five occasions connected by an umbilical delivering primary life support functions. In addition, on four occasions they carried out tethered, stand-up EVAs to retrieve packages from the exterior or to take photographs. During the build-up phase to Skylab missions, discounting Moonwalks in one-sixth Earth gravity, three astronauts (Worden, Mattingly and Evans) conducted umbilical EVAs in weightlessness to retrieve film cassettes on three separate missions returning from the Moon. One astronaut (Schweickart) performed a full EVA wearing an autonomous backpack of the kind that would be used on the Moon. However, in all, NASA had experience of only eight spacewalks in weightlessness.

The lessons learned through the Gemini programme revealed a need to increase the capability of the life support system to remove excess heat and to provide better ventilation, while simultaneously improving the provision of handholds and handrails for the astronaut to move himself around and to provide adequate restraints to anchor him to a workstation. In the Skylab programme there was a requirement for the astronaut to operate tools, undo nuts and open containers. This required external handholds and rails for hand-over-hand access to various locations on the vast expanse of the exterior as well as open grids, foot restraints, toe bars, heel fittings and tethering devices for thigh attachment. There was also a need for restraints for the waste management section and the sleep cubicles.

The triangular openings of the floor grids were designed to accommodate similarly sized plates on the soles of the crew's shoes, by which a crewman could lock himself into a grid opening by a slight turn of his foot. Grids were also provided in the Multiple Docking Adapter, where a significant number of discrete workstations required crew members to work

for sustained periods with their hands free to operate equipment.

Other foot restraints were provided so that crew members could secure their feet in individual strap arrangements, two pairs on the floor of the waste management system (one beneath the hand washer and one in front of the faecal/urine collector) and three on the floor of the wardroom beneath the food table. Each of the light-duty foot restraints was fitted with two Velcro-lined straps with adjustments. A third type consisted of movable toe bars and heel fittings attached to walls and floors.

The OWS platform foot restraints, located under the water tanks in the forward area beneath the dome, were composed of sections of modified grid platforms, rigidly mounted around the periphery of the tank wall. Each section contained the standard hole pattern found in floor grids, cleat receptacles for use with the triangular shoe and open slots for insertion of a bare foot or for handholds. Two portable foot restraints were available for donning and doffing the pressure garment assemblies (PGAs), or space suits, and for drying operations after use.

BELOW Crew restraints were designed on the basis of lessons learned from the Gemini programme of space-walking difficulties, and were as much a stab in the dark as any defined solution to a known phenomenon. Some, such as foot restraints, were useful in only limited areas while others were useful for securing a crew member to a workstation. *(NASA)*

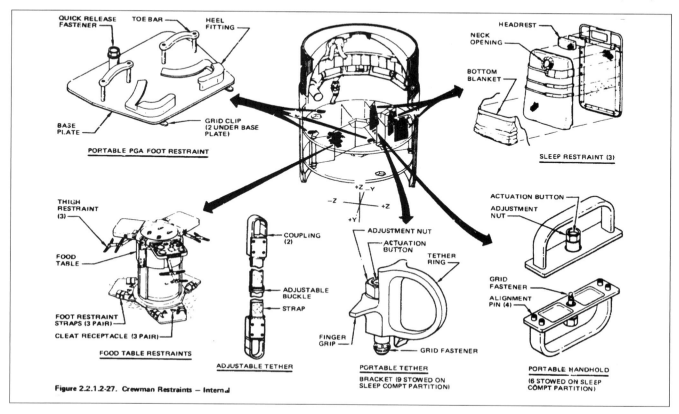

Figure 2.2.1.2-27. Crewman Restraints – Internal

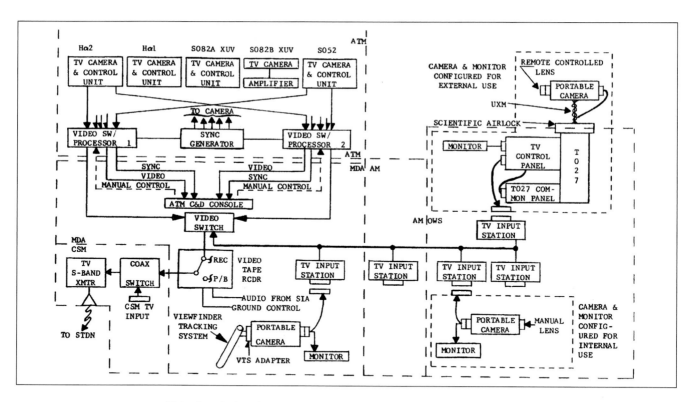

Tethering devices included various restraints, some 30.5cm (12in) in length, another type 66cm (26in) long with various holes for securing at will. Thigh restraints were provided for the food table. Each of these formed a double 'T' at one end, the astronaut placing one leg on each side of the main bar and between the other two bars to achieve secure attachment, leaving the hands free to prepare and eat the meal. Restraints for sleep bags in the private cubicles secured the bag at top and bottom. In addition, a collapsible fireman's pole was provided for moving from one part of the OWS to the other. Secured down the centre of the structure, it provided a useful exercise tool but was infrequently used for moving around the interior.

Waste tank

A considerable amount of waste would accumulate during the mission and any biologically active material would be disposed of into the waste tank using bags that could be used to contain clothing, filters, food cans, tissues, wipes, towels, washcloths and other sundry items. Two types of trash collection were provided, some for disposing of large items and bags that were positioned around

the OWS and used as trash receiving stations. Both types incorporated controlled venting to prevent the build-up of ice crystals, which could have blocked screens in the waste tank into which they were deposited. Eight trash stations were provided: two in the wardroom, three in the sleep compartments, one in the experiment compartment and two in the forward compartment of the OWS.

Trash bags in the wardroom and waste management compartment were replaced daily, the others weekly. After removing a bag from a trash station, a special adhesive-backed diaphragm was sealed and then placed into the trash disposal airlock. The disposal bags were used for urine bags, sleep restraints, food overcans, charcoal filters etc. Large items could be enclosed by Velcro lining or snappers and sealed by a tab before placement in the waste tank. In general, during the mission, the airlock was used about five times a day.

Initially, in the 'wet' workshop configuration, the original plan was to dump urine overboard through a fitting installed by the crew in the side of the liquid hydrogen tank, converted into a work/living area. When tests revealed that this could be damaging to solar arrays, it was decided to have the crew punch a hole in the common bulkhead and install a heated dump probe so that urine could be transferred to the liquid oxygen tank. When the 'wet' workshop gave way to the 'dry' configuration, the LOX tank was found to be a useful place to dispose of all trash.

The OWS waste tank was converted from the manufactured LOX tank of the S-IVB and provided 63,216m³ (2,233ft³) of volume for trash disposal. Solid waste materials were put through the trash airlock assembly that penetrated the common bulkhead. Liquid waste entered the waste tank through liquid dump probes. Non-propulsive vents were added to the waste tank to allow for venting in space. To prevent contamination of the outside of the OWS a series of 10-micron filter screens were added to the waste tank to prevent large particles from leaving the tank through the non-propulsive vents.

The waste tank itself consisted of two domes welded together to form a truncated sphere. The domes were designed with a nominal 330.2cm (130in) radius and the common dome was truncated to a 317.5cm (125in) radius, the maximum height between the domes being 4.525m (14.846ft). The aft dome was a 6.6m (21.67ft) diameter hemisphere made up of nine segments of a sphere. The dome was made from 2014-T651 aluminium and had a minimum thickness of 2.08mm (0.082in), the aft dome being welded to the cylinder. The common bulkhead was a partial hemisphere with a forward aft face of 2014-T651 aluminium, separated by 4.445cm (1.75in) fibreglass honeycomb bonded to each face. The common bulkhead was welded to the aft dome with two circumferential welds, one to each facing sheet. The 'Y' joint at the aft dome intersection was also lock bolted.

The trash screen formed compartments within the waste tank, two screens forming cylindrical segments on a 165.1cm (65in) radius running between the common bulkhead and the aft dome. The cylindrical screens were joined by side curtains that ran radially outboard, supported by a system of longerons running between the aft dome and the common bulkhead. The two non-propulsive vent screens were connected by a 30.48cm (12in) radius half torus that ran around the waste tank at the intersection of the aft dome

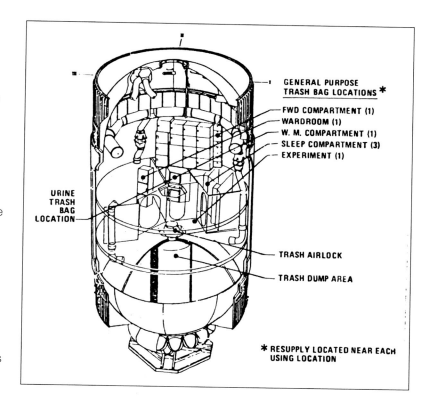

GENERAL PURPOSE
TRASH BAG LOCATIONS ✳
— FWD COMPARTMENT (1)
— WARDROOM (1)
— W. M. COMPARTMENT (1)
— SLEEP COMPARTMENT (3)
— EXPERIMENT (1)

URINE
TRASH
BAG
LOCATION

TRASH AIRLOCK

TRASH DUMP AREA

✳ RESUPPLY LOCATED NEAR EACH
USING LOCATION

and the common bulkhead to equalise pressure between the two vents.

The trash screen was constructed of 2,625 fine 304L stainless steel wires woven in a twilled Dutch weave. Of these, 325 were 0.0355mm (0.0014in) in diameter in the wrap direction, and 2,300 wires were 0.0254mm (0.0010in) in diameter in the chute direction. A section of the trash screen was constructed using 16 x 16 mesh 5056 aluminium screen with a wire diameter of 0.457mm (0.018in). There were two layers of 325 x 2,300 mesh filter screens separating the non-propulsive vent compartment and the liquid dump compartment. These screens were separated by aluminium spacers and stainless steel bolts spaced at intervals of 30.48cm (12in) on centre. A 3.81cm (1.5in) band of aluminised tape ran around the periphery of the screen segments.

The trash screen support structure consisted of a series of angles spanning between the common bulkhead and the aft dome located on a 165.1cm (65in) radius. These angles were 6.35cm (2.5in) square supported by 2024-T4 tee slips bonded to the waste tank domes with polyurethane adhesive. The angles were attached with stainless steel bolts designed with expansion joints so that the tank was not loaded when the

ABOVE **The trash disposal system involved the waste tank, converted from the former liquid oxygen tank when the structure had been fabricated as the S-IVB stage, an airlock for disposing of waste, and trash bags at various locations in the living area.** *(NASA)*

RIGHT The trash bag airlock was attached directly to the top of the converted LOX tank and was operated from the top. *(NASA)*

BELOW Loading the trash airlock with bags involved a simple manual operation from the centre of the living quarters, allowing one-way disposal. *(NASA)*

waste tank expanded due to pressurisation in the ascent mode. The screen was also supported by tee clips bonded to the domes with polyurethane adhesive and the screen was bolted to the tie clips with stainless steel bolts.

The half toroid vent duct was supported by aluminium angle arches located at 15° intervals around the toroid. The arches were attached to the domes with 5.08cm (2in) x 5.08cm (2in) x 0.2387mm (0.094in) tee clips that had been bonded to the domes with polyurethane adhesive. A 15.24cm (6in) x 6.35cm (2.5in) x 0.812mm (0.032in) deflector was attached to the common bulkhead with tee clips to prevent direct impingement of urine on the wardroom water dump probe. The penetrations through the waste tank were all designed using a fitting to feed through the skin. The areas adjacent to the openings in the basic tank structure were all reinforced with appropriate doublers to lower stresses due to discontinuities, the penetrations being doubly sealed with O-rings and a sealant.

The liquid and vacuum dump probe installation through the common bulkhead consisted of a 36.85cm (14.5in) diameter hole for the trash disposal airlock fitting, three holes for the liquid dump fittings, a hole for the waste processor dump fitting and a hole for the refrigeration pump. The trash airlock feedthrough penetrated the centre of the common bulkhead with a two-piece machined fitting that was bolted to the common bulkhead with stainless steel bolts.

A ring with an internal diameter of 35.077cm (13.81in) penetrated through the common bulkhead and supported the trash airlock. A flange was machined into the ring to pick up attachments through the forward skin on the common bulkhead. A support ring was machined from a 7075-T61 aluminium plate and bolted to the ring and the aft skin of the common bulkhead. The cut-out in the common bulkhead was reinforced by two doublers bonded to the common bulkhead skins with polyurethane adhesive and the entire installation was sealed with silicone sealant.

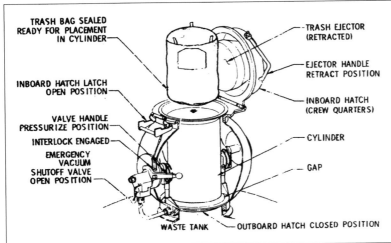

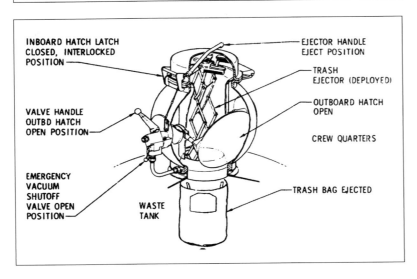

LEFT The trash ejector system involved a 'lazy-tongs' device to lower the bag into the waste container after the operator sealed the lid and evacuated the chamber. *(NASA)*

Skirt assemblies

The forward and aft skirt assemblies were modified from the standard S-IVB stage as installed on the Saturn IB or the Saturn V. The forward skirt assembly was attached to the forward cylindrical section of the OWS and provided a mounting for the Instrument Unit (IU), to which was attached the Fixed Airlock Shroud (FAS). The aft skirt assembly was installed at the aft section of the cylindrical OWS and provided an attachment to the S-II second stage of the Saturn V launch vehicle. The forward skirt was modified from the skirt configuration usually attached to an active S-IVB stage and consisted of a cylindrical shell with a length of 309.9cm (10.167ft) and a diameter of 6.6m (21.67ft).

The basic cylinder was a semi-monocoque aluminium alloy structure of sheet metal skin, external longitudinal stringers and internal ring frames. The forward interface flange of the cylinder provided for a bolted field-joint connection to the Instrument Unit, the circular ring structure that contained all the command and control electronics for directing the sequence of events during ascent. The skin of the forward skirt was 0.812mm (0.032in) thick, consisting of 7075-T6 clad sheet. The external stringers were made from 7075-T6 hat-section extrusions and the frame at the bottom end cylinder was a formed 7075-T6 angle extrusion. It had an outward flange that provided for the bolted connection to the mating flange of the tank cylinder. The frame at the forward end was built up from formed 7075-T6 sheet metal and extruded parts. Two of the three intermediate frames were constructed of formed 7075-T6 sheet, while the aft intermediate frame was formed from a large 7075-T6 hat-section extrusion.

Four pairs of elongated holes spaced approximately 90° apart around the circumference of the forward skirt provided venting of the volume inside the forward skirt void. Each pair of holes in adjacent stringer bays had an area of 241.95cm² (37.5in²) so that the total vent area was 967.8cm² (150in²), with each pair of openings carrying internal rain shields to restrict water entering the interior of the forward skirt in the event of rain showers on the pad.

The umbilical structure for the forward skirt was identical to its equivalent when the structure

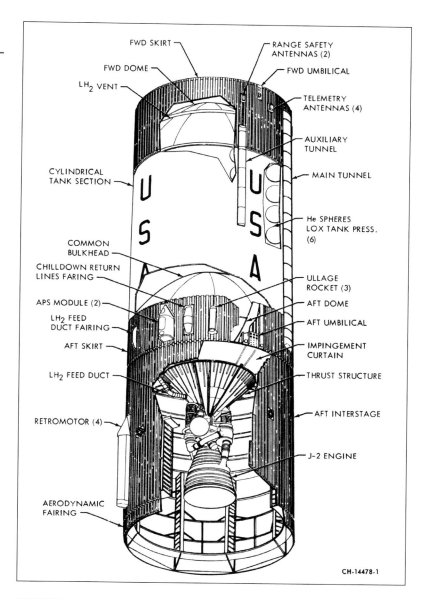

ABOVE The basic S-IVB stage represented here by the configuration typically employed to launch the three crews to Skylab on Saturn IB rockets, demonstrates the significant changes to the structural elements of the vehicle but with the skirt assemblies essentially unchanged. The aft interstage assembly is that configuration which was prepared for AS-212, the basis for the Skylab OWS. (NASA)

was used as a propulsive stage, except for the closing of two unused holes in the umbilical panel. The installation consisted of a sheet metal panel that replaced the skin in a structurally-reinforced area at the forward end of the skirt, just aft of the interface with the IU. It occupied the width of two stringer bays and was approximately 712mm (28in) in length. The umbilical panel was

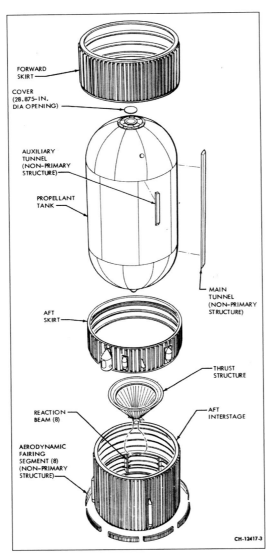

RIGHT Structural elements of the S-IVB stage with the auxiliary tunnel and main tunnel. (NASA)

FORWARD SKIRT

COVER (28.875-IN. DIA OPENING)

AUXILIARY TUNNEL (NON-PRIMARY STRUCTURE)

PROPELLANT TANK

MAIN TUNNEL (NON-PRIMARY STRUCTURE)

AFT SKIRT

THRUST STRUCTURE

REACTION BEAM (8)

AFT INTERSTAGE

AERODYNAMIC FAIRING SEGMENT (8) (NON-PRIMARY STRUCTURE)

CH-12417-3

BELOW The forward skirt of the OWS, formerly S-IVB-212, showing the location of the Solar Array System attachment points and the orientation of those elements with the axial orientation of the skirt, also the auxiliary and main tunnels. (NASA)

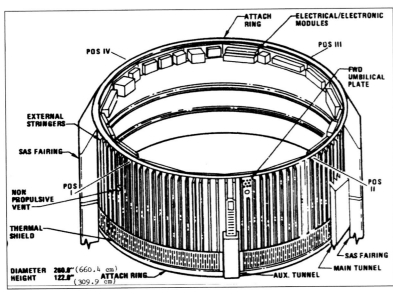

ATTACH RING

ELECTRICAL/ELECTRONIC MODULES

POS IV

POS III

FWD UMBILICAL PLATE

EXTERNAL STRINGERS

SAS FAIRING

POS I

POS II

NON PROPULSIVE VENT

THERMAL SHIELD

SAS FAIRING

MAIN TUNNEL

AUX. TUNNEL

DIAMETER 260.0" (660.4 cm)
HEIGHT 122.0" (309.9 cm)

ATTACH RING

fabricated from 0.254cm (0.100in) thick 7075-T6 aluminium sheet, flat in the central area where the holes for the connectors were located. It was riveted to the skirt's basic structure, replacing an equivalent portion of the skin and the end of one stringer. The rigidity of the panel was increased by internal horizontal stiffeners that were also riveted to the panel. The skirt structure surrounding the umbilical installation was strengthened by additional internal ribs and intercostals.

Electrical and electronic equipment was mounted identical to the S-IVB on panels that in turn were attached through vibration isolators to internal structural support skirt intercostals. The panels were of the same honeycomb design as on the S-IVB stages. Laminate fibreglass epoxy face sheets, 0.812mm (0.032in) thick, were bonded to a 2.86cm (1.125in) thick, glass fabric reinforced phenolic honeycomb core. Glass fabric, 1.60mm (0.063in) thick, Volan finish C-channels were attached at the forward and aft ends of the panel, with Delron inserts installed in the panel for mounting the electrical components. These panels were mounted on two or three isolators, depending on the size of the panel, and on the weight of the electrical components. The isolators in turn were mounted to the forward skirt structure. Some of these panels were thermally insulated on the inboard side and some on the outboard side with a low-emissivity shroud. These shrouds consisted of two to four layers of gold-coated Kapton (a metallised polyimide fibre) with a polyester net fabric between each layer. The shrouds were assembled to the panel by Velcro or tie strings.

Design changes to the forward skirt included the addition of sheet metal channels to strengthen the frames at two stations with machined intercostals between the frames and sheet metal ribs, all of which served as a backup structure at the forward fairing attachment points. Further aft of the forward skirt, just forward of the tank joint, externally mounted fittings were located and the ordnance tie-down/release assemblies were attached to these. A major design change to the basic structure of the forward skirt was the replacement of the sheet metal skin with a chemically milled panel at each end of the two locations. The thickness of the chemically milled panel ranged from 0.812mm (0.032in) to

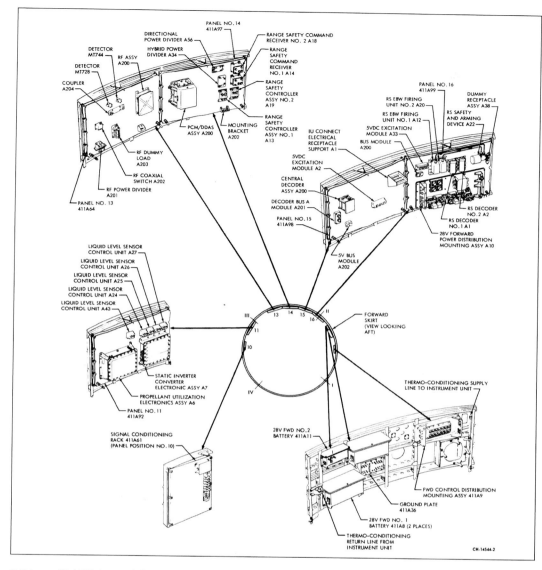

LEFT The components and electronics attached to the inside face of the forward skirt are displayed in this diagram showing relative positions around the circumference of this element. *(NASA-MSFC)*

2.84mm (0.122in), providing increased strength and stiffness.

The thermal shield insulation was added to the structure and extended from the tank joint to the first intermediate forward skirt frame, a length of about 78.74cm (31in), consisting of panels which formed a continuous band around the circumference of the forward skirt, except where interrupted by the solar array wing assemblies. The shield was made of beaded aluminium sheet-metal panels that were attached to fibreglass hat-section supports mounted circumferentially on the forward skirt structure at four stations, 17.22cm (6.78in) apart. The hat-section supports were riveted to the outer face of the forward skirt stringers and the beaded shield panels were riveted to the

outer face of the fibreglass supports. The shield was thus located radially about 3.81cm (1.5in) outboard of the forward skirt skin.

The area immediately forward of the tank joint for a length of approximately 17.78cm (7.0in) was not covered by the aluminium panels. To provide removable panels for access, and to minimise the amount of heat transferred to the shield by conduction and radiation from the tank joint flanges, fibreglass panels were used for the thermal shield in this area. At the forward end of the beaded aluminium portion of the shield, sloping panels of fibreglass were installed between each pair of stringers to provide a ramp-like transition between the forward skirt skin and the surface of the thermal shield.

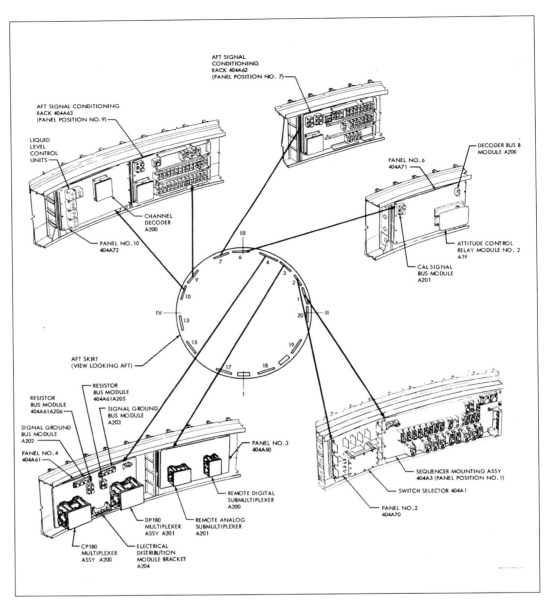

AFT SIGNAL
CONDITIONING
RACK 404A62
(PANEL POSITION NO. 7)

AFT SIGNAL CONDITIONING
RACK 404A63
(PANEL POSITION NO.9)

LIQUID
LEVEL
CONTROL
UNITS

CHANNEL
DECODER
A200

PANEL NO.10
404A72

AFT SKIRT
(VIEW LOOKING AFT)

DECODER BUS B
MODULE A200

PANEL NO.6
404A71

ATTITUDE CONTROL
RELAY MODULE NO. 2
A19

CAL SIGNAL
BUS MODULE
A201

RESISTOR
BUS MODULE
404A61A206

RESISTOR
BUS MODULE
404A61A205

SIGNAL GROUND
BUS MODULE
A203

SIGNAL GROUND
BUS MODULE
A202

PANEL NO.4
404A61

PANEL NO.3
404A60

REMOTE DIGITAL
SUBMULTIPLEXER
A200

DP180
MULTIPLEXER
ASSY A201

REMOTE ANALOG
SUBMULTIPLEXER
A201

SEQUENCER MOUNTING ASSY
404A3 (PANEL POSITION NO. 1)

SWITCH SELECTOR 404A1

PANEL NO.2
404A70

CP180
MULTIPLEXER
ASSY A200

ELECTRICAL
DISTRIBUTION
MODULE BRACKET
A204

The OWS aft skirt was a modified cylindrical structure, 660.4cm (260in) in diameter and 217.17cm (85.5in) in length, with a typical skin thickness of 1.016mm (0.040in) in 7075-T6-clad sheet. A typical stringer was 3.493mm (1.375in) high consisting of a 7075-T6 aluminium extrusion hat-section. The stringers were machined to reduce weight in the intermediate bays where the full section was not required for strength. The ring frames in the aft skirt consisted of two I-section frames made from 7075-T6 aluminium extrusion tees with a cladding of sheet web from the same steel and one hat-section extrusion frame. The forward interface angle was machined from a 7075-T6 aluminium extrusion and bolted to the habitation area tank attach angle. The aft interface angle was a machined component and part of the separation joint.

The aft skirt umbilical was identical to the S-IVB aft umbilical except for minor changes to accommodate revised connectors for the OWS system. Two connector locations were modified for the OWS refrigeration lines and those connector locations not used for Skylab were plugged. These included the holes for the LOX and LH_2 fill and drain system and four fluid connectors. Two pivot points on the aft interstage and three umbilical carrier support fittings supported the umbilical carrier and transferred the carrier loads to the OWS structure.

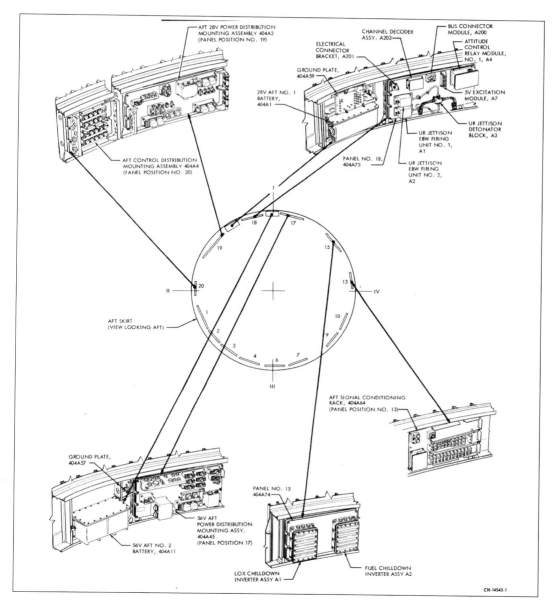

The umbilical plate was machined from a 7.62mm (3in) by 99.06cm (39in) by 121.92cm (48in) aluminium plate with pockets for the connectors and ribs for stiffness to carry the loads from the umbilical carrier and to help transfer the axial load from the habitation area to the aft interstage. The umbilical installation replaced ten typical stringers with five H-section stringers with a heavier section and four short hat sections and H-section stringers. The short stringers reduced hard-point loading on the tank flange and transferred load from the forward interface into the umbilical plate and the full length H-section stringers.

The aft skirt thermal shield was installed 4.445cm (1.75in) radially from the skirt skin on the exterior of the skirt. It extended 83.82cm (33in) aft from the aft skirt-to-tank interface and was fabricated from beaded 7075-T6 clad sheets 0.508mm (0.020in) thick and fibreglass panels 1.524mm (0.060in) thick. The shield was supported by four 1.524mm (0.060in) thick fibreglass hat sections and a fibreglass angle of similar thickness attached to the forward interface angle of the aft skirt. The fibreglass panels extended 0.970cm (0.382in) forward of the skirt-to-tank interface to provide the required shadow for the interface flanges. The shield was sealed,

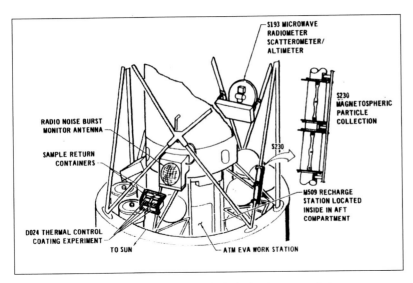

The S193 Microwave Radiometer Scatterometer/Altimeter, S230 Magnetospheric Particle Collection, Radio Noise Burst Monitor Antenna, Sample Return Containers, D024 Thermal Control Coating Experiment, To Sun, ATM EVA Work Station, M509 Recharge Station located inside in aft compartment

ABOVE The forward skirt assembly supported parts of the ATM truss assemblies and some experiments and attachments as shown here. *(NASA)*

except for drain holes to prevent damage and contamination of the gold foil liner on the inner surface.

The equipment mounting panels and support structure was identical to that already described for the forward skirt, except for the Thruster Attitude Control Subsystem (TACS) valves and nozzles which were mounted on fibreglass honeycomb panels approximately 3.175 x

BELOW The Microwave Radiometer Scatterometer was also located on this forward assembly. *(NASA-MSFC)*

BELOW RIGHT This diagram of Skylab's data acquisition systems shows that much of the processing equipment and instrumentation made use of the solid structural foundation for attachments and mounting points. *(NASA)*

44.45 x 45.75cm (1.25 x 17.5 x 18in) and of the same design as the electrical equipment panels. They were mounted on Aeroflex cable-type isolators, six to a panel, which consisted of aluminium cable retainer bars and stainless steel cable. The tangential thruster nozzles were supported by steel fittings mounted to the panel, and the radial thruster nozzle was supported by aluminium fittings. Each protrusion through the skirt skin was sealed with a coated nylon cloth heat-sealable boot clamped around each tube and support fitting with a band.

The Solar Array System (SAS) attachment fittings were installed on the S-IVB aft skirt as part of the conversion to the OWS configuration, with three machined fittings used to attach each beam fairing to the aft skirt. One fitting replaced a stringer and carried the axial loads as well as the SAS loads from the two attachment points. Two separate fittings were used at the other two SAS attachment points and these were installed between existing stringers and existing pick-up attachment fittings, but no internal modifications were necessary.

The OWS separation joint was identical to that employed for the stage as a propulsive element of the launch vehicle, consisting of two 7075-T6 aluminium extrusion angles machined to form an interlocking joint. The upper angle had a groove in its horizontal leg, 0.447cm (0.176in) deep by 2.43cm (0.957in) wide. The lower angle had a mating protrusion that fitted into the groove to transfer shear loads from the skirt to the

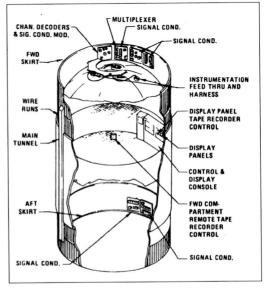

The diagram shows: MULTIPLEXER, CHAN. DECODERS & SIG. COND. MOD., SIGNAL COND., FWD SKIRT, SIGNAL COND., INSTRUMENTATION FEED THRU AND HARNESS, WIRE RUNS, DISPLAY PANEL TAPE RECORDER CONTROL, MAIN TUNNEL, DISPLAY PANELS, CONTROL & DISPLAY CONSOLE, AFT SKIRT, FWD COMPARTMENT REMOTE TAPE RECORDER CONTROL, SIGNAL COND., SIGNAL COND.

interstage. The vertical leg of the lower angle was machined to form a 1.27mm (0.050in) thick band that was severed at separation. A groove was machined into the vertical leg to form a cavity between the upper and lower angles to contain the redundant mild detonating fuses that provided the energy to sever the joint.

Two aerodynamically shaped external tunnels extended from the forward skirt over the cylindrical habitation tank to the aft skirt. One of these was the auxiliary tunnel which was an integral part of the meteoroid shield, the other was the main tunnel, identical to the S-IVB tunnel, being approximately 12.7cm (5in) high and 60.96 (24in) wide, fabricated from several separate sections for the extended length. These sections were stiffened by intermediate J-section frames. Covers in the skirt areas were bolted to the skirt structure and those in the tank section were bolted to clips mechanically attached to star-shaped doublers bonded to the surface of the tank. The tunnel was sealed and vented as per the S-IVB stage.

The main tunnel extended from the forward skirt along the tank to the aft skirt, a total distance of approximately 10.668m (35ft). Internal stiffening frames were spaced every 22.86–25.4cm (9–10in) and covered wiring and tubing that connected systems in the aft skirt with forward skirt components. Wire bundles and tubes were supported at intervals of less than 30.48cm (12in) by Nylafil standoffs bonded to the external tank wall.

Aft support structure and radiator

External to the pressurised work and living space in the adapted liquid hydrogen tank and to the converted liquid oxygen tank, the aft support structure was another legacy from the original design for the S-IVB stage. It was designed to support a single, restartable Rocketdyne J-2 rocket motor that was not installed since the cluster would be carried up into orbit by the first two stages of the Saturn V. As equipped for Skylab, it provided a mounting structure for the Thruster Attitude Control System (TACS) nitrogen gas storage spheres with manifolds and meteoroid shielding and a refrigeration system radiator together with

thermal control panel and all the associated equipment and piping.

Essentially, the aft support structure was a 94° cone fabricated from 7075-T6 aluminium, chemically milled with extruded stringers and clad sheets with an A356 aluminium casting at the apex. Like the S-IVB thrust structure, the Skylab aft structure was attached to a flange on the waste tank aft dome with 96 bolts. Modifications made to the basic thrust structure included replacing two of the three frames with heavier frames and fittings to carry loads from the TACS nitrogen spheres. It was also re-machined to carry the radiator and its shield installations.

New hardware included saddle-type pans to support 23 gas storage spheres installed on the conical surface of the aft structure, each restrained in its pan by four preloaded straps. Manufactured from TI-6AL-4V titanium forgings, each sphere had a 63.5cm (25in) outside diameter with a wall thickness of 0.899cm (0.354in), 22 of the spheres being manifolded together by means of peripherally mounted tubing attached to the aft skirt structure for the TACS system. The other sphere was used for the pneumatic control system. A meteoroid shield covered the 23 spheres and its manifold system, annular in shape and comprising eight identical aluminium alloy segments connected by extruded tees and screws.

The TACS sphere meteoroid shield system was designed so that there would be a very low probability of the spheres being penetrated by a random impact, each segment covering a 45°

ABOVE Taken during the fly-around by the first crew to visit what turned out to be a temporarily crippled space station, this shot from the Apollo spacecraft shows the relative disposition of the radiator and the enclosure housing the 22 Thruster Attitude Control System bottles and the single pneumatic sphere. Note the stuck Solar Array System, held back by debris from the ripped meteoroid shield. *(NASA)*

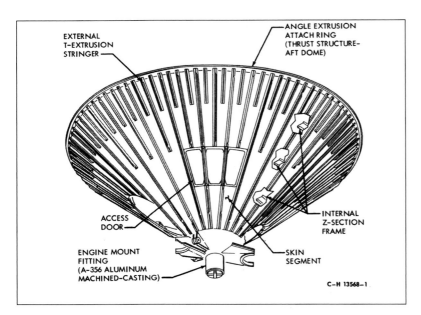

EXTERNAL
T-EXTRUSION
STRINGER

ANGLE EXTRUSION
ATTACH RING
(THRUST STRUCTURE-
AFT DOME)

ACCESS
DOOR

ENGINE MOUNT
FITTING
(A-356 ALUMINUM
MACHINED-CASTING)

INTERNAL
Z-SECTION
FRAME

SKIN
SEGMENT

C-H 13568-1

ABOVE The conical support structure for the TACS/radiator assembly inherited from the basic design of the S-IVB stage, which was designed to carry a single J-2 cryogenic motor as propulsion. *(NASA)*

circular section and consisting of double-wall construction separated by three 5.08cm (2in) extruded frames. The outer compound curved skin was 1.27mm (0.050in) 2014-T6 which was chemically milled after forming to a thickness of 0.99mm (0.039in) to 0.228mm (0.0009in).

The two lower outer skins were beaded 0.812mm (0.032in), 2024-T42 sheet steel and the inner compound curved skin was 2.03mm (0.080in) 2014-T6 material. The two lower inner skins were 2.02mm (0.080in) 2024-T3 material while the two intermediate H-frames were made from 2024-T42 sheet with the lower closing frame being an extruded 2024-T6 channel. Segments were spliced together through a 1.6mm (0.063in) extruded 7075-T6 tee. The segments were bolted to a 1.6mm (0.063in) 2024-T4 Z-section circular support ring which was attached to the aft structure stringers by 52 extruded 7075-T6 T-clips, Hi-locks and bolts.

The TACS sphere meteoroid shield skirt was bolted to the meteoroid shield with a 2.29mm (0.090in) 2024-T42 angle fixture, the skirt proper being of double-wall construction and circular in shape. It was approximately 254cm (100in) in diameter and tapered from 22.9cm (9.00in) to 1.27mm (0.050in) deep to match the slope of the radiator. The outer skin was 0.812mm (0.032in) 2024-T3 and the inner skin was 2.03mm (0.080in) material of the same sheet. The upper cap was a 5.08cm (2in) deep 2014-T62 extrusion channel; the lower cap was a 2024-T42 sheet of the same thickness.

The radiator support structure consisted of an irregular octagon-shaped sandwich structure with four supporting beams on its forward side, attached to and stabilised by eight support struts from the aft structure.

The sandwich structure consisted of a 12.7cm (5in) thick polyurethane foam core with a forward skin 0.635mm (0.025in) thick by 302.3cm (119in) square made from 2024-T3 sheet. Attached to the forward skin were tapered hat-section supporting beams made from 1.6mm (0.063in) 2024-T3 aluminium sheet and tapered from a 5.08cm (2in) depth at the end to a 10.2cm (4.00in) depth at the centre. The aft skin, of 6061-T6 aluminium sheet fabricated into a 0.635cm (0.025in) by 302.3cm (119in) square, had coolant tubes sear-welded to its foam side face. The core consisted of polyurethane foam rigid blocks with continuous fibreglass roving bonded together and polyurethane-foamed in place. A channel, 12.7cm (5.00in) deep, of 1.02mm (0.040in) 2024-T3 aluminium sheet, was bonded to the core around the periphery of the panel assembly. It was also riveted to the forward skin and bolted to the aft skirt.

The eight support tubes made from 2.22cm (0.874in) by 1.65mm (0.065in) wall 347 CRES, had spherical rod-end bearings with an A286 body and a type 718 nickel base alloy ball threaded into each end. One end of each tube assembly was bolted into a fitting made from 2024-T-351 aluminium plate, which in turn was bolted to two radiator support structure beams. The other end of each tube assembly bolted to a fitting from 7075-T7351 aluminium bar which was mounted to the thrust structure casting.

The radiator assembly was bolted at four places at the centre of the thrust structure casting through the fitting assembly, which was bolted to the radiator support structure beams. This fitting assembly was made from A286 DRES that was embedded in glass fibre cloth. A thermal control unit panel assembly supported the thermal capacitors, ground cooling heat exchangers and other units in conjunction with the radiator. The loads were transmitted to the thrust structure by four tubular struts and beams.

The thermal control panel and all the radiator components mounted to it, as well as the installation equipment, was designed to withstand the acoustic and vibration environment. This package was located between the radiator and sloping surface of the thrust structure inside the TACS bottle meteoroid shield. The panel, the same honeycomb design as the electrical equipment panels, had laminated fibreglass epoxy face sheets, 0.812mm (0.032in) thick, bonded to a 2.85cm (1.125in) thick heat- and cryogenic-resistant, phenolic-reinforced, glass fabric honeycomb core.

Glass fibre cloth Volan finish C-channels, 1.6mm (0.063in) thick, were installed around the periphery of the panel. Delron inserts were installed in the panel for mounting the radiator components and the panel was installed on the aft structure by four tabular 2024-T4 struts of 2.22cm (0.874in) outside diameter and approximately 66.04cm (26in) long. These struts were bolted to the aft structure stringers and to an A286 CRES clevis which was in turn bolted to the four corners of the panel. Two 2024-T42 sheet metal beams, located at the outermost ends of the panel, were bolted to the panel and the thrust structure casting. The inboard centre of the panel was bolted to an extended leg of the aft structure casting.

A radiator impingement shield was attached to the radiating surface of the refrigeration system radiator, providing protection from retro-rocket plume impingement from the forward-facing rockets mounted to the interstage skirt. Approximately nine minutes after second-stage separation the shield was jettisoned by the IU automatic sequencer. A backup command was provided through the Airlock Module digital command system. The radiator impingement shield was made from a lightweight 6061-T6 aluminium truss to which insulation covered with Beta cloth was attached. The shield had a single support point at its centre where it was attached to the jettison actuator by a ball release mechanism.

The support truss was a welded and brazed aluminium structure composed of a tubular ring shaped to the peripheral contours of the radiator. Six tapered radial beams supported the ring. The insulation was sandwiched between layers of Teflon-coated Beta cloth that were sewn to the outer ring of the truss. The shield assembly was designed to be jettisoned by

LEFT The exposed TACS bottles seen on the backup Skylab which could have flown as a second space station and is now in the National Air & Space Museum, Washington DC. *(CleOptra)*

a single symmetrical separation force at the centre of gravity. To ensure a central centre of gravity location that was 0.762mm (0.030in) within the theoretical spot, the shield was balanced during assembly. Rotation of the installed assembly about the vehicle's centreline was prevented by two anti-rotation pins. The conical shape of these pins ensured instant disengagement during shield separation.

Separation was accomplished by applying energy to a dual-piston pneumatic actuator that operated the ball release mechanism attached to the centre of the shield. A separation spring mounted in the ball release mechanism provided sufficient force to eject the shield at a velocity sufficient to preclude stage re-contact. A plume impingement curtain located between the aft skirt and the aft structure provided protection from retrorocket plume impingement for the area between the aft skirt and the aft

BELOW The relative placement of the TACS spheres, meteoroid shield, skirt and thermal curtain on the conical aft section. *(NASA)*

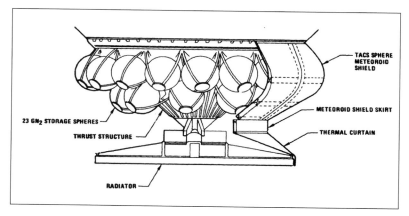

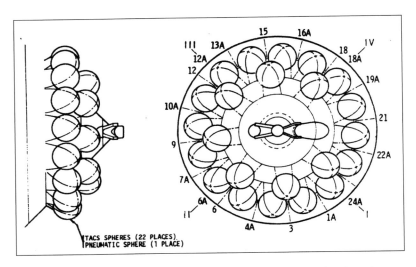

TACS SPHERES (22 PLACES)
PNEUMATIC SPHERE (1 PLACE)

dome. The curtain was subjected to boost acceleration loads, vibrational loads, retrorocket gas impact and adverse thermal environments. This glass fabric curtain was attached to the aft structure/dome joint in a manner that would not constrain movement between the aft skirt and the habitation area of the tank structure.

The curtain's construction provided controlled ventilation of atmospheric pressure from the enclosed volume. Zippers in the curtain allowed access to equipment in the aft skirt area. To avoid loading the tubes and wire bundles that penetrated through the curtain, flexible boots were installed around the penetrations. The curtain itself was made from aluminised, silicone-coated glass fabric, consisting of eight segments joined by leak-proof zippers to form a truncated cone. At the aft skirt attachment

point, the curtain rested against the inner cap of the aft interstage forward frame and to prevent chafing a silicone-rubber tip was bonded to the frame cap.

Aft interstage

This component was a frustum-shaped, semi-monocoque structure designed to connect the S-IVB, or in this case the OWS aft skirt assembly, to the top of the S-II second stage of the Saturn V. It had a height of 577.9cm (227.5in) with a nominal diameter of 660.4cm (260in) at the forward end and a diameter of 1,007.7cm (396.75in) at the aft end. It consisted of 144 externally mounted hat-section stringers, 1.016mm (0.040in) thick sheet metal skin, nine internally mounted ring frames and intercostals in the forward and aft bays with a normal spacing of every third stringer. The major portion of the structure was fabricated from 7075-T6 aluminium alloy sheet metal and extrusions.

The basic cross-section of the ring frames was two extruded Y-shaped (angle shaped on forward and aft frames) caps, a 0.635mm (0.025in) nominal thick sheet metal web and extruded angle stiffeners. The nominal depth of the seven intermediate frames was 40.6cm (16in), the forward and aft frames being approximately 30.5cm (12in) deep.

The intercostals in the forward 48.3cm (19in) were 1.016mm (0.040in) thick sheet metal cut to an X-shaped planform, an extruded stringer attach angle and an extruded I-shaped inboard cap. The aft 48.3cm (19in) bay intercostals were hydroformed 0.813cm (0.032in) thick sheet metal, an extruded stringer attach angle and an extruded T-shaped inboard cap. An access opening, 99cm (39in) long, approximately 90cm (35in) wide at the forward end and 101.6cm (40in) wide at the aft end, located approximately 104.14cm (41in) from the forward end of the aft interstage, provided access into the Orbital Workshop aft skirt and interstage areas. A beaded panel, constructed of two sheets of 1.27mm (0.050in) thick metal riveted back-to-back, was installed in the opening with Camloc high shear type fasteners prior to flight.

Vent openings, provided to control venting of the OWS aft skirt/aft interstage internal area to control the differential pressure loads on the

aft skirt, interstage and S-II forward skirt during ascent and to provide an outlet for the purge gas during ground operations, were located approximately 213.36cm (84in) from the aft end of the interstage. Two sets of eight holes were located 180° apart, each with a length-to-width ratio of 4:1 with the length parallel to the stringer. The area of each opening was 64.5cm² (10in²). Rain shield assemblies were installed inside the aft interstage to prevent moisture entering. A two-by-two 1.6mm (0.063in) diameter wire mesh was installed on the rain shield assemblies to prevent birds and other solid objects from entering the interstage.

A support structure was provided for the four S-II retrorocket installations in the form of two intercostals constructed of a 1.016mm (0.40in) thick clad aluminium alloy sheet riveted to extruded caps and formed clad aluminium alloy sheet angles with a formed clad aluminium alloy sheet support between the intercostals, installed at each retrorocket location. Each retrorocket was supported at the forward end with the two trunnion type 4340 steel fittings and at the aft end by two tubular supports attached to the interstage aft frame inboard cap through two 2024-T351 aluminium alloy fittings.

A fairing with an ejectable nose section was installed at each retrorocket location, the fixed portion being fabricated from 1.6mm (0.063in) thick 2024-T3 clad aluminium sheet, riveted to the exterior of the aft interstage. The ejectable nose section, made of 2.03mm (0.080in) thick 2024-T42 clad aluminium alloy sheet, was attached to the fixed fairing with a hinge and shear pin (rivet) installation. Ejection was accomplished by firing the retrorocket, causing pressure to build up under the fairing until a sufficient load developed to rupture the shear pin. The release point of the hinge was positioned so that the path of the ejected fairing would not strike the OWS or the S-II stage.

The structural tie between the aft interstage and the OWS aft skirt was through 288 equally spaced 0.794cm (0.31in) diameter bolts. Flight separation at this joint was accomplished by fracturing a tension strap on the OWS aft skirt frame by means of a mild detonating fuse. Mating electrical connectors mounted to the OWS aft skirt and the aft interstage forward frame disconnected at separation. The

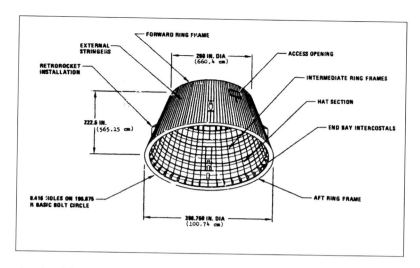

structural tie between the aft interstage and the S-II forward skirt was through 286 equally spaced bolts, each with a diameter of 0.952cm (0.375in). Mating was facilitated by using three equally spaced removable alignment fittings at each of the forward and aft interfaces.

The one difference between the OWS aft interstage and the S-IVB aft interstage was the material and pattern of the thermal insulation coating applied to external areas of the interstage proper. Non-ablative silicone insulation was used on the OWS aft interstage in lieu of the ablative Korotherm insulation used on S-IVB interstages to reduce contamination. The silicone insulation was applied only to highly stressed areas of the interstages that were subject to high heat fluxes due to the OWS aft skirt protuberances and the aft interstage retrorocket fairings.

ABOVE The interstage adapter remained attached to the S-II second stage of the Saturn V when launched into orbit as the Skylab space station. *(NASA-MSFC)*

BELOW The manufacturing plane and separation configuration of the interstage and aft skirt assembly. *(NASA-MSFC)*

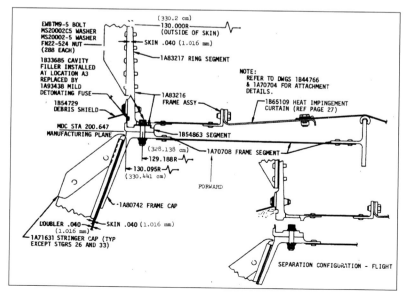

Meteoroid shield

NASA had been worried about the damage which could be caused by fine particles in space impacting the hull of the Orbital Workshop and had already sent into orbit several satellites specifically designed to quantify the risk from micrometeoroid particles and meteoroids, some taking impact counts on various thicknesses of aluminium sheet used for the Apollo spacecraft.

Before that, the first statistically significant penetration measurements were made by the early Explorer series of satellites, notably Explorer 13 launched on 25 August 1961, equipped with pressurised cans of 0.025mm (0.00098in) and 0.050mm (0.0019in) and Explorer 16 sent up on 16 December 1962, which had a useful life of eight months. That satellite recorded data verified by Explorer 23

launched on 6 November 1964, and some members of NASA's Office of Advanced Research and Technology proposed the use of large Saturn rockets to place in orbit more sophisticated devices which could be carried on test launches.

This resulted in Pegasus, a 1,451kg (3,200lb) micrometeoroid monitoring experiment which was carried beneath the boilerplate Apollo Command Module attached to the last three Saturn I flights, SA-8, SA-9 and SA-10. These experiments consisted of a structural mount for a pair of wings, 29m (96ft) across and 4.1m (13.6ft) wide, extended from the folded position and powered by solar cells. Each carried 104 panels with thicknesses varying up to 0.41mm (0.016in) across an area of 210m² (2,300ft²) to detect impacts from tiny particles.

Launched in 1965, on 16 February, 25 May and 30 July, they were inserted in different orbits between 441km (270 miles) and 740km (460 miles). Pegasus 3 lasted until August 1969 but Pegasus 2 remained in orbit until November 1979. Results confirmed expectations that for a sheet of aluminium alloy of 0.4mm (0.00157in), a penetration frequency of 1.3/m²/year could be expected. While there was no qualitative assessment due to the crude nature of the sampling, it was generally agreed that some degree of protection would be required for pressurised, habitable structures, designed to remain occupied for extended periods.

The special case of Skylab arose from its

BELOW The primary components and elements of the Skylab meteoroid shield, which was designed to act as a buffer to protect the surface of the OWS from penetration and depressurisation. It was also required to act as a thermal shield to shade the surface of the tank from direct solar radiation. *(NASA-MSFC)*

BELOW RIGHT Held tight against the surface of the OWS during ascent into orbit, the meteoroid shield was to have been deployed in orbit on stand-off struts to provide separation from the surface of the OWS and prevent conducted heat from solar radiation which has heated the meteoroid shield proper. *(NASA-MSFC)*

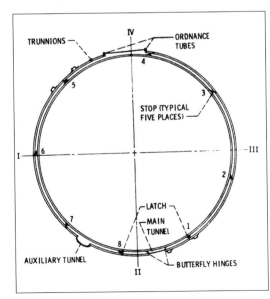

unique size and vulnerability. Developed from the S-IV rocket stage employed with the Saturn I, the S-IVB was an evolved structure that was not expected to resist the effects of long-duration stays in space and was therefore without any protection from meteoroid impact. Moreover, as a pressurised living space and workspace for astronauts, the Orbital Workshop was vulnerable to even minor impact and there were no provisions for repairing a punctured hull. It was imperative, therefore, that some form of protection was provided to ensure that the crew would have sufficient protection to assure safety.

The original meteoroid shield was conceived and developed for the 'wet' workshop, in which the S-IVB would have operated as a propulsive stage to achieve orbit before being occupied and converted into a work and living area in the liquid hydrogen tank. Initial design options focused on a thin shield wrapped tightly around the cylindrical hull of the stage which could be deployed to a standoff 12.7cm (5in) from the surface of the tank in orbit. With liquid hydrogen in the tank, this provided many advantages. The gold coating applied to the tank surface in conjunction with the shield paint pattern and the internal insulation would ensure a simple passive thermal control system would be achieved.

Although there was initially some concern that ice would form to prevent deployment, early tests and analysis indicated that this would not occur. There were also tests to determine the appropriate standoff distance so as to ensure maximum dissipation of impact energy without damaging the surface of the OWS. This was an important feature, and one reason for having a separation between the point of impact and the hull itself; in space there is no blast wave so the only effect of the penetration would be to disperse the single spec of meteoroid, take out much of the velocity and create low-energy fragments easily deflected by the OWS hull proper.

When in 1969 the OWS changed to a 'dry' configuration there was some talk of constructing a fixed standoff shield but that would have compromised other equipment designs, such as the Solar Array System, which could be transferred across to the new fully equipped station. There would also be weight penalties, flutter problems, condensation and

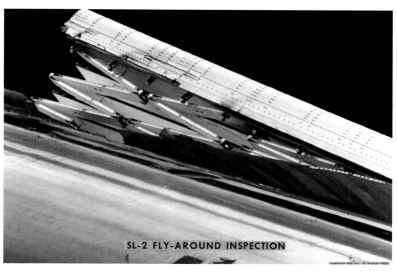

SL-2 FLY-AROUND INSPECTION

aerodynamic stress with a fixed shield. Several small changes were made to what became a direct transfer to the 'dry' configuration. The auxiliary tunnel was designed as a spring to maintain tension in the shield, scroll springs were developed to ensure proper deployed standoff distance at the fold-over panels and the interface with the SAS beam was designed to provide sealing.

As designed and fitted to the OWS the meteoroid shield was fitted tightly around its skin, deployment being achieved by energy stored in 16 torsion bars acting on link arms mounted through the tank-skirt flanges. The linkage mechanism was a series of four-bar linkages in which the shield was a flexible interconnecting bar and the tank flange was a rigid bar. The change in circumference required for deployment was to be accomplished by hinged fold-over panels, located under the ordnance separation joint. The frames of the auxiliary tunnel were designed to act as hoop tension springs to assure intimate contact between the tank and meteoroid shield and also to accommodate growth of the tank due to changes of differential pressure and temperature.

The meteoroid shield was a series of sixteen 2024-T6, aluminium panels 0.635cm (0.025in) thick with a curved radius of 342cm (135in), bolted together through brake-formed flanges at each edge to form a complete cover around the cylindrical section of the habitation area. The weight of the shield at launch was transmitted to the aft tank flange by bevelled 6061-T651 aluminium support blocks located at the panel

ABOVE After the meteoroid shield was torn loose during powered ascent, parts of the torn shade fouled the deployment of a Solar Array System wing. This view shows the gold-coated exterior surface of the OWS that received direct heat from the Sun. *(NASA)*

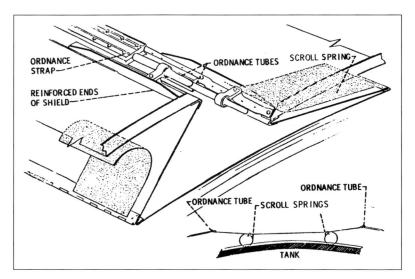

ORDNANCE STRAP

REINFORCED ENDS OF SHIELD

ORDNANCE TUBES

SCROLL SPRING

ORDNANCE TUBE
SCROLL SPRINGS
ORDNANCE TUBE
TANK

joints. The forward and aft ends of each panel had a 7075-T6 closing angle, attached to which was a silicone rubber bulb seal which was adjusted after the shield was rigged to provide ground weather protection for the thermal coating on the exterior habitation area.

Also, attached to the closing angles were 7075-T61 fittings for attaching the deployment links to the panels. At both ends of the individual panels were a series of slotted 0.127mm (0.005in) thick 301 CRES boots preformed to provide an annular closure at both ends of the shield when deployed. This closure was required for meteoroid protection and thermal control on-orbit. When the shield was closed, these boots were pressed between the shield and the tank. The interior surfaces of the panels and boots were Teflon-coated to minimise the coefficient of friction with the tank surface, which had a gold coating. Several of the panels had removable sub-panels to permit access through the rigged meteoroid shield to the viewing window, the side access panels and the two scientific airlocks.

The panel containing the auxiliary tunnel had twenty-eight 6AL-4V titanium alloy frames which acted as springs to maintain a hoop tension load in the shield. They were deflected circumferentially 3.175cm (1.25in) when rigged and were capable of additional deflection to accommodate tank growth due to differential pressure of the habitation area. The frames were attached to a 6061-T651 aluminium base on the panel by dry-lubricated cadmium-plated hinge pins. The tunnel enclosed auxiliary

equipment running the length of the tank and was covered by a three-piece, 0.635mm (0.025in) 2014-T6 aluminium beaded skin that interfaced with the fixed tunnel extensions on both forward and aft skirts.

The folded panel assembly contained the expendable ordnance device and five folded 0.635mm (0.025in) thick 2014-T6 aluminium panels connected at the edges by continuous 2024-T6 hinges with Teflon-coated spacers located between hinge lobes. After deployment, the fold-over panels were held away from the tank by four 0.254mm (0.010in) thick 320 CRES scroll springs which were held flat between the panel fold when rigged.

The shield was attached to the vehicle on both sides of the main tunnel and by sixteen A-286 CRES link arms. A 718 Inconel stud attached each link to a panel and a keyed 718 Inconel shoulder sleeve was pressed into the other end of the link arm and passed through the tank to the skirt flange. The dry-lubricated sleeve rotated in two A-286 CRES blocks mounted on the tank-skirt flange. The sleeve was retained by two A-286 CRES jam nuts. A 6A1-4V titanium alloy torsion bar was passed through each sleeve, mounting the rotatable links, and connected at one end to the sleeve by an indexed spline. The torsion bars were preloaded manually and supplied the energy required to deploy the shield. The anchor end of the torsion bar was an A-286 CRES keeper that slid on to the hexagon of the torsion bar to preload it. The keeper was retained by a 7075-T651 aluminium anchor fitting located between stringers of the forward and aft skirts.

On each side of the main tunnel was a 2014-T651 aluminium full-length hinge attached by dry-lubricated cadmium-plated steel hinge pins to twelve 2014-T651 aluminium tension straps which were bonded to the tank with a polyurethane adhesive. The mating panel hinges were 6061-T651 aluminium and were also joined with dry-lubricated cadmium-plated steel hinge pins. The thrust loads were reacted by aluminium Teflon-coated spacers located between hinge lobes, and tension straps spanned the main tunnel by extending under the wiring and piping that ran between the forward and aft skirts.

The meteoroid shield was preloaded in hoop

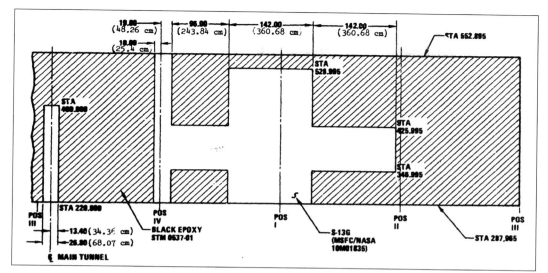

tension by two overlapping panels, each having fourteen 1.016mm (0.040in) thick 7075-T6 aluminium straps attached, joined by A-286 CRES trunnions and 303 CRES take-up bolts. The viewing window was protected at launch by a two-piece, 0.254mm (0.010in) thick 301 CRES Teflon-coated cover. Each piece of the cover was preformed into a scroll. When the shield was rigged, the shade segments were flattened between the shield and the tank. At shield deployment each section returned to its preformed shape, thus exposing the window. A CRES hook was attached to each of the four link arms adjacent to the main equipment tunnel and engaged a latch mounted on a base attached to the tank flange. The latching mechanism stopped rebound of the shield during deployment and the force was achieved by a 302 or 304 CRES compression spring.

When the shield was rigged for launch the shield interfaced with the SAS seals and the auxiliary tunnel on both the forward and aft skirts. The seals interfaced with the panel surfaces in the constant diameter section of the tank. Adjacent to the tank flanges, a ramp was attached to the panel, raising the sealing surface to the height of the sealing surfaces on the forward and aft skirts. The forward end of the meteoroid shield had a Teflon seal interfacing with a flat bulkhead on the aft end of the auxiliary tunnel on the forward skirt. The aft end of the shield auxiliary tunnel was sealed by a silicone rubber seal held in place by a slotted frame that formed around the aft skirt fairing stub.

The frame was attached to the panel with rollers to permit shield-to-tank movement. The shield provided a method of entry into the habitation area through this side access panel, accomplished by removal of a section of the segmented panel after the shield was rigged. After removal of this section the side access panel could be removed. After deployment of the shield, the two cut-outs for the scientific airlocks in the meteoroid shield were approximately centred over the SAL openings in the tank to permit deployment of the experiments. Also,

ABOVE **A view of part of the debris from the ripped meteoroid shield blocking deployment of the solar array wing.** *(NASA)*

(electrical bridge wire) detonators and electronic firing units located on a panel in the forward skirt. A redundant fuse train consisting of the confined detonating fuse extended between the detonation block and the expandable tubes.

The expandable tubes consisted of two flattened 1.25cm (0.5in) diameter steel tubes extending the full length of the shield, each containing 45.9-grain/m (14-grain/ft) RDX mild detonating fuse. The tubes were encased in the tension strap that was severed along its entire length by the expansion of either tube of the redundant system. The folded panels were extended to the deployed position by preloaded torsion bars and springs after the restraining tension strap assembly was severed. Each of the two explosive trains was initiated using an EBW system containing an electronic firing unit and a detonator. The plan was to initiate one system with the other remaining as a backup. The electrical design provided for firing commands from the Instrument Unit (IU), with backup signals from the Airlock Module. This system utilised redundant ordnance trains that were designed so that a single failure did not inhibit shield deployment.

The firing circuit subsystem utilised the IU during the first 7.5 hours of flight, after which both AM Bus 1 and AM Bus 2 power were

the cut-out for the window was approximately centred over the viewing window.

The meteoroid shield was held against the OWS by means of a tension strap assembly that extended along the full length of the shield itself, consisting of six tension straps and two explosively actuated expendable tube assemblies. The strap assembly was installed during manufacture of the shield folded panel assembly, which contained five panels folded on themselves to allow proper retraction to the smaller diameter of the OWS. The release mechanism contained redundant EBW

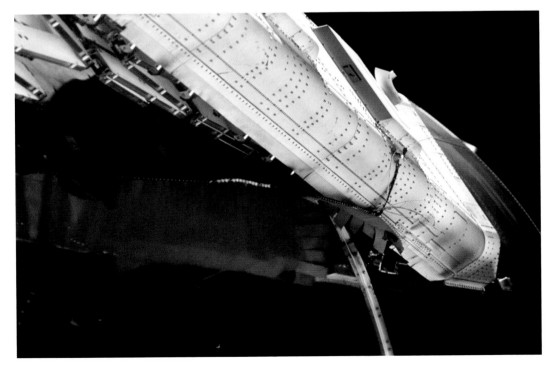

RIGHT **This close-up view of the ripped meteoroid shield shows the extent to which it had blocked the solar array wing, with a metal strap physically restraining the boom. This was cut free during the first manned visit.** *(NASA)*

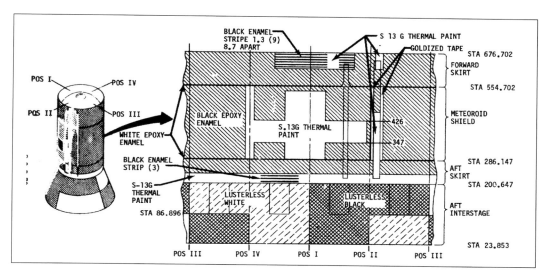

Labels in figure:
BLACK ENAMEL STRIPE 1.3 (9) 8.7 APART
S 13 G THERMAL PAINT
GOLDIZED TAPE
STA 676.702
FORWARD SKIRT
STA 554.702
POS I
POS IV
POS II
POS III
BLACK EPOXY ENAMEL
S.13G THERMAL PAINT
426
347
METEOROID SHIELD
WHITE EPOXY ENAMEL
BLACK ENAMEL STRIP (3)
STA 286.147
AFT SKIRT
STA 200.647
S-13G THERMAL PAINT
LUSTERLESS WHITE
LUSTERLESS BLACK
AFT INTERSTAGE
STA 86.896
STA 23.853
POS III   POS IV   POS I   POS II   POS III

LEFT The thermal paint pattern template with white and black patches was designed to provide passive thermal control operating in conjunction with active elements on the interior of the structure. Paint patterns shown here on this two-dimensional, 360° display include those on the meteoroid shield (see previous section) and the aft and forward skirt assemblies and the interstage section. (NASA-MSFC)

adopted. The primary method of releasing the shield utilised the IU automatic flight control computer to issue proper control commands to the OWS switch selector. Through relay contacts controlled by this selector, AM Bus 2 power was used to charge the firing unit and fire the ordnance, which released the shield. The relays used by this circuit were 10A mag-latch type and 10A general purpose types. The fire command circuit was inhibited by a normally open relay contact controlled by the OWS solar array deployment command. This sequence was required to prevent possible damage to the OWS solar arrays during array deployment. The backup method utilised a ground digital command system to control 10A general purpose relays via the AM and this used Bus 1 power to charge the firing unit and fire the ordnance to permit deployment of the shield.

Instrumentation attached to the meteoroid shield consisted of three break-wires across the ordnance strap assembly, four deployment magnetic switches at the main tunnel and 16 torsion bar strain gauges. The deployment magnetic proximity switches were located on either side of the OWS main tunnel with two of the switches on the forward end and two on the aft end. The switches closed independently of each other when the meteoroid shield deployed. The strain gauges were located on each of the torsion bars that deployed the shield. There were 16 strain gauges, one for each torsion bar, and a measurement of zero degrees rotation corresponded to the meteoroid shield secured position.

Environmental/Thermal Control Subsystem

The specification for the 'wet' workshop concept for environmental conditioning and thermal control was defined at the Marshall Space Flight Center in December 1967, which at that date provided control by fans circulating gas in eight evenly-spaced ducts. These ducts were formed by a series of thermal curtains and rails around the periphery of the habitation area, and the system gave gas temperatures in the range of 12.7–40.5°C (55–105°F). This design was based on the use of a gravity-gradient orientation at Sun-angles met by an orbital inclination of 28.5°. The minimum temperature for safe astronaut entry for a suited crew member after outgassing the active tank was defined as -101°C (-150°F).

During the latter part of 1967 and into 1968, joint studies undertaken by MSFC and McDonnell Douglas delineated advantages for controlling heat leaks in the tank sidewall, tank joint regions, the forward dome and the plenum region including the common bulkhead. These studies led to the gold tape on the external surface, the forward dome high-performance insulation system, the thermal shields on the external joint areas and foam insulation in the plenum region. The addition of foam insulation was not implemented, however, until the transition to the 'dry' workshop.

Hydrogen retention in the tank foam insulation was of concern from the standpoint of habitability and flammability but tests completed in 1968 demonstrated that no problem existed since the passivation sequence allowed sufficient time for outgassing from the insulation.

By mid-1969, when McDonnell Douglas Aircraft Corporation (MDAC) began design analysis on the Environmental/Thermal Control Subsystem (E/TCS) at the request of MSFC, the system concept and design had undergone many changes, but the crew comfort criteria had been defined as achieving a stable atmospheric and mean radiant wall temperature of 18.3–23.9°C (65–75°F), specific and relative humidity levels of 0.018 and 95% respectively, a touch temperature of 12.7–40.5°C (55–105°F) and an atmospheric velocity of 4.6–30.5m/min (15–100ft/min). Temperatures were to be controlled automatically or manually utilising cooling delivered from the Airlock Module ECS and 750W of heater power, with a 500W capability in each of two ducts with fan clusters.

The atmospheric distribution system was to be designed to minimise carbon dioxide and humidity gradients, radiant heaters providing a maximum of 1kW would be utilised for warm-up to provide a -17.7°C (0°F) mean internal temperature at initiation of pressurisation and a 4.4°C (40°F) minimum internal temperature by the time the tank seal and lighting installation was completed. Requirements for shifting from a 'dry' to a 'wet' workshop configuration were reassessed in September 1969, with the mission

now expected to be flown at an orbital inclination of 35°.

Before completion of this assessment, a change to a 50° inclination was made in early 1970, which meant that the E/TCS design had to consider the increased heat loads associated with orbits in 100% sunlight, whereas the maximum previously had been 73% sunlight. Several design changes were driven by this significant alteration of operating conditions and the final configuration was determined on that basis. When the Airlock Module was again redesigned in 1972 heat loads were increased and, based on these changes, the definitive passive and active system evolved.

This design was based on passive thermal control of the OWS environment with augmentation by convective heating and cooling of the atmosphere during manned phases and radiative heating of the internal structure during unmanned phases. It comprised two subsystems: an active thermal control subsystem including ventilation and a passive thermal control subsystem. The atmospheric gas was a mixture of 70% oxygen and 30% nitrogen at 3.45N/cm² (5lb/in²) during habitation.

The active subsystem provided continuous control of the internal environment, with cabin gas temperature controlled by cabin gas heat exchangers in the Airlock Module (AM) and by the convective heaters in three Ventilation Control System (VCS) ducts. Reconditioned and purified gas from the AM was mixed with recirculated gas in the OWS. Prior to habitation, radiant heaters were to be used to maintain temperature above the minimum levels that satisfied food and film storage requirements. The passive subsystem relied on optical properties to control OWS interior and exterior surfaces, high performance insulation on the forward dome, polyurethane insulation lining the inside of the pressure shell and heat pipes attached to structural penetrations of the interior insulation.

The exterior surface finishes and the high-performance insulation (HPI) blankets were to control the net energy balance between the OWS and the external space environment. The heat transfer rates from the habitation area to the meteoroid shield, and from the forward and aft dome areas, were to be regulated by control of the respective finished surfaces. Also,

BELOW The gas supply system for the Skylab cluster operated as an integral provision for all pressurised elements and was not dedicated to any particular modular section. This simplified schematic shows the relevant supply provisions from the separate oxygen and nitrogen bottles and for the intra-vehicular activity (IVA) and extra-vehicular activity (space walking) requirements. *(NASA-MSFC)*

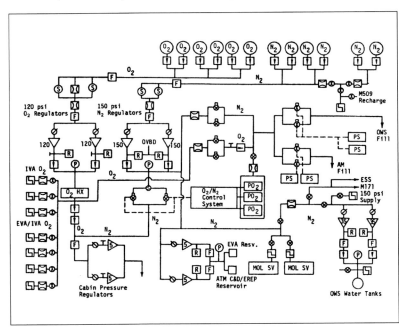

the interior habitation area wall temperatures were to be made more uniform with optical property control of these surfaces and with heat pipes. Because of the warmer habitation area environments after the loss of the heat shield during ascent, the convective heaters in the VCS ducts were never used and the radiant heaters were only actuated once, shortly after insertion and before it was realised that the shield had been torn away.

The entire meteoroid shield was painted with lustreless black paint except for local use of S-13G white paint in selected areas. The thermal control coatings were used to regulate the radiant energy exchange between the OWS and its environment. The white and black paint pattern on the hot side of the meteoroid shield was designed to absorb sufficient solar energy such that the Thermal Control System (TCS) would meet stringent temperature comfort criteria using specified convective heater power. The exterior wall of the OWS beneath the meteoroid shield was covered with a low emissivity coating of gold aluminised Kapton tape to minimise the heat transfer between the wall and the shield. This coating was intended to dampen the amplitude of the internal wall temperature caused by the day/night orbital cycles.

The Kapton tape was provided to ensure a low emittance surface that, in combination with the black-and-white painted meteoroid shield,

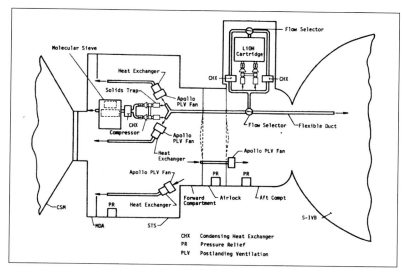

was to have provided the desired heat balance. The 15.2cm (6in) wide strips of tape (Mystic 4017) consisted of 60 angstroms of gold on a 0.0025cm (one mil) Kapton film backed with silicone adhesive and was installed in butted circumferential bands on the habitation area sidewalls. The tape was installed by a controlled application that included removing air bubbles between the tape and surface of the tank sidewall. The gold surface of the tape was protected by a plastic film until just prior to installation of the meteoroid shield in October 1973.

Meteoroid shield boots were designed to reduce the heat loss from the annulus formed by the meteoroid shield and the OWS tank

ABOVE The atmosphere purification system involved air filters, fans, heat exchangers, pumps and lithium hydroxide carbon dioxide removal units. *(NASA-MSFC)*

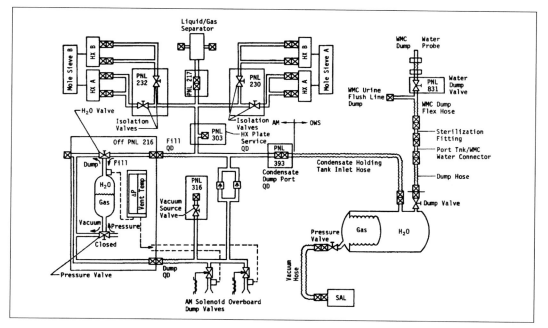

LEFT Water purification concepts were evaluated and changed according to the growth in capability of the Skylab space station from 'wet' design to 'dry'. Two redundant units incorporated molecular sieves and separators. *(NASA-MSFC)*

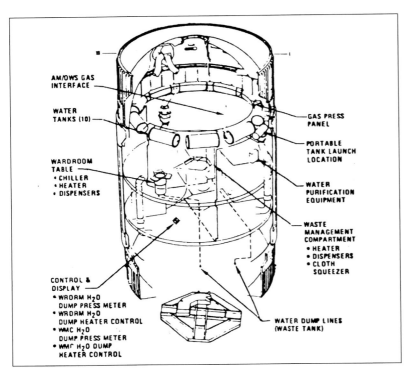

AM/OWS GAS
INTERFACE

WATER
TANKS (10)

WARDROOM
TABLE
• CHILLER
• HEATER
• DISPENSERS

CONTROL &
DISPLAY
• WRDRM H₂O
DUMP PRESS METER
• WRDRM H₂O
DUMP HEATER CONTROL
• WMC H₂O
DUMP PRESS METER
• WMC H₂O DUMP
HEATER CONTROL

GAS PRESS
PANEL

PORTABLE
TANK LAUNCH
LOCATION

WATER
PURIFICATION
EQUIPMENT

WASTE
MANAGEMENT
COMPARTMENT
• HEATER
• DISPENSERS
• CLOTH
SQUEEZER

WATER DUMP LINES
(WASTE TANK)

ABOVE The water
management system
was an integral
operating element
in conjunction with
the water purification
units, and involved
elements of the OWS
where water supply
was contained and
controlled.
(NASA-MSFC)

wall. The low emissivity coatings used on the
skirts and the domes adjacent to the skirt-tank
joints minimised the heat transfer through the
joints. The skirts and domes would have acted
as radiative fins for heat conducted across the
joints if the low emissivity coatings were not
provided. Thermal shields covered portions of
the OWS skirts adjacent to the skirt-tank joint
and protected the coatings in this region from
degradation, both prior to and during flight. The
OWS interior surfaces in the habitation area
had high emissivity to provide thermal radiation
interchange between all walls and partitions.

The VCS consisted of a gas supply duct,
a mixing chamber, distribution container fan

clusters, a plenum, floor diffusers and portable
fans. Conditioned gas was brought from the
Airlock Module to the OWS by the supply duct,
which was attached to the mixing chamber to
the plenum below the crew quarters floor. The
OWS bulk gas flow was maintained by a four-
fan cluster in each duct. The crew quarters floor
was equipped with adjustable diffusers that
allowed the air to circulate through the crew
quarters and back to the forward compartment,
a portion of which was then returned to the AM
for conditioning.

Three portable fan units were included in
the OWS to provide a localised increase in
flow velocity as required by the crew. The
performance of the VCS was dependent
upon the excitation for the fans, the number
of duct and portable fans operating and the
adjustments of the floor diffusers and chambers.
The system designed operating voltage range
was from 24–30VDC. For normal operation
during habitation 12 duct fans were operating
continuously and the three portable fans were
operated as desired by the astronauts. The
range of flow anticipated was 12.7–19.8m³/min
(450–700ft³/min) per duct.

In detail, the supply duct carried conditioned
gas from the Airlock Module Environmental
Control System (AM/ECS) to the VCS mixing
chamber. The duct had a diameter of 20.3cm
(8in) and was designed for a maximum flow of
1.18kg/min (2.6lb/min) at a maximum pressure
differential across the duct of 0.127cm (0.050in)
of water. The conditioned gas from the AM
and the recirculated gas from the OWS were
combined in the mixing chamber and fed into
the distribution ducts. The recirculated OWS
gas entered the mixing chamber through the
screens covering five sides of the chamber.

The three VCS ducts supplied gas to the
plenum below the crew quarters floor. The fan
cluster inlet portion in each duct was a wire-
reinforced two-ply Armalon cloth construction.

LEFT The large-scale movement of fluids,
including water and coolant, required feedthrough troughs breaking the separate structure
at critical locations. Here by example are
the waste processor dump and liquid dump
feedthrough troughs. *(NASA-MSFC)*

MACHINED FITTING 304L
STAINLESS STEEL

7.00 DIA X .040 DOUBLER 7076-T6

SILICON SEALANT

COMMON BULKHEAD

SILICON SEALANT

MACHINED FITTING 304L
STAINLESS STEEL
4.00 DIA X .040
DOUBLER 7075-T6

SILICON SEALANT

4.00 DIA X .063
DOUBLER 7075-T6

7.00 DIA X .063
DOUBLER 7076-T6

SILICON SEALANT

COREFIL

COREFIL

WASHER & NUT

SILICON SEALANT

WASHER & NUT

*17.78 cm DIA x 1.016 mm DOUBLER
**10.16 cm DIA x 1.016 mm DOUBLER

WASTE PROCESSOR FEED THRU

LIQUID DUMP FEEDTHRU

The discharge duct downstream of the fan cluster was a single-ply Armalon construction. A diffuser was placed on the end of each duct to direct the flow in the plenum and provide a uniformly mixed gas supply to the floor diffusers.

The fan cluster in each duct consisted of a baffled resonant chamber, an inlet and outlet muffler and four PLV fans to deliver the conditioned and recirculated gas to the plenum. The fan cluster design provided access to each fan through the four fan access doors for fan replacement, and for that reason it was designed for easy substitution. The fan could be removed by opening the fan access door and squeezing the handle, which retracted the fan retainer pins and released the device.

Two types of adjustable velocity-profile diffusers were provided, one circular and one rectangular. Flow was controlled by the position of the damper and of the diffuser vanes. The position of these vanes was controlled by turning the diffuser vane control to either the narrow or wide-flow pattern. The volumetric flow was controlled primarily with the damper control, although a small change in flow could occur when adjusting from narrow to wide pattern. Flow volume and direction were controlled by manually adjusting the movable diffuser vanes. Locations are shown on accompanying illustrations.

The portable fan utilised the fan in a portable support that could be located on any of the OWS structural grids, the fireman's pole or the handrails, and could be connected to any 3A utility outlet. This portable support incorporated sound suppression and inlet and outlet screens to protect the fan from debris. The fan operated from a three-way switch giving high, low and off positions. The duct fans could be controlled by circuit breakers and the fans in Ducts 1 and 2 were powered from OWS Power Buses 1 and 2. The fans in Duct 3 could be powered from either bus or split between Bus 1 and Bus 2.

The active thermal control subsystem provided continuous control of the OWS internal environment during periods of habitation. The cabin gas temperature was controlled by cabin gas heat exchangers in the Airlock Module and by convective heaters in the three VCS ducts. Conditioned gas from the AM was mixed with recirculated air in the OWS. Radiant heaters were designed to maintain temperatures above the minimum levels that satisfied food and film storage requirements prior to habitation.

The convective heater design power requirement was 500W at 24VDC and was capable of operating over an applied voltage range of 24–32VDC. One convective heater assembly was located in each of the three OWS VCS ducts. In Ducts 1 and 2 the heaters were positioned just above the floor while Duct 3 was located in the forward compartment, just above the living compartment ceiling. Each unit contained two thermostats for high limit temperature control with redundancy. The thermostats were designed to open at 126.7°C (260°F), and close at 115.5°C (240°F). V-band couplings were provided for heater assembly replacement on orbit and a cover over the coupling mechanism was used to provide protection for the astronaut.

The four heater elements were stacked in

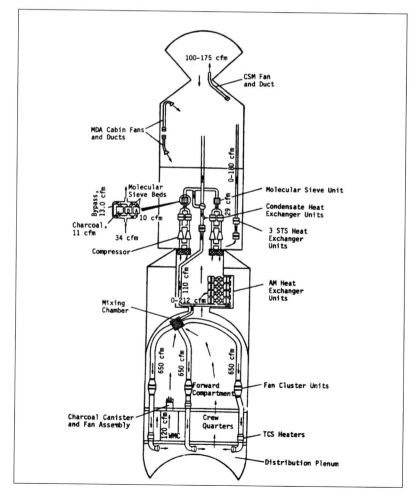

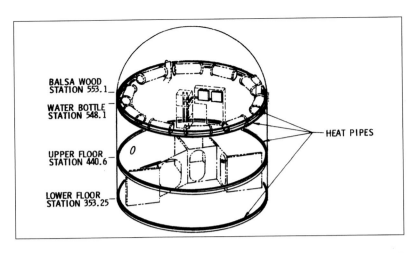

ABOVE Circumferential heat pipes were located around the girth of the OWS below the forward compartment dome and associated water tanks and at the ceiling and floor of the living/experiment compartment. *(NASA-MSFC)*

BELOW Atmospheric mixing chambers were connected to flow distribution bellows leading to pipes circulating fresh air to the separate elements of Skylab. *(NASA)*

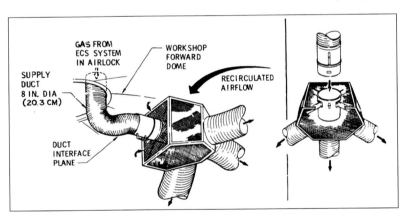

BELOW The atmospheric distribution system was integrated with the heaters and several diffusers, some adjustable and others fixed. *(NASA-MSFC)*

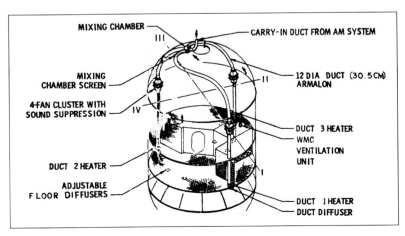

a 15.24cm (6in) diameter, 0.127mm (0.005in) wall aluminium housing, the four units brazed to either side of two spoke assemblies, with eight spokes per assembly, attached to the housing with screws. Each element was of spiral design with a total length of approximately 7.3m (24ft). The outer wall of the 0.318cm (0.125in) diameter element was stainless steel of 0.0635cm (0.025in) thickness. The nickel heater wire within the element doubled back on itself at the centre of the spiral such that both ends terminated at the large radius end of the element. Magnesium oxide was the insulating material used between the nickel wire and the stainless steel sheath. The wiring from an element and its thermostats terminated at one of two junction boxes located on either side of the assembly.

The convective heaters located in the VCS ducts were designed to be used in conjunction with the AM cooling heat exchangers to provide thermal control of the OWS atmosphere during habitation. Duct 1 and Duct 2 heaters were controlled automatically by the Thermal Control Assembly, but they could also be controlled manually by switches located on a control panel. The TCA and the control panel switches were arranged such that heaters could be turned on and off in increments of 250W, while the 250W increments of the Duct 3 heater could be controlled only manually. The convective heater in Duct 3 could be powered by either bus, whereas Duct 1 and 2 heaters could only be powered from Buses 1 and 2 respectively.

The eight radiant heaters were designed to heat the OWS after boost and prior to habitation and also during storage periods between crew visits. They were designed to dissipate a total of 1,000W at 24VDC, three being located in the forward compartment and the remaining five in the crew quarters. The heaters had a semi-circular cross-sectional area and were 78.7cm (31in) in length and 27.4cm (10.8in) in diameter.

The heating element was located beneath the 0.0635cm (0.025in) aluminium shell and consisted of 0.00254cm (0.001in) Inconel. The inner and outer surfaces of the element were insulated with silicone rubber impregnated cloth, and a flame barrier of 0.0305cm (0.012in) fluorocarbon impregnated fibreglass cloth on either side of the insulation was provided.

A layer of 2.54cm (1in) thick polyurethane foam was used to insulate the inner surface of the heater and a 0.05cm (0.020in) aluminium inner shell, while a 0.0076cm (0.003in) aluminium foil outer covering provided fire protection by enclosing the foam. Other structural members of the heater included a 0.477cm (0.188in) base plate and three 0.0813cm (0.0320in) bulkheads.

The eight radiant heaters were provided to maintain the temperatures of the food and film above 4.4°C (40°F) during unmanned periods after orbital insertion and to warm up the habitation area prior to OWS activation. They were designed to be remotely controlled in groups of four, both through the Digital Command System (DCS) and manually through switches in the Airlock Module.

The wardroom window heater was an electrically conductive gold film, 3–5Å thick, vapour-deposited on the outboard surface of the inboard glazing of the window. It was designed to maintain a minimum window temperature of 12.7°C (50°F) capable of operating in the range 24–32VDC. The window had two bus bars bonded to the coating, and when voltage was applied to these bars current flowed to the gold coating on activation of a circuit breaker and a manual switch in the wardroom. The window heater was normally on during manned phases and off at other times, switchable between OWS Bus 1 and Bus 2 and protected by 6A circuit breakers.

The Thermal Control Assembly could activate the heaters or heat exchangers as required to stabilise the cabin gas temperature at the selected level. The allowable temperature deviation was +/-2.2°C (+/-4°F) and if it exceeded that corridor the thermal system was designed to enter a cooling cycle and all four heat exchangers would be turned on. When the gas temperature decreased 1.1°C (2°F) below the set point all four heat exchangers would be turned off, and if the gas temperature increased one heat exchanger would be turned on for each 0.56°C (1°F) sensed above the set point to a maximum of four heat exchangers. When the temperature dropped below the set point by 1.1°C (2°F) the exchangers would be turned off and the TCS would remain in the cooling cycle

until the gas temperature dropped 2.2°C (4°F) below the set point. Then the system would enter the heating cycle and the converse of the cooling cycle would commence.

The heat pipes were designed to provide heat input to internal surface areas which would have had a minimum temperature below 12.7°C (55°F), where areas would have been susceptible to water vapour condensation and would have presented a medium for the growth of bacteria. The basic function of the heat pipes was to provide high thermal conductance paths that allowed heat to be transferred readily from hot areas to raise the temperature of the cold areas. An arterial heat pipe was utilised which had type 304 stainless steel screening for the 0.24cm (0.094in) diameter artery and the wick.

ABOVE The forward compartment provided opportunity for distributing the pipes and plumbing essential to distribution of clean air in an environment where there was no convection and where foul air could accumulate in stagnant areas. *(NASA)*

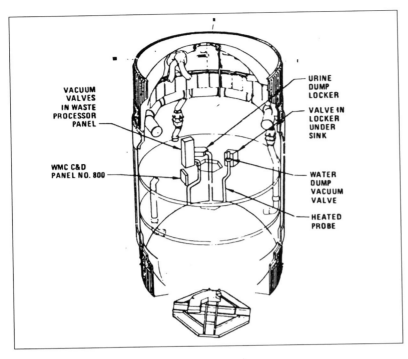

ABOVE Waste management provisions too were integrated within the atmospheric circulation and replenishment system together with the water supplies. *(NASA-MSFC)*

BELOW Feeding back into the general disbursement of habitability provisions described in an earlier section, the Skylab refrigeration system contributed heat from condensers in the freezer system. *(NASA-MSFC)*

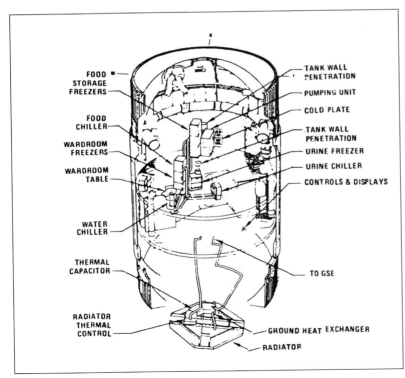

The pipe was made from 6061 aluminium and utilised Freon-22 as a heat transfer fluid.

Two rings of heat pipes were attached to the internal tank wall at each of the four OWS locations. Double rings of heat pipes were necessary since a single heat pipe 20.6m (67.5ft) long (the circumference of the OWS) was not available and would have been too long to install in one piece. The double rings provided the cascading effect (heat transfer continuity between overlapping pipes) necessary to transfer thermal energy from one side of the vehicle to the other. Each heat pipe was 4.06m (160in) long and overlapped the adjacent heat pipe by 50% to achieve the necessary cascading effect.

The thermal requirements dictated that the installation of the heat pipes be different between the hot and the cold sides of the vehicle. On the hot side, which faced the Sun during the solar inertial vehicle orientation, 27 aluminium heat pipes and 0.318cm (0.125in) thick aluminium mounting plates were installed to conduct the required heat from the relatively hot vehicle structure to the heat pipes. On the cold side, which normally faced the Earth or deep space, 66 plates of 0.102cm (0.040in) high conductivity aluminium alloy was used to distribute the heat. The cold side plates covered almost the entire surface area where temperatures below 12.7°C (55°F) were expected without the pipes.

The thermal contact resistance between the cascaded heat pipes was minimised by using DC-340 grease on all thermally critical contact areas and by maintaining a contact pressure of 3.45N/cm² (5lb/in²) with a holding clip. The clip had top and side cantilever springs that forced the heat pipes down on the installation plates and against each other. Good thermal contact between the heat pipes was required to permit cascading in the pipes without impairing overall system performance. The heat pipe installations behind the water bottles and at the upper and lower floors were similar and in these cases the pipes were attached to the wall at 63 waffle intersection points.

The requirement for low thermal resistance between the heat pipes and the tank wall dictated a relatively short and thick high conductivity clip, which had to be flexible to accommodate the tank radial expansion during the boost phase. The movement of the heat pipe attachment points caused by changing vibration, pressure and temperatures during boost required a low stiffness clip to attach the pipes to the tank wall. Consequently, the design of the heat pipe support assembly had to accommodate the conflicting requirements of low thermal resistance and minimal stiffness. A support clip with three U-bends was used to provide this flexible fitting and a low-resistance heat transfer path was provided by the heat transfer strap, which was made of a stack of 36 soft aluminium foils, 0.0076cm (0.003in) thick.

The foils did not contribute significantly to the bending stiffness of the assembly and the support clip was used because the heat transfer strap was not structurally adequate to support the heat pipes during the launch vibration phase. The heat pipes were attached to the heat transfer strap by sheet metal clips with leaf springs that forced the pipes against each other and against the strap for good thermal contact, the contact resistance minimised by the use of DC-340 compound.

A key factor in the heat pipe system was the use of phenolic-fibreglass washers on the bolts to thermally isolate the floor, ceiling and water tank supports from the tank wall on the cold side of the vehicle. Electrical grounding requirements prevented the use of fibreglass washers on all the cold side bolts; thus only about two-thirds of the bolts were so equipped. Heat pipes were also used to transfer the heat dissipated by the logic unit electronics to the back of the forward compartment food freezer, thereby maintaining that surface above the atmospheric dew point temperature.

The heat pipes were installed on the logic unit containers by eight attachment clips equipped with leaf springs similar to those used on the balsa wood area heat pipes. The pipes were attached to the back of the freezer by 25 attachment clips. One of the more significant

mechanical requirements of this installation was the necessity of bending the heat pipes to a 7.6cm (3in) radius, needed to provide a continuous thermal path from the logic boxes to the back of the freezer.

Passive Thermal Control (PTC) was provided through control of the optical properties of interior and exterior surfaces, regulated by the use of paints, coated film and coated tape, in addition to the application of high-performance insulation across the forward dome area. In addition complete circumferential thermal shields covered the longitudinal portion of the forward and aft skirts, and the inside of the OWS was lined with reinforced foam insulation, also contributing to PTC.

The high-performance insulation consisted of ten layers of gold-coated polyimide film, 0.127mm (0.005in) thick, plus nine layers of separator material consisting of 0.1778mm

RIGHT The refrigeration radiator bypass valve, which was to control the flow of water to the radiator and, in so doing, control the balance of thermal energy within the active coolant loop and the flow of heat to the radiator. *(NASA-MSFC)*

BELOW The integration of the refrigeration system with the waste dumps and the habitability functions provided an open-loop system with closed-loop consumables. *(NASA-MSFC)*

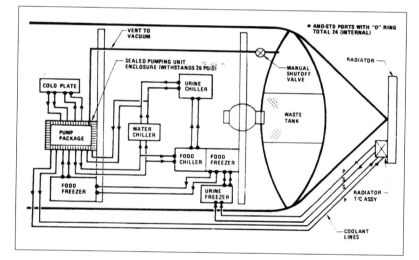

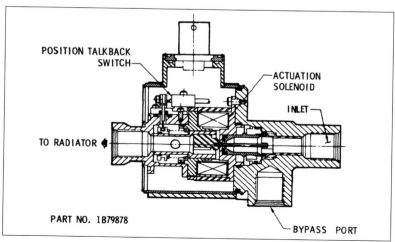

PART NO. 1B79878

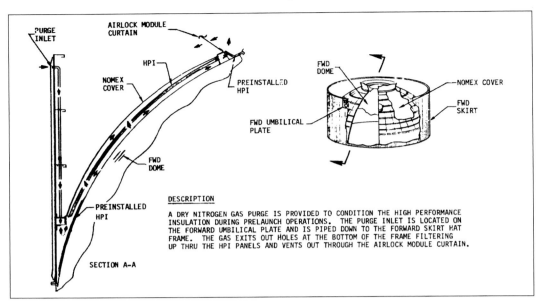

RIGHT Pre-launch and in-flight, the insulation system was responsible for containing the environment within which the structural materials and imported systems were able to operate successfully, a delicate balance between heat and cold. (NASA-MSFC)

DESCRIPTION

A DRY NITROGEN GAS PURGE IS PROVIDED TO CONDITION THE HIGH PERFORMANCE INSULATION DURING PRELAUNCH OPERATIONS. THE PURGE INLET IS LOCATED ON THE FORWARD UMBILICAL PLATE AND IS PIPED DOWN TO THE FORWARD SKIRT HAT FRAME. THE GAS EXITS OUT HOLES AT THE BOTTOM OF THE FRAME FILTERING UP THRU THE HPI PANELS AND VENTS OUT THROUGH THE AIRLOCK MODULE CURTAIN.

(0.007in) thick polyester (Dacron) mesh fabric. A separate layer of closely woven polyester was attached to each side of the composite material, the two cover sheets being reinforced around the edges at 30.5cm (12in) intervals with doubler strips (Dacron) bonded with epoxy resin. The composite panel was held together with a unique plastic fastener, low in conductivity, lightweight and available commercially, providing ease of installation.

The upper high-performance insulation panels were installed over the dome and covered with a grid which supported the wiring. The lower panels were bonded with adhesive tape to the lower portion of the forward dome prior to the attachment of the forward skirt. The major portion of the forward dome was covered with 18 gore-shaped high-performance

insulation panels prior to the vehicle rollout. These were made up of 48 layers of reflector film, 47 layers of separator material and two cover sheets. The reflector films were 0.0038mm (0.00015in) thick Mylar, coated on each side with aluminium and perforated with 1.397mm (0.055in) diameter holes at 0.952cm (0.375in) intervals.

The separator sheets were 0.1778mm (0.007in) thick Dacron net material. This was a loose-weave, lightweight Dacron cloth and formed the structural component of the high-performance insulation panels. Structural integrity was enhanced by doublers impregnated with epoxy resin combined with a cover sheet to form a laminate. The cover protected the high-performance insulation from liquid spillage and from falling tools, retaining the gas purge.

The high-performance insulation on the forward dome was covered with a Hypalon-coated nylon cloth and was made up from six segments that extended from the access kit support ring down to the forward skirt hat section, with each segment made up from three pieces of material woven together. They contained built-in protrusion to cover electrical feeds. These covers had a stainless steel thread sewn into the fabric in a 15.24cm (6in) matrix to electrically ground the fabric to the vehicle. The high-performance insulation was installed with Velcro attachments at the forward edge of the segment, with plastic zippers used for radial splices.

BELOW Insulation materials on the dome of the forward compartment. (NASA-MSFC)

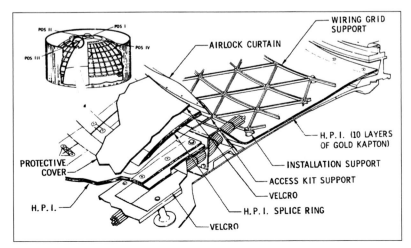

Thruster Attitude Control System

For most of the nine-month-long Skylab mission the primary source of attitude control was the Control Moment Gyroscopes (CMGs), which provided the pointing accuracy and stability essential for many astronomical and Earth resources observations and experiments. This was also necessary for maintaining solar inertial attitude for the Skylab solar arrays. However, a propulsive attitude control system was necessary for controlling the cluster during CMG spin-up in the first ten hours of the mission, for handling docking and attitude transients and large manoeuvres beyond the capabilities of the CMG, to desaturate the CMGs when necessary, and to provide a contingency capability in case of CMG failure.

This Thruster Attitude Control System (TACS) was required to provide a total of 271 x 10⁵N-sec (61,000lb/sec) of impulse. A high thrust level of 222N (50lb) was required at the start of the mission for separation transients, an 89N (20lb) thrust minimum being required for each of the three dockings, and a 44N (10lb) minimum specified for the rest of the mission. Because of the ample payload capability of the Saturn V the design was not subject to the severe weight constraints normally imposed on such a system. This permitted selection of an ambient gas system to minimise development costs and maximise reliability.

Nitrogen was selected as the propellant to minimise contamination of Skylab external equipment and to avoid the complexity of preventing condensation in cold propellant lines that would have resulted from the use of a heavier gas. The system operated in a blowdown mode, with thrust declining proportionate to the remaining volume of propellant in the tanks. The 22 spherical nitrogen bottles stored a total of 622kg (1,372lb) of gas at a pressure of 2.130kN/cm² (3,100lb/in²), +/-69N/cm² (100lb/in²). The TACS had a usable total impulse of 376.996kN-sec (84,752lbf-sec).

In addition, the major components of the TACS consisted of six thruster assemblies, 24 solenoid valves with integral filters (six quad-redundant assemblies), two supply

line filters and a fill disconnect. The thruster nozzle had a 50:1 expansion ratio and a bell-shaped expansion contour, features selected to maximise the specific impulse (Isp), defined as the amount of thrust produced by the consumption of a specified quantity of propellant for one second and as such a measure of the efficiency of the propellant. The average Isp turned out to be 78sec on the hot side and 66sec on the cold side.

The nitrogen spheres were the same as those used in the S-IVB stage ambient helium pressurisation system and were constructed

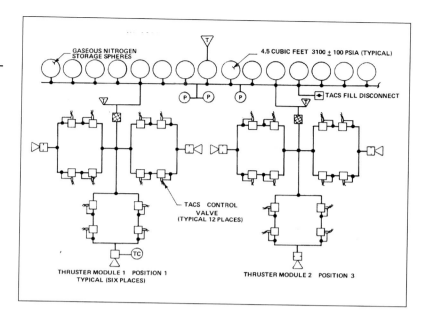

ABOVE The Thruster Attitude Control System consisted of 22 nitrogen gas spheres and associated thruster clusters with control regulators and a fill-disconnect provision for pad operations. *(NASA-MSFC)*

BELOW The general layout and numerical distribution of the 22 TACS nitrogen spheres at the base of the OWS and covered by a dedicated meteoroid shield. *(NASA-MSFC)*

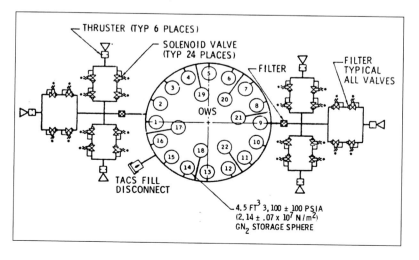

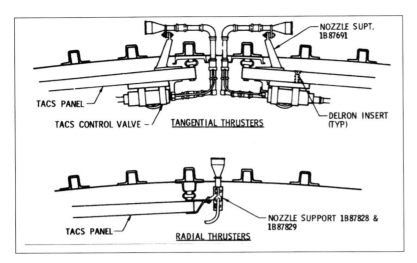

NOZZLE SUPT.
1B 87691

TACS PANEL

TACS CONTROL VALVE

TANGENTIAL THRUSTERS

DELRON INSERT
(TYP)

TACS PANEL

NOZZLE SUPPORT 1B87828 &
1B87829

RADIAL THRUSTERS

LEFT Skylab employed tangential and radial thrusters to expel nitrogen gas and provide reactive thrust for major positional attitude and directional pointing requirements, a system severely stressed by the need to use TACS for maintaining a rigorous attitude-change programme due to the loss of the meteoroid shield and thermal protection. *(NASA-MSFC)*

phase of the mission. It was also required to provide telemetry for Skylab panel display and monitoring requirements. The electrical system used separate redundant circuits and components to protect against single-point failures and employed high reliability parts while ensuring compatibility of command signals, control signals and power measurement signals with the interfacing system.

Solar Array System

Electrical power for the Skylab cluster during orbital activity was provided by solar array systems on the Orbital Workshop and on the Apollo Telescope Mount. This section deals exclusively with the former, the ATM array being described in the section dealing with the latter.

During the design phase of the 'wet' workshop, the Solar Array Wing (SAW) assemblies were designed by NASA for fabrication and checkout at the Marshall Space Flight Center, so that when it was decided to convert from the 'wet' OWS the Solar Array System (SAS) was already partially designed and some of the development testing had been completed. A decision was made to have MDAC take over the SAS design, development and fabrication. At the time of the turnover the plan was to finalise the MSFC design to meet the requirements for launch as a dry workshop. The requirement for articulation was deleted but a decision was made to provide space in the design for incorporation at a future date of an articulation motor and Sun sensors.

At this time the requirement was to provide 11,000W at the S-IVB/fairing interface at the beginning of the mission, at 55°C (131°F) without shadowing. The requirement was evaluated and it was concluded that SAS power at the end of the mission should be specified and that on-orbit

BELOW The pre-flight budget for TACS nitrogen gas consumption showing total impulse in columns (with N-sec across the top) and thrust levels in rows. Thrust levels fell proportionate to consumption due to the reduced pressure from the lower volume within the rigid tanks. Note that spin-up of the Control Moment Gyroscopes (CMGs) accounted for an early consumption rate. *(NASA-MSFC)*

of welded titanium segments. Each sphere had a volume of $0.127m^3$ ($4.5ft^3$) and was pressurised after loading through self-sealing disconnects located at the vehicle skin. The disconnect line was hard-capped to prevent possible leakage. The propellant supply and distribution system was induction brazed at all tubing connect points, also to minimise leakage. A modification to the inlet fitting of each sphere and the addition of a bi-metallic joint provided the capability of 'in-place' brazing. Fluxless induction brazing provided a lightweight and leak-proof joint.

The TACS electrical system was developed to utilise the Airlock Module power, accommodate command or control signals from the Apollo Telescope Mount digital computer, the Instrument Unit flight control computer, the Airlock Module digital command system and the Orbital Workshop switch selector, depending on the mode of operation and the

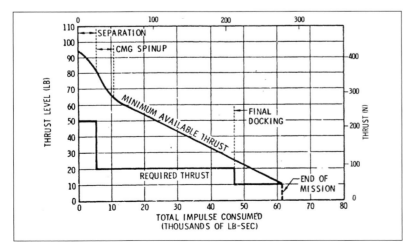

degradation of 6% should be accounted for, shadowing of the ATM solar array and of the OWS structure should also be defined and that the array temperature should be 70°C (158°F). To meet the cluster requirement it was determined that the SAS should provide a minimum average of 10,496W and a minimum 51V. After analysis of the existing MSFC design it was estimated that there would be 8,719W available at the end of the mission.

Previously there had been considerable debate about the use of a dedicated solar power module but it was decided that the SAS attached to the exterior surface of the OWS would be sufficiently effective to meet the defined power requirements; this therefore became the chosen method of providing the primary power for the cluster. In November 1969 the decision was made to subcontract the complete wing assembly except for the ordnance release system, and TRW Inc was selected to do the work, with a contract awarded in March 1970 to build the wings as defined by MDAC.

As designed, the SAS was made up of two separate wings, each consisting of a forward fairing, a beam fairing, three wing sections and mechanical and ordnance systems required to deploy the SAS in orbit. Each wing section contained ten identical active solar panels for a total of 30 panels per wing (60 for the total system). Two additional panels were included in each wing to provide spacing between active panels and the beam fairing; one was a truss panel and the other a dummy panel. Each wing was 945cm (372in) long by 833cm (328in) wide and weighed 1,840kg (4,056lb) including the deployment and stowage structure.

The solar panels were 68.9 x 306.5cm (27.13 x 120.7in) each, weighed 12.7kg (28lb) and contained four separate and electrically isolated solar cell modules. Each solar cell was 2 x 4cm (0.787 x 1.57in) and 0.035cm (0.014in) thick. The 2,464 cells had an aluminium

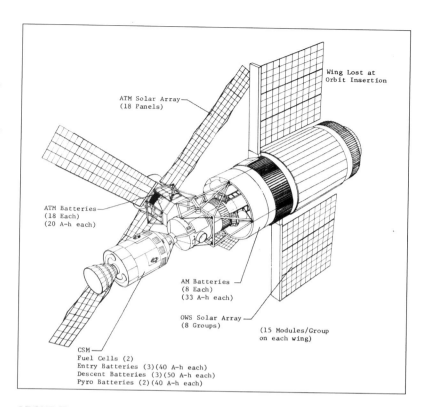

ABOVE The general arrangement of electrical power supplies for Skylab came from the Orbital Workshop Solar Array System (OWS-SAS) and the Apollo Telescope Mount Solar Array System (ATM-SAS), with complementary and supplementary power provided by the Apollo spacecraft fuel cells and battery configurations. *(NASA-MSFC)*

RIGHT Seen by the crew of the second manned visit (SL-3), the OWS retained only one of the two SAS wings, the other having been torn off by rocket motor plumes from the S-II stage retro-rockets. *(NASA)*

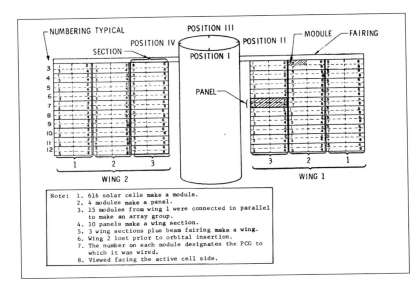

Note: 1. 616 solar cells make a module.
2. 4 modules make a panel.
3. 15 modules from wing 1 were connected in parallel to make an array group.
4. 10 panels make a wing section.
5. 3 wing sections plus beam fairing make a wing.
6. Wing 2 lost prior to orbital insertion.
7. The number on each module designates the PCG to which it was wired.
8. Viewed facing the active cell side.

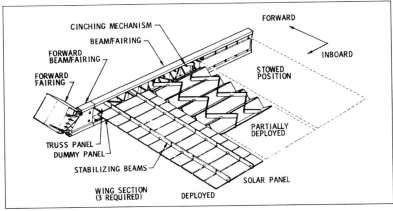

ABOVE The geometry of the sole remaining SAS wing (No 1), with a simplified outline of the basic elements including stabilising beams, cinching mechanism and truss panel. *(NASA-MSFC)*

BELOW This diagram shows a typical wing section retention and release system with the relative juxtaposition of the stowed stabiliser beams and the stowed solar panels. *(NASA-MSFC)*

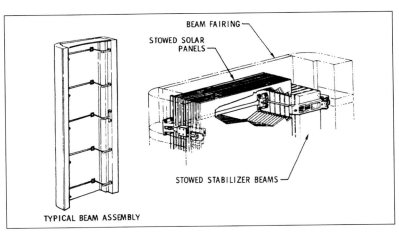

LEFT The OWS Solar Array System configuration as built into Skylab. In total, each SAS wing contained 73,920 solar cells. However, SAS wing No 2 was physically severed from the support structure on the forward skirt assembly shortly after reaching orbit. *(NASA-MSFC)*

face sheet on an aluminium substrate. Each module contained 616 solar cells, 2 x 4cm (0.787 x 1.575in) in area, made up of four parallel strings, each with 154 cells connected electrically in series. The four strings were connected electrically in parallel at the module output terminals. The electrical power was routed from each solar cell module through stabiliser beam channels on the backside of each wing section, inside the beam fairing, and then into the forward skirt of the OWS.

Inside the skirt, solar module power entered the power unit which provided diode isolation and bussing into eight groups of 15 modules each. Power was then routed from the power unit to the OWS/AM interface. The eight module groups from each wing were paired to make eight solar array groups of 30 modules each, each of these in turn being connected to one of the AM power conditioning groups to form the OWS/AM electrical power system.

The beam and fairings were scheduled to be deployed at about 42 minutes after lift-off, release being accomplished by means of an ordnance system. The beam fairings were held against the OWS by six tie-down modules, each of which contained a frangible tension link and explosively actuated expandable tube assemblies. The tie-down modules were installed between the OWS and the beam fairings at the time the SAS was installed on the OWS, mounting holes on the outboard side of the modules mating with fittings on the beam/fairing.

The inboard side of each tie-down module was equipped with a track and slide and had a mounting-hole pattern in the track to mate with the interface-hole pattern on the forward and aft skirts. Beam fairing deployment was actuated and controlled by a viscous damper driven by a compression spring about a skewed hinge axis. A latch was provided to lock the beam fairing in the deployed position, and latching was verified by microswitches.

After the beam fairings had been deployed and latched in the deployed position, the solar array panels would be deployed by means of a damper mechanical system. The folded and stacked panels were stowed in the beam fairing cavity by means of mechanical latches that retained the hinged edges of the stacked panels. The latches at each edge were interconnected by a mechanical linkage to form an assembly that served as a cinching mechanism for the panel stack. Five cinching mechanisms were provided for each panel stack, or wing section, and each mechanism was held in the latched position by means of a frangible link (tension strap).

The panels in the stack were preloaded one against another by jackscrew adjustment provisions incorporated in the latches. This preload was carried in the links of the latching mechanism so that when the tension strap was severed the preload was relieved, springs rotated the mechanism, and the latches released the wing sections to allow deployment. A redundant pair of explosively actuated expandable tubes installed in each wing extended the length of the beam fairing cavity and mated with the 15 tension straps that retained the three wing sections. The hinged solar panels and stabilising beams were released from their restrained position by the ordnance system. Springs throughout the system provided the energy to deploy the solar panels. The deployment rate was controlled by a viscous damper in each wing section. The deployed position of the panels was maintained by positive latches. A rotary potentiometer indicated the position of the panels during deployment.

The SAS vent system consisted of one vent module on each of three sealed beam fairing compartments, an acoustically actuated system designed to preclude beam fairing over-pressurisation during ascent and provide pressure relief during pre-launch nitrogen purge. System actuation and purge venting was designed to occur immediately prior to launch vehicle lift-off. The acoustic device was triggered by the acoustic environment developed by the launch vehicle motors. In flight, during ascent through the atmosphere one of the two SAS wings was torn away, and

the meteoroid shield ripped loose and wrapped around SAS-2, which prevented it being more than marginally deployed in orbit until it could be freed by the SL-2 crew. These actions are described later.

The OWS electrical power distribution system provided the means for distributing power from the Airlock Module to all loads within the Orbital Workshop. In addition to power distribution from the internal OWS buses, power was distributed from airlock power sources to allow operation of external subsystems such as the TACS, instrumentation, etc. The OWS power distribution systems accepted the AM power at the OWS/AM interface, known as the 'octagonal ring', and were located external to the Airlock Module.

For internal systems, power was routed from this ring to hermetically sealed feedthroughs, mounted in the forward dome of the OWS. From these, power was routed to an electrical display and control console located within the experiment compartment of the workshop. This console, in conjunction with remote control panels, contained all necessary switches, circuit breakers and indicators to allow crew control of the OWS electrical system. Power for the external systems was routed from the 'octagonal ring' to various bussed connectors mounted on electrical equipment panels located in the forward and aft skirt of the OWS. The electrical equipment panels contained the necessary fuses and control modules for control and protection of all external systems.

All switching devices were contained in hermetically sealed containers, as specified in the applicable electrical design requirement

BELOW **The Solar Array System beam fairing skirt attachment point relative to the fairing and the tension strap assemblies.** (NASA-MSFC)

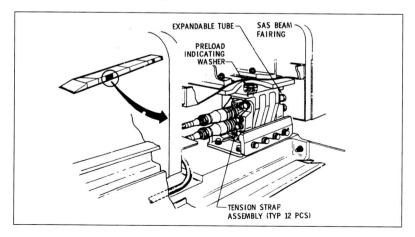

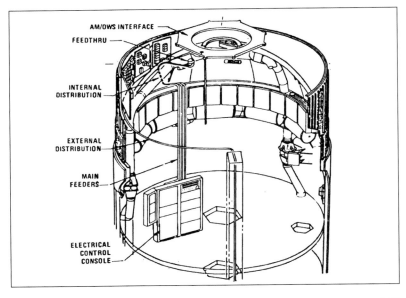

LEFT The geometry of the electrical power distribution system, with the control console located in the living quarters/experiment area, the main feeders rising through the forward dome area to the Airlock Module/Orbital Workshop interface. *(NASA-MSFC)*

CENTRE Command and control of the electrical power system incorporated several interface panels in the area of the forward dome with relay modules and control and distribution equipment installed in the forward section of the OWS. *(NASA-MSFC)*

drawings, and other containers were similarly sealed or encapsulated, where necessary, to protect parts contained within them and to satisfy the system design requirements. All insulated containers were Teflon-covered, nickel-coated stranded copper wire with a 1,000V rating. The conductor insulation was TFE Teflon, as was the jacket material. The shield material was silver-coated copper.

Wire harnesses carrying different bus power were physically and electrically isolated. The power control console was compartmentalised and enclosed to provide flammability and physical damage protection, 1,000V wire being used to provide additional protection against shorts and wire damage. Hard anodise flash was used on the inside of the power control console to provide an additional 500V minimum breakdown protection. Sufficient wire bundle string ties were used to prevent a loose wire from reaching the structure and grounding. Wiring internal to the OWS was routed through a closed trough system for flammability and physical damage protection, consisting of rigid and flexible troughs, interchange boxes, convoluted tubing and

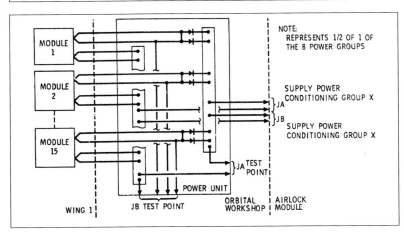

LEFT Eight 15-module groups from each wing were paired to make eight solar array groups (SAGs) of 30 modules each, each of the eight groups in turn connected to one of the Airlock Module power conditioning groups (PCGs) to integrate the OWS/AM electrical system. This diagram shows a typical SAG/PCG interface. *(NASA-MSFC)*

connector boots. Barriers within these devices would cause a flame to self-extinguish. Designated connectors on the wiring harness had tethers attached to prevent the mating of a connector to the wiring receptacle.

The system was designed to provide a 24–30VDC current to all OWS end items, and all subsystems were supplied with power from two buses which were electrically and physically separated. All conductors were electrically and physically protected. In the event of a fault, the sizing of the circuit protection device limited the temperature of the conductor insulation to less than 204°C (400°F) and limited the current to a value less than the fusing current of that conductor. This protection was from the voltage source at the point of connection to the end items. The wiring in the OWS was categorised by its operational function and installed within physically separate locations determined by the position of the consuming equipment.

OWS experiments

Skylab was itself a science laboratory, evaluating the ability of engineers to build and maintain an orbiting outpost for then unprecedented periods of time, also supporting 270 dedicated experiments in almost 300 scientific and technology investigations. The equipment for these investigations was installed or stored in various locations, including the Orbital Workshop, the Airlock Module, the Multiple Docking Adapter and the Apollo Telescope Mount.

A significant number of experiments concerned observations of the human body, in order to understand the effects of prolonged periods of weightlessness. Without that knowledge physiologists could not quantify the risks for missions of extended duration in flights to Mars, nor could engineers plan for spacecraft that may have to incorporate artificial gravity to alleviate the health risks. Back in the 1960s there were indications of permanent and unyielding effects which could not be tolerated if extrapolated to lengthy periods. Consequently there were several important experiments specifically committed to research in this area. Skylab was planned for flights lasting up to 56 days. When it was launched, the world's longest

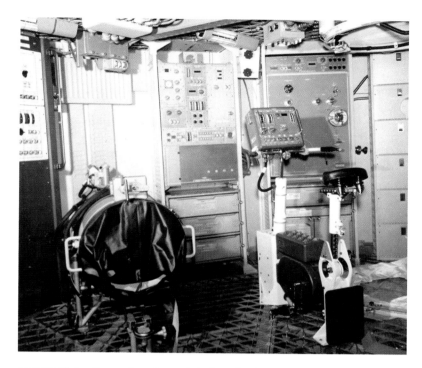

ABOVE Major items of equipment designed to investigate the effects of weightlessness on the human body were installed in the forward section of the OWS before flight, and would provide the first comprehensive analysis of physiological responses to long-duration space fight. Included here are the Lower Body Negative Pressure Device (LBNP) at left and the bicycle ergometer with display and control panel. *(NASA)*

BELOW The LBNP was an instrument for measuring the effects of weightlessness on the body's vascular system by reducing pressure in the lower body and legs. The subject would insert his lower body into the cylinder and secure a flexible pressure seal around his waist for a pre-planned sequence of tests. *(NASA)*

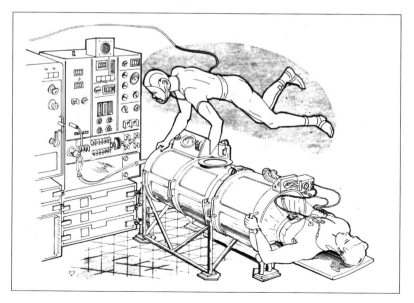

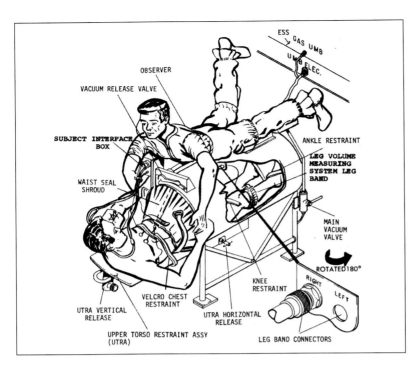

space flight to date had been the 24-day flight
of Russia's Soyuz 11.

One or two prefix letters identified the
affiliation of the experiment to a particular
class of investigation: S0 for solar or space
science observation; M for materials science
or human physiology; D0 for experiments
provided by the Department of Defense; T0
for technology experiments; and ED for Skylab
student experiments designed to encourage
participation from school and university
students. The experiments primarily contained
and used in the Orbital Workshop are described
as follows:

M092

A Lower Body Negative Pressure (LBNP)
apparatus attached to the floor of the forward
dome was designed to provide information on
cardiovascular function in weightlessness. It
consisted of a cylindrical tank with a waist seal
into which the astronaut placed his legs and
hips. Inside the tank, pressure could be reduced
by up to 20% below ambient OWS pressure,
so that leg volume could be measured by
determining the circumference of each leg at
the level of the calf muscle. Conducted by
each astronaut every three days, the entire
experiment took one hour to perform, with
electrodes attached to the body for the first 30
minutes followed by a five-minute rest, followed
by baseline recording of blood pressure,
vectorcardiogram, leg volume and body
temperature. This was followed by 15 minutes
of recording at successively lower pressures
followed by a five-minute post-negative
pressure recording of the same parameters. The
LBNP had a volume of 1.669m^3 (59ft^3) and a
stowed weight of 79.38kg (175lb).

M131

This Human Vestibular Function experiment
measured the response of the semi-circular
canal to show sensitivity to motion for both
acute and chronic responses to induced
motion on zero-g. It made use of the rotating
litter chair, which also supported other medical
experiments. The chair had a volume of
0.8926m^3 (29.2ft^3) with a weight of 115.7kg
(255lb) and was capable of rotating at up to
30rpm (+/-11%) with a control console for
mode, speed, tachometer, timer and control
responses. For testing otolithic function it had
a bite-board for the occupant to hold the test
goggles precisely in position and came with
a reference sphere and magnetic pointer with
three-dimensional readout device.

M171

This Metabolic Activity experiment used a
bicycle to determine the effectiveness of

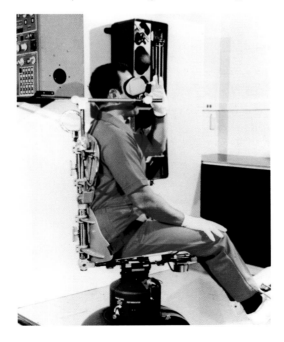

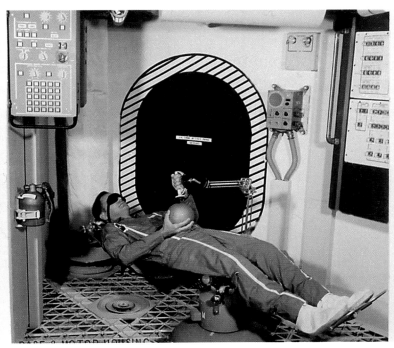

manual work in space, on the evaluation of the muscular system carrying out that work and on conducting measurements of metabolic activity. The complete suite of equipment included the static bicycle, metabolic analyser and a body temperature measurement system, in all a set of hardware weighing 243kg (536lb). The analyser was an inspiration spirometer, a device that measured the volume of air entering the lungs, an expiration spirometer, a mass spectrometer for measuring oxygen, nitrogen, carbon dioxide and water vapour, and appropriate calibration devices recorded on the station's tape recorder for transmission to the ground. Each crew member was to use this device for the M131 experiment five times during the 28-day mission and eight times on the 56-day missions. The bicycle

ABOVE The litter chair support for the M131 human vestibular function set of experiments. At left, the 'oculogyral illusion' (OGI) test subjects the occupant to varying degrees of rotational angular accelerations before opening his eyes and reporting any perceived motion in a target light. At centre, the spatial localisation test exposes the subject to various tilt positions and asks him to record his perceived orientation by setting the direction of an illuminated line in test goggles and by lining up a magnetic indicator rod on a hand-held sphere. In the motion sensitivity test the chair is rotated at a moderate speed before the subject performs a series of prearranged head movements to report sensations. *(NASA-MSFC)*

RIGHT The bicycle ergometer supported the M171 metabolic activity study, in which measurements were made of the subject's heart rate to a programmed loading of 100–200 beats per minute. It was also capable of providing the astronaut with a selectively programmed consistent workload. The ergometer was generally used at evenly spaced test periods and operated in conjunction with the vectorcardiogram and the **LBNP**. *(NASA-MSFC)*

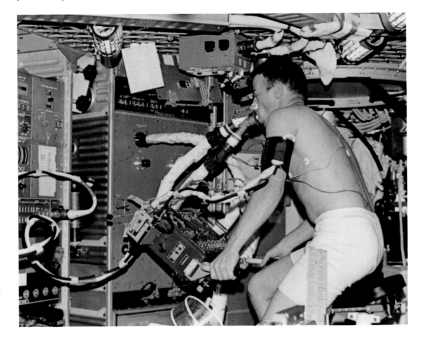

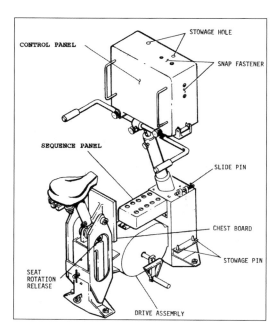

RIGHT The bicycle ergometer was a basic, functional, rotary exerciser, and in zero gravity was capable of being used by feet or hands as an exercise device to maintain muscular strength and to help reduce the levels of atrophy that naturally occur in weightless conditions. *(NASA-MSFC)*

FAR RIGHT The Body Mass Measurement system operated on a linear spring/pendulum principle that measured the level of inertia, the period of oscillation determining the mass measured. *(NASA-MSFC)*

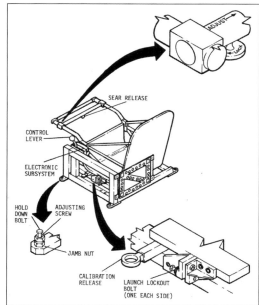

was also used as an exercise machine and for maintaining general physical fitness.

M172

A Body Mass Measurement experiment that tested the feasibility of determining body mass in weightlessness using a linear spring/

BELOW The Body Mass Measurement device was an ingenious way of measuring mass in weightlessness and resulted from intensive studies conducted in the limited volume of earlier spacecraft such as Mercury, Gemini and Apollo, where it became apparent that monitoring of the subject's weight was an important part of understanding what was happening to his body. Oscillations in the chair's motion when unlocked by the seated occupant indicated body mass. *(NASA-MSFC)*

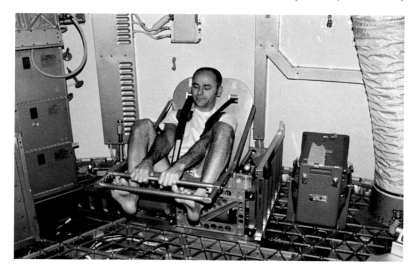

pendulum chair system. When moved, the inertia of the mass caused a pendulum cycle, the period being a function of the mass being measured. It electronically displayed the period of the pendulum and recordings were made of each crewman on a daily basis. The device was a self-contained assembly, measuring 61cm (24in) long by 76.2cm (30in) wide and 50.8cm (20in) high when folded and 98.42cm (38.75in) long by 77.47cm (30.5in) wide and 79.37cm (31.25in) high when set out for use. The device was capable of measuring masses up to 100kg (220lb) and weighed 34.9kg (77lb).

M509

Using Astronaut Manoeuvring Equipment, including an Automatically Stabilised Manoeuvring Unit (ASMU) and a Hand-Held Manoeuvring Unit (HHMU), studies were conducted into astronaut mobility aids within the confines of the forward dome of the OWS. The backpack contained a rechargeable and replaceable high-pressure nitrogen propellant tank, which supplied both units with propellant for thruster jets, and a rechargeable battery. The ASMU was manoeuvred in six degrees of freedom for pitch, roll and yaw via 14 fixed thrusters in various positions on the backpack. Control of the thrusters was achieved by two hand-controllers mounted on arms extending from the backpack.

The HHMU was a small, lightweight manual

RIGHT The automatic blood pressure measuring equipment utilised in almost all medical and physiological experiments was developed specifically for the LBNP and the metabolic experiments. It consisted of the typical cuff and electrical/pneumatic hose connection and electronic controls. *(NASA-MSFC)*

CENTRE The vectorcardiogram consisted of eight electrodes attached to the subject immediately before an experiment run. It was used with the LBNP and the ergometer to provide more information than a standard technique of vectorcardiography could, and enabled investigators to determine the position of the heart within the chest and its change in position at various instants in the beat cycle. *(NASA-MSFC)*

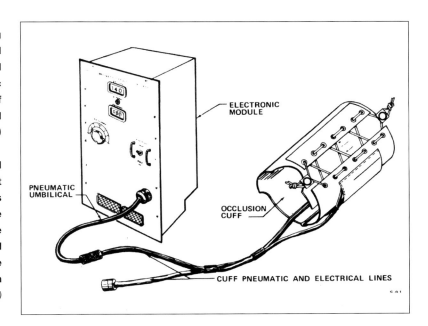

device similar to that used in the Gemini programme for astronauts to manoeuvre around outside their spacecraft. Engineers believed that a manoeuvring pack and a hand-held thruster gun were essential for moving from place to place outside spacecraft and for assembling structures in space. A subset of this experiment (T020) was a foot-controlled manoeuvring unit (FCMU), which was evaluated in association with the ASMU, whereby the astronaut used his feet and toes to activate the thrusters of a separate set of hardware, thereby keeping his hands free.

Overall, the 115.7kg (255lb) ASMU had a welded aluminium frame 68.6cm (27in) wide by 36.8cm (14.5in) deep and the same in height. The 14 nitrogen thrusters were fed from a tank containing 24,585cm³ (1,500in³) of propellant, pressurised to 20,685kPa (3,000lb/in²). Each thruster had a force of 0.45–1.8kg (1–4lb) and was controlled by hand controllers pirated

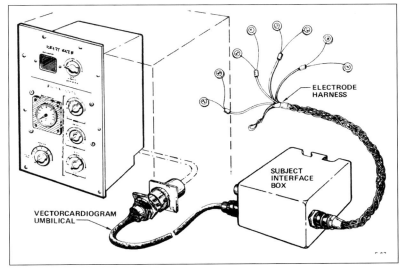

RIGHT The ability of astronauts to move around in space under their own control was considered a vital prerequisite for effective work outside their pressurised habitats, and the M509 Astronaut Stabilised Manoeuvring Unit was considered key to that capability. By using nitrogen thrusters it was possible to conduct a full evaluation inside the pressurised OWS to validate engineering design and operability. *(NASA-MSFC)*

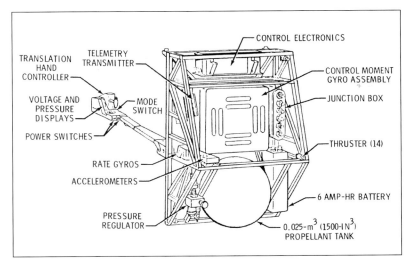

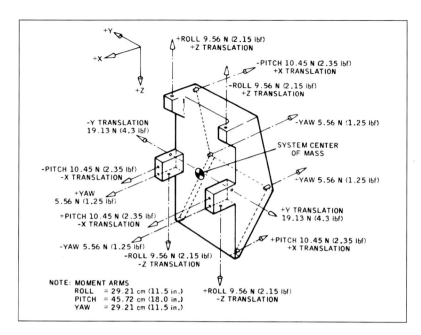

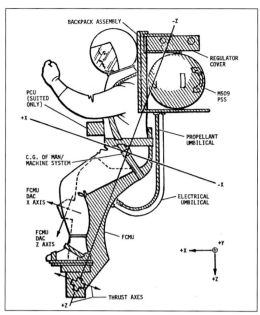

ABOVE The theoretical application of such a manoeuvring device was great and much care was given to providing the right amount of energy available through a range of thrusters on the ASMU. *(NASA-MSFC)*

ABOVE RIGHT As a second alternative to a hand-held manoeuvring thruster unit and the backpack, the foot-controlled manoeuvring unit (FCMU) provided a hands-free position control device through a combination of left and right and up and down movements and toe and foot commands. *(NASA-MSFC)*

from the Block I Apollo Command Module. Three modes were possible: Control Moment Gyroscope attitude hold, with the left control handle performing translation; direct manual attitude (right hand) and translation control; and attitude hold, commanded by the rate gyros and performed with the thrusters and translation under manual control.

The second-generation HHMU was reminiscent of the type flown by Ed White on Gemini IV and Mike Collins on Gemini X. It was a lightweight device incorporating a single 1.36kg (3lb) pusher-thruster and two 0.68kg (1.5lb) tractor thrusters attached to the ASMU nitrogen supply with a 1.2m (4ft) telemetry and delivery line. To operate the device the astronaut used a rocker switch for forward and reverse motion, having positioned it through his centre of gravity. Both the ASMU and the HHMU were parts of a long-term development plan for operational use of a developed system in the Shuttle programme.

S019

UIV Stellar Astronomy experiment, using a reflecting telescope and an objective prism in front of a 35mm camera mounted in the anti-solar airlock of the OWS to obtain photographs of ultraviolet spectra from selected stars. Weighing 90.7kg (200lb) including its container, the instrument's movable mirror protruded past the airlock, gathering spectrographs of higher resolution than a similar instrument in NASA's Orbiting Astronomy Observatory satellite, so that it was able to obtain finer detail and better spectral resolution at the shorter wavelengths.

S020

X-ray and Ultraviolet Solar Photography experiment, to record on photographic film the detailed energy spectrum of X-ray and ultraviolet emissions in weak emission lines of the solar emission spectrum from 10 to 200Å. Mounted in the solar airlock of the OWS, sunlight entering a narrow slit was diffracted into its different energies by a concave grating mounted at a very small angle of incidence to the light beam. Thin metal films in front of the slit blocked light from undesired ultraviolet and visible light. This was the only solar experiment not located in the ATM.

S063

Ultraviolet Airglow Horizon Photography, aimed at a detailed study of the photochemistry of

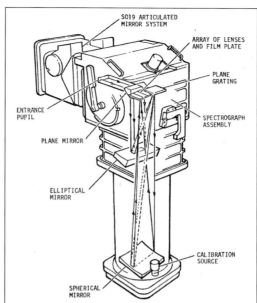

the upper atmosphere in the ultraviolet with the specific objective of quantifying the relative abundances of ozone, oxygen, nitrogen and other gaseous constituents. Two 35mm cameras were provided, one in the visible, the other in the ultraviolet spectrum, and the anti-solar airlock allowed tracking along the flight path. The hardware weighed 53.5kg (118lb) and the exposed film was returned to Earth.

S183

Ultraviolet Panorama, providing a photographic survey in two bands with fine spatial and photometric resolution of star fields previously unattainable. The instrument consisted of a telescope which used the same movable mirror as the S019 experiment and included a grating spectrograph that collected light from the star in its field of view into two 800Å-wide bands centred at 1,800Å and 3,000Å. The astronaut placed either the telescope or camera in the airlock and, using coordinates provided from the ground, pointed the movable, external mirror toward a particular part of the sky, centred the field of view and made a sequence of exposures up to 20 minutes in duration. The photographs were returned to Earth for processing.

S190B

Earth Terrain Camera experiment used to obtain high-resolution data of small fields of view on the

Earth to assist with interpretation of data from the other instruments. This was the first attempt to obtain what was then high-resolution imagery of 11m (35ft) with a ground area coverage of 109km (68km) on a side. It consisted of a single camera operated in the scientific airlock on the anti-solar side of the OWS. An adaptation of the Lunar Topographic Camera carried on the Apollo 14 mission, the Earth Terrain Camera carried a 46cm, f/4 lens and used 12.7cm (5in) film. It complemented several EREP experiments carried by the Multiple Docking Adapter (see page 120).

Airlock Module

The origin of the Airlock Module (AM) dates back to 23 December 1965, when McDonnell Douglas was directed to examine which elements of Gemini hardware could be applied to support the use of a spent S-IVB stage as a habitable living and work area. A request from NASA to MDAC dated 5 April 1966 required the company to present a proposal to design, develop and fabricate a Spent Stage Experiment Support Module (SSESM) that could be used as an interconnecting tunnel and airlock between the Apollo spacecraft and the S-IVB. The proposal was duly submitted on 17 June and NASA gave the go-ahead on 19 August 1966.

The SSESM was to be launched on a Saturn IB with an Apollo spacecraft. It would

(see page 120).

FAR LEFT Representative of a wide range of science experiments, the S193 Ultraviolet Panorama was designed to measure the brightness of a large number of stars. Consisting of a grating spectrograph that collected UV light from a star's spectrum, it was placed in the scientific airlock and was pointed at selected objects by the operator. *(NASA-MSFC)*

LEFT S193 employed a movable external mirror, centring the field of view with a selected star and conducting long exposures. *(NASA-MSFC)*

be installed in the Spacecraft Lunar Module Adapter (SLA), separating the S-IVB from Apollo, a void which could also be used to contain a Lunar Module when the same configuration was fitted to a Saturn V. In its application on a Saturn IB, however, it was a void that could be used to carry the SSESM. After orbital insertion, the Apollo CSM would separate from the SLA, the panels would open, the spacecraft would rotate 180° and move back in to dock with, and extract, the docking adapter. The SSESM consisted of a tunnel/airlock assembly that could provide a habitable structure in itself and serve as an airlock without depressurising the Apollo Command Module.

During activation, a crew member would perform an EVA to remove and stow the S-IVB dome manhole cover, connect a flexible tunnel extension to complete the pressurised passageway and connect oxygen and hydrogen boom umbilicals (see below) to the Service Module. Over 98% of the SSESM components were Gemini flight-qualified hardware and no added qualification testing was to have been performed. Initially, to support additional radiator area and to provide increased pressurised volume for expendables and experiment stowage, the Gemini adapter was replaced with a short cylindrical pressure vessel with an axial docking port and external radiators. This version was designated the Airlock Module and was to be launched with a CSM for a 30-day stay.

Subsequently, in December 1966 the pressurised cylindrical compartment was lengthened and four radial docking ports were added in addition to the axial port. A Solar Array System was also evaluated for airlock installation, and cryogenic oxygen and hydrogen

RIGHT The general configuration of the Skylab cluster was modelled around the launch of a 'dry' workshop, but the existence of the Airlock Module was predicated on the need to access what was originally a propulsive rocket stage vented free of propellant and fitted out in orbit for habitation. The AM would also be employed for spacewalking activities. *(NASA)*

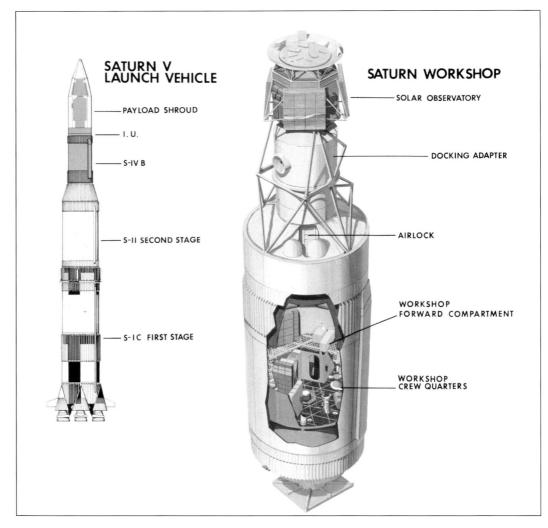

SATURN V
LAUNCH VEHICLE

- PAYLOAD SHROUD
- I.U.
- S-IV B
- S-II SECOND STAGE
- S-IC FIRST STAGE

SATURN WORKSHOP

- SOLAR OBSERVATORY
- DOCKING ADAPTER
- AIRLOCK
- WORKSHOP FORWARD COMPARTMENT
- WORKSHOP CREW QUARTERS

tanks were added so that they could provide reactants to the Apollo CSM fuel cells. A molecular sieve to filter out particles was also added. This upgraded configuration was to be launched unmanned on a Saturn IB, making effective use of the space within the SLA void that would otherwise be occupied by the engine bell at the base of the Service Module, without which there was extra volume.

This maturation of the Airlock Module concept required it to be launched unmanned and followed by a second flight with a crew, which would visit the Apollo Applications Program (AAP) workshop for an initial stay. At this date a third launch would bring up a Lunar Mapping and Survey Station Module (LM&SS) or a Lunar Module/Apollo Telescope Mount (LM/ATM), which would be docked into one of the radial docking ports by remote control.

By mid-1967 a firm workshop configuration had evolved and major changes had been made to the AM and its systems. The forward end of the pressurised cylinder, including the radial docking ports, was removed as part of the AM and a new element, the Multiple Docking Adapter (MDA), had been created (which see). The MDA was to be provided in-house at the Marshall Space Flight Center but the radiators covering the exterior of the MDA were to be added on to the OWS. The mission schedule had also changed and a range of modifications was driven by reallocation of systems.

By mid-1968 the AAP mission had evolved into a single 28-day mission and two 56-day missions, with a 90-day orbital storage period in between; all five launches were to be by Saturn IB: three manned CSM launches, one unmanned OWS launch and one unmanned LM/ATM. But a critical element in the transformation from a 'wet' to a 'dry' station was for the provision of an environmental support and power supply.

The initial requirement dictated by the early AAP concept utilising a 'wet' OWS was to store and supply oxygen at sufficient quantities and flow rates for initial pressurisation, for replenishment of leakage and for metabolic consumption by the three crew members for a 30-day mission, and to provide oxygen and hydrogen for the Apollo CSM fuel cells. The

LEFT The point of entry to the OWS and the exit point from the forward compartment was the dome of the converted liquid hydrogen tank. *(NASA)*

BELOW The 'dollar' closeout on the top of the S-IVB hydrogen tank was modified to provide a hatch that afforded entry to the Airlock Module and a pressure seal when the AM was depressurised for spacewalking, leaving pressurised areas fore and aft. *(NASA)*

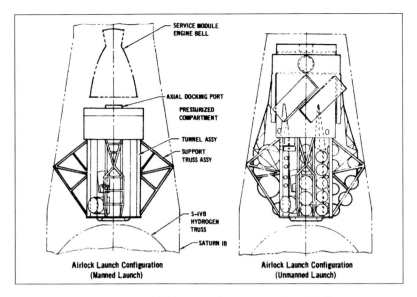

SERVICE MODULE
ENGINE BELL

AXIAL DOCKING PORT

PRESSURIZED
COMPARTMENT

TUNNEL ASSY

SUPPORT
TRUSS ASSY

S-IVB
HYDROGEN
TRUSS

SATURN IB

Airlock Launch Configuration
(Manned Launch)

Airlock Launch Configuration
(Unmanned Launch)

ABOVE The evolution of the Airlock Module tracked the changing nature of the way the station would grow from a 'wet' to a 'dry' workshop. At left, the Airlock Module is small and squat, shaped to fit within the available volume between the Apollo spacecraft and the S-IVB stage, while at right the option to go for an unmanned launch allowed the AM to grow considerably and provide a more spacious support facility. *(NASA-MSFC)*

initial atmosphere was to be 100% oxygen at 3.5N/cm² (5lb/in²), and to contain the fuel cell reactants the plan was to use modified cryogenic tanks from the Gemini spacecraft mounted on the AM trusses. Thermostatically-controlled calrod heaters, installed on the lines downstream of the tanks, would warm the gases supplied to the distribution system. Two 533.76N (120lb/in²) pressure regulators would provide oxygen supply and pressure control.

As the 'wet' workshop was firmed up, the cryogenic tanks were removed from the AM, oxygen and nitrogen to be supplied instead from the CSM for a two-gas atmosphere. Apollo carried two cryogenic oxygen tanks amounting to a total usable load of 290kg (640lb) plus two cryogenic hydrogen tanks for a total load of 25.4kg (56lb), capable of supporting missions up to 14 days. For the planned 28-day and 56-day missions these would be replaced with three cryogenic tanks holding 1,451kg (3,600lb) of oxygen, three cryogenic tanks holding 102kg (225lb) of hydrogen and a single nitrogen tank with a capacity of 385.6kg (850lb).

Oxygen was sufficient for stays of up to a month but the longer-duration missions would require a gaseous mix of nitrogen and oxygen. Theoretically these quantities would allow missions of up to 90 days and the additional tanks from the extended-duration CSMs would provide fuel-cell electrical power throughout, and all the water used aboard Skylab as a by-product. In addition to the main cryogenic gas supply on the CSM, two high-pressure

gaseous oxygen Lunar Module Descent Stage tanks would be carried on the AM to provide high oxygen flow rates for the Astronaut Manoeuvring Unit (AMU), a thruster-equipped backpack for testing in the forward section of the OWS.

When the 'dry' workshop concept launched by the first two stages of a Saturn V was adopted, it permitted a much larger allowable weight and it was thereupon decided to store all oxygen and nitrogen supplies aboard the Airlock Module. Fuel cells in the CSM would no longer provide electrical power and storage as high-pressure gases were selected over cryogenic storage, bringing lower cost, lower development risks, ease of servicing and a greater operational flexibility.

The CSM was to remain as a basic Block II with only a few changes and only two cryogenic oxygen tanks would be carried in the Service Module, instead of the three carried by the CSM for Apollos 14–17 inclusive. All the gas that would have been carried in the extended duration cryogenic tanks in the Service Module for the cluster was placed in high-pressure gaseous oxygen and nitrogen tanks on the exterior of the Airlock Module. There were initially six oxygen and five nitrogen tanks at 20,685kPa (3,000lb/in²) but a sixth nitrogen tank was added later to provide useful capacities of 2,236kg (4,930lb) and 599kg (1,320lb) respectively. The primary power source was to be from solar cells and there was no need for hydrogen following the deletion of fuel cells. Several minor equipment and component changes were necessary, as was the switch to nitrogen instead of oxygen as propellant for the AMU.

While the Airlock Module evolved from the simple SSESM to a highly complex space vehicle over the life of the programme, the primary design requirement of making maximum use of existing flight hardware remained. As it finally emerged through the transition to a 'dry' workshop, the AM involved four elements essential to its primary responsibilities and function: Airlock Module, Deployment Assembly (DA, for the Apollo Telescope Mount), the Fixed Airlock Shroud (FAS) and the Payload Shroud (PS). It was also to provide a pressurised vessel to house cluster controls, allow passage between the OWS and the MDA, to facilitate

EVA and to be a structural support for those other Skylab elements.

The configuration of the AM and the OWS dictated the need for a pressure-tight passageway between these two modules that would accommodate relative deflections with minimum load transfer. A redundantly sealed, flexible tunnel was designed to provide this. A metallic convoluted flexible bellows 107.95cm (42.5in) in outside diameter by 33cm (13in) long formed the pressurised passage and was attached with 60 indexed 1.27cm (0.50in) diameter holes and 0.635cm (0.25in) diameter bolts, centred on a 111.412cm (43.863in) diameter. The oversize holes allowed for alignment tolerances. The mating flanges at the aft AM bulkhead and OWS forward dome interfaces were sealed by a moulded elastomer material. All attaching hardware was selected to remain clamped-up during periods of AM/OWS thermal expansion and contraction. A fluorocarbon coating was applied to the internal surface of the bellows providing a redundant pressure seal.

The tunnel assembly was a pressurised semimonocoque aluminium cylinder 165.1cm (65in) in diameter with a length of 388.62cm (153in). External shear webs, an octagonal bulkhead and the structural transition section (STS) bulkhead provided attachment and shear continuity between the tunnel assembly and the four truss assemblies. Two internal circular

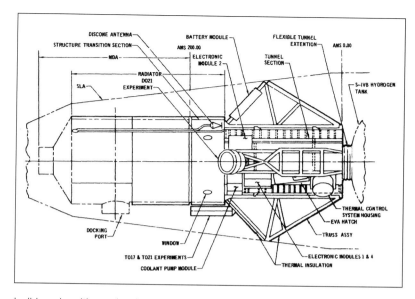

bulkheads with mating hatches divided the tunnel assembly into three compartments. Hatch seals and latching mechanisms were provided in these bulkheads.

At the rear of the Airlock Module, the aft compartment was 106.7cm (42in) in length and provided a housing to support the OWS environmental control system. The centre (airlock) compartment had a volume of 4.81m^3 (170ft^3), was 203.2cm (80in) in length and included a modified Gemini crew hatch for ingress and egress during EVA. The forward compartment was 78.74cm (31in) long and interfaced with the structural transition section. It provided support for stowage containers, tape

ABOVE In one unmanned launch concept, the second flight of an Apollo Applications Program mission (AAP-2) would support the launch of the AM on its own. (NASA)

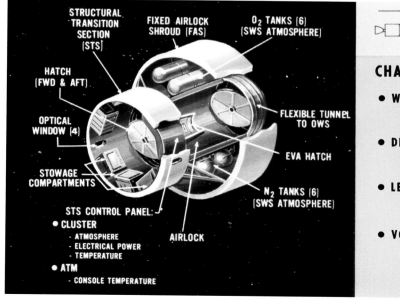

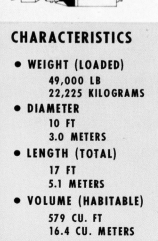

CHARACTERISTICS

- WEIGHT (LOADED)
  49,000 LB
  22,225 KILOGRAMS
- DIAMETER
  10 FT
  3.0 METERS
- LENGTH (TOTAL)
  17 FT
  5.1 METERS
- VOLUME (HABITABLE)
  579 CU. FT
  16.4 CU. METERS

LEFT This schematic prepared by NASA for a briefing on the Skylab programme shows the basic layout with attachment to the Fixed Airlock Shroud, together with location of the EVA hatch and four windows in the forward section. (NASA)

recorders and miscellaneous equipment. The forward and aft internal hatches were designed to seal off the lock compartment from the rest of the Skylab cluster during EVA; however, the OWS hatch was used in conjunction with the Airlock Module forward hatch to perform this function during the mission.

Both AM hatches were machined to a diameter of 125.73cm (49.5in), with stiffeners attached radially. A 21.59cm (8in) diameter dual pane window was placed in each hatch enabling viewing of the lock from both forward and aft compartments. Each hatch was designed to fold open alongside the tunnel wall and to ensure correct latching orientation. A moulded elastomer hatch seal was installed on each bulkhead. Each latching mechanism used a cable that was routed around the compartment bulkhead near the periphery of each hatch, driving nine hatch latch assemblies derived from the Gemini programme. Each hatch was latched when the handle was rotated through approximately 145° with an 111N (25lb) load applied on the handle. A positive lock was included in the handle mechanism on the aft hatch.

The EVA hatch was a modified Gemini design consisting of a titanium structure shaped like a conical section, hinged to the AM torque box by means of four lugs. A moulded elastomer hatch seal was installed on the sill assembly. A single-stroke handle motion through approximately 153° actuated the latching mechanism consisting of a series of gears, links and 12 latches. (This differed from the Gemini hatch in that the Gemini spacecraft configuration used a multi-stroke ratchet-type handle motion.) A double-pane window in the hatch enabled viewing of the aft portion of the EVA quadrant. A tie-down harness was attached to the EVA hatch window frame to restrain a removable machined aluminium protective window during EVA.

The structural transition section (STS) provided the physical connection from the Multiple Docking Adapter (MDA) to the airlock tunnel. The STS was an aluminium pressurised cylinder 119.38cm (47in) long and 304.8cm (120in) in diameter, formed of stressed skin and of semi-monocoque construction. At the forward end a machined ring interfaced with the MDA. Stringers and longerons were resistance-welded externally to the skin to carry bending and axial loads. Intermediate rings added support. Eight internal intercostals along with the truss attachment fittings transferred STS shell loads to the support trusses. The STS

BELOW With the flexible tunnel end through to the OWS at the top in this diagram, essential elements of the Airlock Module can be identified, with structural members for attachment to the FAS. *(NASA-MSFC)*

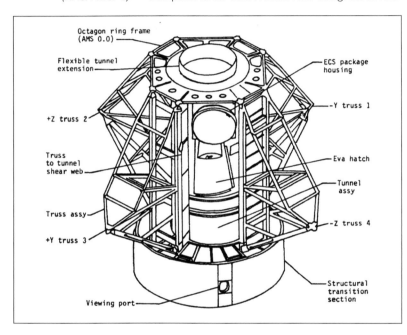

LEFT In this arrangement the flexible tunnel to the OWS is at the bottom, with the attachment interface to the Multiple Docking Adapter at the top. Identified here are the EVA handrail assembly and life-support umbilical connectors. *(NASA-MSFC)*

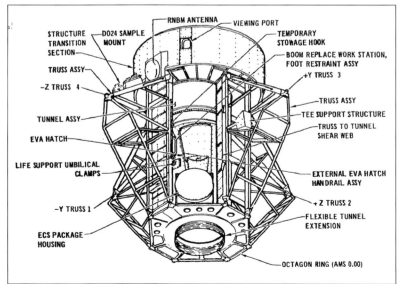

bulkhead provided the transition from 304.8cm (120in) diameter to 165.1cm (65in) diameter to mate to the tunnel assembly. Machined rings were utilised to make a typical flanged, bolted interface.

The STS bulkhead along with the tunnel shear webs and the aft octagon ring provided shear continuity of the Airlock Module and redistributed loads to the AM support trusses. Sixteen radial sheet metal channels and eight machined titanium radial fittings, which included lugs for attaching the STS to the trusses, stiffened the STS bulkhead that interfaced with the AM tunnel. Four double-pane glass viewing ports allowed visibility. Each window was protected when not in use by an external movable cover assembly actuated from inside the STS by a manual crank. The cover served a dual purpose: to minimise meteoroid impacts on the glass and to minimise heat loss from the cabin area.

The Airlock Module radiator panels served as a meteoroid shield for part of the pressure vessel skin in addition to their basic function of removing excess heat. The radiators were mounted on the STS and the Multiple Docking Adapter. To minimise development thermal testing, the panels were designed of the same materials and detail construction as used on the Gemini spacecraft radiator in the adapter section of that vehicle. Existing Gemini bulb-tee shaped magnesium alloy extrusions that provided a flow path for the coolant fluid were seam-welded to a magnesium alloy skin. Each radiator panel was supported 7.62cm (3in) outside the pressure vessel skin by fibreglass laminate angles, which minimised heat conduction from the cabin area. Welded joints connecting most of the radiator coolant tubes minimised the possibility of leakage. Mechanical connectors, utilising Voi-Shan washers for seals, connected the radiator to the coolant loop and joined the radiator panel assemblies together.

The four support truss assemblies were modified from the original configuration to incorporate additional miscellaneous equipment and comprised fusion-welded aluminium tubes with chemical milling applied to save weight. Machined fittings, fusion-welded to the truss tubes, provided attachment to adjoining structures such as the fixed airlock shroud

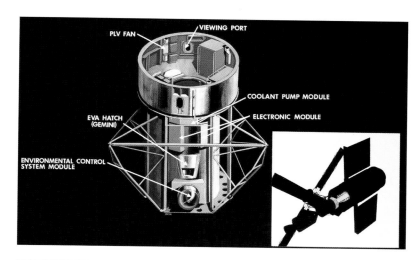

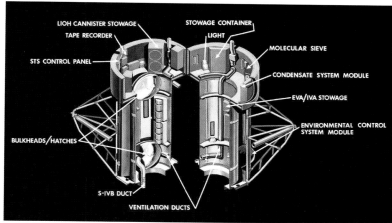

(FAS). The nitrogen tanks were mounted on gimbals to isolate them from truss deflections and resulting loads.

The FAS provided the structural support for the Apollo Telescope Mount, the Airlock Module, the Multiple Docking Adapter and the Payload Shroud during the launch phase. The structural shell consisted of a thick skin and ring construction with local intercostals for structural support of the ATM Deployment Assembly (DA). Two doors were provided in the FAS, one for access to the interior and the ASM EVA hatch during ground operations and the other for access to ground umbilical connectors. Four antennas – two deployable discones and two UHF antennas – were mounted on the FAS. It also supported EVA egress handrails, work platform, film cassette tree supports, film transfer boom (also known as 'the TEE'), a stowage box and lights. The FAS weighed 10,318kg (22,749lb) and had a length of 203.2cm (80in) and a diameter of 660.4cm (210in).

TOP The Airlock Module environmental support equipment is identified in this view showing the external attachments, with fans, pumps and electronic module. *(NASA)*

ABOVE This internal arrangement cutaway of the environmental control equipment also shows ventilation ducting. *(NASA)*

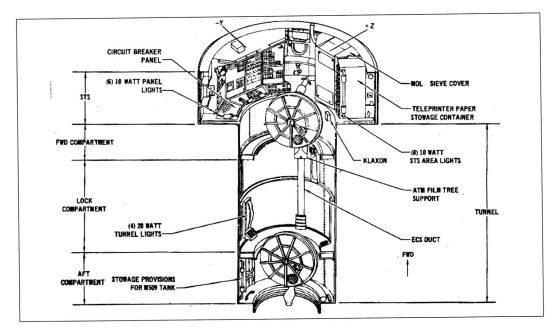

The DA consisted of two tubular aluminium truss assemblies connected by a pair of trunnion joints that allowed the upper truss assembly to rotate through 90° to deploy the Apollo Telescope Mount. The lower truss assembly was made up of bipods with their bases attached to the top ring of the FAS. A framework on top of the upper truss assembly provided mounts for the four ATM attachment points. These rigidising mechanisms were attached to the ATM through four adapter fittings. During ground operations and launch the ATM was supported by the Payload Shroud but only loosely attached to the DA by the rigidising mechanism in the floating position. Following jettison of the PS, the springs in each rigidising mechanism retracted and rigidly attached the ATM to the DA.

The release mechanisms each redundantly released the upper truss to allow rotation, release being accomplished by pyrotechnic pin retractors that were initiated by redundantly interconnected detonating fuses. Two trunnions provided the pivots to rotate the upper truss, each containing a spherical mono-ball bearing and a negator spring that retarded rotation to maintain control of ATM during deployment. Single point failure of bearings was eliminated by making the outer race of the bearing a light fit, thus allowing rotation between the outer bearing race and its fitting should the bearing fail.

The DA rotation system consisted of two redundant springs that retarded rotation and redundant deployment reels, cables, gear trains and motors to pull the ATM into the deployed position. A redundant pyrotechnically operated latch actuator allowed mechanical disengagement of the stabilisation struts, and a spring-loaded latch mechanism retained the ATM/DA in the deployed position. Two deployment reels provided the redundant means to pull the ATM into the deployed position. These reels were mechanically designed to redundantly lock against the cable paying out and were sized to be capable of reeling in all the cable required for total deployment with one reel inoperative.

When the DA reached the deployed position, switches on the latch mechanism were cycled initiating a time-delay relay that cut off power to the reels after they had achieved their full stall load and DA deploy latching was complete. The latch mechanism was used to retain the ATM/DA in the deployed position. Cam action retracted the spring-loaded latch as the ATM/DA approached the deployed position, whereupon spring force latched the hook, eliminating all assembly movement due to thruster attitude control system fittings. A ratchet mechanism made the latch irreversible, locking the structure in position. Redundant switches were cycled initiating turnoff of the deployed reels, sending a telemetry signal that deployment was complete.

The DA included two major wire assemblies to interconnect the cluster electrical power system and to connect the ATM with the ATM control and display panels in the Multiple Docking Adapter. The ATM/DA had an upper length of 309.9cm (122in), a lower length of 492.7cm (194in) and a gross weight of 1,698kg (3,744lb). The weight of the Airlock Module increased from its original design mass of 3,622kg (7,985lb) with the move to a 'dry' workshop, but the added elements attributable increased this to 34,463kg (75,978lb).

The gas supply for the pressurised environment in all three modules (OWS, AM and MDA) consisted of three tanks of oxygen and three tanks of nitrogen. The six tanks were paired in three modules attached to the fixed airlock shroud, each tank constructed with a 5.08cm (2in) thick fibreglass wrap on a thin metallic liner 0.31cm (0.125in) thick and with an internal volume of 1.613m³ (57ft³). Each was cylindrical in shape with elliptical ends and was 114.3cm (45in) in diameter and 228.6cm (90in) in length. Rated pressure was 3,103N/cm² (4,500lb/in²).

A minimum design total of 2,549kg (5,620lb) of oxygen was required, of which 2,240kg (4,939lb) was to be usable at normal design flow rates. The calculated quantity actually loaded was 2,760kg (6,085lb) at pressures of 2,053–2,077N/cm² (2,978–3,013lb/in²) and the margin above the design value was to account for instrumentation inaccuracies at the time of servicing. Because the design usable gas quantities were based on a pressure range of 2,068N/cm² (3,000lb/in²) down to 206.8N/cm² (300lb/in²), a residual 295.7kg (652lb) could not be used.

The six tanks were connected in pairs to a manifold to allow gas to flow simultaneously from all of them and a check valve in a discharge line from each tank prevented back-flow, which prevented loss from other tanks if one should begin to leak. The tank temperatures at launch were 19.8°–22°C (67.7°–71.6°F). The OWS was purged and cooled by circulating gaseous nitrogen until shortly before launch, after which the OWS and waste tank were pressurised with dry nitrogen to 16.2N/cm² (23.5lb/in²) to ensure structural stability during flight through the atmosphere and into orbit.

About 205 seconds after launch, two parallel pneumatically operated, normally closed OWS

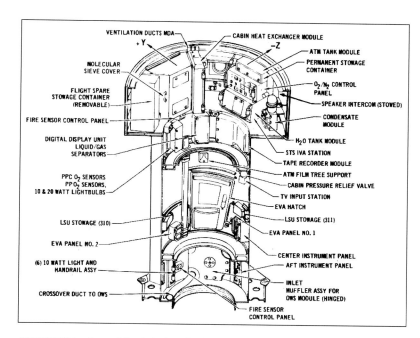

ABOVE This view of the interior displays a wide range of sundry equipment and installations looking out toward the EVA hatch, a much modified design from the type of hatch used in McDonnell Douglas' Gemini spacecraft. *(NASA-MSFC)*

BELOW The Airlock Module in fabrication at McDonnell Douglas. *(McDonnell Douglas)*

LEFT The flight article comes together, alongside a board acknowledging the 18 astronauts assigned to the Skylab programme: Joseph P. Allen, Alan L. Bean, Philip K. Chapman, Charles Conrad Jr, Robert L. Crippen, Owen K. Garriott, Edward G. Gibson, Karl G. Henize, Donald Holmquest, Joseph P. Kirwin, William B. Lenoir, Don Lind, Bruce McCandless II, F. Story Musgrave, Robert Overmyer, Russell L. Schweickart, William Thornton and Richard Truly. Of this total, Crippen and Truly had served as crew members for the cancelled Manned Orbiting Laboratory (MOL). *(McDonnell Douglas)*

Pressurisation flow rates were 10.27kg/h (22.65lb/h) oxygen and 3.15kg/h (6.95lb/h) nitrogen. At these flow rates the minimum time for OWS and AM/MDA pressurisation from $0.34N/cm^2$ ($0.5lb/in^2$) to $3.45N/cm^2$ ($5lb/in^2$) was 9.3 hours and 1.7 hours respectively for the two gases. All solenoid valves were normally closed when Skylab was unmanned, except during the pressurisation sequence. The atmospheric composition was controlled to a partial pressure of oxygen held at $2.482N/cm^2$ ($3.6lb/in^2$), $+/-0.2068N/cm^2$ ($0.3lb/in^2$), close to the atmospheric sea-level pressure of $2.137N/cm^2$ ($3.1lb/in^2$).

The six nitrogen tanks were contained in three grouped modules mounted on the Airlock Module trusses. Each spherical tank had a diameter of 104.77cm (42.25in) and was constructed of titanium with a skin thickness of 1.15cm (0.453in) providing a volume of $0.546m^3$ ($19.3ft^3$). The nitrogen tanks were connected in the same way as the oxygen tanks, except that two of them also served to supply the recharging station for propellant used in the Automatically Stabilised Manoeuvring Unit. The minimum design requirement for 689kg (1,520lb) of nitrogen was met with a loaded capacity of 736.2kg (1,623lb) with tank pressures of $2,002–2,061N/cm^2$ ($2,904–2,990lb/in^2$) at temperatures of 17.72–21.17°C (63.9–70.1°F).

The Airlock Module and its equipment were the engine room of Skylab's environmental control, and the atmospheric control system provided humidity control, carbon dioxide and odour removal, ventilation and cabin

ABOVE This view shows the EVA hatch, windows and key elements on the exterior of the Airlock Module as the flight article is readied for receiving wire bundles. *(McDonnell Douglas)*

vent valves were opened so that pressure was at least $15.16N/cm^2$ ($22lb/in^2$) at maximum dynamic pressure (Max Q) during ascent. Venting continued until the OWS reached $0.779N/cm^2$ ($1.13lb/in^2$). The sphere containing the high-pressure nitrogen for operating these valves was vented down after this so that they could not reopen and were capped *in situ* by the first crew to enter the OWS. Initial pressurisation could be initiated by either ground command or on-board controls with automatic shut-off at $3.45(0.138)N/cm^2$ ($5.0[+/-0.2]lb/in^2$) with that action available by selective operation of the gas supply solenoid valves for pressurising the AM/MDA and OWS separately or together, with either oxygen, nitrogen or the nominal 74/26% ratio.

gas cooling. Moisture was removed from the atmosphere by condensing heat exchangers and molecular sieves located within the STS, ventilation was provided by fans and molecular sieve gas compressors. Acoustic noise suppression was provided by silencers and gas cooling was ensured by condensing and cabin heat exchangers.

The design of the electrical power system for the Airlock Module (AM/EPS) began in a very simple form, since it was originally conceived as performing a supplementary role to the primary provision of electrical power from the Apollo CSM fuel cells and from solar arrays on the Apollo Telescope Mount. For that it was expected to support a small number of silver-zinc batteries, but as the mission became more sophisticated and changed to a solar array/secondary battery system for orbital operation, primary silver-zinc batteries were incorporated for pre-activation power-up. Initially, in this transformational evolution, the Airlock Module was to have supported a set of solar arrays, but when those were moved to the OWS there was greater room to expand their size.

Batteries and power conditioning equipment became subject to trade-off studies and while both silver-cadmium and nickel-cadmium batteries were evaluated it was the latter that were selected. A wide range of solar array/secondary battery system designs was examined with the overriding goal of improving efficiency and reliability. To achieve this some bold and innovative concepts were considered including buck regulation, which is essentially a DC-to-DC converter which steps down voltage while stepping up current from the supply side to the load, for both the battery charger and voltage regulator, while a peak power tracker was incorporated in the charger to extract the maximum power from the array when demanded.

These new, untried and innovative applications of front-line capabilities incorporated into spacecraft design were novel and exciting. The challenges for the AM/EPS were great and demanding, with unprecedented power loads (demand) imposed upon the system. In several ways the electrical power system was the most important new application using known practices and existing technology on a scale which had never been employed

in a space structure before. When the initial design was firmed up, the AM/EPS consisted of four power conditioning groups (PCGs), each consisting of a battery charger, a voltage regulator and a battery.

At this point in the evolution of the AAP, the Apollo Telescope Mount (ATM) was a free-flying vehicle which was intended to dock with the workshop cluster on the third and final manned mission. To this point the cluster was to have been orientated in a gravity-gradient mode, with an articulated solar array providing additional power, but after the ATM docked it was to fly in a solar inertial attitude. Power requirements continued to increase during the early design stage, expanding the area of the solar arrays and increasing the number of

PCGs to eight, resulting in the elimination of the initial silver-zinc batteries.

At first it was planned to use the ATM solar modules for both the ATM and the OWS solar arrays for standardisation but the input voltage of the two systems was different, which would have necessitated wiring the ATM solar modules so that one half of the series string of one module would be wired in series with a second module. Thermal analysis indicated that the maximum array output voltage would be higher than the 110V used for the ATM PCG design. Design requirements for the AM charger and voltage regulator were therefore changed to accept input voltage of 125V maximum to provide some margin above the predicted voltage.

About this time the concept changed to a 'dry' workshop and the ATM became integral with the cluster, transforming the OWS primarily into a space laboratory rather than having it as primarily a propulsive stage. Since the ATM could hold the cluster in a solar inertial attitude there was no longer any need to orientate the OWS array and the articulation systems were removed from the design. An optimised solar array was conceived for the OWS, designed specifically to be used with the AM PCGs as an integrated power system, with uniform minimum and maximum voltages preventing the need for any redesign of the PCGs.

The AM/EPS as flown in Skylab was one of three electrical power systems in the orbital assembly (CSM fuel cells, OWS-SAS and ATM-SAS) with performance requirements compatible with those of the other two and of the consuming elements, configured specifically to accept power from the Solar Array System on the OWS and to condition this power for application to the AM/EPS buses and its batteries. The OWS solar array was divided into eight electrically identical parts (solar array groups, or SAGs) of 30 solar modules, which provided power to either one of two selectable individual PCGs. Each PCG was composed of a battery, a battery charger, a voltage regulator and the associated power distribution and control circuitry.

The function of each PCG was to provide conditioned power to user equipment and to recharge the nickel-cadmium batteries during the orbital daylight period. Various control functions were designed into the AM/EPS to effectively manage each PCG and to apply PCG outputs to the various AM/EPS buses. Appropriate control switching was provided on the STS instrument panels or by ground control via the AM digital command system.

A total of eight PCGs were required in the AM/EPS to efficiently utilise the total energy from the OWS arrays, as well as provide redundancy and increased reliability. Each charger weighed 12.2kg (25lb) and measured 18.4 x 25.4 x 29.3cm (7.25 x 10 x 11.55in), with eight batteries each of 33AH. Each battery charger conditioned the power obtained from an associated nickel-cadmium battery and fed solar array conditioned power, or battery power, to its associated voltage regulator to satisfy maximum load requirement. The battery charger was designed to provide a maximum instantaneous output power of 2,300W and a maximum continuous power of 1,500W at a maximum voltage output of 52VDC.

Each of the eight ATM/EPS batteries consisted of 30 series-connected cells and associated temperature-sensing devices packaged in an aluminium container with dimensions of 17.78 x 20.95 x 69.2cm (7 x 8.25 x 27.25in) and weighing 55.8kg (123lb). Each cell consisted of a parallel-connected group of positive and negative plates packaged in a stainless steel can and sealed with a cell header assembly. All plates were fabricated using a nickel wire-sintered nickel structure into which either active nickel or cadmium material

BELOW The Airlock Module structurally attached to the Multiple Docking Adapter with the crane hoist lowering it to the transportation dolly. *(NASA)*

was impregnated to produce a positive or a negative plate respectively.

Seventeen nickel (+) plates and eighteen cadmium (-) plates, alternately arranged and separated by non-woven nylon made up a cell pack. The header assembly was welded to the cell can to complete the assembly. Each cell was fitted with a self-reseating pressure relief valve. Cell leakage criteria were the same as that imposed on hermetically sealed assemblies.

Each of the 30 cells was taped and then epoxy potted into one of the 30 individual compartments in the battery containers. Each battery also contained three nichrome wire temperature sensors with two sensor assemblies containing three thermistor elements and a normally closed thermal switch. The sensing devices were placed in such a way that the temperature at the top of the cell case was monitored rather than using terminal or cell interconnect temperatures to minimise or preclude terminal and/or cell interconnect heating effects. The container was compartmentalised to provide heat transfer from five surfaces of each cell to the container cold-plate mounting surface.

The function of the peak power tracker circuit was to automatically adjust the battery charger output voltage so that the power demand on the associated solar array group was limited to its available power. Without the tracker a load demand in excess of the available peak power would cause a sharp drop in the solar array output voltage and therefore a sharp drop in output power. The circuit sensed the array

output of voltage and current, determined the relationship of the operating power point to the peak power point, and generated an appropriate signal to the battery charger regulator circuit to control the charger output voltage and the output power.

The amp-hours (AH) meter circuit continuously computed the state of charge of the associated battery and provided charge

ABOVE **The combined flight articles, Airlock Module and mated Multiple Docking Adapter, being readied for tests prior to delivery for flight.** *(NASA)*

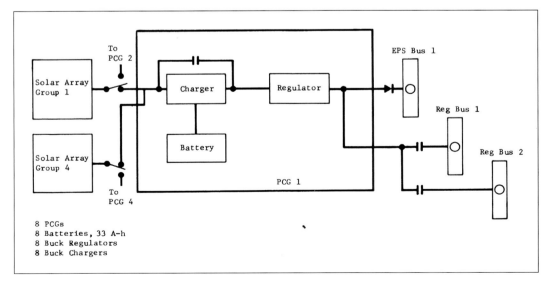

LEFT **The configuration of the general operating schematic for the Airlock Module electrical management systems including eight power conditioning groups (PCGs).** *(NASA)*

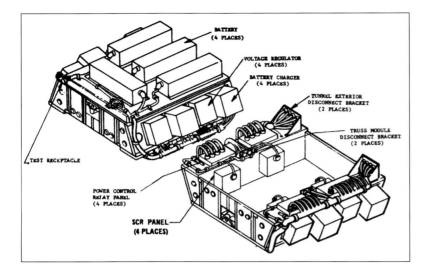

Labels on diagram:
- BATTERY (4 PLACES)
- VOLTAGE REGULATOR (4 PLACES)
- BATTERY CHARGER (4 PLACES)
- TUNNEL EXTERIOR DISCONNECT BRACKET (2 PLACES)
- TRUSS MODULE DISCONNECT BRACKET (2 PLACES)
- TEST RECEPTACLE
- POWER CONTROL RELAY PANEL (4 PLACES)
- SCR PANEL (4 PLACES)

ABOVE The power conditioning group packages contained batteries, regulators and power relay panels. *(NASA-MSFC)*

control signals based on the computed value. This was accomplished by monitoring the battery discharge in AH during dark periods and the battery recharge in ampere-hours during daylight periods. The battery status at any time was then computed in percentage state-of-charge, starting at 100% with a fully charged battery.

The primary control signal, generated when the computed state-of-charge reached 100%, terminated the voltage limited charge mode and initiated the current limited charge mode. An analogue signal indicating the computed state-

BELOW No better indication of the liberating effect caused by moving to an all-up 'dry' workshop can be had than this graph that tracks Airlock Module weight changes. Note the major step up in allowable mass with the decision to launch on a Saturn V, pegged here at the beginning of the last quarter in 1969. *(NASA-MSFC)*

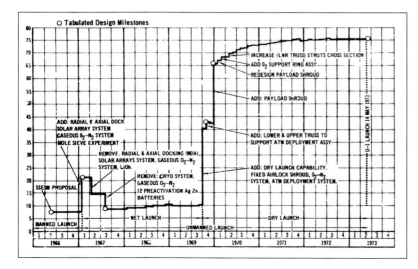

of-charge was also generated in the ampere-hours meter for telemetry and display purposes. However, only one of these circuits provided battery charge control signals at any one time. Selection of either the primary or secondary circuit for control purposes was made by a digital control signal command or by a crew manual switch.

The instrumentation system in the Airlock Module was derived from the Gemini programme where applicable, or by modifying other designs to accommodate requirements. New designs were only used where available hardware could not be made to satisfy needs. The initial system for the 'wet' concept consisted of 238 channels of pulse-code modulation (PCM) telemetry with a single tape recorder capability. Several changes and improvements were made to the multiplexer/encoder equipment in the Airlock Module and an interface box was added to the PCM equipment so that a total of 37 multiplexers could be accommodated. This also provided three additional separate portions of the real-time data available for recording, which allowed housekeeping and experiment data to be available via delayed time.

As the concept evolved and moved to a 'dry' workshop, one major change was to provide an increase in telemetry channel capacity to 625 channels with 535 allocated. The multiplexers were located in the Airlock Module and in the OWS. Subsequently, further changes included reallocation of multiplexers and the usual changes resulting from the evolution of the programme. The final flight assignment provided 1,297 telemetry channels of which 1,076 were used; remote multiplexers were located only in the AM and the OWS. Data signals from the Multiple Docking Adapter and selected measurements from other modules were wired across the appropriate vehicle interface and accommodated by multiplexing and encoding hardware in the Airlock Module.

Overall, items attributable to the Airlock Module included the AM itself, the structural transition section, the fixed airlock shroud, the ATM deployment assembly and the Payload Shroud. Gross weight of the Airlock Module at launch was 6,879kg (15,166lb) providing a working volume of 17.263m³ (610ft³) and an overall length of 537.3cm (211.54in).

Multiple Docking Adapter

The Multiple Docking Adapter (MDA) was first conceived in the summer of 1966 during development of the 'wet' workshop for the Apollo Applications Program when it was required to have two radial docking ports and one axial port. It was to facilitate a docking position for the Apollo CSM for replacement crew members and to have the structural rigidity to support the Lunar Module/Apollo Telescope Mount and the Lunar Mapping & Survey System (LM&SS). In the original MDA design, the shell had a length of 96.5cm (38in) and a diameter of 165cm (65in).

In November 1966 the radial tunnels had a length of 142.24cm (56in) and a resupply module was incorporated into the mission plan, located at the second radial port 180° opposite the LM/ATM. Each port was to have a diameter of 86.4cm (34in) and incorporate passive thermal control with a pure oxygen atmosphere provided by the Airlock Module. With a weight of 408kg (900lb), the MDA at this stage was entirely passive, receiving electrical wiring from

the AM to the docking ports. A third evolution in 1966 extended the main tunnel to a diameter of 292.1cm (115in) and a diameter of 213.4cm (84in) with the radial tunnels possessing a length of 50.8cm (20in) and weight now increased to 907kg (2,000lb). Significantly expanded, it would have lighting and communications equipment and the ability to store consumables for transfer to the main workshop.

In March 1967 the MDA entered preliminary design and now had a main tunnel with a diameter of 304.8cm (120in) and a length of 457.2cm (180in) and four radial ports. Shortly thereafter it got new running lights and two ports were deleted when the LM&SS and the resupply module were cancelled. New experiment locations were added and the module was listed as a candidate for consideration as a workshop study in its own right. In 1968 the design grew to include fans, ducts, heaters (sixteen wall, three port and two window) and two vent valves. Electrical equipment expanded to include four auxiliary power outlets and power distribution capability and, temporarily at least, an Experiment Support System.

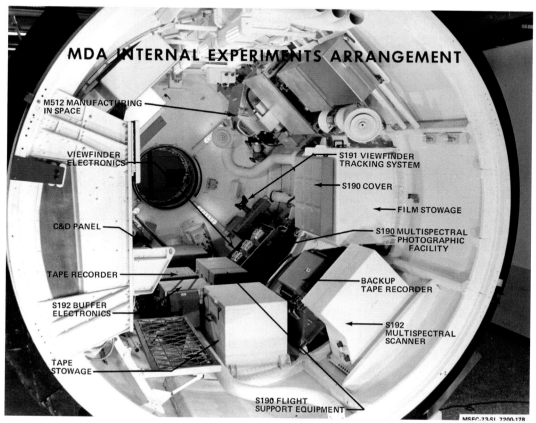

LEFT The Multiple Docking Adapter was an integral part of the stations proposed under the Apollo Applications Program because there was no other means by which crew members could access the OWS – either 'wet' or 'dry' – and the range of alternative concepts was wide. Functionally, for Skylab, the MDA served as a docking facility for the Apollo spacecraft and to house several materials processing experiments as well as the control panel for the Apollo Telescope Mount and its experiments. *(NASA)*

With the shift to a 'dry' workshop in 1969 everything changed, including the prelaunch installation of OWS equipment rather than having to pass it through the Airlock Module hatch had the S-IVB stage been used to place itself in orbit prior to outfitting and habitation. The MDA now received a control and display console for the Apollo Telescope Mount, film vaults, a multispectral photographic facility (S190) and a materials processing facility (M512). Three of the four radial ports were removed, only one remaining for contingencies.

As built for Skylab, the MDA had a total length of 4.78m (15.67ft), a diameter of 3.05m (10ft) and a volume of 32m³ (1,140ft³). It consisted of a cylindrical section with a length of 4.139m (13.58ft) and a conical section with a length of 0.64m (2.1ft). Added to these dimensions was an axial docking port with a length of 0.515m (1.69ft), to which the Apollo CSM would dock, increasing the total length to 5.29m (17.36ft). An additional radial docking port was added to the precursor 'wet' configuration to which the LM/ATM would have been attached and was retained as a back-up for Skylab, centred 2.6m (8.58ft) up from the bottom of the cylindrical assembly. Both docking ports were 83.8cm (33in) in diameter with a length of approximately 50.8cm (20in).

Originally the longerons were designed to accommodate equipment that was to be transferred to the OWS in orbit, but the heavier weight of the ATM control and display console, the EREP equipment and experiment packages for the 'dry' Skylab required major structural redesign, which reinforced them with longitudinal splices. The docking port frames were strengthened and an intermediate frame was added between the ports and the structural transition section interface frames. The outside shell also supported the S194 L-Band antenna for the EREP equipment.

The basic structural shell was fabricated from 2219-T87 aluminium with a nominal skin thickness of 0.635cm (0.25in), and a minimum thickness of 0.193cm (0.076in). In the docking area the skin ranged from 1.143cm (0.45in) to 1.65cm (0.65in) thick. Eight longerons and five ring frames were used in the cylindrical section to stabilise the skin and to provide mounting surfaces for internal components. Two ring frames were welded to the skin to form part of the pressure shell, other frames and longerons being attached to the skin with mechanical fasteners. To minimise leakage, sealing washers were installed under the heads of all skin-penetrating fasteners and sealant was applied to the surface of the longerons and frames that came in contact with the shell.

The longerons were designed to provide two parallel-facing surfaces on adjacent longerons to facilitate the attachment of intercostals. Each

RIGHT A simplified layout showing the principal experiments contained within the MDA, including those shown here in blue for materials processing research and those in orange for the Earth Resources Experiments Package (EREP), flown coincidentally with the first Landsat satellite. Also shown is the Apollo Telescope Mount control console and the radial and axial docking ports. *(NASA)*

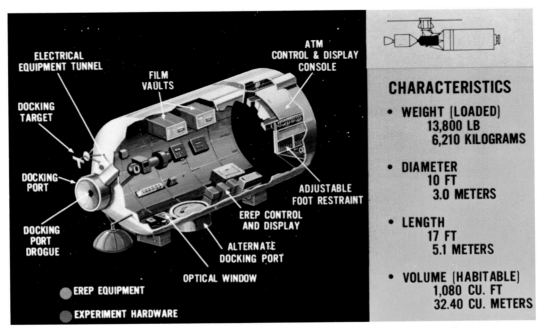

CHARACTERISTICS
- WEIGHT (LOADED)
  13,800 LB
  6,210 KILOGRAMS
- DIAMETER
  10 FT
  3.0 METERS
- LENGTH
  17 FT
  5.1 METERS
- VOLUME (HABITABLE)
  1,080 CU. FT
  32.40 CU. METERS

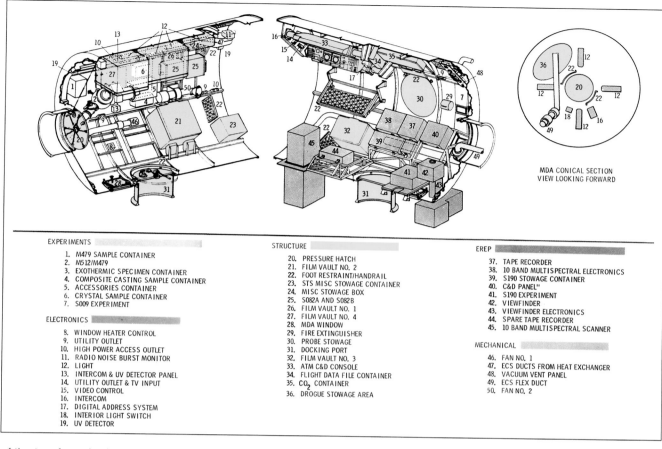

MDA CONICAL SECTION
VIEW LOOKING FORWARD

EXPERIMENTS

1. M479 SAMPLE CONTAINER
2. M512/M479
3. EXOTHERMIC SPECIMEN CONTAINER
4. COMPOSITE CASTING SAMPLE CONTAINER
5. ACCESSORIES CONTAINER
6. CRYSTAL SAMPLE CONTAINER
7. S009 EXPERIMENT

ELECTRONICS

8. WINDOW HEATER CONTROL
9. UTILITY OUTLET
10. HIGH POWER ACCESS OUTLET
11. RADIO NOISE BURST MONITOR
12. LIGHT
13. INTERCOM & UV DETECTOR PANEL
14. UTILITY OUTLET & TV INPUT
15. VIDEO CONTROL
16. INTERCOM
17. DIGITAL ADDRESS SYSTEM
18. INTERIOR LIGHT SWITCH
19. UV DETECTOR

STRUCTURE

20. PRESSURE HATCH
21. FILM VAULT NO. 2
22. FOOT RESTRAINT/HANDRAIL
23. STS MISC STOWAGE CONTAINER
24. MISC STOWAGE BOX
25. S082A AND S082B
26. FILM VAULT NO. 1
27. FILM VAULT NO. 4
28. MDA WINDOW
29. FIRE EXTINGUISHER
30. PROBE STOWAGE
31. DOCKING PORT
32. FILM VAULT NO. 3
33. ATM C&D CONSOLE
34. FLIGHT DATA FILE CONTAINER
35. CO_2 CONTAINER
36. DROGUE STOWAGE AREA

EREP

37. TAPE RECORDER
38. 10 BAND MULTISPECTRAL ELECTRONICS
39. S190 STOWAGE CONTAINER
40. C&D PANEL"
41. S190 EXPERIMENT
42. VIEWFINDER
43. VIEWFINDER ELECTRONICS
44. SPARE TAPE RECORDER
45. 10 BAND MULTISPECTRAL SCANNER

MECHANICAL

46. FAN NO. 1
47. ECS DUCTS FROM HEAT EXCHANGER
48. VACUUM VENT PANEL
49. ECS FLEX DUCT
50. FAN NO. 2

of the two faces had two rows of blind nuts installed on 7.62cm (3in) centres, providing the capability to install support hardware at any location in the MDA.

The cone consisted of four machined panels welded together, 0.635cm (0.25in) thick in the weld lands and around a vent cut-out, and 0.317cm (0.125in) thick in the remaining areas. A ring bolted to the forward end of the cone was used to attach the docking port and hatch ring. The cone was attached to the cylinder by welding a common frame to the aft end of the cone and the forward end of the cylinder.

The two docking ports were built-up cylinders consisting of machined aluminium rings at each end with a centre filament-wound fibreglass cylinder to provide thermal isolation. All mechanical joints were sealed to minimise leakage. Both docking ports had provisions to install a drogue and provide the proper interface for CSM docking. The axial port had provisions for transferring power, communications and instrumentation between the MDA and the docked CSM. The radial port did not have these

provisions since it was intended for rescue purposes only.

As built, the two docking hatches had a diameter of 81.3cm (32in) and were 3cm (1.2in) thick, held in the closed position with six over-centre latches controlled by linkages attached to a central shaft. Handles were attached on both sides of the hatch, allowing opening and closing from either side. The handles were restrained in the closed position during launch and orbital storage periods by a launch lock, which was locked from the outside only but could be unlocked from either side. Each hatch was operated by moving the operating handle through an angle of about 60°, a typical operating force being 2.7kg (4lb) although any force up to 11.3kg (25lb) was permissible. A ball plunger detent device held the handle in either the open or closed position but after the hatches were released the hatch was free to swing open on hinges to the full open stowed position, where it was restrained by ball plungers in the hinges. A force of approximately 3.17kg (7lb) was sufficient to free the hatch from this stowed position.

ABOVE This sectionalised view shows the internal arrangement of equipment, systems, subsystems and experiment support equipment.
(NASA-MSFC)

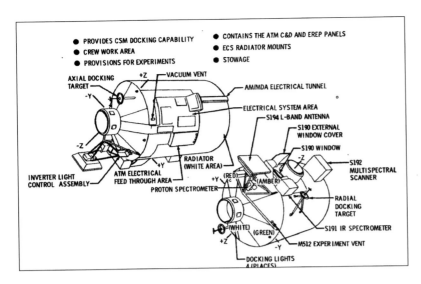

Labels on diagram:
- PROVIDES CSM DOCKING CAPABILITY
- CREW WORK AREA
- PROVISIONS FOR EXPERIMENTS
- CONTAINS THE ATM C&D AND EREP PANELS
- ECS RADIATOR MOUNTS
- STOWAGE

AXIAL DOCKING TARGET
+Z — VACUUM VENT
-Y
+Y
-Z
INVERTER LIGHT CONTROL ASSEMBLY
ATM ELECTRICAL FEED THROUGH AREA
PROTON SPECTROMETER
+Y
+Z
-Y
(WHITE)
(GREEN)
RADIATOR (WHITE AREA)
(RED)
(AMBER)
AM/MDA ELECTRICAL TUNNEL
ELECTRICAL SYSTEM AREA
S194 L-BAND ANTENNA
S190 EXTERNAL WINDOW COVER
S190 WINDOW
-Z
S192 MULTISPECTRAL SCANNER
RADIAL DOCKING TARGET
S191 IR SPECTROMETER
M512 EXPERIMENT VENT
DOCKING LIGHTS 4 (PLACES)

ABOVE This diagram shows the external location of science equipment, engineering systems and structural layout. *(NASA-MSFC)*

BELOW Structural dimensions and engineered layout of the MDA as built for Skylab. *(NASA-MSFC)*

The edge of the hatch was a lip that depressed a silicone rubber seal in the MDA shell docking-port ring to achieve a press-tight closure. The amount of seal indentation was limited by six mechanical stops to prevent overstressing. The axial hatch included a toolbox mounted on the Apollo CSM side with tools for contingency opening of the hatch in the event of a mechanical malfunction or a hatch-to-seal sticking problem. The seals were held in their retaining rings by a pressure-sensitive adhesive that enabled the crew to replace a seal during the mission if required.

The MDA contained four single-pane windows installed in the structural shell. The one designed to support the S190 experiment was the largest, and whenever the camera was rotated back to its stowed position a removable transparent cover was installed over the interior surface to protect the glass from accidental damage and to act as a redundant pressure seal in case the window failed. A second window was used with the viewfinder tracker to locate EREP targets and point the S191 Infrared Spectrometer at them. The other two windows were used to pass visible and infrared light rays through the MDA wall from the external sensor of the S192 Multiband Scanner to the internal detector.

In detail, the S190 window was a single pane of borosilicate crown glass, 4.06cm (1.6in) thick by 45.72cm (18in) by 58.42cm (23in) square, mounted and sealed in an aluminium frame installed directly above the radial docking port. The window incorporated a heating system. The safety shield for the window was a removable external cover positioned against the inside of the window frame and hand-fastened there by a crewman whenever the S190 experiment was rotated into the stored position, back away from the window. The shield consisted of a high-strength Corning Chemcor 0315 high-strength glass panel, 0.736cm (0.290in) thick, mounted and sealed in an aluminium frame. The frame included an O-ring on its mounting surface to provide redundancy for the S190 window.

The window was stowed for launch in its allocated position on the aft end of film vault 4. The external cover was a curved fibreglass honeycomb panel 2.54cm (1in) thick and approximately 50.8cm (20in) by 76.2cm (30in) square, with metal fittings integrally bonded to the panel for hinge attachment and latch engagement. Multilayer insulation was installed in a fibreglass pan attached to the internal surface of the cover. The cover, including the pan, was painted black for thermal control

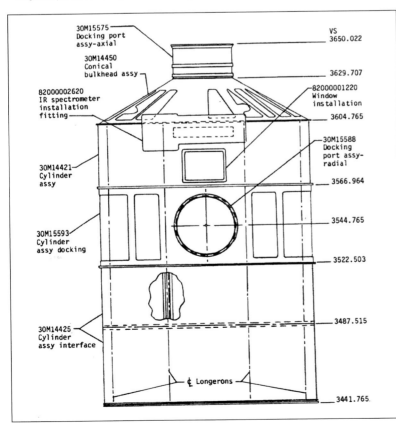

30M15575 Docking port assy-axial
30M14450 Conical bulkhead assy
82000002620 IR spectrometer installation fitting
30M14421 Cylinder assy
30M15593 Cylinder assy docking
30M14425 Cylinder assy interface
VS 3650.022
3629.707
82000001220 Window installation
3604.765
30M15588 Docking port assy-radial
3566.964
3544.765
3522.503
3487.515
℄ Longerons
3441.765

and to minimise reflected light on the window. A resilient foam seal around the cover edge closed the gap between the cover and the meteoroid shield to prevent dust and other contaminants from reaching the window.

The circular S191 window was a single pane of borosilicate crown glass 10.16cm (4in) in diameter and 1.22cm (0.48in) thick, installed with an elastomeric seal in the mounting fitting for the S191 experiment. Its function was to maintain structural and pressure leakage integrity of the MDA and to act as a viewing port for the crewman when pointing the experiment at the selected target.

There were two S192 windows, each 7.62cm (3in) in diameter and 0.635cm (0.25in) thick installed with elastomeric seal in separate openings in the S192 experiment mounting. One window was of fused silica, the other of germanium, which permitted certain infrared rays to pass into the S192 Internal Scanner/ Processor; the fused silica (Infrasil) window performed the same function for visible light.

Four film vaults were located and supported in the MDA at locations deemed best suitable for crew operation and to sustain launch loads. The vaults were fabricated from 6061-T6 aluminium. The doors were attached to the basic box with a continuous piano hinge and locked in place for launch with expander pins. During activation by the SL-2 crew these pins were replaced with pip pins. The doors were equipped with a friction device to control inertia forces on the door used during zero-g operations.

The vaults contained cameras, canisters, film magazines and other miscellaneous equipment including communications umbilicals, power cables, the S190B Earth Terrain Camera and a hatch seal. Each vault was a unique shape: vault 1 weighed 117.94kg (260lb) and measured 58.4 x 60.96 x 101.6cm (23 x 24 x 40in); vault 2 weighed 205kg (452lb) and measured 81.28 x 58.4 x 73.66cm (32 x 23 x 29in); vault 3 weighed 224.5kg (495lb) and measured 53.34 x 60.96 x 76.2cm (21 x 24 x 30in); vault 4 weighed 136.98kg (302lb) and measured 86.36 x 71.12 x 66.0cm (34 x 28 x 26in).

The MDA hosted seven purpose-built stowage containers used to store a variety of items such as carbon dioxide absorber

ABOVE The structural test article for the MDA comes together at the McDonnell Douglas facility, where it was subject to a wide-ranging examination of the engineered design. *(NASA-MSFC)*

BELOW Fabrication of the flight MDA took place at the Marshall Space Flight Center, after which it was delivered to Martin Marietta for outfitting. *(Martin Marietta)*

ABOVE Clad in insulation, the flight rated MDA is moved for testing, following which it will be mated to the Airlock Module. *(NASA)*

BELOW The forward docking tunnel area with strip lights in the conical fore dome and axial hatch area. *(NASA)*

canisters, flight manuals, crew communication equipment, experiment support equipment, contingency tools and in-flight maintenance tools and equipment. Several containers employed Mosites fluorelastomeric closed cell foam as a cushioning material for stowed equipment. The containers were numbered in series according to their location and each container lid had a decal listing the items and the quantities stowed. Six of the seven containers were rectangular while one was cylindrical.

While the MDA did not carry any life-support gas atmosphere supplies, it had a ventilation system that consisted of three fan/muffler systems, two adjustable diffusers to control air distribution in the module and ductwork to direct air from the Airlock Module to the MDA and from the MDA to the Apollo CSM. The MDA environmental control system (MDA/ECS) carried atmospheric gas from the structural transition section area into the MDA when the AM/ECS fans were switched on. The AM introduced cooled atmosphere into the MDA when the fans in the Airlock Module were turned on. Ambient air was introduced to the Command Module by the CSM-to-fan/duct system and recirculated back to the MDA through the docking port tunnel.

The molecular sieve introduced fresh air, scrubbed of carbon dioxide and odours, to the MDA and one or two compressors could be used to deliver the conditioned air. The atmosphere would be diverted to the MDA or the OWS depending upon the damper position located in the structural transition section duct. The interface of that duct was at the AM/MDA mating splice. The velocity of the atmosphere at the crew stations was controlled by operating one or both of the MDA cabin fans at high, low or off settings and by adjustment of their attached diffusers, which established the direction and shape of the existing atmospheric flow.

The outside of the MDA was protected from meteoroid impact by radiators and a shield, conforming to the mission requirement for a 0.995% probability of no penetration of the pressure or electrical wiring. The radiators covered approximately 75% of the exterior surface and were constructed of 0.076cm (0.030in) magnesium, with coolant tubes attached, and finished with a special reflective white paint. The radiators were bolted to 7.62cm (3in) high fibreglass standoffs attached to the shell of the module. The entire exterior was covered with a meteoroid shield, the cone having a 0.127cm (0.050in) aluminium cover and was protected by a 0.051cm (0.020in) aluminium cover over areas not protected by the radiators. The shield sections were bolted to 7.62cm (3in) standoffs attached to the shell. Exposed electrical wiring was protected by tape wrapping.

High-performance insulation was made into individual blankets manufactured to fit between the fibreglass standoffs, consisting of 91 layers of aluminised Mylar separated by 90 layers of Dacron netting. A fibreglass frame that had 'boat hooks' installed on 10.2cm (4in) centres was attached to the outside surface of each blanket. Velcro was stapled to the edge of the inner surface of each blanket and the total blanket was held together with Swiftachments, essentially nylon I-shaped parts normally used in the 1970s to attach price tags to clothing in American stores. The shell contained a layer of Velcro bonded to the exterior to accept the blankets with 'boats hooks' attached to holes drilled through the fibreglass standoffs on the frames. The blankets were then installed by pressing the mating Velcro together and by wires tying 'boat hooks' on adjacent blankets pressed through holes provided in the standoffs.

Prior to entry, the pressure between the CM and the MDA was equalised by means of a manually operated pressure equalisation valve and a differential pressure gauge that were located in the axial hatch. The valve provided an atmosphere flow path through the hatch for pressure equalisation and for atmosphere sampling on SL-2. A pressure cap provided a redundant seal to the equalisation valve and was installed on the outer (CM) side of the hatch. The cap was removed prior to valve operations and the system was operable from either side of the hatch after the pressure cap was removed. A similar system was located in the radial docking hatch to provide the crew the same equalisation with a radial docking.

The differential pressure gauge was a bourdon type with a range of -6.895kPa (-1lb/in²) to +6.895dkPa (+1lb/in²) and consisted of two units mounted back-to-back in a bracket

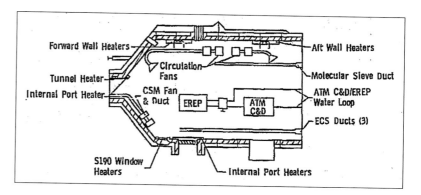

ABOVE Elements of the active thermal control system essential for maintaining a comfortable working environment, with wall and window heaters, fans and ducting. *(NASA-MSFC)*

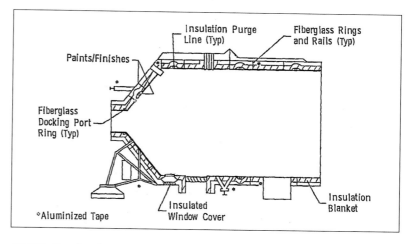

ABOVE Passive thermal control systems included tape, various paint patterns and finishes and fibreglass coverings. *(NASA-MSFC)*

BELOW Careful placement of heaters throughout the MDA resulted in a balanced thermal environment, which, despite problems down in the Orbital Workshop, was maintained at comfortable temperatures. *(NASA-MSFC)*

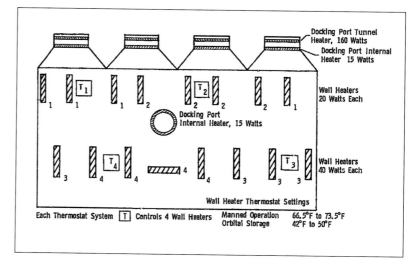

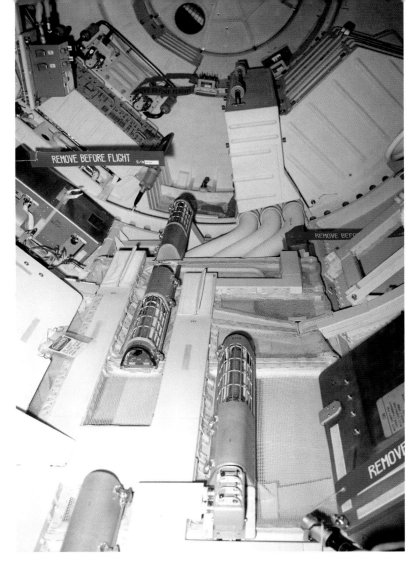

which was then installed through a hole in the hatch. The inside of the coiled bourdon tube of each gauge was exposed, via a sensing tube, to the atmosphere on the opposite side of the hatch, while the outside of the bourdon tube was exposed to atmospheric pressure on the near side. A difference in pressure across the bourdon tube would cause the tube to coil or uncoil, thereby causing the dial pointer to move.

The MDA had a passive and an active thermal control system (TCS) for maintaining an average wall temperature of 15.5°–32.2°C (60°–90°F) during the manned portion of the mission and 4.4°–32.2°C (40°–90°F) during unmanned phases. The passive system controlled the overboard heat loss from the MDA interior to a value that allowed the active TCS to control internal temperatures. It consisted of insulation blankets, use of fibreglass as structural standoffs and spacers, aluminised tape and thermal control paints and coatings.

The insulation blanket consisted of 91 layers of perforated double-aluminised Mylar separated by Dacron netting. The blankets were held in position on the MDA exterior by using lacing and 'boat hooks'. The multi-layers were held together by the use of nylon Swiftachments. The insulation blanket was placed between the MDA pressure shell and the radiator/meteoroid shield, the design of the blanket allowing the multi-layer Mylar to act as a radiation shield that retarded the flow of heat from the MDA.

Fibreglass standoffs had low thermal conductivity and took the form of circumferential rings and longitudinal rails to thermally isolate the MDA pressure wall from the external meteoroid shield. The use of low emissivity aluminised tape and paints and coatings having special thermal properties also retarded heat transfer overboard. Low emissivity tape was used principally on the L-band truss and the fibreglass standoffs to reduce heat leak in potentially high-loss areas. Tape was also used in several other local areas such as the S192 and S191 penetrations for optical viewing.

The insulation purge system was used only prior to flight, providing dry gaseous nitrogen distribution for conditioning the insulation blanket and S190 window at various times during ground operations, storage and transportation. The exterior of the pressure shell was encircled with a network of perforated tubing, located beneath the MDA insulation blankets, forming the gas distribution system. It was used for purging the insulation blankets and the exterior of the surface of the S190 window.

The active thermal control system included electrical and MDA/ECS hardware, the electrical hardware consisting of heating systems for the MDA wall, internal docking port area and the axial docking port tunnel. During periods of low internal heat generation the thermostatically controlled MDA heater systems provided heat to allow the MDA to meet specified temperature limits. During manned operation the plan was to set the heaters to 21.1°C (70°F) and during orbital storage to a 7.2°C (45°F) control mode. The MDA heating systems were inactive during manned occupation due to thermostat cut-out and cooling was provided by introducing cooled air from the Airlock Module via the ECS ducts. The cabin fans were used to provide

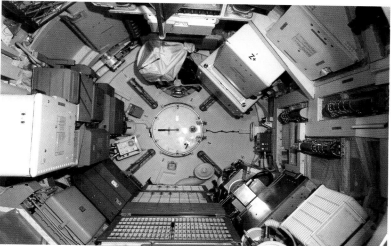

CENTRE A view looking forward in the MDA toward the hatch that would be used to allow the crew access to the Skylab space station. *(NASA)*

satisfactory atmosphere circulation and gas velocities at crew stations.

Eight 20W and eight 40W wall heaters were located in the interior barrel section of the MDA pressure shell to heat the MDA. Each heater had a primary and a secondary, redundant, heater element. An over-temperature thermostat was electrically in series with each heater element. Four wall heater 21.1°C (70°F) thermostats and four 7.2°C (45°F) thermostats were provided to control the internal temperature during manned and unmanned periods respectively. Each thermostat had a redundant set of points.

Each docking port had a 15W heater to make up the heat lost through the docking port itself, each heater possessing a primary and a secondary, redundant, element. An over-temperature thermostat was electrically in series with each heater element and each circuit had an inline thermostat to control the docking port temperature between 15.5°C (60°F) and 21.1°C (70°F), with thermostats equipped with primary and secondary contact points.

Two semi-circular 80W strip heaters were installed around the external surface of the axial docking tunnel, each heater having a primary and secondary, redundant, element. The system was used to provide a shirt-sleeve environment for crew entering the docking tunnel and in addition it assisted on the overall thermal control of the vehicle during orbital storage and manned mission modes. An over-temperature thermostat was electrically in series with each heater element. Two thermostats were provided

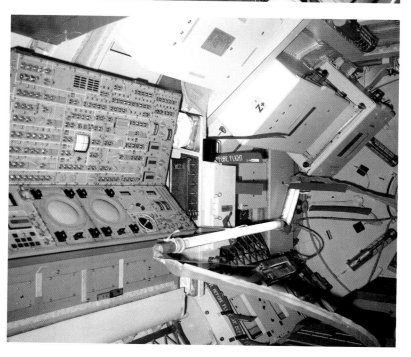

RIGHT Again looking forward but from further back, the sidewall of the MDA supported the Apollo Telescope Mount control console that would provide considerable work time for solar observations on all three crew visits. *(NASA)*

ABOVE Vance Brand checks out switch positions at the ATM control console, utilising a pull-out tray support. *(NASA)*

BELOW A view of the ATM control console from the other end, with Paul Weitz at work during the first manned visit. *(NASA)*

to control the temperature of the tunnel to between 15.5°C (60°F) and 23.3°C (74°F) and each thermostat on this installation had primary and secondary contact points too.

The S190 window heater contained a 40W electrical conductive film heater on the glass outer surface. Two 100W frame heaters were mounted in the glass support frame. These three heaters contained a total of four temperature sensors for heating control and three sensors for over-temperature. The purpose of the window heating system was to control the window temperature so that the glass temperature gradients were minimised and moisture condensation was removed.

The MDA electrical system provided four 1A utility outlet assemblies that supplied voltage to low-power portable equipment and two 12A high-power assemblies which supplied voltage to high-power portable equipment. The low-power outlets provided 28VDC power with a single on/off switch and zero-g connector that interfaced with the portable equipment cable connectors. Four power distribution assemblies were installed in the MDA, two to control the tunnel heaters, docking port heaters and the lights and the other two controlling MDA wall heaters. Each of the identical units received power/control inputs from the Airlock Module from separate power buses to provide redundancy and reliability.

The MDA electrical cabling consisted of stranded and coaxial wire. The standard wire types were constructed from a polyimide-coated Teflon insulation over a silver-plated copper conductor. The shield jacket was extruded Teflon. Feedthrough connectors were used to provide hermetically sealed skin penetrations. Eight interior general illumination floodlight assemblies provided crew workstation illumination with four on the forward dome and

LEFT Skylab was unique in that its design and layout retained the conventions of living and working on Earth, this chair seat providing a location for the ATM operator to remain seated – in weightlessness! Note the unsecured belt straps flowing free. The Russians would not adopt this design and the International Space Station would certainly not have seats. *(NASA)*

four along the air ducts. Each of the eight lights had a local switching capability of off, low and high. Each light had an output of 315 lumens minimum before installation into the light fixture. A switch panel for on/off lighting control was sited near the axial docking port of the MDA for easy selective control during astronaut ingress or for all eight lights simultaneously. For proper operation the lights had to be in 'high' or 'low' position.

The MDA lighting control system was designed so that all the Airlock Module remote control switches were independent of each other and functioned in pairs of two lights per control. Control power switching of the lights was accomplished through latching relays in the power assemblies. The two lights above the Apollo Telescope Mount control and displays panel were provided with removable and adjustable light filters for the purpose of attenuating illumination levels. Two lights functioned as emergency lights and were controlled from the Airlock Module.

The MDA caution and warning system monitored the CSM, Airlock Module, Apollo Telescope Mount and Orbital Workshop for malfunction conditions categorised as caution, warning or emergency, and identified malfunctions by visual and distinctly coded audible alarms. Functionally, it was divided into a caution-and-warning (C&W) and emergency subsystem. The C&W monitored the orbital assembly performance parameters categories as caution and warning conditions; the emergency subsystem monitored fire in the MDA, AM and OWS, and a rapid decrease in pressure within the orbital assembly. Each subsystem was further divided into two subsystems, providing redundant parallel parameter monitoring and malfunction indicators. The C&W system was only active when the assembly was manned and no ground control of the C&W system was provided.

The components used to detect and initiate a caution and warning alarm (high or low limit detection) consisted of C&W sensors, C&W detector module and C&W signal conditioning display converters. Emergency condition detection was provided by two delta-pressure sensors located in the structural transition

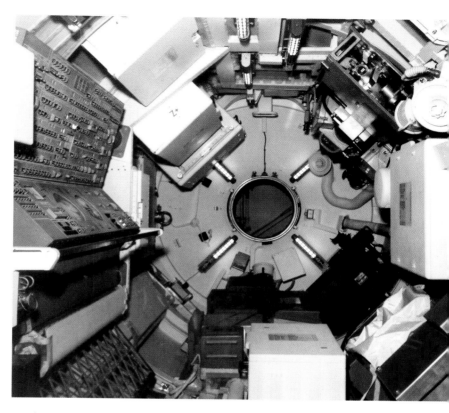

section and 22 fire sensors installed throughout the orbital assembly. The two fire sensors, one fire sensor control panel and the master alarm lights located on each speaker intercom assembly made up the caution and warning system in the MDA.

ABOVE Looking aft toward the Airlock Module, with the full internal layout of the MDA on display. *(NASA)*

BELOW Commander of the first manned visit to Skylab, Charles 'Pete' Conrad evaluates the materials processing equipment on the opposite wall of the MDA during pre-flight familiarisation and training. *(NASA)*

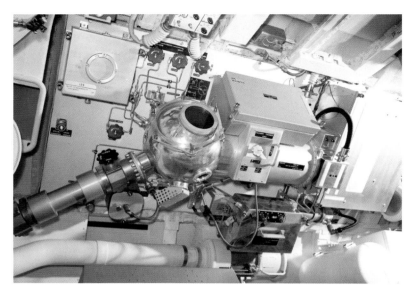

ABOVE The materials processing suite of experiments involving crystal growth, metals research, welding and general metallurgical studies was packaged in a relatively compact and well-designed collection of equipment for conducting a wide variety of tests. *(NASA)*

BELOW The work chamber and control panel for materials processing experiments are depicted here in this annotated breakdown of equipment. *(NASA-MSFC)*

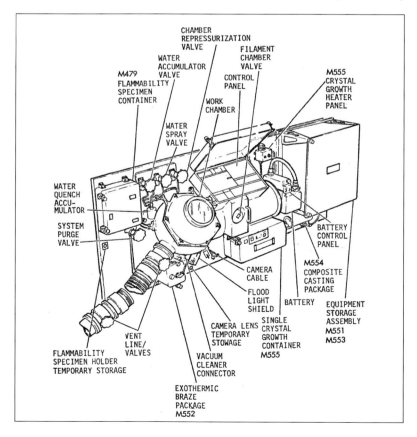

MDA experiments

In addition to supporting the control and display console and operating equipment for the instruments in the Apollo Telescope Mount, the Multiple Docking Adapter also housed a major suite of experiments and their supporting equipment generalised under the category of 'materials processing in space'. From an early stage in planning orbital activities, engineers thought about the requirements for building large structures in space. Because of the limitations on volume and mass available in rockets and launch vehicles of the foreseeable future, it made sense to carry into orbit the essential materials required for space stations and bases in orbit rather than assemble them on the ground. That would call for assembling metal structures that in turn would require welding in the weightless vacuum of orbital flight.

Beginning around 1963, engineers at NASA's Marshall Space Flight Center began designing compact electron-beam welding equipment and an experiment to be carried into space was proposed the following year. In December 1966 it was approved as one of the emerging experiments for the Apollo Applications Program, and thus into Skylab by 1969, in a bid to determine how best to assemble metals in zero gravity. The potential for manufacturing in space appeared to have intrinsic advantages that emphasised the value, and not the negative medical aspects, of weightlessness. This positive effect of near zero-g became self-evident in the preparation of purer and larger semiconductor crystals, in the possible production of purer vaccines, and in the preparation of a wide range of materials of value to humans on Earth.

As NASA moved toward the development of permanently manned space stations serviced by shuttlecraft routinely connecting them to the Earth with frequent visits and the return of material to Earth, Skylab came to be seen as a precursor research facility for exploring all these possibilities. The materials processing in space facility (M512) provided a basic apparatus for investigating the possibility of rearranging the molecular composition of materials unimpeded by the dominating influence of gravity. On Earth the density differences caused by the change in temperature resulted in convection, which is a hindrance; in space there were no variations in temperature and no convection.

The M512 facility was hard-mounted in the MDA and consisted of a work chamber with associated mechanical and electrical controls. Initially planned as a facility for experimenting with the feasibility of joining metallic materials with heat through electron beam and exothermic processes, it grew into a general-purpose facility for materials research and manufacturing, with six individual experiments inside the redeveloped pressure chamber, and a controls and display panel.

The vacuum chamber was a 40cm (16in) diameter sphere with a hinged hatch for access. It was connected to the space environment by a 10cm (4in) diameter line containing two gate valves. The electron beam subsystem was mounted to the chamber so that the beam traversed the sphere along a diameter parallel to the plane of the hatch closure. The chamber wall contained a cylindrical well accommodating small electric furnaces where the M555 crystal growth experiment was carried out. Here single

crystals of gallium arsenide would grow, from a solution dissolved in liquid gallium metal at 750°C (1,382°F) to seed crystals at the relatively cooler end at 550°C (1,022°F).

A receptacle above the well provided power and instrumentation connections to the control panel with provisions for a floodlight and a 16mm data acquisition camera. There was also a subsystem for spraying water into the chamber during, for instance, runs of the zero-g flammability tests (M479). The electron beam operated nominally at 20kV and 80mA with focusing and deflection coils operated directly from the control panel so that the position and size of the beam impingement could be adjusted by the operator.

The four specific experiments associated with the M512 facility included metals melting (M551), exothermic brazing (M552), sphere forming (M553) and gallium-arsenide crystal growth (M555). Separately, a Multipurpose Electric Furnace System (M518) consisted of three main units: the furnace, a control package, and 33 cartridges consisting of 11 experiment sets. The furnace had three

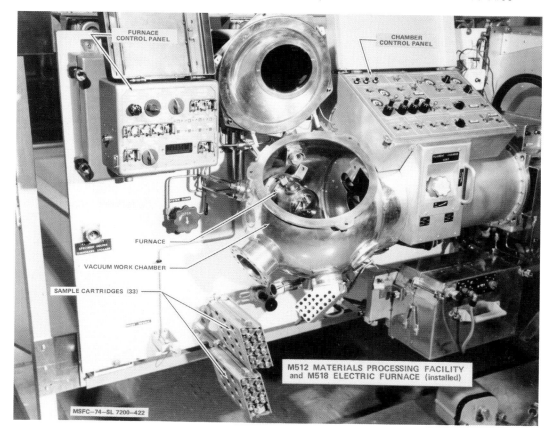

FURNACE CONTROL PANEL

CHAMBER CONTROL PANEL

FURNACE

VACUUM WORK CHAMBER

SAMPLE CARTRIDGES (33)

M512 MATERIALS PROCESSING FACILITY and M518 ELECTRIC FURNACE (installed)

MSFC—74—SL 7200—422

LEFT The interior view of the vacuum work chamber and furnace with disposition of control equipment in the Multiple Docking Adapter. *(NASA-MSFC)*

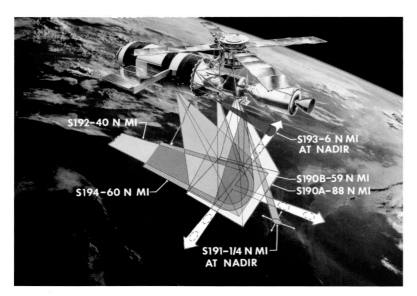

S192–40 N MI

S193–6 N MI
AT NADIR

S190B–59 N MI
S190A–88 N MI

S194–60 N MI

S191–1/4 N MI
AT NADIR

ABOVE This annotated diagram shows the several separate remote sensing experiments and their viewing angles and footprints. *(NASA)*

Technology Satellite (ERTS-1) was launched to a 1,000km (600-mile) polar orbit in July 1972, providing images of the Earth in several bands encompassing infrared and visible portions of the spectrum. Skylab observations were designed to build upon those.

Physically supported on the MDA structure, the 979kg (2,159lb) Earth Resources Experiments Package (EREP) was the next technological step, embracing visible and infrared photography, infrared spectroscopy and microwave radiometry. Some 300 proposals for scientific experiments to be included in the Skylab EREP package were submitted from institutions in the US and abroad, from which 146 were selected and further divided into 170 individual tasks, several in numerous sectors, in 32 areas of application. The facility included six sensors with associated support equipment including data handling, a control and display panel and primary and spare tape recorders. These experiments each required unique sets of equipment as follows:

specimen cavities so that three material sample cartridges could be processed simultaneously. It was designed to provide a constant temperature hot zone of up to 1,000°C (1,832°F), a gradient zone ranging from 20°C (68°F) to 200°C (392°F) and a cool zone where heat was conducted out of the system.

The MDA was also responsible for supporting a set of instruments designed to conduct remote observation of the Earth in various spectral bands, largely in support of an increasing interest by NASA in the use of satellites for geological, geographical and resource mapping and categorisation. The first Earth Resources

S190A Multispectral Photographic Camera

– designed to include photographs of the Earth's surface extending from the visible into the near infrared with sufficient definition and resolution to allow localised analysis and interpretation. One portion consisted of an array of six 70mm

RIGHT The attitude orientation for remote sensing observations placed Skylab in the local vertical (Z-LV) mode, which was also used for rendezvous activity during unmanned periods. This diagram shows the manoeuvre for EREP observations and back again to solar inertial. *(NASA-MSFC)*

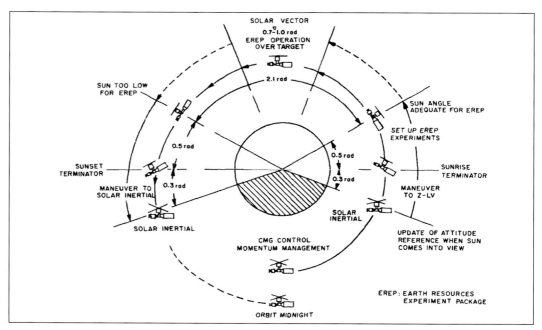

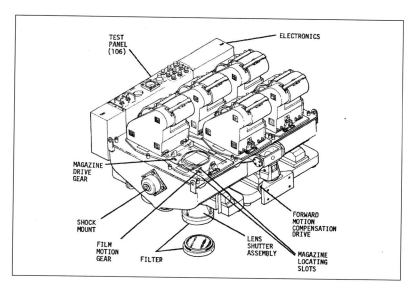

cameras precisely boresighted for accurate overlay of the same features in different parts of the spectrum. They had a focal length of 15.2cm and an aperture of f/2.8, lenses producing square fields of view 163km (100 miles) on a side with an optional combination of black and white and colour filters for comparison with the S192 experiment and with the ERTS images. The camera array was mounted behind a 42 x 56cm (16.5 x 22in) optical glass window just forward of the radial docking hatch in the MDA and weighed 135kg (296lb).

S191 Infrared Spectrometer

– designed to make a fundamental evaluation of the effects of strong atmospheric water vapour on attenuating the infrared signature of features on the ground, and of the effectiveness of this means for determining the health of crops. The instrument was known as a filter wedge spectrometer because it allowed measurements of relatively high spectral resolution, corresponding to a ground resolution of 0.434km (0.270 miles). A Malakar closed loop cooling system used helium gas in a refrigerator cycle to cool the infrared detectors in the spectrometer to -196°C (-321°F). The instrument was 48.3 x 50.8 x 129.5cm (19 x 20 x 51in) in size and weighed 190.5kg (420lb). The spectrometer had the ability to point 45° forward, 10° aft and 20° to the side of the

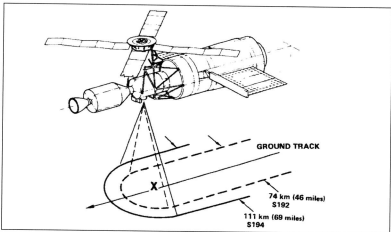

GROUND TRACK

74 km (46 miles)
S192

111 km (69 miles)
S194

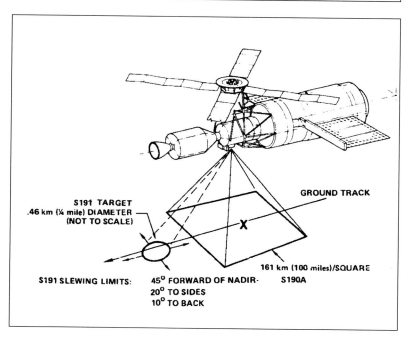

S191 TARGET
.46 km (¼ mile) DIAMETER
(NOT TO SCALE)

GROUND TRACK

X

161 km (100 miles)/SQUARE
S190A

S191 SLEWING LIMITS: 45° FORWARD OF NADIR-
20° TO SIDES
10° TO BACK

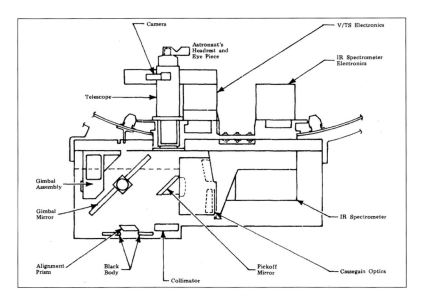

portion of the spectrum with high atmospheric transmission. The fundamental principle behind the instrument was that of an optical mechanical scanner utilising an object plane nutating scan mirror with a folded 30.48cm (12in) reflecting telescope, used in this instance as a radiation collector. The instrument had a ground resolution of 79.2 x 79.2m (260 x 260ft), better than that of S191 largely due to the coarser spectral resolution of the scanner which gave a better signal-to-noise ratio despite smaller field stops. The scanner provided a swathe per scan of 79.2m (260ft) by 41.8km (26 miles). Here, too, a Malakar cooling system provided a temperature of -180°C (-290°F). The instrument had a volume of 0.549m³ (19.4ft³) and a weight of 61.7kg (136lb).

ABOVE The S191 infrared spectrometer split the incoming radiation into short and long wavelengths, radiation in both channels passing through a chopping wheel that allowed intermittent comparison with known calibration sources. A filter wheel spectrometer allowed the intensity of the image in various spectral bands to be measured and enabled the operator to view and photograph the ground site using the mechanism shown here. *(NASA-MSFC)*

ground track. The astronaut played a major part in aligning the instrument for a range of pre-selected targets with data recorded on magnetic tape for return to Earth.

S192 Multispectral Scanner

– designed to provide information for assessing the viability of remote sensing of Earth's resources from space and to align the spectral signature identifying agricultural targets such as forestry, as well as hydrology and oceanography. The scanner operated in 13 spectral bands, each relatively wide, in that

S193 Microwave Radiometer/ Scatterometer/Altimeter

– designed to complement S191 and S192 in extracting useful information about the surface of the Earth and its resources by making simultaneous measurements of the radar differential back-scattering cross-section and passive microwave thermal emission of the land and the ocean. Data from this instrument was useful in providing information about seasonal changes in snow cover, gross vegetation and seasonal changes in topography including

RIGHT The S192 multispectral scanner provided high-resolution, quantitative data on radiation reflected and emitted by selected test sites in 13 discrete spectral bands of the visible-near-infrared, and thermal-infrared regions of the spectrum. *(NASA-MSFC)*

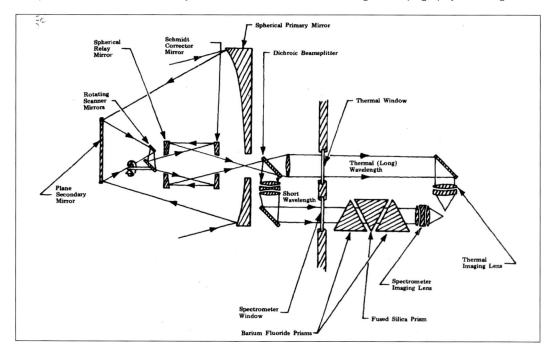

flooding, soil-type measurement, heat from urban areas and ocean characteristics. It consisted of an external antenna on a gimbal assembly attached to an aluminium mounting plate, secured to the ATM deployment assembly. The transmitter operated at a frequency of 13.9GHz with the tilt mechanism providing a maximum forward and sideways pointing angle of 48°, with a ground area coverage straight down of 11.1km (6.9 miles) diameter.

S194 L-Band Microwave Radiometer

– to measure the brightness temperature of the Earth's surface adopting essentially the same operating principle as the radiometer part of S193, except that the operating frequency was changed to 1.42GHz, effectively supplementing that other instrument by incorporating clouds on the radiometric measurements. The equipment was based on instruments then being used on NASA's Lockheed NP3A Orion earth resources aircraft and consisted of a receiver and antenna, weighing a total 22.68kg (50lb). Fixed in an Earth-pointing local vertical, the instrument surveyed ground swathes 111km (69 miles) wide and recorded data on magnetic tape at 200 bits per second.

Apollo Telescope Mount

In 1965 the US National Academy of Sciences made a recommendation that NASA should conduct a concerted effort to understand the way astronauts could advance the capabilities of large manned telescopes in Earth orbit. The Academy wanted to follow an existing programme, known as the Orbiting Solar Observatory (OSO) programme, with a more advanced project paving the way for a large space telescope that could be used by

BELOW The Apollo Telescope Mount (ATM) dominated the visual appearance of the Skylab space station and provided Southern Astrophysical Research (SOAR) astronomers and physicists with unprecedented access to information obtained from outside the Earth's obscuring atmosphere. (NASA)

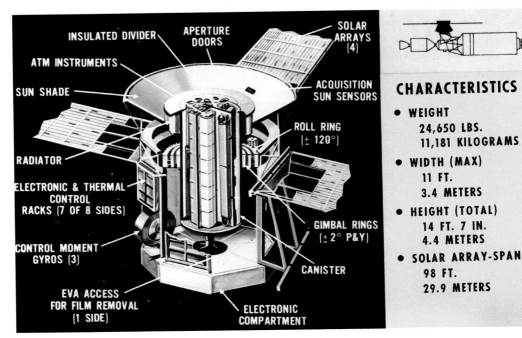

SOLAR ARRAYS (4)

APERTURE DOORS

INSULATED DIVIDER

ATM INSTRUMENTS

SUN SHADE

ACQUISITION SUN SENSORS

RADIATOR

ROLL RING (± 120°)

ELECTRONIC & THERMAL CONTROL RACKS (7 OF 8 SIDES)

GIMBAL RINGS (± 2° P&Y)

CONTROL MOMENT GYROS (3)

CANISTER

EVA ACCESS FOR FILM REMOVAL (1 SIDE)

ELECTRONIC COMPARTMENT

CHARACTERISTICS

- **WEIGHT**
  24,650 LBS.
  11,181 KILOGRAMS
- **WIDTH (MAX)**
  11 FT.
  3.4 METERS
- **HEIGHT (TOTAL)**
  14 FT. 7 IN.
  4.4 METERS
- **SOLAR ARRAY-SPAN**
  98 FT.
  29.9 METERS

RIGHT This simplified drawing shows the external canister into which were inserted the instruments, also the location of the Control Moment Gyroscopes (CMGs) utilised for pointing and orientation of the entire station. *(NASA)*

BELOW In this cutaway, electrical, instrumentation, communication and elements of the pointing control system are visible with the solar arrays, folded on one side and deployed on the other. *(NASA)*

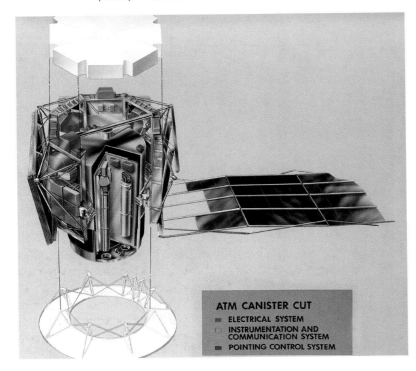

ATM CANISTER CUT
- ELECTRICAL SYSTEM
- INSTRUMENTATION AND COMMUNICATION SYSTEM
- POINTING CONTROL SYSTEM

scientists in orbit. It suggested a joint effort between NASA's Office of Space Science and Applications (OSSA) and the Office of Manned Space Flight (OMSF) to expand both the spatial and spectral bandwidth available to scientists.

The OSO programme was designed around a requirement to more fully understand the dynamics and structure of the Sun, both for its intrinsic value in better understanding the solar environment and its interaction with Earth's atmosphere, and as a contribution to astrophysics and the life and evolution of stars in our galaxy. They were small satellites, weighing between 200kg (441lb) and 300kg (661lb) depending upon the specific model launched. Built by Ball Brothers for the Goddard Space Flight Center, OSO 1 was lifted into orbit by a Delta rocket on 7 March 1962 and was followed by OSO 2 on 3 February 1965, and subsequently by a further six satellites, the last (OSO 8) in June 1975.

When the Academy issued its recommendations for a more advanced, manned successor, it was on the back of the first two highly successful satellites in the OSO series, initial flights of which were designed to study solar radiation in the ultraviolet, X-ray and gamma-ray regions of the spectrum. Measurement of the Sun from space was one of the earliest of NASA's space science objectives, the OSO being included in its 'Ten Year Program' issued on 17 August 1959.

Work was by then already under way with Ball Brothers on development of this exciting programme, a launch then being tentatively planned for 1960. From its inception, OSO was known as a 'streetcar' satellite because it could carry an interchangeable set of scientific instruments. OSO opened a new era in solar astronomy but its proposed successor, the

Advanced Orbiting Solar Observatory, was cancelled on cost grounds in 1965.

In January 1966 OSSA asked NASA's field centres to contribute facility skills to the use of a three-axis orientated solar telescope in the vacant sector 1 of the Apollo Block II Service Module. The system was to be capable of resolving solar features of about 5 arcsec in size, to hold selected alignments to within 5 arcsec in pitch and yaw and to within 1 arcsec of roll during data acquisition. Three months later, the Marshall Space Flight Center carried out trade-off studies of this and a solar telescope array mounted to an unmanned derivative of the Lunar Module (LM), originally designed for conveying two astronauts from lunar orbit to the surface of the Moon but seen as a potential workhorse for a variety of manned and unmanned missions in the gradually evolving Apollo Applications Program.

The studies swung opinion toward the Lunar Module Apollo Telescope Mount (LM/ATM) and Marshall received a further request from the OSSA to study that further and the results were delivered in late June. On 11 July NASA decided on the LM/ATM concept and assigned Apollo Telescope Mount hardware and experiment management to the Marshall facility. In the project development plan submitted on 25 July, an experiment package of up to four telescopes would replace the LM Descent Stage, the box-shaped structure containing the LM descent engine and the four landing legs.

The mission profile would have the three-person Apollo CSM launched first followed by the LM/ATM a day later. After rendezvous and docking, two astronauts would enter the Ascent Stage, undock and occupy it for seven days of scientific observations. Re-docking

BELOW The experiments were inserted into the equipment canister that supported the Solar Array System and the mounting plates for the film cameras and the access doors at the top of the ATM. *(NASA-MSFC)*

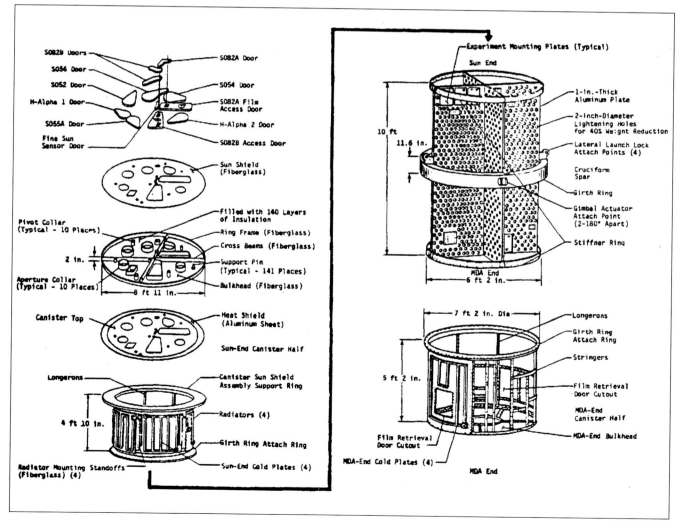

BELOW In this cutaway of the ATM structure the Sun end is at the bottom, the area closest to the Multiple Docking Adapter being at the top. Notice the structural supports, intercostals and outrigger assemblies, in no small measure reminiscent of the Descent Stage of the Lunar Module, from which the ATM evolved when Skylab adopted the 'dry' workshop concept. *(NASA-MSFC)*

with the CSM, one astronaut would exchange position with the third astronaut followed by undocking and a further seven days of observations. Mission duration was 14 days with the potential to extend it to 28 days. At the time of this conceptual planning, NASA was well into the operational flight phase of the Gemini programme and was adopting a policy of doubling up space-flight time, having gone from four days on Gemini IV to eight days on Gemini V and 14 days on Gemini VII. Missions of 28 and 56 days were considered a natural progression for AAP missions.

The initial concept envisaged a universal rack previously designed for Project Thermo and the Payload Module Project, initial technology exploitation efforts that had been cancelled. The rack would provide support for experiments, for batteries and for the Control Moment

Gyroscopes to maintain high pointing accuracy and stabilisation. It would also serve as a mount for the Ascent Stage and its docking ring, the assembly of which would fit within the same payload volume as that available to a standard, unmodified Lunar Module.

The octagonal planform truss structure was to be 246.4cm (97in) across the longitudinal direction within a prescribed circle of 289.6cm (114in). A 152.4cm (60in) diameter payload support ring would be located at the centre of the aft plane for the rack to which the experiment package would be attached, parallel to the thrust axis. The overall dimensions of the octagonal planform structure was 152.4cm (60in) in diameter by 304.8cm (120in) in length. This structure would be capable of accepting a single large telescope up to 127cm (50in) in diameter or, with the installation of a cross-frame spar, several smaller telescopes.

However, two alternative concepts were evaluated at the development meeting on 25 July 1966. One envisaged a modification allowing the experiment package mounted in the LM Descent Stage to feature a package of instruments extending into the Ascent Stage where the engine would normally be located. This would necessitate the installation of additional hard-points on the Descent Stage that would support the CMGs and other supporting modules. Solar arrays would be fixed to the landing leg attachment points. The second option was to keep the LM/ATM attached to the CSM for the duration, thereby allowing much equipment necessary for autonomous flight to be removed, saving weight and providing more spacious accommodation between the Command Module and the Ascent Stage.

During this time several concepts for the further use of Apollo hardware in the proposed AAP missions challenged the independent application of LM/ATM/CSM missions and for a while during early 1967 a tethered concept was mooted in which the ATM would be tethered, undocked, to the CSM by umbilicals carrying fluids, electrical power and oxygen etc.

But it was the configuration of LM/ATM docked to the CSM that was favoured, despite increasing complexity of the ATM components, which grew to require their own active fluid cooling system, solar arrays, gimbal system

Star tracker cutout
Plug plate
Fiberglass angle
Alum. angles
1/2 in. alum. honeycomb panels plus 30 layers of super insulation
Thermal shield MDA end

Outrigger assemblies (4)
Payload shroud support fittings (4)
Intercostal
CMG mounting bay (3)
Equipment mounting panel (3) (alum honeycomb)
OBMM mounting panel (3)
Diagonal strut (3)
Solar shield assy mounting ring
ATM-DA attach fitting (4)
Vertical "I" beam (8)
Center work station bay
Canister bay
Octagonal ring
Solar array wing attach points (6) (typ 4 places)
Rack Sun end

Cutout for acquisition sun sensor viewing point
.062 alum plate
140 layers of super insulation
Fiberglass standoffs
Additional structure for sun end work station platform
Open area for canister sun end
Mounting trusses (8)
L. stringers
Outer ring
Panels
Inner ring
Cutout for EVA translation handrail
Solar shield

and attitude control and pointing equipment. As the ATM package itself grew in complexity and potential autonomy, the essential components of the ATM as flown began to evolve into the definitive configuration. The only unresolved issue was the platform on which the ATM would fly, which became entangled with the concept of the 'wet' workshop from a modified S-IVB stage. This evolved further to the cluster configuration and on into the 'dry' workshop and Skylab.

The decision to fly a 'dry' workshop was approved by NASA Administrator Tom Paine on 18 July 1969, and on 9 September the ATM was given responsibility for total cluster attitude control, followed on 4 December by a requirement to parallel the ATM electrical power system with the rest of the cluster, which necessitated putting additional wires across the interface. As events would demonstrate, this single decision would save Skylab and allow the ATM electrical production systems to supplement the power-starved workshop after one of the two Solar Array System solar cell wings was torn away shortly after launch.

One of the effects of the evolving application of the ATM was the weight effect. Established initially when the baseline configuration was to adopt the LM Ascent Stage to support a universal rack carrying scientific instruments, the total estimated weight of the LM/ATM on

23 October 1966 was 6,941kg (15,302lb), but when the Ascent Stage was deleted for application to the 'dry' workshop cluster the discounted weight of that stage, 2,268kg (5,000lb), and the life support items' 626kg (1,380lb) produced an initial baseline of 4,047kg (8,922lb). At launch on 14 May 1973 the ATM would have a mass of 11,200.3kg (24,692lb), displaying an overall growth factor of 2.768.

In fairness, the several changes to weight estimates were influenced by numerous modifications, additions and revisions resulting from the transformation of the ATM's operating profile, as well as the additional responsibilities attached for cluster operations. A significant weight growth occurred in wiring mass estimations, increasing by 939.4kg (2,071lb) due to the added requirements. There was also a consequential effect from the changes to design philosophy after the Apollo fire on 27 January 1967. In January 1968 the more realistic mass of the ATM had been assessed at 8,437kg (18,600lb) set against a final control weight of 11,181kg (24,650lb), exceeded by 19kg (42lb).

The final design configuration consisted of two major parts of the ATM, an outer structure or rack and an inner section, the canister, which supported the solar telescopes. For launch the ATM was positioned along the long axis, encapsulated by the Payload Shroud, on a

ABOVE LEFT The experiment mounting arrangement, with the girth ring clearly visible in this photograph of the ATM thermal test structure. *(NASA)*

ABOVE The spare flight unit receives the experiment canister and displays the vertical placement of the several instruments and solar telescopes. *(NASA)*

support structure rotating 90° in orbit to place the assembly in a radial orientation to the long axis of the cluster. This effectively cleared the docking path for the Apollo CSM so that the spacecraft could attach to the axial port on the Multiple Docking Adapter. This also positioned the ATM to point its instruments at the Sun and to deploy four Solar Array System wings, the ATM-SAS, for producing electrical energy.

The octagonal rack structure had a diameter of 3.3m (11ft) and a length of 3.6m (12ft), to which were attached a thermal shield assembly at one end and a solar shield at the other, four canister support assemblies and four outrigger assemblies. The frame consisted of two large octagon-shaped aluminium rings open in the centre and separated by eight 2.54cm (1in) aluminium vertical beams attached to the corners. Panels for equipment were mounted in seven bays between these beams. One bay was open for access to the canister film retrieval doors and designated as the centre workstation. Three bays were braced by a tubular diagonal strut and four bays were braced by outriggers attached to the octagonal rings. A smaller third ring, also octagonal and open in the centre, was attached to the Sun end of the frame by open truss work. This ring provided support for the solar array and the mounting for the solar shield assembly and

support points for ground transportation. A small, trapezoid-shaped structure extended down from one side of the small ring to provide a mount for the acquisition Sun sensors.

The thermal shield assembly was an octagonal structure 50.8cm (20in) deep and 340.4cm (134in) across the flats. It was made up from eight triangular truss structures attached to a ring in the centre and connected by channels at the flats. This structure was covered by 1.27cm (0.5in) thick aluminium honeycomb panels for thermal protection, overlain by 30 layers of superinsulation. The thermal shield assembly was attached to the MDA-end of the frame structure.

At the other end, the solar shield assembly consisted of a cone-shaped ring with an outside diameter of 436.9cm (172in) and an interior diameter of 248.9cm (98in), creating an open, circular, centre area for the Sun end of the canister and its telescopes. It was 38.1cm (15in) deep and covered with thermal panels and mounted on a 63.5cm (25in) high open truss structure. It was attached to a small octagonal ring at the Sun end of the rack to protect equipment from direct solar radiation. A series of eight mounting trusses located the shield on the main octagonal body of the rack, with a cut-out for Sun-sensor view angles and another on the opposite side for the EVA translation

RIGHT The experiment canister is lowered precariously into the outer rack. *(NASA)*

FAR RIGHT The vibration test model of the ATM shows the principle elements, including the outer rack and the mounts for structural attachment to the fixed airlock shroud. *(NASA)*

handrail. There was an additional structure to support the workstation platform. The thermal shield was covered with 0.157cm (0.062in) aluminium plate, fibreglass standoffs enclosing 140 layers of superinsulation.

The four outriggers were open truss tubular assemblies that provided support for the ATM in the Payload Shroud (which see) during launch. Two were attached at one end to the corners of each of the two large octagonal rings and at the other end to the Payload Shroud support fitting. During orbital operations the only rack structural assemblies interfacing with the canister were the support roller assemblies, which were functionally a part of the experiment pointing, control-roll positioning mechanism discussed later in this section.

The experiment canister provided a support structure for the telescopes and instruments and was located within the rack assembly. It also provided the structure for attaching the thermal control system cold plates, the radiators and associated fluid-transfer hardware. It was composed of a spar, an MDA-canister half and a Sun-end canister half.

The spar was a cruciform structure made up from 2.54cm (1in) thick aluminium plate, 304.8cm in length, and perforated with 5.08cm (2in) diameter holes to reduce the weight by 40%. Stiffener rings, with a maximum diameter of 187.96cm (74in), were located at the opposing ends of the structure and a girth ring, 29.46cm (11.6in) high and 218.44cm (74in) in diameter, was attached midway along the length of the structure. This served as an attachment point for the Sun-end canister half at the top and the MDA-canister half at the bottom. The spar was wrapped with insulation and the experiments and rate gyros were mounted on low-conductance mounts. The spar itself was similarly isolated from the canister by low-conductance mounts.

The MDA-canister half had a maximum length of 157.48cm (62in) and a maximum diameter of 187.96cm (74in). It consisted of an aluminium ring of L-shaped cross-section and a machined aluminium bulkhead supported by stringers of T-shaped cross-section. Short spacers separated the stringers. Eight cold plates for the active Thermal Control System (TCS) were attached to this framework. The

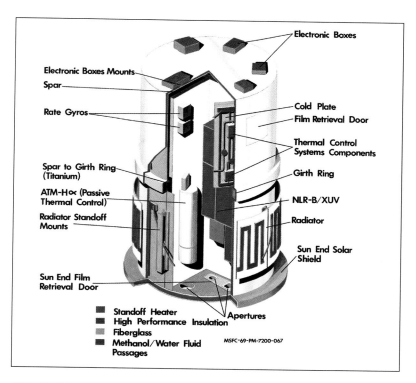

ABOVE This ATM cutaway diagram displays the levels of insulation, coolant passages for active thermal control, the position of the rate gyros and the electronic control boxes. *(NASA)*

BELOW The Fixed Airlock Shroud contained the support trusses for the ATM deployment rig, this diagram showing the launch position with the ATM forward. Note the relative location of the Airlock Module, the Multiple Docking Adapter being absent in this view for clarity. *(NASA-MSFC)*

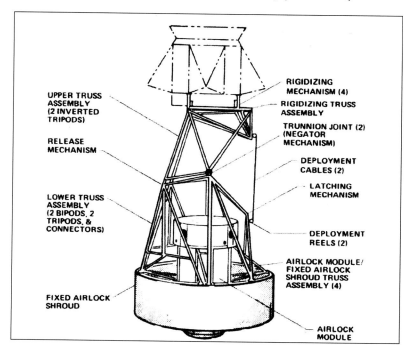

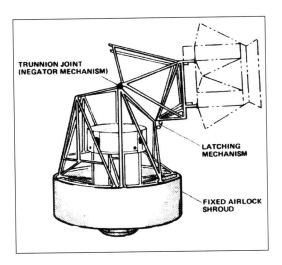

TRUNNION JOINT
(NEGATOR MECHANISM)

LATCHING
MECHANISM

FIXED AIRLOCK
SHROUD

active TCS components were mounted on standoffs on some of the cold plates while others had openings for experiment film retrieval doors. Some subsystem equipment was mounted on the outside of the machined aluminium bulkhead. The MDA-end canister half was slipped over the upper spar and spare mounted experiments and attached to the girth ring. The outside was covered with insulation.

The Sun-end canister half was constructed in the same manner as the MDA-end canister half

but without the openings in the cold plates. It had a length of 157.32cm (58in) and a diameter of 218.4cm (86in). Four TCS radiators were mounted on I-beams outside with cold plates. A machined aluminium bulkhead covered the Sun end of this canister half with bulkhead openings for each experiment. The bulkhead was formed from cross-beams within a ring frame with a diameter of 271.78cm (107in) and a depth of 5.08cm (2in) filled with 140 layers of superinsulation and carrying 141 support pins. The ten aperture collars were paired with ten pivot collars.

Two one-way vent valves were attached to the bulkhead. The purpose of these was to passively vent the canister whenever differential pressure built up inside; they were designed to maintain a Δ pressure of 3.44kPa (0.5lb/in^2) to meet the design requirement. A fibreglass Sunshield was attached on the outboard side of the bulkhead, with mounting provisions for each experiment aperture door and its associated operating mechanism together with a door for the fine Sun sensor. This half of the canister was also slipped over the spar and attached to the girth ring.

The experiment-pointing control-roll positioning mechanism (EPC-RPM) provided a three degrees of freedom mount for the ATM experiment canister within the rack. It consisted of two concentric welded aluminium rings, four actuator assemblies, a roll drive and brake assembly, a roll position indicator assembly, two orbital lock assemblies, a roll stop assembly, four lateral launch lock assemblies, a torsional launch lock assembly and four support roller assemblies.

The four support roller assemblies were attached to the rack structure and supported the outer or roll ring by means of a cluster of three rollers at four locations. The roll ring was attached to the inner or gimbal ring by two actuators for right/left motion. The gimbal ring was attached to the canister girth ring for up/down motion. A ring gear on the roll ring was driven by the roll drive and brake assembly for roll motion. The roll ring gear drove the roll position indicator. One orbital lock locked the roll ring to the canister girth ring. Four launch locks were provided to prevent all canister motion during launch and were released by pin pullers operated by explosive devices.

DA/ATM
interface

Deployment
reel

Forward

Pivot point

Upper truss
Lower truss

Deployment
reel

DA/FAS
Interface

The EPC actuator assembly consisted of one mechanical flexure bearing assembly, one torque motor and one multispeed electrical resolver. The mechanical flexure bearing provided a support system with a limited mechanical rotation similar to ball bearings but did not require lubrication since there were no rubbing parts. The torque motor drove the flexure bearing to provide the required maximum +/-2° motion. The roll drive and brake assembly consisted of torque motors, two tachometers and a two-coil solenoid-operated brake. The motors, tachometers and solenoid coils were arranged for electrical redundancy and the unit was rated for one unit to be operational at a time. The motors drove the ring gear on the roll ring to rotate the canister +/-120°. The brake assembly provided the braking force for positioning accuracy and to maintain the desired position. The tachometer measured the rotational speed of the motor shaft.

The roll position indicator assembly was attached to the rack by a spring-loaded bracket and engaged the roll ring gear by means of a small pinion gear. The assembly provided an electrical indication of the roll axis position and consisted of a tandem installation of two fine and four coarse resolution resolvers. The fine resolvers were driven by the input shaft and rotated at 16 times the roll axis speed. The coarse resolvers comprised two coarse resolution units and two coordinate transformation units and were driven by a reduction gear train and resolved at roll axis speed. The coordinate transform resolvers were not used. The pairs provided electrical redundancy.

The roll stop assembly limited the canister rotation to +/-120° and dampened the impact forces when the canister was stopped at its limits. The pawl on the roll stop assembly was engaged by one of two stop blocks on the roll ring, compressing the spring and thus preventing further canister rotation in that direction. The orbital lock assembly caged the experiment canister to the gimbal ring and the gimbal ring to the roll ring. It consisted of a roller mechanism driven by one or other of two redundant brush-type DC motors and a set of rails.

The roller mechanism motors were attached to the gimbal ring and the rails were attached to the canister girth ring and roll ring. To cage

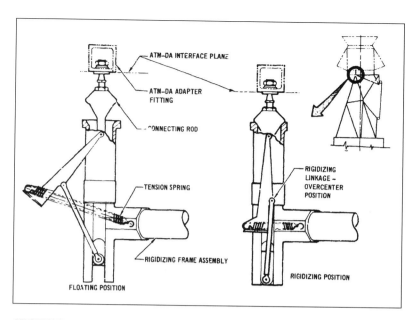

ABOVE The rigidising mechanism for locking up the deployed ATM, important for attitude control as well as alignment of the ATM experiments. (NASA)

the canister the torque motor rotated the roller mechanism until the rollers contacted the stops on the rails. In the caged position the rollers were slightly over 'top dead centre' with respect to

BELOW The ATM rack and canister assembly being prepared for thermal testing. (NASA)

ABOVE, BELOW AND BOTTOM Views of the Apollo Telescope Mount in varying degrees of completion showing the separate sides of the ATM outer rack assembly. *(NASA)*

the rails and were firmly compressed, preloaded, between the rails. The pitch and yaw orbital lock centre lines made a 23° Sun angle which resulted in an equal moment arm for both axes.

Five door openings penetrated the side of the canister, four for film retrieval during EVA and a fifth for ground access to one of the scientific instruments and for monitoring contamination prior to launch; this last was a double door with a latching mechanism on one side and fixed handle on the other. All doors incorporated a launch lock mechanism, latch, door position indicator, magnetic latches and rim seal. The latch had spring-loaded lock pins to hold the latch pins in their retracted position. To open the door the crewman first released the launch lock by pulling a 'D' handle far enough to break the lock wire and allow the split handle to be rotated and snapped into the stowage clip. The launch lock was not used again.

The door would open by pushing the handle into the dust boot, which rotated the cam and retracted the latch pins. The pin locks dropped into the detent section of the latch pin shaft to keep them in a retracted position and the door was pulled open to overcome the magnetic latches at the top and the bottom of the door. A friction device kept the door open using the friction of a spring against a curved rod. The door hinge pin was dry film lubricated to prevent cold welding in the vacuum of space. When the door was opened, a spring-loaded pin in the door indicator released allowing a red flag to drop into the housing. When the door was closed, it was held by the magnetic latches until the handle was pulled out, which rotated the cam in the opposite direction forcing the latch pins outward into holes in the door sill, which pushed in the pin on the door open indicator, raising the red flag up out of the housing and into view.

There were two film retrieval doors on the Sun shield for the two spectroheliography instruments. The three aperture doors that covered the film retrieval doors had to be opened from the centre workstation before the film retrieval doors could be opened; however, the canister also had to be rotated into the proper position so the doors would be accessible from the Sun-end workstation. The two film retrieval doors were manually operated and had no position indicators. The door assemblies were composed of a fibreglass shell filled with aluminised Mylar insulation, latch mechanism, lock mechanism, friction device and seals.

The latch mechanism was unlocked by depressing the lock release button on the top of the handle. This pushed the spring-loaded inner shaft down far enough to allow the locking pins to clear the retaining slot. The lock release leaf spring then rotated the cam and shaft far enough to prevent the lock release button spring from pushing the locking pins back into the retaining slot. The handle was then rotated, causing the cam to rotate and retract the latch pins from holes in the door sill. A friction device kept the door open using the friction of a spring against a curved rod. The door hinge pins were coated with a dry film lubricant.

If the handle was rotated in the wrong direction when trying to unlatch the door, the lock pins would be forced back into the retaining slots again. The door could not be unlatched until the lock release button on the top of the handle was depressed again. The door latched by rotating the handle in the opposite direction, causing the cam to rotate and force the latch pins into the holes in the door sill. The latch release button spring then forced the locking pins into the retaining slots to lock the door latches.

ATM experiments and the fine Sun sensor viewed the solar disc through openings in the Sun shield, which were covered by doors to protect the instrument and fine Sun sensor when not in use. The two spectroheliographs also had internal aperture doors, described later. The doors consisted of fibreglass shells filled with aluminised Mylar, with a shaft attached to one corner and a tapered ramp opposite the shaft. This ramp fitted into a U-shaped ramp latch attached to the Sun shield. Each door had a ramp latch that provided support during the launch phase. A 4° sloping ramp around the Sun-shield opening aided in sealing the doors. The door-operating mechanism consisted of redundant 28VDC torque motors driving a common jack screw shaft, a carriage, a lever, a mounting bracket and four limit switches. The mechanism was attached to the inside of the Sun shield and the lever was attached to the door shaft.

The door control circuits were basically the same. When commanded, the selected torque motors rotated the jack screw moving the carriage and lever. The lever rotated the door shaft to open it and when the carriage reached full travel it activated the door-open talkback indicator circuit and the door-open telemetry indicator. The door-closed circuit operated in a similar manner. The aperture doors could also be operated manually to preclude loss of mission objectives if the electromechanical doors failed. The EVA astronaut could remove the tee-shaped EVA pin from the door opening assembly and manually translate and lock the door in the open position.

The ATM experiment canister was purged on the ground with gaseous nitrogen, carried through a retractable fitting from the rack to the canister. The ground support line was disconnected at the rack prior to lift-off but the retractable fitting between the rack and the canister was not, this fitting being released when the crew rotated the canister in a clockwise direction the first time in orbit.

Initially, the thermal control system for the ATM encompassed a combined passive/semi-passive concept, tailoring high-performance insulation, reflective and non-reflective surface coatings and low-conductance mountings with a semi-passive management, including proportional heaters with sensory temperature controls. As the design of the ATM evolved, with the spar and experiments enclosed within a canister, thermal analysis revealed a need for a positive high-load thermal management system

BELOW The geometric configuration and panel identification of the ATM Solar Array System (ATM-SAS) with the direction to the OWS at the bottom in this orientation. Each panel contained 20 modules, except for the inboard panel, which had 10. (NASA-MSFC)

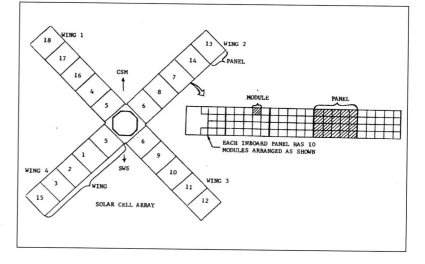

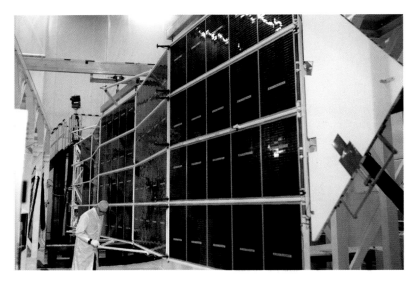

to maintain the stringent temperature gradient for the scientific instruments. From this emerged the active fluid TCS concept with related cold plates and radiators in addition to the passive/semi-passive control system.

In 1967 the firm decision was made to use the liquid TCS concept for canister thermal management and studies began considering the use of Freon or a methanol/water mixture as the coolant fluid. A mixture of methanol/water at 80/20% was utilised in the final design of the system, a decision based on existing hardware whereby the Apollo CSM used a glycol coolant, similar to methanol/water. The basic design criterion was established for maximum use of available off-the-shelf

hardware, maintaining a thermally stable spar temperature within 10–21°C (50–69.8°F) and that touch temperatures should not exceed 121°C (249.8°F). No boiling or freezing of the coolant was permissible and the radiator fluid temperature was to be constrained to a range not below -73.4°C (-100.1°F) and not at or above 10°C (50°F). The maximum canister heat load was to be 500W.

Throughout the early design phase of the TCS, only two significant problems were posed: flow instability and pump shaft seizure. Flow instability problems early in the test phase forced relocation of the modulating flow control valve and its associated equipment and there was some talk of replacing it with a thermal mechanical valve to solve the problem. Although the thermal mechanical valve performed satisfactorily, the modulating flow control valve mixing concept was the preferred default option, if only because it had consistently proved viable through exhaustive testing and it was felt that an impact on the schedule which would be caused by substitution was not warranted. The second difficulty was solved by increasing the clearances between the pump shaft and the bearing.

All the essential components of the thermal control system were supplied by vendors. The radiators and cold plates were manufactured by machining flow channels in a thick plate, cold forming that to the contour of the canister and welding a matching faceplate to the machined surface. The flow channels had an inside diameter of 1.57cm (0.62in). Three methods of securing the faceplate to the machined plate were tested. The bonding and fusion welding concepts were deleted in favour of a resistance roll seam welding process. Special fixtures were developed to assure stability of the machined plate and faceplate as the welding operation was accomplished. Prior to the start of each welding operation a series of sample weld runs was completed, then tested before adjustments could be made to the welding equipment to produce high-quality production weld seams.

The TCS tubing was assembled by using Aeroquip Spacecraft fittings with Aeroquip brazing equipment. The brazing material was 82% gold and 18% nickel with the brazing function at 1,038°C (1,900°F). NASA chose the Aeroquip method because of its high reliability and low strength-to-weight ratio but at first minor problems were encountered, as the tube cleaning process deactivated the tubes' acceptance of the brazing process. This problem was resolved by plugging the tubes after chemical cleaning, sand blasting the brazing area and then cleaning the external surface by the ultrasonic process. Special fittings were developed to connect the tubing to the TCS components, a design based on a four-bolt flange with O-ring compression concepts.

The TCS cold plates were mated with the ATM canister structural framework and the radiators were attached to the cold-plate mounted standoff hardware. The fluid transfer hardware was then mounted and the connecting tubing routed to their respective components. Special tube-routing jigs were utilised to ensure correct tube length prior to the brazing operation. After cutting and fitting of the fluid tubing, the tubing was braze-assembled in place. The Aeroquip method was found to be completely satisfactory and much was learned from this programme about potential applications in the fabrication of other systems and subsystems for other programmes.

The ATM Solar Array System (ATM-SAS) eventually flown on Skylab was very different to the method of providing electrical power for the telescope assembly envisaged at the beginning of the programme. A primary battery system was recommended as the most feasible and economic approach for the proposed 14- and 28-day missions. The total electrical power requirement for the ATM and the Lunar Module was estimated to be 1,247W during Sunlight and 1,325W during darkness, with a total capacity of 800kWh needed for the 28-day operating period. It was predicted that up to 20% of the anticipated loads could be reduced by power management procedures.

Several battery configurations were considered, with the final proposal being a total of 62 silver-zinc batteries in four packs on four sides of the rack in a symmetrical pattern. The total battery weight was expected to exceed 3,629kg (8,000lb), more than half the then total weight of the ATM, projected to be 6,350kg (14,000lb). Two ATM battery

packs were allocated to the LM through a rack-mounted distributor and four main buses to the relay junction box in the LM, with distribution through the existing LM system. The other two ATM battery packs were centralised into two buses for distribution to the ATM systems and experiments. Power system controls and monitoring were to be located on the ATM control panel in the LM Ascent Stage. Some thought was given to recharging the ATM batteries from the Apollo CSM fuel cells when in the docked mode but this idea gained little traction.

The networking system was based on the same concept as that eventually used in the final ATM configuration, with the exception of the power paralleling requirement which evolved later, that is, a combination of hardwire commands and binary commands via the ATM control panel, switch selectors, power logic distributor and measuring distributors. Since the major components to be used were already available from the Saturn programme and their individual capabilities were known, only the quantity of components required was dependent upon the final ATM systems configuration.

When the shift was made to abandon the idea of an ATM attached to an LM Ascent Stage in the 'wet' workshop cluster configuration, the 'dry' configuration introduced the need for a dedicated rack and experiment canister for use on extended missions. In lieu of primary batteries, now excluded on grounds of weight and storage capacity, a four-wing solar

ABOVE Folded against the side of the ATM rack, the Solar Array System performed flawlessly on the three manned visits to the Skylab space station and was an essential source of power following the loss of an OWS-SAS wing during ascent. *(NASA)*

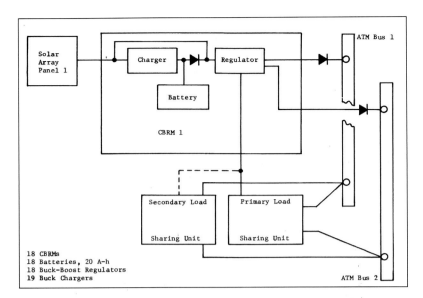

Solar Array Panel 1

Charger

Battery

Regulator

CBRM 1

ATM Bus 1

Secondary Load Sharing Unit

Primary Load Sharing Unit

18 CBRMs
18 Batteries, 20 A-h
18 Buck-Boost Regulators
19 Buck Chargers

ATM Bus 2

ABOVE A simple schematic of the ATM electrical system with a single charger battery regulator module (CBRM) connected to ATM bus 1 and a share unit to bus 2. *(NASA-MSFC)*

array was introduced as the only alternative, nuclear power sources – already being adopted for planetary and deep-space missions – being unacceptable due to the proximity of humans. Moreover, the plutonium 238 dioxide fuel for the Radioisotope Thermoelectric Generator (RTG) technology, such as that envisaged for the Apollo Lunar Surface Experiments Package (ALSEP), was unavailable in the quantities that would be required for the power demanded.

In designing the solar cell array, it was necessary to size the system for two and a half times the load required, to allow for charging secondary batteries to supply power during Earth occultation periods. Readily available and with a proven record, solar cells were particularly attractive on Sun-orientated missions because of the availability of 90° incident solar radiation without the need for an ancillary array pointing system. The choice for the secondary batteries was nickel-cadmium, desirable because of its low weight and volume and proven lifetime, and existing secondary battery designs already included 28V, 20AH batteries of this type.

The major spacecraft constraint was the requirement for passive cooling of the power system components, high power conversion and energy efficiencies being necessary to

reduce the amount of heat generated. Other constraints imposed included minimum weight and volume and no single point failure that could disable an entire system. These constraints and the need to have passive cooling requirements, plus the desirability of having the electronic power conditioning as an integral unit with the battery to simplify interconnection, led to what eventually became the charger battery regulator module (CBRM).

The maximum load required of each CBRM was calculated on the basis of the battery amp-hour rating and the allowable depth of discharge for the batteries to assure sufficient cycle life to meet the mission lifetime requirement. The electrical load requirement and reliability considerations indicated the number of CBRMs required, originally calculated as 24 when the mission was for 18 months of operation with a 20% allowable depth of discharge. When the mission requirement was changed to two months of operation at 25% discharge, the number of CBRMs was reduced to 20 and then to 18, and subsequent analysis showed that this was sufficient for the final 'wet' workshop requirement of six months of operation at 30% depth of discharge.

All of the CBRM requirements analyses were based on continuous Sun orientation of the solar array and supplying power to the ATM and LM only, subsequent requirements involving the other elements of the cluster predicting a power requirement with paralleling capabilities between the ATM/LM and the Airlock Module power systems of 2,500W in either direction. Conversion to the 'dry' workshop, which disposed of the Lunar Module and hard-mounted the ATM to the AM/MDA/OWS via a deployable truss assembly, resulted in little theoretical change to the basic power system or the design of the networks. However, inversion of the ATM, discarding the LM and relocation of the control and display console to the Multiple Docking Adapter did require extensive physical redesign. Analysis confirmed that 18 CBRMs were still sufficient for the mission requirement of eight months' operation and 30% depth of discharge.

As defined for the revised configuration, the basic design specification required the system to be powered by a solar array/nickel-cadmium battery capable of operating in parallel with the

Airlock Module power system. The electrical system was to be capable of operating for 4,000 cycles, defined as 94-minute day/night cycles, which included pre-flight testing and eight months of operation. It was required to be capable of continuously supplying 3,716W at a nominal +28VDC to the cluster loads while in the solar inertial (SI) mode, 3,000W in the local vertical (Z-LV) mode, and 1,300W in the Z-LV rendezvous mode. It was required to have a peak load capability of 5,574W, with a 3,716W orbital average. It would be designed to an isolated two-bus system with power loads grouped on sub-buses, and power feeders were to be provided capable of carrying 2,500W in either direction.

The initial concept for the ATM-SAS was based on requirements for the 'wet' cluster outlined in the development plan signed on 13 April 1967, where the size of the array was largely determined by the ATM rack size and the capability to mount the array in the launch configuration within the Lunar Module adapter cone on top of the Saturn IB. The choice of using solar cells for power generators on the ATM evolved early in the programme from initial project power conditioning trade-off studies which favoured four solar wings, each of which would support six panels. Further analysis allowed a downsizing to five panels per wing and finally to four full panels and a half-panel inboard on each wing. The final total configuration was 4.5 panels per wing for a total of 18 panels and associated CBRMs. The size and type of array and cells was agreed on 22 November 1968.

Early solar cell module environmental tests established the maximum of 114 cells connected in series per module but tests revealed that at extreme low temperatures, predicted for the ATM array, high module/panel output voltages were experienced. These were of such a magnitude that damage to components, principally capacitors, within each ATM system could occur. The limits on solar cell series connection strings were set for a maximum panel output of 115–120V at the expected orbital temperatures and the size and number of module parallel connections were set to maintain sufficient current for proper operation of equipment. However, the final

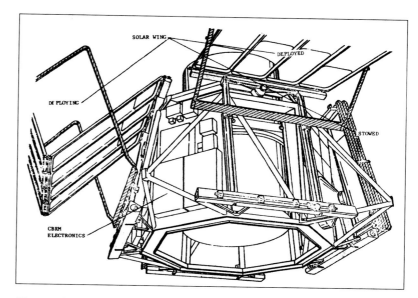

18 panel/CBRM configuration power output capability was still in excess of the expected ATM systems' requirements.

To obtain the required surface area for the solar wing and to maintain a capability for retraction, to maintain docking loads, the cruciform pattern was chosen to minimise those retraction forces, with the deployed wings orientated 45° to the X-axis of the cluster for minimum shading of other elements of the station and to fit within the launch payload envelope atop the launch vehicle. The mechanical, electromechanical and structural design requirements were established in a definition and specification signed on 15 April 1969, with the requirements finalised on 9 May.

With the decision to go to a 'dry' workshop, the cinching and deployment system became a one-time operational action, with the primary purpose of deploying the wing from launch to orbital configuration only once. The solar wing mounting structure provided the basic support for the entire wing assembly and was the interface to the AM rack. The inboard half-panel interfaced with the mounting structure through five hinge points at the ATM Sun end, and the inboard scissors arms interfaced with the mounting structure through two sliders and tracks. The wing assembly's five solar panels were tightly cinched against the mounting structure, forming an integral package that could be handled and transported independently of other ATM hardware.

Each wing contained 20 solar cell modules

ABOVE In this drawing the deployment sequence for the solar arrays wings are shown stowed (right), during deployment (centre) and deployed (top). *(NASA-MSFC)*

and was capable of supplying its respective CBRM with 580W. Each cell module contained either 684 Type A cells, each 2 x 2cm (0.787 x 0.787in), or 228 Type B cells, each 2 x 6cm (0.787 x 2.362in). The solar cell modules were each 50.8cm (20in) long by 62.48cm (24.6in) wide with a thickness of 1.27cm (0.5in). Each panel was 265.43cm (104.5in) wide by 264.92cm (104.3in) long and weighed 66.2kg (146lb). Each wing had a length of 13.233m (43.417ft) with 20 individual and 18 'actual' panels. When deployed, the wings spanned 29.87m (98ft) tip to tip across the ATM structure. The total power output was rated at 11,224W at 55°C (131°F), 10,298W predicted available power. There were 360 modules, 90 per wing.

The main ATM-SAS support structure was fabricated from 6061-T6 aluminium with two vertical tracks, one upper and one lower box beam with stiffeners and braces. The ATM/wing interface had six attachment points symmetrical about the wing longitude centreline with two turnbuckle fittings as dark-end attachment points. The support structure for the solar panels consisted of a rectangular frame of five parallel tubes interconnected at the ends by hinge fittings and short tube sections, 2.54 x 5.08cm (1 x 2in) and 0.152cm (0.06in) wall thickness. The inboard half-panel was fabricated from heat-treated 4140 steel; the other panels were extruded aluminium 2219-T-87.

The panel-to-panel interface consisted of five sets of male/female clevis joints with Teflon

lines and spherical bearings on male halves. The shear plates consisted of five sets of male/female plates mounted adjacent to the hinges. The deployment system consisted of five sets of scissor arms, end attachment hinges incorporating tension springs. The centres incorporated pivot (flange journal bearing) points that attached to the panel outboard centres. The material consisted of 2.54 x 5.08cm (1 x 2in) and 0.152cm (0.06in) wall thickness, except for the inboard pair that had a thickness of 0.317cm (0.125in). The inboard second and third pairs were fabricated from steel, the fourth and fifth pairs from aluminium. All the hinge fittings were aluminium castings and the scissor-arm cross-beams were fabricated from 6061-T6 aluminium.

The deployment mechanism consisted of a dual closed loop cable/slider 7.467m (24.25ft) long consisting of a standard 0.3175cm (0.125in) aircraft cable with 0.792cm (0.312in) diameter swaged steel balls spaced 5.97cm (2.35in) apart and secured via turnbuckles at both ends to track beam sliders. There were eleven cinching ties, seven at the Sun end and four at the dark end, mounted on a fifth outboard panel and retained at the main structure by a ball-end rod which was seated in a standard torque tube rotary ball seat. It primarily consisted of an arm, clevis, turnbuckle ball-end rod, pivot bolts and tension springs.

The pyrotechnic thrusters and torque tubes comprised two dual piston and cylinder assemblies utilising two CDF 2000 pyrotechnic cartridges. The pistons were secured to a crank, which in turn was secured to the torque tubes. The deployment system incorporated triangular panel assemblies hinge-mounted to the outboard end of the fifth half-panel. Each wing was deployed by dead position torsion springs, retained by a pre-tensioned cable activated by a spring plunger and shear pin. Wings 3 and 4 carried a dipole antenna assembly, nestled in a Teflon-lined cradle bolted to the outboard end of the fifth half-panel. It was deployed by torsion springs, retained by cinching strap and pre-tensioned cable, also activated by a spring-loaded plunger and shear pin.

Accurate and consistently precise pointing was crucial for the ATM to do its job of supporting the instruments and telescopes it contained. The

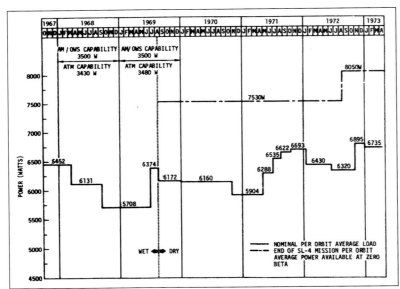

evolution of the Attitude Control and Pointing System (ACPS) began in June 1966, after various proposals and concepts for using Control Moment Gyroscope (CMG) based systems were studied. From ground rules drawn up the following month, when the ATM was conceptually attached to the Ascent Stage of a Lunar Module, control was based around a CMG design originating at NASA's Langley Research Center. Requirements for extremely precise attitude control during long-duration use eliminated conventional reaction jet control systems as being too imprecise and inconsistent with precision control over the desired arcsec range. Also, propellant consumption would have required more than could be carried in the ATM/LM.

A momentum exchange device, the CMG was chosen as the controlling device since it offered the advantages of precision pointing control and avoided contamination of optics from thruster efflux. Based on these ground rules, the ACPS design of 1966 consisted of a fine and coarse Sun sensor, a single analogue control computer with switching and logic, three CMG units, associated electronics and inverters, three rate gyros, a hand controller and analogue meters. This system did, however, still require a reaction control system for manual dumping of CMG bias and visual pointing of the experiments, and that evolved as the OWS TACS (which see).

A CMG is based on the principle of the conservation of angular momentum and consists of a spinning wheel with high mass connected to a gimbal fixture which can tilt the angle of rotation and thereby change its angular momentum. In the near-weightlessness of orbital space flight, this tilting action will cause the space vehicle to rotate in response to that torque in the direction of the energy. If three such CMG wheels are set at orthogonal axes to each other, the attitude of the entire spacecraft can be controlled. All that is required is that they are supplied with electrical energy for providing power to the gimbal torque motors. CMGs differ from reaction wheels in that the latter operate through changes to the speed of rotation but these require much more electrical energy and are not as efficient as the CMG.

Changes to the specified requirements for the ACPS were brought about when the

concept went to the cluster phase, where the ATM would be docked to the radial port of the Multiple Docking Adapter. Increased CMG momentum was required due to the vehicle's moments of inertia and a roll-positioning capability was added. The enormous expansion of mission capability brought about by the switch to a 'dry' workshop changed ACPS requirements still further and the definitive ACPS was born. It was at this point that the TACS emerged; the role of the computer increased and the dedicated ATM control computer was relinquished.

Further changes were brought about by the addition of the Earth Resources Experiment Program (EREP), and while this was not related to the ATM itself it did impose requirements on the ACPS due to the Earth-pointing requirement. Initially, attitude manoeuvres were to have been handled by the TACS. With the EREP on board, the –Z vehicle axis was required to be co-linear with the local vertical and with the principal axis in the vertical plane. Neither TACS nor ACPS was capable of accommodating the new manoeuvre requirements and a solution was found by using the CMGs to assist with making manoeuvres while the TACS would be available if the CMGs were momentarily unable to control Skylab. With vehicle inertia increased the CMGs became marginal, so the rotational speed of the CMG wheels was increased 14% to expand momentum storage capacity.

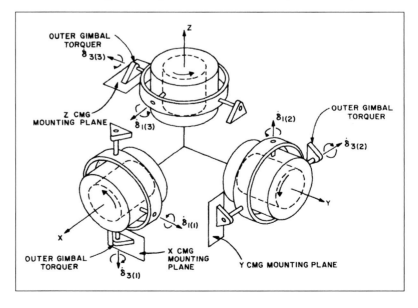

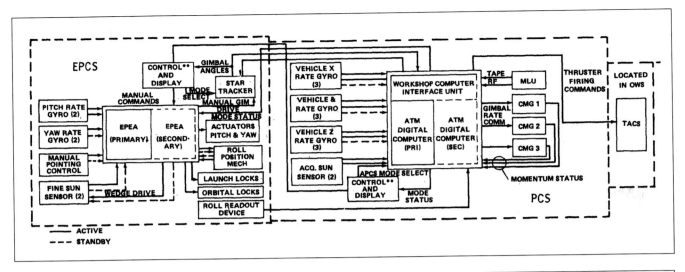

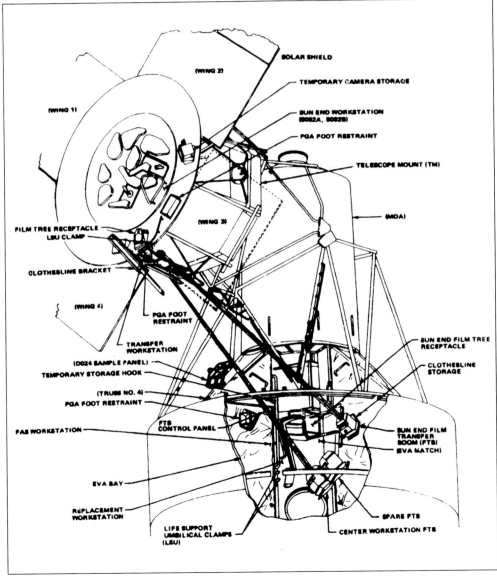

ABOVE The Attitude Control and Pointing System (ACPS) consisted of the Experiment PCS (EPCS) and the PCS proper. At the heart of the EPCS was the Experiment Pointing Electronic Assembly (EPEA), which contained the electronic functions to command the flex-point actuators, closing the control loop. The EPEA also provided an interface between the star tracker and the manual pointing controller (MPC). The PCS was a digitally implemented combination for the CMG momentum exchange and reaction jet control system. *(NASA-MSFC)*

RIGHT Extracted from the astronaut training manual, this somewhat poor quality reproduction shows the foot restraints for the space suits (or pressure garment assemblies – PGAs) and the clothes line used to lower film canisters from the Sun end of the ATM in readiness for returning them to Earth. *(NASA)*

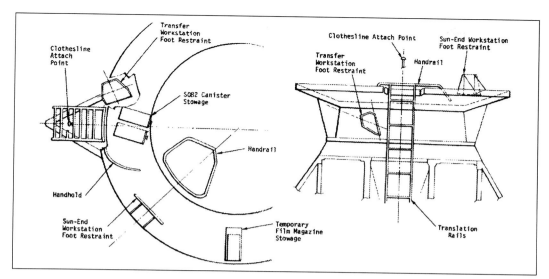

LEFT The transfer and Sun-end workstation arrangement for astronaut access to the telescope instruments. Note the translation rails. (NASA)

As designed and installed on Skylab, the CMG wheels each had a mass of 110kg (242lb) and were 55.9cm (22in) in diameter spinning at 9,000rpm, each wheel set in a separate 99cm (39in) diameter sphere on three sides of the ATM. The bearings ran in an oil bath and telemetry indicated oil temperature, wheel speed and the electrical load drawn by the motors. The CMGs were designed to electrically disconnect if the temperatures exceeded 93.3°C (200°F) or the spin speed exceeded 15,000rpm.

The ATM control and display console were located in the Multiple Docking Adapter, and commands from the crew to ATM systems were provided by toggle and rotary switches, a manual pointing controller and the digital address system. Status lights, confidence lights, alert lights, dual scale vertical meters, time-shared digital displays and TV displays allowed the crew to monitor systems. Controls were also available for power distribution overload protection, lamp testing and lighting. Because of its dependency on the accurate attitude control and pointing system, the requirements of the ATM were closely linked to the development of Skylab's computer system.

Because of the unique nature of its mission, NASA chose to break with the traditional legacy computer system used for Apollo, which had its origin in the Polaris missile system, and to go instead for a central processor using commercially available IBM 4Pi series processors. This was a descendant of the System 360, which had been developed in the early 1960s, with some applications seen in

aircraft of the late 1960s. Skylab used the TC-1, a 16-bit word processor with a destructive readout core memory (erasing bits as they were read) of 16,384 words in two modules of 8K words each. Addresses ranged from 0 to 8K with a hardware switch to determine which module was accessed.

The two processors were attached to a single workshop computer interface unit (WCIU), each with an input/output section but only the one actively connected received power. The common section contained a 64-bit transfer register and a timer associated with redundancy management, which were the only parts that consisted of triple modular redundant (TMR) circuits. This sent signals to separate channels that then voted, the one output representing either two or three identical inputs. An added component to the computer as it evolved was the Memory Load Unit (MLU). This had been helpful in handling memory overloads in the computer's predecessor, which had been developed for the Gemini programme. The Skylab MLU had a 16K software load and another, 8K, load that could be written into either module of either memory. This alone raised reliability from 0.87 to 0.96.

IBM delivered the first of ten such computers on 23 December 1969, two being flight versions. It represented an intermediate step in computer and software design between the somewhat limited Gemini system and that which was already being considered for the Shuttle programme. Tests showed high reliability levels, with significant levels of performance outstripping expectations, completing a 271-day simulation of a full three-visit Skylab mission without recourse to the MLU, which had to be switched on just to show that it worked! However, some problems arose because of an irritating tendency for NASA to issue the specification for the hardware before writing the software.

Cautiously, IBM used a multiplicity of aerospace contracts to conduct development work on operational computer systems, thereby advancing the state-of-the-art positively to the advantage of the customer. This was so with the 4Pi, the top model being the AP-101 that would be used in the Shuttle. IBM kept its teams small and top-flight software managers such as Harlan Mills and Frederick Brooks drove the company philosophy and its growing reputation among customers. On the Skylab system, no more than 75 people were involved and no more than six were directly involved in reactivation software.

But Skylab was unique among space vehicles and the development programme became more difficult with the complexity of the control moment laws. Engineers working on the design of the CMGs had to work with the hardware and software people at IBM to restructure the way the gyros would work, so as not to overload the demands of the software, which, because NASA had already set the memory limit, was all too readily exceeded. In this way, computer memory – and not processing power – became the prime consideration.

BELOW The film transfer boom and hook assembly used to recover the film cassettes. *(NASA-MSFC)*

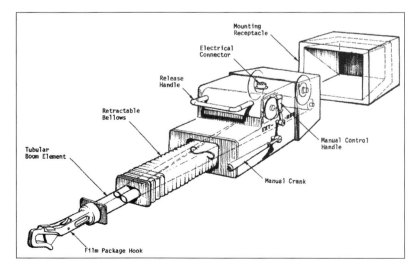

ATM experiments

As noted elsewhere, the Apollo Telescope Mount was conceived as a means of following research begun by the Orbiting Solar Observatory, studying the connection between Sun and Earth and the interaction of the charged particles of the solar wind regulating the behaviour of the Earth's outer atmosphere. This was an early justification for the Apollo Applications Program. As flown, the ATM contained instruments for five separate categories of observation, as follows:

S052 White Light Coronagraph

– designed to measure the brightness, form and polarisation of the Sun's corona from 1.5 to 6 solar radii and correlate those observations with sunspot and solar flare activity. This instrument viewed the corona by taking photographs on to 35mm film at varying rates, usually twice daily but up to one every 13 seconds if required, capturing rapidly moving material as it moved away from the Sun, a region of very high temperatures of more than a million degrees and very low pressure where most atoms are ionised and large numbers of free electrons are present which are capable of reflecting the light from the surface of the Sun. The instrument was 3.05m (10ft) long and 45.7cm (18in) across with a weight of 142.4kg (314lb).

S082A/S082B Ultraviolet Coronal Spectroheliograph/ Spectrograph

– built to obtain high-resolution pictures of short-time variations in the solar atmosphere. Two separate instruments and respective housings provided photographs of the Sun in selected ultraviolet wavelengths for scientists to study and discriminate hotter regions of the solar atmosphere. Previously, ballistic sounding rockets sent up through the outer atmosphere before falling back to Earth had been able to take 'snapshots' of these phenomena, but even the OSO satellites had not been able to provide high-resolution imagery. Skylab provided long periods of sustained observation and returned film taken of areas of interest to which the

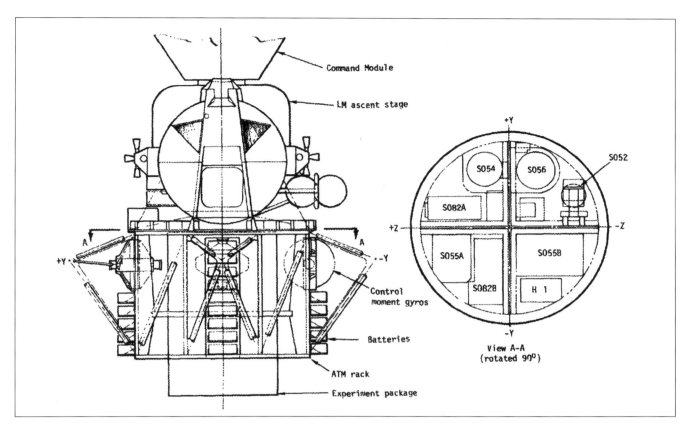

View A-A
(rotated 90°)

instruments had been directed as the solar events occurred. Instrument A was 3.05m (10ft) long and 30.5cm (18in) in cross-section, weighing 114kg (252lb), and consisted of a concave grating which separated ultraviolet light from 150 to 650Å. The B instrument consisted of a mirror and entrance slit for selecting portions of the solar disc, a set of two gratings spreading the ultraviolet regions from 970 to 3,940Å to photographic film. Essentially the same size as instrument A, the spectrograph weighed 169kg (373lb).

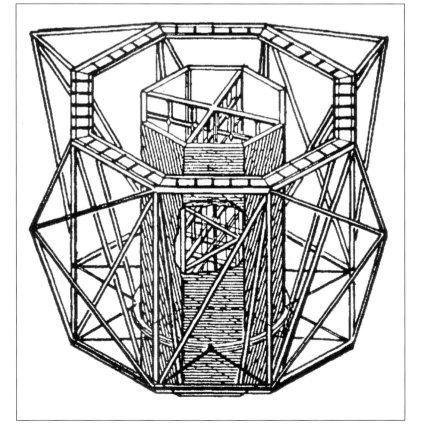

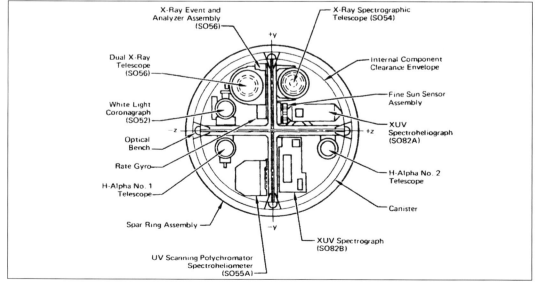

X-Ray Event and Analyzer Assembly (SO56)

X-Ray Spectrographic Telescope (SO54)

+y

Dual X-Ray Telescope (SO56)

Internal Component Clearance Envelope

White Light Coronagraph (SO52)

Fine Sun Sensor Assembly

-z

+z

XUV Spectroheliograph (SO82A)

Optical Bench

Rate Gyro

H-Alpha No. 2 Telescope

H-Alpha No. 1 Telescope

Canister

Spar Ring Assembly

-y

XUV Spectrograph (SO82B)

UV Scanning Polychromator Spectroheliometer (SO55A)

ABOVE AND RIGHT

The battery of telescopes identified by the adjacent diagram of the specific instruments as deployed in the experiment canister.
(NASA-MSFC)

S054 X-ray Spectrographic Telescope

– designed to study flares in soft X-ray with high spectral and spatial resolution so as to understand flare mechanisms. X-rays emitted by the Sun had been observed for several years and OSO spacecraft were already observing spectra of X-ray emissions, but their intensity associated with solar flares was greatly enhanced during periods near the solar maximum, which is when the Skylab missions operated. The X-ray telescope consisted of two concentric mirrors of highly polished metal alloys to intercept the X-radiation and focus it at a grazing incidence. Filters of beryllium, aluminised Mylar and other materials of varying thickness allowed selection of the wavelength band to be photographed. The telescope was 3.05m (10ft) long, 45.7cm (18in) in diameter and weighed 138kg (300lb).

S055A Ultraviolet Spectrometer

– for monitoring discrete ultraviolet lines to study the mechanisms of activity in the photosphere and chromosphere. The extreme ultraviolet region of the solar spectrum is generated in the chromosphere and the lower corona. This instrument provided simultaneous observation of both phenomena by capturing radiation from the Sun, reflected by a mirror moving along both axes and adjusted to place the desired segment of the solar surface on to a spectrometer grating that broke the light into spectral components, with the EUV region received by seven detectors. An eighth detector saw light at all wavelengths. No film was used with this instrument, which was 3.05m (10ft) long and 0.6 x 0.6m (2 x 2ft) in cross-section and weighed 156.5kg (345lb).

S056 X-ray Telescope

– to measure the intensity of solar flares with spatial and temporal resolution so as to understand the dynamics of the solar atmosphere. This instrument covered much the same region as S054, and the proportional counters on the X-ray event analyser provided spectral information with good time resolution. This complemented data from other experiments and helped establish the detailed nature of flare emissions and other X-ray events. The instrument consisted of a double reflecting grazing incidence mirror that focused X-radiation

on to photographic film. Two proportional counters covered ten channels of the spectrum providing spectral and temporal information on X-ray events. X-ray activity was displayed in analogue form on the control panel in the Multiple Docking Adapter. The total package was 2.75m (9ft) long and 45.7cm (18in) in diameter, with a weight of 160.6kg (354lb).

Two instruments, the H-alpha telescopes, became the 'eyes' of the astronauts, one with a beam splitter for simultaneous pictures and TV transmission and the other for TV operations only. Both carried a Fabry-Perot filter that allowed direct observations at any desired wavelength with a zoom capability to reveal selected portions of the solar disc in detail. As the most abundant element on the surface of the Sun, hydrogen is one of the most observed from Earth, but during flares the white light emission remains about the same while the amount of H-alpha emission increases greatly and becomes a measure of the magnitude of the flare itself.

The H-alpha telescopes were the primary means of boresighting the ATM experiment package and provided the means by which the operating astronaut could target and track active regions. One telescope had a length of 2.74m (9ft) and a diameter of about 30.5cm (12in) and weighed 86.2kg (190lb). The second telescope had a length of 1.5m (5ft), a diameter of 30.5cm (12in) and a weight of 49.9kg (110lb). As with the other instruments recording images on film, the containers were retrieved by astronauts on EVA.

BELOW Astronaut Owen Garriott from the second visit to Skylab, viewed from the Airlock Module at the Sun end of the ATM with the film retrieval boom. *(NASA)*

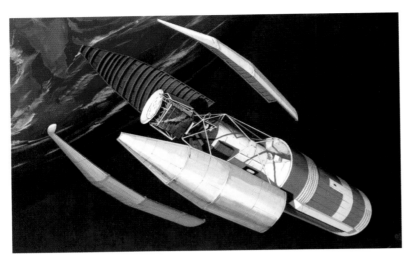

Payload Shroud

The design of the Payload Shroud (PS) was selected from two options: an over-the-nose concept which would have been jettisoned using axial thrusters; and the segmented concept, whereby four 90° segments would be pyrotechnically separated and detached radially outward, away from the ATM. The overall design of the PS was designed to provide an aerodynamic fairing for the OWS, a structural support for the Apollo Telescope Mount, an environmental shield with purge capability and a non-contaminating separation and jettison system. The PS was a critical element, since without its successful jettisoning the Skylab space station would be unattended and inoperable.

Axial loads and bending moments were calculated to provide a safety factor of three to eliminate testing to ultimate loads, although a factor of 1.25 was acceptable in the rebound direction for ATM attachment bolts. Calculations based on stress measurements showed that it actually had a factor of safety of 5.77 relative to the bending moment and 3.24 in respect to axial compression loads. The basic structural requirement was for the PS to support a telescope mount weighing between 9,072kg (20,000lb) and 11,340kg (25,000lb). The maximum mass of the PS was 11,804kg (26,024lb) and at launch it weighed 11,544kg (25,473lb).

In the final decision about which concept to adopt, the segmented design concept was selected. It had a total length of 17.12m (56.17ft), divided into three sections: a cylinder section at the bottom, 6.6m (21.67ft) in diameter and with a length of 8.89m (29.17ft); an aft cone tapered at a constant angle of 12.5° to a top diameter of 5m (16.42ft) along a length of 3.6m (11.83ft); a forward cone tapering at a constant angle of 25° to a diameter of 1.016m (3.33ft) along a length of 4.29m (14.08ft); plus a rounded nose cap 32.9cm (1.08ft) in length stiffened with rings and intercostals (all numbers rounded). Skins on both nose section cones were 0.635cm (0.250in) thick 2024-T351 aluminium sheets stiffened with internal rings from 7075-T6 aluminium. The cylinder frames were formed from 7075-T73 aluminium I-beam extrusions and spaced about 58.4cm (23in) apart.

Telescope mount loads were supported at 90° intervals on the forward end of the cylindrical section, a support link secured between fittings by semi-cylindrical slots providing attachment of the telescope mount outrigger fittings through eccentric

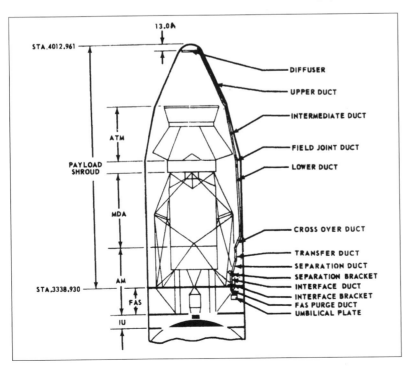

bushings with 0.3175cm (0.125in) radial adjustment. During jettisoning of the PS, movement of the support fittings at 45° to the axes of the shroud released the telescope mount. The support link was designed to remain attached to the telescope mount during subsequent operations.

A critical part of the specification was that there should be continuous purging with conditioned air and that the PS should provide a waterproof environment on the inner face, but during a rainstorm at the Kennedy Space Center prior to launch some leakage was observed. Inspection showed that there was no sealant around the cap-to-cone interface. This was rectified with an application but a further rain shower showed that it had failed to completely prevent leakage. Because the launch pad damper arm was attached to the PS, it was not possible to prevent all movement between the two sections and, therefore, it was not possible to completely leak-proof the joint.

The separation system incorporated two non-contaminating longitudinal thrusting joint assemblies and eight discrete latches, four at the base and four at the upper ring of the PS cylinder. Eight backup, or redundant, discrete latches were also in the system and at separation the thrusting joints imparted a radial velocity to each Payload Shroud quarter segment of about 6m (20ft) per second. Two ordnance systems were used for separation and jettisoning: the discrete latch system and the longitudinal system. With the OWS in the nose-down attitude, signals from the Instrument Unit on top of the OWS (and below the Fixed Airlock Shroud) caused detonation of the ordnance. This created a pressure wave that retracted pins in the latch actuators and circumferentially unlocked the quarter sections. Seconds later an IU signal would be sent causing longitudinal separation into four segments by expandable bellows with a linear explosive inside. When the longitudinal separation was initiated, the bellows expanded by internal pressure from the linear explosive, causing the longitudinal rivet joints to shear. The bellows continued to expand, imparting a velocity to the PS quarter sections that caused them to move away.

ABOVE Separation dynamics of the Payload Shroud are tested at the Plum Brook Station facility. At the time this was known as the NASA Lewis Research Center, Cleveland, Ohio. In 1999 it was officially renamed the John H. Glenn Research Center at Lewis Field. *(NASA)*

BELOW The separate manufacturing components of the Payload Shroud which will come together and which separated along the four linear seams equipped with pyrotechnic cutters. *(NASA-MSFC)*

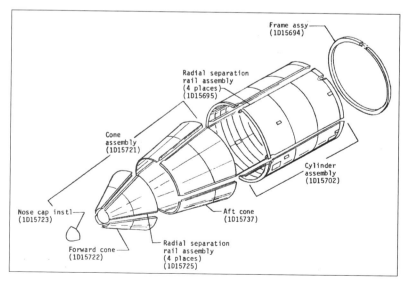

Chapter Three

The missions 1973–74

Skylab was the most ambitious human space-flight programme that NASA had embarked on to this date. As flown, the three expeditions to the orbiting space station would exceed the total accumulated time of NASA's previous 27 manned space flights. But more than that, it demonstrated that humans could work productively in space, creating new materials and carrying out a wide range of scientific experiments.

OPPOSITE The launch facilities for the Skylab missions made use of the Kennedy Space Center and three primary elements: the Vehicle Assembly Building (VAB), the Launch Control Center (LCC) and Launch Complex 39 with its two pads. Here, the two-stage Saturn V AS-513 is moved from the VAB to pad LC-39A. *(NASA-KSC)*

When the decision was taken to fly the 'dry' Orbital Workshop the mission prefix designations changed from AAP to SL and the phasing of the flights changed too. SL-1 would launch the Skylab cluster on the first two stages of AS-513 from LC-39A, to be followed approximately a day later by SL-2 on Saturn IB AS-206 and CSM-116. The first crewed flight was scheduled to last 28 days. Ninety days after the return of that crew, SL-3 would launch on AS-207 and carry the second manned expedition to Skylab aboard CSM-117 on an expedition lasting 56 days, this to be followed by a further unmanned period of 90 days. The launch of SL-4 on AS-208 and CSM-118, on another 56-day mission, would conclude the Skylab operational programme. All CSM flights would take place from LC-39B. The gap between manned occupancy was dictated by the need for a minimum 84-day turnaround on the pad and a 96-day limit constraint so as not to unduly stretch consumables by extending the total length of the operational phase.

Initial planning for the 'wet' workshop concept in March 1968 was to have the cluster go to a gravity gradient stabilisation attitude for the Apollo CSM rendezvous phase, with the long axis pointing directly down at the centre of the Earth and remaining in this attitude due to the pull of the Earth's gravity. The primary attitude for the rest of the mission was to be in solar inertial (SI), whereby the X-axis of the station would be perpendicular to the orbital plane (X-POP). Between manned occupancy, Skylab was to be put in a gravity gradient stabilisation mode. The second manned mission was to use the same docking attitude and was to be performed with the cluster primary attitude being SI, with the X-axis in the orbit plane (X-IOP). In October 1968 it was decided to align the cluster in an X-POP attitude with the Z-axis along the local vertical, for all rendezvous and docking activity.

LEFT Modifications to the Launch Umbilical Tower (LUT) – the fixed structure which carried propellant, hydraulic, pneumatic and electrical needs to the stack – allowed the Saturn IB/Apollo spacecraft to be launched from LC-39B atop a unique pedestal dubbed the 'milk stool'. *(NASA)*

BELOW A view showing the open structure below the launch vehicle that allowed the Saturn IB rocket motor emissions to vent freely. *(NASA)*

When the 'dry' cluster was adopted, the primary mission attitude was refined as SI, X-IOP, which became the baseline for all missions and storage periods, so as to maintain the rendezvous and docking attitude. The Z-LV attitude was selected for all Earth observation passes with the EREP equipment (which see). In October 1971 this planning was modified so that the primary attitude would be SI with the X axis in the orbital plane, pointing along the velocity vector at orbital noon, with the +Z axis pointing toward the Sun. For rendezvous, Skylab would go to the Z-LV(R) attitude, where Z local vertical was with the X geometric axis in the orbit plane and –X axis was in the direction of the velocity vector with the –Z axis pointing toward the Earth.

The orbital lifetime of Skylab was determined by its mass and drag. Increasing the mass would tend to lengthen the life of the station while increasing drag would shorten it. Drag would be dependent on the altitude of the orbit and on the density of the atmosphere at that height above the surface. Higher levels of solar energy output would cause the upper atmosphere to expand and have the same effect as a lower orbital altitude in times of solar quiescence. The final orbit selected was 435km (270.4 miles) to provide an altitude compatible with rendezvous and docking and to ensure that its orbital decay (due to drag) would not degrade the orbit below 389km (242 miles) at the end of the eight-month period between the launch of SL-1 and the return of SL-4, thus assuring an orbital lifetime of about 2,050 days.

In the overall mission as run, the use of trim burns to repeat ground tracks meant that at the end of the planned eight-month period (mid-January 1974) the station was still expected to be very close to the insertion altitude of 433km (269 miles). This allowed an extension of the orbital lifetime prediction by 700 days and

BELOW Both Saturn V AS-513 and the three Saturn IBs used to carry crews to the Skylab space station were erected and checked out in the Vehicle Assembly Building. This layout shows where the various vehicles and their stages were worked on. *(NASA)*

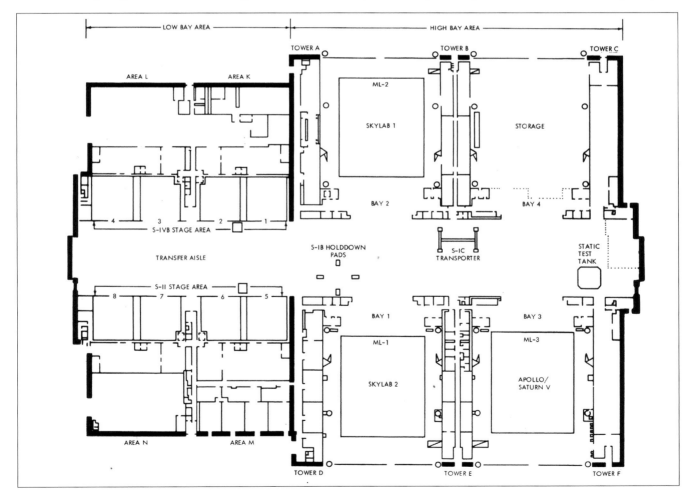

BELOW Mobile Launcher 1 was modified to support the Saturn IB/ Apollo spacecraft during final pad checkout and launch. The available Saturn IB launch pads had been retired by this time and there was no other facility to support launch operations with this rocket and its payload. (NASA)

modified the end-of-mission decay prediction to 2,730 days (7.5 years) from the launch on 25 May 1973, taking the survival time out to the end of November 1980.

The orientation of the orbital plane relative to

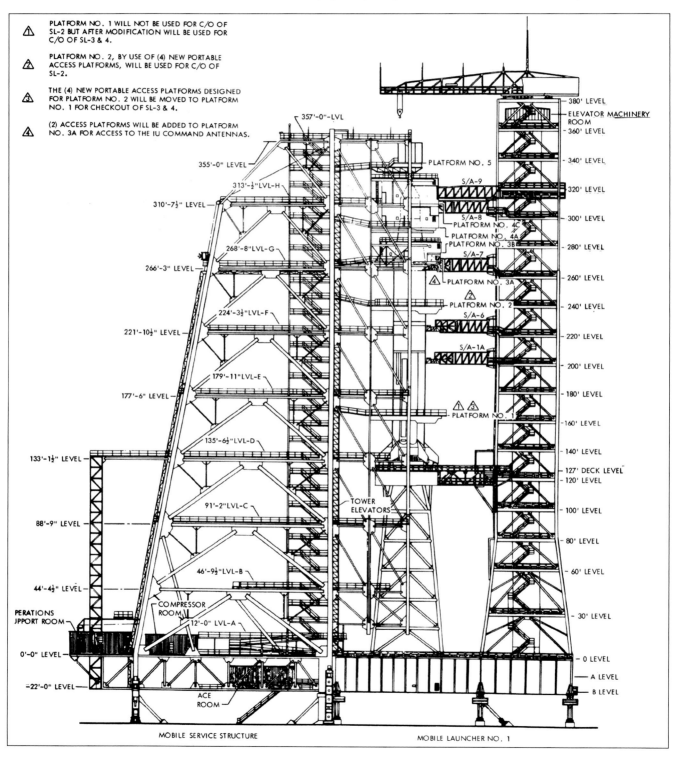

⚠1 PLATFORM NO. 1 WILL NOT BE USED FOR C/O OF SL-2 BUT AFTER MODIFICATION WILL BE USED FOR C/O OF SL-3 & 4.

⚠2 PLATFORM NO. 2, BY USE OF (4) NEW PORTABLE ACCESS PLATFORMS, WILL BE USED FOR C/O OF SL-2.

⚠3 THE (4) NEW PORTABLE ACCESS PLATFORMS DESIGNED FOR PLATFORM NO. 2 WILL BE MOVED TO PLATFORM NO. 1 FOR CHECKOUT OF SL-3 & 4.

⚠4 (2) ACCESS PLATFORMS WILL BE ADDED TO PLATFORM NO. 3A FOR ACCESS TO THE IU COMMAND ANTENNAS.

357'-0"-LVL
355'-0" LEVEL
313'-1½"LVL-H
310'-7½" LEVEL
268'-8"LVL-G
266'-3" LEVEL
224'-3½"LVL-F
221'-10½" LEVEL
179'-11"LVL-E
177'-6" LEVEL
135'-6½"LVL-D
133'-1½" LEVEL
91'-2"LVL-C
88'-9" LEVEL
46'-9½"LVL-B
44'-4½" LEVEL
PERATIONS JPPORT ROOM
COMPRESSOR ROOM
12'-0" LVL-A
0'-0" LEVEL
-22'-0" LEVEL
ACE ROOM

TOWER ELEVATORS

380' LEVEL
ELEVATOR MACHINERY ROOM
360' LEVEL
PLATFORM NO. 5
340' LEVEL
S/A-9
320' LEVEL
S/A-8
300' LEVEL
PLATFORM NO. 4C
PLATFORM NO. 4A
PLATFORM NO. 3B
S/A-7
280' LEVEL
⚠4 PLATFORM NO. 3A
260' LEVEL
⚠2 PLATFORM NO. 2
240' LEVEL
S/A-6
220' LEVEL
S/A-1A
200' LEVEL
180' LEVEL
⚠1 ⚠3 PLATFORM NO. 1
160' LEVEL
140' LEVEL
127' DECK LEVEL
120' LEVEL
100' LEVEL
80' LEVEL
60' LEVEL
30' LEVEL
0 LEVEL
A LEVEL
B LEVEL

MOBILE SERVICE STRUCTURE

MOBILE LAUNCHER NO. 1

the Earth and the Sun was used in designing the Skylab passive and active thermal control systems, the solar power systems, attitude control systems and the planned mission and experiments utilisation profile. The orientation to the orbital plane is known as the beta ( ) angle, in which beta is the angle between the Sun and the orbital plane in a plane perpendicular to the orbit plane that includes the Earth-Sun line. In the Skylab programme, beta was considered positive when the Sun was north of the orbit plane.

The beta angle was crucial for several reasons: the length of orbital daylight and darkness determined when various experiments could be used; the availability of sunlight directly affected the amount of electrical energy produced by the solar arrays; the scheduling of EREP passes was dictated by the beta angle on the station; and the procedures for attitude change when entering the rendezvous (Z-LV(R)) orientation so that if the beta angle was greater than 50° the station had to be biased about the X axis so that the approaching Apollo spacecraft's transponder antenna could view the station antenna.

On the ground the plot of the beta angle was a sinusoidal curve whose amplitude was bounded by the sinusoidal envelope that follows the seasonal motion of the Sun. The origin of the envelope is dictated by the date of the launch, while the origin of the beta curve depends on the time of launch. Therefore the beta history for Skylab depended on the integrated choice of launch date and time.

The orbit of the target vehicle (Skylab) established the framework within which planning for the Apollo spacecraft launch was calculated, taking into account the available delta-velocity (ΔV) in the CSM, plus

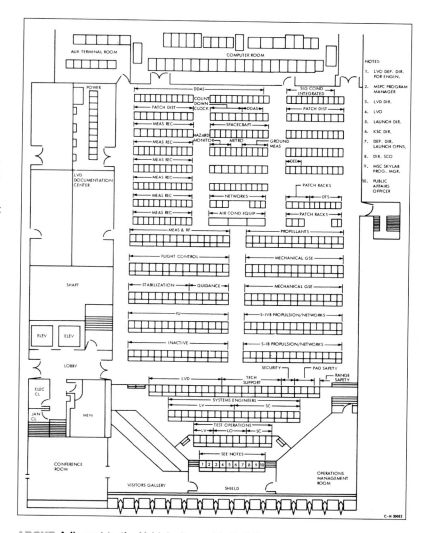

ABOVE Adjacent to the Vehicle Assembly Building and connected to it by a covered walkway, the Launch Control Center housed more than 400 people focused on flight preparation and launch operations, controlling both the unmanned launch of Skylab and the flight of the three manned visits. *(NASA)*

RIGHT The continuous operation of the three manned visits to Skylab brought special pressure to Mission Control in Houston. Generally, from midnight through 08:00 hours mission planners were writing up the tasks for execution two days later. In space, the crew ran on a normal 24-hour clock and maintained a routine which at times brought conflict with mission control teams on the ground, most notably the 'rebellion' on the last visit in which the crew took control of their schedules and summarily declared a day off. *(NASA)*

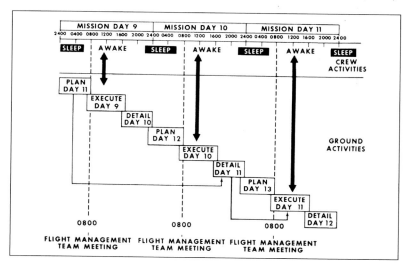

the criteria for lighting and abort constraints. To accomplish a successful rendezvous, each launch opportunity of the chase vehicle had to take place in the appropriate launch window and at the time of the proper phase angle with Skylab. Moreover, the launch and insertion into orbit had to occur with minimum propellant consumed by the Saturn IB and at a time when the launch window was sufficiently wide to allow for the increasing use of propellant

for yaw steering to match the shifting orbit of the station. The duration of the launch window determined the maximum weight of the booster propellant to be allocated for yaw steering and dictated a specific loss in the amount of payload that could be inserted into orbit.

SL-1

When NASA decided to opt for a 'dry' workshop, the Saturn V rocket was selected to lift the converted S-IVB stage, MDA, AM and ATM to orbit from where the smaller Saturn IB would deliver three crews for rendezvous and docking.

Designed specifically for sending Apollo spacecraft and the Lunar Module to the Moon, the Saturn V first flew on 9 November 1967 and had completed three flights to Earth orbit and nine to trans-lunar trajectories supporting six landings. All but the Saturn V assigned to Skylab consisted of three stages (S-IC, S-II and S-IVB) but AS-513 would comprise only the first two. Moreover, this would be the first flight in which the S-II stage would be called

BELOW This view of the Skylab launch facilities shows the Crawlerway leading from the Vehicle Assembly Building to the two launch pads. The nearest, LC-39A, was for launching the two-stage Saturn V/Skylab, while LC-39B, to the left, was assigned to the Saturn IB/Apollo flights. Note the slight kink in the Crawlerway to LC-39B. The original alignment of the road was to have supported a third pad (LC-39C), an equal distance to the left, but this was abandoned after the Crawlerway was laid down. Intriguingly, at first they were designated A, B and C in reverse order to the assignment for the pads as built. Pads A and B were originally designated B and C with LC-39A as the pad farther north which, along with Pads D and E still farther to the north, were never built. The launch of SL-1 on 14 May 1973 was the last use of LC-39A before extensive modifications allowed the Shuttle to fly from this pad for the first time on 12 April 1981. *(NASA)*

FAR LEFT On its way to LC-39A, the Saturn V/Skylab vehicle makes slow progress, a unique configuration but one which had been investigated as the launch vehicle for the core module of a permanently manned space station, much bigger than Skylab and with a diameter of 10m (33ft), which NASA envisaged for the mid-1970s supported by winged shuttlecraft. *(NASA)*

LEFT AS-513 lifts off on 14 May 1973 but within a minute it would be doomed by an imperfect design for the meteoroid shield wrapped tight against the hull of the Orbital Workshop. *(NASA)*

LEFT Another view from the opposite side. Note the paint patterns, more precisely identified earlier in this book. *(NASA)*

upon to place itself and its payload in orbit. On all previous flights it was left to the S-IVB third stage to deliver the final 10% of orbital velocity.

On a typical Moon flight, the weight delivered by the S-IC and the S-II stages would be approximately 171,300kg (377,716lb), comprising the S-IVB stage and the assembly of Apollo spacecraft as the payload. The S-IVB would fire to propel itself and its payload into Earth orbit while the S-II stage fell back through the atmosphere and was burned up. For Skylab, the first two stages of AS-513 would lift 89,441kg (197,180lb) directly into orbit with the S-II stage left circling the Earth after separating from the station.

Skylab (SL-1) was launched at 17:30:00 UTC (13:30 EDT) on 14 May 1973 and while for the first minute all appeared well, a potentially catastrophic sequence of failures very nearly doomed Skylab before it reached orbit and created a cascade of events which could have caused the first failure of a Saturn V rocket to deliver its payload to orbit. At ignition the AS-513 stack had a weight of 2,852,959kg (6,289,699lb), some 109,371kg (241,163lb)

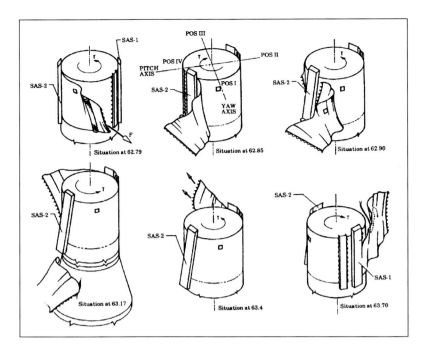

ABOVE An artist's impression of the appearance of the failed meteoroid shield that ripped away from the fixture adjacent to the SAS-1 array 62.79sec into the flight. In the ensuing sequence, culminating in the dislodging of the SAS-1 array 0.11sec later, it took less than one second to doom Skylab and render it potentially inoperable. *(NASA-MSFC)*

BELOW A schematic of the affected area, where insufficient design around the auxiliary tunnel and the lack of capping on two hollow stringers caused air pressure to start a cascading sequence of destruction. *(NASA-MSFC)*

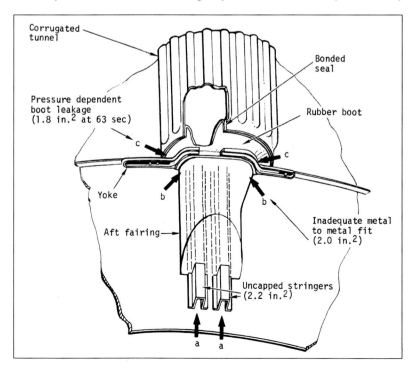

lighter than the preceding Saturn V (AS-512) which, with three stages, had launched Apollo 17 to the Moon in December 1972. The five F-1 engines in the S-IC stage delivered a thrust of 33,586,850kN (7,551,000lb).

The launch was nominal up to 60sec into flight when telemetry indicated a change in electrical demand on the S-II stage, followed at 63sec by several indications that there had been early deployment of the OWS Solar Array System and loss of the meteoroid shield. The vehicle was at a height of 8,717m (28,600ft) and going through the speed of sound. Strong disturbances were noted in the dynamic motion of the vehicle, with abnormal accelerations, vibration and irregular temperatures and voltages. Telemetry indicated that a portion of the micrometeoroid shield had come away, striking the forward S-II/Skylab interstage adapter, according to post-flight analysis opening a hole of up to 0.186m² (2ft²) in area.

Completely unknown at the time, but discovered during the post-flight analysis, omission to cap two hollow structural stringers during assembly, and inadequate fitting between the auxiliary tunnel and two stringers to which it was secured, caused pressure to build in the auxiliary tunnel and stress a very unforgiving design. As air pressure built up it lifted the meteoroid shield fixture and tore it loose, breaking the SAS No 2 tie-downs and allowing the boom to lift from the aft end.

The vehicle continued to ascend with only very minor perturbations to the trajectory brought about by the loss of the meteoroid shield and the partial deployment of SAS No 2. The centre engine shut down at 140.42sec followed by the four outer engines between 158.16sec and 158.23sec as planned. The stack was now at an altitude of 85km (52.8 miles) and travelling at 2,800m/sec (9.188ft/sec), about 37% of the speed it would need to attain orbit. The stage separated and the eight S-IC forward-facing retro-rockets, located in pairs in the semi-conical shrouds over the outer F-1 engines, fired as scheduled at 159.9sec. This was so as to retard the forward acceleration of the inert mass and prevent it bumping into the S-II second stage. The five J-2 engines of the S-II were ignited at 163.6sec and the command to separate the interstage adapter, which had held the S-II on top of the S-IC, was given at 189.9sec. The interstage was 10.05m (33ft) in diameter, the same as the S-IC and the S-II stage that it connected, and 5.56m (18.25ft) tall with a weight of 3,900kg (8,600lb).

At that time a pyrotechnic device should have severed 199 ties holding the interstage to the S-II but debris from the mangled meteoroid shield damaged the explosive charges that should have simultaneously broken the ties and cut the steel forming the circular lip of the interstage section. The ties were severed but the electrical line that should have triggered the detonation of the physical connection was broken by the now loosely suspended adapter. Ironically, previous Saturn V rockets had a single linear detonation string but on this one they had two separately connected command channels. As a result of the hang-up, the interstage was carried all the way up into orbit until the S-II shut down, the centre engine at 314.05sec and the four outer engines at 589.2sec, a powered flight phase lasting 6min 39.3sec for the second stage.

It had been a near thing. The base heating caused by the interstage adapter remaining in place brought the S-II stage close to complete failure, with rupturing of critical lines caused by the high temperatures encountered on the base area only seconds away. Thermal energy trapped within the area shrouded by the interstage ring caused the heating rate to increase at a higher level than ever seen before and temperature sensors on the thrust cone supporting the five J-2 engines reached 73.9°C (165°F) compared to a maximum temperature of 30°C (-1°F) previously seen on Apollo launches. Moreover, the temperatures continued to increase and were within several seconds of causing a catastrophic failure, bringing about the destruction of the rocket, had the vehicle not achieved the desired altitude and velocity and shut down on time.

But it was not over. As the assembly reached orbit SAS No 2 was already partially deployed, and had it not been possible to fully deploy it for some reason it would, theoretically, have been possible for the first visiting crew to have conducted an EVA and completed deployment. Two seconds after S-II shutdown, at 591.2sec the stage separated from the cluster and the four forward-facing retrorockets attached to

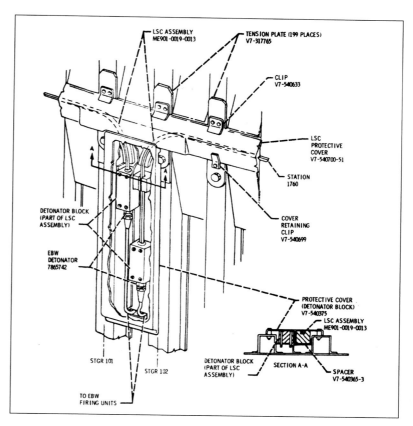

the S-II/OWS adapter fired. These delivered a total thrust of 622.72kN (140,000lb) for two seconds to retard the momentum of that stage and prevent it from striking Skylab as the two moved away from each other at 18.8m/sec (57ft/sec). The blast from the forward-facing rockets impinged on the underside of the partially deployed boom on SAS No 2 pushing it out, up and over, tearing it free from the side of the Orbital Workshop. In orbit now with a mass of 88,474kg (195,052lb) including the Payload Shroud, Skylab was potentially doomed.

The Payload Shroud was jettisoned at 920.4sec, and the Apollo Telescope and its mount began to deploy at a mission elapsed time of 16min 39sec as planned during the first orbit. The command to deploy the ATM arrays was given at 24min 52sec. Ground control confirmed that the ATM telemetry had switched on at 36min 49sec. Believing there to be two good OWS solar arrays, Skylab automatically manoeuvred to a solar inertial attitude for maximum power generation. But when the signal was sent to deploy the solar arrays at 41min 5ec, SAS No 1 was released – but stopped after only a few degrees of deployment.

ABOVE At three locations in the timeline of the AS-513 ascent trajectory, both launch vehicle and Skylab were threatened with potential destruction. One was the result of a failure to execute second-plane separation when the S-IC/S-II interstage adapter remained attached. This drawing shows the interface for second-plane separation that almost brought the Skylab programme to an abrupt end. *(North American Aviation)*

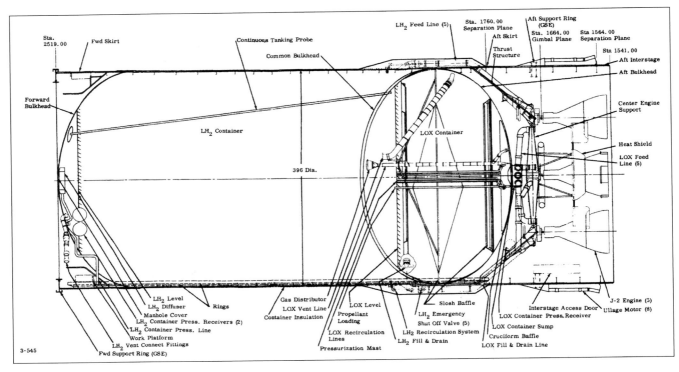

Sta. 2519.00 — Fwd Skirt — Continuous Tanking Probe — Common Bulkhead — LH₂ Feed Line (5) — Sta. 1760.00 Separation Plane — Aft Skirt — Aft Support Ring (GSE) — Sta. 1664.00 Gimbal Plane — Sta 1564.00 Separation Plane — Sta 1541.00 — Aft Interstage — Aft Bulkhead — Thrust Structure — Forward Bulkhead — LH₂ Container — LOX Container — Center Engine Support — Heat Shield — LOX Feed Line (5) — 396 Dia. — LH₂ Level — LH₂ Diffuser — Rings — Manhole Cover — LH₂ Container Press. Receivers (2) — LH₂ Container Press. Line — Work Platform — LH₂ Vent Connect Fittings — Fwd Support Ring (GSE) — Gas Distributor — LOX Vent Line — Container Insulation — LOX Level — Propellant Loading — LOX Recirculation Lines — Pressurization Mast — Slosh Baffle — LH₂ Emergency Shut Off Valve (5) — LH₂ Recirculation System — LH₂ Fill & Drain — Interstage Access Door — LOX Container Press. Receiver — LOX Container Sump — Cruciform Baffle — LOX Fill & Drain Line — J-2 Engine (5) — Ullage Motor (8)

3-545

ABOVE **This cutaway shows the geometry of the S-II stage, with the S-IC/S-II interstage adapter to the right. When the adapter failed to separate it allowed heat to reach critical levels, threatening to shut the stage down.** *(North American Aviation)*

Instead of delivering 12kW, the ground received signals indicating a level of only 25W!

At the time, however, nobody on the ground knew the precise state of Skylab, though there were already some very worrying signs of deep trouble. At 96min 4sec, with Skylab back over the United States at the end of its first orbit, the automatic command to deploy the non-existent meteoroid shield was sent as scheduled. Radar tracking of the spent S-II stage showed that at an elapsed time of two hours, the two structures were 298km (185 miles) apart, with the S-II in an orbit of 443 x 372km (275 x 231 miles). Skylab was in an orbit of 434 x 431km (270 x 268 miles). Weighing 35,835kg (79,000lb), the S-II re-entered the atmosphere on 11 January 1975.

With the loss of the meteoroid shield approximately 63 seconds after lift-off, Position I of the habitation area sidewall was subjected to continuous direct solar exposure after the vehicle was inserted into orbit and attained a solar inertial attitude. As a result, the temperature of the gold surface on the solar side increased rapidly, attaining an estimated maximum temperature of 138.9°C (300°F) at the external surface and 93.3°C (200°F) on the internal surface of the 2.5cm (1in) polyurethane foam.

After about one and a half days in orbit, a series of pitch manoeuvres was performed to reduce the solar incidence angle of the gold surface and lower the sidewall temperatures. Eight days after launch the temperature of the habitation area was stabilised to a mean value of 51.7°C (125°F) with a maximum external temperature of 92.3°C (200°F).

Immediately after orbital insertion the main problem was in evaluating the optical properties of the gold tape that surrounded the outer surface of the OWS tank hull. The instrumentation on that side of the wall was off-scale high because of the higher than expected boundary temperatures for the OWS heat balance. Two methods were employed to determine these properties. A small-scale thermal model was used to analyse the large transient response of the Position I internal and external temperature data before their respective maximum temperature scales of 48.9°C (120°F) and 87.8°C (190°F) were exceeded. Also, the OWS temperature evaluation extrapolation model was run to correlate the temperature readings with the remaining on-scale data points.

By taking readings at three locations along the length of the OWS the estimated optical properties were arrived at, data which consisted of the outboard and inboard surface temperature responses of the tank sidewall foam insulation at a time when sunlight was directly incident on the area. Utilising a solar flux model of 1,325W/m² (419Btu/hr-ft²), and an albedo of 0.3, it was found that the temperature derivations were quite accurate and could be used for thermal modelling of the extrapolated response of inboard and outboard temperature gradients under varying beta angles of solar incidence. This was vital information from which Mission Control could derive attitude angles for minimal thermal impact.

Because of these uncertainties, the launch of the SL-2 crew – which was to have taken place a day after SL-1 – was delayed at least ten days, and several NASA field centres were asked to conduct various analyses to try to close down uncertainties regarding the condition of the station. Temperature conditions in the film vaults, the food lockers and on the polyurethane foam inner wall lining of the OWS were of particular concern. Film could fog, food could be ruined and the outgassing from decomposing foam could produce a toxic atmosphere. Skylab was initially manoeuvred to an SI attitude with the plane of the solar arrays normal to the Sun for maximum power generation.

At 13 hours into the mission the cluster was pitched up toward the Sun to reduce the incident angle on the OWS. This attitude further reduced the power production capability by taking the ATM arrays off-line to the Sun. A delicate balance was necessary to achieve maximum power production for minimum solar heating on the hull of the workshop, and that continued for ten days. ATM power was further compromised by the need to cycle power regulator modules to prevent overheating caused by these unscheduled attitudes.

Within 24 hours of launch, temperatures inside the OWS were at 38°C (100°F) and attention focused on the design and fabrication of a shade which could be placed over the solar-facing side of the OWS. In Houston, the

crew, who had been at the Kennedy Space Center to watch the launch of SL-1, began to work on an abbreviated flight plan, but 36 hours after launch word came that the temperatures had reached 46°C (114.8°F) only hours before problems were encountered with one of the Control Moment Gyroscopes. At present, in unmanned mode, there was sufficient power from the ATM arrays to run Skylab, but as analysis verified that SAS No 1 had been completely torn away, work to provide the crew with a means of deploying SAS No 2 from its stalled position was crucial to getting power up.

Two days after the launch, NASA field centres, government research establishments and several contractor teams were working on options for a shade and on a means to deploy the remaining solar array on the side of the OWS. Engineers were flown in from Hawaii and Japan to bring expertise, and emergency repair plans were being formulated for a launch

BELOW The design of the base loading area of the S-II stage required complete exposure to the vacuum of space for thermal balance and energy dissipation. This is how that area should have looked had the interstage adapter separated as planned. *(North American Aviation)*

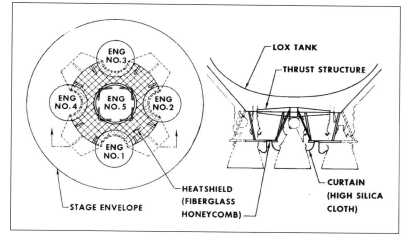

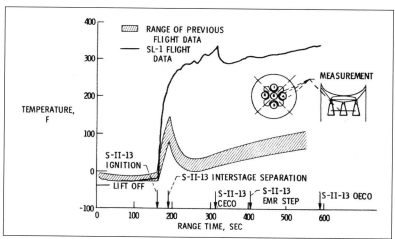

RIGHT When the adapter failed to separate, temperatures began to rise in the base area, rising far above the levels previously measured (hatched area), which brought the stage to within seconds of catastrophic failure. *(NASA-MSFC)*

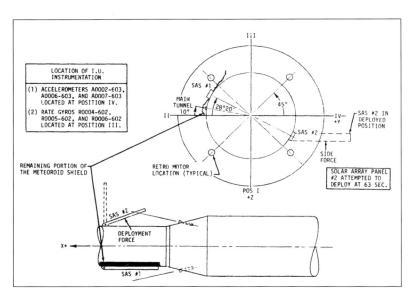

LOCATION OF I.U.
INSTRUMENTATION

(1) ACCELEROMETERS A0002-603,
A0006-603, AND A0007-603
LOCATED AT POSITION IV.

(2) RATE GYROS R0004-602,
R0005-602, AND R0006-602
LOCATED AT POSITION III.

III

SAS #1

MAIN
TUNNEL
10°

28°20'

45°

II

IV
+Y

SAS #2 IN
DEPLOYED
POSITION

SAS #2

SIDE
FORCE

SOLAR ARRAY PANEL
#2 ATTEMPTED TO
DEPLOY AT 63 SEC.

REMAINING PORTION OF
THE METEOROID SHIELD

RETRO MOTOR
LOCATION (TYPICAL)

POS I
+Z

SAS #2

DEPLOYMENT
FORCE

X+

SAS #1

ABOVE This graphic shows the way in which the SAS-2 array, which had been dislodged 63 seconds after lift-off, was blown back against its hinge point and completely severed at 593 seconds when the OWS/S-II interstage adapter fired retro-rockets to back the stage away from the station. *(NASA-MSFC)*

of SL-2 on 20 or 25 May. Due to the orbit of Skylab, launch windows for the first manned visit would cycle back around every 72 orbits, at five-day intervals.

Moreover, as temperatures in the OWS crept up to 55°C (131°F) a new pointing angle rationale emerged so that thermal management could adopt a more cyclical approach. On one 93.4min orbit the cluster would be aligned broadside to the Sun, maximising power generation from the ATM arrays, followed by the next orbit flown with the longitudinal axis pointing at the Sun (Docking Module forward) to minimise thermal exposure of the OWS

and allow it to cool somewhat. With each orbit providing only 50 minutes in sunlight, the alignment of the ATM arrays for solar power production only 50 minutes in every three hours of two full orbits was placing great demands on the storage CBRMs. But it started to work when temperatures in the OWS began to stabilise around 39°C (102°F).

During the early planning phase for Skylab, NASA had planned a second cluster and the S-IVB from the last production Saturn V (AS-515) had been fabricated as a duplicate station with that in mind, in-house documentation referring to this as Skylab B. At some point during all these deliberations the prospect of launching the backup Skylab B hardware was considered, but the $325 million cost of launching it was beyond NASA's means. It would eventually end up in the National Air and Space Museum in Washington DC, where it can be seen today.

Several schemes for erecting a shade were proposed and tried out in the neutral buoyancy facility at the Marshall Space Flight Center and an early candidate involved a two-man crew carrying a large thermal curtain in a box occupying the location of the centre seat in the Apollo Command Module, but that was rejected. Another idea involved four 3.6m (12ft) long rods secured end-to-end to form a 14.6m (48ft) pole deployed down the side of the OWS by a space-walking astronaut. End-tubes would spring out to form a 'T', and a crew member would use a lanyard to haul a thermal curtain back up to the workshop to lay out a square 7 x 6.1m (23 x 20ft) shade.

On the third day after launch MSFC had assumed responsibility for deciding on the shade, restrained in options by the 41kg (90lb) which could be added to the existing load in the Command Module for each of up to three solutions. Three were to be carried, two as backups. The prime method selected would be a parasol that had been devised by Jack Kinzler, the director of the Technical Services

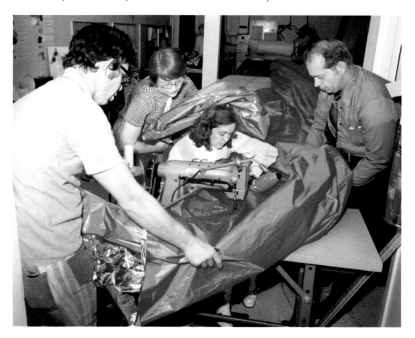

LEFT Seamstresses and technicians work on sunshades to protect the external hull of the Orbital Workshop from the searing effect of the Sun on the unprotected surface. *(NASA)*

FAR LEFT Testing deployment schemes for erecting a sunshade over the exposed Skylab OWS hull. *(NASA)*

LEFT Feverish work under way at the Manned Spacecraft Center to stitch together alternative sunshades that the first crew to visit Skylab would use. *(NASA)*

Division at the Johnson Space Center, which could be packaged in a spare T027 canister for the scientific airlock (SAL) consisting of a box 21.6 x 21.6 x 134.6cm (8.5 x 8.5 x 53in). It employed rods that were the same type as those used for deploying experiments through this square-shaped airlock on the solar side of the OWS.

Major components consisted of a 6.7 x 7.3m (22 x 24ft) aluminised Mylar/nylon laminate canopy partially opaque to solar thermal energy, a mast, mast hub with deployment springs, four telescoping deployment rods, seven extension rods and the T027 canister support tripod. The

canopy was a lamination of orange-coloured rip-stop nylon bonded to 0.05mm (0.002in) aluminised Mylar with a hem around the periphery of 2.52cm (1in) nylon tape and 0.635cm (0.25in) centre diameter PBU line sewn in.

The nylon side of the canopy would be deployed facing the Sun, with the reverse side of the aluminised surface providing low emittance to reduce thermal radiation between the canopy and the hull of the OWS. The back plate of the canister contained provisions for mast and extension rods and disconnecting devices for the telescoping deployment rod tip retainers. The plate also supported O-ring

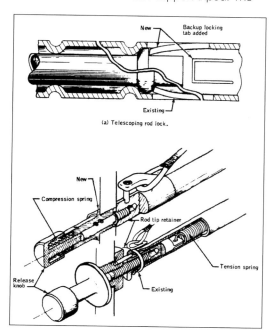

FAR LEFT The telescoping rod lock and tip design for the parasol umbrella which was the initial and preferred means of lowering the internal temperature, typical of a range of complex engineering equipment developed specifically for the job. *(NASA)*

LEFT New tools from old as bolt and wire cutters are adapted for the demanding tasks ahead in freeing the sole remaining SAS wing and restoring some power to the OWS electrical system. *(NASA)*

seals to maintain pressure on the inside of the workshop, and a friction brake prevented turning or overextension of the canopy.

In addition to the parasol as prime candidate, the Command Module would also carry a SEVA shield, as deployed from an Apollo spacecraft during a stand-up EVA, and the twin-pole shield. Unknown, and more difficult

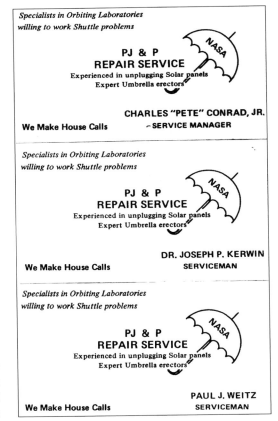

to plan for, was the type and magnitude of the restraining debris from the meteoroid shield preventing deployment of SAS No 1, the sole remaining OWS solar array. Special shear-type sheet metal cutters were prepared, modified for longer handles and, after testing in the neutral buoyancy facility, these together with cable cutters and a universal tool were shipped to the Kennedy Space Center for packing in the Command module for SL-2.

During the unmanned period venting and repressurisation was initiated to purge the workshop of potential toxic gases, outgassing from material subject to high temperatures. Three full nitrogen purging/repressurisation cycles took place, with the last cycle venting to 4.137kPa (0.6lb/in²) and the final pressurisation of 34.47kPa (5lb/in²) prior to crew entry at a nitrogen/oxygen mix of 28/72%.

SL-2

NASA chose veteran astronaut Charles 'Pete' Conrad Jr to command the first visit to Skylab, along with rookies Paul J. Weitz and Joseph P. Kerwin, an all-Navy crew. Conrad had flown the Gemini V mission in August 1965, the Gemini XI mission in September 1966 and had commanded the Apollo 12 flight to the Moon in November 1969. Diminutive in stature, Conrad was a jocular giant among the very best the astronaut corps had on its books who many had tipped to be the first man on the Moon. All that resolute steadfastness and determination would be called upon to get Skylab repaired, protected from the Sun and up and running for a successful series of visits.

The Saturn IB was the obvious choice for launching Apollo spacecraft to Skylab and had been embedded as the workhorse of choice from the inception of the Apollo Applications Program. A man-rated development of the Saturn 1, the first of ten of which had been launched on 27 October 1961, the Saturn IB had essentially the same S-I first stage as its predecessor but the more powerful S-IVB upper stage. In this configuration, the first Saturn IB had been launched on 26 February 1966, followed by three more equally successful flights supporting development of Apollo CSM vehicles and qualifying the S-IVB for its role as the restartable third stage of the Saturn V. The first Apollo spacecraft had been launched by a Saturn IB on 11 October 1968 when it carried astronauts Schirra, Eisele and Cunningham on the ten-day flight of Apollo 7.

However, the plan to use the Saturn IB posed a daunting challenge for the launch support infrastructure at the Kennedy Space Center, since there had been a decision to mothball the Saturn IB launch pads at LC-34 and LC-37. After Apollo 7, when the decision was taken to shift Apollo operations from the Saturn IB to the Saturn V, cost savings demanded a drawdown of personnel because, at that time, the AAP flights had been put back to 1970 at the earliest and it was too expensive to maintain those pads at LC-37 in a launch readiness condition. Officials began to consider moving the AAP launches to the Saturn V complex and its two pads – LC-39A and B. But that brought its own problem.

Saturn V was assembled in the Vehicle Assembly Building (VAB) more than 5km (3 miles) from the launch site. There would be no difficulty launching Skylab on the first two stages of a Saturn V from the existing launch vehicle support infrastructure, but the two stages of the very much smaller Saturn IB were designed to be stacked directly on the pad. Moreover, because they were designed specifically for the giant Saturn V stages, the swing arms at LC-39 carrying fluid, pneumatic, hydraulic and electrical umbilicals from the ground facilities to the launch vehicle were of a completely different configuration and size.

The original plan was to fly the AAP, all Saturn IB missions, from LC-34, a very old structure built by the Army in 1960 and from which the first flight of a Saturn I took place on 27 October 1961. It was old, inadequate and had been modified several times after NASA took over the Saturn programme. As for LC-37, it had received all the benefits of a more adaptable design concept that made it applicable to Saturn IB and its more powerful S-IVB stage; but it had never supported manned operations, and modifications would take two years and cost heavily.

The solution was to use a special pedestal 39m (128ft) tall, on a standard Mobile Launch Platform on which would be erected the two

ABOVE Left to right, astronauts Joe Kerwin, Pete Conrad and Paul Weitz, the crew of the SL-2 mission. *(NASA)*

BELOW The Saturn IB, ready for lift-off and a rescue mission that will cool the interior of the Orbital Workshop and raise the available electrical power levels. *(NASA)*

separate Saturn IB stages and its Apollo CSM payload. The pedestal took the form of a truss structure with a platform on top to which the first stage would be mated. It looked like a milking stool, which is what it was soon known as! By raising the Saturn IB the S-IVB and the Apollo CSM were able to connect up to the umbilicals usually used for Saturn V, which had those same upper elements as the larger rocket, only the Saturn IB first stage requiring adapted umbilical positions.

The milking-stool pedestal had to be

designed to withstand engine exhaust efflux temperatures of up to 2,760°C (5,000°F) and to resist 200kph (124mph) hurricane strength winds without a launch vehicle, and to support maximum wind velocity of 59.4kph (37mph) winds, the highest at which the Saturn IB could be launched. Perched high above the pad it was vulnerable, and there were concerns that it would not be sustainable.

With the launch delayed ten days due to the problems necessitating new tools and fixtures to get Skylab working as designed, there was a certain haste to meet the rescheduled launch date of 25 May. If missed, it would be another five days before the window opened again. Preparations were tight and the parasol was packed aboard a NASA Lear Jet on the afternoon of 23 May, supported by other equipment that was to be flown out from Houston in a Lockheed T-38. The countdown was already under way and the crew were at the Kennedy Space Center when the equipment arrived. The atmosphere there was tense but expectant, and the mood was bright, if tinged with a little uncertainty that the station could be put in good working order.

SL-2 would use AS-206 and Apollo CSM-116, the latter modified considerably from the Block II flown previously. Because the CSM would only be required to carry out rendezvous and docking and de-orbit burns, it would not require the propellant to put the entire CSM/LM into Moon orbit and fire the CSM back home.

Typically, a lunar mission would call for velocity changes totalling 1,900m/sec (6,230ft/sec) while a Skylab mission would involve 200m/sec (656ft/sec) of manoeuvres at most. Consequently, two of the Service Propulsion System (SPS) propellant tanks were removed from sectors 3 and 6, leaving fuel in the sector 5 tank and oxidiser in sector 2. One of two helium pressurisation tanks was removed from the centre tunnel running down the middle of the Service Module and an additional tank was added. It had the capacity for 245kg (540lb) of excess water produced from the two fuel cells, which were retained in sector 4, one less fuel cell than with standard Block II spacecraft. Total SPS engine propellant loaded for a Moon mission was about 18,389kg (40,540lb) in the four tanks, but the two remaining tanks for SL-2 were partially loaded and contained only 2,270kg (5,005lb) of propellant.

The standard Block II Service Module carried four thruster quads, for attitude control, at 90° intervals around the outside of the Service Module, each with two fuel and two oxidiser tanks for a total propellant capacity of about 608kg (1,340lb), mounted to the outer panels of sectors 2, 3, 5 and 6. These were retained, but the capacity of the propellant tanks was increased by 689kg (1,519lb) through the addition of a propellant storage module in the otherwise vacant sector 1.

The module contained five oxidiser and four fuel tanks, three spherical helium tanks 31.42cm (12.37in) in diameter, and associated plumbing connecting these propellants to all 16 thrusters on all four quads. Each titanium propellant tank was 32cm (12.6in) in diameter and 98.55cm (38.8in) in length. The provision of this additional propellant allowed the thrusters to be used to boost the orbit of Skylab. On the first manned visit, 572.4kg (1,262lb) of thruster propellant was consumed.

Electrical power was primarily provided by the two fuel cells, supplemented by three Lunar Module silver-zinc Descent Stage batteries, each with a capacity of 500AH at an open circuit voltage of 37.1V. Each battery weighed 111kg (245lb), two of which could provide all the power necessary for undocking and the de-orbit sequence. All three could provide power for up to 18 hours of autonomous CSM operation. During the pre-launch countdown, at 17:24 EDT the day before flight the SL-2 mobile service structure was struck by lightning, but retests found no reason to hold the flight.

CSM-116 was launched on AS-206 at 13:00:00 UTC (09:00:00 EDT) on 25 May 1973 with a thrust of 8,149kN (1,832,069lb), achieving orbit 9min 46sec later. At lift-off the stack had a mass of 586,353kg (1,292,666lb), of which the spacecraft weighed 19,982kg (44,060lb). On achieving orbit after releasing the launch escape tower, the weight was 14,023kg (30,920lb).

RIGHT Lift-off, early afternoon local time on 25 May 1973 as the first Skylab crew head for orbit. (NASA)

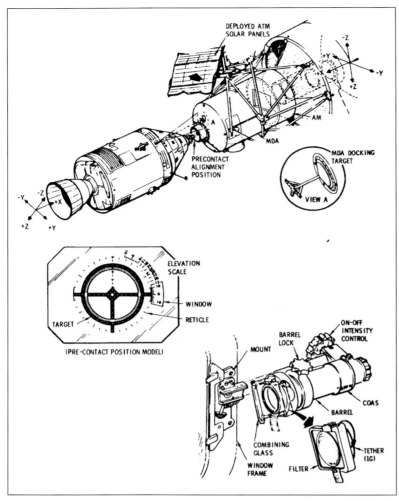

Several experiments designed to fly with SL-2 in the Command Module had been removed to make room for the shields and the tools but additional cameras were carried for a fly-around visual inspection and a spare TV for coverage of the ATM EVA. Initially, the orbit achieved was 357 x 156km (221.8 x 96.9 miles) with the CSM 1,445km (898 miles) behind and below Skylab. A series of four rendezvous manoeuvres brought the spacecraft to Skylab at 16:30 EDT over the Guam tracking station in the Pacific Ocean, an orbit of 424 x 415km (263.5 x 255.7 miles), with the spacecraft weight now 13,386kg (29,516lb) after consumption of rendezvous propellant.

Over the United States the crew televised views of the damage in a 15-minute session as they flew around the station on their fifth orbit, verifying that SAS No 2 array was missing and that SAS No 1 was only partially deployed. At 21:14 UTC, Mission Control gave the word for Conrad to conduct a soft-dock with the axial docking port on the Multiple Docking Adapter at 21:25 UTC. A soft-dock is where the extended probe latches on to the receptacle at the centre of the drogue but does not complete retraction of that probe to achieve a hard dock by triggering 12 latches around the circumference of the docking collar. A hard dock was not advisable since it would require the complete

ABOVE The crewman optical alignment sight (COAS) employed to aid in docking with the Multiple Docking Adapter. *(NASA)*

RIGHT Attenuation clearances for the Apollo spacecraft stowage and crew couches in the Command Module were reworked for the SL-2 mission due to the additional supplies and equipment carried aboard for repair tasks. *(NASA)*

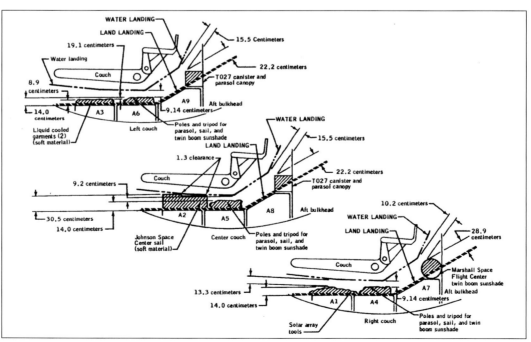

removal of the probe to reset the latches, a time-consuming activity. At this stage, after consumption of manoeuvring propellant, the CSM weighed 13,276kg (29,273lb).

The next activities confirmed, at about 23:04 UTC the crew were given the word to undock from the MDA, a simple step of unlatching the probe and backing away. They were advised to fly to the rear of the OWS and make an attempt to cut away a 2.54 x 1.9cm (1 x 0.75in) piece of 7075-T6 aluminium angle iron. More than one hour passed before the complex was back in communication, with the crew conducting a 35-minute SEVA and working with boat hooks and other tools in an unsuccessful attempt to clear the debris. Weitz pulled so hard he disturbed the stability of Skylab, causing the gyros to steady the motion, the oscillations threatening to pull him out of the hatch. Struggling to get back in, Weitz twice rammed the long poles against Conrad's helmet, sending him diving under the couches for cover, chafing against switches and dials bringing a string of expletives from Kerwin!

Out of radio contact again, the crew had trouble getting a hard dock with the MDA and four attempts were required to spring sufficient latches to get a firm connection between the two, finally achieved at 03:50 UTC on 26 May.

RIGHT On attempting to re-dock with the MDA after failing to free debris snaring the solar array wing, the Conrad crew encountered difficulties with engaging the docking latches. *(NASA)*

After a sleep period in the CSM, the crew began to open up the Multiple Docking Adapter at about 16:30 UTC on 26 May, approximately 27hr 30min after launch. They reported that the MDA, which had been insulated from the hot OWS due to its isolation and both passive and active thermal control, was a cool 10°C (50°F).

Most of the second day was spent preparing the parasol deployment, gathering and connecting the separate tubes of diminishing size which was extended gradually, rod by rod, out through the +Z scientific airlock on the solar side. Deployment of the parasol began and was accomplished by attaching the extension

ABOVE LEFT During the fly-around of Skylab the crew were able to obtain a clear view of the exposed hull of the OWS and the restrained SAS wing. *(NASA)*

ABOVE The scientific airlock through which a parasol shade would be extruded and opened to cover the sunlit side of the OWS. *(NASA)*

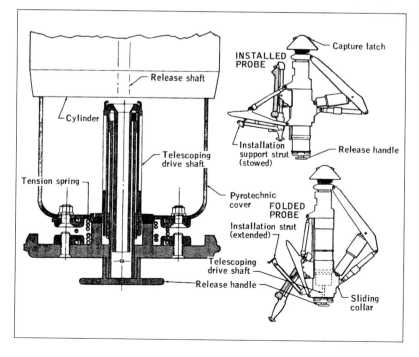

RIGHT The parasol would be deployed through the scientific airlock and extended from a folded position once free of the deployment box. *(NASA)*

PARTIALLY DEPLOYED

BELOW The parasol consisted of a complex set of telescoping rods, extension rods, deployment mechanisms and the canopy proper. *(NASA-MSFC)*

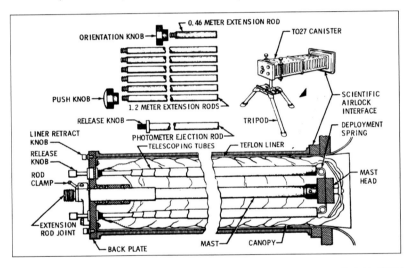

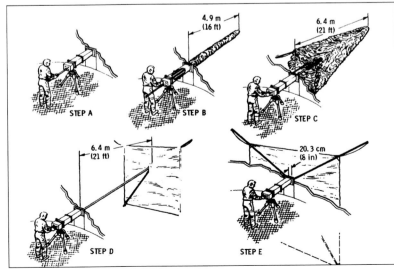

rods to the mast and pushing the rod assembly outward. As the mast hub was extended to 4.9m (16ft) above the opening, the telescoping deployment rods were released. The mast hub was then extended to 6.4m (21ft), allowing the rod tips to swing free of the SAL opening and deploying the canopy. The parasol was then retracted to its final position a few centimetres above the hull of the OWS.

During retraction the long extension rods were removed, one by one, leaving only the short rod in place. Upon deployment, workshop temperatures started dropping immediately with a steady decline to a stabilised 28.5°C (83°F). Deployment was completed by about 00:30 UTC in the morning hour of 27 May, about 35hr 30min into the mission. The deployment rods were withdrawn by around 02:00 but the parasol was not perfectly aligned and required some adjustment. To try and provide better thermal control the parasol was rotated slowly, but when it was it was noted that this raised the temperature in the sleep compartment, so it was turned back.

The first full EVA began at 15:23 UTC on 7 June, Day 14, with repressurisation followed by

LEFT The general deployment sequence used by the crew from the inside of the Orbital Workshop using the T027 canister and supporting tripod, which would be used to provide a mounting and deployment stand. *(NASA-MSFC)*

the Airlock Module hatch being opened before Conrad moved to exit the CM three minutes later, working his way into the Fixed Airlock Shroud, followed by Kerwin. At 16:40 he began assembling poles and tools before resting as Skylab passed into the night side of Earth. At an EVA elapsed time of 1hr 3min Conrad had moved down the boom and was configuring the poles to work the cutter, which took him about 20 minutes. At 1hr 31min Conrad was attempting to cut the strap holding SAS No 1 against the OWS.

By 2hr into the EVA, Conrad was forced to rest on the dark side of the Earth awaiting sunrise at 2hr 32min. The debris around SAS No 1 array was cut free and Conrad muscled the wing out and it began to deploy at 17:59, 2hr 36min into the EVA. Slowly at first, inching its way gradually to the fully deployed position, the array wing began to unfold while Conrad disassembled the poles before stowing them in the airlock at 3hr 2min. At this point Kerwin worked his way up to the Sun end of the ATM to look down across the OWS and observe the shape and configuration of the parasol. The EVA lasted 3hr 23min.

Much of the success of this activity had been due to the ability of Mission Control to send lengthy and complex procedures to the Skylab crew via the onboard teleprinter, relieving the crew of having to copy down, and read back, lengthy lines of procedures and sequences. The absence of such a device had always been a tiresome and troublesome inconvenience on all previous manned flights and the long periods spent out of communication made the necessity for such a device all the more evident. In this, as in many other ways, Skylab was a true pioneer for new technologies, effectively bridging the gap between eras in human space flight.

For the first 14 days of the first visit the ATM continued to supply all Skylab power requirements, the average load managed at 4kW, with the CSM powered by its fuel cells. On Day 6, during the first Earth-pointing mode for the EREP pass, the ATM batteries were excessively discharged and two CBRM were lost completely, leaving 16 serviceable for the rest of the mission. On the three additional EREP passes the crew and Mission Control imposed better power management

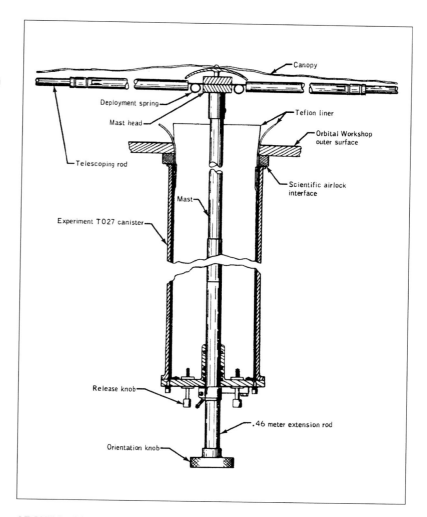

ABOVE In this view, the general orientation of the parasol is seen in proximity to the scientific airlock. *(NASA)*

BELOW Pete Conrad on the bicycle ergometer. *(NASA)*

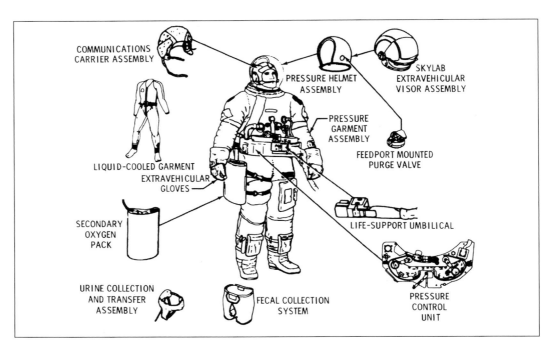

RIGHT Based on the Apollo A7LB extravehicular mobility unit, the Skylab pressure garment assembly provided the occupant with an umbilical connection from the Airlock Module for oxygen and electrical power, while a secondary oxygen pack was available for emergency use if the umbilical failed. *(NASA)*

RIGHT An artist's impression of the work effort required to release the SAS wing after cutting away the debris that had held it tightly down from deployment. *(NASA)*

BELOW Pete Conrad gets a little dental check, a capability for which each crewman was trained. *(NASA)*

techniques. After deployment of OWS SAS No 1 on Day 14, however, average load requirements went up to 4.7kW and to 5.8kW after CSM fuel cell shutdown. Operating in parallel, the capabilities of the ATM and OWS arrays were more than sufficient to provide a positive power level for each SI attitude. As

BELOW Kerwin conducts experiments on fluids inside the Orbital Workshop, part of an integrated series of tests and evaluations to determine the reaction of various fluids to weightlessness. *(NASA)*

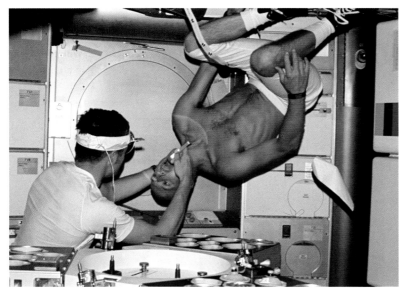

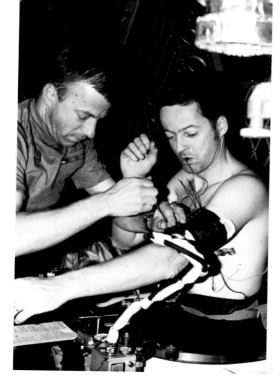

anticipated, ATM solar array degradation levels averaged 0.9%/month.

The second and last EVA for the first manned visit occurred on Day 26 (19 June), beginning at 10:56 UTC and lasting 1hr 36min, during which Conrad and Weitz retrieved film from the ATM S052, S054, S056 and H-alpha experiments, bringing some 30,242 frames back into the OWS for return to Earth. A stuck relay in CBRM-15 was made to work through the judicious use of a hammer being struck against its mount! The S052 and S054 cameras had failed and were replaced so as to allow images to be taken during the period between manned visits. This was the sole spacewalk that had been planned before Skylab entered the flight phase with the eventful launch of SL-1.

Two orbital trim manoeuvres had been performed, one on Day 4 to stabilise the ground track 92.6km (57.5 miles) west of the pre-planned track, which compensated for a westerly orbital drift. The second had been conducted on Day 24, a trim burn to correct a cross-track error of 4,530m (14,864ft) and to place Skylab in the correct path for the launch of SL-3.

Day 29 (22 June) saw the end of the first manned mission, starting with reactivation of CSM-116. Its fuel cells had been shut down on Day 21, having operated continuously for 485 hours since launch. In fact, FC-1 had

operated for 1,072 hours and FC-3 for 562 hours, inclusive of pre-launch and testing. Separation from the MDA occurred at 08:55 UTC followed by a fly-around of the cluster for TV and photographic coverage for 45min. A 10.9sec shaping burn was conducted by the SPS engine at 10:05:40 UTC followed by the 7.5sec de-orbit burn at 13:11:54 UTC.

The spacecraft landed at 13:49:49 UTC, at 24.76°N by 127.67°W, and was recovered by the USS *Ticonderoga* some 38.5 minutes after splashdown. The crew travelled by ship to San Diego, California, from where they were flown

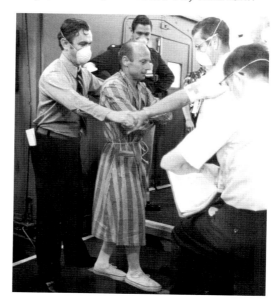

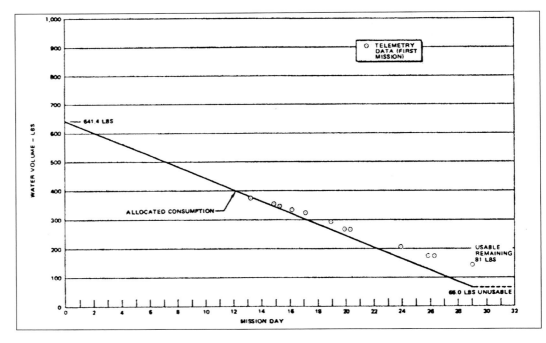

BELOW The crew for SL-3 consisted of (left to right) Owen Garriott, Jack Lousma and Alan Bean, seen here in the MDA training facility at the Johnson Space Center, Houston, Texas. *(NASA)*

to Ellington Air Force Base, Texas, on 24 June. Of the total SPS propellant loaded, 1,160kg (2,557lb) or 51%, remained at SM separation after the de-orbit burn and of the total Service Module RCS propellant, 611.9kg (1,349lb) or 47% of loaded total, was still in the tanks when the SM burned up in the atmosphere.

Despite the problems encountered and the workaround procedures made necessary by the high temperatures and the stuck solar array wing, some 80% of the pre-planned solar data was obtained as well as 12 of the scheduled 15 Earth resources data runs. All 16 medical experiments were completed and data was taken on all the other science experiments carried, with the exception of those few which would have used the scientific airlock, playing host to the parasol and therefore unavailable.

SL-3

The second Skylab mission was in two parts: an unmanned phase from 22 June to the launch of SL-3 on 28 July 1973 (Skylab day 76), and the manned phase beginning with the launch of SL-3 for a scheduled visit duration of 56 days for the second crew. During the unmanned period temperatures increased somewhat due to the increased time spent in sunlight during each orbit but the plan to deploy a twin-pole sunshade, carried to the OWS by the SL-2 crew, would, it was believed, correct the temperature variations during the next unmanned period after SL-3. An improved parasol shield was also carried up on SL-3 in the event that the twin-pole shade could not be deployed.

Due to the excessive use of TACS caused by the continuous attitude changes only about 44% of the pre-mission propellant total remained. TACS use for the second and third visits was expected to be minimal. ATM solar

observations were carried out as expected but the primary up-down rate gyro failed and observations ceased despite some corrective procedures being successfully applied. Nevertheless, a package of six supplementary rate gyros, called the 'six-pack', was prepared for installation during the second visit. Three units were prepared: one for fit checks on the backup MDA with Martin Marietta in Denver, Colorado; the second to the Marshall Space Flight Center for dynamic testing; and the third to the Kennedy Space Center, where it arrived five days before the launch of SL-3.

The electrical power system performed well, average power when the SL-2 crew departed being 6.7–8.5kW with cluster loads being around 4.7kW, or 5.9kW when CSM-117 arrived. Only minimal consequences affected power operation, although one CBRM remained inoperative and one of the solar cell modules had a 10% degradation. Pre-mission flight preparations commenced about 40 hours before the launch of SL-3 with depressurisation to 4.48kPa (0.65lb/in²) with immediate re-pressurisation to the nominal 34.47kPa (5lb/in²) by T-20 hours.

The configuration of Saturn IB AS-207 and CSM-117 was almost identical to that of the SL-2 vehicles, with approximately the same relative quantities of propellant in launch vehicle and spacecraft as described above for the first manned visit. The crew for this mission were Commander Alan L. Bean, US Navy, formerly Lunar Module Pilot for Apollo 12 and the fourth man to walk on the Moon, Science Pilot Doctor Owen K. Garriott and Pilot Major Jack Lousma (US Marine Corps), both making their first flight. The launch had been advanced by 20 days due to the deteriorating condition of the rate gyros and of the parasol thermal shield, which was exhibiting decay. Because of that, the nominal mission duration was extended by three days to bring the ground-track more favourably into alignment with the desired splashdown point.

Lift-off from LC-39B occurred at 11:10:50.5

RIGHT The Saturn IB for the SL-3 missions at LC-39B. Note the elevated pad, which could not be dug down into the ground due to the high water table in the Cape Canaveral area. *(NASA)*

UTC (07:10:50.5 EDT) on 28 July 1973. S-IVB second stage cut-off occurred at 9min 53sec with orbital insertion at 10min 2.5sec into an initial orbit of 231.2 x 154.7km (143.6 x 96.1 miles). With an in-orbit weight of 14,168kg (31,240lb), CSM-117 separated at 17min 59.4sec for a nominal five-orbit rendezvous, after which a fly-around was undertaken to take pictures of the exterior. The CSM was taken so close to the parasol that it caused exhaust from the thrust to impinge on the fabric surface, causing it to flap and rebound before the crew prudently backed away. During the manoeuvres to dock with the MDA a leak was discovered in Service Module RCS (Reaction Control System) quad B. It was isolated for the rest of the mission.

Docking occurred at 8hr 21min (19:32 UTC), but shortly after orbit insertion Lousma had suffered from space sickness, a feeling of nausea, and this persisted after entering Skylab, a motion sensitivity quickly affecting all three crew members which slowed them and delayed activation. The first EVA, to deploy the twin-pole sunshade on Day 4, was deferred for four days beyond the scheduled date and the sickness impacted the entire operational flight plan, reinforcing the value of real-time planning and the use of the teleprinter for uplinking revisions without overly tying up crew time.

On 2 August, Day 6 of the second visit and Day 81 for Skylab, the crew discovered a leak in Service Module quad D, oxidiser venting within the engine housing, when an alarm sent them scurrying into the Command Module. It was isolated by closing the propellant isolation valves and plans to use this system for trim manoeuvres to set up a repeatable ground track were abandoned. This second RCS quad failure brought some concern on the ground and opened discussion as to whether to activate AS-208/CSM-118 as a rescue mission.

Skylab programme director William Schneider ordered a full activation of the rescue plan and astronauts Vance Brand and Don Lind, backup crew for a two-man rescue flight, went into the simulator to perfect their procedures. The earliest a launch could take place would be 5 September, Day 40 of the SL-3 mission. The final decision came down to Chris Kraft, former flight director and now director of the Manned

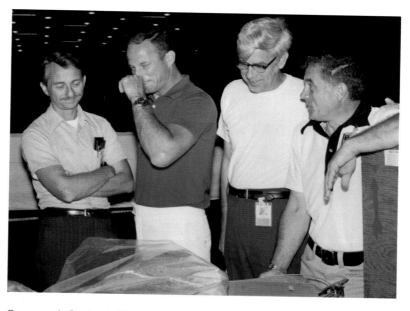

Spacecraft Center (which would became the Johnson Space Center in a special dedication on 27 August), who decided that the situation was stabilised and that the normal mission could continue, for the present – but with SL-4 in accelerated flow, ready for launch if needed.

Activity with the Service Module thruster quad delayed the first EVA by a further two days. Three EVAs were performed, on mission Days 10, 28 and 56, and each required two fully

ABOVE Before the flight, even while the first crewed flight was under way, the SL-3 crew worked on the twin-pole shade which they would deploy to provide a more extensive cover over the hull of the OWS. Here (left to right) Owen Garriott, Jack Lousma, Jack A. Kinzler and Carl Henize discuss deployment prospects. *(NASA)*

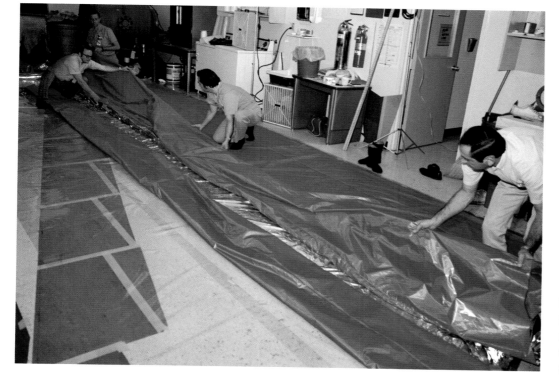

LEFT Technicians pack the sunshade ready for installation in the Command Module. *(NASA)*

suited crew members and one partially suited member in the MDA on standby. The first EVA occurred on 6 August and involved Garriott and Lousma. It included the erection of the twin-pole sunshade to further protect the OWS, ATM film installation, installation of particle collection experiments and various inspections of the exterior looking for leaks etc. On activating Skylab, the crew had spent considerable time trouble-shooting several annoying problems with various systems, none of which were terminal but all requiring concerted attention.

The first EVA began at 17:30 UTC, 6 August, with initial focus on deploying the new shade. The hardware included 24 poles, each 1.5m (4.9ft) long, stowed in two pallets; a 7.4 x 6.8m (24.2 x 22.3ft) sunshade stowed in a bag; a pole base, two clothes lines (also on pallets) to serve as halyards; and a portable foot restraint adapter to use with a universal foot restraint from the OWS. The shade consisted of an aluminised Mylar fabric treated with a special zinc-oxide thermal coating to reflect 75% of the solar energy falling across its surface. In preparation for deployment, the parasol was lowered to within 20cm (8in) of the OWS to allow sufficient room for the twin-pole shade to lie across it.

First, equipment was located in the fixed airlock shroud and Garriott moved to the area where the sunshade EVA workstation was to be mounted on an ATM truss. Next, foot restraints, the sunshade base plate and the sunshade bag assembly were transferred to Lousma at

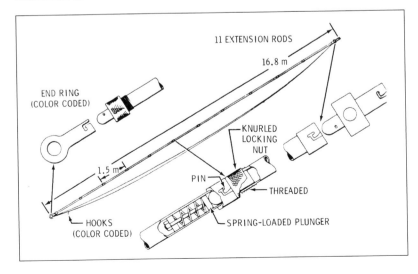

11 EXTENSION RODS
16.8 m
END RING (COLOR CODED)
KNURLED LOCKING NUT
1.5 m
PIN
THREADED
HOOKS (COLOR CODED)
SPRING-LOADED PLUNGER

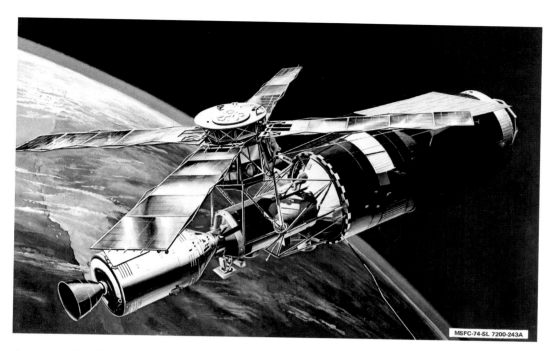

LEFT The deployment of the twin-pole shade was largely responsible for the endurance of both the second and third visits, together with the extension to the last visit. Ultraviolet light was degrading the parasol, which would not have lasted the full mission duration had it not been supplemented. *(NASA)*

the workstation through the transfer boom. Subsequently, the foot restraint and base plate were attached to the truss.

The astronaut in the FAS area assembled the poles and transferred them to the other crewman who placed them in the base plate. Then the sunshade was attached to the halyards on the pole assemblies and was deployed along the poles. Finally, the crewman positioned the forward edge of the sunshade against the OWS after-skirt and parasol, tied off the reefing lines to the ATM truss and returned to the airlock. Almost immediately the temperatures inside the OWS started to come down, indicating the considerable improvement in shading made possible by this assembly.

The entire operation required a lot longer than estimated and took up most of the EVA time, solving minor problems with deployment and smoothing wrinkles in the sunshade. The crew carried out a visual inspection of the exterior and observed the thruster quads to look for signs of leakage from the failed units, but found none. They removed a ramp latch for the S055 telescope aperture door when it stuck using a box-end wrench from the OWS toolkit and modified it by building up the handle with tape. They installed a particle collection experiment and retrieved and replaced film cassettes from the S056 and Hydrogen-alpha 1 telescope. The EVA lasted 6hr 31min.

On 13 August, Day 17, Bean had given the ASMU its only workout on this second visit, strapping himself into the backpack for a scheduled 3hr 15min fly-around, calibrating fore, aft, left, right and up and down motion followed by translating from one side of the OWS forward dome. With an acceleration rate of 0.09m/sec^2 (0.3ft/sec^2) he was unable to reach a speed that could cause a damaging collision with any of the workshop structure and rarely got up to more than 0.15m/sec (0.5ft/sec). After Bean, Lousma got a ten-minute workout on the ASMU, at the end of which OWS pressure had increased to 35.85kPa (5.2lb/in^2) due to expelled nitrogen gas from

BELOW The general configuration of the twin-pole shade as deployed across the top of the parasol. *(NASA)*

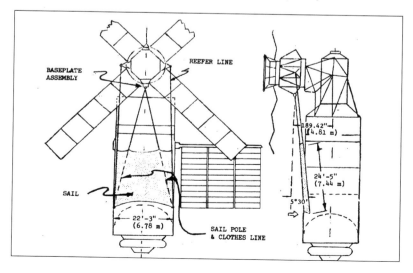

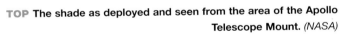

TOP The shade as deployed and seen from the area of the Apollo Telescope Mount. *(NASA)*

ABOVE Owen Garriott gives Alan Bean a haircut, with the suction tube capturing pieces of floating hair. *(NASA)*

ABOVE RIGHT Alan Bean flies the backpack using the hand-held manoeuvring unit for position control. *(NASA)*

the back-pack. A second run, with suits on to simulate an EVA use of the ASMU/HHMU, took place on 15 August.

The day before (14 August), a crawler-transporter had rolled through the doors of the Vehicle Assembly Building at the Kennedy Space Center to pick up AS-208 and its payload, CSM-118 on the 'milk stool', and carry it to LC-39B, accelerated by the possibility of it having to fly to Skylab to bring the SL-3

crew home, abandoning CSM-117 due to two thruster quad failures. What could have been dubbed SL-R reverted to SL-4 preparations when word came that the examination of telemetry and other analysis showed that a normal re-entry using CSM-117 was safe. Had the SL-4 stack been used as SL-R, it would have cost NASA another $45 million to prepare AS-210 to serve as a potential rescue vehicle for AS-209, which in that event would have been used to launch SL-4, the last manned visit.

But the decision as to how to fly AS-208 was nuanced by another issue. Due to problems with Skylab's primary coolant loop, the condensate tank and the rate gyro processors, Schneider evaluated the possibility of launching SL-4 on 24 September, one day prior to the return of the SL-3 crew, and docking CSM-118 to the radial MDA port to allow its crew to move in without having to go through a period of deactivation/reactivation, which was felt to stress the systems. Alternatively, they could launch on the 25th before SL-3 separation, station-keep until CSM-117 departed, and then dock to the axial port. The third option was to stay on schedule.

16 August brought seminal news: the backup hardware would stand down as a potential Skylab B, the firm decision having been taken not to fly a second cluster. There had been considerable talk in recent months about the possibility of a second station. The hardware for a second Skylab was in a very high stage of completion and while it would have drawn funds from an already diminishing budget, by late 1973 the first flight of the Shuttle had been put back to no earlier than 1979 – at least four years after the joint flight with the Russians, the Apollo Soyuz Test Project, scheduled for 1975. By demonstrating its ability to repair a damaged and potentially crippled cluster, the Skylab team had hoped to garner support for a second Skylab.

On 19 August, Day 23, Bean got a workout on the T020 foot-controlled manoeuvring unit (FCMU). This device consisted of a saddle-mounted structure with support arms connected to a foot-board at the base and a backpack fixture at the upper end. It incorporated the same type of tank as that in the ASMU, feeding four 0.45kg (1lb) and four 0.22kg (0.5lb) thrusters located at the upper end of the foot-board. To operate the FCMU, Bean seated himself on the saddle and strapped on thigh and waist tethers. A rocking motion of the foot-board produced four-axis manoeuvrability versus the six degrees of the ASMU. Bean found it difficult to control, unstable and complained that it kept slipping off his back.

The second EVA began at 16:24 UTC on 24 August, mission Day 28 (Skylab Day 103) of the second visit, and was conducted by Garriott and Lousma. The immediate task was to replace the troublesome rate gyros with the 'six-pack' which had been sent up with the crew. The pack was mounted inside the vehicle but had to be connected to the control system during EVA. That involved removing and replacing electrical connectors with special pliers specifically developed for this task, and

ABOVE Alan Bean tries out the M509 backpack while wearing the full pressure suit to impose a realistic test on how it might be applied during spacewalking. *(NASA)*

BELOW Owen Garriott during a medical test with respiration and exhalation measure while providing continuous blood pressure readings. *(NASA)*

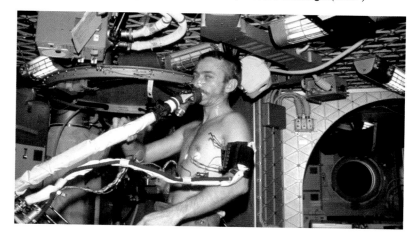

THIS PAGE Owen Garriott going about the business of retrieving film cassettes from the Apollo Telescope Mount, a vital part of mission operations in the days before digital download and continuous communications. *(NASA)*

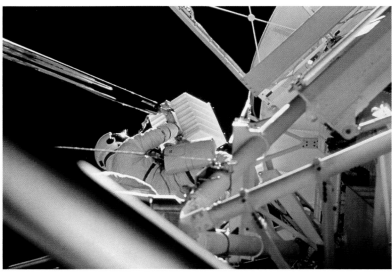

running a 7.3m (23.95ft) cable to the computer interface on the ATM. If the rate gyro processor had failed, mission termination would have been imminent.

Sticking ramp doors on S056 and S082A aperture doors necessitated the removal of the ramp latches, achieved by the same method used on EVA-1. The ATM film magazines were replenished and in an attempt to measure the degradation of solar exposure to the parasol, two pieces of that material were attached to a clipboard and fastened to a handrail on the structural transition section (STS) in full view of the Sun. During rate gyro installation the vehicle drifted off attitude about 9° but a return to solar inertial attitude was accomplished satisfactorily.

EVA-3 began at 11:18 UTC on 22 September, Day 57 of the second visit (Skylab Day 132), involving Bean and Garriott. This was a trouble-free activity involving a planned film change-out procedure but with some additional tasks, including retrieval of the parasol sample material from the STS. This EVA was conducted using air cooling rather than liquid cooling, due to the failure of the primary coolant loop in the Airlock Module leaving only the secondary to carry the load. There was no visor fogging and the astronauts paced themselves so as not to overwhelm the ability of the life support system with unacceptable energy levels. Lousma was cooled in the AM using the vacuum cleaner blower connected by hose, air being pulled into, rather than blown out of, the suit. The third EVA lasted 2hr 41min.

Its fuel cells deactivated since 16 August, Day 20, the CSM was powered up for its final free flight and return to Earth on 25 September, Day 60 (Skylab Day 135). Because re-entry was to take place at an hour which required a very early rise, on Day 51 they began a sleep session shifting back from the usual start at 23:00 EDT (10:00 CDT, Houston time) at two hours per day to 17:00 EDT (18:00 CDT) by Day 53. Wake-up times were advanced by the same proportion from 07:00 EDT (06:00 CDT) to 03:00 EDT (02:00 CDT). They remained at those advanced times thereafter, acclimatising to them to ensure an alert and healthy, rested crew by re-entry day.

Woken at 03:00 EDT on 25 September the crew prepared for return, suiting up, powering up the CSM and sealing the MDA hatch, which was completed at 10:30 EDT followed by undocking at 15:34 EDT. Because of the problems with the two thruster quads the planned fly-around was cancelled. Separation occurred as planned followed by the de-orbit burn at 17:38:18 EDT (21:38:18 UTC). Splashdown occurred at 18:19:54 EDT (22:19:54 UTC), 402km (250 miles) south-west of San Diego, California, setting a new US space-flight record of 59 days 11 hours 9 minutes 4 seconds.

Overall, Skylab was in good shape. The electrical system had been providing between 6.3kW and 8.4kW during flight with demand averaging 4.8–6kW when power was fed after CSM shutdown. Sixteen of the 18 CBRM were

BELOW LEFT Alan Bean displays the pressure garment assembly together with the new controls and displays. *(NASA)*

BELOW Time and motion studies and ergonomic analysis was made possible for on-board activity using cameras in the forward dome and at lateral locations. *(NASA)*

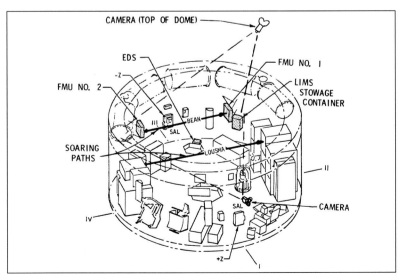

still working, battery capacitance tests showed a degradation to 12AH with the PCG groups fed from the single solar array wing averaging 33AH. These eight units were well up to expectation and overall the electrical systems were capable of exceeding original mission requirements.

Environmentally, Skylab had 1,905kg (4,200lb) of oxygen remaining and more than 410kg (905lb) of nitrogen. Temperatures were holding well at about 23.3°C (74°F) and the coolant loops had stood up well to the extremes handled during the early phase until deployment of the parasol on Skylab Day 14. The primary loop had failed on SL-3 Day 30 of the second visit (Skylab Day 138) but the secondary had been used for the balance of the stay and plans were already being made to re-service the primary. Carbon dioxide levels were holding well, with a maximum 5.8mm/Hg sustained by the molecular sieves.

A broad range of minor problems were being sorted out by Mission Control and the government-industry support teams, to whom great credit must be given for pioneering sustained station operations on a 24-hour basis for two months on continuous engineering monitoring and control. In this they were a world leader, far eclipsing the maximum of less than 24 days in space of the Soyuz 11 crew who visited Salyut 1 but died during re-entry. Not until 1979 would the Russians exceed the record that would be set by Skylab on the third manned visit. Continuous monitoring allowed engineers on the ground to command corrective switching without bothering the crew, who were not required to actively participate.

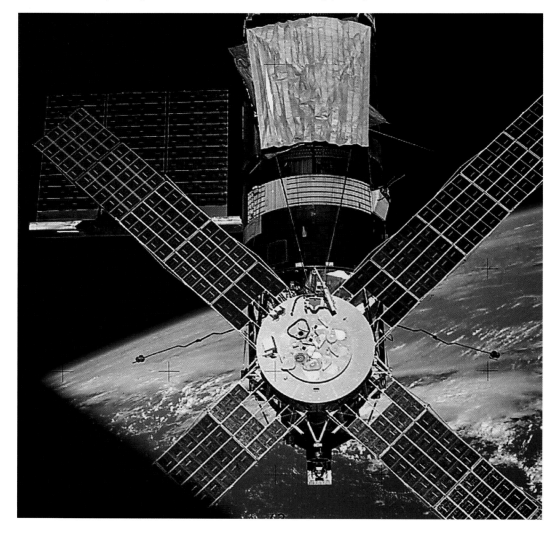

RIGHT As the SL-3 crew depart to return home, they see the fruits of their efforts in deploying the A-frame shade, seen here covering the parasol deployed on SL-2. *(NASA)*

RIGHT The last crew to visit Skylab included (left to right) commander Gerald P. Carr, Edward G. Gibson and William R. Pogue. (NASA)

SL-4

On 16 August 1973 the decision had been made to launch SL-4 on the last manned visit on 9 November (Skylab Day 180) so as to have the crew occupy the station with minimal unmanned activity and to get in position to capture images of the Comet Kohoutek, which would present a unique opportunity to observe the event above Earth's atmosphere. The prime viewing period for Kohoutek would be around 4 January 1974, Day 50 of the mission and Skylab Day 236, and scientists wanted the station to turn into an observatory.

The AS-208/CSM-118 stack had been moved to LC-39B on 14 August as a result of an acceleration in work hours to a continuous round-the-clock operation, in case it was required to bring back the SL-3 crew. The vehicle was eventually brought to a level of readiness where it could be launched within nine days of the go-ahead. However, on 15 August the mobile launcher received several lightning strikes that which damaged systems within the CSM, and these had to be replaced. A retest of the Saturn IB showed no effects on the launch vehicle but cracks were found in the lower web of an upper aluminium 7178-T6 E-beam forging on 27 August. Repairs were completed by 3 September.

By late September the launch date had migrated to 11 November but sustained tracking of the Skylab orbit shifted that up by one day and a late morning launch. On 6 November, four days before the revised launch date, final inspection of the vehicle's structure revealed cracks in the aft attachment fittings of fins at the base of the first stage. AS-208 had been out of post-manufacturing checkout for more than seven and a half years, and cracks had first been observed on AS-209 in the

RIGHT The launch of SL-4 on 16 November 1973 marked the penultimate flight of a Saturn IB. (NASA)

Vehicle Assembly Building, sending engineers checking AS-208 on the pad.

Each fin weighed 220kg (485lb) and consisted of a front and rear spar, a hold-down fitting and two diagonal strengthening tubes and ten vertical ribs. The hold-down fitting passed compression loads through the fourth rib position from the structural interface, with fin attachment provided by front and rear bolt blocks at respective spar positions where they butted with the thrust structure E-beam assembly. Cracks were found in all eight fin attachment fittings with two cracks on seven fins and one on the eighth, the longest measuring 3.8cm (1.5in).

The decision was made to replace all eight fins, and by the early hours of 7 November the launch had been put back to mid-morning on 15 November. Work to remove the first fin began at 14:33 EST on 8 November and was completed 35 hours later. The target was the start of the countdown for the revised launch date, now set to begin at 02:30 EST on 13 November. Then, late morning on the day before the countdown start, another structural problem emerged when cracks were discovered in seven of the eight reaction beams joining the first and second stages. Because these new cracks were in compression and not tension there seemed

ABOVE On arriving at the space station, the SL-4 crew found a surprise stowaway waiting for them, left by the previous crew. *(NASA)*

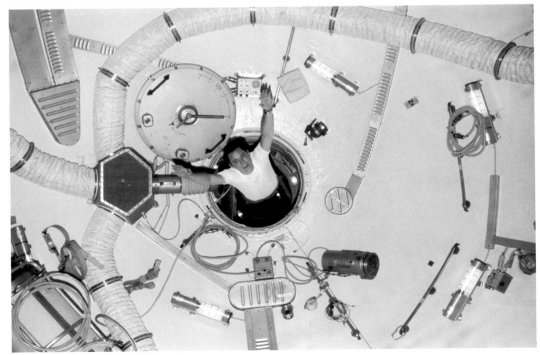

RIGHT Ed Gibson displays the freedom of movement on entering the spacious volume in the forward section of the Orbital Workshop. *(NASA)*

little necessity to perform work on those beams. Although up to 6.35cm (2.5in) long, stress analysis indicated that the cracks still carried a safety factor of 1.5, just inside the minimum required factor of 1.4. Nevertheless, that analysis put back the launch to 16 November.

By 07:04 EST on 13 November, all eight first-stage fins had been removed and reinforcing blocks installed before the mounting bolts at each fitting. This would ensure an adequate load path if cracks developed in the bolt fittings after final inspection. Because previous Saturn IB launch vehicles displayed flight loads of 35% of the limit value, and because the fully fuelled vehicle produced higher equivalent fin loads, it was deemed necessary to restrict the launch to 50% of the normal design limit.

Corresponding to 165,905.94kg-cm (144,000inch-lb), half the flight load mentioned here, it is clear that with a free-standing fully loaded condition at 188,948.4kg-cm (164,000in-lb) the fins were providing stress levels only 87.8% of the flight load, or a ratio of 1:1.139. It was, therefore, either mischievous or as a product of ignorance that the media created such a scare-flap at the Kennedy Space Center that many uninformed citizens berated NASA for risking astronauts' lives! Simply by not crumbling and falling over the stack proved it was safe to

fly. Paradoxically, it was technically unnecessary to reinforce any of the fins.

While proving challenging to sustain in terms of adaptive, real-time flight planning, both first and second visits had demonstrated the ability of the crew to adapt and to find their own level of work, sometimes at variance with ground controllers, flight planners and flight support personnel. There was a sense of independence on the part of all crews that frequently crossed the legitimate intentions of Mission Control, staffed with decision-making engineers and scientists who had never been into space.

ABOVE As viewed during EVA, the Apollo spacecraft (CSM-118) is shown docked to the MDA with characteristic paint patterns for passive thermal control. *(NASA)*

LEFT Carr and Gibson pausing to have their picture taken, the grid floor/ceiling dividing the two areas in the OWS clearly visible. *(NASA)*

RIGHT Carr and Pogue disposing of trash at the airlock on the floor of the living/ experiment area. *(NASA)*

FAR RIGHT Apparently balancing Pogue on his finger, Carr demonstrates the counter-intuitive poses made possible by weightlessness. The spacious nature of Skylab gave space-watchers a new reality only hinted at in Hollywood movies up to this time. *(NASA)*

Yet there had been a considerable amount of pressure brought by experienced astronauts from the Gemini and Apollo programmes to more effectively understand the operating environment of the crews in space. It did not always work and the third manned visit was an example of that, where the crew had to reverse the decision-structure and take control of their own work/rest balance and find their own optimum flow pattern which, ultimately, was to the benefit of personnel on the ground. Before the third crew got to reach Skylab, however, mission planners ramped up the anticipated work schedules to create difficult and challenging goals and objectives.

Because of the successes of the first two visits, mission managers decided to run the final visit as an open-ended flight, planning for a nominal 56 days but progressively approving extensions to 69 days and then to 84 days, subject to careful monitoring of the crew's physiological condition. Weekly reviews would be held by the physicians to approve recommendations to the Mission Director. Because of that potential extension, an additional 72kg (159lb) of food was packed aboard CSM-118, of which 26.7kg (59lb) comprised high-density products. It was also

carrying the S201 experiment, a far ultraviolet electronographic camera for observations of comet Kohoutek. New to Skylab, it was the backup camera for the far-UV telescope that had been carried to the Moon on Apollo 16, together with two film magazines capable of a total of 350 frames. In addition a primary coolant loop servicing kit weighing 39.5kg (87lb) was added.

The crew selected for SL-4 consisted of Commander Lieutenant Colonel Gerald P. Carr (US Marine Corps), Science Pilot Doctor Edward G. Gibson and Pilot Colonel William R. Pogue (US Air Force). None had flown before and they would not fly again. Both Pogue and Carr would probably have made it on to the Apollo 19 crew, one of two Moon missions cancelled in September 1970. Instead, the gap until the Shuttle flew was widening, and several astronauts were finding careers elsewhere.

Carrying CSM-118, the penultimate Apollo spacecraft launched, AS-208, the penultimate Saturn IB, lifted off from LC-39B at 14:01:23 UTC (09:01:23 EST) on 16 November (Skylab Day 187). At lift-off this was the heaviest Saturn IB of the Skylab programme, weighing 587,969kg (1,296,228lb). Second stage shutdown occurred at 9min 47sec followed by orbital insertion, at 14,889kg (32,830lb) the heaviest CSM of the Skylab programme. A standard five-orbit rendezvous ensued and docking came after three attempts at an elapsed time of 8hr 1min.

Because Pogue had already become seriously affected by space sickness, and as a result of experience with the SL-3 crew who had moved too quickly into the weightless void of Skylab, the SL-4 crew remained in the CSM until the second day. But air-ground relations got off to a very bad start when the crew left their data storage device on 'record', which, when dumped to the ground, revealed private discussion never intended for relay to Houston. Believing it to be private, they had discussed hiding the true nature of Pogue's sickness and dumping the vomit bags in the trash can rather than preserving them for medical analysis as required. Alan Shepard made a personal call to the crew, chastising them and calling for a more open attitude.

By Day 3 the crew were beginning the process of activation and un-stowing the Command Module, although despite repairs to the coolant loop accomplished on Day 4 it still left a further two days to fully reactivate the station, the schedule being delayed by crew sickness.

Conducted by Gibson and Pogue, the first EVA began at 12:42 EST on 22 November (Day 7) and incorporated a wide range of tasks and new activities, including installation of a coronagraph contamination measurement experiment which was to have used the -Z scientific airlock now containing the parasol set up on the first visit – it had been thought unwise to remove the parasol prior to setting out the twin-pole shade for fear it could not be done and either one of the shades would have precluded use of that airlock for its designed purpose. Other EVA tasks included inspection and repair of the S193 antenna pointing system, which had malfunctioned and which required portable foot restraints, and special mounting brackets to access an area not supported with handrails and installed foot restraints. In addition to installing film magazines in several ATM experiments, the crew attached sample materials for exposure to the Sun and a magnetospheric particles collector. The EVA lasted 6hr 34min.

ABOVE Carr photographs Gibson during an EVA to retrieve film cassettes from the Apollo Telescope Mount. *(NASA)*

Early the following day, while the crew were still asleep, the Honeysuckle tracking station in Australia reported that CMG No 1, controlling the X-axis, was overheating with a current exceeding 2A, more than twice the normal load. Just 38 minutes after loss of signal at Honeysuckle, Skylab came in view of the Bermuda station which reported that the wheel speed had gone from 9,027rpm to zero. A free-spinning wheel would take 30 hours to run down and Mission Control ordered its immediate shutdown. This would place greater demand on TACS propellant for attitude changes but as the probability of one CMG failing was 20% and the probability of two failing was 0.3%, there was some reassurance. But should a second CMG wheel fail, with only 133.447kN-sec (30,000lbf-sec) of nitrogen gas remaining in the TACS, this would, at a daily consumption rate of 2.2241kN-sec (500lbf-sec) to control Skylab, result in loss of control after only four or five days. There was no real assurance that engineers could adequately estimate the position with at least one other CMG. On 28 May, Day 4 of the first visit, the CMG No 3 wheel speed transducer had failed, showing a telemetered reading of 3,774rpm, which was clearly wrong. There was little way of knowing if there was something insidiously threatening in that wheel.

The immediate impact of the problem was to conserve TACS propellant and a planned 90° roll manoeuvre for Day 9 was cancelled, although there were plenty of other opportunities to conduct scientific observations on the object and hand-held photographs were taken on Day 9, ostensibly an off-duty day for the crew. Over the next several days observations of both the comet and of Earth through the EREP instruments were curtailed and Skylab limped along in a semi-operational mode while flight controllers wrestled with the attitude control options to limit TACS consumption.

Further problems emerged on Day 17 when two back-to-back EREP passes had Skylab go to local vertical and back to solar-inertial in a planned, rapid attitude change, but in going to the first local vertical orientation the cluster flew away at 0.1°/sec, nine seconds going by before guidance officer Ronald Lerdal noticed and uplinked a thrust command. Taking ten seconds to execute, the thrusters fired hard on and consumed 3.047kN-sec (685lbf-sec). Total consumption for the day was 5.711kN-sec (1,284lbf-sec), leaving just 124.550kN-sec (28,000lbf-sec). The limiting redline for end-of-mission emergencies was 44.482kN-sec (10,000lbf-sec) but several options were being worked and on Day 21 the decision was made to lower the redline level to 26.689kN-sec (6,000lbf-sec).

On 3 December, Day 18 (Skylab Day 204), AS-209 was rolled out to the pad in case it

was required for a rescue, but this was part of the pre-launch plan for SL-4 and was not in response to the problems with CMG No 1. Next day the fuel cells on CSM-118 were shut down, the ATM arrays feeding the Apollo spacecraft with 1kW of electrical energy henceforth. But ominous indications of a potential problem with CMG No 2 came on Day 20 when a 50% decrease in speed was noted, an event which had been spotted preceding the failure of CMG No 1, but only when engineers conducted a detailed analysis of the telemetry.

Now there was a plan that could extract more life out of the system should a second wheel fail. A new guidance logic would minimise thruster firings and preserve TACS gas. With a 24° roll deadband, Skylab would use 7.117kN-sec (1,600lbf-sec) per day, which would provide sufficient fuel for 14 days, after which the Apollo spacecraft could provide a further ten days of attitude control from the quad thrusters. But CMG No 2 gave further cause for concern on Day 30 (15 December) when speed dropped from 8,912rpm to 8,870rpm, albeit with a consistent temperature at the lower end of the permissible band. But with the second EVA coming up on Day 40, attention once again focused on the TACS remaining, now at 115.653kN-sec (28,000lbf-sec).

The EVA began on Day 40 (25 December) as planned, with Carr and Pogue leaving the Airlock Module at 18:00 UTC (12:00 CST). This and a planned third EVA were scheduled four days apart so as to capture photography of Kohoutek prior to and after perihelion, its closest pass around the Sun. Again there was the usual exchange of sample materials, attention to ATM experiments, the replacement of a filter wheel on the S054 experiment and the use of the S021 instrument for Kohoutek in a spacewalk lasting 6hr 53min, about two hours longer than planned. Unexpected attitude drift in pitch again drew excessive use of the diminishing TACS propellant, some 17.210kN-sec (3,869lbf-sec) being used, leaving 103.643kN-sec (23,300kgf-sec), or 76.954kN-sec (17,300lbf-sec) remaining for mission use above the new and reduced redline.

Kohoutek reached perihelion at 22:24 UTC on 28 December, when it passed within 21.2km million (13.2 million miles) of the Sun, 167.1km million (103.9 million miles) from Earth travelling

BELOW **Ed Gibson works at the ATM console in the Multiple Docking Adapter.** *(NASA)*

at 403,859kph (251,000mph). Next day, the crew spoke directly with the comet's discoverer, Czech astronomer Doctor Luboš Kohoutek.

The third EVA involved Carr and Gibson and began at 17:00 UTC (11:00 CST) on 29 December (Day 44/Skylab Day 230) and involved retrieval of a sample of sunshade material installed during the second EVA on the first visit, retrieval of a sample cover material from the Airlock Module, installation and retrieval of photographic experiments from ATM instruments and temperature measurements on the S020 experiment. When CMG No 2 unexpectedly hit the gimbal stops an even greater proportion of TACS propellant was used, reducing the remaining quantity by 1.7187kN-sec (3,864lbf-sec) and leaving approximately 83.626kN-sec (18,800lbf-sec) in the tanks, almost one third of which was allocated to a redline limit for possible contingencies. The EVA lasted 3hr 29min.

Now more than halfway through their mission, the determination of the crew to map their own work schedules, and to use flight plans generated on the ground as guidelines only, had reached levels of tension not seen since the fractious dialogue between Houston and Apollo 7 in October 1968 when Commander Walter M. Schirra flatly refused to adhere to schedules he believed were unrealistic and intrusive on the astronauts' decision-making capabilities. A very long message was uplinked via the teleprinter and much of the evening of 30 December was spent in very frank discussion.

Attracted to the high performance of the first two crews to visit Skylab, mission planners had sought to raise the bar too high, believing that even higher performance levels could be achieved without due regard to the myriad of small, unexpected and seemingly simple but irritating onboard tasks frequently skewing the pre-planned timeline. The ability to constantly modify the flight plan and uplink new versions daily only compromised the ability of the crew to carry out increasingly demanding workloads. For their part, the crew had been silent too long and were reluctant to voice their concerns before compromising tasks impossible to carry out. Skylab itself was an experimental laboratory and meaningful lessons were being learned on

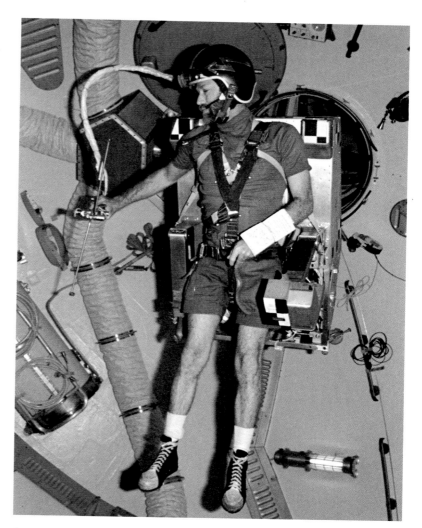

the ground as well as in space, but the reality of that was hard won.

As the mission progressed the unremitting struggle to conserve TACS propellant and continuously monitor the performance of the remaining CMG units was accompanied by a more judicious balance of time-sharing among the crew and a more realistic and achievable set of objectives on the daily flight plan. On Day 73, 27 January 1974, Skylab passed within 5.6km (3.5 miles) of OV32, a Department of Defense satellite which had been launched on 28 October 1966.

The fourth and final EVA of the Skylab programme began with Carr and Gibson leaving the Airlock Module at 15:19 UTC (10:19 CDT) on 3 February, Day 80 (Skylab Day 266) of the third visit, with more than 20 separate tasks awaiting them. Six ATM experiment film magazines were retrieved and samples

ABOVE Gerald Carr 'flies' the M509 backpack using the hand-held manoeuvring unit that expelled nitrogen gas for propulsion. *(NASA)*

left outside on previous EVAs to measure the results of exposure were retrieved. The EVA lasted 5hr 19min and the crew left in place a cassette of particle collection samples in case of a revisit on an early Shuttle flight. Mercifully, TACS use during this extensive activity was well down on projected consumption, with 31.137kN-sec (13,000lbf-sec) available in total.

For the next two days the crew packed the Apollo Command Module with items for retrieval and the last activities with the materials processing experiments was carried out with the burning of 30 different materials in the furnace, left until the end of the mission for fear of contaminating the environment when the gases were vented. During the third and final visit there had been three significant trim burns conducted by the Service Module RCS thrusters: mission Day 9 (24 November 1973), 88sec, 1.8m/sec (5.8ft/sec) retrograde; mission Day 27 (12 December 1973), 17sec, 0.34m/sec (1.1ft/sec) posigrade; mission Day 83 (6 February 1974), 180sec, 3.7m/sec (12ft/sec) posigrade.

On mission Day 83 (6 February), the crew took sleep medication and advanced their sleep time by two hours, starting their rest at 20:00 CDT – Houston time – and then advanced it by a further seven hours the next night so as to be on an early wake-up at 21:00 CDT on Day 84 ready for return to Earth on Day 85. On re-entry day, 8 February, the crew closed out the MDA tunnel at 07:30 UTC (02:30 CDT) and undocked the Apollo CSM at about 11:28 UTC (06:28 CDT).

A brief fly-around inspection of Skylab preceded the firing of the SPS engine for an 89.6m/sec (294ft/sec) shaping manoeuvre begun at 12:32:54 UTC (07:32:54 CDT) lasting 12.14sec, prior to the de-orbit burn, a 56.4m/sec (185ft/sec) manoeuvre begun at 14:25:59 UTC (09:35:59 CDT) and lasting 7.97sec. Command Module 118 splashed down in the Pacific Ocean at 15:16:54 UTC, 289km (179.5 miles) south-west of San Diego, California. The mission had lasted 84 days 1 hour 15 minutes 31 seconds. The total flight time for the three visits had been 4,117hr 14min 24sec.

The end of the Skylab programme was marked by the start of a period of testing that began at 11:20 UTC (06:20 CDT) on 8 February with a series of engineering checks. Power was

applied to CMG No 1 and bearing temperatures monitored, but it refused to move. All Airlock Module batteries were discharged to 30V one at a time and the ATM power-sharing circuitry was cycled off. Radiator subsystem tests were performed, but degradations previously noted could not be corrected. The six unpowered rate gyros originally installed were powered up but the ones that had shown defective performance were still in poor condition. One by one the systems and subsystems were turned off, and the cluster was shut down with a final command sent up at 20:09:05 UTC (15:09:05 CDT) on 9 February, Skylab Day 271.

The cluster had been vented but it would take up to two months for it to completely evacuate all internal atmosphere. There was approximately 1,515kg (3,341lb) of oxygen and nitrogen left, the limiting gas being oxygen which, at a use rate of 12.7kg (28lb) per day, would have supported a further 222 days of occupation, the surplus due to the cluster

having a much lower leak rate than predicted. Water supplies were also on the high side, with 775kg (1,710lb) remaining in the tanks, sufficient for a 90-day occupation.

Despite the extreme temperature conditions shortly after launch, the water tanks survived unscathed and apparently without problems despite a temperature in the tanks of 54.4°C (130°F). On initial activation, tanks 1 and 7 were connected to the wardroom and the WMC distribution systems and on initial occupancy by the SL-2 crew there was some unwarranted concern that the nitrogen supply line from the

Airlock Module may have been damaged when the meteoroid shield was lost. Verification of its integrity was assured by use of the gas side of the portable water tank to monitor pressure through the gauge. This was the only time that tank was used. The urine flush system was not used at all on any visit.

The waste management compartment water dump system performed normally during the first manned mission but the heater probe failed during the second visit due to icing. It was replaced by a spare unit and then operated normally. Additionally a pressure transducer failed, causing

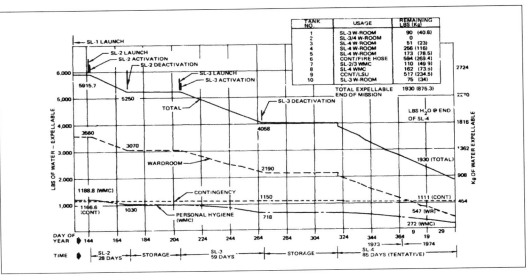

the pressure gauge to read off-scale high. The crew was instructed to vent it overnight and then activate the system. Several minor irregularities were noted during all three visits but the general technical condition was at a high standard and the crew were able to make observations that helped determine the minor improvements that would make life more comfortable.

The first crew found the use of the shower to be effective, despite taking a lot longer than planned to clean it up. The second crew disliked the shower, complaining about the inadequate flow of air and the amount of time spent drying off, the water tending to stick to the body and to surfaces in weightlessness. The third crew felt the shower-head was inadequate and insufficiently flexible but were supportive of the concept, as was the second crew. General observations were that the water flow could be better, greater quantities being required for its effective use, and that the temperature could be higher along with a higher velocity of warm air.

The TACS had a loaded capacity for 376.996kN-sec (84,824lbf-sec) at launch but the frequent use of this system to resolve problems encountered during the early phase of the mission resulted in the total mission expenditure of 340.311kN-sec (76,505lbf-sec), some 133.447kN-sec (30,000lbf-sec) more than had been redlined as a worst-case situation. The number of orientation changes necessitated by the Comet Kohoutek observation, together with problems encountered with the rate gyroscopes and CMG No 2, accounted for the excessive usage. Nevertheless, at SL-4 use rates, there was sufficient propellant remaining for an additional 30 days.

End of days

At the end of the manned period Skylab was expected to remain in orbit for up to nine years, extending its orbital life to at least November 1979 and at best March 1983. By late 1977 it was apparent that Skylab had experienced a significant increase in orbital decay due to an unexpected sharp increase in solar activity, advancing the predicted demise of the station to between late 1978 and early 1979. NASA believed it could use an early Shuttle flight to deliver a teleoperator system

LEFT The SL-4 Command Module can be seen on display at the National Air and Space Museum, Washington DC. *(David Baker)*

and placed a contract with Martin Marietta to build such a device, essentially a propulsion module to dock with the axial port and push Skylab to a higher orbit.

On 6 March 1978 contact was made with Skylab and reactivation began on 24 April when NASA sent reactivation commands to place the vehicle in an attitude that would extend its lifetime in orbit, adding up to 12 months to a predicted uncontrolled re-entry as early as mid-1979. The plan was for the second Shuttle mission to add the Martin Marietta Teleoperator system to boost its altitude and greatly extend

BELOW NASA planned a Skylab re-boost mission that would have raised the orbit of the station to prevent it decaying into the atmosphere and extend its lifetime to a date when the Space Shuttle could be used to reoccupy the facility. It was hoped that the second Shuttle mission could deliver the unit. The formal approval to build the Shuttle came in January 1972 and by 1977 the first flight was expected in 1979. *(NASA)*

SKYLAB BOOST MISSION

Skylab Boost Mission Configuration

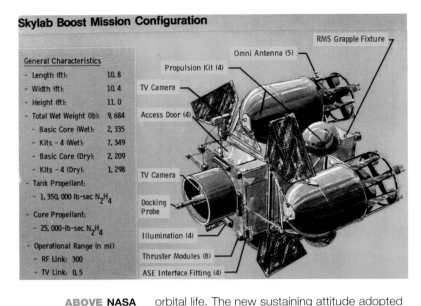

General Characteristics	
- Length (ft):	10.8
- Width (ft):	10.4
- Height (ft):	11.0
- Total Wet Weight (lb):	9,684
- Basic Core (Wet):	2,335
- Kits - 4 (Wet):	7,349
- Basic Core (Dry):	2,209
- Kits - 4 (Dry):	1,298
- Tank Propellant:	
- 1,350,000 lb-sec N_2H_4	
- Core Propellant:	
- 25,000-lb-sec N_2H_4	
- Operational Range (n mi)	
- RF Link:	300
- TV Link:	0.5

Labels on diagram: RMS Grapple Fixture; Omni Antenna (5); Propulsion Kit (4); TV Camera; Access Door (4); TV Camera; Docking Probe; Illumination (4); Thruster Modules (8); ASE Interface Fitting (4)

ABOVE NASA contracted with Martin Marietta to produce a propulsion unit that would have greatly extended the lifetime of the Skylab station. *(NASA)*

RIGHT Ambitious plans were made to exploit Skylab, to add power production and experiment modules and to establish a replenishment system for consumables which could be provided by Shuttle visits. NASA's ambitious plan to build a 12-man space station and a Shuttle in parallel had long disappeared, only the Shuttle being approved by the Nixon administration. With uncertainty as to when a space station could be funded, NASA looked to Skylab to provide an interim solution. *(NASA)*

orbital life. The new sustaining attitude adopted between June 11 and 28 used the TACS to place the MDA in the direction of travel with the longitudinal axis parallel to the Earth's surface (Earth Orbit Velocity Vector, or EOVV mode). The SI mode was activated on 19 July. By December, with difficulty securing funds for such a mission, NASA abandoned plans to place it in a higher orbit, or to conduct a controlled re-entry. President Carter accepted a recommendation from NASA on 15 December

that all future Skylab options be dropped.

Concern over an uncontrolled re-entry resulted from analysis which showed that up to 22,680kg (50,000lb) of the Skylab's 79,380kg (175,000lb) structure could remain intact through the atmosphere, spread through 400–500 pieces falling along a 6,400km (4,000-mile) ground track and 80km (50 miles) either side. However, about 75% of Skylab's ground track was over water and the probability of debris falling on a populated area was low. After spending $23.5 million on the retrieval system, NASA cancelled the contract with Martin Marietta on 18 December 1978. As then projected the earliest a Shuttle mission could have been sent to Skylab would have been February 1980, with a more likely date two months later. In fact, the first Shuttle flight did not occur until 12 April 1981, the second – the earliest for deploying a Skylab boost system – on 12 November that year.

On 25 January 1979 NASA placed Skylab back in a high-drag solar-inertial attitude to hasten re-entry and examined a wide range of options for potentially being able to control the orbit on which it burned up so as to avoid land. By June, increased solar activity made this less possible but plans were put in place to exercise

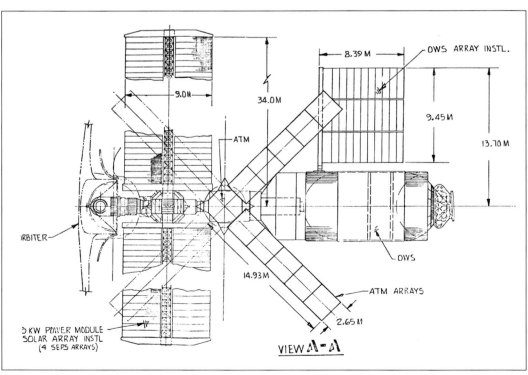

a so-called 'torque equilibrium' attitude in which the orientation of the station could be changed so as to delay, or advance, the precise orbit in which re-entry occurred, and this manoeuvre began on 20 June. At 07:45 UTC on 11 July a tumble command was sent to Skylab from the Madrid, Spain, tracking station to shift the point of re-entry away from Canada and the US eastern seaboard.

Re-entry occurred at 16:37 UTC on 11 July, on Skylab's mission Day 2,249. The impact footprint extended from 46.9°S by 94.4°E to 26.0°S by 131.2°E, an area extending across a linear range of 3,960km (2,460 miles) across a sparsely populated area of south-western Australia. The OWS cluster and Airlock Module debris was centred at 32°S by 124°N, with the Apollo Telescope Mount around 28.5°S by 128.5°E.

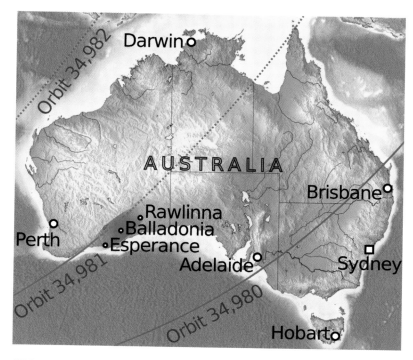

BELOW Extended utilisation of Skylab would have seen removal of the existing Apollo Telescope Mount solar arrays and replacement with a 25kW power module, plus docking ports and airlocks for general expansion into a permanently manned facility, crew replacement being made by the Shuttle. *(NASA)*

ABOVE At the end of 1978 the decision was made to abandon Skylab and all plans for re-boost and further use were cancelled. Budget pressures and delays to the Shuttle programme left no confidence in being able to save the station before it decayed back down through the atmosphere, which it did during orbit 34,981 over south-western Australia on 11 July 1979. So ended the operational phase of Skylab, the sole survivor of the Apollo Applications Program. *(NASA)*

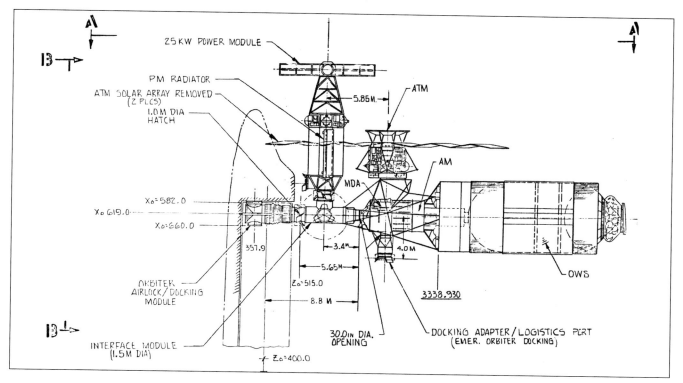

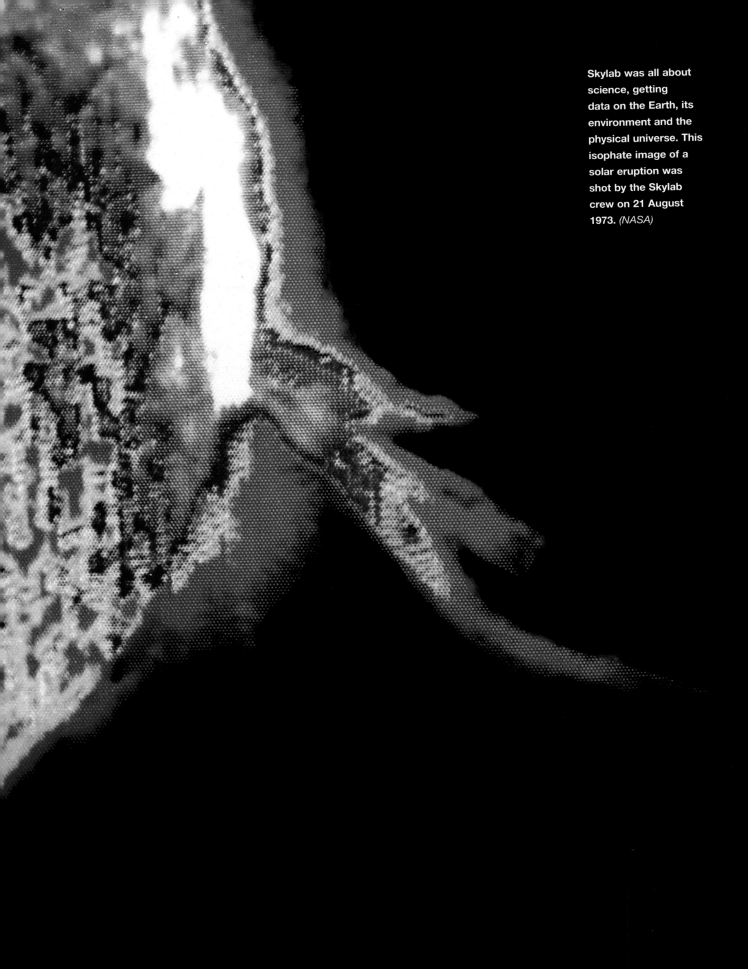

Skylab was all about science, getting data on the Earth, its environment and the physical universe. This isophate image of a solar eruption was shot by the Skylab crew on 21 August 1973. *(NASA)*

Appendix

Skylab man-hours utilisation

	First visit (SL-2)	Second visit (SL-3)	Third visit (SL-4)
Duration[1]:	672:49:49	1,427:09:04	2,017:15:31
Medical experiments	145.3 (7.5%)	312.6 (8%)	366.7 (6.1%)
Solar observations	117.2 (6.0%)	305.1 (7.8%)	519.0 (8.5%)
Earth observations	71.4 (3.7%)	223.5 (5.7%)	274.5 (4.5%)
Corollary/student experiments	65.4 (3.4%)	243.6 (6.2%)	156.0 (2.6%)
Sleep, rest, off-duty	675.6 (34.7%)	1,224.5 (31.2%)	1,846.5 (30.5%)
Pre-/post-sleep	403.4 (20.7%)	837.6 (21.3%)	974.9 (16.2%)
Lunch	73.7 (3.8%)	138.1 (3.5%)	409.1 (6.8%)
Housekeeping	103.6 (5.3%)	158.4 (4%)	298.9 (4.9%)
Physical exercise and hygiene	56.2 (2.9%)	202.2 (5.2%)	384.5 (6.4%)
Other operations[2]	232.5 (12%)	279.7 (7.1%)	571.4 (9.4%)

[1] Expressed in hours:minutes:seconds.
[2] These include EVA, activation and deactivation and television transmissions.

BELOW The standby "rescue" launcher should the final flight have required the flight of a second Apollo spacecraft to bring the crew home, AS-209 stands in the "rocket garden" at the Kennedy Space Center. *(Stig Nygaard)*

Appendix

Abbreviations and acronyms

A – Amps/amperes.
Å – Angstroms.
AAP – Apollo Applications Program.
ACPS – Attitude Control and Pointing System.
ACS – Active Control System.
AH – Amp/ampere hours.
AM – Airlock Module.
AM/ECS – Airlock Module Environmental Control System.
AM/EPS – Airlock Module Electrical Power System.
AMU – Astronaut Manoeuvring Unit.
ASMU – Automatically Stabilised Manoeuvring Unit.
ATM – Apollo Telescope Mount.
ATM/EPS – Apollo Telescope Mount Electrical Power System.
ATM-SAS – Apollo Telescope Mount Solar Array System.
BIS – British Interplanetary Society.
C&W – Caution-and-warning.
CBRM – Charger battery regulator module.
cm – Centimetres.
CM – Command Module.
CMG – Control Moment Gyroscope.
CSM – Command and Service Module.
V – Delta-v, measure of velocity.
D0 – Department of Defense experiments.
DA – Deployment Assembly.
dB – Decibels.
DC – Direct current.
DCS – Digital Command System.
EBW – Electrical bridge wire.
ECS – Environmental Control System.
ED – Student experiments.
EDT – Eastern Daylight Time.
EPC-RPM – Experiment-pointing control-roll positioning mechanism.
EPCS – Experiment Pointing and Control System.
EPEA – Experiment Pointing Electronic Assembly.
EREP – Earth Resources Experiments Package.
ERTS – Earth Resources Technology Satellite.
E/TCS – Environmental/Thermal Control Subsystem.
EUV – Extreme ultraviolet.

EVA – Extra-Vehicular Activity.
FAS – Fixed Airlock Shroud.
FCMU – Foot-controlled manoeuvring unit.
FMS – Food management system.
ft – Feet.
ft³ – Cubic feet.
ft/min – Feet per minute.
ft³/min – Cubic feet per minute.
ft/sec – Feet per second.
g – Measure of gravitational force.
GHz – Gigahertz (billions of cycles per second).
HHMU – Hand-Held Manoeuvring Unit.
HPI – High-performance insulation.
hr – Hours.
in – Inches.
in³ – Cubic inches.
Isp – Specific impulse.
IU – Instrument Unit.
IVA – Intra-vehicular activity.
kg – Kilograms.
kg/h – Kilograms per hour.
kg/min – Kilograms per minute.
kN – Kilonewtons.
kN/cm² – Kilonewtons force per square centimetre.
kN/m² – Kilonewtons force per square metre.
kN-sec – Kilonewtons per second.
kPa – Kilopascals.
kph – Kilometres per hour.
kV – Kilovolts.
kW – Kilowatts.
kWh – Kilowatts per hour.
lb – Pounds.
lbf-sec – Pounds force per second.
lb/h – Pounds per hour.
lb/in² – Pounds per square inch.
lb/min – Pounds per minute.
LBNP – Lower Body Negative Pressure Device.
lb/sec – Pounds per second.
LCC – Launch Control Center.
LM – Lunar Module.

LM/ATM – Lunar Module/Apollo Telescope Mount.
LM&SS – Lunar Mapping and Survey Station Module.
LOX – Liquid oxygen.
LUT – Launch Umbilical Tower.
m – Metres.
M – Science or human physiology experiments.
m³ – Cubic metres.
mA – Milliamperes.
MDA – Multiple Docking Adapter.
MDAC – McDonnell Douglas Aircraft Corporation.
MDA/ECS – Multiple Docking Adapter Environmental Control System.
min – Minutes.
ml – Millilitres.
MLU – Memory Load Unit.
mm – Millimetres.
mm³ – Cubic millimetres.
mm/Hg – Millimetres of mercury.
m/min – Metres per minute.
m³/min – Cubic metres per minute.
MOL – Manned Orbiting Laboratory.
mph – Miles per hour.
m/sec – Metres per second.
MSFC – Marshall Space Flight Centre, Alabama.
N – Newtons force.
N/sec – Newtons force per second.
NASA – National Aeronautics & Space Administration.
N/cm² – Newtons per square centimetre.
N/m² – Newtons per square metre.
OMSF – Office of Manned Space Flight.
OSO – Orbiting Solar Observatory.
OSSA – Office of Space Science and Applications.
OWS – Orbital Workshop.
OWS-SAS – Orbital Workshop Solar Array System.
PBI – Polybenzimidazole.
PCG – Power conditioning group.
PCM – Pulse-code modulation.
PGA – Pressure garment assembly (space suit).
ppm – Parts per million.
PS – Payload Shroud.

PTC – Passive Thermal Control.
RCS – Reaction Control System.
rpm – Revolutions per minute.
RTG – Radioisotope Thermoelectric Generator.
S0 – Solar or space science observation experiments.
SAG – Solar array group.
SAL – Scientific airlock.
SAS – Solar Array System.
SAW – Solar Array Wing.
sec – Seconds.
SEVA – 'Stand-up' EVA, where astronaut works from an open hatch without fully leaving the spacecraft.
SI – Solar inertial.
SL – Skylab.
SLA – Spacecraft Lunar Module Adapter.
SOAR – Southern Astrophysical Research.
SPS – Service Propulsion System.
SSESM – Spent Stage Experiment Support Module.
STDN – Spacecraft Tracking and Data Network.
STS – Structural transition section.
T0 – Technology experiments.
TACS – Thruster Attitude Control System.
TCA – Thermal Control Assembly.
TCS – Thermal Control System.
TFE – Tetrafluoroethylene.
TMR – Triple modular redundant.
UHF – Ultra High Frequency.
UTC – Coordinated Universal Time.
V – Volts.
VAB – Vehicle Assembly Building.
VCS – Ventilation Control System.
VDC – Volts of direct current.
W – Watts of electrical energy.
WBS – Whole body shower.
X-axis – Longitudinal (roll).
X-IOP – In the orbital plane.
X-POP – Perpendicular to the orbital plane.
Z-axis – Vertical (yaw).
Z-LV – Local vertical.

Appendix

Index